'In the hyperbolic issue of gun control, comparisons of gun habits across nations are too often made based on too little credible analysis. Squires's sensible cross-national examination of the gun issue from a truly international perspective brings welcome sobriety and thoughtfulness to this pressing and timely subject.'

Robert J. Spitzer, Distinguished Service Professor of Political Science,
the State University of New York College at Cortland, USA

'Peter Squires's impressive new book provides a rigorous and authoritative examination of recent developments in gun crime and gun control and their inter-relationships. Applying a criminologist's perspective, the book not only provides a detailed and revealing analysis of trends in gun crime and control measures in the contrasting cases of the USA and UK, but also situates these in the wider context of firearms deaths and injuries across the world, in developed, industrializing, fragile and conflict prone states, and of global efforts to improve regulations on gun flows. Strongly recommended.'

Owen Greene, Director, Centre for International Co-operation and Security,
University of Bradford, UK

'Admirable for its international perspective and scope of thought, this is a "must-read" for anyone who wonders where the world is heading with guns. Squires examines current debates: gun crime and spree shootings, domestic violence and "gun culture", the UN and global gun trafficking – then breaks open emerging discussions: the militarization of self-defence and the neo-liberalization of firearm ownership. This is the breadth of canvas we need to draw effective policy.'

Philip Alpers, GunPolicy.org

GUN CRIME IN GLOBAL CONTEXTS

Every year around three-quarters of a million people die (directly or indirectly) as a result of gun violence, with most deaths occurring in the poorest, yet also most highly weaponized, parts of the world. Firearm proliferation – 875 million global firearms – is a direct contributor to both regional conflicts and to crime. This book attempts to understand the inter-related dynamics of supply and demand which are weaponizing the world.

Now over ten years after Peter Squires's *Gun Culture or Gun Control?*, the issues pertaining to gun violence and gun control have developed dramatically. With *Gun Crime in Global Contexts*, Peter Squires offers a cutting-edge account of contemporary developments in the politics of gun crime and the social and theoretical issues that surround the problem. This book contains:

- an innovative political analysis of neo-liberal globalization and weapon proliferation;
- an overview of recent gun control debates and gang strategies in the UK;
- an updated analysis of US gun politics: self-defence, race and the 'culture war';
- a critical analysis of US school and rampage shootings, how they have impacted the gun debate and how different societies have responded to mass shootings;
- an examination of the UN's development of an Arms Trade Treaty (2001–2013);
- a discussion of weapon trafficking;
- discussions about youth gangs around the world, including those in Brazil, Kenya, West Africa, Mexico and South Africa.

With its interdisciplinary perspective and global reach, this book will be important reading for academics and students interested in youth and gang crime, violent crime and comparative criminal justice, as well as peace and security studies and international relations.

Peter Squires has been a Professor of Criminology and Public Policy at the University of Brighton since 2005, having worked at the University of Brighton since 1986. He has published ten books (single or jointly authored, or edited), and has made numerous contributions to journals and other media. Professor Squires has a significant media profile, contributing regularly to TV, radio and news media debates on crime and criminal justice, and was profiled in *The Guardian*'s 'leading academic experts' series in 2007 [http://www.guardian.co.uk/education/2007/oct/16/academicexperts.society]. His teaching and research interests extend across many sub-divisions of contemporary criminology, but specifically gun crime and gun control, gangs and youth crime. Professor Squires recently joined the ACPO Police National Independent Advisory Group on Criminal Use of Firearms.

GUN CRIME IN GLOBAL CONTEXTS

Peter Squires

Routledge
Taylor & Francis Group

LONDON AND NEW YORK

First published 2014
by Routledge
2 Park Square, Milton Park, Abingdon, Oxfordshire OX14 4RN

and by Routledge
711 Third Avenue, New York, NY 10017

First issued in paperback 2015

Routledge is an imprint of the Taylor & Francis Group, an informa business

British Library Cataloguing in Publication Data
A catalogue record for this book is available from the British Library

Library of Congress Cataloging-in-Publication Data
Squires, Peter
Gun crime in global contexts / Peter Squires. – First Edition.
pages cm
1. Gun control. 2. Firearms–Law and legislation. 3. Firearms and crime. I.
Title.
HV7435.S68 2014
364.2–dc23
2013048555

ISBN13: 978-1-138-93739-0 (pbk)
ISBN13: 978-0-415-68859-8 (hbk)

Typeset in Bembo by
GreenGate Publishing Services, Tonbridge, Kent

CONTENTS

FIGURES

TABLES

PREFACE AND ACKNOWLEDGEMENTS

This book began as a proposal to update my book, *Gun Culture or Gun Control*, first published in 2000. The premise of that original book had been to explore the differing reactions of Britain and America to the tragedies represented by Dunblane and Columbine. These two school shootings both had, although for quite different reasons, major impacts upon politics, culture and debates about gun violence and public safety in their respective societies. Situating the analysis of these very different reactions within culture, law and history went some way to explain the differences, but it became increasingly clear that this was only part of the story. Updating that story, ten years on, of two countries sharing a common language but with *increasingly divergent* attitudes and approaches to guns seemed to offer the opportunity to reflect upon how and why our two societies were moving further apart with respect to firearms crime and violence.

Much had happened in the intervening years and, if anything, America's exceptionalism had seemingly grown as first 'concealed carry' licensing, then later 'Castle Doctrine' and 'Stand Your Ground' laws began to feature in the USA, further empowering individual gun owners to confront and, if necessary, to shoot offenders – even as overall levels of crime appeared to be falling. These issues, as we shall see, were little to do with America's past, but much more to do with fear of crime and disorder, contemporary concerns about race and impatience with Government. Britain, meanwhile, even having prohibited handgun ownership, had witnessed a sudden rise and then a fall in recorded gun crime and had passed through a distinct 'moral panic' about youth violence and street gangs. A series of terrible gun rampages occurred in the USA, individual states were introducing purchase checks but major loopholes remained in their databases, while the assault weapons ban, introduced in 1994, lapsed. A third spree shooting occurred in the UK in 2010 and in the USA, the same year, the second of two Supreme Court rulings, struck down the relatively long-standing handgun ban in Chicago (Washington, DC's handgun ban already having been found unconstitutional in 2008). This was a busy time for firearm politics.

Moreover, many other societies were experiencing some very similar problems with the gun. Rampage killings were certainly not confined to the USA, numerous other modern, civilized, democratic societies experienced mass shootings (Canada, Australia, Norway, Finland, Germany, Switzerland amongst them), but horrific and inexplicable as they were, these occasional outbursts of armed rage were minute compared to the havoc wrought by guns in a wide range of failed states and conflict zones, where weaponization appeared both cause and seeming consequence of the chronic violence and instability. Furthermore, gun violence and social disorder, just as it had in the US homeland, was invariably accompanied by a demand, on the part of 'law-abiding citizens', for firearms for self-protection (the privatization of armed force) and so the wheel of weaponization turned, neo-liberal gun culture spinning out globally. US advocates of armed self-defence represented the 'right to bear arms' as a global human right, all the more so as, under the auspices of the United Nations (UN), and drawing together many emerging threads of work on arms control, research, peace building and economic development, an international small arms (and light weapons) control movement began to take shape.

Rather than simply update *Gun Culture or Gun Control*, the project became one of attempting to embrace the new global agendas represented by neo-liberal weaponization and the social and political challenges facing global gun control. The aim was to explore these various tensions in the context of a range of different societies: beginning in those where gun misuse is still, primarily, a criminological question (UK and most of Europe), extending to the USA where gun ownership and use runs to the heart of core principles of contemporary neo-liberal governance and, finally, moving on to an exploration of the dilemmas represented by firearm proliferation in failed and failing states, broken societies and war zones. But then, by way of an alternative, we conclude with a review of the ways in which a number of societies, having experienced their own gun tragedies, have sought to reform their own domestic gun laws, culminating with a review of the way in which the UN has similarly sought to restrict and constrain the illegal proliferation of small arms.

While I have described the book's origins as a personal project, many people have helped me to formulate and develop the analysis which follows. Foremost amongst these were the participants at an excellent international workshop on *Guns, Crime and Social Order* organized by James Sheptycki, at York University, Toronto, in 2008. Four very worthwhile days of intense discussion and debate allowed for a very fruitful exchange of ideas. Thanks are especially due to James, and also to Martin Innes, Adam Edwards, Simon Hallsworth, Phil Cook, Chris Lewis, Wendy Cukier, Biko Agozino, Gavin Hales, Daniel Silverstone and Peter Klerks who participated. Philip Alpers 'gun policy news' service and the www.gunpolicy.org database hosted by the University of Sydney have also been invaluable.

Colleagues at Brighton and friends at other universities have also helped maintain my momentum on this project, both discussing the issues arising, and tolerating my tendency to see guns and firearm-related politics in the strangest places. Many parts of the book have been worked out in the course of lectures and seminars, at Brighton and elsewhere. Particular thanks are due to John Lea, Peter Kennison, Carlie Goldsmith, Craig Johnstone, Roxana Cavalcanti (who prepared her own very fine analysis of the Brazil 2005 referendum) and Phil Haynes. I am also especially grateful for the support of friends and colleagues in the UK Gun Control Network, especially Gill Marshall-Andrews, Mick North, Georgina Mortimer and Chrissie Hall. In 2006, while acting as an external examiner for the University of Essex, the opportunity to read Christine Allen's splendid thesis, an ethnography of gun rights activism in the USA, *Living the Second Amendment*, was also particularly useful.

Working with Roger Grimshaw, Enver Solomon, Will McMahon and Arianna Silvestri (all at the Centre for Crime and Justice Studies (CCJS)) was very helpful in developing the analysis of British gun crime 'evidence and policy', and I am grateful to Owen Greene for allowing a criminologist to escape to Brussels and a European seminar on international weapons trafficking, my first, quite fascinating, encounter with 'arms control' researchers.

I would also like to thank the Equality Trust for giving me permission to reproduce Figures 1.1, 1.2 and 1.3 in Chapter 1 and Gill Marshall-Andrews and GCN for allowing me to use their images from the replica gun advertising campaign in Chapter 2 (Figure 2.5).

That said, any faults, flaws or problems of interpretation are down to me and I sincerely hope that no-one's inputs or contributions have been overlooked.

Two, it has to be said, very much earlier versions of parts of this book have been published as short encyclopaedia entries. The first 'Weapons Smuggling' can be found in the *Encyclopedia of Transnational Crime and Justice* (pp. 457–461), edited by Margaret E. Beare (Sage, 2012); the second 'Gun Control' is in Volume 2 (pp. 718–723) of *The Social History of Crime and Punishment in America: An Encyclopedia*, edited by W.R. Miller (Sage, 2012). It goes without saying that I was very grateful to be able to make those contributions.

During the time that the idea for the book was forming and, later, as it was being written, the opportunity to participate in a number of academic/political engagements came to me. The first involved attending the American Criminology Association annual meeting in Denver in 2003, where I endured the whole of the 'firearms stream' with its sometimes strange mixture of firearms advocacy and 'criminological science'. In 2005, I was invited (by Don Kates) to George Mason University in Arlington, for a fascinating symposium on the 2nd Amendment and the 'human right' of self-defence. Arguing the distinction between asserting a right to kill in self-defence, as opposed to reducing the need to do so, can seldom have seemed so perplexing. However, nothing could be quite so perplexing as my live TV debate with Wayne La Pierre of the National Rifle Association (NRA), filmed in London in March 2012. An account of this debate, and maybe the film itself, might be accessed from my website. I think it went quite well.

I would especially like to thank Thomas Sutton, Nicola Hartley and Heidi Lee at Routledge Criminology: Thomas for agreeing to go ahead with the project in the first place and Nicola and Heidi who were patient and supportive at times when I despaired of ever finding the time to finish the manuscript.

Thanks also, as ever, to Kathy.

ABBREVIATIONS

ACPO	Association of Chief Police Officers
ASB/ASBO	anti-social behaviour/anti-social behaviour order
ATF	Bureau of Alcohol, Tobacco, Firearms and Explosives
ATT	Arms Trade Treaty
BASC	British Association for Shooting and Conservation
CAAT	Campaign against the Arms Trade
CPS	Crown Prosecution Service
CSJ	Centre for Social Justice
DDR	disarmament, demobilization and reintegration
DTO	drug-trafficking organization
EUC	end-user certificate
FCC	Firearms Consultative Committee
GCN	Gun Control Network
GMP	Greater Manchester Police
GSS	General Social Survey
HMRC	Her Majesty's Revenue & Customs
IANSA	International Action Network on Small Arms
IRS	Inland Revenue Service
MMAGS	Manchester Multi-Agency Gang Strategy
MPA	Metropolitan Police Authority
MPS	Metropolitan Police Service
NABIS	National Ballistics Intelligence Service
NAFTA	North American Free Trade Agreement
NCRS	National Crime Recording Standard
NICS	National Instant Check System
NRA	National Rifle Association
NSPOF	National Survey of Private Ownership and Use of Firearms

PCA	Police Complaints Authority
PoA	Programme of Action
RTC	Right to Carry
SALW	small arms and light weapons
SIPRI	Stockholm International Peace Research Institute
SOCA	Serious Organised Crime Agency
TARN	Trauma Audit and Research Network
TGAP	Tackling Guns Action Programme
UNODC	United Nations Office on Drugs and Crime
VCRA	Violent Crime Reduction Act
WFSA	World Forum on the Future of Sport Shooting Activities

PART 1

Introduction

1

GUNS AS A GLOBAL ISSUE

A spectre is haunting civilization, the spectre of an indiscriminate proliferation of small arms and light weapons (SALW).

Gunfire as a *social* relationship

Any analysis of the global context of gun crime is inevitably related to a series of further questions regarding the design, production and marketing of firearms; the distribution of them – who gets them; and the uses, or misuse, to which they are put. Finally, in the global context, it concerns the places in which they are most often used or misused. But this raises a further question, given that a firearm is most dangerous precisely when it is used as it is *designed* to be used (Springwood, 2007a): what is it to 'misuse' a gun?

Some of our earlier questions are technical, even scientific: for instance *ergonomic* (how does the gun handle?); *structural* and *metallurgical* (what is it made of and how robust are the components?); *design related* (what does it look like?); and *ballistic* (how does it shoot?). Other questions involve the law, rights, control and governance (and their limits): who gets to have a gun and what can they do with it? The issues pursued by this book, however, are more obviously social and moral, in part, because what a firearm does, what it is designed for, has largely been predetermined. Modern hunting weapons and shotguns are generally fit for purpose: hunting or target shooting. Contemporary production handguns, however, are now generally closely modelled upon (or are identical to) military combat weapons, while the growing enthusiasm of the US gun-owning public[1] for military-style assault rifles, and the proliferation around the globe of the ubiquitous AK-47 and its derivatives, is achieving what many commentators (see for example Diaz, 2013) have referred to as a 'militarization' of civilian firearm ownership, beginning, arguably, to collapse a distinction between 'criminal' and 'conflict' firearms (Marsh, 2012: 13).

The significance of this 'militarization' of civilian gun ownership and, more broadly, the weaponization of communities around the world, lies in the fact that contemporary firearms are very good at what they are designed for – dispensing bullets rapidly and efficiently, in other words, killing quickly. So the issue of gun misuse is not a question of technical capacity, despite occasional malfunctions, for many incidents might testify to the efficient killing power of modern firearms (this is, after all, what they were designed to do), for example efficiency, durability and ease of use were amongst the reasons for the global success of the AK-47 as compared with the original American M-16s (Chivers, 2010); even children can and did use them. So the question of gun misuse is not related to its capacity to fire bullets quickly and efficiently, rather, the real questions are about *who* gets to do this? Who uses the gun, against whom and under what circumstances? These are irretrievably social, moral and, for my own part, *criminological* questions; and they foreground profoundly *social* relationships.[2]

It is important to start here, in part because when, in later chapters, the discussion turns to weapon proliferation and the weaponization of homes, communities or even whole societies; weaponization conceived as a dangerous vector of neo-liberalism or an ominous dimension of risk globalization, the argument is not one about a kind of technological determinism where guns 'cause' violence. Rather, weapon technologies, gun use and misuse are socially embedded and socially meaningful (Greene and Marsh, 2012b: 9). Gun enthusiasts, critics of gun control, often complain that it is wrong to focus exclusively upon firearms as a supposed *cause* of problems but, as Currie has argued, this claim misses a more important sociological point: 'the role of guns in violent crime cannot be considered in isolation from other conditions that influence the likelihood of violence, such as the degree of inequality, the depth of social exclusion, and the erosion of family and community supports' (2005: 106–107). Even the US NRA, an organization with which this book finds relatively few areas of agreement, sometimes get close to recognizing this. A gun may be a tool, although never just a tool; 'guns don't kill people; people kill people', they argue. Although NRA spokesmen seldom go on to acknowledge the corollary: that while guns may not *cause* violence, they do tend make it more likely, more lethal, more widespread, more harmful, more protracted, more entrenched and more likely to recur. As Currie concludes, it is 'hard to avoid the conclusion that, in conditions that are otherwise conducive to breeding violent crime, the wide prevalence of guns compounds and "lethalizes" those problems' (2005: 108). But these violent outcomes are the result of human behaviours and social and political relationships; the efficacy of firearms is a result of the uses to which humans put them (Ashkenazi, 2012: 229); guns just make killing really simple. One of the central questions explored in a recent book edited by Greene and Marsh, *Small Arms, Crime and Conflict* (2012a) precisely concerns the extent to which the availability and proliferation of SALW represent 'significant independent variables in processes of armed violence, conflict, security or development' (Greene and Marsh, 2012d: 250). Much research on violence and conflict merely views weaponization as a symptom of conflicts driven by deeper or wider social, political, economic or ethnic or ideological processes. Here, however, in common with Currie and Greene and Marsh, and developing the concept of weaponization in specific local contexts, our argument concurs with their remark that 'variations in the characteristics, availability and flows of arms can significantly affect the wider risks, dynamics, extent, and lethality of armed violence, conflict, insecurity and obstacles to development' while, traversing the academically distinct fields of conflict and crime, 'the ready availability of handguns or automatic weapons can qualitatively affect the lethality, scale or implications of violence, with enduring consequences' (Greene and Marsh, 2012d: 250).

Variety and difference in local contexts should not be overlooked either, everywhere is not the same, there is no such thing as a 'global gun culture' (Ashkenazi, 2012: 231); there are distinct local cultures in which firearms and weaponization exert a different, perhaps more or less powerful, influence. There may be tightly controlled or chaotically uncontrolled 'gun cultures'; moreover 'control' in this sense is not reducible to the law and its enforcement, informal social controls, traditions of firearm ownership and use, personal responsibility or self-discipline, can all help keep the negative consequences of firearm proliferation in check. Warring groups can negotiate a cease-fire; urban gangs may agree a truce and most social groups, to some degree, regulate the behaviour of their members. Even in violent gang and gun cultures, most young men do not act violently most of the time (Greene and Marsh, 2012d: 254). There was always something mistaken in the popular misconception that gang communities were awash with firearms and the young men in them chaotically and uncontrollably violent, in fact weapon discharges were still relatively rare and a form they often took, 'drive-by shootings', although seemingly wanton and indiscriminate, generally only targeted doors or windows, buildings or cars. In other words, this was shooting as ritual, performance or communication: a message in a bullet or ballistic graffiti (Squires, 2011a).

Later on I introduce the notion of 'regime' analysis in order to characterize different degrees of effective governance over violence and disorder. Simply put, strong states generally manage levels of violence and disorder, they develop strong disincentives to weaponization which reduces the overall demand for guns and therefore prevents the influx of firearms which might destabilize law and order. Weaker or failing states, by contrast, or 'post-conflict' societies, may find themselves caught in a vicious circle whereby they cannot achieve a monopoly of armed force within their own territory and cannot dampen the demand that brings an illicit supply of firearms to armed factions, organized criminal groups or gangs which, in turn, render law enforcement ineffective. They therefore cannot even protect their own citizens. A sudden massive influx of weapons into either types of society is unlikely to represent a positive development, but while the former may have the infrastructure to contain the criminal violence which might ensue, in the latter extra weapons may simply widen and deepen the conflict.

Synthesis and innovation

In diverse global contexts SALW are employed in both conflict and crime, indeed as I have already noted, these types of violence may no longer seem so distinct: war itself is a major facilitator of criminal violence; terrorism and political insurgency are often funded by the proceeds of crime, narco traffickers exercise regional governance via corruption, assassination and force of arms, civilians are acquiring military specification weapons and the 'new' forms of asymmetric or 'fourth generation' warfare have blurred distinctions between civilians and combatants – as both casualties and perpetrators (Newman, 2004: 174–175). That said, the scope of the book, even as it begins from traditional criminology, has to embrace the full range of ways in which weaponization fuels criminal violence and conflict. One ambition of the book, therefore, is intellectual and academic synthesis.

Firearm use and misuse certainly features in criminology but, in societies such as the UK, where gun crime (as presently defined) represents only some 0.25 per cent of recorded crime, it is far from being a mainstream issue, notwithstanding its more symbolic significances (Squires, 2008a). Criminology itself generally engages with firearms at the 'end-game' – at the crime scene where guns have been illegally fired, but tries, occasionally, to shift its emphasis upstream into trafficking and criminal supply. In the US, by contrast, a vast body of quantitative criminology exists, often rather inconclusively mining the impact of any number of diverse firearm acquisition restrictions upon rates of weapon misuse.[3] Rather more useful sociological analyses have focused upon the contexts and social relations of gun use and misuse, the meanings associated with gun possession by those who use them (Wilkinson, 2003; Kohn, 2004b; Harcourt, 2006; Pogrebin et al., 2009; Carlson, 2012; see also Chapter 5).

Arms control scholars, on the other hand, tend to start from the supply side, focussing upon the production and distribution of weapons. Their work engages with criminological issues at the lower ends of these supply chains where illegal weapon trafficking, close to the actual contexts of criminal firearm misuse, occurs (Spapens, 2007; De Vries, 2011). It was once assumed that illicit supply, by shady international weapons dealers and brokers[4] or 'rogue states', was the source of most of the weapons that were criminally misused, but more recent research shows that patterns of illicit global weapon supply mirror very closely the patterns of supply for legal small arms (Lumpe, 2000; Bourne, 2007). The real regulation issue, then, becomes one concerning the slippage of weapons from the legal to illegal spheres. This issue has been of particular interest and concern for scholars of international relations. Although small arms regulation only represents a small part of a complex field of inter-state relations, the work of international relations (IR) specialists has contributed a great deal to our understanding of the role of international treaties, international law, arms embargoes and end-user certification, and the ways in which the global architecture of governance, such as the UN and other, more regional, inter-state bodies (for example the EU, NATO, the Organization of American States and the Economic Community of West African

States) has contributed to the outlawing of certain types of weapons (chemical weapons, land mines and cluster munitions), and has helped contain the proliferation of small arms, while attempting to guide errant or conflict states to higher standards of governance (Sands, 2005).

Finally, from the fields of peace and development studies, there has emerged a vast array of local and regional case studies of disarmament, demobilization and reintegration (DDR) and social and economic redevelopment. A good deal of such work has developed around the work of NGOs involved in development and peace building (the Red Cross, Oxfam, Amnesty International or International Action Network on Small Arms (IANSA)) and has necessarily focused upon the role of weapons, widely diffused into communities as a result of recent conflicts, hampering the rebuilding of trust or achieving reconciliation. Case studies with a more anthropological perspective have often been able to throw much light upon the local consequences of weaponization (Richards, 1996; Goldstein, 2003). Weaponized violence may have brutalized whole communities, undermined social cohesion, discouraged investors and eliminated more traditional structures of authority (Greene and Marsh, 2012c: 100–102); young men who have spent their early teens carrying a gun and participating in terrible acts of violence (even if coerced) may find it difficult to revert to civilized living (Louise, 1995). Other armed groups, having become accustomed to carrying firearms and getting their way, may feel somewhat reluctant to give them up – as in Nigeria (Ikelegbe, 2005). In such settings, the local practicalities of disarmament, as social and economic redevelopment, or crime prevention, or peace building, need to be continuously alert to arms control matters and the dangers of renewed weapon supplies which might trigger further outbreaks of violence.

It follows that, in this book, one aim is to bring some synthesis to these four dimensions of the global gun question, four dimensions that have often pursued their own agendas quite separately, even down to a focus upon different kinds of weapons. For as Marsh (2012: 13) has noted, handguns have typically been the choice of the criminal whereas anyone contemplating conflict or civil war needed assault rifles or more automatic weapons. By contrast, as Greene and Penetrante (2012: 151) observe, misuse of sporting guns has seldom contributed to political conflict. As we shall see, however, these distinctions are breaking down. Furthermore, in the context of globalization, weapon trafficking, and other crimes committed to facilitate further crime, connects many areas of an increasingly globalized criminology: the crimes of states, political crime, organized crime, cross-border crime, genocide and human rights violations, international policing and law enforcement, peace and conflict studies. Synthesis alone, around these many dimensions of global gun crime, is a tall order raising important questions.

Greene and Marsh have likewise pointed to a number of gaps between the study of gun crime in settled, advanced, liberal-democratic societies, chiefly the preserve of criminology and gun violence in fragile, broken or developing states, often conducted alongside the work of NGOs and arms control organizations. It is likely that there are important, transferable knowledges and important lessons to be learned across these differing contexts; about the community consequences of weaponization, about masculinity, young men and the attractions of firearms, about gangs and armed criminal groups and about the impact of weapons on families and gender relationships. There are also lessons to learn about public safety and policy change; how might gun regimes be changed, what works in other societies. I will be exploring these issues later, but there are often problems when criminologists venture abroad, especially when they travel to wholly different types of societies where the rule of law and systems of governance are compromised or fragile, and law enforcement non-existent, or corrupt, or just one of the parties in a conflict. In many of these respects a genuine cross-cultural criminology is still in its infancy, but its research agenda needs to develop quickly; the various research communities have much to tell to one another and plenty to learn (Greene and Marsh, 2012c: 103–104; 2012d).

This leads to the, perhaps, more ambitious, aim of the book. Beyond synthesis of existing work, the book aims to offer a theoretically innovative and multi-disciplinary approach to the phenomenon of weaponization in the context of a globalizing, neo-liberal world. Findlay (1999) has earlier described how both trans-national crime and crime control can be seen as forces of globalization, here, by extension, I am also treating weapon trafficking as a vector of neo-liberalization bringing sovereign capacity to human agents through their firepower. In a revised take on the claim attributed to Samuel Colt, producer of the first repeating revolver, guns are not so much 'equalizers' or 'peacemakers', rather they transform through empowerment, turning powerless subjects into citizens and players, decision-makers for the neo-liberal world. In one sense, just as Marx described the creation of the working class as labour power, made up of many millions of factory 'hands' (Bauman, 1982), so weapon proliferation and weaponization give us the elusive 'gunman', the citizen/combatant of 'asymmetrical' or 'fourth generation' warfare in an insecure 'global South'.

Older commentaries on military discipline, illustrated, for example, in Foucault's work (1977: 135–141) revealed how a training in firearms 'made the man'; here, by contrast, I am exploring how weaponization 're-makes' masculinity, militarizing the mind (Muggah, 2001) and attaching a lethal capacity to youthful immaturity, with often terrifying consequences. Jacklyn Cock, for example, writing of the reconstruction of armed masculinity amongst the gangs of South Africa, refers to the ideology expressed in the American bumper sticker: 'An armed man is a citizen; an unarmed man is a subject' (Cock, 2000: 90). This illustration appears in a chapter in a three volume series of books produced by the Institute for Security Studies in South Africa, titled *Society under Siege* (Gamba and Meek, 1997–2000). The work characterizes post-apartheid South Africa as besieged by organized crime, weapon flows, armed gangs, opposition militias and local 'cultures' of gun use and misuse. Similarly, despite the reticence of some commentators, this book will employ the notion of gun culture, always in specific local contexts, as an outcome of weaponization, just as Cukier and Sheptycki (2012: 4) describe 'pistolization', the way in which the carrying of firearms turns 'good guys' into 'potential killers', and Carr (2008) depicts 'Kalashnikov Culture' where society and sociability are transformed, rendered insecure, by firearm proliferation. Cukier and Sheptycki (2012) have recently argued that the global 'carriers of gun culture', by which they refer to 'technology, media and ideology' not least amongst which are featured Hollywood violence, television cop shows, violent video games and music culture (Bascuñán and Pearce, 2008: 8, 15), have worked to '(re)produce the links between masculinity, affluence and firearms'. For example, as the anthropologist Paul Richards discovered in his research with the young fighters involved in the Sierra Leone civil war, repeated viewings of *Rambo* videos seemed a particular, if perverse, source of inspiration to them (Richards, 1996). In this book, while attempting to draw together the diverse perspectives on gun violence, referred to already, in a new cross-cultural criminology, I am simply acknowledging an inevitable corollary; the global dissemination of market liberalism has also diffused gun culture.

As a highly marketized and desirable personal technology, firearms have appealed to police and security forces and both the law abiding and the criminally inclined alike: from the fearful citizen of a gated community in upmarket Pretoria, thinking that security rests with the gun under his mattress, to the 14-year-old gang-banger, hiding down a dark alley, waiting to rob the local drug dealer with the aid of a junk pistol borrowed from his cousin. However, the more the latter have them, the more the former feel the need for them; and the more that the former acquire them (generally speaking) the easier it is for the latter to acquire them also. Yet it does not end there, for policy transfer in law enforcement and criminal justice has also been a significant feature of neo-liberal globalization. The types of policies, typically pioneered in or by North America and which have translated as core foundations of neo-liberal governance (Wacquant, 2009), include: anti-gang strategies and mass incarceration in parts of Europe; SWAT unit policing methods (the 'mano dura', or iron fist policing methods) in Central and Latin America; RICO (Racketeer Influenced and Corrupt Organization) inspired control strategies for tackling criminal gangs and organized crime groups in South Africa; not forgetting direct military interventions (invasions, military assistance, peacekeeping missions and regime change). It seems fair to say that, with few exceptions, all have been characterized by levels of weaponized violence or resistance on such a scale and at such a cost that they generate demands for further weapons, promote illicit weapon supplies, multiply criminal opportunities, exacerbate the collateral victimization of innocent civilians while compromising the effective implementation of the original policies and threatening the longer-term safety and security of the regions in which they are applied. Each of these dimensions of violent, gun-enabled illegality, resistance or insurgency (or armed law enforcement, peacekeeping, gang suppression or militarized crime control) might *separately* be claimed for the discipline of criminology, but seldom are they considered together. This is the more ambitious aim of the book, to connect the dynamics of weaponization to the cultural contexts of gun use and misuse, the relations of firearm supply and demand, and crime prevention, law and policy-making and law enforcement. The objective is also to shift the focus cross-culturally to see how these social relations of the gun play out differently (whether resolved or not) in a variety of societies. Foucault once argued that, above all else, the discipline of criminology needed to 'escape the prison', to abandon the task, metaphorically, of counting heads and embrace, instead, the question of the power to criminalize. This vision was also the clarion call of *The New Criminology* in 1973 (Taylor *et al.*, 1973).

In this book, the ambition is similar, by walking away from the crime scene itself: the victim, chalked in outline onto the sidewalk, the shell casings and ballistic traces, and the young perpetrator, handcuffed, seated in the back of a police cruiser, I concentrate instead on the social dynamics that brought them face to face, the cultural context in which their personal motivations made 'sense', the community in which their identities were formed, the local demand for weapons and the criminal networks that delivered a gun, perhaps from half-way around the world, the international relationships or conflicts that shaped this supply, and the gun control regime that permitted – or at least failed to prevent – this level of weapon ownership, this weaponization.

Googling a gun?

Perhaps the ultimate breakthrough in 'globally indiscriminate' firearm ambitions arrived in March 2013. An American designer had put the digital blueprints for a '3D printable handgun', onto the internet. Anyone with a compatible 3D printer could download the instructions, 3D-print the separate parts of the weapon before assembling them, with the aid of a small nail and an elastic band (Woollaston and Murphy, 2013). Accessing suitable ammunition, fortunately, might be a different matter. The Wisconsin company producing the software, revealingly named *Defence Distributed*, scored an international media coup with a YouTube film clip purporting to show the gun being fired several times. In fact, however, the clumsy plastic gun that was produced is hardly likely to have endeared itself to many gun enthusiasts, for whom the 'look' of a handgun (alongside a range of other qualities) is important. By contrast, the plastic gun was bulky and ugly, a cross between a chunky water pistol and something made out of coloured *Lego*. Even so, the gun could fire a .38 calibre bullet, so it could certainly kill. It could also explode when fired; Australian police tested the weapon, a Police Commissioner for New South Wales commenting: 'being on either end of this weapon can be lethal' although he acknowledged that the 3D printing technology and materials were bound to improve from the early and rather crude weapons currently available (Vincent, 2013).

The weapon's designer named the gun the *Liberator*, though he did not spell out what it was that the gun's potential users were to be liberated from; maybe liberation from 'gunless subjection' or perhaps the name was in homage to the single-shot handguns intended to be dropped into occupied France, for the Resistance, during WW2. We may never know, the point about this firearm was the novelty of its potential distribution. This was a lethal weapon that could travel through the fibre-optic cables of the internet, crossing borders and jurisdictions, and potentially available to anyone with access to a, by now, relatively familiar 3D printing capability. In the first two months of their availability, the printable gun software instructions had been downloaded, apparently, over 100,000 times. Answering questions from journalists about his invention, the gun's designer, a self-proclaimed 'libertarian', sought to justify releasing the software with the suggestion that 'everyone should have access to guns'. Later, demonstrating precisely the anti-social dynamics of danger and weaponization that I will be exploring throughout the rest of this book, he added, in sentiments very reminiscent of remarks attributed to Mikhail Kalashnikov: 'I recognise the tool might be used to harm other people ... it's a gun. But I don't think that's a reason not to do it' (Woollaston and Murphy, 2013).[5] The US Government, however, did not agree and ordered the company (albeit, 100,000 downloads too late) to remove the blueprints from the internet (Legge, 2013).

The weapons and the numbers

SALW, as a wide range of statisticians and researchers working in international relations, arms control, the UN, the WHO and a number of disarmament and development NGOs repeatedly tell us, are the weapons *most likely* to be used in criminal violence, domestic conflict, organized crime, terrorism and politically motivated violence. Although, as Jackson and Marsh (2012: 105) concede, 'the extant research does not conclusively show a *causal* relationship between [firearm] availability and homicide or crime' (emphasis added), the role of SALW proliferation in facilitating criminal violence, de-stabilizing fragile political systems, promoting and sustaining conflict, arming militants and terrorists and empowering drug cartels, ethnic warlords, urban gangs and criminal militias, is well understood (Cukier and Sidel, 2006; Bourne, 2007; Stohl *et al.*, 2007). As Paul Collier (2008, 2009) has noted from his development research in Africa, arms proliferation, likened to a disease vector, sustains the weaponization of communities, resourcing the chronic, recurring and endemic violence that reproduces perpetual conflict traps, gripping countries and entire regions in brutal poverty. While Collier refers to 'conflict traps' precisely because of the stranglehold they exert upon the economic development potential of whole countries and regions, undermining peace building operations, disrupting the supply of aid and making effective governance impossible, Bourne (2007) refers to 'conflict complexes' in order to draw particular attention to the structures, channels and processes by which regional weaponization takes place. As the Small Arms Survey (2002) has noted, firearm supplies need to be seen as an 'independent variable' in conflict zones, or 'situational facilitators' of a full spectrum of violence, from domestic abuse to gang violence and civil war.

The best available, most reliable, research evidence tends to suggest a figure of around 200,000 homicides each year resulting directly from firearm misuse outside of warfare and militarized conflict (Cukier and Sidel, 2006; Jackson and Marsh, 2012). The figure has a history and (in keeping with a large majority of the empirical evidence on the 'consequences of firearms proliferation') is contested, for example, by US firearm advocates Kopel *et al.* (2003, 2010). In 2004 these authors took the 200,000 figure to task, producing a much lower estimate of their own, although basing their estimates on limited sources of information[6], in 2010 they took as their target the higher figure of 740,000 annual deaths reported in the 2008 Geneva Declaration, *The Global Burden of Armed Violence* (Small Arms Survey, 2008). This report makes it clear, however, that the figure, 740,000 deaths, comprised both direct militarized killings, criminal homicides and indirect conflict deaths arising from the famine and disease frequently associated with violent conflict. Furthermore, the figure also recognizes that war, civil war and conflict represent *extremely* crimogenic conditions by virtue of the wider offences and harms that they encourage or facilitate: robbery, revenge, sexual abuse or sadism: 'if only due to the frequent absence of effective law enforcement' (Kreutz and Marsh, 2012: 47). Casualties arising from such behaviours may not be calculated as conflict deaths or injuries.

Amongst the wider indirect casualties of small arms proliferation are

> the displacement of civilians; the militarization of refugee camps; the erosion of sustainable development; the restriction of access to health services, education, and food security; land denial; contributing to obstructions in humanitarian assistance, as well as the use of these weapons to threaten the lives and well-being of humanitarian, development and health workers ... [Furthermore] hundreds of thousands of people survive armed violence with injuries, permanent disability and mental health problems.
>
> *(Buchanan, 2004: 2)*

And, while not overlooking the involvement of 'child soldiers' (or adolescent gang members) in a great deal of the global small arms violence (Bellos, 2003; Dowdney, 2003; Honwana, 2006; Wessells, 2006;), young men being typically both the perpetrators and the most frequent victims of gun violence, the prevalence of armed young men invariably poses major threats to gender relations and the safety of women and children. As Honwana remarks, violent social conflict means that 'social order is almost entirely disrupted, and defenceless civilians, especially women, children and the elderly are particularly vulnerable' (Honwana, 2006: 1).

For purposes of comparison, the 2011 Geneva Declaration report (Small Arms Survey, 2011) suggested a lower figure of 526,000 direct and indirect deaths, comprising organized and collective violence and criminal and interpersonal violence (not that these categories are absolutely watertight). The 2008 report also argued that a majority of killings occur outside of militarized conflict settings (war zones) and that 396,000 of the total number of killings represent 'intentional homicides' some 60 per cent of these committed with firearms (Small Arms Survey, 2008: 5) ranging from as much as 77 per cent in Latin America to as few as 19 per cent in western Europe.

Civilizing and weaponizing?

Stephen Pinker's much lauded recent book, *The Better Angels of our Nature* (2011) strays, perhaps inadvertently, into this very dispute. Pinker's primary aim appears to be to establish the truth of Norbert Elias's thesis on the 'civilizing process' (Elias, 1939) and, in particular, to show that rates of interpersonal violence, homicide and brutality correspond to a historically progressive downward sweep over many centuries (from the thirteenth to the twentieth century). The evidence, meticulously compiled by Gurr (1981, 1989) relating, respectively, to England, Europe and America, confounds, according to Pinker, 'every stereotype about the idyllic past and the degenerate present' (Pinker, 2011: 72). Pinker develops his case, specifically about the decline and marginalization of European violence, in relation to both psychological changes and state formation which, he argues, complemented and reinforced one another (2011: 93). A similar process, he contends is observable in the settled, north-eastern seaboard of the USA. In the lawless American West, by contrast, 'annual homicide rates were fifty to several hundred times higher than those of eastern cities or midwestern farming regions' (2011: 122). And, he continues: 'The causes were right out of Hobbes. The criminal justice system was underfunded, inept and often corrupt' (2011: 123). Nevertheless, even the 'wild west' was tamed, not so much by 'flinty-eyed marshals and hanging judges' but by an 'influx of women' (2011: 125–126).

Yet civilizing processes were neither uniform nor necessarily one-directional around the world, places 'civilized' at different times, and speeds, adopted different routes and sometimes turned back upon themselves. Fletcher (1997), for instance, identifies aspects of a 'de-civilizing' process in Elias's work centred upon the world wars and genocides of the twentieth century, and Rodger (2012) connects the question of 'de-civilization' to Wacquant's work on 'advanced marginality' and the new 'urban outcasts' (Wacquant, 2008a, 2009; Squires and Lea, 2012a). Further, Muchembled (2012), in the final chapter of his sweeping account of violence and pacification, ominously titled 'the return of the gangs', points to old inequalities and new disequilibriums through which globalized patterns of violence are sustained; Bauman (1989) goes even further, describing the 'civilization thesis' as one of the myths of modernity. Pinker himself, carefully selecting the data for each stage of his magnum opus, even admits of elements of a *de*-civilizing turn in the developed western world in the aftermath of WW2 and the social and cultural revolutions that followed, developments that often become conflated with the 'sixties counter-culture'. Many recent conservative-leaning politicians, commentators and social scientists have also repeatedly defined the 'liberal' sixties, with their alleged permissiveness; the supposed sexual revolution; the championing of social and civil rights; broadly interpreted 'anything goes' behavioural freedoms and implied 'loosening' of personal moralities, as the seedbed of many of our contemporary crime and disorder problems (Newburn, 1991). This 'demoralization thesis' (Himmelfarb, 1996) is closely associated with the rightwards shift in politics characterizing the 1970s (Hall and Jacques, 1983) where (in the UK especially) resorting to old-fashioned 'Victorian values' was deemed necessary to stop the rot of moral relativism and the allegedly impoverishing and dependency creating consequences of supposedly 'over-generous' welfare programmes.

While accepting that the origins of America's contemporary 'culture war' had its roots in the 1960s (see also Melzer, 2009; Sandbrook, 2011), Pinker allies himself with a number of neo-liberal, essentially conservative-individualist commentators advocating a new rationalist common-sense of free-markets, low taxation, flexible labour, limited and conditional welfare (and later workfare), zero-tolerance of delinquency, disorder and incivility, personal responsibility, strong law and order and tough punishment. For Pinker, these elements of the neo-liberal political turn were the essential building blocks of a new, *re*-civilizing phase of history making itself apparent from the early 1990s. Correspondingly, recorded violent crime, including gun violence, appeared to peak in 1993, in both the USA and the UK. From this date overall violent crime and gun crime rates (with just a few exceptions) have tended to track downwards; criminologists have generally not disputed this as a phenomenon but have mostly confined themselves to arguing about its causes (Blumstein and Wallman, 2000; Zimring, 2007; Van Dijk *et al.*, 2012). However, underpinning all of these generic political discourses in the USA was an implicit politics of race (Miller, 2008; Tonry, 2011), also factored into this picture (*especially* in the USA, but by no means only there) was a resurgent politics of fear, firearms and self-determination. Many of these issues are developed further in later chapters of the book.

Melzer (2009), for example, describes the conservative social movement for gun rights – white, middle class and middle aged – as embracing the culturally and historically specific form of 'frontier masculinity' but it was a social movement that is no less 'modern' for all that. For whereas Pinker has argued that the eventual 'peaceful triumph' of the west had derived from its ability to banish violence beyond its frontiers, social and economic changes in late modern America began to establish and reproduce domestic and internal frontiers in its inner cities, ghettos and hyper-ghettos, and across racial, ethnic and cultural divides, as newer forms of precarious life (Standing, 2011) or 'advanced marginality' (Wacquant, 2008a, 2009; Squires and Lea, 2012a) began to manifest themselves. Around the world the 'older inequalities and newer disequilibriums' depicted by Muchembled 2012, accelerated by rapid social changes in countries and regions as diverse as Latin America, South and Central Africa, eastern Europe and the 'Middle-East', continued to generate conflict, acting as magnets for illegal weapon trafficking, sources of political instability and catalysts of organized crime, terrorism, gangs and warlordism.

These new frontiers, domestic and foreign, served two purposes: on the one hand they drove the firearm economy, generating a demand for weapons, both legal and illegal. They became the test beds of a new armed and dangerous individualism where a new breed of modern necessity became the foundation for a new human right – self-defence. Weapons would become a currency in these conflicted regions, the price of weapons representing an index of social and political instability (Carr, 2008; Collier, 2009; Small Arms Survey, 2007, 2010). This was not so much a case of 'have gun will travel' in the older American idiom, but rather 'have gun, might survive'. The dark and dangerous, hostile, world that these conflict zones and trouble spots came to represent, nightmares to our safe European home, demanded an essential weaponization of the self and the culture, an enhancement of human capacity and the new values and outlooks to accompany and support it. On the other hand, while this weaponization of the self and the social became a direct driver of firearm production and distribution, the fear of these conditions and a strongly allied desire to keep them at bay, to restrict them to the margins and beyond the frontiers translated into effective advertising copy (de facto neo-liberal political propaganda) for the domestic firearm industries. In simple NRA speak, when guns are everywhere and the 'bad guys' are tooling up, common sense dictates you – the 'good guys' – do likewise. The world's conflict zones and their violent criminal 'hotspots', with their darker, dusty-skinned and invariably heavily armed occupants become variants of the 'universal other' against whom a defence must be maintained. In this contemporary, racialized neo-liberalism, class, race, corporation, culture, self and society coincide: all are now armed. This is the real, contemporary meaning of SALW proliferation in our culture: the gun as metaphor, facilitator, tool, currency, threat, solution, icon and life preserver comes of age.

With the exception of a short discussion of Weissner's anthropological study (2006) of the impact of weaponization on the indigenous peoples of New Guinea, Pinker scarcely engages specifically in the discussion of contemporary global small arms proliferation and its consequences. He notes the phenomenon described by other quantitative scholars of international violence trends (LaFree and Tseloni, 2006) or development studies (Collier, 2009) that 'transitional democracies' (it appears to matter less what the society may be transitioning from: apartheid, colonialism, dictatorship, communism or primitive accumulation) appear to be the most murderously unstable, and most prone to violent crime, corruption, terrorism and disorders up to and including civil wars. With the weakening of older forms of social order and copious supplies of weapons, potentially unrealistic aspirations about what the new democracies might deliver often outrun commitments to democratic processes and institutions (such as human rights). And as we shall see later, highly weaponized cultures typically have profound consequences for gender relations (Cukier, 2002; Farr et al., 2009). Aside from a brief mention of these dilemmas of democratization in the world's most dangerous places, Pinker avoids engaging with the hard to calculate death and violence rates in failed and failing states and bases his civilization argument, instead, upon violence trends in developed and democratic societies or wars between them. This, as the SALW analysts have already told us (Cukier and Sidel, 2006; Small Arms Survey, 2011; Jackson and Marsh, 2012; Kreuzt and Marsh, 2012), is barely half of the story. As Newman has argued, while more quantitatively minded scholars may have concluded that there have been significant global declines in violence levels since the ending of the Cold War, 'there is less room for optimism about other forms of low-intensity conflict and serious violence which falls outside conventional definitions of civil war' (Newman, 2009: 256). Accordingly, attention must return to the proliferation of weapons beyond the state and into the hands of private individuals, whether these are, in NRA speak, 'good' guys or 'bad' guys.

The chief reason for US firearm advocates' discontent with annual armed violence death rate calculations lay in their argument that the supposedly inaccurate and inflated figures served as 'the empirical foundation of the push to ratify an Arms Trade Treaty' (Kopel *et al.*, 2010: 676). Firearm rights advocates in the USA have tended to view the proposed UN Programme of Action (PoA) on SALW, subsequently the Arms Trade Treaty (ATT), as a generalized proposal for global civilian disarmament and, ultimately, as a threat to the USA Second Amendment's presumed 'right to bear arms'. Such claims are manifestly false; I discuss them in greater depth in Chapter 8. However, prominent NRA spokesmen and activists have rallied to the cause, describing the ATT as a UN conspiracy to institute a 'global gun ban' (La Pierre, 2006), their chief complaint turning on the fact that the Obama administration, following the presidential election of 2008, and in marked contrast to the preceding Bush administration, had committed the USA to participate constructively in the ATT negotiations as opposed to obstructing them at every turn. Unhappy with the progress made during the UN sessions in New York, gun rights advocates have sought to undermine (albeit rather tediously and unsuccessfully) the evidence base upon which the case for controlling the illegal trafficking, transfer and stockpiling of SALW has been based. Disputing the scale and nature of the global problem of firearm-related violence is, to firearm advocates, a necessary first step in resisting the case for 'gun control', although Kopel and his colleagues had it in mind to go rather further than query evidence. Their broader argument, developed in a different article (Kopel *et al.*, 2008) is that gun control – or, in the case of the UN initiative about which they are concerned – 'gun confiscation', can itself amount to a human rights abuse. The implied corollary, although sometimes, in unguarded moments, it is also *explicitly* stated by firearm rights advocates, suggests that unrestricted firearm proliferation – 'an assault weapon in every home' – is the best guarantee of personal security and human freedom.

Another commentator (Smith, 2006) has drawn upon the civilization thesis in a discussion of attitudes to guns and gun control in the UK, although the implications of his argument are truly global. Smith suggests that in the face of gun control initiatives in the UK, reaching back to the early twentieth century, firearm ownership has become subject to a process of 'sportization' (2006: 720). This process is both reflected in the way the shooting lobby represents itself and has become central to the ways in which modern firearm possession is rendered legitimate in a civilized society. The process is in part a deliberate tactic of lobbyist positioning and the attempt to ideologically 'sanitize' (McCarthy, 2009, 2011: 320) firearms from criminal violence (one of the reasons the field sports shooters found it easy to drop the handgun shooters after Dunblane) and partly a political consequence of the practical and institutional development of shooting (around leisure interests, game shooting, target shooting). Sanitizing shooting has taken many forms; it is akin to the civilization process described by Garland (2005, 2010) in respect of the death penalty in the USA. The ultimate punishment was retained even though many of its apparently cruel and gratuitous features (publicity, pain, disfigurement, arbitrariness) were supposedly removed. In the case of British shooting, humanoid targets were replaced, sports competitors were discouraged from dressing in military surplus and camouflage gear and, as Smith has noted, there are even occasional calls from members of the Clay Pigeon Shooting Association to drop the word 'pigeon' from the organization's name; 'killing even a *symbolic* pigeon' (Smith, 2004) is a trigger pull too far for some.

Smith's account, however, is only partially correct in depicting a 'sportization' shift in British shooting activities. As I show later in Chapter 8, offered the chance, after 2001, to detach their sporting interests from the violence legacy associated with global firearm proliferation, British shooting interests, and no doubt badgered by their American fellows at a World Federation of Sports Shooting Activities meeting in London, circled their wagons around a defence of combat handguns and semi-automatic assault rifles as 'sporting' weapons. The only SALWs they excluded from the 'sport firearms' category were fully automatic machine guns. 'Sporting purpose' has often been something of a flag of convenience for some gun owners whose motives might suggest a little more ambiguity in practice (Squires, 2000). The same ambiguity might be displayed in magazines and periodicals designed for the 'sports shooter'; it is not uncommon to see articles or legal advice directed at the 'sporting gun owner' regarding self-defence, reasonable force and confronting burglars[7], while shooting's more political representatives occasionally surface in debates about reforming the law on self-defence, as in the periodic efforts to revive interest in the UK in a supposed 'householder protection' bill, a distant shadow of US 'Castle Doctrine' laws. Nevertheless, one can appreciate the anger and frustration of sports shooters when their hobby of choice is forever dragged back to the bloody scene of the crime by strange, deranged or lonely men 'with a passion for guns' (Collier, 1998). Most of the time shooting lobby commentators are keen to erect watertight categories between 'good' and 'bad', or safe and responsible gun ownership and the homicidal misuse of illegal firearms in the inner cities (Smith, 2006: 729). Currie has already referred to this as a peculiarly 'myopic' viewpoint afflicting contemporary thinking about crime and violence (Currie, 2005: 8); I will develop a critique of this myopia in subsequent chapters.

However, in Smith's discussion of the 'spectre of violence' hovering behind gun ownership, notwithstanding the firearm lobby's rather chequered attempts to exorcise it, we might find a broader recognition of the multiplex power of the gun. After every shooting, after every heroic rescue by armed law enforcement, after every military encounter and, especially, as these are replayed (as both fact and fiction) across a variety of media where gallant cowboys, cops or soldiers fight the good fight with their weapons, the power of the gun is vindicated. Kantola *et al.* (2011) make a similar point regarding 'armed masculinity' and redemption as the good guys (the police) intervene to restore the order and security that the 'bad guys' have imperilled. But this power of the gun transcends the merely *legal* status of the weapons: we know very well that 'those without access to … weapons (the 'unarmed') are forced to cede a potentially very unequal power ratio to those who do' (Smith, 2006: 728). Springwood, likewise, refers to the 'seductive transformation that a body, grasping and shooting a gun, undergoes' (2007a: 3). And, as McCarthy concedes, 'guns are empowering when possessed … guns permit their owners a sense of uniqueness and individuation … they are the ultimate extension of self' (McCarthy, 2011: 321). That, of course, will be true 'whether firearms are held legally or illegally … guns are guns' (Smith, 2006: 728). This may all be an unfortunate by-product of the violent legacies to which firearms are tied and about which we are daily reminded, or it might be a more psycho-social and political calculation. We know what a person with a gun can do, we know they become powerful. In the risk society, this might be associated with the idea that gun owners represent additional dangers or that they cannot be trusted.[8] In its turn, this way of thinking might contribute towards the development of especially exacting (high) standards of responsibility and accountability for regulating firearm ownership but, prior to this, it also has a wider global and analytical resonance in acknowledging firearm ownership as a critical social relation; the gun as an aspect of human capacity, weaponization as selective human empowerment. I return to these issues, realist dilemmas of the gun, throughout the book and by way of conclusion.

History, philosophy and an ethic of armed citizenship

The philosophical ideas underpinning claims about self-defence, security and individual rights seldom engage directly with these 'realist dilemmas' of weaponization and instead they reach backwards to the political theory of John Locke, conceptions of the 'state of nature' and 'natural rights'. There is an obvious historical connection between notions of the 'state of nature' and contemporary myths of the American frontier (Slotkin, 1973, 1992), the conditions that prevailed there and the conception of 'frontier masculinity' (Melzer, 2009) considered necessary to survival prior to the coming of civilization and the law. A good deal of US culture has continued to celebrate this vision of American history; taming the frontier, 'winning' the west and making the man. Subsequently, Hollywood turned its approving lens on this phase of US history, and tall, vigilant cowboys stalked our TV screens, bringing justice through superior firepower, followed later by subsequent genres of cop, war and crime-fighting heroes (Gibson, 1994). There is, as Jeffords (1989) has argued, no surprise that in later years as the US looked to address the criminal and military problems confronting it on all sides, and as newly contested frontiers open up at its own borders and even in its own cities[9], it turned to cultural role models steeped in tough and resourceful maverick masculinity. After all, the frontier was the state of nature where a war of 'all against all' might prevail and therefore, as Brown has argued, in the last resort, the frontiersman needed his gun (Brown, 1975, 1991). Society may have changed in the intervening years but gun rights activists stand firm on two principles: in the first place asserting a simple right of personal (and familial) self-defence against personal aggression (shooting criminals); and, in the second place, they assert a right of armed resistance against political tyranny and the Government they distrust (shooting hostile enemies – British 'redcoats' in the eighteenth century, troops of a foreign power or even the agents of an over-zealous Federal Government, more recently).[10] That said, many felt that NRA leaders had gone too far in the 1990s when it referred to Federal Agents of the Bureau of Alcohol, Tobacco, Firearms and Explosives (ATF) as 'jack-booted government thugs' (Anderson, 1996). The NRA later apologized, even though the logical consequence of their underlying political philosophy would necessarily pit the firepower of free individuals against the might of an overbearing, distrusted state. In one sense this helps explain the enthusiasm for 'assault weapons' amongst US gun advocates. On the one hand, criminals have obtained them and, on the other, state agents (police and federal agencies) are certainly issued with them. Accordingly, free individuals certainly feel the need to be as well armed as their potential opponents and, in any event, this is precisely what *their* strict reading of the US Second Amendment guarantees.

Unfortunately, the flaws in the natural rights philosophy lying behind this vision of a seemingly defeatist, self-defensive, republican libertarianism are not unlike the weaknesses exposed by Nozick (1974) in relation to social contract theory's advance from the state of nature. On the one hand, powerful states exist and modern societies have developed far more effective, peaceful and, ultimately, more productive means of negotiating with and within them, than by effectively 'declaring war' on every occasion they overstep their perceived authority. Second, just as successful entrepreneurs, starting out as small craftsmen producers, may amass wealth that far exceeds the stock of other entrepreneurs, eventually compelling the smaller craftsmen to work for the larger, so a parallel accumulation of weapon power might similarly undermine the sovereignty of free individuals. Finally, where large enterprises come to act malevolently, utilizing their accumulated weapon power for criminal or exploitative purposes, a disparate mass of individual gun owners is unlikely to provide effective resistance. It may be a comforting historical myth that the 'Minutemen' and informal militias were the key to the American colonists' victory in the US War of Independence, but it is some way from the truth (Brown, 1981) as even contemporaries George Washington and Samuel Adams appeared to acknowledge: the continental army rather than citizen militias made the decisive difference (Wills, 2002).

Despite such philosophical flaws and historical inaccuracies, this ethic of universal firearm ownership, of personal empowerment for self-defence and freedom, the foundation stone upon which all other human rights are supposed to rest (Malcolm, 1994), is firmly rooted in a political philosophy of western neo-liberalism. In that respect, the aims of this book might be further developed: in one sense it seeks to chart the proliferation of SALW around the globe as part of an ethic of neo-liberal governance in which firearms are both practical and symbolic facilitators of a version of competitive individualism; in another sense the book will seek to explore the ways in which the philosophy and ethics of neo-liberalism establish the ideological framework for an ethic of armed citizenship.

The notion of armed citizenship will be explored in relation to ideas about justice, crime and safety. One theme that does emerge concerns the relationships between fear of crime, the rise of populist punitiveness and personal self-defence. The demand for personal defence firearms arises especially where citizens fear crime and disorder (and do not trust strangers) but lack faith in the capacity of government to offer protection (McDowell and Loftin, 1983; Carlson, 2012). That said, as we shall see, tolerant attitudes towards crime, disorder and 'otherness' stand counterposed to more intolerant and punitive viewpoints and are generally more pronounced in societies that are less unequal (Wilkinson and Pickett, 2010). It follows, therefore, that more unequal societies generally exhibit less tolerance, but greater fear, and they harbour more punitive attitudes and personal enmities, while cultivating less trust and confidence in government and, accordingly, generating greater demands for self-defensive firearms. In turn, a proliferation of firearms is likely to accelerate rates of criminal violence. It is important to be clear at this point. It is not being claimed here that simple numbers of firearms, *alone*, produce higher rates of gun violence (although, all other things being equal, it is certainly probable that where there are more firearms there will be more firearm injuries and deaths[11]; just as it is likely that some proportion of any given demand for firearm ownership is likely to be dubiously motivated), rather, the point is that the factors to which gun ownership is often a response (inequalities and social divisions, fear of crime, intolerance and punitive attitudes, personal enmities and distrust of strangers) are themselves likely to intensify the criminal risk posed by a given firearm stock. And in these kinds of cultures, as we have seen, firearms are both powerful and purposive signifiers while also helping realize a sovereign capacity associated with neo-liberal individualism; enabling particular forms of (legal and illegal) human action. Thus, when guns are associated with a particular kind of 'gun culture', criminal problems are likely to follow. On the contrary, when a gun culture is of a particularly 'elite' character, such as is associated with Scotland and the 'Glorious Twelfth', the greatest risks are likely to be run by the unfortunate grouse (but that is another story). With this in mind, the book will be concerned with relating the changing patterns of firearm distribution to changing political cultures, popular attitudes, crime trends and political instabilities.

A more general objective of the book is to assess the consequences of the global proliferation of firearms and gun ownership 'regimes' and the 'gun crimes' that are facilitated or, perhaps, prevented. These consequences are explored in the safe European homelands of Britain and northern Europe; in the cauldron of neo-liberal gun rights advocacy, the USA, where many people – although by no means all, or even necessarily a majority – subscribe to an equation that guns ownership equals freedom; and in the wider world of developed, developing and underdeveloped societies, where guns often wreak havoc and condemn many of the poorest people on the planet to unrelenting cycles of poverty and conflict (Collier, 2008). Here gun ownership may help some people feel safer, defended and even 'more free' (although one would have to ask, 'from what?'). For, just as arming the *powerless* might provide them with a certain self-defensive capacity (the Colt '45, from the days of the 'old West' as 'Equalizer', or 'Peacemaker' springs to mind), firearm proliferation seems just as likely to embolden the powerful, violent and aggressive. As we have already seen, this is the fatal flaw in much of the gun rights libertarian-ism discussed already. Any culture that permits widespread firearm ownership and possession can expect there to be a large illegal weapons pool, easily available to the criminally inclined. While there is an 'infamous', even oxymoronic, NRA bumper sticker which asserts 'If guns are outlawed, only outlaws will have guns', it is no less true that where guns are not outlawed (or controlled), the aggressive, violent and disreputable, the mentally ill, convicted felons, organized criminals, gangsters and terrorists are likely to be even better armed and equipped.

In that sense, one issue taken up by the book comprises the attempt to bring together two strands of political discourse that constantly weave themselves around one another but, for the most part, fail to engage directly. For instance, in much academic scholarship on the US Second Amendment, perhaps the foremost and probably the best-known statement of armed citizenship,[12] essentially philosophi-cal, legal and juridical, claims are made about what the Second Amendment *really* means and what the 'Founding Fathers' *really* intended, although these discussions seldom engage directly with the more empirical consequences of widespread fire-arm ownership (the uses and misuses to which firearms are actually put) or the cultural experiences that are entailed when living in communities where firearms are prevalent. These latter questions are more generally the terrain of social sci-ence (sociology, criminology and ethnography), and while they *might* contribute to improved public safety policy-making (Cook and Ludwig, 2004; Hemenway, 2004; Webster and Vernick, 2013), as indeed the 'common-sense gun laws' initia-tive of the Obama administration attempted, the US gun debate really does define the limit of positivism. Even in a social scientific culture where positivism appar-ently reigns supreme, evidence is not allowed to trump ideology. On the other hand, it is true, there have been a number of speculative, flawed and, sometimes, downright unscrupulous attempts to show that what the 'Founding Fathers' sup-posedly intended – citizenship coterminous with gun ownership – does contribute to improving public safety but, for a variety of methodological or analytical reasons (here one thinks of the 'defensive gun use' debate, or the 'more guns, less crime' controversy, both of which I consider later in the book), the results seldom stand up to scrutiny. A still wider peculiarity of the US gun control debate (although it is not unknown elsewhere) concerns the tendency of the political allies and representatives of gun lobbyists to do everything in their power to weaken and undermine gun control legislation as it is being formulated, then subsequently complain that it does not 'work'. The US gun control debate is a prime example of David Garland's astute observation (2001a: 26) that 'crime control strategies are not adopted because they are known to work'. Instead they are the outcome of politi-cal horse-trading, the competition of vested interests, often ill-informed, media-led public preferences, deep-rooted political ideologies and personal convictions, con-temporary moral panics, popular fears and even relentless advertising and political propaganda. The late swing in voting intentions that altered the outcome of 2005

Brazilian referendum on firearms controls might be a case in point. NRA money and advertising know-how, late entrants to the debate, swung the result, seemingly convincing the fearful middle classes that they had a lot to lose if they gave up their guns (Goldstein, 2007a; Cavalcanti, 2013).

Yet in attempting to bring together the political and philosophical discourses on firearm ownership and findings from empirical social science research, the purpose of this book is analysis not prescription. The book does not have a policy to promote; its main aim is to explore the ways in which neo-liberalism provides an accommodating political climate for widespread gun ownership – weapon proliferation – and how weapon proliferation serves to accelerate neo-liberaliz*ation*, at the same time as it exposes inherent flaws and tensions in this mode of governance. At the same time, and just as the book will draw upon some recent developments in both cultural and 'regime' change theories (Esping-Anderson, 1990; Garland, 2001a; Cavadino and Dignan, 2006; Wacquant, 2009), so it will also be at pains to argue that weapon proliferation alone is not the only relevant cause of gun violence. Indeed, as I shall argue, while there is compelling evidence to show that the more extensive firearms ownership is, or the higher proportion of gun owners there are in a given population, the more frequent firearm misuse will be, a number of important social and cultural factors have an important influence on rates of firearm violence. These same factors also shape how different forms of gun violence are perceived (for example, in the hermetically sealed mindset of the NRA leadership, 'good guys' shooting 'bad guys' is a far less troubling phenomenon, than 'bad guys' shooting 'good guys', but in the real world those conceptions of good and bad may be far less hard and fast). Contrary, again, to the alleged wisdom of an NRA bumper sticker – or Alan Ladd in the 1953 film *Shane* – a gun is not *just* a tool, and it comes loaded with far more than bullets (Springwood, 2007). As McCarthy remarks, 'there is magic, mystery and meaning residing in guns … craftsmanship honed with measured singular purpose, however its use and misuse have elevated this machine to almost mythical status' (2011: 321). Firearms, their ownership, possession, display and use, embody many attributes and values; they are associated with manliness, frontier spirit, rugged independence, freedom, discipline yet self-determination, power and authority (Harcourt, 2006; Melzer, 2009). These are often precisely the attributes drawn upon in firearms industry marketing; values and qualities are even attributed to particular weapons. For example, in 2010 a Bushmaster Firearms advertisement accompanied a photograph of their .223 semi-automatic, assault-style rifle pointing menacingly outwards from the page with the caption '**CONSIDER YOUR MAN CARD RE-ISSUED**' (Waldman, 2012b). Bushmaster assault weapons had, apparently, been employed in at least four rampage killing incidents since 1999 and, after the Sandy Hook, Connecticut, school shooting in December 2012, the company were pressured to withdraw their advertisement.

The reference to both 'cultural' and 'regime' issues and changes represents an attempt to connect the explanation developed in this book to recent attempts to theorize and explain changing criminal justice cultures, policy discourses and forms of governmental intervention. Debate about firearms in society, and the consequences of weaponization, may not be exclusively related to questions of crime and justice, accordingly criminology may not be the only – or even the primary – academic discourse to be brought to bear upon firearm proliferation (in a more global context, international relations, war studies or peace and development studies may well have more to offer – as we shall see later). However, for the moment the close connections between conceptions of gun ownership and social order (deterrence and self-defence), gun misuse and criminal violence, gun control and crime prevention, firearm proliferation and illegal trafficking, amongst others, do give criminology some important traction on the gun question – if not the only relevant perspective. So, in view of the practical centrality of 'the gun question' to much of the core content of applied sociological criminology, I will begin by exploring some important parallels between firearm rights and wrongs in sociology and criminology and the articulation of contrasting 'regimes' and 'regime' and 'cultural changes' in criminal justice policies and politics.

Process questions and 'regime' issues

In an important contribution to understanding the social processes and mechanisms by which social order degenerates into violence and disorder, American criminologist Elliott Currie has outlined what he refers to as a 'mid-range theory of post-industrial violence' (Currie, 1997). He subsequently developed this analysis in a short book attempting to set 'violent crime' in a 'global perspective', a work that is very much a precursor to the analysis developed here (Currie, 2005). There are some similarities with the better known, much travelled 'Broken Windows' theory of Wilson and Kelling (1982) except that the latter theory tended to imply that communities break down (degenerate or implode) as a result of social forces peculiar to themselves and their populations. This implies they, largely, have only themselves to blame, that the forces of decay are there, already, waiting in the wings, to overrun the ever diminishing, watchful forces of decent resilience. In short, urban decline is the fault of the urban poor; they alone are responsible for the violent mess they have made for themselves. We have, of course, heard this all before, the story lies at the heart of many classic 'blaming the victim' or 'bashing the poor' narratives of welfare dependency cultures reaching back well before the nineteenth century, although these ideas certainly assumed their modern form in the early nineteenth century (Golding and Middleton, 1982; Taylor-Gooby and Dean, 1992). Currie's account, by contrast, emphasizes the structural pressures external to the community; communities do not degenerate under their own steam, they are broken down from the outside, typically by forces beyond their control. The process often entails that, political or economic, decisions have been explicitly taken or priorities set. The importance of this observation lies in the recognition that so-called 'regeneration strategies' focussing primarily upon the perceived personal and social deficiencies of communities themselves will be unlikely to succeed (Loney, 1983; Flint and Robinson, 2008).

The first dimension to Currie's conception of 'post-industrial violence' entailed the 'progressive destruction of livelihood', in particular the loss of mainstream jobs and employment opportunities as industries closed and would-be investors went in search of cheaper or more flexible labour supplies. This invariably leads to a second phenomenon, 'the growth of extremes of inequality and material deprivation'. Reflecting these processes, the rhetoric of 'fiscal crisis' or 'austerity' and 'overspent' or 'over-generous' welfare budgets provides political cover for and contributes to an incremental 'withdrawal of public services and supports', although ultimately these are political decisions. Aside from the direct consequences of inequality and deprivation, a growing distinction between 'haves' and 'have-nots' encourages the growth of divisive and discriminatory attitudes and social distinctions (in the USA, especially, racialized divisions) prompting the strain and envy that often accompanies perceptions of undeserved relative deprivation (Webber, 2007). In turn, as Currie argues, the new attitudes and, especially, the spread of an increasingly individualized and 'materialistic and neglectful' culture, part of what Harvey describes as a new neo-liberal common sense (Harvey, 2005: 3), locates the primary responsibility for poverty with the poor themselves (their lack of effort, skills, employability, or – the latest – magic ingredient of successful self-promotion, 'social capital' or 'resilience') while serving to corrode any emerging informal networks of mutual support. Networks of mutual support in poor communities often entail illegalities (which attract often disproportionate policing attentions). Economic activities that are 'off the books' (Venkatesh, 2006), or networks in contraband goods and services, represent forms of 'social crime' (Lea, 1999) in which people sell what they can, not what is necessarily legal. These activities are often supplemented by unreliable, often highly conditional and scrupulously policed (in marked contrast to tax frauds) welfare claims (Bryson and Jacobs, 1992; Gustafson, 2011). In the American context, Currie continues, another factor 'the deregulation of the technology of violence' or 'easy access to firearms', personal and community weaponization, has added ever further dangers to these marginal criminal economies that are policed internally by violence and hierarchies of status and respect (Short, 1997; Bourgois, 2003; Mullins, 2006) and externally by often heavy-handed policing interventions fighting the war on drugs, the war on gangs or the war on crime (Kraska and Kappeler, 1997; Balko, 2006). Currie's final observation acknowledges the fact that, in such de-stabilized communities, so much time and effort is devoted to day-to-day crisis management that there is no scope for the development of more strategic social and political alternatives (Currie, 1997; Kennedy, 2011).

Currie's theory of 'post-industrial violence' depicts the rise of violence as a consequence of increasing disorder occasioned by social and economic decline, rising inequality and state withdrawal – or the failure to deliver needed social and infrastructure services and supports. It sets the outcome, violence, as the culmination of a process of compounded social decline. As the social infrastructure of the society changes so, likewise, do its essential qualities and characteristics. Currie gives us a theory that not only shows how this process of social change works dynamically, he also demonstrates how each stage of the process might be associated with different social and personal characteristics, value systems, attitudes and beliefs. People may be more or less socially minded, or more selfish. They might be welcoming of strangers or fearful, guarded and defensive: they might pity the poor or condemn them; seek to rehabilitate and reintegrate offenders or brand them indelibly with the mark of the delinquent. Social institutions, similarly, might be inclusive, generous and universal, in their service and coverage, premised upon concepts of right, or punitive, stigmatizing and selective, grudgingly allocating the bare minimum (or maybe less) according to the achievement of certain demeaning behavioural requirements.

On a more general scale, Wacquant's study *Punishing the Poor* (2009), subtitled the 'neoliberal government of social insecurity' has sought to depict these transitions in the US governance of welfare and order in the decades at the end of the twentieth century. There are undoubtedly debates about the extent to which Wacquant's model 'fits' or 'explains' developments in a range of other societies (see Lacey, 2008; Nelken, 2010; Squires and Lea 2012b) or, indeed, how well it translates to other cultures (something I will discuss later). Nevertheless, in broad terms, Wacquant traces the shift, in the USA, from an incomplete US 'welfare state' to the 'workfare state' and, finally, to what he calls a 'prisonfare' state, in which a substantial part of the life-world and experiences of the poorest sections of society (inner city African–American populations in particular) are determined by the criminal justice and correctional system. As Tonry (2011: ix) has confirmed,

> American drug and crime control policies since the mid-1970s have disabled poor young black men from successful participation in American life and thereby damaged not only them, but also their children, their families and their communities ... one in three black baby boys born in 2001 will spend part of his life as an inmate of a state or federal prison. At any time in the first decade of the twenty-first century one third of young black men in their twenties were in jail or prison or on probation or parole.

In short, young black men appeared more likely to spend time in the criminal justice and correctional systems than in higher education, while the coming of mass incarceration in the final decades of the twentieth century significantly expanded racial inequalities in the USA (Justice Policy Institute, 2002; Western, 2002: 542).

Wacquant also adopts the metaphor of a benevolent and caring 'left hand' of the state counterposed to the harsh and more punitive, authoritarian 'right hand'. The final decades of the twentieth century, he has argued, have witnessed a rolling back of the nurturing 'left hand' welfare functions and a corresponding rolling out of the more punitive features. This is not a change in the scale of governance, but rather in its nature, content and consequences or 'government through crime' in Simon's telling phrase (Simon, 2007). Illustrating this change, the 2002 Justice Policy Institute report, cited above, recorded the state-by-state change, between 1985 and 2000, in funding on higher education as compared with spending on prisons. The rate of increase of the former was dwarfed by that of the latter, this evidence broadly corresponding with similar spending pattern shifts reported by Wacquant regarding corrections spending compared with welfare (Aid to Families with Dependent Children), food stamps and public housing (2009: 159–160). To this extent, Wacquant's work has broadly been seen as a contribution to a growing range of scholarship relating to the 'punitive turn' in penal systems and cultures (Pratt *et al.*, 2005; Pratt, 2011), the onset of mass incarceration (Garland, 2001b; Parenti, 1999; Drake, 2012), the neo-liberal transformation of criminal justice (Bell, 2011; Whitehead and Crawshaw, 2012) and accelerated patterns of criminalization (Healy, 2004; Scraton, 2007; Rodger, 2008; Squires, 2008b).

A variety of commentators (see Squires and Lea, 2012b) have grappled with Wacquant's depiction of the supposedly ambidextrous (left and right handed); or roll-out/roll-back; or free economy – strong state (Gamble, 1988); or even the two-faced 'Centaur' state ('liberal and permissive for the middle and upper classes, but disciplining and controlling for the poorest': Mayer, 2010: 94), but what they embrace in common is a profound politics of differentiation, an increasingly selective application of the power to criminalize, punish or exclude (Young, 1999; Cowling, 2012). But more than this, for the distinctions established stand in close relation to acknowledged social distinctions between rich/poor; white/black; citizen/alien – or, more colloquially, 'good guy'/'bad guy'. The language of 'strivers and skivers' adopted by the Conservative-led coalition in the UK, for instance, in justification of its austerity-led welfare cuts during 2010–2013 would be another case in point.

Campbell (2010: 60), developing Wacquant's analysis, describes the onset of this selective or discriminatory governance as comprising four features: (i) economic deregulation; (ii) welfare retraction and recomposition; (iii) an expanded and intrusive penal apparatus; and (iv) 'the development of the cultural trope of individual responsibility'. Furthermore, as Whitehead and Crawshaw (2012: 2) note, these structural characteristics of neo-liberalism are experienced as the regular common sense of daily life: deregulated markets and responsible individuals share common ideological cause in disavowing a responsibility for the poor, other than by way of disciplining them or punishing their transgressions. Economic deregulation and personal responsibility extend to civil society; good citizens share a duty to police the poor and augment the authority of law and property rights. Here, one might even go further, when Prime Minister Blair spoke of 'rebalancing' the criminal justice system in favour of the responsible 'law-abiding majority' (Tony Blair, cited in Tonry, 2010), he was simply nudging wider a gap between human rights and political realities. In due course Conservative leader David Cameron thrust caution to the wind by asserting, not unlike the USA 'Castle Doctrine' or 'Stand your Ground' laws, that the freedom of property owners consisted, ultimately, in the right to kill intruders; burglars apparently 'left their human rights at the door' (Prince and Whitehead, 2010). One American commentator, keen to find some vindication for the tough household defence strategies being adopted by a number of US states wrote, somewhat wishfully, of a 'worldwide popular revolt against proportionality in self-defence law', while concluding (apparently oblivious to the decade-long downwards trajectory of serious crime in most 'developed' societies) 'unless governments are willing and able to seriously reduce criminality, they can expect continued popular pressure to expand the permitted use of force in self-defence'. It is not hard to see where this is going, for *even if* crime rates were to fall, 'citizens' intuitions about the proper scope of self-defence [might] lead them to want to reform current law' (Lerner, 2006: 363). What else might be shaping *citizens' intuitions* is left unconsidered.

The key issue seems to be, some ideological creeds, in this case a kind of competitive individualism, given the right circumstances, opportunities and inducements, can effectively overwhelm others, becoming the new 'common sense'. When the economy is shedding 'surplus' labour, yet fiscal pressures are squeezing the welfare budget and neo-liberal discourses of individual responsibility filling the airwaves and transforming poverty into a personal moral failing, it becomes easier to view the poorest as an alien threat and their behaviour unacceptable. This is especially so when the poorest are themselves closely allied with groups long regarded with a combination of mistrust, fear and contempt, such as (in the USA) African–Americans, ghetto-dwellers and offenders. It then becomes just a small step to regard these groups as non-citizens, or even 'enemy-others' (Steinert, 2004), for whom public policies must be redesigned and about whom personal precautions must be taken. Whether, as a consequence, 'rolling out' or 'rolling back', including or excluding, extending welfare or expanding incarceration, public policy is intimately implicated in the governance and reproduction of social relations and the rearticulation of social values. Different forms of governance can achieve fundamentally different purposes.

These observations about the contrasting political purposes of public policies (and the social values they reflect or mobilize) take us some way back to a fundamental insight arising from the very 'golden age' of the 'welfare state'. In 1964, Richard Titmuss wrote,

> there is an assumption that the establishment of social welfare necessarily and inevitably contributes to the spread of humanism and the resolution of social injustice. The reverse can be true. Welfare can serve different masters. A multitude of sins may be committed in its appealing name … welfare may be used to narrow allegiances and not to diffuse them … what matters then, what indeed is fundamental to the health of welfare, is the objective to which its face is set: to universalise humanistic ethics and the social rights of citizenship or to divide, discriminate and compete.
>
> *(Titmuss, 1964, cited in Squires, 1990: 4)*

Titmuss employed this insight in developing his argument that there was not, in fact, one but three welfare states (Titmuss, 1963). Subsequent commentators, in the first place Frank Field (1981), extended Titmuss's *three* welfare states to five, comprising: the benefits welfare state; the tax allowance welfare state; the company welfare state; the inheritance welfare state; and the private market welfare state. The point about these differing 'welfare states' was that, to some degree, while they all existed simultaneously, at different times, people might transition between them depending upon the changing circumstances of their lives, furthermore some of these forms of 'state' were more dominant. Titmuss's original point was not just about the different ways in which the various layers of the 'welfare state' distributed income and opportunities (for example direct pension transfers to the elderly, or benefits for the unemployed compared with the role of offshore and overseas banking services in minimizing the exposure of the incomes of the rich and multinational companies to UK tax liabilities) he was also concerned (along with Marshall, 1963) in the *quality* of citizenship values embraced by and embedded in these various layers of the 'welfare state'. Titmuss's insight was not simply that the private market welfare state provided for its clients a much better standard of living than the benefits welfare state but that it also treated them rather better: furthermore, services exclusively *for* the poor, tended to become *poor services*.

In time, policy analysts have developed this exploration of welfare states, drawing attention to the different characteristics of contrasting welfare 'regimes'. Amongst the first, Swedish academic Esping-Anderson (1990) initially differentiated between: broadly liberal, conservative corporatist and social democratic 'welfare state regimes'. Subsequently many other public policy commentators came to engage in these debates[13] although the principles upon which they differentiated between various policy regimes remained fairly consistent. These included the degree to which social goods and services had been marketized or commodified (in other words, the extent to which consumers paid market prices); the extent of social stratification (or inequality) in the society in question; and the balance of public, private or voluntary provision (Bambra, 2007). Yet just as Titmuss and Field had pointed to the underlying values and the quality of citizenship entailed by particular arrangements for the delivery of social goods and services to different groups of the population, so also, embedded in the contrasting structural characteristics of the various welfare regimes, were a range of ideological values regarding freedom, inequality, personal responsibility and culpability for social problems (Levitas, 1996). More recently, Rodger (2008) has undertaken a similar classification of the prevailing policy discourses in play in different conceptions of criminal and social problems.

This ideological, even psycho-social, dimension to policy regimes became more explicit when commentators, in particular Cavadino and Dignan (2006; but see also Lappi-Seppala, 2007), extended the political economy conception of regime analysis into the fields of penality and law and order. But not only did these authors echo the broad tripartite regime distinction first constructed by Esping-Anderson (neo-liberal, conservative corporatist, social democratic), they also added another regime type ('oriental corporatist') while explicitly acknowledging (bringing some recognition of the deeply ideological character of 'law and order' politics; Reiner, 2007) the role of cultural and political factors in the definition of the regime. For our present purposes, however, the typology developed by Cavadino and Dignan, while it extends the conception of 'regime purpose' to take account of Titmuss's observation that the 'direction of travel' of governance matters, it limits the range and type of regimes. Accordingly, the typology presented below, while it borrows from Cavadino and Dignan (2006: 15), also reflects a framing predicated upon the governance of violence and the nature and extent of weaponization in different political and cultural contexts. While the first regime typologies addressed 'welfare', and Cavadino and Dignan added issues relating to legality and penality, Table 1.1 attempts to grapple with the material and ideological framing of contrasting 'violence regimes'. It also imagines the potential, as described by Currie and Wacquant, for these regimes to mutate dynamically into different regime types and/or vary their relative investments in welfare, penality, security or violence (Lappi-Seppala, 2007, 2012). This is important; after all, the violent and crimogenic character of societies in transition is well known (Koonings and Kruijt, 2004, 2007; Lemanski, 2004; Collier, 2009; Alba and Guzman, 2010; Rawlinson, 2010). Accordingly, the typology developed attempts to extend beyond simple regime descriptions based simply upon notions of political structure and social spending, in order to embrace welfare, conflict, security and violence; legality, order and penality; political cultures and values (including social inclusion/exclusion and personal protection choices); while not overlooking issues of regime development and change. As Currie has argued,

> the sharp stratification of violent death has been with us for a long time; if anything it has increased in recent years, so that we are now seeing an even more pronounced pulling away of the high-violence countries from the rest.
>
> *(Currie, 2005: 33–34)*

In similar fashion, even in relatively affluent societies, violent crime is increasingly concentrated in the poorest neighbourhoods. Overall, Currie offers a distinctly more critical perspective on the future of global violence than Pinker, especially its tendency to stack up the body count in the most unequal corners of the weaponized, neo-liberal world. In the conflict traps and gang territories of failed governance even the 'better angels' might find a measure of comfort and security with a Glock in their belts and an AK-47 slung over their shoulders.

Yet this is not simply a phenomenon in regimes that have 'failed', even in some the more apparently secure regions of neo-liberal governance, there has been extensive privatization or 'outsourcing' of policing and security functions, not to overlook the private military companies (Blackwater or Titan Corporation), acting as de facto agents of US foreign policy in Iraq and Afghanistan (Singer, 2007); private security agencies protecting the oil installations of Nigeria (Abrahamsen and Williams, 2010) or simply the new 'Minutemen' flocking to the Arizona–Mexico border to lend their vigilant firepower to the effort to prevent illegal immigration (Chavez, 2007). As Pratten and Sen (2007: 2) have argued, 'seen on a macro scale, the global political order wrought by neoliberalism has created unparalleled opportunities and motives for citizens to take the law into their own hands'.[14]

TABLE 1.1 Violence regimes: guns, values and security

	Social democratic	Conservative corporatist	Neo-liberal	Oriental, colonial, dictatorship, racial	Failed or failing state	Frontier or war zone
Characteristics						
Social and economic organization	Universal welfarist	Status-related selection	Free market individualism	Regime-related infrastructure	Scarcity, conflict	Militarized confrontation
Social and economic differentials	Largely egalitarian	Hierarchical, traditional	Formal equality but extreme income inequality	Regime-related inequality	Inequality, conflict	Subordinated to military authority
Citizen–state relations	Social democracy	Corporatist democracy	Utilitarian democracy	Regime inclusivity	Conflicted, lawless	Martial law, warfare
Dominant ideological discourses	Equal opportunity	Traditional (i.e. qualified) meritocracy	Individualism, freedom, marketized	Regime-related pragmatism	Social Darwinism, survival	Warlordism, warrior culture
Citizen inclusivity/exclusivity	Social inclusion	Traditionally limited inclusions/exclusions	Social exclusions	Regime-related exclusions	Clan, gang, cartel or group related, vigilantism	Victim or enemy
Political orientation	Left	Traditional, elite conservative	Neo-liberal/right	Regime centred, hierarchical	Arbitrary, conditional, corrupted	Hierarchical, military command
Penal culture	Human rights, rehabilitation	'Order through law'	'Law and order' priority, part privatized	Regime selective enforcement	Arbitrary, corrupt	Enemies, combatants
Form of punishment	Reparative	Traditional symbolic	Exclusionary	Regime protective	Delegated or private violence	Elimination

Rate of punishment, victimization	Low	Medium	High	Regime selective	High, arbitrary	High collateral victimization
Regime security	Social security	Traditional rule of law	Rule of law	Regime protection	Compromised, corrupt, private	Military control
Degree of 'weaponization'	Relatively low (exceptions: Finland, Norway, Switzerland), legal gun ownership	Limited, legal/ traditional, elitist, duty	Relatively high, legal and illegal, personal protection choices	Regime related, often strict controls (e.g. Japan, Singapore)	High, unregulated, illegal gun ownership predominant	High, illegal, ownership normalized

Note: The table draws upon the typology in Cavadino and Dignan (2006: 15) but with a number of additional elements. The fifth and sixth (additional columns) combine a more eclectic attempt to characterize the 'broken' or 'failing state' and the war zone.

However, while a typology provides the bare structure for describing and differentiating between types of societies, it needs to be complemented by evidence of the observable qualitative differences between cultures; the degree to which societies that are differently labelled share contrasting collective characteristics. In this regard, Wilkinson and Pickett's work in *The Spirit Level* (2010) is especially informative. In their book, Wilkinson and Pickett attempt to correlate a wide range of social issues and problems with the degree of inequality found in a range of societies. Having plotted their comparisons in respect of a range of societies, they repeat the exercise in respect of the 50 American states, finding, as predicted, a strong correlation between inequality and social problems. However, that is not all.

Figure 1.1, one of many scatter-plots developed by Wilkinson and Pickett (2010), outlines the overall case that their research advances: taken as a whole, the more unequal and given society, the more health and social problems the society will exhibit.

This is a relationship that sustains across a wide variety of social problems, including a range of crimogenic influences, although not crime itself (with the exception of homicide) although it does impact upon rates of imprisonment.[15]

Taking any given range of social problems, even before aggregating them into a single scale is likely to pose a range of definitional questions at the very least,

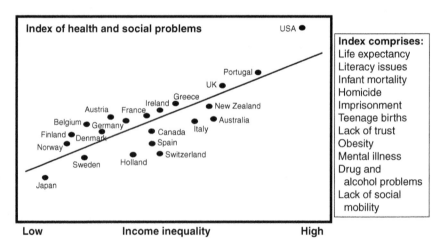

FIGURE 1.1 Health and social problems are generally worse in more unequal societies

Source: Wilkinson and Pickett (2010). Thanks to the Equality Trust for their kind permission to reproduce this figure.

but turning to the singular and rather more reliable variable, criminal homicide, Wilkinson and Pickett show that this phenomenon, too, varies in relation with inequality. The relationship they describe is supported by a wide range of evidence, including a meta-analysis of 35 studies undertaken in 1993 (Hsieh and Pugh, 1993). Broadly speaking, 'as inequality increased, so did violent crime' (Wilson and Pickett, 2010: 135). The line of correlation produced (see Figure 1.2) is not without certain anomalies which they note. In particular, for our purposes, they remark: 'international relationships between gun ownership and violent crime are complicated' (Wilson and Pickett, 2010: 136). This complication includes the fact that there appears to be a significant relationship between gun ownership and female homicide victimization, but less so for male homicides (Killias *et al.*, 2001). Likewise, Finland appears as a similarly rather aberrant case. Finland is an affluent and relatively egalitarian culture where a welfare ethic and social spending have endured more successfully than in many comparable European societies. Furthermore, during the second part of the twentieth century Finland experienced a noticeable movement away from the global norm of ever-increasing penal incarceration and, during the past two decades, appears to have resisted the tide of international punitiveness already discussed (Lappi-Seppala, 2007, 2012). As Lappi-Seppala summarizes (2012: 206): 'Finland enjoys an internationally high level of social security and equality, high social trust and political legitimacy, and low levels of penal repression.' I will turn to the question of social trust shortly, for the moment it is Finland's status as the society with one of the highest rates of legal household gun ownership which concerns us.

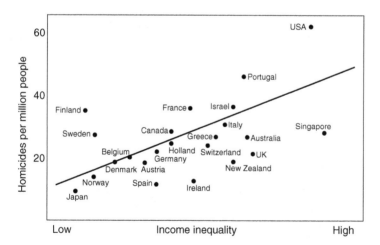

FIGURE 1.2   Homicide rates (per million) and inequality

Source: Wilkinson and Pickett (2010: 135). Thanks to the Equality Trust for their kind permission to reproduce this figure.

Clearly, for its degree of inequality, Finland has a high homicide rate (especially when compared, for example, with other Nordic societies and Belgium) and gun ownership may play some part in this, but it also has to be acknowledged that the cultures and social relations of gun acquisition and use also play an important role here too. Finland has a tightly controlled culture of gun ownership (including traditionally low estimates of illegal, unregistered firearms) almost entirely organized around hunting and sport shooting; unlike the USA, where the issue of self-defence has come to dominate gun politics. Furthermore, gun owners cannot legally trade weapons in the gun store parking lot or at 'gun shows' and 40 per cent of weapon transfers do not take place 'off the books'. Accordingly, gun cultures vary considerably in their relative lethality.

Similar qualifications apply in respect of Singapore, for given its degree of inequality, Singapore has a particularly low homicide rate. It also has one of the lowest rates of firearm ownership in the world, the Small Arms Survey putting Singapore 169th in a list of 178 countries judged in terms of their rates of gun ownership, with less than one firearm per 200 people (Karp, 2007). Tight regulation of firearms and a very low rate of firearm homicide in Singapore (only one gun homicide in 2006) also reflects the restrictive culture of a disciplined society, a form of oriental paternalism, as illustrated in Figure 1.2 above. As Chua (2013) remarks:

> Singapore is a highly regulated state that has restrictive laws members of the more liberal western world disdain or cannot accept … The right to private defence in Singapore is not something overtly encouraged by the law, unlike the strong emphasis placed upon this right in [the USA]. A balance has to be struck between freedom and safety, and sometimes the best of both worlds is unattainable. Singaporeans appear to be tolerant of, or are accustomed to, the restriction of some rights for the greater good and the safety of society.

Even so,

> the younger generation, often complain of the stifling environment we find ourselves in due to paternalistic laws, [although] we should, at the very least, appreciate that some of these compromises in personal liberty serve a greater good. The flipside of greater freedom is always the danger of people abusing that freedom. This principle extends beyond gun control and applies to areas such as freedom of speech as well.
>
> *(Chua, 2013)*

Another aspect of highly unequal societies is demonstrated in Figure 1.3; higher inequality is associated with declining levels of trust and mutuality. Here the idea of interpersonal trust refers to confidence, reciprocity, safety, a sense of common destiny, shared ideals of citizenship and community, and a cluster of values often misleadingly lumped together under the rubric of 'social capital' (Fine, 2001).

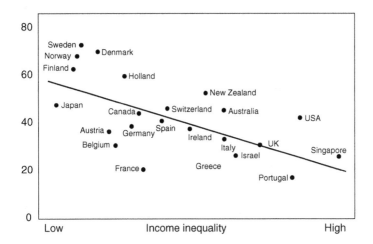

FIGURE 1.3   Trust and inequality

Source: Wilkinson and Pickett (2010: 52). Thanks to the Equality Trust for their kind permission to reproduce this figure.

Figure 1.3, for Wilkinson and Pickett, purports to show the relationship between inequality in society and the extent to which people feel they can trust one another. Their presentation of data regarding trust is prefaced by a short discussion of inequality, social change and anxiety in modern societies. The argument developed is similar to aspects of Merton's 'Strain Theory' (Merton, 1957) namely that increasing inequality renders individuals vulnerable to anxieties and diminished self-esteem for which people seek compensations. Furthermore, in an increasingly competitive culture, inequalities generate status aspirations and differences and tend to exacerbate class prejudices and stereotypes. In other words, inequalities erode 'fraternity' while fostering coping strategies often premised upon assertiveness and hierarchy. Criminologists have identified these psycho-social, 'self-defensive' strategies operating in adolescent gang cultures where a currency of 'respect' is aggressively policed, with often murderous consequences (Bourgois, 2003; Millie, 2009). Street gang cultures may (in many respects) represent a particularly low point in terms of convivial social relationships but, as Rose (1999) has noted, just as the twentieth-century policy sciences rediscovered 'community' as a solution for the ills of modernity, it was also in recognition of the fact that these re-imagined communities had largely ceased to exist. Subsequently, considerable efforts have been devoted to reconstructing secure communities of identity, behind walls and gates (Atkinson and Blandy, 2006) although with rather mixed results. The unfortunate cases of South African paralympian Oscar Pistorius and Florida neighbourhood watch coordinator George Zimmerman each, in their own way, illustrate that residence in a gated community might not provide the safety and reassurance sought after.

Building walls and erecting defences (even 'psychological stockades') is hardly a new response to ontological insecurities (Davis, 1990; Caldeira, 2000; Brauer and Van Tuyll, 2008) but the cult of personal responsibility underlying contemporary neo-liberal individualism often fosters a distrust of strangers and others, facilitating a shift in explanations of crime and social problems away from structural causes and back to personal issues (bad choices, bad behaviour, bad people) while also representing a fertile seedbed for intolerances based upon racism, class or xenophobia. In such an environment, as Caldeira has noted, discourses of fear and intolerance simultaneously justify a withdrawal from a more socialized existence and legitimate the construction of fortified enclaves 'for residence, work, leisure and consumption'. She continues, noting that the discourses of fear that necessitate this withdrawal and social distancing are frequently about crime and violence, 'but they also incorporate racial and ethnic anxieties, class prejudices, and references to poor and marginalized groups … where talk of crime feeds a circle in which fear is both dealt with and reproduced and violence is both counteracted and magnified' (Caldeira, 2000: 1, 19). Caldeira's point is also about social change or, to refer back to Table 1.1, 'regime changes', and the ways in which new social and economic imperatives reshape values and attitudes, alter policies, re-build environments, unearth new risks and dangers, fabricate new 'folk-devils' and pose different personal and political choices. In due course poverty becomes 'idleness', the poor a burden and welfare turns to disciplining; the social contract fractures, the rich withdraw to their gated lifestyles and the firepower of their private security guards. The welfare state becomes the punitive society, corrections become containment and criminal records mark an indelible and irreversible shift in social worth. The rich purchase a little extra security, never confident that the police will arrive on time (also assuming certain risks), in the form of a firearm in the closet or a handgun in the bedside cabinet; below the radar, the poor embrace even greater dangers, where they can, by doing the same. Weaponization has begun; lifeworlds change and, like George Zimmerman, we shoot strangers around here. The gun in the glove compartment ratchets our choices and opportunities dangerously upwards. What Caldeira describes as the ideological and psychological processes of urban segregation (leading to fortification) might just as easily describe the rise of weaponization. As she notes,

> talk of crime works its symbolic reordering of the world by elaborating prejudices and creating categories that naturalize some groups as dangerous. It simplistically divides the world into good and evil and criminalizes certain social categories. This symbolic criminalization is a widespread and dominant social process … it stimulates the development of two novel modes of discrimination: the privatization of security and the seclusion of some social groups in fortified and private enclaves. Both processes are changing concepts of the public and of public space that used to be dominant in western societies.
>
> *(Caldeira, 2000: 2)*

However, Caldeira's formulation is incomplete; neo-liberal weaponization is not solely founded upon a *retreat* from the public sphere, it also comprises a more aggressive challenge to the threatening external environment: like a manifest destiny of the neo-liberal self, it seeks to *tame* the frontier and win the war on crime. Asserted more forcefully as a 'right' of self-defence, it asserts a right to kill. The American Second Amendment, perhaps the most unconditional expression of armed citizenship, delegates the power of lethal force to private individuals, yet the less competent that states appear to be in protecting their own citizens, the more unequal they become, and the more they fail to deliver safety and security, so the more insistent the weaponization demand becomes. This suggests that weaponization, inequality and state failure are closely related.

In the wake of the Newtown, Connecticut, shooting on 14 December 2012, a series of analyses were posted on the internet attempting to examine the relationships between firearm prevalence in a society and gun deaths (Reid, 2012). Reid's work was responded to by Kingsbury (2012) who made the valid point that scatter-plots attempting to show correlations between gun prevalence and gun deaths are often influenced more by firearm suicide deaths than firearm homicides.[16] From a public health perspective, the precise 'cause' of death may be of less consequence, but it seems clear that, publicly and politically, homicides count for more. A second issue concerns the adequacy of the records relating to gun prevalence; illegally held weapons are responsible for the greater proportion of criminally motivated gun violence, but their precise numbers are much harder to ascertain. Furthermore, as we shall see, the states in which firearm homicides are most prevalent tend to have the least reliable record-keeping arrangements. It is acknowledged that these influences can run in contrary directions: on the one hand states might 'fail' because of the widespread misuse of illegal firearms; on the other hand, citizens might arm themselves because they fear the insecurity of a failing state. In order to explore this issue further, and to return to the theme of inequality and weaponization, it is instructive to consider Kingsbury's scatter-diagram exploring the relationship between income inequality.

Figure 1.4, drawing upon data from a number of sources and based upon the scatter-plots posted on the internet by Kingsbury (2012), shows an interesting correlation between income inequality and firearm homicide; the graph also confirms a number of the distinctions implied in the regime analysis typology in Table 1.1. Japan remains in its familiar place as one of the least armed and least murderous societies, followed closely by a cluster of social democratic European cultures, or former socialist societies. Singapore I have already considered, while Australia and New Zealand conform more closely to the 'European' model than that of post-colonial, 'frontier' societies where firearm ownership is often politically significant. By contrast, Canada, India and Israel lie closer to the USA.

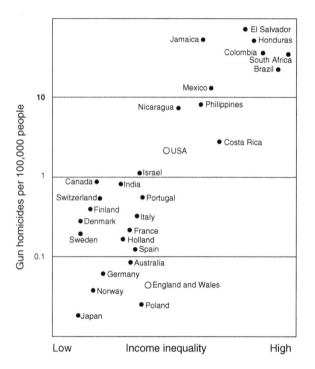

FIGURE 1.4 Firearms homicide and income inequality

Sources: Compiled from data including Alpers *et al.* (2013); Currie (2005); Kingsbury (2012); Wilkinson and Pickett (2010).

The USA lies close to the centre of the distribution, if we wanted to make a controversial point, we might say it lies half way between the failed states and the real democracies, for beyond it are only a number of Latin American societies – some of these, still violent, were relatively late to democracy (Chevigny, 1995; Koonings and Kruijt, 2004; Pereira, 2005; Arias and Goldstein, 2010) – and a couple of African states. The diagram corresponds to a similar ranking in Currie's 'global violence' book (Currie, 2005: 25) where the USA sits uncomfortably between a range of safe European societies and a considerably more dangerous clutch of transition societies from eastern Europe and Latin America. African societies are largely excluded from the diagram for reasons to do with the availability and reliability of their data. As Currie remarks, however, the already 'anomalous' matter of the USA's level of violence 'is even more striking if we focus upon the group at greatest risk – young men' and he goes on to comment,

> the USA comes closer, in this respect, to the pattern that is usually found in
> some of the poorer countries; its level of youth violence more closely resembles
> that of some third world countries than it does the rest of the advanced world.
> *(2005: 28–29)*

This is a theme I return to in later chapters, especially Chapter 7.

As the data analysts Reid and Kingsbury remark, however, it is manifestly not the case that a simple, single relationship prevails between gun prevalence and homicide rates. For as Wilkinson and Pickett (2010) have shown, different degrees and dimensions of deprivation are correlated here and when a number of the social and cultural relationships often associated with inequality are factored into the picture, a more compelling analysis emerges, vindicating the regime categories sketched out earlier. Inequalities and, in particular, failures of governance relating to economic, social and personal safety and security are related to the nature and frequency of violence and, as a recent US study has attempted to show, this is even observable at state level. Gerney *et al.* (2013) compared all 50 US states against 29 different 'gun control policy' standards. The measures included policies such as 'background checks for all gun sales, banning assault weapons and high-capacity magazines, and requiring applicants to demonstrate the need for a concealed weapon before being issued a permit to carry one' (2013: 28). Two lists of ten states with what were judged to be, respectively, the weakest and the strongest gun laws were produced. A close relationship between the lists is apparent; eight out of the ten states with the worst gun violence records also fell amongst the 25 states with the weakest gun laws. Somewhat completing the picture, six of the ten states with the worst gun violence scored highly amongst Wilkinson and Pickett's 'greater inequality' states (although the picture is not simple, New York state, evidencing the greatest degree of inequality, benefits from the relatively restrictive gun control policies in New York City). An analysis by Florida in 2011, however, confirms an earlier point: culture, politics and economic and social relations *all* conspire to produce different violence regimes. Poverty, inequality and unemployment were all significantly associated with high levels of firearm deaths, as was the related matter of having an economy dominated by working-class jobs. In these areas there were also more drug problems and more young people recorded as carrying weapons to school. Weaponization proceeds by degree and takes a number of forms. The only issue more likely to be associated with higher gun violence rates was a Republican political affiliation. By contrast, voting Democrat, having a high proportion of college graduates in the workforce, living in a jurisdiction with one or more key gun control measures (safe storage, trigger locks and an assault weapons ban), higher scores for well-being, happiness and standard of living, and having a higher than average number of immigrants in the population were all associated with lower levels of gun violence (Florida, 2011).

The plan of the book

In the chapters that follow I pursue many of these arguments centring upon the exceptionalism of US gun policy, but also in the context of a more global perspective on gun ownership, trafficking, use and misuse. Chapters 2 and 3 are preoccupied with the United Kingdom, a society (but three distinct firearm jurisdictions: England and Wales, Scotland and Northern Ireland) with one of the lowest international rates of gun violence and a relatively low rate of firearm ownership.

However, the UK has certainly been impacted by the weaponizing world and, for the two decades from the early 1990s, became convinced that it was facing an unprecedented gun crime crisis. Prompted undoubtedly by the terrible shootings at Dunblane Primary School, in Scotland, on 13 March 1996 (Britain's second rampage shooting incident), British politicians and police leaderships eventually (and not all at once) adopted a range of measures that substantially began to impact the supply of legal and illegal firearms, in time, significantly reducing year-on-year rates of recorded gun crime. This is not the whole of the British story, however, for tragedies have continued and gun law loopholes remain and, while most informed commentators now appear to believe that the gun crime problem is moving in the right direction in the UK, there is no place for complacency in a global and weaponized world. Gun violence, as I have already noted is not just about the *availability* of weapons, it is also about the social and economic relations associated with their use and misuse. Accordingly Chapters 2 and 3 attempt to examine the numbers and the gun crime trends impacting in the UK. Chapter 3 explores the social and cultural relationships of gun misuse, specifically those areas in mainland Britain where firearm misuse appears to be the most prevalent. A good part of this discussion, and certainly the greater part of the policy responses, strategies and media commentaries, relate to the activities of violent street gangs, although this is not the whole of the story. In another sense, Chapter 2 could be seen, more conventionally, as a *criminology* of gun crime prevention; a case study of the control of weapon-involved crime in a society where gun crime remains relatively rare. None of this entails, however, that there is no criminological critique to be developed of the policy-making or the policing practices that have ensued. The very fact I am viewing these issues through the lens of criminology rather than, for instance, 'conflict studies', however, says important things about society, legitimacy and consent and the construction of these issues.

Chapters 4, 5 and 6 deal with broadly American issues: Chapter 4 explores the numbers and key trends in gun violence and gun ownership, while Chapter 5 explores a series of the tensions, the cultural and political debates and differences underlying the politics of guns in the USA. Chapter 6 then turns to consider a series of events – school shootings and mass or 'rampage' killings – that, unlike more 'routine' levels of gun crime, resulting in around 80 people being shot and killed each day, appear to be able, on occasion, to propel the gun control debate forwards, even if the forward momentum achieved is typically far less than many advocates might wish for. A focus on the USA is necessary for reasons related to the evidence suggested by Figure 1.4. America is a significant 'outlier' in relation to its rates of gun violence when compared with other advanced, liberal-democratic societies; it is also renowned for its liberal regime of firearms controls and unusual in regard to the constitutional status claimed for gun ownership. America is also unusual in relation to the wealth of academic scholarship devoted to firearms issues, the results of which may, or may not, be translated to other societies and settings.

As the chapters will suggest, many contemporary US debates concerning firearms are often a foil for a range of other issues, something that also surfaces in the activist politics of US gun advocates in other parts of the world.

The final part of the book turns to four issues that give gun violence and small arms politics a truly global resonance. In Chapter 7, I consider trends and patterns of gun trafficking around the world and consider the extent to which illicit firearm supplies, the process of 'weaponization' itself, represents a direct cause or facilitator of conflict, crime and violence. In the second part of Chapter 7 I explore the broader circumstances and legacies of gun violence in these highly weaponized conflict zones, the frequent involvement of marginalized and disaffected young men and the highly gendered and often misogynistic form taken by much of the violence. I also look at attempts by these societies, often unsuccessful, to address this gun driven violence.

Chapter 8 then follows this policy response perspective to explore how a number of societies (including case studies of Canada, Australia and Brazil) have responded to their own 'gun crises', typically following a mass shooting. America does not have a monopoly on 'rampage shootings', they have occurred in many other countries of the world, although most other societies experiencing them have done rather more to ensure that the frequently voiced reactions of 'never again' do not become the unfortunately hollow rhetoric they have become in the USA (despite the valiant efforts of many lobby groups). Finally, building out from these national initiatives in gun control, the final section of Chapter 8 connects with the United Nations' effort to curtail illegal firearms trafficking and the localized efforts of peace and development organizations (NGOs, charities and UN development bodies) working in some of the world's most violent conflict zones to build an international framework for global arms control. This effort culminated in the UN ATT, adopted in 2013, an aspect of the PoA on Small Arms and Light Weapons which the global arms control community has been developing through the UN since 2001.

Notes

1 Even as they become a relatively smaller percentage of the US population, see Chapter 4.
2 Consider, perhaps, the intricate etiquette surrounding a nineteenth-century duel between gentlemen, the elaborate routines, roles and responsibilities and their embracing codes of honour and moral courage, preparatory to the singular act of aiming a pistol and pulling a trigger (see Squires, 2000: 38). In his film *The Big Country* in 1958, director William Wyler plays with these codes of 'manliness', pitting a gentlemanly Gregory Peck against the shallow cowboy bravado of Chuck Connors. The ensuing action embraces several contrasting – positive and negative – dimensions of masculinity as well as honour, courage, cowardice, civilization, justice and redemption, a thoroughly social exchange of bullets.
3 Much evaluation of US gun control measures involves complex quantitative time-series testing of regulative measures that are not often especially strong in themselves and whose effects are often difficult to disentangle from those of a range of other influences. Kleck (1991, 1997) and Jacobs (2002) have drawn rather sceptical conclusions about the policy utility of much of this work. However, amongst the better attempts to draw reliable,

evidence-based conclusions from the accumulation of gun policy research findings are works by Ludwig and Cook (2003) and Hemenway (2004). This research, however, has become practically inconclusive for another reason, the growing disinclination of politicians, judges and opinion-formers to engage with evidence at all, as gun politics has become increasingly driven by ideology and emotion.

4 The arms control literature presents us with case studies of the careers of a few of these infamous characters: Victor Bout, who played his part in the arming of large parts of Africa, or Sarkis Soghanalian, otherwise known as the 'merchant of death', who has claimed that many of his deals were sanctioned by the CIA (see Stohl *et al.*, 2007). These issues are further developed in Chapter 7.

5 Mikhail Kalashnikov, the inventor of the ubiquitous AK-47 which, along with its variants is the world's most numerous and widespread firearm, is alleged to have voiced regret that his firearm had been used to kill so many people: 'I created a weapon to defend the borders of my motherland. It's not my fault that it's being used where it shouldn't be. The politicians are more to blame for this … I always wanted to construct agricultural machinery.'

6 As Jackson and Marsh (2012) have argued, both the definition of 'firearm deaths' and the methodology for calculating these is crucial here. Calculating those deaths arising only *directly* from shootings, outside of militarized conflict (warfare) and not including deaths resulting from the famine, disease and poverty that so typically accompany violent conflict, will inevitably produce substantially different figures. Jackson and Marsh demonstrate that no single data source provides comprehensive coverage of global firearm deaths, so they advocate a 'mosaic' model, drawing data from different sources to build a more complete picture. They note that this is an established method of proceeding (Krug *et al.*, 2002; Richmond *et al.*, 2005), acknowledging that the capacity to produce an accurate death toll diminishes in the more destabilized, conflict-torn and 'ungovernable' regions (Soares, 2004).

7 Although seldom so forcefully argued as by Greenwood in *Guns Review* in the early 1990s. See Squires (2000: 2–3).

8 Chapman (1998/2013: 18) describes a similar phenomenon during the Australian gun control debates following the Port Arthur shootings in 1996:

Night after night on their televisions, Australians saw and heard embittered, belligerent men whose main purpose in life appeared to be ensuring that they could keep military-style and rapid-fire weaponry capable of blowing apart all in its path. This was a far cry from any sentimental notions of rustic farmers bagging a few ducks, rabbits or kangaroos that many Australians might have visualised when the subject of shooting had arisen in the past. At worst, many of these [anachronistic] men rapidly came to signify a subterranean, angry and potentially dangerous side of Australian life.

9 See, for example, Courtwright (1996: 272) describing the modern hyperghetto:

[V]ice-ridden combat zones in which groups of armed, unparented, and reputation conscious young bachelors, high on alcohol, cocaine and other drugs menace one another and the local citizenry, undeterred if not altogether untouched by an entropic justice system.

10 Diaz (2013: 137–140) shows how the US state of Indiana passed a law in 2012 extending the 'Castle Doctrine' or 'Stand your Ground' laws adopted by many US states in order to allow private citizens who reasonably suspected that police interventions (eg. forced entry into a home) was *unlawful* might threaten and use lethal force to resist them. As Diaz notes, the implications of such a law are particularly far-reaching.

11 Two new international studies, both of them first published in late 2013, analysed the relationship between rates of firearm ownership and firearm death and injury rates or 'gun victimization': Bangalore and Messerli (2013) and Van Kesteren (2014). The former authors concluded, 'the current study debunks the widely quoted hypothesis that guns make a society safer', while Van Kesteren noted: 'Analysis of the data from 26 countries show that owners of a handgun show increased risk for victimization by violent crime.'

12 'A well-regulated militia being necessary to the security of a free state, the right of the people to keep and bear arms shall not be infringed', although even the meaning of this sentence is contested. These issues are more fully elaborated later in Chapter 5, for the moment I am simply acknowledging that one view of the interpretation (the individualist or 'standard' interpretation) of the 2nd Amendment asserts that it guarantees an individual right to bear arms.

13 Other commentators have included: Leibfried (1992); Castles and Mitchell (1993); Kangas (1994); Ragin (1994); Bonoli (1997); Korpi and Palme (1998); Navarro and Shi (2001); Bambra (2007).

14 These developments are broadly understood within the supposed 'great transformation' in policing outlined by Bayley and Shearing (1996) and Jones and Newburn (2002). Ultimately, as Pratten and Sen remark, 'vigilantism is a cheap form of law enforcement' (2007: 3).

15 Snowden (2010) in his critique of Wilkinson and Pickett, *The Spirit Level Delusion* points out that the correlation between inequality and *imprisonment* is reversed when one looks at inequality and *crime*. Perhaps surprisingly, he notes, affluent egalitarian societies, including the Scandinavian welfare societies, have higher rates of crime (2010: 73). Snowden is keen to refute the inequality/social problem relationship by pointing out that imprisonment is a political choice rather than an independent statistical variable. Although he is keen to argue that low rates of imprisonment (rather than inequality) cause high rates of crime, effectively reversing Wilkinson and Pickett's correlation, he fails to recognize that crime rates are themselves social constructs and the product of many personal and political influences, and a variety of reporting and recording practices.

16 Both commentators added substantial caveats to their analyses, and neither made strong claims for the reliability of the data they accessed which was drawn from 'readily available' public sources on the internet. Reid added:

> At no point have I ever claimed that this is even close to a rigorous analysis. I have not attempted to use these plots to draw any kind of conclusion about the relationship between gun ownership and gun deaths. Indeed, I do not think there exists a simple explanation. All I intended to do was attempt to shed some light on a … possible correlation.
>
> *(Reid, 2012)*

PART 2

Safe European home?

2

GUN CRIME IN THE UK

The supply-side story

According to the typology developed in Chapter 1, the UK ranks as a high control, low tolerance society so far as gun ownership is concerned. The following two chapters, however, address the rise and fall of gun crime in mainland Britain as an illustration of the ways in which such a society engages with an emerging firearm proliferation problem, most obviously confined to a relatively defined number of inner-urban areas, during the 1990s. What we might call a rising profile of 'routine' gun crime, however, was not the issue that most prompted Britain's most sustained explicit engagement with gun control politics. Instead, the triggering incident was the awful massacre at Dunblane Primary school, although the policies that emerged in the wake of that incident were, arguably, long overdue. The detailed story of the more immediate response to Dunblane has been told already (North, 2000; Squires, 2000) and those issues will not be substantially revisited here. Rather, in the present chapter I will primarily examine the 'supply side' to the UK gun crime problem: the sources of small arms proliferation and weaponization and how legal changes and policing practices have addressed the problem; in Chapter 3 I will address the social contexts in which a demand for firearms originates and the ways in which this has been responded to.

Neither the beginning, nor the end: gun crime trends to 1996

It is difficult to overstate the significance of the events of 13 March 1996 in terms of British attitudes to firearms and the related idea of a 'gun culture'. When Thomas Hamilton walked into Dunblane Primary School carrying four handguns and some 700 rounds of ammunition and proceeded to shoot dead 16 children and their teacher, seriously wounding 13 more, his appalling actions and the reaction to them fundamentally crystallized an attitude and a politics that, to a large extent, still prevails. These attitudes were echoed in the wake of the Sandy Hook elementary school shooting in Connecticut, USA, especially as commentators contrasted the reforms brought in the UK with the stubborn intransigence of pro-gun legislators in the USA. In 1996, Conservative MP David Mellor had taken (rather unusually amongst his party colleagues) a strong positive stance in favour of tougher gun controls and sought to persuade his parliamentary colleagues that 'handguns have no positive role in society ... They bring no benefits whatever to a wider public' (Mellor, 1996a). An editorial in the same paper added, 'there is no justification for individuals owning powerful handguns like those amassed by Hamilton. These were not small bore target pistols, but military-style killing machines.' Rather later in the year, Mellor coined the phrase that struck to the heart of the issue: 'If we import the American way of life, we must expect the American way of death' (Mellor, 1996b).

His phrase resonated with significance; it pointed both to a dangerous American future that Britain would do well to avoid; recognized certain important differences between our two societies and implied that, while we could, Britain should grasp the opportunity to legislate for a safer future without (so far as was possible) civilian possession of handguns. It has to be said, Mellor's arguments were not without their critics – especially, but not only, in the USA. Nevertheless, sustained by a powerful tide of public support, Britain moved very quickly to abolish, first the higher calibre types of handguns such as employed by Hamilton in his murderous spree, while, subsequently, the incoming Blairite, New Labour Government of 1997, honouring a high-profile election pledge, banned a further series of smaller handguns, down to and including .22 calibre weapons.[1]

In legislating in this fashion Parliament had gone substantially beyond the carefully measured recommendations of Lord Cullen's Judicial Inquiry into the incident (Cullen, 1996) as well as the unfortunate recommendations of a conservative dominated Home Affairs Select Committee which had specifically rejected banning some or all calibre types of handguns (House of Commons: Home Affairs Committee, 1996).[2] Public reactions had well and truly trumped politics and negotiation, leading to a degree of recrimination in some quarters about 'knee-jerk reactions', supposedly ill-considered political decisions reached in haste and the rather 'event-led' character of gun control legislation in the UK. The phrase surfaced once again, for instance, adopted by the prime minister in the parliamentary debate following the shootings in Cumbria in 2010. Another view is possible, this voiced by Chris Mullin MP at the Home Affairs Select Committee in 1996. He remarked upon the conspicuous failure of government to act decisively following the 16 firearm killings in Hungerford some nine years earlier in 1987. Proposing a ban on handguns in 1996, he argued, was no 'knee-jerk reaction'. In 1987, 'the opportunity to strike at the gun culture in a big way was lost to general inertia ... the opportunity afforded by the tragedy at Dunblane should not be missed; if action is not taken after such a disaster, it never will be' (House of Commons: Home Affairs Committee, 1996: xl, para 9).

Clearly, however, while Dunblane and the legislation that followed was a critical turning point for attitudes to firearms and a vital watershed for gun control policy in the UK it was by no means the *beginning* of a recognizable gun (crime) problem in the UK – and nor were the events at Hungerford nine years earlier for that matter. More to the point, while Dunblane and the legislation that followed may have represented a terrible chapter in the UK gun control debate they were far from being the end of the story.

Interpreting gun crime trends

As we have seen, while Dunblane and the legislation that followed represented a significant chapter in the UK gun control debate they were far from being the end of that story (see Figure 2.1). This is an interpretation also borne out by the data on 'crime involving firearms in the UK' although, as we shall see, even that criterion raises difficulties which were, for some time, to bedevil the interpretation of gun crime trends. At face value, Home Office statistics[3] suggested a rapidly increasing rate of handgun misuse (an eight-fold increase) in England and Wales between the mid-1970s and the early 1990s, followed by a sharp fall after 1993. Interestingly, 1993 was also the peak year for recorded firearm homicide in the USA although this coincidence across two quite different cultures of firearm use and misuse has attracted rather little commentary. Likewise, the fact that, at the time of the Dunblane killings (in Scotland), gun crime in England and Wales had actually been falling for three years also went rather unremarked. There was also a small increase to 1993 (followed by a decline) in crime involving shotguns, although the trend for handgun offences causing injury – perhaps a more reliable underlying indicator of actual handgun misuse – revealed a four-fold increase between 1988 and 1993 in England and Wales (see Squires, 2000: 11–13).

However, notwithstanding the apparently simple and rising trends – until 2002 – implied by Figure 2.1, there are a number of difficulties in making appropriate sense of British gun crime figures. The first problems concern questions of emotion and of scale. To begin with 'gun crime' now only represents approximately some 0.3 per cent of all police recorded crime (11,227 offences in 2010–2011). When crime committed with air weapons is set aside this figure falls by about one-third to just over 7,000 offences or around 0.2 per cent of recorded crime; subtracting *known* imitation firearms[4] leaves a total of around 5,500 gun crimes each year in England and Wales (Lau, 2012). Moreover, as the Home Office has been pleased to point out, since 2001–2002 in England and Wales, overall gun crime trends have been falling.

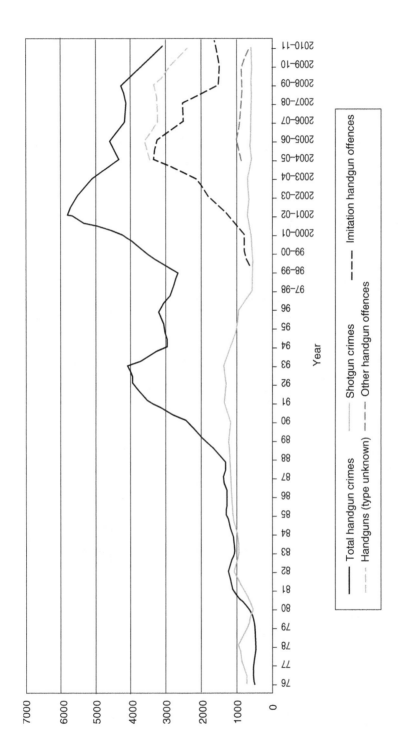

FIGURE 2.1 Selected firearm offences in England and Wales, 1976–2011: handguns, shotguns and 'other handguns'

Sources: Smith *et al.* (2012); Squires (2000: 11).

In contrast to the most recent figures for England and Wales, the five years after 1996 saw a substantial overall reduction in crimes involving handguns in Scotland, approximating 80 per cent, but these numbers began to rise again after 2004 (see Figure 2.2). The picture is undoubtedly complicated by the role of imitation firearms (and, although not separately represented in the graph, 'unidentified firearms') in the data. With imitation firearms apparently falling when handgun offences rise and rising when handgun offences fall, then alongside the 'unidentified firearm' figures, there is clearly some scope for mis-identification here. In common with the English and Welsh data, greater recognition of the imitation firearm issue and better – certainly more consistent – analysis of recovered weapons has meant that a more reliable – although substantially more complex – picture of the mixed economy of firearms available on British streets has begun to emerge (see Figure 2.4). For example, the large increase in handgun-involved offending depicted in Figure 2.1 between 1987 and 1993 is likely to have included a significant proportion of imitation/replica weapons, although data on these was not separately available until after 1998. Finally, offences involving shotguns in Scotland fell dramatically after 1993 and have remained on a low, largely flat, trajectory since 1998.

Two media reports recycling press releases from, first, the Strathclyde Police in 2002 and, second, the Scottish Government indicate the difficulties associated with making a too-hasty commentary upon volatile crime trends. In 2002, it was suggested that 'serious' shootings were 'soaring' in Strathclyde, and that 'almost all were a result of battles for control over drug supplies' (BBC Scotland, 2002). The latest incident involving a man shot in the face with a gas-powered air weapon, 'part of an on-going gangland feud over drug dealing' (BBC Scotland, 2002). By contrast, in October 2011 Kenny MacAskill (2012), Scotland's justice minister, announced that gun crime had fallen to a 32-year low. The good news needed to be set in context, a substantial portion of this reduction involved apparently falling rates of air weapon misuse.

However the clearly divergent patterns relating to the recording of air weapon offences in England and Wales and Scotland requires a further comment. Figure 2.3 shows the relatively low, and falling, profile, over 20 years, for air weapon crime in Scotland, although the trend is dwarfed by the rise, then fall, in air weapon-involved crime in England and Wales.

To give the Scottish air weapon figures some further context, at the beginning of the period represented by the graph, air weapon offences accounted for roughly two-thirds of Scottish gun crime but by 2010–2011 they accounted for only one-third. In other words, firearms *other than air weapons* were accounting for a more substantial proportion of recorded Scottish gun crime.

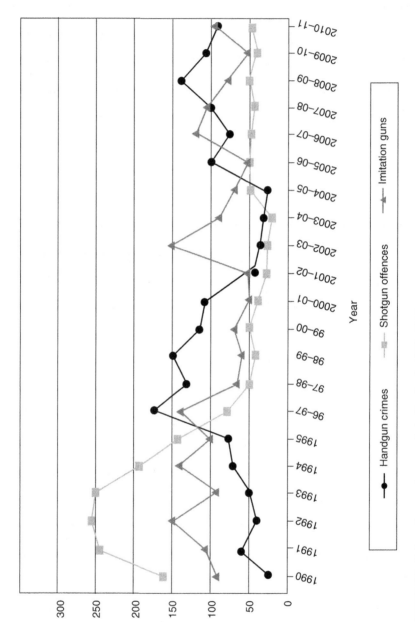

FIGURE 2.2 Selected gun crime trends in Scotland, 1990–2011

Source: Scottish Government Statistical Bulletins.

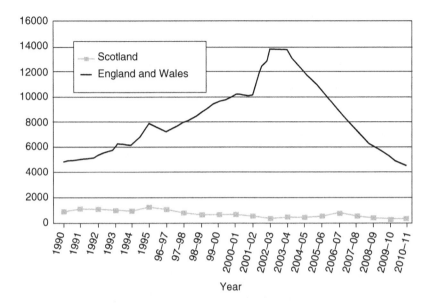

FIGURE 2.3 Air weapon offences: England, Wales and Scotland, 1990–2011

Sources: Home Office Supplementary Firearm Crime Data and Scottish Government Statistical Bulletins.

A similar, although less marked, shift in the share of gun crime attributable to air weapons (from a half to just over one-third) is observable in relation to England and Wales. These trends, and especially the numbers of offences to which they relate, have an important bearing upon the interpretation of gun crimes. Including or excluding the air weapon figures can lead towards quite different kinds of conclusions, especially where, as in the England and Wales figures, the trend appears to rise or fall significantly. Air weapon crime figures also introduce other levels of complexity into the analysis, in one respect because as some commentators suggest – perhaps erroneously – that they represent a 'less serious' form of gun crime and, relatedly, because they generally reflect a different *pattern* of criminal misuse.

Despite some suggestions that air weapon offences are less serious, they have typically been responsible for a greater overall number of firearm injuries. Furthermore ten people (more frequently children) in England and Wales were killed by air weapons in the decade up to 2010. Air weapon misuse is more usually recorded as an offence *when the weapon is fired*. In 2010–2011, air weapons were fired in 84 per cent of the air weapon offences recorded (Lau, 2012) whereas more conventional firearms are more often used to threaten (handguns were fired in only 12 per cent of recorded handgun offences in 2008 (Kaiza, 2008)).[5] These differences in patterns of use go some way towards explaining, in part, the historically higher rate of air weapon injuries, although these patterns are also changing. Around three-quarters of air weapon offences only involve criminal damage offences and total air weapon injuries have fallen by more than 50 per cent since 2004, which is also the year during which the rate of air weapon injuries was overtaken by injuries resulting from more powerful weapons.

When such remarkably different trends emerge from the recording of essentially similar crime phenomena in two jurisdictions (air weapon misuse in England and Wales, and Scotland) explanation necessarily turns to the process of crime recording itself. It seems clear that, until 2002, guidance to police in England and Wales was to treat air weapon offences, especially those involving any injury, as *firearm* offences. With the significant increases in recorded gun crime after 1996, the compilation of rising gun crime figures, including the air weapon offences, was beginning to cause significant political embarrassment. However, recoding practices appear to have changed in 2002–2003 coincident with the passage of the 2003 Anti-Social Behaviour Act, part five of which (sections 37–39) specifically dealt with the possession of air weapons (and imitation firearms, a point we return to later) in public places. After 2003, therefore, charges for the misuse of air weapons (unless air weapon misuse resulted in serious injuries) came to be recorded as 'anti-social behaviour' incidents (or offences) as opposed to gun crimes. The significance of this change, evidenced in Figure 2.3, will become more apparent in due course (its impact was also evident in Figure 2.1). The 2010 Home Affairs Select Committee noted, with some satisfaction, the decline in air weapon offences, but nowhere appeared to recognize that it may well have resulted from a simple change in record-keeping (House of Commons: Home Affairs Committee, 2010: paras 6–12).

Such questions about what the crime statistics really mean certainly complicate the analysis of gun crime trends and especially so when the social practices – and especially the crime recording practices – surrounding gun use are themselves relatively opaque and/or changing. Both these considerations apply to the analysis of police recorded gun crime figures. For example, it is well understood that most crime goes unreported to the police (Garside, 2006) and in 2006 Allen and Ruparel calculated that only some 42 per cent of crimes recorded by the 2005–2006 British Crime Survey were actually reported to the police (Allen and Ruparel, 2006). Furthermore, in the case of gun crime there are additional reasons why victims might not report these offences. Fear of reprisals might be a significant factor; in addition, statistically speaking, those groups most likely to be victims of gun offences are young men themselves involved in gang-related, criminal activities.

Research by Bullock and Tilley in Manchester (2002), by Pitts in Tower Hamlets (2007a) and the Home Office survey by Hales *et al.* (2006), not to mention a wide range of American research, confirms the fact that victims of gun crime are typically from very similar social groups, geographical areas, social circumstances and lifestyles as the perpetrators of gun crime. In Pitts' terms gun violence is often 'symmetrical': 'victims and offenders are similar in terms of age, ethnicity and class' (Pitts, 2007a, 2008; Hayden *et al.*, 2008: 165). In Bullock and Tilley's Manchester study many of the sample of gun crime victims had previous arrests or convictions for weapons offences and a number were known to police for their gang affiliations and involvement in shootings. In all, 43 of their sample of gun crime victims had previous arrests (an average of 11 per person), this was not a cohort particularly enthusiastic about dialogue with the police. On the flip side of the equation, of the rather smaller sample of Manchester gun crime offenders, eight (of 26 with previous firearm possession arrests) had previously been shot at and, between the commencement of the research and the completion of the report, three were subsequently shot dead (Bullock and Tilley, 2002). Two years later Bennett and Holloway reported that while younger men (more than older men) identified firearms as a useful means of protection for their illegal drug dealing and, while there were statistical associations between drug dealing, weapon carrying and gang membership, ethnicity on its own did not appear to be related to firearm possession (Bennett and Holloway, 2004). The authors concluded that such patterns of gun ownership and use appeared to reflect in the UK 'the broader characteristics of the new forms of youth crime that developed in the United States during the 1980s and 1990s' (2004: 251).

One aspect of this new criminal culture is a frequently remarked reluctance (often underpinned by a fear of reprisals on the part of many gun crime victims – and their wider communities) to provide evidence to the police, not to mention the powerful 'no grassing' conventions in gang cultures. Accordingly, it is likely that much 'gun crime' (especially incidents involving only minor injuries, firearms discharges resulting in no injuries or situations where weapons are simply brandished to threaten) goes unreported. On the basis of their interviews with 80 convicted firearm offenders in prison, Hales *et al.* (2006: 37) concluded that 'victimisation generally only came to the attention of the police in the case of fatalities or serious injury requiring medical attention … Otherwise, interviewees reported a preference for taking personal retributive action and a fear of being labelled a grass'. This conclusion also reflected the findings of the Jill Dando Institute's *Rationalisation of Current Research on Guns, Gangs and Other Weapons: Phase 1*, which further suggested that under-reporting 'may be due to negative attitude towards the police, fear of retribution for "grassing", or a culture of enacting informal retribution' (Marshall *et al.*, 2005: 14). But perhaps the more extreme manifestations of this non-reporting, extending to denial of involvement in gang and gun-related offending, are revealed in the case of gun crime victims who have sustained injuries but still refuse to cooperate with the police. Data provided to the *Magnet* Research team by Greater Manchester Police's (GMP) specialist intelligence-led Operation Xcalibre, intended to tackle the city's gun crime problems, reveals numerous instances of uncooperative gunshot victims. Thus, taken from the anonymized Operation Xcalibre intelligence briefings:

Whilst walking home on Cedar Walk, TT6 heard three bangs which sounded like fireworks and then realised he had an injury to the rear of his right knee cap. This later transpired to be a single gunshot wound. The round was imbedded in his leg. The round is to remain in his leg due to its proximity to an artery. There are numerous inconsistencies in the account as given by TT6 whose cooperation is to say the least minimal.

(Tactical Criminal Use of Firearms Threat Assessment, Presentation 28/09/05)

At approx 04:21hrs reports were received by the Police that males were firing shots on Smith Avenue, Old Trafford. This resulted in the discovery of AW, the brother of KW and DW with a gunshot entry wound to his thigh and exit wound to his buttock. A bullet head was recovered in the doorframe of Branden Way. AW was taken to MRI hospital and later discharged himself. At this stage AW is being uncooperative with Police enquiries.

(Tactical Criminal Use of Firearms Threat Assessment, Presentation 10/01/06)

At 23.15hrs Police were called to the above address. Three unknown males approached the address and discharged a shotgun twice before making off running onto Paving Road where it is believed they have got into a small black possibly Fiat Punto type car and drove off. No one was believed present in the flat at the time. Damage was caused to the front door and a window consistent with a shotgun being discharged. A short time after the incident the occupier HS arrived. He was reluctant to speak to police and refused to make any complaint. HS is the cousin of RS. When asked regarding a possible motive he intimated that he was under threat because of RS's activities.

(Tactical Criminal Use of Firearms Threat Assessment, Presentation 03/08/05)

This particular incident relates to an earlier point about the intentions behind 'drive-by' shootings. They are not always motivated by a desire to kill or injure, but sometimes simply to 'send a message'.

The victim AW of Coxen Street, Moss Side, presented himself at the MRI (Manchester Royal Infirmary) with a gunshot wound. He stated that he was at a car park at a block of flats on Richards Road Chorlton, when he was approached by two males who attempted to rob him. As AW refused to cooperate he was shot in the leg. Two friends were with him at the hospital and they were spoken to: DB and LG. Initially all three were reluctant to talk and their stories have changed and are inconsistent. AW has indicated he does not wish to provide any assistance to the Police and has since been uncontactable. Of note, AW is associated to JR, who was also shot on Davis Road, Hulme, in November 2005.

(Tactical Criminal Use of Firearms Threat Assessment, Presentation 26.04.06)

Fascinating as they may be, such police intelligence reports are surpassed by the case reported by three radiologists in *The Lancet* in February 2009 (Fallouh *et al.*, 2009). Since 2003 the General Medical Council has recommended that A&E doctors report all gunshot injuries to the police (at Government behest, adding the reporting of knife crime injuries to this arrangement in 2009), thereby posing a dilemma to injured offenders who are in need of medical care but have no wish to be interviewed by police. The radiologists reported two cases where the injured persons denied having been shot only for X-ray examination to reveal bullets still lodged within their bodies. The patients remained uncooperative, one of them even escaping from the hospital during the early hours, taking all his hospital notes with him. In Canada, such developments have led some doctors to question both the ethics and presumed effectiveness of mandatory gunshot reporting by A&E departments: 'mandatory reporting would only serve to discourage [gunshot wound] patients from seeking medical care' (Mackay, 2004; Pauls and Downie, 2004). I later consider some further light that A&E data might throw upon our understanding of these gun crime trends.

Less dramatic, but of possibly greater significance in influencing apparent rates of firearm misuse, were crime recording changes resulting from the implementation of the National Crime Recording Standard (NCRS) by police forces on 1 April 2002 and which influenced the numbers of crimes recorded during 2002–2003 (Hales, 2006). The changes also brought further 'improvements' in recording practices leading to statistical increases, in particular regarding violence against the person and criminal damage offences, during the following two years. A number of firearm offences were amongst the categories, such as criminal damage involving an airgun, which were most likely to have been affected by the NCRS (Coleman *et al.*, 2007: 32).

Beyond this it should also be noted that local policing activities and priorities affect the levels of reported and recorded violent crime. Walker *et al.* have cited research by the Cardiff Violence Research Group which reaffirms the argument that police data primarily reflects changes in policing activity against violence rather than measuring changing underlying levels of violence. For example, their study showed an association between the introduction of CCTV surveillance and increased police detection of violence (Walker *et al.*, 2006: 50). In a similar fashion Squires and Kennison (2010) have shown how the adoption of an intelligence-led, anti-gang strategy by Manchester police appeared to increase the apparent size and scale of the 'gangs and guns' threat facing the city, driving a more proactive policing strategy which, at times, both intensified gang conflicts and rivalries and produced more gang violence.

Beyond this there are still further questions about the adequacy of existing gun crime statistics, in particular the ways in which the very definition of 'gun crime' influences patterns of crime recording. For example, the Home Office criminal statistics only record offences involving the *criminal 'use' of a firearm* rather than simple offences of illegal firearm possession or transfer (Hales, 2006: 5). Even though a mandatory five-year prison sentence now applies for illegal firearm possession, there are further ambiguities involved in the interpretation of the notion of firearm 'use'. Very often the type of firearm employed in an offence remains unknown, especially when the weapon is neither fired nor retrieved; likewise only the supposed 'principal firearm' identified in an incident are recorded for each offence in which a firearm is used (others present at an incident, brandished or carried may be overlooked), meaning that potentially important intelligence data may be lost (Hales, 2006). Such problems with offence definition and recording inevitably contributed to intelligence gaps and crime prevention problems precisely because it is often the breach of the more 'technical' firearms control and licensing laws that put firearms into the hands of the people more likely to use them criminally. Since the introduction of the National Ballistics Intelligence Service (NABIS) in 2008, police forces are referring the majority of weapons recovered for forensic analysis and intelligence tracing but this is unrelated to the process of crime recording.

There are as many as 55 firearm offences that can be committed even before a gun is pointed and fired. While many of these are apparently technical in nature and non-newsworthy (although also including offences such as 'sawing-off' a shotgun, or filing away a weapon's serial number, as well as many licensing offences or the failure to keep weapons securely) it is the commission of such offences that often puts firearms (and ammunition) in the hands of offenders who will actually use them. In 2005–2006 there were over 4,000 such offences recorded by the police but these are not gathered together as part of the headline 'gun crime' figures (Walker *et al.*, 2006). If these additional offences against the Firearm Acts were included in the reported 'crimes involving firearms' statistics, then the gun crime figures for England and Wales would rise by around 50–60 per cent (Barrett, 2008). It is understandable why no Government would wish to contemplate such an increase 'on its shift'; it is also clear that shooting lobby organizations around the world are usually keen to maintain the comforting illusion that gun offences are the exclusive preserve of career criminals, but the evidence rather suggests otherwise. For example, Seiber's diligent recording of, at least scores of, *gunfire graffiti* incidents around the country where road signs in particular, often on major roads and motorways, are peppered with shotgun pellets or holed by high velocity rifle fire, is clearly indicative of fairly widespread firearm misuse (Seiber, 2011). This practice, criminal damage by firearm, is familiar in the USA, where it is sometimes regarded as a joke, even as it suggests that gun owners may not all subscribe to the high standards of behaviour sometimes claimed.[6] So there is no absolutely watertight distinction between firearms used for sporting and agricultural purposes and those used in crime even though an overwhelming majority of handguns used in the furtherance of criminal activities are unlikely to have ever been legal weapons in the UK (although the same is not true of shotguns, air weapons and converted or imitation firearms, however).[7] One consequence of these various definitional and recording anomalies is an incomplete picture of the scale, extent and nature of the gun crime problem.

The underlying issue here became particularly absurd following the passage of section 28 of the 2006 Violent Crime Reduction Act (VCRA) which made it an offence to use another person to 'mind' or 'look after' a firearm. The legislation also criminalized: the possession of a firearm with intent to injure; possession of firearms with intent to cause fear of violence; carrying a firearm in a public place; and trespassing in a building with a firearm. The new firearm laws had been specifically amended following rising concerns about the carrying, circulation and 'minding' of illegal firearms by street gang members. However, despite this and the fact that the illegal activities they sought to address were presumed to be directly related to UK gun problems, offences committed against these new provisions are still not included in the overall totals for 'gun crime' in England and Wales. Accordingly, we have a very incomplete picture of the problem. The same was true in 2008 of 'knife crime', when media and government alike began to express growing concern about stabbings. Although the social profile of stab victims was very similar to that of gunshot victims, Home Office data gave only a very limited handle on the scale of the problem – even to the point of being unclear about whether the number of stabbings was actually rising or falling (Squires *et al.*, 2008; Squires, 2009b; Squires and Goldsmith, 2010).

Notwithstanding the problems inherent in the available data already referred to, one of the most striking developments (revealed in Figure 2.1) is undoubtedly the significant increase – by almost 105 per cent – of handgun-related offences during the three years after 1998 when handguns had been banned. How much of this may have been triggered by greater, post-Dunblane political sensitivities and proactive policing remains an open question, although the contribution of imitation firearms (and the new mixed economy of illegal weapons, see Figure 2.4), concealed by the 'unknown handgun' figure is likely to have been significant. After 2002, not unlike the air weapon figures referred to already, the 'total handgun crime' figure turns downwards, continuing on a downward path until 2010–2011. From 2003–2004, the picture complicates, reflecting the growing sophistication of the analysis of police recovered firearms: a fuller picture of imitation firearm misuse is emerging and a new category isolated of 'unidentified handgun'.[8] Not unlike the data on air weapons in Figure 2.3, the evidence suggests that imitation firearms are being diverted from 'firearms crime' recording and into the new anti-social behaviour categories.

In Figure 2.4, the pie chart and the percentages show the respective shares of different categories of firearms making up the illegal gun inventory of England and Wales – insofar as it has come to light via police crime recording. The lists in the boxes provide the actual numbers of the types of firearms in each category. It is important to acknowledge that this is not, for reasons discussed already, a complete picture of firearms circulating on the streets of our cities. Furthermore, fully 9 per cent of these firearms being recorded as misused in criminal activity during 2010–2011 remain 'unidentified' and over three-quarters of handguns used in crime are 'type unknown'. Put another way, almost one-third (30 per cent) of English and Welsh crime guns are unknown, and a further 20 per cent are a motley collection of junk 'other firearms' or known to be imitations, while a further 37 per cent are air weapons. Similar proportions were found in the national study of convicted firearms offenders undertaken for the Home Office in 2006. Eighty offenders accounted for 106 firearms, 34 of which comprised a motley collection of conversions, blank firers, imitations and BB guns (Hales *et al.*, 2006: 40). This represents a particularly complex, multi-layered, illegal weapon inventory and while it demonstrates a certain criminal inventiveness in acquiring, adapting and utilizing a variety of weapons, it also points to the need for a similarly diverse set of control, prevention and response strategies. Insofar as the strict controls upon factory quality, purpose-built firearms – in particular handguns – are concerned, the variety of firearms now comprising the illegal mixed economy of weapons in England and Wales probably indicates the degree to which several forms of weapon displacement have occurred in the UK, perhaps more significantly so following the handgun prohibitions after Dunblane and the availability of new types of criminal firearms (especially imitations, reactivations and conversions) from the mid-1980s. It is certainly arguable that recent concerns about 'knife crime' in the UK are also reflective of another aspect of this process of weapon displacement (Squires, 2011a).

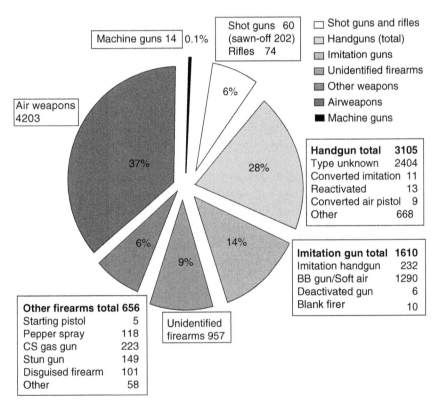

FIGURE 2.4 The diverse mixed economy of illegal firearms: figures relate to England and Wales, 2010–2011

Source: Lau (2012).

The diverse mixed economy of weapons: a 'sub-prime', junk-gun market

Imitation firearms

Figure 2.1 revealed a rapid apparent growth up to 2004–2005 and a significant fall off in the misuse of imitation firearms. The sharp decline in imitation misuse corresponds closely with the fall in air weapon offences and both are likely to reflect the effect of section 37 of the 2003 Anti-Social Behaviour Act which made it an offence to carry an imitation firearm, or air weapon, in a public place so as to cause 'harassment, alarm and distress' to members of the public. The new provision provided police with a less serious charge for these offences, moreover one which was not included in the Home Office recorded gun crime data. In effect both the rapid apparent growth and equally dramatic decline of British gun crime is likely to reflect the crime recording anomalies associated with imitations. This is certainly not to be complacent and imitation firearms are far from being the entirety of the problem, but they (and the recording of them) are likely to account for a substantial proportion of the recent trend fluctuation.

Concern about misuse of imitation – or replica firearms – began to surface in the 1980s (see Squires, 2000; Squires and Kennison, 2010). Imitation firearms took a number of forms, some were incapable of firing anything, other 'Airsoft Guns' fired small plastic pellets at low velocity, different varieties of air weapons or BB guns could fire air pellets or small ball-bearings while, at the top of the range, gas cylinder-powered weapons could fire pellets at a much greater velocity, some of these being powerful enough to take them into the 'prohibited' category.[9] In addition to this variety were also a range of athletics starting pistols, blank firers, 'alarm' guns and CS gas firers. In a more innocent time, some of the weapons listed above, especially the less powerful ones, may well have shaded to some degree into the 'toy' category. The 2004 Metropolitan Police Authority (MPA) Gun Crime Scrutiny report agreed: 'replica weapons can range from children's toys to easily convertible, sophisticated pieces of machinery' (MPA, 2004: 52), going on to recommend that clear distinctions be made between 'toys' and weapons capable of discharging any form of shot, pellet or bullet.

Unfortunately such advice ran somewhat counter to the newer marketing of these 'quasi' weapons, some indeed were marketed precisely for their 'collectable' or 'playful' characteristics and it was only the 2006 VCRA that raised the age for purchasing an air or replica weapon to 18. Other types of replica weapon were advertised in the pages of a variety of shooting magazines or a range of other more euphemistically titled 'male interest and leisure' magazines (Taylor and Hornsby, 2000).

Such firearms have also sustained the establishment of new sports and leisure activities enjoyed by many, such as paintball and 'airsoft skirmishing'. Akin to Bauman's characterization of 'liquid modernity' (Bauman, 2000), underpinned by newly marketed products, neo-liberal cultures of individual rights and choices and new technologies, these developments have, according to Taylor and Hornsby, helped to disrupt established and traditional conceptions of 'legitimate sports shooting' and 'play'; notions of lethality and non-lethality, safety, danger and display, legality and illegality, protection and aggression, and distinctions between weapons and 'toys' in ways that established legal discourses on crime and public safety. They argue that:

> Discussions about firearms law in Britain, as currently constituted, still very often carry forward the assumption that there is an orderly relationship between the list of weaponry defined as being 'prohibited' or, alternatively, categorised as 'Section 1' firearms and lethality, but the concern in many quarters is that fast changing technology is allowing for the modification of many weapons which might have first been sold purely as leisure-sport style air pistols.
>
> *(Taylor and Hornsby, 2000)*

During the 1980s, apparently concerned that their primary sales markets were saturated, a number of firearms manufacturers had, during a phase of 'horizontal and vertical product diversification', licensed their design patents to other manufacturers, creating a wholly new replica firearm market (Diaz, 1999). Low powered, air-powered, toy and 'collectable' firearms began, increasingly, to resemble the real thing. In due course they began to be employed in criminal activities.

In 2004, the MPA Gun Crime Scrutiny report suggested higher proportions of replicas and conversions were finding employment in criminal activities: 'a significant amount of firearm offences in London are committed with replica and converted weapons', anything up to 50 per cent (MPA, 2004: 48; Wheal and Tilley, 2009: 174). Researchers reported evidence that anything between 40–50 per cent of 'armed robberies' in England were undertaken using 'imitation' firearms (Morrison and O'Donnell, 1994, 1997; Matthews, 1996; Rix *et al.*, 1998). Gill's later study of commercial robberies (interviews with 341 convicted armed robbers) found that only 39 per cent were carrying a real gun and only 26 per cent had potentially lethal firearms (Gill, 2000: 74–76). Apparently with softer targets (shops and commercial premises) an imitation weapon could be a sufficient 'frightener', whereas robbing banks (according to the offenders) appeared to require a more capable firearm. Even so, Matthews (2002) detected a quite mixed range of factors motivating weapon choice for offenders: replicas were cheap and easier to come by and could often do the job. And while real firearms may have carried more 'weight', or threat potential, there was the risk that they might be fired either accidentally or impetuously and thereby considerably raising the stakes in ways an offender might have hoped to avoid (a point made also by Hales *et al.*'s (2006) interviewees).

Bennett and Holloway's study between 2000 and 2002 using the NEW-ADAM (the New English and Welsh Arrestee Drug Abuse Monitoring programme) arrestee database found that, for arrestees claiming to have employed a firearm in their criminal activities, one-third of the weapons they referred to were either air weapons or replicas; the type of a further 8 per cent of the firearms was not specified, although converted weapons were not separately counted (Bennett and Holloway, 2004: 243).

Drawing together a range of such evidence, Wheal and Tilley (2009: 176) conclude that official crime figures 'very substantially understate the significance of imitation weapons'. In due course, the Association of Chief Police Officers (ACPO) and the Police Federation began to lobby for controls on such weapons (Fry, 1989, 1991). The MPA also called for an outright ban on the production and sale of replica firearms (MPA, 2004).

Concern about what Taylor and Hornsby (2000) referred to as a 'new frontier in the gun market' began to manifest itself and not just in the UK. For example, a study of firearms recovered by police in five Canadian cities found that 21 per cent of these firearms were replicas as against 20 per cent genuine handguns (Department of Justice Canada and Canadian Association of Chiefs of Police, 1997). Raising especial concerns on grounds of both cost and danger to the public were incidents where the police officers were confronted by apparently armed suspects. Senior police officers interviewed have argued that some 25 per cent of armed response call-outs involved incidents involving imitation firearms – tragedies waiting to happen. Research in Nottingham (Schneider *et al.*, 2004, cited in Wheal and Tilley, 2009) found that 46 per cent of firearms recovered by Armed Response Vehicle crews were not capable of firing live ammunition. In 2003, following concern about the number of suspects shot by police but found to be carrying (only) replica firearms, the Police Complaints Authority (PCA) published the results of its own survey of all suspects shot by police between 1998 and 2000 (PCA, 2003): one-third of these were carrying replica firearms (see Squires and Kennison, 2010: 159–163 for a fuller discussion). Professionals engaged in intelligence gathering on illegal weapons have likewise argued that, even after the 2006 VCRA, firearms controls have 'failed to keep pace with the spread of gun culture in this country and its complexity' (Luck, 2009).

Hales and his colleagues summarize the changes that their research suggests have impacted upon the new complex mixed economy of illegal weapons, crosscutting and disrupting the familiar landscape of firearm ownership and use:

- the innovations of converted imitation firearms and home-made ammunition and the re-circulation of firearms that have been used in crime;
- the availability of highly realistic imitation firearms has increased; these are sufficiently realistic to facilitate crimes relying on the threat of violence, such as armed robbery;
- illegal firearms have become increasingly accessible to younger offenders who appear more likely to use those firearms recklessly;
- the entrenchment of a competitive consumer culture has placed increasing pressures on young people to conform to explicitly materialistic social norms;
- the growth and increasing normalisation of illegal drugs markets and other offending has provided a credible alternative career path to the legal mainstream for some individuals, particularly in many economically deprived communities, and has stimulated violent crime;
- in many areas, the operation of the local criminal economy has become conflated with cultures of gang membership.

(Hales et al., *2006: 113)*

In turn, each of these factors has further consequences, driving the gang-membership, which both catalyses and sustains conflict and violence, generating a demand for weapons which, again in its turn, fosters violent expectations, facilitating violent problem-solving and the cultural and psychological conditions in which a violent reputation ('respect') becomes a key (albeit, as we shall see in Chapter 3, a deeply problematic one) to self-preservation (Squires, 2008a, 2009a). In the USA, drawing upon their research on young people's narratives of weaponized encounters, Fagan and Wilkinson have described these self-perpetuating violence contexts as 'lethal ecologies' (Fagan and Wilkinson, 1998, 2000; Wilkinson, 2003). I will consider their work more fully in Chapter 5.

From around 2002 the UK Gun Control Network (GCN) also began to lobby for the prohibition of imitation firearms, its campaign materials (reproduced below in Figure 2.5) making the point that: imitation firearms could not easily be distinguished from the real thing and that the trauma was genuine even if the firearm was not real – imitation firearms were undoubtedly a part of the UK's gun crime problem. According to Heal (1991), replica firearms carried as virtual 'fashion accessories' by wannabe gangsters (a complaint voiced by a number of senior police officers) were not just a problem at the level of appearances, their very proliferation encouraged offenders to contemplate obtaining real firearms. In due course section 36 of the 2006 VCRA prohibited the manufacture, import and sale of 'realistic imitation firearms'.

Unfortunately, despite the passage of the 2006 VCRA, a number of flaws and weaknesses – 'loopholes' – accompanied the framing and implementation of the new legislation in respect of 'realistic imitation' firearms. Wheal and Tilley (2009) have gone some way to account for these problems. There were problems in defining precisely what a 'realistic imitation' firearm was (as opposed to toys, paintball or airsoft weapons); Home Office officials (some of whom were rather sceptical anyway) claim that the relevant clauses were rushed rather than fully consulted. Regarding implementation there are suggestions that agencies such as Her Majesty's Revenue & Customs (HMRC) did not give tackling imitation weapons the priority given to intercepting real firearms, and that front-line officers were slow to act; the wide opportunities for sourcing imitation weapons (from market stalls and shops to the internet) meant that distribution was difficult to contain especially following the successful lobbying by historical re-enactment, paintball and skirmishing associations as well as dramatic and theatrical societies to exempt their 'weapons of choice' from the legislation by way of allowing legal defences for the manufacture, distribution, sale, purchase and carrying of 'realistic imitation' firearms. Wheal and Tilley concluded that the VCRA 'did not dent the stock of imitation firearms which might be accessed and used by offenders' while the legislation's loopholes meant that 'a determined offender will not find it difficult to acquire a new "realistic imitation" firearm to use in crime' (2009: 179–181).

FIGURE 2.5 UK Gun Control Network posters for the imitation firearm campaign

Source: Thanks to the UK Gun Control Network for their kind permission to reproduce these images.

Converted firearms

However, imitation firearms were not the only new niche market feeding into
Britain's gun crime problems. A range of converted and convertible firearms also
began to make their appearance. Also during the 1980s, evidence had emerged
that offenders were 'exploiting a loophole in the law by buying replica [and blank-
firing] weapons and then converting them to fire live ammunition' (Heal, 1991).

Likewise, evidence emerging from Operation Trident in 2003, the Metropolitan Police initiative to address 'black-on-black' and gang-related armed crime in London, has revealed that something like 75–80 per cent of 'guns' recovered as a result of police investigations 'did not start out as purposeful firearms' (Brown, 2003; MPA, 2004: 50) but rather comprised 'conversions', 'reactivations' or outright replicas. However, most significant of all, an astonishing 80 per cent of the Trident incidents in which firearms were used causing injury involved air- or gas-powered weapons, which had been illegally converted to fire a live bullet, or were otherwise 'converted'. GMP likewise reported that almost half of the firearms capable of live firing recovered during 2003–2004 were converted, adding that 'scarcity in supply [of real firearms] means that criminals will invest significantly in conversion' (GMP, 2006). The GMP briefing paper also provided details on two successful police operations to intercept, first, 30 Cuno Melcher Sportwaffen ME90 gas alarm pistols legally manufactured for sale in Germany for self-defence purposes but illegally converted in Lithuania to fire live ammunition and equipped with silencers and, second, an operation to intercept 274 lawfully manufactured 'gas guns' modelled on Smith & Wesson, Luger and Glock templates, which were purchased on the European mainland and transported for conversion in a Manchester machine shop.

As well as scarcity and the difficulty of accessing factory quality, purpose-built firearms, Hales et al.'s (2006) interviewees also cited the importance of price. They noted, on the basis of their interviews with convicted gun offenders, 'the overall impression is that converted firearms are more widely available and cheaper than purpose built firearms' (2006: 52). Converted firearms were also thought to be less easy for the police to trace. Indeed exactly one-third of the 66 offenders who claimed to know people with guns mentioned 'converted weapons'. Interesting, also, were their observations on the variable quality of the conversions:

- They're shit; it's just a ball bearing on the end of a blank cartridge innit. Them guns ain't meant to fire fucking live cartridges (London);
- [A] lot of them were blank firers, converted ... and they're pieces of shit, blow your hand off (West Midlands);
- [T]hey always used to jam (West Midlands).

(Hales et al., 2006: 52)

These are widely acknowledged problems with low-price, 'junk' firearms. Although the USA might be presumed to have a ready supply of factory quality handguns, in fact there are significant firearm 'quality' parallels with the British stock of junk firearms (Cook et al., 2007). For instance, not unlike the sub-prime credit market there are long recognized problems associated with the sub-prime gun market: the 'poor man's gun' – the 'two-dollar pistol' or

'Saturday night special' (Squires, 2000). Furthermore, the sub-prime gun market carries extra risks:

> [A] converted pistol is both less reliable and also potentially dangerous for the user since the materials used are not designed by the manufacturer to withstand the much higher gas pressure that occurs with live ammunition ... the work of the converters, of course, does not meet the quality standards that the regular manufacturers apply. And, last but not least, these weapons are not tested ... a converted gun can thus be considered a poor man's alternative, [despite this] such weapons circulate on a large scale among criminals.
>
> *(Spapens, 2007: 366)*

As De Vries (2011: 212) has added, such weapons are dangerous and unreliable, 'their popularity must be due to their availability and low price instead of their performance'. However, perhaps the most dramatic evidence of the fallibility of the converted firearm was provided by a shooting crime scene in South London where police found not just a victim with bullet wounds but also the severed fingers of the shooter whose gun blew up in his hand (O'Neill, 2008). Perhaps the ultimate danger represented by the use of a junk firearm, however, is the risk of being confronted, and shot by armed police officers. Squires and Kennison (2010: 160) report evidence from a 2003 PCA analysis of 20 police fatal shootings in England and Wales from 1998–2000. Over one-third of the total number of incidents (seven out of 20) involved a replica/imitation firearm, rising to over half (seven out of 12) of the cases where a supposed firearm was involved. In other words, none of the handguns were real, only three air weapons and two shotguns were 'genuine firearms'. Two years later, the dangers of junk or replica firearms for police and suspects alike were revealed when officers from CO19 performed a 'hard stop' in Mill Hill, North London, on a silver VW Golf containing three armed men believed to be on their way to rob some drug dealers. In two bursts of rapid fire from a HK G36 carbine, one police officer fired eight shots, six of which struck Azelle Rodney, the final four in his head. In the car with Mr Rodney was a deactivated Colt semi-automatic pistol (showing signs of an amateurish and unsuccessful attempt to reactivate it), a Baikal CS gas pistol that had been converted to fire live ammunition and a converted 'key fob' gun (Holland, 2013: 39).[10]

Weapon conversions can take a number of forms. Over a five-year period between September 2003 and September 2008, the National Forensic Science Service undertook a review of the 8,887 firearms submitted for forensic analysis and recorded upon its National Firearms Forensic Intelligence Database (NFFID). On an annual basis an average 21 per cent of the firearms submitted were converted weapons (Hannam, 2010).

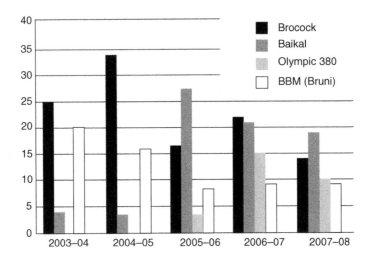

FIGURE 2.6 National Firearms Forensic Intelligence Database Survey, 2003–2008: selected converted firearms submitted for analysis

Source: Hannam (2010).

Hannam's analysis also revealed the different 'waves' of converted firearm types finding their way to Britain. In the late 1990s and early 2000s the Brocock and Bruni BBM pistols were the most frequent types appearing (respectively 477 and 244) submitted during the five-year assessment period. In 2004, the MPA noted that: 'Since the ban on real handguns in 1997, Brocock guns have become a weapon of choice for criminals in cities across Britain' (MPA, 2004: 48). Apparently company executives had acknowledged that 'their entire range of airguns … could easily be turned into lethal weapons' (MPA, 2004: 48). Brococks and other 'air cartridge' firearms became prohibited weapons in 2003. Seven years later, a converted Bruni semi-automatic pistol, was thought to have been acquired by Mark Duggan on or around 4 August 2011. Intelligence about this gun led to his fatal shooting by the police (the incident which 'sparked' the 2011 riots). The weapon was discovered several yards from the vehicle he had been travelling in (Dodd, 2011). The Inquest jury appeared to accept that he had thrown the gun away before being shot. Later the Baikal pistol types and the model 'Olympic 380' revolver (a starting-pistol 'blank firer' also manufactured by Bruni) arrived on the scene (Gill, 2008; O'Neill, 2008; Luck, 2009). An Olympic .380 pistol had been buried in the garden of a house in Manchester owned by the former girlfriend of a gang member. Whether she had been coerced into hiding the weapon, or had volunteered, was never entirely clear. However, the weapon was later found by the woman's teenage son who, playing with it one day, accidentally shot and killed his sister (Allison, 2007).

As each type of conversion surfaced in significant numbers, the particular make of convertible firearm could be added to the prohibited list. NABIS now monitors the recovered converted firearm trends reporting to ACPO and the Home Office on any weapons appearing as an emerging crime threat. In 2011, NABIS produced a report detailing its operation in respect of the Olympic .380 which had attracted attention following 179 converted Olympic .380 revolvers being seized by 13 police forces in England and Wales between 2007 and March 2010, 157 (88 per cent) of these in the Metropolitan Police area (NABIS, 2011).

A series of events followed: liaison with the gun trade and the manufacturers in Italy and testing of the ease of convertibility of the firearm; subsequently, plans were set in motion to prevent further importation of the firearm and withdraw those already here; followed by a targeted amnesty for the remainder. The 'intelligence-led' bespoke amnesty ran from April (when the weapon became prohibited) to June 2010, during which time almost 800 Olympic .380s were handed in (and a quantity of ammunition), just over one-quarter in London. Around 100 further assorted blank-firers were handed in. Overall, only seven of the amnesty returned weapons had been converted, a considerably lower proportion than had hitherto come to light via police action and underscoring previous understandings that amnesties tend to pick up the more low-risk guns, not those involved in criminal activity (Warlow, 2007: 118; Wheal and Tilley, 2009). As NABIS acknowledged, however, the entire operation and related policing activities had netted some 1,300 Olympic .380 BBMs, removing from circulation a significant number of convertible firearms already known for their criminal misuse. Reflecting upon the success of the Olympic .380 Operation, NABIS acknowledged that although it had been a very successful piece of intelligence-led, proactive partnership police work it was still the case that: 'Criminals are entrepreneurial and will look to replace the Olympic .380 BBM with another blank firer' (NABIS, 2011: 24). More consistency in police recording of firearm types recovered was urged and an urgent need for changes to section 39 of the 2006 VCRA was proposed, in order to establish clear standards and specifications for blank firers especially relating to their potential for criminal convertibility.

Work of this nature by NABIS is triggered by the emergence of particular crime guns (in this case converted weapons) on British streets although there are layers of security, prior to trafficking and criminal misuse, that require prior attention. Dutch criminologist Toine Spapens, writing in 2007 on trafficking in illicit firearms in Europe, acknowledged that at least 95 per cent of the firearms seized by the Dutch police during 1998–2000 were originally produced quite legally (Spapens, 2007). He then went on to identify six primary routes by which these firearms slipped into illegality:

- leakage directly from the factory to the illicit circuit;
- fake exports, sometimes via intermediaries;
- conversion of non-lethal firearms;
- recycling of discarded weapons or re-use of the surplus parts;
- theft from legal dealers or private owners of legal firearms;
- fraud by private owners of legal firearms.

(2007: 365)

Here we are especially interested in the third of the routes identified; the others, aspects of a much more complex analysis of weapon trafficking, I will leave for Chapter 7. For the moment, it is enough to acknowledge the various layers and types of facilitation: from failing states, political compromise, regulatory weaknesses and open border 'free markets', legal ambiguity, policing failures, security deficits, resistance, corruption, geo-political and paramilitary alliances, parallel criminal organization and smaller-scale criminal inventiveness and entrepreneurism by which the supply of and demand for illegal firearms functions. In this respect it is worth noting that many of Europe's firearm trafficking problems are especially associated with small arms overproduction and stockpiling in former Soviet states; the trafficking to and oversupply of weapons in the former Yugoslavia; disharmonies in gun law regimes across European members states; distinctive national gun cultures in European societies and the scale and character of weapon production and brokering in different societies. Layered onto these structural political factors are a series of more fluid relationships relating to post-colonial cultural associations, patterns of immigration and people movement. Questions of race, racism, social exclusion and marginality almost inevitably follow and, with them, concerns about organized criminality, terrorism, contraband trafficking routes and networks and, more recently, gangs. In this regard, the particular significance of Holland – in relation to the UK – was clear to Spapens, 'the United Kingdom was already an important destination country for narcotics being transhipped via the Netherlands' (2007: 370). The strengthening of firearms laws in Britain combined with a criminal demand capable of inflating the price of a junk euro-firearm served to create a new criminal opportunity, thus 'it was obvious that the Netherlands would also begin to play the role of transit country for illicit firearms' (Spapens, 2007: 370).

Another Dutch researcher (De Vries, 2011) reviewed evidence that, between 2002 and 2006, around 1,000 converted firearms were seized by the Dutch police, the majority of which were of Italian and Turkish origin, but most of the conversions had been undertaken in Portugal, from where the weapons had travelled to Holland, some of them moving subsequently to the UK. In Holland most of the weapons' end users were young men from ethnic minority groups. De Vries' analysis revealed the difficulty of addressing the problem effectively by only tackling the criminal 'end use' of the weapons: 'fighting the problem by its tail instead of its roots' (2011: 215). As a national policing agency the Dutch police, acting alone, could neither prevent converted firearms reaching its borders nor tackle the prior trafficking processes that brought them there. Accordingly, her analysis drew attention to the trans-national determinants of the crime: the political, legal, social, ethnic and criminal networks sustaining the trafficking, generating the demand and providing the supply. Crucial to the trafficking and conversion were links between Turkish and Portuguese criminal groups in Italy, Portugal and the Netherlands. Beyond the trafficking of the converted weapons lay questions about the lack of harmony in EU laws regarding firearm production and inadequate regulation of original sales (from initial producers to criminal converters).

As De Vries (2011: 214) noted,

> the lack of border controls within the European Union in combination with differences in the firearms legislation of individual EU member states concerning the purchase of gas pistols interfere[s] with the ability of one national police force to fight this specific type of cross-border crime.

EU Directive 91/477 (18 June 1991) had sought to regulate weapons transfers within the EU but had not addressed the then relatively unknown problem of converted firearms. A new Directive of European Parliament of 21 May 2008 (European Commission, 2008) noted that 'police intelligence evidence shows an increase in the use of converted weapons within the Community. It is therefore essential to ensure that such convertible weapons are brought within the definition of a firearm for the purposes of Directive 91/477/EEC'. The problem remains that without further harmonization of firearms laws, strategic policing initiatives to tackle the trafficking of what, in some EU member states, is perfectly legal firearm production, transfer and ownership are likely to be very difficult. For countries such as Holland and the UK, which have some of the toughest firearms control regimes in Europe (which has, in part, helped create the criminal converted weapons market), gun law harmonization will inevitably look like a watering down of their existing gun control regimes. Because of these differences, and a survey of EU member states in 2009, the European Commission announced they were not convinced that the problems associated with the trade in replicas were so serious as to justify subjecting all the manufacturers, dealers and owners of replicas to the rigorous obligations contained in the Weapons Directive. Accordingly, 'inclusion of replicas into the scope of application of Directive 91/477/EEC appears to be neither possible nor advisable' (European Commission, 2010). The British Government European Scrutiny Committee, on the one hand, recognizing that statistics on the extent of converted firearm involvement in crime was not especially reliable and, on the other, noting that it was possible, within the terms of the EU agreement, for individual states to ban the particular firearms that were the most readily convertible (such as the Brocock, BBM and Olympic .380), consoled itself with the news that crime committed with 'realistic imitation' firearms appeared to be falling (House of Commons: European Scrutiny Committee, 2010).

However, as Hannam's (2010) Firearms Forensic Intelligence Database Survey (Figure 2.6) revealed, just as some types of converted firearms appeared to be declining in use, others, also reflecting other important European geo-political, legal and criminal legacies, were apparently growing in availability or popularity. The stories behind particular weapon types reveal classic global–local dynamics at work.

A young black man, aged 16, was shot twice in the back at point-blank range at Streatham Ice rink in February 2007. Over 300 people were attending an event at the venue, but five years and as many as 18 arrests later, no-one has identified the shooter and no-one has been convicted of the killing. The identity of the gun involved was, apparently, rather more quickly revealed, the Baikal IZH-79 had the words 'made in Russia' stamped on the barrel (although this may have been to mislead). It was originally (apparently) manufactured as a tear gas-firing, self-defence weapon for the European market in the Russian city of Izhevsk, home of the Soviet Kalashnikov AK-47 assault rifle and Makarov pistol (the standard Russian military and police side arm), and part of the new Russia's post-Cold War product diversification in that town. The weapons were described as 'a step up from personal rape alarms … designed to fire a cloud of tear gas at an attacker' (O'Neill, 2008). Accordingly, in an intriguing 'American' touch the weapons were marketed in glossy brochures showing young women pulling handguns from handbags to fend off muggers and rapists (O'Neill, 2008). However, the Streatham weapon had been converted in a Lithuanian workshop to shoot live bullets. The weapon was apparently smuggled into Britain and sold to the armourer of a South London gang. According to *The Times* (O'Neill, 2008): 'Three years ago no one had heard of the Baikal. Today it is the gun of choice in gangland Britain.'

In 2007, four men were convicted of smuggling converted Baikal pistols, converted in Lithuania, and sentenced to a total of 56 years imprisonment at Manchester Crown Court. When Lithuanian police acting in conjunction with the GMP raided a veterinary practitioner's house in Kedainiai, two-hour's drive north of the capital Vilnius, they found over 100 'gas guns' in process of conversion. The weapons (perfectly legal in Lithuania) had been purchased from Baikal for the equivalent of around £10 each, they were re-modeled to fire live ammunition and were sold, some fitted with silencers), for around £300 each and trafficked to Manchester where they were thought to fetch over £1,000 each (Connolly and Cobain, 2007). Five men (Lithuanian traffickers and known British organized criminals) were sentenced at Southwark and Blackfriars Crown courts in related cases. The following year, seven men were imprisoned, again in Manchester, for their parts in what was described as the 'biggest gun-running operation ever uncovered in the UK'. Fifty-six converted Baikal firearms, described as 'assassin's kits' with an estimated street value of £1,700 each, and 856 rounds of ammunition were seized (BBC News, 2008). According to news reports, Lithuania was becoming a destination of choice for European gunrunners. Michael Campbell, brother of one of the men allegedly behind the Omagh bombing, was apprehended in Lithuania after travelling there allegedly to source firearms for the Real IRA (Walker, 2009). Two years later in Manchester, three women were convicted and sentenced to seven and eight years imprisonment each, for storing illegal firearms in their homes, the weapons in question were converted Baikal pistols (GMP press release, 2011). The scale of the illegal converted gun trade was such that the Lithuanian police were said to joke that their criminals had joined the European Union several years before the rest of the country (O'Neill, 2008).

Reactivated firearms

If factors critical to the supply of converted weapons lay in Europe's political and military past and, not least, its history of small arms production, a key issue for reactivated weapons has been the domestic demand for deactivated firearms. Warlow (2007) notes how: 'In response to increasing customer demand for examples of military arms' during the 1990s it was common to see 'advertisements for all manner of deactivated firearms in the shooting press' (Warlow, 2007). Attention had already been drawn to the emerging interest of gun collectors in exotic foreign and military firearms, after all Michael Ryan took a modified Kalashnikov AK-47 assault rifle on his Hungerford killing spree in 1987; few people realized such a weapon could be legally owned in Britain. Prior to 1995 deactivated weapons could be held by collectors without a firearms licence although that year, upon the basis of evidence that deactivated weapons were being brought back into use and sold into criminal circles, the deactivation specifications were tightened up. Nevertheless there is evidence of a sizeable backlog of pre-1995 deactivated firearms still available for sale in the UK and, obviously, even greater quantities abroad.

Forensic scientists examined a major cache of reactivated weapons seized by Belgian police in the late 1990s (Migeot and De Kinder, 1999) while, in Britain, police were beginning to unravel a supply chain of reactivated Mac-10 machine guns feeding the criminal underworlds of Dublin, Manchester, Glasgow and London (Walsh, 1999). The weapons were eventually traced to a rented workshop in Hove, East Sussex where a police raid found 40 deactivated Mac-10s and a collection of components to restore them to full working order. The Forensic Science Service went on to link the workshop to more than 50 reactivated guns used in numerous shootings, seized from criminals or recovered from crime scenes around the country. In their deactivated form the weapons could be purchased for around £100 each, reactivated they could be priced at ten times that amount. The lure of easy money seems to have been what enticed the two men behind another cottage industry criminal gun reactivation enterprise in Derbyshire in 2003. Thousands of deactivated firearms passed through the pair of men's hands – and the kits to reactivate them – in what police described as the country's most prolific gun reactivation business. Following the arrests, police were still trying to trace some 3,000 firearms sold on by the business. Apparently 'guns supplied by the [pair] have been recovered from at least eight murder scenes, gangland shootings and a loyalist paramilitary arms cache … and traced to at least 65 crime scenes' (Townsend, 2007; Warlow, 2007). NABIS cited the case in calling for tougher controls on reactivated weapons.

Yet if the domestic demand for 'deactivated/reactivated' firearms explains something of the context of this particular dimension of the British gun crime problem, difficulties in regulating the national and international trade definitely form another. Warlow (2007) describes how his forensic weapon examination duties brought him into contact with two Smith and Wesson .38 calibre revolvers involved in two murders. The first had originally been purchased by the Hong Kong police, later when decommissioned by the police it was sold as one of a batch to a registered firearms dealer in London. The dealer's records falsely claimed the weapon had been deactivated (deactivation would have significantly lowered its resale value). A second Smith and Wesson .38 was found at a murder scene in the West Midlands where a man had been shot five times and killed. Forensic analysis revealed that the weapon had originally been in a consignment sold over 20 years earlier to Strathclyde police. When the weapons were taken out of service they too were sold to the same London-based registered firearms dealer. Warlow acknowledged the inventiveness of criminals to evade restrictions and in breaking laws but seemed to reserve his particular frustration for what he referred to as the 'present near-draconian standards [of] enhanced firearm deactivation and the constant tightening up of British firearms legislation' (2007: 118). He continued, somewhat overlooking the victims of shooting themselves,

> law-abiding sportsmen and target shooters have become the inevitable victims of these restrictive controls … Legitimate shooting pursuits previously enjoyed by many law-abiding citizens have been curtailed, or even brought to an abrupt end. Decent and respectable members of the gun trade have become the inevitable victims of the decline of their industry.
>
> *(Warlow, 2007: 118)*

The complaint is familiar and closely associated with a complacency sometimes associated with the national and international gun trade and, as we shall see in later chapters, allied with notions of 'self-defence rights', 'sporting and business interests' and 'legitimate commercial activity' helps to shield much of the business of firearm production and marketing from public scrutiny, facilitating shady deals and, ultimately, criminal enterprise supplying the 'grey' and 'black' firearms markets of the world (Karp, 1994).

In a similar vein, responding to a Home Office consultation paper on Controls on Deactivated Firearms issued in 2009, the British Association for Shooting and Conservation (BASC) expressed its doubts about the scale of the criminal misuse of reactivated weapons and the 'flimsy' evidence used to justify the proposed new controls. The Home Secretary, they suspected, was intent on tougher controls whatever the outcome of the consultation. In turn, the BASC resolved that any decision on the question ought to be deferred 'until a report has been received from NABIS – based on at least two years evidence – which gives a proper assessment of the criminal use of deactivated firearms' (BASC, 2009). Of course, quite why a sports shooting and conservation association (sports shooting and conservation has often seemed a rather anomalous pairing to many commentators) should be so emotionally invested in the preservation of what they refer to as 'heritage firearms' is an open question. We might ask *whose* heritage is being preserved. Furthermore, the heritage value of former military weapons shadily traded around the world in military junk bucket shops (the sub-prime gun market) seems questionable at best. 'Heritage' seems a rather grand and beguiling concept when applied to the continuing legacies of crime, death and injury, abuse and conflict perpetuated by such firearms in large parts of the world.

Antique firearms

In addition to conversion and reactivation, evidence has also come to light of offenders, facing an apparent shortage of serviceable weapons, acquiring, using and adapting antique weapons for criminal purposes. According to Faiola, the supply of illegal firearms in Britain bears no relation to that of the US. Reporting for the *Washington Post* in early 2013, he noted:

> When police on a weapons raid swarmed a housing project after London's 2011 riots, they seized a cache of arms that in the United States might be better suited to 'Antiques Roadshow' than inner-city ganglands. Inside plastic bags hidden in a trash collection room, officers uncovered two archaic flintlock pistols, retrofitted flare guns and a Jesse James-style revolver.
>
> *(Faiola, 2013)*

British firearms regulations do not specify precisely what constitutes an antique; instead the definition rests upon a number of factors including age, but also whether the weapon calibre is obsolete, the firing mechanism and the loading and propulsion systems. Thus a number of old, but otherwise fully serviceable, and therefore potentially lethal, firearms dating back to WW2, WW1 and beyond might be bought legally as antiques but adapted to fire contemporary ammunition – alternatively offenders might adapt modern ammunition to fit it to the older calibre weapons. A weapon seized by West Midlands police during the 2011 riots was originally designed for French army officers in the 1870s, similarly a number of small and highly concealable Derringer-style pistols have been recovered. Police commentators have remarked that 'a number of burglaries at antiques weapons collectors' homes across the country may have been ordered by gangs who are desperate to source new guns and rifles' (Mackie, 2013). Officers from the Metropolitan Police Operation Trident have similarly encountered WW2 handguns in raids on 'gang armouries'; according to a police spokesman, 'gangsters are exploiting a "grey area" which means antique or old weapons owned by legitimate firearms dealers are being passed on to street gangs' (Davenport, 2013). The fact that a weapon is re-used or of a rather rare or even unique calibre may make it rather easier for ballistics experts to trace occasions on which it has been used. The number of publicly evidenced cases of antique weapon use in criminal activity remains low, however, and shooting lobby commentators have cautioned against bringing wide-ranging legal changes affecting the antiques trade on the back of, thus far, relatively infrequent incidents (Harriman and Perring, 2012). How 'exceptional' such incidents really are remains an open question; however, evidence of a rather more complex relationship between gun ownership, antiques, firearm collecting and criminal enterprise has arisen in a number of police raids. A former Commissioner of the Metropolitan Police, Sir Paul Condon, had argued about patterns of illegal weapon supply, implicating the licensed firearms trade, in the 1990s, although few well-evidenced figures were ever supplied (Squires,

2000: 110). A raid by Strathclyde police in December 2012 netted some 90 fire-arms including AK–47s, handguns, air weapons, replicas, reactivated weapons and antiques owned by a presumed weapons and ammunition 'collector'. Devon and Cornwall police likewise unearthed the largest cache of illegally held weapons they had ever encountered, over 300 firearms including sub-machine guns, when they raided the home of a man who declared himself as a collector 'fascinated by guns', in November 2012 (Watt *et al.*, 2012).

Sharing the guns around

The role of criminal armourers (sometimes individuals working around the edges of the legal firearms trade, see Squires, 2000: 110), supplying firearms 'to order' for domestic criminal use, has long been an understood feature of the supply networks, often operating within relatively closed, personalized or localized markets (Wright and Rossi, 1986; Morselli, 2012), such as, in the British case, in provincial cities. This is, moreover, a recognized feature of illegal weapons markets and supply chains in other parts of the world (Cook *et al.*, 2007); the 'straw purchaser' phe-nomenon, for instance, is well understood in the USA (Braga and Kennedy, 2001; Brandl and Stroshine, 2011). Although, also acknowledging important differences, a number of US commentators have expressed scepticism about the potential effec-tiveness of purely *supply-side* constraints in keeping guns away from adolescents and other unauthorized users in the USA, given the prevalence of firearms – and alternative sources of supply – available (Koper and Reuter, 1996). In Cook *et al.*'s more recent work (2007), however, the 'thinner' the market (the more effective the existing 'formal' gun restrictions, or the more resistant the community itself to a culture of gun ownership), the more restricted the supply points.[11]

In England and Wales, of the 80 convicted firearms offenders interviewed by Hales *et al.* in 2006, at least 12 claimed to know 'armourers' who converted, sold or loaned firearms. As one of their interviewees put it, 'there are a couple of people like that who sell guns. If I wanted a particular sort of gun now I'd know where to go in Birmingham' (Hales *et al.*, 2006: 46). The authors noted, however, that the nature of the relatively closed criminal markets in which firearms circulated meant that 'supply is patchy and [offenders] are forced to buy whatever is on offer' (Hales *et al.*, 2006: 60). This explained the resort to converted, reactivated or otherwise unreliable 'junk' firearms, and guns of unknown provenance that may well have been used in earlier serious crimes and for which the current, unwit-ting possessor of the firearm might well be charged. The practice of sharing guns around, like the use of unreliable conversions, is a reaction to weapon scarcity and reinforces the importance of police enforcement action continuing to be addressed to weapon supply issues. Especially in gang networks, and even across them, many more offenders might have *access* to firearms than actually own them. As Hales *et al.* (2006: 60) concluded, 'relatively few illegal firearms may have a considerable impact on violent crime and perceptions about levels of illegal firearms ownership'.

These issues come directly into play in the wake of the continuing decline in recorded gun crime after 2002 in England and Wales. Police commentators have claimed that the falling crime figures also reflect the diminishing availability of illegal firearms – the result, in turn, of better, intelligence-led policing operations, more effective surveillance, automated number plate recognition (ANPR) and improved community links. But amongst the consequences of this, alongside the resort to antique firearms and homemade ammunition, according to police reports from the West Midlands, has been a greater sharing of firearms between gangs and groups of offenders (Peachey, 2013). There are real issues for offenders in renting a firearm, but the practice also fits with the evidence that only 12 per cent of recorded gun crimes involve the weapon being fired. Weapons appear to be acquired, for the most part as 'frighteners' and not for shooting. If they are fired, they leave potential forensic ballistic evidence that can compromise the resale value of the gun or the 'deposit' an offender may have to pay to an armourer. Interviewed in 2013, Hales remarked that the retention of used, compromised or 'hot' firearms, guns that were used and then 'sold back into the market', represented another indication of scarcity: 'That marked a break in tradition, in a previous decade a gun used in a shooting would have been disposed of immediately' (cited in Peachey, 2013).

On the one hand, when renting a weapon, the offender offsets the risk of being subsequently caught with the weapon, on the other he may be vulnerable if someone comes after him for retaliation – maybe even with the same gun. Evidence has already exposed the practice of gang members having others (young people or girlfriends) to 'mind' or transport their firearms. Perhaps this practice, specifically criminalized via section 28 the VCRA represents the best of both worlds for the offender, swift access to the weapon without possession of it. Following growing evidence of the role of criminal armourers in weapon supply and pressure from ACPO and NABIS (House of Commons, Home Affairs Select Committee, 2010, paras 120–122) the Government announced its intention to introduce a further offence to target weapon suppliers and criminal armourers. A case in Manchester in 2011 involved a 'criminal quartermaster' prosecuted for renting firearms. A cache of weapons was uncovered when his home was raided, including a sub-machine gun which was reported to have been used in five shootings over a period of five years in the North West (Peachey, 2013). NABIS representatives have argued that tackling suppliers was a key to keeping a lid on the gun problem, the new law 'possession of a firearm with intent to supply' being likely to affect between 10 and 20 offenders per year.

A more tragic case involving a much recycled firearm came to light in 2011 following the random killing of a 16-year-old girl as she queued, waiting for a take-away pizza, in Hoxton, East London. The shooting was part of an alleged revenge attack by two local gang members who were responding to a beating handed down to one of their friends. The gun they used, however, an Agram 9mm sub-machine gun, was originally manufactured in Croatia. The weapon, capable of firing 800 bullets a minute and notoriously difficult to control, spraying bullets everywhere, when firing fully automatic, had been used in six previous shootings across London by a variety of gangs, from Croydon to Enfield. Ballistic tracing of the weapon discovered the following sequence of known shootings, most of them said to be 'gang-related', beginning in January 2009:

28 Jan 2009	Fired in the street in Berriman Road, Holloway.
8 Mar 2009	Fired in Cavendish Road, Haringey.
22 Mar 2009	Fired outside a nightclub in Upper Clapton Road.
10 May 2009	Fired in Ockley Road, Croydon.
28 Aug 2009	Fired, with two other guns, outside a snooker hall in Enfield.
30 Sep 2009	Fired by a Turkish gang member at two men in Tottenham, both survive.
14 Apr 2010	Fired killing 16-year-old Agnes Sina-Inakoju in Hoxton.
21 Apr 2010	Found, along with other weapons, in a rucksack dumped by a 17-year-old male trying to escape the police in London Fields.

(Summers, 2011)

Aggregated NABIS data has likewise revealed that 700 firearms offences, or 34 per cent of just over 2,000 recorded, were followed by further offences involving the same weapon, 11 per cent of these committed in a different police force area. A small number of weapons were recorded as used on ten or more occasions (Gibson, 2012: 32). Apparently converted blank-firing weapons were the most likely weapon type to be re-used, which might indicate something about the demographic primarily accessing such weapons. Re-use of the Agram sub-machine-gun in London, above, appears rather more frequent that the average, 210 days between incidents, reflected in the NABIS database (Gibson, 2012: 35). Although it needs to be borne in mind that 'use' in this sense entails 'use resulting in a ballistic trace', if the gun is not fired, for instance in the course of a robbery where it is used to intimidate, no trace will result.

Gun-smoke, mirrors, ballistics and statistics

The creation of complex, low-level mixed economy of illegal firearms as so far described – the 'sub-prime', 'junk-gun' market comprising low-powered air weapons, non-firing replicas and imitations, conversions, reactivations, antiques and rented weapons – but also some very serious and lethal weapons is, itself, a response to what is, in many respects, effective, intelligence-led policing and gun control strategy. As I have already suggested, the current strategy that appears to be driving down rates of gun crime did not arrive, all at once and fully formed. It has developed over time and now engages the origins of the supply chain, including the points where legally produced or held firearms shift into illegality. This is followed by questions concerning importation, trafficking, conversion, reactivation, assembly, criminal distribution and eventual end-user supply and recycling. It also concerns the contexts generating a *demand* for illegal firearms and the circumstances, conditions and inter-personal relationships associated with their misuse; in many parts of the world this often involves the behaviour, affiliations and identities of relatively deprived, or marginal, young men in peer groups, often referred to as 'gangs'. Despite huge differences in scale and lethality, there are still some constants, disadvantaged and unattached young men are often the most frequent users of illegal firearms and typically the most frequent victims of gun crime.

In Chapter 3, I turn to consider the contexts surrounding the 'demand' for illegal firearms in a number of British towns and cities, exploring the range of police, multi-agency and social crime prevention strategies that have been adopted – both successfully and unsuccessfully – to suppress demand for guns and curtail the activities of gangs. In subsequent chapters of the book, I review essentially similar gun demand contexts in other parts of the world. In the present chapter, however, I have been reviewing the effectiveness of these policing and 'gun control' mechanisms in a society that is, by international standards, a highly restrictive regime as far as firearms are concerned. But it is important to recall, gun control, just like crime control more generally, is not simply about laws, it also concerns social and inter-personal relationships and supports, the role of families, key institutions and culture shaping the behaviour and outlooks of young people – especially those 'at risk' – and about societies capable of offering young people more positive and rewarding opportunities than a life of criminality and the dangerous lifestyle of the gang. Yet it is also about law, about having the prohibitions and regulations around which police enforcement activity can focus. The British response to a perceived gun crime crisis from the late 1990s has embraced both approaches: empowering communities and passing new laws, the two arms of this approach have worked together. In more fragmented and unequal societies, communities are less capable of resisting weaponization, and such gun control laws as exist are harder to enforce; in more explicitly neo-liberal cultures, where crime is considered commonplace, weaponization is often difficult to resist because gun ownership appeals to both the law abiding and the criminally inclined. Finally, in the most fragmented and failing societies law enforcement and governance are themselves compromised and resisted; weaponization may be equated with self-determination.

As I have noted in the foregoing discussions, the creation of the sub-prime junk market in firearms is itself the outcome of effective restrictions imposed upon weapon supply. Clearly a demand for illegal firearms still exists and the underlying issues influencing patterns of serious youth violence, evidenced by the growth in concern with knife crime from around 2007 (Eades et al., 2007; Squires et al., 2008; Squires, 2009b), remain significant. Nevertheless, the overall apparent reduction in recorded gun crime certainly suggests a move in the right direction even if, as we have noted, a substantial part of this reduction reflects a change in the processing of air weapon and imitation offences; that is charging these under anti-social behaviour legislation and recording them as anti-social behaviour offences rather than as 'firearms offences'. Without a detailed excavation of offence handling patterns it is difficult to draw a precise conclusion about how much of the apparent reduction in gun crime is attributable to the changed charging and recording practices, but the evidence we have from earlier research (Morrison and O'Donnell, 1994, 1997; Matthews, 1996; Rix et al., 1998; Hales et al., 2006) and that comprised in Figure 2.4 allow us to set some parameters.

As we have seen, a number of earlier studies and Home Office data (as reflected in Figure 2.4) put the proportion of gun crime involving air weapons and/or imitation firearms at 51 per cent with a further 15 per cent margin of uncertainty relating to 'other weapons' and 'unidentified firearms'. Correspondingly, Gill's (2000) study of armed robbers found that as few as 39 per cent were carrying a real gun and only 26 per cent had a potentially lethal, loaded firearm. Taken together with the evidence in Figure 2.4, this suggests that fully two-thirds of the increase in gun crime in England and Wales between 1998 and 2002 could have been attributable to replicas and air weapons and on that basis it does not seem unreasonable to suggest that, with increasingly sophisticated analysis and cataloguing of recovered weapons, up to two-thirds of the fall in the gun crime figures is similarly accounted for. When the Home Affairs Select Committee considered these issues in 2010, it drew attention to the falling rates of gun crime, but, despite some of the evidence presented, it failed to fully recognize or appreciate why this was happening. The Committee, responding to the concerns of gun lobby groups anxious to distance gun crime from lawful gun ownership, pointed out that 'there is no direct correlation in recent UK history between levels of gun ownership and gun crime trends' (Home Affairs Select Committee, 2010: para 35) without acknowledging that the reason for the lack of a correlation involved the 'sub-prime', junk weapon market (air guns and imitations) which comprised up to two-thirds of the gun crime total.

However, quite rightly, the committee also went on to commend the role of 'well-designed legislation to regulate and restrict the legal supply of firearms' which, in conjunction with effective, intelligence-led policing 'can reduce gun crime' (para 35). The Select Committee were convinced by representatives from NABIS that 'the UK's gun controls "significantly constrain" the ability of criminals to obtain lethal Firearms' (para 31) and by 2013 NABIS were reporting still further success. In the wake of debates about the impact of comparative gun control measures, following the December 2012 mass shooting at Sandy Hook school in Newtown, Connecticut, attention turned to the impact of the measures taken in Britain after Dunblane. A NABIS spokesman confided in a reporter for the *Washington Post*, 'ballistic tests indicate that most gun crime in Britain can be traced back to fewer than 1,000 illegal weapons still in circulation' (Faiola, 2013). This is the first time police have ever put such a figure into the public domain, even if the figure was only reported in the USA. It is also the first time police have ever had the comprehensive database from which to make such a statement and, above all, it is the first time that that any such estimate of the scale of the illegal weapons inventory has been so low. At face value the '1,000 criminally active, potentially lethal, firearms' figure tells a story of police and law enforcement success, it corroborates much of the picture developed already of the sub-prime junk weapons market to which offenders are having to resort, so constrained has the gun supply become. However, the figure is a police intelligence construct and, while nothing that follows is intended to detract from the successes achieved in the control firearms in Britain, it is important to understand how the figure is constructed in order to better appreciate what it means.

NABIS has established and operates a ballistic intelligence database. Every time a firearm is reported used in a criminal offence a record is created, every bullet or cartridge case recovered from a crime scene (or retrieved from a victim) is screened and run through the database; every firearm recovered is test fired and the ballistic material also compared to the database. Using this methodology NABIS can calculate the number of criminally active firearms. Every time a firearm is recovered by police and the database comparison reveals a number of 'hits' indicating that the gun has previously been used in a crime, the total number of criminally active firearms can be reduced by one. Many of the firearms on the NABIS database are 'inferred' firearms, this can occur in two ways. First, ballistic evidence can be retrieved but not the gun itself; second, credible intelligence can also indicate that a particular gang or individual is known or believed to possess a firearm. Combining these figures produces the intelligence construct that is the known number of 'criminally active firearms'. For obvious reasons the number is not a complete count of criminal firearms, illegal weapons that are not 'active' will not appear on the list unless other intelligence confirms their existence; weapons that are not fired may likewise not appear in the count. Establishing a figure of 'criminally active firearms' recreates a problem familiar to international firearms control researchers. The latter distinguish between 'black' and 'grey' firearms markets (Karp, 1994). The former entail those in direct possession of criminals, insurgents and terrorists, the latter are those weapons to which the criminally inclined might have relatively easy access. It is likely that the latter significantly outnumber the former and the same is likely to be true in Britain. Accordingly the antique, sometimes dubiously legal, firearm collections of enthusiasts, stored in private homes, such as some of those referred to already,[12] or the carelessly stored shotguns of farmers may easily slip into illegality if stolen. For instance, a Freedom of Information Act request to Cambridgeshire police revealed that 89 firearms had been stolen in the county during 2008–2009 and 64 during 2009–2010. Such firearms are not automatically entered into the 'criminally active firearms' database unless they become criminally active; furthermore many are likely to have been shotguns which are difficult to trace and compare (Brown, 2011). Between 2007 and 2011, almost 3,000 firearms, over 2,000 of them shotguns, and some 380 rifles, were lost or stolen in England and Wales as a whole, according to Home Office data (Beckford, 2012).

Another issue with the count of criminally active firearms, as with much police intelligence gathering, is that the size and scope of the database is often a product of the amount of effort and resources devoted to the production and maintenance of the database and effective information sharing. The NABIS database has been operational since 2008, so it is at least arguable that it is still developing as a resource. Finally, as the foregoing arguments have shown, a critical question for any effective gun control (domestically and internationally) concerns the ease of weapon slippage 'from grey to black'. I have highlighted a number of issues here. All this being said, the '1,000 criminally active' and potentially lethal firearms figure is not an unreasonable estimate (acknowledging the limitations to which I have already drawn attention). As we shall see in Chapter 3, the main contexts in which firearms are most often misused are well understood; most gun crime is recorded in five or six police force areas, London and the major conurbations, which have dedicated firearms crime intelligence units each with a detailed database of gang members and their affiliates (see Squires and Kennison, 2010). The Home Office 'Tackling Gangs Action Programme' (TAGP) which ran between 2007and 2008 in four intervention areas (Metropolitan, Greater Manchester, West Midlands and Merseyside) identified 774 active gang members with an average of 11 previous convictions each (see Squires et al., 2008: 102). There is no suggestion that the number of 'criminally active' firearms will necessarily equate to the number of 'criminally active' gangsters, but at least the numbers are in the same ballpark. I return to these issues, the contexts of firearm demand and use, in Chapter 3.

Shootings, victims and other legacies

As the BASC noted in 2009, successive Home Office ministers have been pleased to report year-on-year reductions in the total numbers of recorded offences involving firearms. This applies both to air weapons and to other 'more dangerous' firearms, including the modern criminal's supposed 'weapon of choice', the handgun. If only things were so simple. Here I turn to consider certain other legacies of the criminal fringes of a flourishing gun trade.

As we have already seen in discussion of the data in Figures 2.1 and 2.4, while there are good reasons for scepticism about the accuracy of recorded crime statistics, this applies just as much when they are rising as when they are believed to be falling – although for different reasons. There are some suggestions that recorded crime rates tend to be inflated during a period when crime is thought to be rising (defined up) and similarly under-counted (defined down) after a crime trend has peaked and is thought to be falling (Van Dijk et al., 2012). In some ways this is similar to the more familiar crime/media reporting cycle which draws attention to crimes that are 'new and newsworthy' only to lose interest when these become more routine. It is difficult to avoid a conclusion also that there are political and institutional pressures that cannot be divorced from resource lobbying pressures (as crime rises) and law enforcement performance issues (as crime is subsequently seen to fall). Beyond this, just as we acknowledged that recorded gun crime does not necessarily reflect accurately the scale of criminal gun possession and misuse, so it is also important to appreciate that falling gun crime figures do not necessarily reflect falling rates of gun involved criminal activity. The earlier discussion of shooting victims and their frequent reluctance to cooperate with the police tells us something about possible under-reporting; it is likely that threats involving firearms are far less frequently reported. The same goes for firearm discharges (shots fired) when no-one is injured.

Evidence from GMP's Operation Xcalibre provided to the Magnet project team (referred to earlier) similarly suggests how many police intelligence records relate to shootings, many of which may not have been recorded as crimes. These involved incidents in which cars, buildings, doors and windows *rather than people* had been fired at (Squires, 2011a). Such incidents, colloquially referred to as 'drive-by shootings', despite the seemingly reckless irresponsibility with which they are carried out, are manifestly not an indication of a ruthless and unambiguous intention to kill. Rather, as Sanders' (1994) path breaking study of this issue in California has pointed out, such actions have a number of possible meanings, these include: sending messages, issuing warnings, making territorial claims, making challenges and so on. A similar picture emerged in more recent Metropolitan Police evidence. For example, during Autumn 2009 the Metropolitan Police Service released figures showing that of 985 firearms seized in the capitol from January to July 2009, less than one-quarter (22 per cent) were 'live-firing' weapons, the others were said to be air weapons, BB guns, replicas or other non-firing guns. Accompanying the release of the figures was an MPS 'warning' to the effect that 'young gang members were carrying out non-fatal shootings to inflict "war wounds" or issue threats to their rivals' (Davenport, 2009). In other words, as we have noted before, although undoubtedly violent or potentially violent, firearm attacks were sometimes more ambiguously motivated and not necessarily always attempts to kill – sometimes, for example, they were carried out with less powerful weapons that were unlikely to kill (Davenport, 2009). Furthermore, as Lau (2012) notes, a clear majority of firearm offences (79 per cent) resulted in no injury at all. This finding is also somewhat corroborated by NABIS firearm offending data on more serious incidents (number 2,370) where shots were actually fired; of these, 42 per cent involved no injury. Of a smaller sub-set (number 1,039) involving multiple use firearms, some 52 per cent involved no injury (Gibson, 2012: 24, 34). Unearthing such hidden layers of meaning concerning violence, gang behaviours and gun possession is an important aspect of exposing a fuller picture of gun crime and street violence beyond the portion captured and represented in Home Office and official figures.

Another way of triangulating the evidence on gun victimization, even though it brings its own difficulties, is to use hospital A&E admissions figures, although these will only pick up incidents where injuries have resulted and, given the mandatory reporting of gunshot injuries by A&E doctors, it is likely that a proportion of less serious shooting injuries never make it to A&E in the first place. Figure 2.7 provides evidence on particular types of shooting injury victims entering English A&E departments during the decade 1997–2007; from 2002–2003 the data was available with a racial classification.

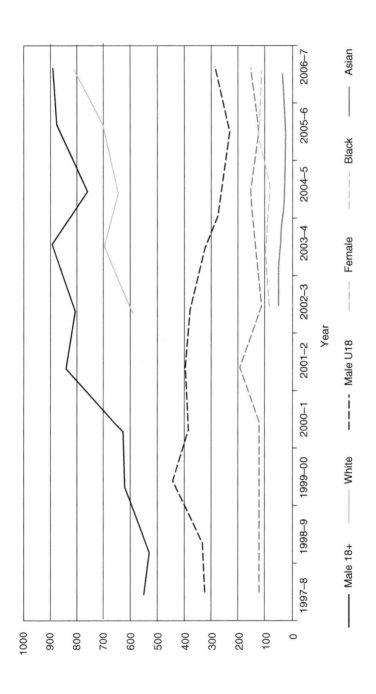

FIGURE 2.7 Gunshot victims reporting to hospital A&E departments, 1997–2007

Sources: Department of Health (2008a, 2008b).

Clearly the visibly upward trend during this period is sustained primarily by white male gunshot victims aged 18 and over. Comparing this graph with the recorded crime statistics in Figure 2.1 exposes an interesting contrast. In Figure 2.1, total handgun crime could be seen to rise to 2002, then fall back, whereas in Figure 2.7 the increase is more consistently upwards. This evidence (bearing in mind the different numerical scales in play) might suggest the role of imitation or low-powered firearms in inflating 'low-level' gun crime figures alongside a continuing more serious gun violence problem (offenders in possession of real weapons and willing to use them) affecting the rates of more serious firearm injury. On the other hand, Lau, reviewing the Home Office data for 2010–2011, notes that

> serious [gunshot] injuries decreased by 18 per cent from 404 in 2009/10 to 330 in 2010/11, *continuing the long-term downward trend* … [while] firearm offences involving any type of injury decreased by 7 per cent, from 2,568 in 2009/10 to 2,399 in 2010/11. The number of injuries recorded each year as a result of firearm offences has fallen by more than half since they peaked at 5,402 in 2004/05.
>
> *(Lau, 2012: 55, emphasis added)*

It is difficult, at first sight, to reconcile these conclusions, although findings emerging from a recent retrospective analysis of serious gunshot hospital admissions (covering 1990–2007) held by the Trauma Audit and Research Network (TARN) throws a little more light on the issue. TARN is the largest national database of serious trauma injuries.[13] The data was extracted to examine trends in firearm injuries reported to A&E and the demographic characteristics of gunshot injury victims (Davies *et al.*, 2012). Of nearly 250,000 of the 'most serious' trauma cases recorded on the database, 656 (0.28 per cent) were due to firearm injuries. The study followed previous locally based A&E studies, for example Persad *et al.* (2005) in inner London, which noted a four-fold increase in gunshot injury admissions to their A&E department between 1998 and 2002 (this being the period during which gun crime figures rose by 105 per cent).

Between 1995 and 2007, TARN evidence showed a five-fold increase in the *proportion* of serious trauma injuries attributable to gunshot wounds. Consistent with a number of other UK studies (Porteous *et al.*,1997), demographic analysis of the data showed that young, black males appeared to be at disproportionate risk. A study published in 2004 reviewing 187 'live referrals' to A&E involving 247 bullet injuries, found that 66 per cent of the victims were aged under 25 and nearly three-quarters of the admissions were outside 'normal working hours' (Cowey *et al.*, 2004). Eighty-three of the admissions required surgery although 76 had rather more minor injuries. Although the purpose of the study was primarily to assess the cost and preparedness of A&E departments for gun-shot injuries, such data still tells us something about the very mixed and wide-ranging character of firearm injuries and the relative lethality of the weapons used (less than half requiring surgery). The picture would be incomplete, however, unless we also acknowledge that four of the gunshot victims in Cowey et al.'s (2004) study, arriving alive at A&E, died there.

One key towards understanding the different evidence presented here seems to lie in the distinctions drawn between 'serious' and 'less serious' firearm injuries. Figure 2.7 details A&E attendances only, whereas TARN data collates serious injuries requiring three or more days of hospitalization. Neither data set deals with fatalities. Davies et al. (2012: 13) conclude that the overall evidence 'lends support to media concerns that more people are being injured through firearm crime in the UK … [although] the number of deaths by assault remains relatively stable'. Finally, reiterating my earlier points about the very variable mixed economy of illegal firearms available in the UK and the sometimes conflicted and ambiguous motivations of those with access to them, they note that 'this may reflect the diminishing relative lethality of the firearm stock in England and Wales or a growing reluctance of those using them to intentionally maim rather than cause death' (Davies et al., 2012: 13).

Rather confirming these findings, Davies and his colleagues undertook a follow-up study repeating a project first undertaken in 1997 to examine the frequency and characteristics of civilian gunshot wounds in a urban environment in the UK (Davies et al., 2011). All patients presenting to the Emergency Department (ED) of King's College Hospital (KCH) with gunshot wounds from 1 January 2003 to 31 December 2004 were identified. A total of 46 patients arrived with firearm injuries, the majority being from ethnic minority groups with an average age of 24 years. Thirty-two of the patients were admitted to hospital and although all of the injuries were due to 'assault by low-energy projectiles', six of these admitted patients eventually died from their injuries. Overall, the research showed little increase in firearm injuries seen over the ten-year period at KCH, although 'predominately young, black males continue to be the victims'. The majority of wounds inflicted were thought to suggest a 'desire to maim rather than kill', while 'the absence of high velocity injuries may reflect the UK's stringent gun control legislation' and the relatively poor quality or lower-powered firearms mostly available to the groups of offenders perpetrating such assaults (Davies et al., 2011: 13–14). As we have seen, however, diminishing attendance at A&E facilities might also reflect the disinclination of victims to report their injuries and thereby becoming involved with the police.

The supply story: cautious optimism

A key aim of much of the preceding discussion has been to add some greater accuracy and empirical complexity to the picture of gun crime in England, Wales and Scotland. The purpose was to better understand the structure and composition of the UK gun problem in order that it might be more effectively analysed, proportionately addressed and appropriately dealt with. Understanding criminal gun use more sociologically might in this sense help us to quash two quite inconsistent media narratives of contemporary gun crime. The first is that the country is awash with illegal firearms and the second is that the criminal gangs with access to firearms are addicted to wanton and uncontrolled, random, brutal violence. Both narratives cannot be true; British gun crime is far too uncommon. Either the country is not awash with illegal firearms or those who mostly misuse them do so with a measure of restraint. We would be making progress if we could move to a more dispassionate and informed understanding of the problem. A more balanced understanding might lead to more effective policies.

In this chapter, I have reviewed the evidence relating to British gun crime, offering an explanation that connects domestic and international developments in the establishment of a unique, mixed economy of firearms which have driven the peculiarly British 'gun culture' and the weaponization of some of its poorer and more marginal communities. I have accounted for the significant fluctuations in British gun crime trends over the past decade and a half, finding answers in the novelties of that mixed economy of firearms, changing gun control policies and new legislation as well as the policing innovations, changes in crime recording practice, intelligence development and analysis. Encountering all of these developments, offending behaviour has continued to shift and adapt, invariably throwing up new challenges and new weapon choices. However, overall, the 'supply story' regarding the attempt to constrain illegal firearm supply into mainland Britain is one of cautious, qualified success, involving some effective new laws, new crime prevention successes and effective, intelligence-led and inter-agency policing – but also some fortuitous statistical recalculation and offence re-categorization.

Finally, I have begun to connect this 'supply story' with a series of issues of more global significance concerning crime, firearms ownership rights and the slippage of weapons from legal into illegal possession. I will develop these points more extensively later in the book, particularly in Chpater 7. A discourse about firearm rights has scarcely taken hold in Britain, although the country has not been entirely immune to the broadly neo-liberal attitudes regarding personal security, self-defence and weaponization. This phenomenon, and the gun 'culture' that often accompanies it globally, has taken strongest root in the criminal communities facing the highest risk of violent victimization where it generates a demand for firearms. In Chapter 3, I turn to consider the demand side of this equation and the policies that have sought to address it.

Notes

1 By virtue of the Firearms (Amendment) Acts, handguns of all calibres (with relatively few exceptions such as antiques) became section 1 'prohibited' weapons.
2 The six Conservative majority members of the committee subsequently underwent a bitter campaign of press vilification for their perceived 'insensitivity'. See Squires (2000: 142–149) for fuller discussion.
3 The Home Office publishes, each year, a supplementary volume of statistics covering: Homicides, Firearm Offences and Intimate Violence. The 2012 edition, edited by Kevin Smith, Sarah Osborne, Ivy Lau and Andrew Britton, was published in January 2012 as *Supplementary Volume 2 to Crime in England and Wales 2010/11*.

4 Furthermore, as Figure 2.1 makes clear, in every annual statistical publication of the past decade the majority of handguns used in offences have been recorded by police as 'type unknown'. If the *type* of weapon is unknown a question arises as to whether the weapon is a real firearm.

5 Much reporting of gun (and gang-involved) criminal activity is written as if the perpetrators were, by nature, uncontrollably violent, anti-social and chaotic. Along with our later discussion of typical 'drive-by' shootings in the UK, however, the evidence that guns were only fired in 12 per cent of recorded handgun offences suggests a high degree of restraint in firearm misuse, a picture at odds with much 'conventional wisdom'.

6 Later in the chapter I consider further instances of legality/illegality overlap in firearm ownership in relation to firearm collections, hunting and sport shooting. For the moment, reference to the following recent case will suffice to illustrate the point. In November 2013, a five-year-old Essex boy was seriously injured after being shot in the face at home by an eight-year-old. Arresting an 18-year-old man, police reported that the discharged weapon was illegally held, but also recovered a number of legal and licensed weapons from the property (Meikle, 2013).

7 These issues relate to wider and deeper definitional questions. I will discuss the particular problems involving different types of firearms and the various forms of criminal misuse to which they are put, in England and Wales later in the chapter. Wider developments are referred to in Chapter 1 regarding the distinction between 'civilian' and 'military' firearms, the 'militarization' of the US civilian market (Diaz, 2013) and UN efforts to regulate illicit small arms trafficking by differentiating between 'civilian sporting' and 'military' weapons. Rather complicating the picture, especially for the more moderate sports shooting enthusiasts, the US NRA-led World Sports Shooting lobby has always insisted upon the widest definition of a 'sporting firearm' which included military specification assault rifles and semi-automatic combat pistols. Refer to the discussion in Chapter 8.

8 This category is likely to decline as more *retrieved* weapons are submitted to NABIS for analysis, although handguns used in offences that are not recovered (perhaps only described or identified by victims, or 'inferred' from ballistic traces or intelligence intercepts) will often remain 'unidentified'. Even while formally unidentified, however, a weapon will come to acquire a police intelligence history.

9 The energy threshold for an illegal weapon at section 1 applies to air rifles or air guns capable of discharging a projectile which, on discharge from the muzzle, has a kinetic energy exceeding 12 ft. lb., or 'an air pistol discharging a projectile as above with a kinetic energy exceeding 6 ft-lb' (Sandys-Winsch, 1999: 25).

10 Following police intelligence and evidential disagreements, the Azelle Rodney shooting, in 2005, was eventually the subject of a judicial inquiry chaired by Sir Christopher Holland, which reported in 2013. The inquiry found that the police use of force was not appropriate ('there was no lawful justification for shooting Azelle Rodney so as to kill him') in that the officer who fired the fatal shots did not have reasonable grounds for discharging lethal force (Holland, 2013: 87, para 21.13).

11 Cook's work was set in Chicago where, by US standards, restrictive controls have been applied to handguns since 1982. There were also very few firearms retailers in the city and, again by US standards, a relatively low rate of overall gun ownership. Furthermore the state of Illinois required any would-be gun owner to obtain a firearm owner's ID. The net effect of these regulations was to limit legal firearm supply within the city while thereby restricting illegal firearm supplies. This 'containment' effect may well now be jeopardized by the 2010 Supreme Court decision in *Macdonald V Chicago*. We discuss these issues in Chapter 4.

12 A routine online search of news reports throws up many further 'weapons stash' discoveries by police. An SA-80 British army rifle, two AK-47 rifles, two handguns and a shotgun as well as around 10–15 magazines of ammunition were recovered from farm buildings in Scotland (*Huffington Post*, 13 April 2012); the former chairman of a

Worcester gun club was prosecuted in 2011 for possession of an illegal semi-automatic rifle and had 30 further weapons and a quantity of ammunition confiscated from his home (*Worcester News*, 19 October 2011); hundreds of firearms, some of them illegal types, were found in a raid by officers from Operation Trident on the home and business premises of a firearms dealer with links to London gangs in September 2006 (BBC News website, 13 September 2006); a stash of weapons (over 30 shotguns, a semi-auto pistol and three revolvers) greased and wrapped in newspaper for long-term storage were found behind a plasterboard wall in Dinas Powys outside Cardiff. The newspaper wrappings were dated 1996 (*Daily Mirror*, 24 January 2013).

13 TARN covers approximately 50 per cent of trauma receiving hospitals in England and Wales, collecting data on patients attending participating hospitals who receive an injury resulting in immediate admission to hospital for three or more days, admission to an intensive care or high dependency unit, or death within 93 days. However, TARN only records data on patients reaching hospital alive.

3

CONSEQUENCES OF UK GUN CRIME

Politics, policy and policing

While the previous chapter sought to examine the 'supply-side' questions relating to firearms crime in mainland Britain, this chapter moves to consider the contexts in which a demand for, typically illegal, personal firearms arises, and the wider consequences of community weaponization. The key themes and issues around which debate concerning firearms ownership turns in a 'high control' and 'well-ordered' regime differ markedly from those that characterize more disrupted and failing regimes. In particular the legal niceties of 'ownership' and sports shooting (Smith, 2006) play a role here that might seem something of a luxury in a culture where gun possession is more concerned with self-defence and survival. In this chapter I also explore the public and political reactions, the policies that emerged and the policing practices that developed, to address the emerging gun crime problems facing Britain. As I have already noted, the gun crime problem as it first presented itself in the wake of Dunblane and the handgun ban that followed, especially the apparent doubling of handgun-involved crime after 1998, was a major driver of subsequent reactions, but it was not the only issue. In any event, the way the phenomenon was initially understood was not an especially evidence- or 'intelligence-led' (or even accurate) picture of either the real nature or extent of the problem.

That said, 'gun crime' is never just a question of statistical trends and this has to be reflected in our discussion of the issue, both in understanding perceptions of the problem and in the responses to it. 'Gun crime' is perhaps best regarded as a particular 'signal' crime (Innes, 2004), important not just in and of itself, but also for the kinds of messages it relays about violence and danger in urban areas, about the breakdown of community safety and about the risks and vulnerabilities of modern living. Such issues were often reflected in a great deal of the media reporting of 'gun crime'. For example, following the gang-related, 'drive-by' killing of teenagers Charlene Ellis and Latisha Shakespeare at a New Year party in Birmingham, media attention focussed upon what the media called 'a new breed of young killers with no conscience' (Oliver, 2003). According to a senior police commentator, such offenders

> see guns, the bigger the better, as status symbols and engage in 'disrespect' shootings sparked by as little as someone making fun of their haircut or spilling their drink ... There is no consideration of the consequences of using these firearms. These are not trained killers – these are people who are completely unaware or don't care about the damage the firearm can cause. The types of people who now have access to firearms are immature people with very potent weapons. They have no social conscience, no restraint and are completely unaware of the consequences of their actions.
>
> *(Oliver, 2003)*

In this way an interpretative moral folklore of the new street gang is layered onto the popular understandings of the gun crime problem, culminating in what Hallsworth and Young (2008) have labelled 'gang talk'. The key elements of this 'gang talk' paradigm, reflecting themes going back to Thrasher's first 'sociology of the gang' back in 1927 (Thrasher, 1927; Squires, 2012), comprise: sensational and (often) inaccurate media coverage (often led by law enforcement definitions and commentaries), not unlike Cohen's original account of 'moral panic' (Cohen, 1972); an underdeveloped or incomplete evidential case demonstrating the supposed truth of the gang phenomenon; and the adoption of emotive, moralizing and sensational language bringing a range of 'ideological baggage' – dangerous and leading inferences and assumptions – into play, such that commentators who begin by talking about 'gangs' invariably end by asserting the need for gang 'suppression' as a policy response (Hallsworth and Young, 2008). Along the way, a range of academic contributors can also be found embellishing the gang story. What gave the British gang story even more ideological weight was its seeming associations with firearms, race and 'American' criminal practices. For, as we have seen with gun crime, despite evidence to the contrary, the problem is invariably seen as becoming worse; Britain is frequently said to be becoming more like the 'Wild West' (Squires, 2000). Even when the evidence fails to tell this inexorably worsening story, the relative youth of the perpetrators, the innocence of the victims or the casual, supposedly 'senseless' brutality of the offence and the ways that weaponized and gang-related 'post-code wars' can tear fearful communities apart, often speaks far louder than mere statistics. I will return to these issues later in the chapter.

Continuing official caution

As we have seen, the tragedy at Dunblane was followed by a public inquiry led by Lord Cullen (Cullen, 1996) and a report by the Home Affairs Select Committee (House of Commons: Home Affairs Committee, 1996), the conclusions of both being rather swept aside by the tide of popular public opinion that led to handguns of all calibres becoming prohibited in England, Wales and Scotland.[1] Another Home

Affairs Select Committee inquiry was launched in 1999 (House of Commons: Home Affairs Committee, 2000), just two years into the 'New Labour' Government. The reason for the new inquiry concerned both the 'generally increasing trend' of gun crime and the scale and range of firearm misuse – from 'petty vandalism and casual cruelty' to homicide. Both ends of the gun crime spectrum gave rise to public safety concerns, although the committee claimed to have no particular agenda, noting only that the existing firearms controls were 'unacceptably complex [and] inconsistent' and not apparently designed with public safety uppermost (perhaps a particularly damning observation). Moreover the regulations were said to be 'difficult to understand and administer', failing to deliver the safeguards that the public had the right to expect even as they imposed burdens upon firearms users (House of Commons: Home Affairs Committee, 2000, paras. 2–3).

The committee report addressed a range of issues regarding firearm safety and control, including basic principles of public safety and the rights of firearm owners and users; they considered the dangers posed by firearm misuse and the evidence available relating to misuse of legal and illegal (unregistered/unlicensed) firearms. For obvious reasons, there being no real tradition of research in gun crime in the UK, there was relatively little 'criminological' input to these discussions other than a memorandum of evidence by Broadhurst and Benyon (2000) of the Scarman Centre, at the University of Leicester. Nevertheless an attempt was made to discuss the problem profiles presented by legal and illegal weapons – so far as the evidence allowed, even as it was acknowledged that this evidence was rather incomplete. The discussion of these issues occupied several pages of the committee's final report, which also comprised a discussion of the evidence submissions from a number of interests including the GCN, the British Shooting Sports Council, the Firearms Consultative Committee (FCC) and independent firearms Consultant Colin Greenwood.[2] A fairly limited range of social science evidence was actually employed in the committee's deliberations and even that which did appear tended to be stacked up on either side of criminology's fundamental paradigm divide between, on the one hand, a perspective rooted in neo-classical rational individualism privileging the motivated offender and, on the other, a more empirical perspective acknowledging social causation and context (social positivism). For the latter position, US research exemplified by Zimring and Hawkins (1997) was employed to draw attention to the role of weapons as *facilitators* of potentially lethal violence and, allied with the work of Kellerman (1993) and Killias (1993), contributed to a view that rates of firearm ownership were positively correlated with rates of firearm homicide, injury and suicide. To the firearm lobbyists, on the other hand, such supposedly 'circumstantial' considerations were of little importance, for where firearms were rationally chosen and legally acquired by responsible people, few harmful consequences were said to result. Furthermore, responsible gun owners were not to blame for the actions of criminal ones; Greenwood went even further to deny any relationship between the numbers of firearms circulating in a society and the rates of homicide, such things, he suggested, 'cannot be correlated' (1999: 18) as if the objects themselves – firearms – and not the social relationships surrounding them, were all that mattered. Such an approach reflects a 'sovereign' approach to gun rights, in which gun control laws are unnecessary because responsible gun owners do not need them and (committed) criminals will only ever break them. A more intellectually stunted analysis would be hard to imagine and, as we have seen in Chapter 2, 'legal' and 'illegal' are seldom such watertight compartments.

A realist criminology could contribute a great deal to this debate, its first task would be to demolish the neo-classical, pseudo-rationalism apparently distinguishing 'good' and 'evil' while recognizing the accumulated marginal, 'messy' and ambiguous social contexts within which weapons were most often misused. Debates about human rights and sporting freedoms or knowledge of the law are unlikely to tell us much about street weapon usage and how it might respond to interventions of various kinds (although the 'targeted deterrence' described by Kennedy (2011) for Boston's Operation Ceasefire, does offer a contrary example, of a sort). An informed appreciation of the realities of actual firearm misuse is more likely to lead us to a real politics of firearms control as opposed to merely perpetuating a practice of arming the 'good guys' and thereby implicitly tolerating the inevitable slippage of firearms from legal to illegal hands which would, and often does, follow (refer to Chapter 7). In the event, therefore, the committee's deliberations really only reiterated the artificial integrity of a distinction between legal and illegal firearms, thereby rather playing into the hands of those taking shelter behind such manufactured distinctions.

Some significance was placed upon evidence from both the Leicester study and the answers of the Minister of State (Charles Clarke) representing the Home Office view, that

> the fundamental risk to public safety in relation to firearms arises from illegally held rather than legally held firearms ... I do not think there is *significant evidence* that legally held firearms in this country provide a significant risk to public safety.
>
> *(Charles Clarke MP, vol. 2: Minutes of Evidence, para 388, page 53, emphasis added)*

Even so, the minister drew a telling distinction between the adequacy of the available evidence of the risk posed by legally held weapons and the risk itself. Evidence in the Leicester submission drew upon a paper prepared for the Cullen Inquiry suggesting that, when *stolen* firearms were also taken into account, then weapons legally held by private citizens may contribute to some 20 per cent of firearm homicides (Broadhurst and Benyon, 1999, para 5.9, page 157). Unfortunately, this particular finding did not make its way into the committee's eventual report.

In other respects, the committee's eventual report mapped the contours of the emerging British gun debate even as, in a number of places, they lamented the lack of clear evidence about the 'provenance' or sources of illegal firearms, the composition of the illegal gun stock and the growing contribution of different types of firearms (replicas, air weapons, conversions and reactivations) to this. Accordingly, the committee proposed a comprehensive examination of the firearms recovered by the police. They went on to consider the process of weapon licensing and reviewed the risks that were thought to be associated with different firearm types. Their conclusions were broadly framed by the suggestion that 'a well regulated system of firearms controls should allow the legitimate possession of firearms for lawful activities which do not threaten the public safety' (House of Commons: Home Affairs Committee, 2000, paras 112, 220). How realistic such an aspiration may be, might be gauged from an American perspective, a place where the gun question has been far more extensively debated and where the country's leading gun control academics have cast considerable doubt as to 'whether the gun market *can* be segmented in this way' (Cook *et al.*, 2007: F588–589, emphasis added).

In many respects, therefore, checks and balances were the order of the day, but even as the committee articulated this cautious conclusion they seemed to sense the perilous state of their consensus and the foundations upon which it rested: 'the patterns of firearm use have substantially altered, and new threats, either actual or perceived, have arisen' (House of Commons: Home Affairs Committee, 2000, para. 218). One conclusion *might* have been that considerations of public safety with respect to firearms control also needed to change, but committee members could find no substantial agreement here and largely confined themselves to questions of practical detail, the simplification and consolidation of the law and also recommending that a wider range of public safety interests be incorporated into the Home Office FCC. They did gave some attention to rising levels of gun crime, the emerging criminal 'gun culture' and its weapon supply, although the next shooting tragedy to hit home ultimately had a greater step-changing impact on the UK gun debate than the cautious output of the committee.

Constructing 'illegality'

In this regard the Home Affairs Select Committee of 2000 largely echoed the impact of its predecessors. Gun control policy is often criticized for being 'event driven', a series of knee-jerk reactions to tragedies. One of the reasons for this may well be the fact that the work of parliamentary inquiries and other consultative bodies has been so conservatively minded and interest dominated that little other than cautious progress is ever made. In some respects this can be considered a virtue, in others it certainly inhibits an ability to react quickly to new and emerging threats. The new threat was emphatically signalled by the drive-by clatter of a reactivated MAC-10 machine pistol fired from a moving vehicle outside a hair salon party in Birmingham early on 2 January 2003 (Benetto, 2004). The shooting caused the deaths of two young women, largely consigned the Select Committee's careful balancing act to history, while bringing a new urgency and new issues to the British gun debate.

The Birmingham shooting focussed the British gun control debate much more tightly around the problem of *illegal* guns in criminal hands and the gangs and criminal groups through which these illegal firearms circulated. However, before the decade was out politicians had several more opportunities to reflect upon the other side of equation: the misuse of legal or licensed firearms. Gun lobby representatives are often keen to draw a firm line between 'legal' and 'illegal' firearms; in reality it is seldom so simple.

On 2 June 2010, Derrick Bird, a self-employed taxi driver in west Cumbria, shot and killed 12 people, injuring 11 others, with a legally owned shotgun and rifle. He was subsequently found dead, a presumed suicide, in a wooded area. A month later, near Newcastle, Raoul Moat, recently released from prison, became the subject of a high-profile, week-long manhunt (Rowe, 2013) after he shot three people with a sawn-off shotgun (wounding a former girlfriend and killing her partner, and blinding a police officer by shooting him in the face – the officer later committed suicide). Moat was eventually contained by armed officers before, following a six hour stand-off, shooting himself, as darkness began to fall and police deployed taser equipment attempting to arrest him. In August 2008, failed businessman Christopher Foster had killed his wife and daughter and slaughtered all the family's horses and dogs with one of a number of shotguns he owned legally, before setting his home alight and killing himself (Graef, 2009). These incidents re-ignited a hitherto relatively dormant debate about the risks associated with legal (or licensed) firearms. Accordingly, the House of Commons Home Affairs Select Committee embarked upon another investigation into firearms controls (HASC, 2010). It solicited written submissions of evidence and took oral evidence during the Autumn of 2010, with many of the usual 'interests' contributing to the debate. The committee's evidence gathering also coincided with the deliberations of the Mark Saunders Inquest. Saunders was a London barrister shot and killed by police in May 2008 following a five-hour siege during which, caught in a deep alcoholic depression, he had begun firing a licensed shotgun from the window of his London flat (IPCC, 2010). These incidents re-ignited a hitherto relatively dormant debate about the risks associated with legal (or licensed) firearms. Even this third Select Committee Inquiry failed to 'resolve' the domestic gun safety questions, however, for on New Year's Day 2012, a Durham man, the licensed owner of six firearms, shot and killed three female family members before turning his shotgun on himself. Other members of the household made desperate escape attempts through an upstairs window.

In view of the types of incidents, none being obviously 'gang-related', the inquiry focused its attention upon issues surrounding the use of legal firearms in criminal activity (including air weapons) and what it called 'the relation between gun control and gun crime'. It addressed the 'fitness for purpose' of existing firearms laws and the process of information sharing between police and health agencies when considering firearm licence applications and renewals and the risk assessment of licensees. The committee's report was published in December 2010 thereby predating the Durham incident, which once again reawakened concerns about firearms stored at home and domestic violence. The committee had devoted some attention to these issues however in its evidence gathering and discussions.

It transpired that Derrick Bird, the Cumbria shooter, had previous convictions including drink driving and a suspended sentence for theft, he had also come to police notice in respect of allegations of violence towards a girlfriend and that he had made threats 'demanding money with menaces', although he had retained his firearm licence since the 1970s. There were also allegations of mental instability, financial concerns and on-going grudges with family and friends, although his entitlement to own firearms had not been called into question. Likewise, the perpetrator of the later Durham shooting had previously faced a temporary refusal of his shotgun licence renewal, amidst allegations of alcohol misuse and domestic violence, although this decision had later been overturned by a senior officer. During the Select Committee hearings, a great deal of emphasis was, perhaps understandably, devoted to the process of police scrutiny and decision-making in respect of firearms licensing; there were obviously very specific decisions about licensing entitlement that needed to be reviewed as well as more general questions about gun control and public safety.

The committee was assisted in their consideration of the former issue by a report prepared by Assistant Chief Constable Adrian Whiting, chair of the ACPO Firearms & Explosives Licensing Working Group (Whiting, 2010: parts 1, 2). Whiting concluded, in the first part of his report concerning the specifics of the licence renewal decision, that

> the current licensing system was properly operated by Cumbria Constabulary. There do not appear to be any features of this case that provide a clear opportunity to improve the system in such a way as to have prevented these events.
>
> *(Whiting, 2010: parts 1, 2)*

But he then went on (in part 2 of his report) to consider a number of wider recommendations not directly linked to the particular case that might improve domestic firearm security and firearm licensing. These included: formal information exchanges between health authorities and the police in order 'to be able to alert police to concerns regarding certificate holders'; making more extensive enquiries as to the suitability of firearm licence applicants (including, with the domestic violence issue in mind, present and former family members); reconsideration of the scope of the 'prohibited person' (prevented from owning firearms); and the simplification of the licensing process by adopting a single licence system for both shotguns and other firearms (Whiting, 2010: 3).

Unfortunately while detailed, Whiting's report was rather conservative and somewhat parochial, even including a plug for the reinstatement of the former Home Office FCC, the body through which the shooting lobby had once hoped to be left alone to regulate itself (Whiting, 2010: 9). Elsewhere a tone of self-censorship pervades his report and, indeed, in the oral evidence given by Whiting and Craig Mackey (Chief Constable of Cumbria) to the Select Committee on 16 November 2010 (HASC, 2010: 25, Evidence 37–38). Both officers sought to bracket off what they referred to as the 'fundamental question of the private ownership of firearms' (Whiting, 2010: para 3.5) from their considerations. 'The hard truth', Whiting continued,

> is that the system of certification is designed to reduce the risk of lawfully possessed firearms being misused criminally, not to eliminate it altogether. To achieve the latter would require a very different approach from Parliament and a different agreement between a government and the people it governs.
>
> *(Whiting, 2010: para 3.6)*

Implicitly linking the issue to the cherished tradition of British 'policing by consent', Whiting commented that the police service was not 'well placed' to comment on such far-reaching changes. Perhaps it goes without saying, but police leaders have seldom been so reticent to speak on political issues[3] for, as Punch (2010) has noted, ACPO very much took the lead (raising major questions of public accountability) in crafting the framework for police armed response policy development. Waddington, also discussing the police use of firearms, has earlier remarked upon what he referred to as the 'impotence of the powerful' (Waddington and Hamilton, 1997) whereas our more recent example suggests a rather more *selective* impotence, or reticence.

In the event it was left to other contributors to raise the wider issues in the Select Committee's terms of reference. As Cukier and Cairns (2009: 18) have noted, while the legality of the firearm hardly matters to the victim, it represents a significant area of public policy failure if licensed firearms, held in public trust, are misused. Gun control advocates have continued to raise the issue concerning the role of legal or licensed weapons in criminal violence. For many years the UK GCN has been collating published information on legal firearm misuse, this information is available on the GCN website (http://www.gun-control-network.org/IN0612i.htm). A breakdown of these figures is given in the Select Committee's submission of evidence (HASC, 2010: Evidence 77): thus some 40 per cent of recorded gun crime involved air weapons; around 14 per cent (based on the Home Office's own assessments) is accounted for by known licensed weapons; and a further 8.5 per cent could be attributed to other (not illegal) weapon types, producing a figure of 62.5 per cent of gun crime deriving from misuse of legal – or, at least, not illegal – firearms. This is not just a matter of semantics, although it may be objected that the substantial part of this total does relate to (generally less serious) air weapon misuse. One of the issues here concerns the notion of legality itself. Many commentators and firearm lobbyists alike tend to discuss legality as if it were an inherent characteristic of the weapon itself; some gun control regimes *prohibit* certain weapons, other societies with firearms registration attach this notion to the idea of an 'unregistered' firearm that may be illegal to possess, but legality is not inherent in the weapon itself. Rather, 'legality' rests in the relation between a person and a firearm; when a licensed shotgun is stolen it does not change, we might argue that the risk of its misuse increases, but its status is a 'stolen firearm' not an illegal one. The Government's own response to the Select Committee report and recommendations spoke of 'illegally held' weapons (in the same fashion we might refer to 'illegally used' firearms) (HM Government, 2011b). So when gun lobbyists metaphorically circle their wagons around the idea of 'legal firearms' they are protecting a fiction and misrepresenting the messy reality of firearm misuse (many weapons employed in criminal activity (e.g. air weapons and replicas) lie outside the licensing system, something of a grey area between 'legal' and 'illegal', their misuse or unlawful possession constitutes the crime). Likewise, the weapons with which Michael Atherton killed members of his own family on New Year's Day 2012 were licensed and in lawful possession, they did not change when he pulled the trigger, they were misused. The distinctions are important. First, they substantially grey the distinction often crafted by gun lobbyists between 'legal' and 'illegal' firearms and, second, they underpin the argument that (all other things being equal) where firearms are prevalent they are generally more frequently misused.

Supporting this argument, the Select Committee was given evidence illustrated by the case of 44 'domestic firearms incidents' reported in national and local media between 1 January and 30 September 2010 (but *excluding* the 12 murders, 11 attempted murders and single suicide in Cumbria). Those 44 incidents comprised nine further murders (including three murder-suicides), nine further attempted murders (including one attempted murder followed by suicide) and 23 other incidents involving threats, wounding, assault/ABH and animal cruelty (HASC, 2010: Evidence 78). Basing an estimate on evidence submitted by the Home Office Research and Statistics Directorate to Lord Cullen's Inquiry, after Dunblane in 1996 (Home Office RSD, 1996), which revealed that 18 out of 42 domestic homicides involved a legally held firearm and fully 70 per cent of domestic murders involved shotguns, it is not unreasonable to suggest that between one-third and a half of those 44 incidents is likely to have involved a legal firearm. The GCN data for the first half of 2012, this time including suicides (Figure 3.1), further reinforces the contribution of legally held weapons to firearm tragedies. The GCN noted that there were 32 recorded shooting deaths in the first six months of 2012 (15 of these occurring in non-metropolitan areas); in 19 cases (59 per cent), the weapon used was either known to be legal or highly likely to have been in legal ownership given other evidence available; 12 deaths (38 per cent) were apparent suicides, four of these appearing to be murder-suicides where ten lives were lost. Finally, all six of the female victims appeared to have been victims of domestic violence (http://www.gun-control-network.org/GCN02.htm). Such evidence confirms the global picture reviewed by Cukier and Cairns (2009: 22–25) that the presence of firearms in the home is a significant risk factor for domestic homicide.

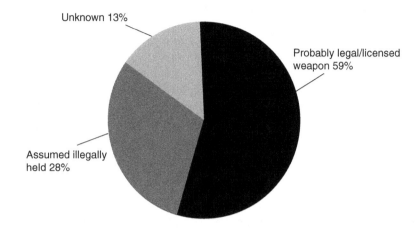

FIGURE 3.1 Firearm deaths in the UK by legal status of the weapon

Source: Gun Control Network website.

Evidence submitted to the Select Committee regarding domestic firearms and licensed weapons also pointed to what it called 'a particular pattern of licensed weapon misuse', here referring to domestic firearm homicides (or sometimes murder-suicides or 'dyadic murders') which often represent the culmination of many years of domestic abuse (as in the later Durham incident). Furthermore, the earlier Home Office findings were consistent with a series of studies undertaken between 1993 and 2007 which reviewed the circumstances of domestic homicide and domestic murder/suicide in England and Wales (Milroy, 1993, 1998; Barraclough and Harris, 2003; Travis *et al.*, 2007) and with a range of other international studies indicating firearms 'readily available in the home' and therefore often legally owned continued to account for a significant proportion of domestic murder and murder-suicide incidents (Alpers and Morgan, 1995; Carcach and Graborsky, 1998; Mouzos, 2000). One further reason for the reluctance of many people to acknowledge domestic shootings as 'crimes' – especially murder/suicides – concerns the extent to which they become cloaked in a language of 'tragedy' rather than of 'crime'. The phenomenon has been noted earlier in respect of mass shootings (see Chapter 6 which follows and, for example, Squires, 2000, Chapter 5) where the tragic scale of the killing often seems to eclipse the legal status of the crime. In the process, attention shifts from the facilitator of the incident, frequently a firearm, and settles instead upon the suffering of the victims and their families, the (often) troubled psychology of the perpetrator, the dysfunctional relationship between perpetrator and victim(s) or, as in the case of the Breivik massacre in Norway 2010, the neo-Nazi political or terrorist sympathies of the killer. In the face of such intimately human trauma and tragedy, questions of gun control can become sidelined.

Nevertheless, the accumulation of such national and international evidence did at least prompt the Select Committee to reflect back upon the *processes* for validating firearm licence applications and the information sharing and 'good practice' employed internationally when doing so. Representatives of the British medical profession were reluctant to be drawn into predicting the 'future dangerousness' or mental stability of firearm licence applicants (HASC, 2010: 28–2, Evidence 42) but accepted that a procedure recently adopted in Canada which involved a current partner or recent ex-partner countersigning the application form of any person applying for a firearms licence might have some merit (Cukier and Cairns, 2009). ACPO representatives appeared to agree (HASC, 2010: 33–34).

Overall, the Select Committee rather declined to more fundamentally engage with the problem of legal firearms in crime, including air weapons, where its attitude seemed to be one of 'wait and see' (HASC, 2010: 55) regarding the recent section 46 of the 2010 Crime and Security Act (allowing persons under 18 to have access to air weapons), although it did acknowledge the problems associated with deactivated and convertible firearms. Therefore, not unlike its predecessors and its policing advisors and, no doubt, bolstered by the reassurances of an inner circle of shooting lobby interests, it rather echoed the cautious pragmatism of earlier Select Committees.

In this regard, at least, the Select Committee's proposals corresponded closely with the Government's own thinking. The Government response to the Select Committee's report (although appearing a mere two months after the shooting tragedy in Norway[4]) accepted many of the cautiously conservative recommendations made, seeing many of the issues as resolvable by better guidance, effective information sharing, tighter process and the dissemination of best practice. It declined to propose extending the category of 'prohibited person' with respect to gun licence applications, preferring to see this as an issue for police discretion, but did accept a recommendation about allowing police 'intelligence' to inform firearm licensing decisions, for example prior arrests or repeated complaints (not leading to convictions) for domestic violence, although further consultation was proposed regarding the Canadian countersignatory idea. The broad principle of a 'public health' perspective on criminal violence was accepted and referred to the ongoing work in early intervention, 'tough enforcement' and community engagement to tackle gangs and weapon-involved violence then being developed by the Home Office and Department of Health: '[T]he Government is committed to tackling violence and gun crime as well as the gang culture which, in some instances, drives them' (HM Government, 2011b). Finally, returning to 'gun crime' directly, the Government's response endorsed the popular (although, as we have now seen, rather more doubtful) view that 'the vast majority of crimes involving firearms are carried out with illegally-held[5] guns' while returning to the gang question: 'the Government is committed to tackling gun crime and the gang culture which is a known driver of it' (HM Government, 2011b).

I now turn to address the development of policies intended to address this gang culture, a 'known driver' of gun crime, in the critical decade-and-a-half after civilian ownership of handguns became substantially prohibited in Britain.

The gangs and guns connection

Opening to the sound of gunfire down a Birmingham street, 2003 was a year bracketed by shooting incidents. The year drew to a close with the shooting of two police officers in Leeds on Boxing Day (26 December) following what police described as a 'routine' traffic stop (one of the officers died). During September and October, further fatal shooting incidents had occurred, keeping gun crime in the spotlight. Jewellery shop owner Marian Bates was shot and killed in Nottingham during an attempted robbery; a few days later, in what police described as 'targeted professional shootings', five people were injured in two separate incidents in the Reading area. An Asian business man, Amratlal Kanabar, was shot and killed following a 100mph motorway chase in an incident containing elements of both robbery and hate crime, although by far the greatest public outrage was reserved for the 'cold-blooded', execution-style murder in September of seven-year-old Toni-Ann Byfield (Boffey, 2004; Pallister, 2006), shot in the back in order to prevent her identifying the killer of her father, a known crack cocaine dealer. Key themes in the reporting concerned the ongoing drug gang vendettas sustaining such collateral violence; another involved the idea of gun crime spreading from its dangerous urban core.

New year 2003 was certainly not the first of the contemporary gangs and guns connections in Britain; Walsh, for instance, takes us back almost two decades to an emerging street gang scene in South Manchester (Walsh, 2003) where a combination of poverty, racism, cultural resistance, drug dealing and conflict (especially with the police) was shaping the patterns of local violence. Silverman (1994) and others (Small, 1995; Davison, 1997) have similarly described the influence of a new Jamaican 'Yardie gang culture' (McLagan, 2005) dominating the distribution of crack cocaine in the late 1980s and early 1990s. By the mid-1990s senior police officers, including the Commissioner of the Metropolitan Police, Paul Condon, were warning of the new street gang culture where firearm carrying brought power, respect and street credibility. By July 2000 Operation Trident, the Metropolitan Police specialist operation to tackle 'black-on-black drugs and gang-related violence' was launched and gang and gun crime had been officially and controversially racialized (Pitts, 2007a). Between April and October 2002, for example, there were said to have been 33 'black-on black' gun attacks in Birmingham (Burke et al., 2003).

In one sense, the social construction and political over-determination of black gun crime follows similar contours to the construction of the (black) 'mugger' described so thoroughly and effectively by Stuart Hall and his colleagues over 30 years ago in 1978 (Hall et al., 1978). But as Hall et al. then emphasized, the real story was not about 'black crime' as such, but about poverty, racism, social exclusion, the toughening climate of law and order politics, the emerging neo-liberal political agenda, and the role of the media in crystallizing popular fears and urban insecurities around the image of the demonized, violent, black offender. In a related fashion, the more recent construction and representation of the black street gangster (even aside from the many prior examples provided by the USA, the 'ideological baggage' referred to by Hallsworth and Young, 2008) fixes the issue as a problem of an 'alien/external' black culture and of dangerous individuals (Gilroy, 2003; Fitzgerald and Hale, 2006; Palmer and Pitts, 2006). Prime Minister Blair forayed into these debates during April 2007 following a spate of shootings in London where the perpetrators and victims were thought to be unusually young. Blair expressed the unfortunate view that the murders were not caused by poverty but by a 'distinctive black culture' (Wintour and Dodd, 2007). Although, on this occasion, the Prime Minister's assessment set him at odds with his Home Office minister Baroness Scotland who, a month earlier, had told the House of Commons Home Affairs Committee that while she accepted there was a problem with 'gun crime', there was no evidence that it was specifically a black issue (Baroness Scotland, 2007).

The question of cultural construction appears perhaps the most clearly in the bizarre twist added to the 2003 gun crime story by Culture Secretary Kim Howells' assertion that 'gangsta rap' and 'hip hop' music were instrumental in the production of a culture of urban armed violence. Only three days after the Birmingham shootings, commenting upon an earlier story where senior police officers had attacked rap music for contributing to the alienation of marginal young men (Goodchild, 2003), Howells referred directly to the Birmingham shootings: 'For years I have been very worried about the hateful lyrics that these boasting macho idiot rappers come out with. It is a big cultural problem ... It has created a culture where killing is almost a fashion accessory' (cited in Gibbons, 2003). I can only briefly touch upon these issues here, but recognize they are part of a much wider debate in the field of media effects and influences (Zylinska, 2004), one that has already played out in the USA (Hamm and Ferrell, 1998; Armstrong, 2001), even culminating in a series of congressional inquiries. A Centre for Social Justice (CSJ) report, even as it drew upon critical cultural theory, for example Hagedorn's work referring to the wider global dimensions of rap music as part of a resistance identity, a cultural response to a world of oppression, danger and exclusion (Bascuñán and Pearce, 2008; Hagedorn, 2008), still voiced its fears about 'the impact [the music] has on our most disadvantaged young people ... [and] the genre's glamourisation of gang violence and its accompanying style ... 'bling', drugs, killing, crime and womanising' (CSJ, 2009: 91–92). Fortunately, Howell's fellow Labour MP, Diane Abbott, brought some closure and perspective to the issue with her comment: 'let's not pretend that ending gun criminality on the streets of Hackney or Birmingham is as simple as getting people to sing different songs' (BBC News, 2003a).

Back in the more mainstream language of criminology, Robert Reiner has argued that a fear of racialized violence has likely been heightened by 'emotionally charged reporting' (Reiner et al., 2003) which has the effect of focussing upon the personal and individual aspects of extreme violence rather than its structural determinants. As we shall see, as the Government's gang strategy developed, similarly personalized and emotionalized – even fictional – case histories have likewise made their way into Government policy literature, begging further questions about the balance of ideology and evidence in policy-making. Similarly, moving into the policy and response debates, Barry Goldson (2003: 392) has complained of the ways in which, not unlike the debate taking place within the Home Affairs Select Committee, 'material circumstance[s] are impatiently dismissed as an excusing distraction within a crude anti-intellectual aetiology rooted in spurious constructions of morality and individual responsibility.' In the USA, Franklin Zimring even went so far as to argue that violence and criminality had become 'the primary lens' through which contemporary youth problems were viewed. This, he argued, had the consequence of distorting public policy and encouraging the projection of 'negative stereotypes and cartoon superficiality' onto the motives and character of young people' (Zimring, 1998: 181). Such insights are important keys to understanding the entire 'gangs and guns' policy industry as it has lately emerged in the UK, aping its American predecessor, even as the US gang suppression industry failed to achieve a significant purchase upon angry, marginal and armed young men in the new urban wastelands of American cities (Hagedorn, 2008; Wacquant, 2008a).

Prior to outlining British Governmental responses to the Birmingham shootings, it is worth sketching in outline some of the broad contours of the preceding US debate. This is not because the British debate was *predestined* to follow it (even if that was a distinct possibility[6]) but simply to gain a sense of the structure of this debate and the way that fundamental understandings of the 'gang violence' problem are related to policy development. First of all, however, it is important to acknowledge that there is an immense literature on gangs, gang cultures and violence in US social science. This work has, in turn, been rather selectively appropriated in US policing and policy documents, FBI 'threat assessments', crime prevention strategies and gang intervention projects. This is not the place to review that work in any detail, although it is important to acknowledge the perceived significance that both policing agencies (National Alliance of Gang Investigators Associations, 2005) and some researchers placed upon the issue. Malcolm Klein, a leading US gang researcher, even implied that the 'gang problem' had largely eclipsed the distinct threats posed by communism, organized crime and urban terrorism in the eyes of the FBI (Klein, 1995).

The dominant, although profoundly restricted, framing of the US gang violence debate in terms of morality, responsibility and individual choice left little place for policy interventions that went beyond either deterrence or responsibilization and, allied to the populist conceptions of youth 'deviance' identified by Zimring, actively cultivated discourses of misunderstanding and othering. Together they pointed to the truth of Garland's (2001a: 26) argument that 'crime control strategies and criminological ideas are not adopted because they are known to solve problems'. By contrast

> the programmes and ideas that are selected are those that fit with … dominant structures and the cultures they support. They are the ones that mesh with the most powerful institutions, allocate blame in popular ways, and empower groups that currently command authority, esteem and resources.
>
> *(Garland, 2001: 26)*

Accordingly the populist conceptions of gang cultures, violence and – in particular – of firearm misuse, which have tended to prevail in debates on either side of the Atlantic, systematically exclude both socio-economic and structural variables (inequality, unemployment, social exclusion, race and discrimination) as well as the pressures of context and experience that these bring (experiences of policing, racism, criminalization, prison, abuse and victimization), culminating in the self-fulfilling process of 'gangsterization' (Squires, 2011a, 2012). Yet just as the authorities bemoan the existence of the gang and its violence so their discourses, policies and policing practices produce yet more gangs, even more violence and still further resort to firearms. One of the crucial ironies here is that this paradox was recognized by Thrasher back in 1927 (Thrasher, 1927). The conclusion has been subsequently reaffirmed by more recent research and analysis. Reiterating the core messages from the evidence, Malcolm Klein made the point: although they are often very popular because they resonate with contemporary punitive responses to youth violence,

> most gang intervention programs can be shown to increase gang cohesiveness ... increasing gang cohesiveness also increases group morale and productivity. One of the products of gangs is crime ... [therefore] most gang intervention programmes, without meaning to, have the net effect of increasing gang crime.
>
> *(Klein, 1995: 7–8)*

Such a finding is reinforced by later findings from a Justice Policy Institute study published in 2007. The authors note that while gang suppression 'remains an enormously popular response to gang activity', gang experts are concerned that 'such tactics can strengthen gang cohesion and increase community tension ... Heavy-handed suppression efforts can increase gang cohesion and police-community tensions, and they have a poor track record when it comes to reducing crime and violence' (Greene and Pranis, 2007: 7).

So much for deterrence and suppression: but what of responsibilization? It is often overlooked that what is sometimes characterized as a distinction between the 'iron fist' and the 'velvet glove' is not, in the context of the present discussion, a distinction at all. Both deterrence (the attempt to – sometimes blindly; sometimes targeted – influence the behaviour of potentially rational actors by threats of punishment) and responsibilization (the attempt to rationalize, incentivise and educate and thereby influence the behaviour and choices of would-be sovereign individuals) are in fact simply aspects of the *same* side of a single criminological coin. As Bell has convincingly argued, responsibilization and criminalization are closely tied together (Bell, 2011: 68). The consequence of failing to moderate one's behaviour, or act responsibly, is punishment – as if deviancy were nothing more than a simple choice – and, in turn, much of the punishment then delivered consists in the effort to influence future behaviour and future choices (though not to understand why they are made). Beyond *a priori* universalized understandings of error, greed and human frailty, none of the foregoing provide even the very least explanation for the supposedly deviant or violent behaviour itself. Accordingly the real alternative, a significant contribution to our understanding of gang culture, violence and the allure of (or demand for) firearms and weapons has to be rooted in the material structures and psycho-social experiences of young people, their relationships, identities and affiliations. Such a qualitative 'gang sociology' has certainly begun to emerge (see for example Venkatesh, 1997, 2008; Anderson, 1999; Bourgois, 2003; Mullins, 2006; Pogrebin *et al.*, 2009; Garot, 2010). A number of these writers have explicitly linked their analyses to street gang 'gun cultures' (Fagan and Wilkinson, 1998, 2000; Wilkinson, 2003; Harcourt, 2006) but this work has so far achieved relatively little purchase on the public policy debate. I will return to these issues in Chapter 7, exploring the phenomenon of chronically violent cultures or global 'conflict complexes' and the roles played by armed young men and gangs within them.

The preceding remarks, less about the *substance* of the US gangs, guns and violence phenomenon and more attentive to the media constructions and political appropriation of the issue, are a useful prerequisite for grasping the major ways in which, after 2003, the salient themes of the British 'gangs and guns' debate were initially pulled together, then crystallized within (implicit) discourses of race and class before, finally, being deployed politically in governing strategies.

Connected: signal crimes and symbol politics?

The gravity and significance of the Birmingham shootings could hardly be overstated, they connected immediately with the statistical evidence I have earlier examined of apparently rapid increases in gun crime in the four years after 1998. David Bamber, writing in the *Daily Telegraph* (Bamber, 2002), pieced the global jigsaw of gun crime together, connecting the 'flood of Jamaican cocaine' to Britain with a plentiful supply of eastern European and former Yugoslavian firearms to produce 'soaring rates' of drug-fuelled gun violence. David Taylor, in the *Evening Standard*, employed the same phrase, 'soaring gun crime' (Taylor, 2003). A 2003 headline in *The Sun* asked: 'Are we losing the war on Gun Crime?', while BBC journalist Dominic Casciani described urban gun crime as a 'national crisis' (Casciani, 2003). Guns were said to be 'ruling communities' with the innocent 'hiding in fear' (Burke *et al.*, 2003). Senior police officers entered the fray: Greater Manchester's Deputy Chief Constable (and ACPO lead on firearms) Alan Green described gun crime as 'a cancer' and, tellingly, he added, 'impacting particularly in our black communities' (BBC News, 2003b), while Nottinghamshire's chief constable described his force as 'over-run by gun crime' (Britten, 2003). The more partisan ramifications of the issue were not lost on commentators with Steele noting, for the *Daily Telegraph*, that 'gun crime' had doubled 'since Labour took office in 1997' (Steele, 2003).

The party politics of this issue were not lost on the UK Government, after all Blair's New Labour had only recently wrestled the 'party of law and order' label from the Conservatives; an authoritative response was called for. Home Secretary

David Blunkett made three announcements: a new firearm amnesty (which ran to the end of April 2003); a proposal to introduce minimum mandatory five-year prison sentences for carrying illegal firearms; and the establishment of a wide-ranging communities and cross-governmental 'summit' meeting to explore the emerging gun culture in Britain's more deprived communities, and to galvanize and empower those communities and to seek solutions. The mandatory five-year sentence (for those aged 18 or over) was incorporated in s.287 of the 2003 Criminal Justice Act, although only after a compromise, agreed to placate opposition in the House of Lords. The Lords had been opposed to the complete abrogation of judicial autonomy on this issue and an agreement was reached that 'in exceptional circumstances' the five-year minimum sentence could be waived, where the judge considered it appropriate (Travis, 2003). Like the US jurisdictions discussed earlier, having been symbolically 'tough on crime' and having waved its deterrent stick, the Government now turned to its companion strategy, the community responsibilization agenda. As I have already noted, these approaches represented complementary wings of an emerging neo-liberal governance of urban marginality and chronic community violence; they engaged with similar aspects of communal, familial and individual problems as their US predecessors but, just as inevitably, did not touch the more structural, economic and political problems disadvantaging these very communities. Even in their earliest manifestations, the Connected: Tackling Gun Crime Summits (summits *plural*, for there were a number of them to follow) both anticipated and inflected the developing shape of British neo-liberal crime strategy, although even this only followed after a fairly selective reading of the initial summit outputs.

The first such summit, Connected: Together We Can Tackle Gun Crime, was held in Birmingham in January 2004, a year after the murders of Charlene Ellis and Latisha Shakespeare. The government strategy centred on 'community empowerment' against the 'gang and gun culture' said to be developing in a number of cities and on rebuilding trust and confidence in community policing in excluded and vulnerable urban communities. The core focus of the event comprised an attempt to understand the emerging street gun culture in order to understand the *demand* for firearms and thereby *prevent* or *suppress* the emerging British gang culture. In practice policies rather oscillated between the two approaches. Participants at the event 'included young people, officers from local authorities, police officers, teachers, central government civil servants, activists on gun issues, youth workers and others (including victims and bereaved family members) with direct experience of gun crime' (Home Office, 2004).

The invited membership of the summit closely resembled the familiar 'joined-up', community-led, largely experiential approach to gun and gang crime that had become the hallmark of new Labour communitarianism (Squires, 1999; Hughes, 2007). Significantly, a research and evaluation dimension was largely absent from the event. While the report emerging from the summit undoubtedly took up a broad-based understanding of the gang and gun problem, drawing upon the experiences of many community groups and sharing and disseminating good practice in youth mentoring and diversion, there is also a sense in which the conference was, implicitly, endorsing a strategy of social and moral renewal and 'capacity building' at the community level, aided and abetted by community policing. Taken together, the strategic direction identified by the summit anticipated the growing preoccupation with overcoming perceived 'social capital' deficits in deprived and 'marginal communities', not unlike the Government's wider 'Respect' agenda emerging simultaneously (see Squires, 2008b). Above all, focussing upon this constellation of community interests, brought together especially for a summit on gangs and guns, tended to endorse a governmental assumption that the problems arising were, first and foremost, problems of the communities themselves. The inadequacies of such a perspective rested upon two erroneous assumptions, assumptions that had been made explicit over 25 years earlier. These were: 'firstly, that it was the "deprived" themselves who were the cause of "urban deprivation". Secondly, the problems could best be solved by overcoming people's apathy and promoting self-help' (CDP, 1977: 4).

Such assumptions are very similar to the 'community cohesion' and 'capacity building' agendas embodied in initiatives such as Labour's *New Deal For Communities*. Both agendas located social pathology and lack of motivation within the communities concerned seeing these as the major sources of social deprivation, marginality, conflict and violence. Such ideas also connected with those emerging in the Government's response to the Bradford riots of 2001, highlighting a number of important adjustments being made to ideas about communities, responsibility and policy development (Flint and Robinson, 2008). The new watchwords were 'inclusion', 'cohesion' and 'social capital', all underpinned by neo-liberal conceptions of governing whereby communities would become less costly in terms of state expenditures, more resourceful for themselves and more attractive to business in the global marketplace. For example, in the aftermath of the 2001 riots, John Denham MP, reviewing the investigations into the causes of those riots, posed the issue in terms of the need 'to understand the obstacles that prevent some ethnic minority communities from being more successful in local labour markets' (Denham, 2002: para 2.36). Part of the received answer at least was that such communities had become too insular and inward looking and lacked motivation to make themselves attractive to business. In the words of the Ousely report into the Bradford riots, the ethnic minority (Asian) community was characterized by negative features of 'self-segregation … driven by fear of others' (Ousely, 2001: para 2.5.5). This, apparently, made the areas unattractive to inward business investment and restricted social and economic development (Flint and Robinson, 2008).

Similar issues surfaced a few years later in a 2007 inquiry of the Home Affairs Select Committee into Young Black People and the Criminal Justice System (HoC: HASC, 2007). Here the issue was not uneconomic 'self-segregation' prompted by fear culminating in riot but rather a toxic combination of racism, discrimination, social exclusion and violent victimization prompting fear, leading to a safety in numbers approach to street socializing (frequently misunderstood as 'gangs') and a dangerous resort to weapon carrying for personal safety. According to the committee report, the 'evidence does point strongly to a much greater likelihood of young black people falling victim to violent and weapon-enabled crime, including homicide'. Several witnesses before the committee noted how many

> young black people live in sustained fear of victimization ... Many people live in absolute terror, and they have armed themselves in response to that terror ... the safety of young people traveling to and from schools is an issue which comes up 'continually' in some schools.
>
> *(HoC: HASC, 2007: paras 35, 39–40)*

Notably, it was reported that 'young black people primarily fear being attacked by someone of the same ethnicity' (HoC: HASC, 2007: para 41) and 'young black people's fear of crime is typically to do with them being attacked by other young black people' (HoC: HASC, 2007: para 42). Lee Jasper, the then Mayor of London's race adviser, 'highlighted a "specific crisis" in black communities as regards the level of violence and death by guns and knives' (HoC: HASC, 2007: para. 58), but has been criticized by Palmer and Pitts on the grounds that suggestions about calling upon the black community to 'work with the police to tackle gun crime' betrays both historical amnesia and profound misunderstanding concerning 'the decades long legacy of mistrust between the police and local residents which characterise the neighbourhoods in which gun crime is a problem' (Palmer and Pitts, 2006: 16).

The first Connected Summit linked this alleged 'crisis' to a gun and weapon culture developing in some British communities. A major concern expressed involved young men 'who have or use guns because they believe that guns give a person "respect", power, and/or protection' (Home Office: Connected, 2004). Notably, as we have seen (and as the argument in Chapters 4 and 5 develops), these claims were not inconsistent with many of the messages in much US gang research; young people who felt they were at risk of violence took precautions, sometimes this involved acquiring weapons – just like white householders, this *was* the American way. British research soon began to tell a similar story (Hales *et al.*, 2006; Marfleet, 2008; Squires, 2009b, 2011).

Summit participants went on to identify a range of factors – stretching from global trends to personal circumstances – contributing to this street level weaponization and leading to gun crime. Specific issues identified included: the disintegration of communities and families; a widening gap between rich and poor; the failure of public services to address increasing deprivation and rising violence; school failures and social exclusion; young men's apparently diminished life skills; unemployment, racism and discrimination; the lack of affordable youth services, facilities and opportunities; and lack of positive and appropriate male role models for young men. Finally, reference was made to a diminishing sense of respect for self and others, the need for greater self-discipline and the rise of a culture of selfish individualism (Home Office: Connected, 2004). The issue here was not a lack of consensus about the causes of social exclusion, urban marginality, violence and weapon carrying but rather that addressing these more structural and material contexts and influences lay beyond the scope of what neo-liberal government thought it could, or should, seek to do.

Therefore, having identified the discourses, assumptions and social contexts establishing gun and gang violence as *problems of* the community rather than *problems for* the community, then the kinds of policy proposals arising from the Connected Gun Summit – solutions to be found within the communities themselves primarily by galvanizing their members into action – become perhaps more understandable. Specific proposals included:

- rooting initiatives in local communities;
- finding and funding local solutions to local problems;
- supporting strong local partnerships;
- building sustainable, cohesive, socially inclusive, thriving communities;
- encouraging active citizenship – promoting empowerment and responsibility;
- encouraging and supporting parents to take responsibility and ownership of their children's life chances, and helping make sure that children and young people get the support and care they need;
- encouraging and supporting positive role models and mentoring schemes;
- providing accessible, appropriate and responsive youth provision;
- including young people in setting local agendas, developing policies, planning services, advocacy, peer mediation.

(Home Office, 2004: 14)

While such proposals did not lack ambition, they were generally stronger on aspirational rhetoric about community capacity building and partnership development, all the way punctuated with participants 'hopes' and 'pledges' (Home Office, 2004: 27–28) than they were on mainstreaming the practical policies to address poverty, educational disadvantage, social exclusion, racism and lack of economic opportunities. In other words, the very issues that academic and policy research has consistently and over many years shown to be strongly associated with inflated rates of crime, anti-social behaviour, violence, victimization and murder (Social Exclusion Unit, 1998; Dorling, 2005; Pitts, 2007) were sidelined in favour of social and community 'capital' building.

A second Connected Summit event was held in Oxford in May 2006 (Home Office, 2006), which, while it could not be faulted for its breadth and enthusiasm, suffered from an equivalent lack of practical focus. Although it recommended developing 'a robust understanding of the issues that need to be addressed, by talking to people directly affected and other stakeholders' (Home Office, 2006: 22), the highlighting of such homespun truths such as 'a biblical lifestyle will change gun and knife crime' (Home Office, 2006: 23) and Home Office Minister (later Attorney General) Baroness Scotland's proclamation 'I want all my dreams to come true – that is not easy, but it is doable' (Home Office, 2006: 24) suggest that something far removed from traditional policy-making, building upon a conventional evidence base, was going on at the first two summits.

Following a third summit in 2007, the new Home Secretary John Reid announced a new 'three-point plan' to tackle gun crime comprising policing, new legal powers and prevention. Specific proposals included: a wide-ranging review of the legislation relating to guns, gangs and knives; and consideration to be given to making gang membership an aggravating factor when judges were passing sentence in gun and knife crime cases. Politicians also wanted to emphasize the mandatory five-year sentence for possession of an illegal firearm, while a new offence of 'minding a weapon' was proposed, designed to address the practice of younger gang members, family members or girlfriends carrying gang guns for older offenders, confident in the knowledge they were less likely to be searched by police (an interesting example of gang offence displacement). The new offence described in sections 28–29 of the 2006 VCRA provided for sentences of up to ten years for offenders aged 16 or over. In sections 36–41, the VCRA also prohibited the manufacture, sale and importation of 'realistic imitation firearms' (Home Office, Press Release, 22 February 2007; *The Guardian*, 23 February 2007) although, as we have already seen, a number of issues remain with both the definition, loopholes in the law and the availability of 'realistic imitation' air weapon models of regular firearms as advertised in the shooting press (see Animal Aid: *Gunning for Children*, 2012: 9).

Progress with the Home Secretary's new 'policing, powers and prevention' strategy was provided in May 2008, in the form of the Violent Crime Action Plan (Home Office, 2008b) and the Tackling Gangs Action Plan (including a 'Practical Guide': Home Office 2008c). The former contained an enforcement-led package of policing measures including:

> [working] with the police to develop state-of-the-art imaging technology to provide information and intelligence on firearms used in crime … new controls on deactivated firearms… identify[ing] key gang members; enhanc[ing] the use of covert surveillance; and implement[ing] targeted, multi-agency crackdowns.
>
> *(Home Office, 2008b)*

Developments in policing gun crime, or 'policing in a gun culture' (Squires and Kennison, 2010: Chapter 6) were influenced also by the MPA Gun Crime Scrutiny (2004) and two high-profile ACPO conferences in 2006 and 2007. The ACPO events were largely devoted to managerialist responses to support police enforcement, investigation, intelligence development and inter-agency working in order to streamline relationships between the police, Crown Prosecution Service (CPS), HMRC and other agencies. The first event in 2006 saw the public launch of the NABIS programme, shared good practice while taking the opportunity to lobby for (potentially controversial) changes in evidence and procedure to make it easier to bring offenders to justice or to protect victims and witnesses. The conference also outlined proposals for the extension of 'super ASBO' (anti-social behaviour order) provisions for gang-related serious offenders, the amendment of rules relating to evidence disclosure and provisions to ensure witness anonymity. Once again there was little external academic input to the agenda, as if policing were best left to the police, and that tackling gun crime was best responded to by policing anyway. The assumption that the skills, insights and evidence base to address 'gun crime' problems were all available 'in house', within the police and criminal justice system themselves and that durable solutions for crime problems might lie beyond the police and criminal justice system merits some attention (Garside, 2006).

Earlier, an all-Party Parliamentary Inquiry on Gun Violence, chaired by Diane Abbott MP (APPG, 2003) had produced a report attempting to strike a balance between a robust and effective, enforcement-led police response in weaponized urban environments while avoiding a seemingly irreversible shift to more routinely armed policing. Balancing these competing pressures led the MPs' inquiry team to recommend increasing the numbers of authorized firearms officers (AFOs) and enhancing Armed Response Vehicle (ARV) cover while still committing itself to a routinely unarmed policing and a broad-based community preventive approach (APPG, 2003). Unfortunately, some two years later, the mistaken shooting of Jean Charles de Menezes at Stockwell underground station in the wake of the London 7/7 bombings threw the Metropolitan Police, and armed response policy more generally, into a major critical turmoil and exposed a number of dilemmas in police armed response policy, management and practice which, arguably, remain still unresolved (Squires and Kennison, 2010; Punch, 2010). The acute pressures and difficulties in policing a gun culture, working within weaponized environments and facing potentially armed confrontations with offenders hugely ramps up the demands from victimized communities and the risks facing police officers just as it magnifies the consequences of police actions under a spotlight of critical public scrutiny. Police shootings of reportedly armed and allegedly gang-involved offenders Azelle Rodney (in 2005), Terry Nicholas (in 2007) and Mark Duggan (in 2011, the police shooting that was the flashpoint for the August 2011 riots in England) indicate something of the tensions and dilemmas here.

Each case throws up a number of critical issues: following two attempts on his life, one of which he survived only by virtue of the bullet-proof vest he was wearing, Nicholas was offered police protection. He refused any police assistance, commenting that he would 'sort it out himself' (IPCC, 2009). Police received information that Nicholas was aiming to acquire a firearm, either for protection or revenge, and planned an operation to intercept this transaction. When confronted, according to the IPCC Inquiry Report, Nicholas opened fire and three police officers returned fire. Nicholas was hit by at least 20 shots, mainly in the head and neck and he died of multiple gunshot wounds. At the inquest questions were asked about the police tactics when approaching Nicholas. IPCC Commissioner Deborah Glass acknowledged that 'Terry Nicholas's family and friends believe that he would not have fired if he had known the people approaching him were police officers' (Summers and Jackson, 2009).

Legal controversy also surrounded the case regarding certain evidence disclosure issues relating to the source of police intelligence about Nicholas's intention to obtain a firearm. Similar questions arose in the Azelle Rodney case, closure of which was delayed for over seven years while legal issues relating to the police intelligence intercepts were addressed. In the event, an official inquiry was commissioned in 2010, reporting some three years later in July 2013 (Holland, 2013). Critical questions were posed during the inquiry regarding whether the police officer engaging with Rodney on the rear seat of a VW Golf absolutely needed to fire eight shots at very close range. The incident bore certain similarities to the shooting of Jean Charles de Menezes at Stockwell underground station less than three months later. Finally, the disorderly consequences of the shooting of Mark Duggan were compounded by the failure of the local police to communicate effectively with community members and the IPCC issuing an incorrect and misleading statement concerning the circumstances of the shooting. An IPCC press release had suggested that Duggan had fired his (converted pistol) first, whereas the bullet that hit a police officer's radio was, in fact, a ricochet initially fired from another police officer's weapon. In such intense, dangerous, fast-moving and difficult scenarios the pressures of policing armed crime will almost inevitably generate profound dilemmas and difficulties, rendering all the more important the 'prevention' side of the Government's strategy which was still developing.

The second Home Office document issued in 2008, *The Tackling Gangs: Practical Guide* (Home Office 2008c) comprised guidance on a wide range of measures that were either already in place (in the Manchester, London, Birmingham or Liverpool areas) as well as proposals for future measures for local agencies to pursue. Illustrative examples included:

- effective enforcement strategies for dealing with gangs;
- section 60 stop and search initiatives;
- armed checkpoints;
- ANPR initiatives (to track gang members' movements);
- gang disruption operations;
- crack house closures;
- witness intimidation initiatives;
- ASBOs and injunctions for use against gang members.

(Home Office, 2008c)

As Gordon Brown was preparing to replace Tony Blair as Prime Minister, early indications regarding his strategy for 'gun crime' came in a speech to ACPO in June 2007. An uncompromising, zero-tolerance approach to weapon carrying was announced.

The clear message needs to go out to young people: carrying weapons will not be tolerated. No matter the circumstances, no matter the peer pressure, no matter what anyone else is carrying ... Five years for carrying a gun, two years for a knife – there will be no let up on our efforts to bear down on these crimes.

(Brown, 2007)

This characteristically 'tough' stance was maintained by the Prime Minister's response to the shooting of 11-year-old Rhys Jones in Liverpool in August: 'Where there is a need for new laws, we will pass them, where there is a need for tougher enforcement we will make sure that that happens' (Prime Minister's Office website, 23 August 2007). Jacqui Smith, the Home Secretary, added that she would also be considering legislation to compel witnesses of 'gun crime' to give evidence to the police and the courts (Travis, 2007). In September 2007, the Home Office announced a renewed initiative, the TGAP, a police-led, multi-agency initiative to tackle 'gun crime' in areas identified by the police as 'suffering disproportionately from problems with criminal gangs ... involved in gun crime' (Home Office, Press Notice: 145/2007, 9 September 2007). TGAP operated in London, Liverpool, Birmingham and Manchester, where the gang and gun violence problems were mostly concentrated. When the results were eventually published, they raised some interesting questions about the effectiveness of the strategy as well as about race and the police targeting of gang members and the quality of the weapons available to gangs (see Squires *et al.*, 2008).

Finally, in recognition of the apparent difficulty of getting gang members to leave the gang lifestyle, or victims and witnesses to report gang crime (for fear of reprisals), commitments were made to ensure support for victims and witnesses – 'the best possible protection from the earliest stage of the criminal justice process' (Home Office, 2008c) – as well as mentoring and support for those seeking to exit gangs. The range of proposals here included: the use of covert operations and surveillance against targeted gang members; high visibility police presence on the streets ('robust reassurance') in target areas including on routes to and from schools; the use of civil orders to restrict gang members; provision of safe houses for victims, witnesses and those seeking to leave gangs; the establishment of mediation services for gang members; and greater witness protection including, following discussions between ACPO and the CPS, proposals for witness anonymity in gang cases.

This tough, policing-led response was reaffirmed during Gordon Brown's speech at the 2007 Labour Party Conference. In selected areas, he said the police would be undertaking high-profile stop and search operations to deter gun carrying by offenders. Action on these priorities followed on 28 November 2007 when, as part of the TGAP initiative, a coordinated day of action, four police forces, working with HMRC and the Serious Organised Crime Agency (SOCA), executed 67 search warrants and arrested 118 people, in the process seizing over 1,300 'firearms'. Interestingly, however, only ten of the firearms seized were capable of live firing (and four were air weapons), confirming yet again the rather doubtful quality of the UK illegal firearms inventory and the significance of replica weapons within it (Home Office, Press Release, 29 November 2007).

TGAP had become part of the new Tackling Violence Action Programme, overseen by a central ministerial taskforce on guns and gangs, chaired by the Home Secretary' (Home Office, Press Release, 19 December 2007). The core of the new strategy comprised policing, target-hardening, intelligence development, technology, education and social crime prevention, although there was still very little reference to research or learning capacity, nor was much said about sources of illegal gun *supply*. By contrast, examples were presented to illustrate the kinds of educative, anti-gang and anti-violence work designed to reduce *demand* for guns in key communities. The action plan documented the work of the Manchester Multi-Agency Gang Strategy (MMAGS) (Home Office, Press Release, 19 December 2007: 17), while the Home Secretary praised the work of Lambeth's X-it project which aimed 'to reduce offending behaviour among young people who are directly at risk of joining gangs or who want to leave gangs' by using ex-gang members as mentors for young people (Home Office, Press Release, 19 December 2007).

Finally, however, early 2008 saw the long-awaited launch of NABIS, enhancing the police's forensic tracing and intelligence management capacity for criminal firearms and other ballistic materials, while there were also suggestions that SOCA might be raising the priority given to firearm trafficking into the UK, although there were few specific details. By 2010, therefore, substantial resources had already been put into intelligence gathering, policing, policy development and strategy implementation in respect of gangs and gun crime in the UK. The broad outlines of this strategy, comprising the *tough on crime* policing arm and the *tough on causes* community empowerment agenda, which emerged in the course of the various Connected Summits and related policy fora between 2004 and 2008, can be clearly discerned. The change of Government in 2010, and the riots of 2011 (initially and opportunistically, although also rather incorrectly, attributed to 'gangs and gang culture' by leading politicians – Hallsworth and Brotherton, 2011) following the police shooting of Mark Duggan added further shape and direction to this evolving programme.

Gangs, guns and the 'broken society'?

In 2009, the right-of-centre 'think tank', the CSJ, chaired by former Conservative party leader Iain Duncan Smith, published a substantial report *Dying to Belong*, and subtitled an 'In-depth Review of Street Gangs in Britain' (CSJ, 2009). In a very direct sense, the report paved the way for the cross governmental report *Ending Gang and Youth Violence* published late in 2011(HM Government, 2011a) where, as Secretary of State for Work and Pensions, Iain Duncan Smith contributed one of two ministerial forewords. This document made ever more explicit the transition from a social scientific understanding of youth violence, gang culture and weaponization to a neo-liberal and profoundly individualist conception of criminality (Bell, 2011); of individuals exercising poor judgement, making poor choices, as they negotiated the risky landscapes of 'Broken Britain'. The narratives are now about individual journeys rather than social and economic conditions, material circumstances and structural constraints; they are occasional stories of dreams realized, success or redemption where even 'get rich or die trying' strikes a chord, contrasting markedly with the huge silences surrounding poverty, suffering and social exclusion.

All the same, one has to be careful in not overstating the paradigm shift in criminological explanation; it hardly amounts to a U-turn. Rather, over two decades this transition has culminated into a profound individualization of dominant perspectives on 'criminal career' development, underpinning culturalist conceptions of gang formation, the use of weapons and the exercise of violence. Even more dramatically, as we shall see, this individualized and culturalist perspective exercises a near total hegemony in the policy and practice intervention discourses. Commentators from the practice communities often make critical reference to the fact that the greater part of current anti-violence strategies are designed more to address the risk that young people *pose*, rather than the risks they *face* (Fitch, 2009: 3) but, for all that, the language is primarily of risks to be negotiated or managed by individuals rather than social problems solved or risks lowered.

This transition was certainly reflected in the Connected Gun Crime Summits between 2004 and 2008, but the process did not begin there. It certainly had its American origins, acknowledged earlier, and, not least, via the 'broken windows' (Wilson and Kelling, 1988) 'broken society' connection, the debate was tilted in a moralist direction which Tony Blair's self-acknowledged 'crusade' (Squires, 2008b) against 'anti-social behaviour' did much to further strengthen, disseminate and popularize (Tonry, 2004; Squires and Stephen, 2005; Bell, 2011). As far as the demonization, criminalization and 'new punitive' responses towards youth were concerned, the murder in 1993 of James Bulger was certainly a critical catalyst, but the way it was seized upon (see for example Goldson, 2000, 2001, 2003) to herald the wayward marginality and criminal disrespect of the young, urban, working class reveals a fairly direct lineage through to the vitriolic outpourings of contempt concerning the supposedly 'mindless' and 'feral' rioters of August 2011 (Squires, 2011a) which, in turn, was reflected in the severe sentencing. Even so, this 'line of infamy' was punctuated by further episodes in the criminology of weaponization where still further American influences over policy and practice are discernible.

In Manchester, where firearm-involved gang crime had been an early subject of Home Office research and analysis (Bullock and Tilley, 2002), a version of an apparently successful gun crime initiative, Operation Ceasefire, had been adopted to tackle the city's gang problems (see Squires and Kennison, 2010: 138–142). The initiative had first been developed in Boston, and the primary goal of the initiative was to target inter-agency police, criminal justice and social service partnership energies and resources upon the relatively small number of priority offenders (who were often *also* gang violence *victims*; Bullock and Tilley, 2002; Pitts, 2008; Ralphs *et al.*, 2009), thought to be primarily responsible for the large majority of urban gun violence problems in the city (Braga, 2008). On the other hand, the Manchester initiative, MMAGS, was also rooted in a youth-work practice tradition (Shropshire and McFarquhar, 2002) of working with young people at risk and, in this sense, while it was never intended as a response to the wider structural inequalities, exclusions and deprivations of South Manchester, it certainly reflected an approach centred upon empowering, mentoring, capacity building, family intervention and community capital enhancement, all underpinned by effective inter-agency support. Similarly, in Glasgow, which had its own particular legacy of sectarian, weaponized gang violence going back many years, Strathclyde Police had also been piloting targeted interventions on known gang members, along the lines of Boston's Operation Ceasefire (Adams, 2008; Campsie, 2008; Knight, 2010).

In 2008, the Government's new Youth Crime Action Plan (HM Government, 2008) unveiled a 'triple-track' approach initially outlined in the Youth Taskforce Action Plan (DCSF, 2008) and comprising a familiar strong emphasis on early intervention, with tough measures of enforcement backed by sanctions where problems persist, alongside a supposedly 'non-negotiable' theme of family-centred support. Likewise, both the Manchester and Strathclyde violence initiatives involved targeted, community-based, early intervention methods and 'wrap-around' (or 'team around the child') risk management and support services, not unlike those developed in respect of anti-social behaviour (ASB) and youth crime more generally (Brand and Ollereanshaw, 2008; Home Office, 2008: 55; Knight, 2010).

The work of MMAGS took place under a particular research spotlight comprising both Home Office researchers (Bullock and Tilley), following up their original gang study published in 2002, and an ESRC funded team of gang researchers from the University of Manchester, the latter project exploring the role of parenting support (Aldridge et al., 2011) and mentoring (Medina et al., 2010) establishing an evidence base to contest the enforcement-led approach that has otherwise dominated British gang policy (Aldridge et al., 2011). Unfortunately, as I have noted already, enforcement and a combination of capacity building and responsibilization have not represented alternative strategies. Bullock and Tilley's evaluation of the implementation of MMAGS suggested that its initial efforts to engage with the socio-economic factors underpinning the reasons why youths join gangs represented an 'impractical strategy' and that this had diverted attention from the enforcement aspect of the project (Bullock and Tilley, 2008) with potentially significant net-widening (criminalizing) consequences for the generation of local youth perceived to be 'at risk' of gang involvement. The concern was that such responses might be less likely to 'nip' potential gang membership 'in the bud' and – as occurred with the Blair government's ASB (anti-social behaviour) strategy (Squires and Stephen, 2005) – more likely to mobilize a self-fulfilling ('gangsterization') prophecy which over-identified and labelled potential gang members, installing still further obstacles in the path of marginalized young people seeking to negotiate their transitions to adulthood (Medina et al., 2009; refer to Hagedorn's (1988) discussion of this process).

In due course, however, even as the youth and community safety professional 'practice' communities continued their advocacy for inter-agency, community and supportive interventions (APYCO, 2008; Brand and Ollereanshaw, 2008; Fitch, 2009) against a more police-centred and enforcement-led approach, the wider socio-economic contexts of poverty and inequality, racism and discrimination, unemployment and social exclusion became overlooked and sidelined; they simply became just risks that could, with willpower, effort, practice and some support, be managed or handled. The problems were not the inequalities, disadvantages and exclusions themselves; it was, instead, a question of the capacity of individuals to cope with them. Inequalities and social problems were just 'opportunities' that effort, ability and a magic ingredient – personal, social or community 'capital' – could overcome. As Fine (2001, 2010) has noted, there is great significance in this neo-liberal economic reading of personal and social capacity, it implied no less than that individuals and communities had to work upon their value and profit potential in the new market landscape. For only if they represented more potential value to others, their skills or their investment potential, in society as a marketplace, would wider society (of employers, investors, buyers) come to value *them*. The route to social inclusion and success was via employment, this was employment-based social inclusion (Levitas, 1996; Rodger, 2008) or the workfare culture (Wacquant, 2009) to which contemporary conservatives had grafted the wider demoralization discourse of the underclass. To endorse the analysis, that 'work is the most sustainable route out of poverty' (CSJ, 2009: 190), conservative commentators were keen to deploy the slogan of the Los Angeles gang diversion project, Homeboy Industries, 'nothing stops a bullet like a job', its marketing literature promised (CSJ, 2009: 210).

One particular policy report, embracing the Conservative-led coalition's 'Big Society' agenda, even alluded to the need to free deprived communities from the 'dark social capital' within which they were trapped (Fisher and Gruescu, 2011). This 'dark social capital' appears rather like one's own, personalized, negative equity (a negative equity of the self') and, in that sense, not unlike a house now worth less than its mortgage, dark social capital is simply a new take on the notion of 'stigma' or, more dynamically, of the 'dependency culture'. Dark social capital converts social and moral worth to economic value and tells us that the poorest have little or none, but then as 'dependency' this diminished value is read-off as a personal characteristic or failing (Taylor-Gooby and Dean, 1992).

The Conservative–Democrat coalition Government clearly did not invent this perspective on the problems of the poorest communities and in some respects the shift from New Labour gang strategy to Conservative–Democrat gang strategy was relatively seamless. Launching the practitioner guidebook that accompanied Labour's 2008 *Tackling Gangs* initiative (Home Office, 2008c), Home Secretary Jacqui Smith referred to what she called the 'successful', 'new and innovative approaches to tackling gangs' which she felt 'show[ed] the affected communities that we *can* tackle this problem and together we can fight the culture of despair that gangs prey on' (Home Office, 2008: 1). Note especially the culturalist reading of the problem; a 'culture of despair' is undoubtedly an aspect of that 'dark social capital' about which we have been warned. In other ways the document presented a rather unbalanced picture of the existing gang violence strategy deployed by Labour. For example, the 'successes' referred to by the Home Secretary referred almost entirely to police-led and criminal justice interventions (high-visibility police operations, deployment of weapon search technologies, police gang disruption strategies, targeted anti-gang injunctions, NABIS, coordinated CPS prosecution strategy and the dawn-raids TGAP of the 'day of action' referred to already). By the same token by far the most extensive section (Section 8) of the document concerned itself with police enforcement action: 'Targeting Gang Members', including everything (alphabetically) from 'armed police checkpoints', gang ASBOs, stop and search initiatives, vehicle seizures, the execution of search warrants and strategies to address witness intimidation. Onto this exhaustive catalogue of enforcement-led activities the Government sought to graft a more locally focussed sequence of approaches addressing families, youth peer groups, 'third sector' (or voluntary) agencies and communities designed to prevent young people from joining gangs and becoming involved in violence, while encouraging communities to resist gangs and help young people leave them.

Experience drawn from the Strathclyde Violence Reduction Unit (VRU) (established in 2005) was also influential in shaping the emerging national gang strategy. For although the Strathclyde region suffered the lion's share of Scottish gun crime, it was knife crime, in particular, for which Glasgow had its unwanted reputation (CCJS, 2008). Responding to the high levels of weapon-involved and gang-related violence, the region had established a multi-agency violence reduction strategy: 'High levels of knife carrying, gang violence and feuds between rival criminal gangs are common features, often fuelled by alcohol' (Strathclyde Police, *Public Performance Report* 2006/07). At the same time it was also acknowledged that criminal violence was under-reported by some 50–70 per cent. More generally, the evidence pointed to a pattern of chronic, concentrated and 'symmetrical' (Pitts, 2008) violence, with police estimating that there were over 160 gangs in the Glasgow area. In an overwhelming majority of gun and knife crimes, both victims and perpetrators tended to be white Scottish males, aged 14 to 18; the victims of violent attacks also knew their attackers in over three-quarters of cases, and repeated exposure to violence and victimization was common (Brown and Bolling, 2007).

The originality of the Strathclyde VRU lay in its explicit adoption of a 'harm reduction' public health approach to violence. Its work, also drawing upon the Boston gang project experiences has, in part, also centred upon multi-agency partnership working to develop an effective evidence base of risk factors relating to violence. This is supported by prompt enforcement, early intervention and prevention in families and attitude and behaviour change programmes. Culture, attitudes and family and community failure stand out amongst the factors picked out by the VRU: including cultural norms accepting the use of violence and weapons and the perceived legitimacy of violence as a means to settle disputes. In addition a profound, often 'sectarian' territorialism, along with a dearth of aspiration, were said to overwhelm social relationships. Although, despite passing reference to poverty, deprivation and unemployment, the resulting lack of opportunities was not seen as either *prior to* or *causal* in this catalogue of cultural failure, it was just another factor. As in other areas of the country a familiar itinerary of risk factors: poor parenting skills, violent and abusive families, criminal peers, a lack of positive role models, poor communication or impulse control skills, social and educational exclusion, nutrition and health issues and alcohol or substance misuse problems described a context in which violence and conflict were endemic (CCJS, 2008).

In 2008, a Street Weapons Commission, commissioned by Channel 4 television and chaired by Cherie Blair QC, looked very positively on the Strathclyde VRU strategy, recommending that a VRU, established on similar lines, be established within the Home Office (SWC, 2008: 82). It also largely adopted the Strathclyde VRU synthesis of 'societal, community and individual risk factors', recognizing the damaging relationships between people in such anti-social environments in its model for future policy development. Perhaps most significantly of all, it framed its intervention strategy within a perspective that saw weapon carrying and violence as an entirely individual choice or decision – undoubtedly a choice influenced by particular contexts and experiences, but a choice nonetheless: 'any attempt to address issues of violence must take into account key factors that influence an *individual's decision* to become involved in gun or knife crime' (SWC, 2008: 67, emphasis added). The commission also rejected an argument, put to them by a number of witnesses, that saw a crucial distinction between enforcement-led action and prevention. On the contrary, the commission insisted, enforcement, support and intervention each had a role to play in shaping choices and decisions as those at the greatest risk embarked upon their troubled life-course.

The developing New Labour strategy, Tackling Gangs, announced by Jaqui Smith was strong on recommendations about inter-agency working protocols, developing professional practice and information sharing – it was, after all, a management document designed to prompt Crime and Disorder Reduction Partnerships (CDRPs) to raise their game in the battle against gangs, guns and violence – but compared to the Street Weapons Commission and the CSJ report (CSJ, 2009) it was rather light on research. Evidence-led policy development had lost out to bureaucratic management and drilling delivery agencies into line. Where Tackling Gangs was light in terms of any a real understanding of the gang problem that had to be confronted, the CSJ report situated its approach in the context of a cultural appreciation of marginal young men in urban Britain literally *dying to belong*. Yet, like the connected conferences that preceded it, this starting point did not prevent the CSJ, ultimately, turning socio-economic contexts, growing inequalities and social exclusions into personal narratives of avoidable risk.

Even more strikingly, like the right-wing 'culture of dependency' theorists from the earlier history of the New Right (as discussed, for example, by Taylor-Gooby and Dean, 1992, and Morris, 1994), the CSJ inverted the chain of causation and, in his Think Tank Report's foreword, CSJ chairman, Iain Duncan Smith, wrote of the need to 'better understand what was happening on our streets' and of the danger 'of losing yet another generation as they plunged through violence and criminality to hopelessness and despair' (CSJ, 2009: 9). To underpin this interpretation, that 'violence and criminality' *leads to* 'hopelessness and despair' (and not the other way around) Duncan Smith advanced a culturalist argument centred upon what he called five key *pathways to poverty*. These supposed pathways were 'family breakdown, economic dependency and worklessness, educational failure, addiction and personal indebtedness' (CSJ, 2009: 9). By abrupt sleight of hand, the overwhelming weight of social scientific evidence (see for example Wilkinson and Pickett, 2010) is summarily ignored and the consequences of poverty and inequality are read as its causes. For Duncan Smith, the broad sweep of the argument is concluded with the claim that

> Britain's gangs are the product of these pathways and are found in our most deprived and marginalised communities. They are most commonly found in areas of high family breakdown, addiction, unemployment and worklessness. The modern gang is perhaps the best illustration of how broken Britain's society is.
>
> *(CSJ, 2009: 9)*

This notion of 'pathway' is important and instructive, it focuses attention upon the individual journey and the experiential narratives of these journeys and the risks encountered and negotiated along the way. It resonates with a discourse of youth transitions (Smith and McVie, 2003; McAra and McVie, 2010), from the supposed safety of childhood, through the dangerous 'adolescent' years and into adulthood. It implicates notions of identity formation and moral compass for the traveller on their pathway; each one has his or her own path to take, their own individual decisions to make. It has to be acknowledged, the report, in its entirety, is both substantial and thorough, drawing upon an extensive array of available research, comment and informed practitioner and community opinion. It introduces a wide range of different perspectives to underpin recommendations in relation to youth outreach, peer support, mentoring, diversion, early intervention in troubled families and disadvantaged communities, committing itself to tackling 'the *drivers* of gang culture, not just the symptoms' (CSJ, 2009: 31). At the same time the report is sociologically informed and supported by a wealth of research evidence.

Making choices and living with risk

The report is organized around three substantial sections: first, examining the emerging 'definitions' of gang activity and exploring the state of existing knowledge about gangs in the UK; second, broadly repudiating the notion that there exist any 'quick-fixes' to the problem; and third, reviewing existing gang strategies, projects, and interventions and making recommendations. Any summary of such a substantial report will necessarily be fairly selective (the report runs to over 200 pages) but in the following few paragraphs an attempt will be made to draw out the salient themes relating to gun crime, weaponization and gangs in the context of the wider argument of this chapter.

From the outset the report makes a clear acknowledgement that the 'drivers' of 'gang culture' represent a 'parallel … alternative society' and its constituent elements, 'a desire for status, respect, material wealth and sense of belonging' (CSJ, 2009: 35–6), have to be understood. The core 'gang' question here is presented in terms of how 'young people from dysfunctional families who live in deprived areas of high unemployment, crime and violence and who are marginalized from mainstream society' (CSJ, 2009: 36) can realize these essentially normal ideals, and secure their 'safety, identity respect and protection' through gangs because mainstream legitimate opportunities are denied them. Significantly, the report also adopts the language of 'pathways', detailing in a series of case studies how young people's 'personal experiences and the opportunities open to [them] can dictate the path they follow' (CSJ, 2009: 36). The report devotes some space to American gang definitions, parallels and precursors, acknowledging (like much of the sociological literature; Hagedorn, 1988) that gangs are often 'over-defined', even voicing concerns about inflammatory media reporting 'fuelling hysteria', unleashing moral panic, creating fear and by virtue of this even encouraging the very weapon carrying it otherwise sought to condemn (CSJ, 2009: 68). Ultimately, however, having warned of the dangers of this 'over-gangsterization' the report largely follows the path from denial to recognition acknowledged by previous gang researchers (Klein, 1995; Hagedorn, 1998, Klein et al., 2000; Aldridge et al., 2008). Further chapters summarize the available UK data on the scale, nature and impact of gang activity and, although recognizing that relatively little reliable research evidence existed, the report then attempted to 'profile' British gang membership. Here they deal with the question of ethnicity, refuting the often expressed view that 'gang culture is … a "Black problem" while acknowledging that problems do exist, profoundly exacerbated by patterns of policing, police malpractice, police units formally dedicated to "black-on-black" violence and recent histories of "policing without consent"' (CSJ, 2009: 115–117). The report acknowledges instead that the evidence (see for example CCJS, 2008) shows that territory trumps ethnicity.

> The ethnicity of gang members tends to reflect the ethnicity of the population living in that area. Hence the gangs of Easterhouse estate in Glasgow are White, whereas the gangs of Brixton are predominantly Black. The higher proportion of Black gang members reflects the disproportionate presence of Black communities in deprived inner city neighbourhoods.
>
> *(CSJ, 2009: 76)*

The report also situates its analysis of the rise of the modern gang 'in contexts of globalisation, social exclusion and the widening socio-economic divide', while acknowledging a tradition of sociologically informed gang research reaching back to Thrasher in the 1920s (Thrasher, 1927) and, later, Hagedorn (1988), thus 'street gangs are the products of deprivation and marginalisation' (CSJ, 2009: 81). A political economy model of labour market globalization, segmentation and ('immediate and conspicuous') consumerism is distilled into an explanation of the precarious 'advanced marginality' (Wacquant, 2008a; Standing, 2009; Squires and Lea, 2012a) fostering contemporary gang culture. It becomes hard to imagine that the report's authors or sponsors, especially with their added critique of 'penal populism' (CSJ, 2009: 104) could have anything to do with the simplistic condemnations of contemporary youth culture emerging in the wake of the 2011 English riots. Joan Moore's work, in particular, was drawn upon to underscore the roles of poverty, inequality and the absence of social mobility opportunities as catalysts of illegality, discontent, gang culture and disconnection. She argues,

> periphalization means that in developed nations, large segments of both new immigrants and the old working class increasingly function outside of the main economic life of cities. Ladders of mobility are virtually inaccessible. The gap between the rich and the poor increases. Long term unemployment is not much alleviated by the creation of low paid dead-end jobs. An informal economy flourishes, with strong illicit components.
>
> *(Moore, 2008, cited in CSJ, 2009: 81)*

It is this substantially social and economic analysis that the CSJ's Chairman flipped around, preferring to see poverty, inequality and unemployment as a *consequence* of illegality, marginalization and dead-end jobs rather than as the *cause* of it.

Perhaps even more notable, when the report writing team drew together these various antecedents of the contemporary gang context, youth identity and culture, the report reiterated the key factors to which policy-makers would need to turn. The list is instructive: family breakdown and dysfunction; the lack of positive role models; educational failure; mental and emotional health problems; an (alleged) absence of aspirations; unemployment and underemployment; discrimination and stereotyping; and poverty (CSJ, 2009: 215). Each of the factors identified, although, rather tellingly, not the last two, received their own specific policy prescriptions and proposals. Even though the report made a point of endorsing Heale's 'fallacy of autonomy' – the idea that 'we can separate parenting ability from the circumstances in which parenting is undertaken, is the cruelest [sic] misconception about gangs there is' (Heale, 2008) – a particular emphasis was placed on family failure and dysfunction and, especially, in a familiar echo of an older 'underclass discourse' (Morris, 1994), single-parenthood was cited as a driver of gang membership in deprived areas. Thus, 'family breakdown is helping to drive gang culture' (CSJ, 2009: 96) and

> not only is it near impossible for many lone (usually) mothers to supervise their children to the level necessary in gang-impacted neighbourhoods, it is also a huge challenge for the children to stay out of gangs – whether because of the attractiveness of gang life, or because they feel they simply have no choice in order to be safe.
>
> *(CSJ, 2009: 97–98)*

Finally the report closed with a renewed emphasis on families, early intervention and encouraging communities themselves to take a greater 'ownership' of these issues.

The broad continuities in policy and analysis with the earlier Connected Summits are clear but, equally, the conception of 'gang culture' as a precarious *pathway* consisting of choices on a risky journey through failing and dysfunctional families, educational exclusion, impoverished childhoods and violent adolescence and, not least, sudden trips, slips and stumbles through the ever-growing holes in the welfare safety net, takes on a firmer shape. Elsewhere the CSJ report cites 'gang-involved young people' as having 'slalomed through the system' (2009: 121). This is not the place to embark upon a wider critique of the broader criminal career paradigm (Farrington, 1996, 2002; Graham and Bowling, 1995; Loeber and Farrington, 1998) which continues to inform the new 'pathways' perspective, except to note, first, that the latter tends to focus attention on the active subject, making simplified moral choices, rather than upon the contexts in which these are made. Intriguingly, one of Heale's former gang member interviewees likens his personal biography to the choice between the light and the dark side made by Anakin Skywalker in *Star Wars*. 'That's all the road is', he notes, 'an illusion … The way I've told it, it looks like the road chose me. It didn't, I chose the road. Ain't got no-one to blame but myself' (Heale, 2008: 12).

Such an emphasis on choices overlooks the major theoretical advances of the 'new' gang studies emerging since the 1980s concerning the ways in which 'the gang becomes an institutionalised feature of some poverty communities' (Hagedorn, 1988: 38) where it functions to reproduce a particular lifestyle, becoming a permanent and structuring feature of poverty/excluded communities (Hagedorn, 1988: 49–50). Second, the pathway focus tends to reduce street life and gang culture to its discrete and isolated elements (personal choices, individual narratives, risk and experiences) and neglects both structures and contexts. A particular illustration of this might lie in Heale's observation that 'in some cases they [gangs] barely exist at all, except in the way that chemical reactions exist: a mixture of dangerous elements that occasionally react and then disappear' (Heale, 2008: 65). But while gang contexts may be fluid and the social relations within them transient and fleeting, nothing considered here makes them any less real. However, as the choice and pathways, early intervention and family-focussed analysis of the CSJ crystallized still further into the Conservative–Democrat Government's approach to *Ending Gang and Youth Violence* (HM Government, 2011a), the gap between analysis and strategy became even wider. The CSJ working group's parting shot that, 'success rests on the implementation of the full range of policies outlined below: this is not a pick and mix. Implementing the short term recommendations without the long-term proposals' they argued, 'or the enforcement tactics without the intervention and prevention models will lead, at best, to limited success' (CSJ, 2009: 9). Nonetheless, the Government, however, had other (rather more traditional, symbolic, populist and – it has to be said – parsimonious) ideas.

A central paradox of the Government strategy document lay in the way, drawing upon research by Bellis *et al.* (2011), it presented clear evidence (see Figure 3.2) of the overwhelming impact of area deprivation on assaultive injury rates in England but then, following the 'pathways approach' I have earlier referred to, focussed its strategy almost entirely around individual choices, decision-making and the 'life stories that lead to murder' (HM Government, 2011a: 11–12). The case study of 'Boy X' presented in the document bears a close resemblance to the young violent offender 'profile' employed by the Strathclyde VRU and reported by Knight (2010: 211–213). A footnote in the Government Strategy document acknowledged that:

> Boy X isn't a real person, but the things that happened to him and his family are based on real events presented to the review team over the past two months and discussions with frontline experts on gang violence. It illustrates how, unchecked, harmful events can damage individuals and families.
>
> *(HM Government, 2011a: 12)*

This use of fictional life stories and case histories raises interesting questions for a Government policy document, for the moment the issue is simply the manner in which the account provided underscores the sense of closure that has enveloped government gang strategy. Poverty, deprivation, unemployment and social exclusion will continue; there will also be 'broken communities' and dysfunctional and failing families but it will no longer, apparently, be a core objective of government policy to reduce the level or seriousness of the risks arising from these contexts and circumstances. In that sense this aspiration of government policy has been definitively 'rolled-back'. In its place a 'small minority of violent young people' will be systematically targeted in their families, communities, peer groups and schools (should they still attend them) and a network of statutory and non-statutory agencies surrounding and supporting them – including the new Troubled Families team, will be charged with working smarter and more systematically to 'prevent, target and enforce' while also educating, reducing harm, stopping people 'falling through the cracks' and preventing life stories ending in tragedy (HM Government, 2011a: 14–15).

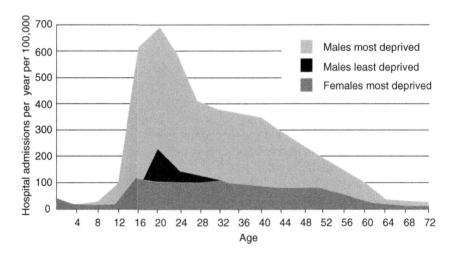

FIGURE 3.2 Admissions to English NHS hospitals for assault

Sources: Bellis *et al.* (2011); HM Government (2011a: 16).

The remaining document echoes throughout with the fictional story of Boy X, and even while reporting the marked social deprivation profile associated with violent victimization, the strategy document prefers to address

> the factors lying behind these graphs [which] can be seen in the individual stories of boys like Boy X ... the same themes recur time and again: early childhood neglect and abuse; ill health in the family, including mental ill health; parental violence and drug addiction; school exclusion and early conduct disorders; violent victimisation and repeated hospital visits; early involvement in local gangs; and early and repeat offending, inadequately punished or prevented.
>
> *(HM Government, 2011a: 16)*

Furthermore, the document continued, even beyond these factors were 'community attitudes' – to the illegal economy, the police and violent dispute resolution – all requiring appropriate attention. Tracing the path of its imaginary Boy X through his foundation and primary years, early childhood, teenage years and early adulthood, the strategy document completed the metamorphosis of criminological understanding into a neo-liberal vision of a sovereign, decision-led, risk narrative. Wider social change, or social investment, is neither contemplated nor proposed; early intervention, effective targeting of the problematic minority, prevention, prosecution and punishment are the watchwords. We have come some way, moving in stages, from the social and cultural reading of the first Gun Crime summit although, in retrospect, the changes seem consistent and purposive.

The longer-term irony of this may be that, in fabricating this sovereign, risk-managing life course decision-maker, as both an identity and a prescription for neo-liberal citizenship, Government might well be further eroding the foundations of political order and consent. Having made clear its reluctance to engage with the social and material foundations of collective social citizenship in order to avert many of the risks of inequality (in the same way that in the 1980s an earlier neo-liberalism abdicated responsibility for employment levels) Government may find individuals making their own choices. We have already found evidence that those who consider themselves at the greatest risk carry weapons – 'for protection' – they typically say (Hales *et al.*, 2006; Marfleet, 2008).

The wider ramifications of this question might suggest that fearful neo-liberal 'individuals' may no longer choose to seek safety and security through the social contract or the state's provision, just as countless others have made alternative arrangements for their welfare, happiness, health and well-being. Neo-liberalism in personal defence choices, as in many other areas of community or 'civic' life, erodes its own foundations. The sum total of private decisions, the promise of market liberalism, may not lead to the greater good, it may polarize the distribution of risks and benefits, undermining rather than enhancing the very security envisaged or aspired to. This has always been a particularly American inflected debate, becoming especially marked after the 1960s. I will turn to explore these themes in subsequent chapters. The issues arise first in our discussion of society, guns, crime and self-defence and politics in the North American context and, second, in the global/local debates arising in the chronic violence complexes suffering most from the global proliferation of SALW.

This concludes our discussion of the demand side of the 'gun culture' equation, and of the British Government's efforts to 'empower' communities and the individuals comprising them to resist 'gang culture' and the weaponization associated with it. These are undoubtedly the crime control interventions and policies of a very restrictive gun control regime still manifesting a marked intolerance of the criminal gun culture observable overseas. Yet, this is not social crime prevention and it brings potentially profound consequences in its wake. In practice, the policies adopted have largely entailed neo-liberal inspired, individually targeted, enforcement-led, conservative realist, neo-classical and deterrent-oriented crime control strategies which, in their entirety, have already gone some way to entrench the problems of social exclusion and marginality. They have blamed the poor and punished the delinquent, within a number of largely inner city communities marked especially by deprivation and inequality, a lack of opportunities and, all too often, racism and discrimination. Transferred from the USA where many of the gang suppression strategies adopted have similarly failed to deliver sustainable solutions for the problems of urban youth violence, British gang intervention strategies may have already gone some way to reinforce the problems they are seeking to solve, sustaining a demand for guns even as the supply may tighten. And finally, by attaching their colours to the mast of personal responsibility and individual choice, just as global neo-liberalism has underpinned the proliferation of self-defence firearms in many parts of the world (a theme I return to), so the idea of investing in a little portable personal protection may appeal to those who believe that the best solutions may not be legal ones. In Chapter 4, I turn to explore these issues in the USA, a significantly more liberal firearms regime, where a presumed 'right to bear arms' has become increasingly central to the politics and practice of 'law and order' – with many quite troubling consequences.

Notes

1 Different arrangements applied to Northern Ireland where as a legacy of 'the Troubles' several thousand individuals, including law enforcement, criminal justice and judicial personnel are permitted to keep personal protection firearms.
2 The GCN were represented by Gill Marshall-Andrews, Dr. Mick North and Professor Ian Taylor; the FCC is an advisory body established by section 22 of the Firearms (Amendment) Act 1988 (passed after the Hungerford shooting). The FCC, represented by David Penn, consists primarily of firearms lobby and law enforcement interests and was intended to advise the Home Secretary on firearm safety and not 'gun control' – the distinction can be important (see Squires, 2000). Colin Greenwood was a firearms consultant who had been a special advisor appointed to the unfortunate 1996 Conservative-dominated Select Committee which had advised against any further controls on handguns after Dunblane.

3   Senior police officers, and former police officers, as both Reiner (1991) and Caless (2011) have noted, have become in recent decades a prominent influence upon criminal justice policy. Senior officers speaking out on a wide range of issues from the death penalty and police powers to public morality, corruption, public order and sentencing.

4   Anders Breivik, a Norwegian neo-Nazi sympathiser, detonated a home-made bomb near government buildings in Oslo, killing eight people, before embarking on a shooting spree targeting young people at an adventure holiday camp. He killed a further 69 young people and seriously injured many more.

5   Reference to 'illegally held' firearms, although a far more satisfactory expression than implying that 'illegality' represents a characteristic of a firearm itself, still evades the key issue at the heart of 'gun control' where the question of *how* the guns come to be 'illegally held' is paramount.

6   After all, the broader 'broken windows' perspective and the ensuing 'incivilities' debate had profoundly shaped the emerging British anti-social behaviour policy agenda which had particularly demonised youth, while British gun crime problems were frequently referenced back to the USA: the 'American nightmare' (Squires, 2000). Similarly, 'gang culture' was often deemed to be a uniquely American import and, in due course, crime control strategies: dispersal and curfew initiatives, gang injunctions, mediation projects, mentoring schemes, school security projects and the like, were all to follow.

7   In this regard perhaps we should not be surprised by the provocative currency of 'respect' as it operates in gang cultures, how different after all is it from this idea of social capital so enthusiastically embraced by the disciples of 'new community development'.

PART 3

The land of the free and the home of the gun

4

AMERICAN EXCEPTIONALISM?

Weaponizing the neo-liberal homeland

Gunfare states and gun-fire cultures

As the 'firearm regime' analysis developed in Chapter 1 indicated, the USA occupies a somewhat exceptional position amongst the range of societies depicted. While we have become familiar with seeing the USA topping lists of 'liberal democratic' and/or 'developed' nations in respect of gun ownership or firearm involved deaths, Chapter 1 (and especially Figure 1.4) provide a wider perspective. Yet America's supposed 'exceptionalism' is not just a quantitative and comparative construct, it also has to do with how America sees itself and how a particular cultural politics centred upon firearm ownership, weaves together notions of tradition, freedom under law and individualism (Melzer, 2009). When these issues are played out in the grinder of daily politics, some interests and issues are prioritized, others subordinated. As I will argue in this chapter, however, in an attempt to set a broad agenda for discussing the apparent exceptionalism of American gun laws, these questions are not primarily about America's past, rather, they form a very substantial foundation of the neo-liberal common sense that has already established a form of global and emotional hegemony in the face of popular perceptions of crime, terror and violence. While Wacquant (2009) identified the drivers of a penal populism establishing the punitive governance of the poorest, its close corollary is the doubtful weaponized freedom aspired to by the US gun lobby. Neo-liberal weaponization entails a profound and fundamental statement of politics, national identity and purpose, running to the heart of a flawed and corrosive vision of personal freedom and individual responsibility; perverse rights and lethal injustice with enormous consequences for human societies. Where Wacquant described successive shifts from the 'welfare' to the 'workfare' and finally the 'prisonfare' state, in its broadest outline, this chapter marks the emerging possibility of the 'gunfare' state and, where the state is failing, of 'gunfire cultures'. Weapon proliferation is a critical facilitator of this new neo-liberal politics, weaponization the vector along which its 'new' wars, conflicts, insurgencies and criminal violences travel. But it is always a process reflecting human choices, capacities and decisions and not just an abstract and inevitable mechanics of neo-liberalism (Gutierrez, 2010). Yet even failed states and conflict complexes can renounce violence and surrender weapons if they can be given reasons to do so. Even America might tire of the rhetoric of 'never again' in the wake of another mass shooting and submit its gun laws to substantial reform. The particularly liberal regime of law and policy by which US firearm ownership is currently managed is a creation of late twentieth-century US politics. It was put together, it might be taken apart, and in the two chapters that follow I will critically explore how it has come to be established, what continues to hold it together and what its consequences are.

The American gun control debate, which bursts back into life, albeit often only temporarily, in the mainstream news media, following each new US shooting tragedy, has lately become rather inextricably linked with the debate on the Second Amendment. After the Sandy Hook school shooting in Connecticut, where 20 young children and six school staff were killed by a rampaging gunman with an assault rifle, President Obama declared his support for action to attempt to prevent such atrocities in the future. After a week, the NRA responded including the claim that the president's proposals were an attack on the US constitution, specifically the Second Amendment. Yet these issues have not always been so closely and tightly impacted. There was a time when policies to promote public safety were not *inevitably* seen as contrary to the 'right to bear arms' (Winkler, 2011; Squires, 2012), these measures were, in their own ways, times and contexts, 'sensible gun controls' and a great deal still rests upon the definition of that idea.

A dark night for the Dark Knight

Around midnight in the Denver suburb of Aurora, a failed research student, 24-year-old James Holmes, wearing a gas mask and body armour, burst into the crowded midnight premiere of *The Dark Knight Rises*. He threw a gas canister into the packed auditorium and began shooting fairly randomly into the audience. In all, during the 90 seconds it took police to respond following the first 911 calls, 12 people were killed and many more were critically injured. Holmes was carrying an AR-15 assault rifle, a 12 gauge shotgun and a Glock .40 calibre handgun. Having later arrested Holmes, who surrendered to police in the cinema car park, officers found a further Glock .40 calibre handgun in his car (Coffman and Simon, 2012). When Holmes' apartment was identified, police found it to be wired up with a complex range of explosive booby traps, intended to kill anyone entering. The whole incident exposed a wide range of issues that have run throughout the US gun debate over several decades. The issues, almost inevitably, connect to one another but first I will try to identify the salient issues in relation to the Aurora incident and then having made a few observations about the cultural and political context of the US gun debate develop these, each in turn, more extensively in the second part of the chapter.

... and the nightmare before Xmas

There is always a danger in crafting the theme of a discussion around events that recur – and rampage shootings certainly do recur with dismal regularity in the USA. Even so, the scale and ferocity of the awful killing spree at Sandy Hook Elementary School, in Newtown, Connecticut, on Friday 14 December jolted the American conscience in ways that few previous mass shootings had managed. And yet, many of the elements of this tragedy were utterly familiar: there were 26 innocent victims, rather more than usual; most of them only five or six years old, rather younger than usual; there was an assailant with multiple firearms, notably a Bushmaster .223 semiautomatic rifle, carrying large capacity ammunition magazines. And as police and journalists unearthed the back-story to the terrible incident, evidence began to emerge of the perpetrator's troubled psychological profile, of his difficult relationship with his mother and estranged father, and of his mother's gun collection.

Reacting to the news, a visibly upset President Obama committed himself to action. 'This time,' he said, 'words need to lead to action', for too often before, they had not (Brady Campaign), and before the week was out he had announced the formation of a task force, headed by the Vice President, Joe Biden, to tackle gun violence. This taskforce hosted a gun violence prevention conference at the Johns Hopkins University, Bloomberg School of Public Health, which, by April 2013, had produced a report Reducing Gun Violence in America (Webster and Vernick, 2013). The president promised that his January 2013 inauguration speech would contain proposals for addressing gun violence, although substantial legal and political obstacles will always inevitably confront gun policy reform. For its part the NRA maintained an official silence until a week after the Newtown shooting, its website merely noting 'we were shocked, saddened and heartbroken by the news of the horrific and senseless murders in Newtown. Out of respect for the families, and as a matter of common decency, we have given time for mourning, prayer and a full investigation of the facts before commenting', then adding 'the NRA is prepared to offer *meaningful contributions* to help make sure this never happens again' (emphasis added) (NRA website, 20 December 2012, http://www.cbsnews.com/news/nra-promises-meaningful-contributions-to-avert-another-newtown/). What these *meaningful contributions* might be remained to be seen.

The NRA might have been keeping its powder dry, although other firearm advocates were not so reticent. Failing to acknowledge their own twitching knees, gun lobby advocates the world over are often quick to denounce gun control groups for their 'knee-jerk reactions' in favour of greater gun regulation following shooting incidents (see for example HASC, 2010: Evidence 74). Larry Pratt, director of the more militant *Gun Owners of America* lobby group asserted on the organization's website that 'gun control supporters have the blood of little children on their hands'. He continued, 'federal and state laws combined to ensure that no teacher, no administrator, no adult had a gun at the Newtown school where the children were murdered. This tragedy underscores the urgency of getting rid of gun bans in school zones'. For some time this more absolutist reading of so-called Second Amendment rights has been winning the arguments. Certainly since the Virginia Tec tragedy in 2007 an NRA affiliated student organization *Concealed on Campus* has been campaigning for the right of students to carry guns on college campuses while, only a week before the Sandy Hook massacre, the state of Michigan passed a law allowing gun owners to carry concealed firearms in schools (McGreal, 2012). Many Texas school boards have permitted teachers to carry concealed firearms into the classroom for some time (McKinley, 2008). After the Sandy Hook shooting, firearm advocates and the NRA proposed rolling out *Operation School Shield*, advocating that armed officers should be attached to all schools (Hutchinson, 2013).

However, in one of the more poignant resonances of the week's events, while the 13 or so mass public shootings occurring in the USA during 2012, with their 80 fatalities, prompted the same old debates and the same old political stalemate on gun control and public safety, an 11-year-old boy in Utah wasn't for waiting. He took his parents' handgun to school, fortunately unloaded, subsequently explaining to police that he had done so in order to protect himself if the school was attacked (Gorman, 2012).

In the meantime, just as they do after any major shooting incident, riot or public order problem, firearms and ammunition literally flew from the gun store shelves. Whether from fear of crime, a desire to own 'notorious' weapons, maybe to beat any potential ban that a particular weapon might attract or perhaps just for their investment potential (the assault weapon ban introduced by the Clinton administration in 1994 only prohibited production and sale of *new* assault rifles, those in private hands were unaffected, except that scarcity increased their value). As Barrett (2012) has noted, in a crowded gun market, notoriety is itself a selling point. Walmart was said to have sold out of whole ranges of guns in many of its stores, including assault rifles. Out of respect for the bereaved family members of the Newtown shooting, the company had removed the Bushmaster .223 from its website but reported that, despite this, demand for the weapon was especially strong (Neate, 2012). This state of affairs might provoke many interesting reflections upon the economic consequences of gun control and the Second Amendment in the land of the free and the home of the market.

Groundhog Day in Denver

Aurora is a suburb of Denver lying some 17 miles from Littleton, another Denver suburb, where the Columbine High School, scene of a school 'rampage' shooting in 1999, is located. The Columbine killings, perpetrated by two disaffected school students, represented a significant step change in US gun politics (Cullen, 2009; Newman *et al.*, 2004). It was not that Columbine represented the first school or campus shooting, far from it; nor was it the most murderous rampage killing (and there was certainly more and worse to follow) but it did appear to represent a growing new menace of school violence; it suggested something very troubling about disaffected (white) teenagers, even as the major urban gun crime problems of the USA were seen to be associated with African–American gang members and career offenders; furthermore it polarized debates on school and community safety, and the broader public policy responses; while posing new challenges for the police. That another mass shooting should occur in the same city, reviving memories of an earlier tragedy, added further poignancy to the grief, commentaries and reflections emerging following the cinema shooting incident.

However, while the accelerating presidential electoral race was reined back in Colorado to allow the rival candidates to voice their commiserations and extend their sympathies to the bereaved and wounded, neither appeared at first willing to budge one inch on the central gun control questions. In gun politics, tradition, recent history, political culture and interests do weigh heavily. Mitt Romney, then still the Republican front-runner, despite having supported some gun control measures in the past (for instance in 2002, while governor of Massachusetts, Romney had banned assault weapons such as the AR-15 used in the 2012 cinema shooting. At the time he had described assault weapons as 'instruments of destruction with the sole purpose of hunting down and killing people' (Borchers, 2012; Gabbatt, 2012b) but, since seeking the Republican presidential nomination, he had not been quite so forthright). By 2012 and fronting a political party with strong ties to the NRA and its affiliates, he was unlikely to say or do anything to disengage his apparently rather lukewarm base of support.

President Barack Obama, on the other hand, was thought to have rather burned his fingers on the hot gun issue during his previous election campaign, referring in 2008 to a strand of red-neck American parochialism, the embittered people who 'cling to guns and religion'. This apparently off-the-cuff remark, added to his earlier support for 'responsible gun control', reinforced a sense that Obama would not see eye-to-eye with the NRA leadership on many issues. Obama's views were articulated both in his autobiography *The Audacity of Hope*: 'I believe in keeping guns out of the inner cities, and that our leaders must say so in the face of the gun manufacturers' lobby' (Obama, 2007: 215), as well as during his acceptance speech at the Democratic National Convention in 2008: 'The reality of gun ownership may be different for hunters in rural Ohio than they are for those plagued by gang violence in Cleveland, but don't tell me we can't uphold the Second Amendment while keeping AK-47s out of the hands of criminals' (Obama, 2008). Somewhat confirming his pro-control image, the Brady Campaign to Prevent Gun Violence greeted Obama's election with a booklet, *Guns and the 2008 Elections*, picturing the victorious president-elect waving to the crowd, alongside his vice-presidential running mate Joe Biden, below a sub-title declaring 'Common sense gun laws won, the NRA lost and what it means' (Brady Campaign, 2008). As has been noted, however, until 2012 there had been rather less evidence of actual 'common sense gun legislation' emerging from the Obama White House.

Nevertheless, the publication of a poll in August 2012, sponsored by the organization Mayors Against Illegal Guns (MAIG, 2012) and carried out before the Aurora shooting, appeared to suggest, contrary to much conventional wisdom, that there may still be some political leverage around a number of so-called 'sensible' gun laws and that even gun owners, as well as past and present NRA members, did not share the implacable positions, resolutely opposing any and every gun control proposal, adopted by the NRA leadership (C. Allen, 2006; Gabbatt, 2012a; MAIG, 2012). Although, the NRA, like many large-scale membership organizations, comprises many shades of opinion, the rank and file are generally far less 'radical' than the inner core (C. Allen, 2006; Melzer, 2009). On the other hand, critics have also commented that many of the actual gun control proposals announced by Obama following the Aurora cinema shooting emphasized closing a number of loopholes within *existing* laws, for example regarding collaboration between federal and state authorities on firearm purchase background checks or information gaps in the National Instant Check System (NICS) relating to records on mental health, and drug and alcohol misuse (MAIG, 2011). The president appeared to be avoiding proposing any more potentially controversial proposals such as those concerning possible bans on large capacity magazines or on assault weapons themselves, both being proposals that are currently advocated by MAIG.[1]

As regards the particular weapons carried by Holmes in his cinema rampage, particularly the AR-15 assault rifle and the Glock .40 semi-automatic pistol, each has now acquired its own 'history' within the US gun story. The AR-15, for example, even came to international prominence when one was used in a killing rampage leaving 35 people dead and 23 wounded in Port Arthur, Tasmania, in 1996. This incident led to a significant tightening of Australian gun laws, to be discussed later. For ten years, following the passage of the Violent Crime Control and Law Enforcement Act of 1994 under the Clinton presidency, the manufacture and sale of assault weapons (for civilian use) was prohibited. The ban, however, had what is known as a 'sunset clause' and the law was allowed to lapse in September 2004. However, the ban had only applied to weapons manufactured *after* the date the law was passed. Any already existing weapons – 'grandfathered' in US parlance – could still be used and traded, a major hole in the regulatory effort (Koper, 2013) creating a situation not dissimilar to insider trading whereby firearms scheduled for prohibition flew off the gun store shelves (often stockpiled by gun industry insiders themselves; Barrett, 2012) purchased by customers who knew that prohibition would inflate significantly the re-sale price of the firearms in question.

There was more than a little symbolism about the law, 'assault weapons' were never precisely defined, but the phrase related to military-'style', semi-automatic rifles and sub-machine guns. A series of, in some respects, relatively 'cosmetic' weapon features (bayonet attachments, flash suppressors, pistol grips) were itemized to describe a 'military assault rifle' rather than a rifle primarily designed for hunting. Although in the years before the ban 'assault weapons' were involved in only a relatively small proportion (less than 5 per cent) of American gun crime (Koper, 2004, 2013), a number of high-profile 'mass shooting' incidents,[2] and including occasions where responding police officers were reportedly outgunned (Brady Center, 2004, 2011), had given these firearms an inflated threat level. Furthermore, rather like the 'Tommy Gun' had become the iconic gangster weapon in the 1920s and 1930s (Helmer, 1970), assault weapons were thought likely to be especially attractive to criminals and gang members. California had banned a number of assault weapon types in 1989 after the Stockton shooting and other US states had followed suit. Even so, debate continued regarding the effectiveness of the bans, Kristen Rand of the Violence Policy Center arguing in 2004 that the gun industry easily found ways around the law and that most of the weapons that Congress had sought to ban subsequently became available in virtually identical 'post-ban' versions once the 'superficial' militaristic identifiers had been removed (VPC, 2004). The Brady Center's (2004) own evaluation was more positive about the value of the legislation in preventing the production of copy-cat, assault-type weapons for the civilian market, although both organizations were critical of the efforts of a 'cynical' gun industry to ignore the intentions of Congress and evade the law. Koper has recently concluded the most significant effect of the assault weapon ban may have been the restriction on large capacity ammunition magazines (2013: 162–169).

Another weapon employed by Holmes in his cinema rampage, a Glock .40 semi-automatic pistol, has lately been described as America's best-selling gun (Barrett, 2012). In that respect there may be little, beyond the wider Glock story itself, especially remarkable in the fact that a rampage killer should acquire a best-selling and popularly available firearm with which to perpetrate his atrocity. After all, Glock pistols had been employed in previous rampage shootings: George Hennard used a Glock 17, in October 1991, after driving his pickup truck into a Luby's cafeteria in Killeen, Texas, and fatally shooting 23 people and wounding a further 20; Seng Chui Ho used Glock pistols in his murderous assault killing 32 (fellow students and a teacher) at Virginia Tec in 2007; and Jared Loughner used a Glock pistol to kill six and wound 13 more (including Democratic Party representative, Gabrielle Giffords, shot through the head) in a shopping centre car park in Tucson, Arizona, in January 2011. Perhaps the greatest irony regarding the use of Glock pistols in these incidents concerns the subsequent surge in sales reported by gun dealers. These seem to happen for two reasons: on the one hand such incidents appear to ring an alarm bell regarding the dangers of violent crime, prompting more people to buy guns for personal protection; on the other hand other people seem to believe that 'notorious firearms' are more likely to face state or federal bans and, as Barrett (2012) has described at length, the Glock did have something of a checkered reputation here, so people purchase more of them before any such ban can be announced. In effect, any firearm outrage prompting political or law enforcement attention turns into a win–win situation for gun production and retail; for firearm marketing there seems no such thing as bad news.

Such issues extend well beyond any particular type of pistol employed in any given shooting incident. Glocks are not just the 'most popular' models of handgun, they also been adopted by more official police and security agencies than any other firearm (Barrett, 2012).[3] In turn, this double aspect to the personal firearm – both part of the *problem* and part of the perceived *solution* – crosscuts the entire debate about gun ownership in the USA. No sooner had the sirens stopped wailing in the wake of the Aurora cinema shooting than firearms lobbyists began to argue how, if other members of the cinema audience had been carrying concealed defensive firearms (as Colorado state law permits) they might have been able to intercept (shoot) the shooter, thereby stopping the attack and reducing the overall number of fatalities. Irrespective of the almost unthinkable dangers of a shoot-out in a crowded cinema, the point being made was that, without a means to defend themselves, the cinema audience were no more than 'sitting ducks', a point also made in respect of school shootings (Kopel, 2009). When campus gun bans or other 'gun-free zones' are illegally breached by angry students (or, indeed, anyone else) bringing guns to college, everyone complying with the law is rendered immediately, and perhaps fatally, vulnerable. Gun-free zones are effectively 'defence-free zones' argued a concealed carry campaign spokesman (Soderstrom, 2012a, b). One consequence of such arguments has been the emergence, gathering momentum since the Virginia Tec shooting, of an NRA-backed campaign 'Concealed Campus' Students for Concealed Carry (http://concealedcampus.org) disputing the constitutionality of campus gun bans and seeking to overturn local laws and ordnances. While Utah has been the only state not to exempt college campuses from its permissive statewide concealed carry laws, a number of states are now facing pressure on their campus 'gun-free zones'. The Colorado Supreme Court recently upheld a challenge to the University of Colorado's campus firearm prohibition (Burnett, 2012). The new ruling will apply to all of Colorado's public college campuses, where students will now be able to take their guns to class.

The debate about college and campus 'gun-free zones' is itself just a microcosm of the far wider debate about gun control, defensive gun use and 'concealed carry' policies in the USA. This is a fraught and contested issue and, like much of US gun politics, while it generates much contrasting (and sometimes rather partisan) research and endless (sometimes questionable) data, often seems to produce rather more heat than light (Spitzer, 1998). However, these issues are important and cannot – and should not – be ducked. Debates around these issues have sharpened in recent years following a number of important developments. In turn, these help to set the context for our following discussions.

Altered realities: a brief history of the gun control idea

A first issue to consider here concerns the ways in which the very idea of gun control has changed in the final decades of the twentieth century (Winkler, 2011). Discourses concerning gun ownership and gun control have substantially polarized, yet for most of its history the Second Amendment to the Constitution had been considered entirely compatible with a number of laws, policies and police powers designed to prevent crime and ensure public safety. Nowadays, however, every restriction on gun ownership or gun owners is fought tooth and nail by gun rights advocates who have, apparently, come to believe in the Second Amendment as an absolute principle and that every measure of control represents the start of a slippery-slope ending in firearm confiscation, totalitarian government and political servitude.

How this has come about serves as a wider but indispensable backdrop to the more specific examination of the evolution of gun control laws in the USA. Much of the early history of gun control, which was never so conflicted as it is today, can be seen as somewhat 'event driven'. In recent years, however, the growth and influence of the NRA and its partner gun rights organizations have been much more significant. The organization was first established in the 1870s as a special interest firearms membership and training organization, however the NRA evolved in the 1970s and 1980s into a much more hard-nosed political lobby, and establishing a 'legal affairs' department to use the courts and the political system to press a stronger case for shooters' rights. Recent Supreme Court judgements (2008 and 2010) substantially reflect this more assertive firearm rights advocacy, as do the shifting parameters of US gun control policy, and the altered meaning of 'gun control', which we have already noted.

Any discussion of gun control must also deal with both the intense political controversy now surrounding this issue as well as the loaded philosophical character of the concept. Contemporary interpretations of the Second Amendment now emphasize the second part of this much contested statement, that 'the right of the people to keep and bear arms, shall not be infringed', in what is referred to as the 'standard' or individualist interpretation (Squires, 2000: 70–73). Even so, it is often acknowledged that there are many thousands of gun control laws, regulations and ordinances at federal, state and municipal level, regulating the ownership, possession, purchase and transfer, carriage and use of firearms. Many such laws remain relatively uncontroversial, designed to restrict the access of children, convicted felons or persons with a history of mental illness, to firearms. In today's altered realties, such laws would be regarded as laws *against firearm misuse* rather than *gun control*. This distinction has become vitally important. Gun control, in this sense, is not considered incompatible with widespread, but responsible, gun ownership: on the contrary, responsible ownership is seen as the most important form of gun control: the 'careful' gun culture. As a famous NRA bumper sticker would have it, 'Gun Control means using Both Hands'. Furthermore, more guns, it is claimed, can mean less crime, as the 'good guys with guns' deter the 'bad guys' or guard schools or supplement the overstretched '911 Emergency Response' of the police, or confront terrorists or illegal immigration, although the evidence here remains intensely contested.

The issue has not just preoccupied contemporary social scientists; legal and constitutional historians have also entered the fray. For example, intense debate has surrounded the question of the extent of civilian firearm holdings prior to the US War of Independence (1775–1783) and, then again, after the American Civil War (1861–1865) (see Bellesiles, 2000; Lindgren, 2002; Lindgren and Heather, 2002) and likewise concerning the differences between American and European cultures and their traditions of gun ownership (Malcolm, 1994). Demonstrating widespread ownership of firearms *before* the Civil War lends credence to a claim that those responsible for the drafting of the Second Amendment sought to give constitutional protection to individual, as opposed to militia-based, ownership and use of weapons.

However these thorny questions are resolved (refer to the intense debate surrounding Michael Bellesiles' *Arming America* research),[4] the notion of the US citizen's unique and unrestricted right to possess firearms still requires qualification.

What some scholars regard as the 'second thesis' of Bellesiles' (2000) book, the proliferation of firearms in the context of the Civil War and the historical contribution of this weaponization to the gun ownership and violence traditions of the US, might even be detached from his 'problematic' first arguments about the meaning of the Second Amendment in the eighteenth century. His second thesis offers a remarkably useful and prescient observation of direct relevance to the analysis of the more global weaponization, which is pursued later in this book (Chapters 7 and 8): wars diffuse weapons into civilian cultures, establishing and perpetuating chronic conflicts and violent instabilities that are, often only with difficulty, pacified. Furthermore, while, after the Civil War, widespread firearm ownership had become much more established, white Americans were still keen to prevent African–Americans (former slaves) and indigenous peoples amongst others from owning firearms (Boyle, 2004). While firearms ownership in old Europe was overlain by restrictions of rank and religion, in America they were coloured by race, ethnicity and social class.

Following the Civil War and the westwards expansion of the population, many new and disorderly frontier towns established regulations forbidding the carrying of weapons within the town limits. Ordinance #9, introduced in Tombstone by Wyatt Earp on 19 April 1881, is perhaps the best known. Such measures, anticipating the 'police powers' public safety and crime prevention provisions later adopted in many local jurisdictions, were not initially seen to contradict firearm rights but simply imposed restrictions on the places and occasions firearms might be lawfully and safely carried. When ranch hands came to town after weeks on the trail, to let off steam and spend some of their hard-earned money on drinking, gambling and prostitutes, the presence of a firearm was considered an avoidable danger. Such questions have lately become more controversial with some commentators seeing them as an fundamental infringement of Second Amendment rights. Thus debates have arisen concerning the legitimacy of restricting firearm carriage in shopping malls, college and university campuses, in the vicinity of schools, at airports and at leisure and entertainment venues. Given the fact that large numbers of Americans now carry firearms for self-defence and that over 40 states permit concealed firearm carriage, NRA backed campaigns, and several law suits, have lately begun to question whether it is right or lawful to ask citizens to risk going unarmed when visiting such locations. In September 2013 one company flipped the other way. Howard Shultz, CEO of the Starbucks coffee chain, advised that concealed carry firearms would 'no longer be welcome' in the company's coffee shops. His comments fell short of a ban, however, he was not looking to incite legal action and no 'guns prohibited' signs were going up (Horovitz, 2013).

One early twentieth-century piece of conventional gun control legislation conforming to the 'police powers and public safety' regulative discourse was the Sullivan Law (named after its sponsor, state senator Timothy Sullivan). The law was passed in New York State in 1911 following the shooting of the city mayor and amidst a wave of anti-immigrant and criminal gang hysteria. The law even gets a brief name check in the 1954 film *On the Waterfront*. Although passed as a crime prevention measure, typical of many similar provisions, the law closely reflected the social prejudices implicit in earlier gun prohibitions. It put control of firearm licensing in the hands of the local police and city authorities and allowed them free rein to discriminate against undesirables, the underclass, immigrants and non-Americans. An underlying problem was the ready supply of cheap pistols, so-called *Niggertown Saturday Night Specials*, in high-crime, slum neighbourhoods, establishing an urban gun culture in poorer areas and has preoccupied law enforcement ever since. The Sullivan Law and many similar localized gun control ordinances have subsequently drawn criticism that they are both un-American and un-constitutional, although at the time when many of these laws were passed 'Americanism' was itself the strongly defended preserve of the white, Anglo-Saxon and protestant elites (often explicitly allied with the Ku Klux Klan) seeking to defend jobs, homes and neighbourhoods from the northwards migration of American blacks and the immigration of impoverished Europeans (Boyle, 2004). The Sullivan Law may yet encounter a similar fate to similar restrictions in Washington, DC and Chicago, although the politics of New York point in a different direction. New York state was one of the first states to implement a package of 'common sense' gun laws (including an assault weapon ban, gun registration and limits to magazine capacity), similar to those proposed by Barack Obama, in the wake of the Sandy Hook shooting. Firearm rights advocates were said to be planning legal challenges to the new law.

Until the later twentieth century, gun control was not a particularly important policy area for federal legislators. The 1919 War Revenue Act had established a federal manufacturer's excise tax on firearms, the first use of fiscal measures to serve public safety goals by restricting firearm distribution and placing responsibility for this area of policy within the Department of the Treasury. In the following years, reflecting state and municipal concerns about criminal access to cheap handguns, the first federal gun controls were introduced in the 1920s and 1930s. They initially sought to restrict the sale and transfer of weapons by mail order. Later came bans on the private ownership of machine guns and other so-called 'gangster' weapons (National Firearms Act 1934) and on interstate weapon trafficking (Federal Firearms Act 1938). Passed shortly after the repeal of alcohol prohibition, the legislation reflected growing disquiet about the violent activities of organized criminal bootleggers and gangsters (including the St Valentine's Day Massacre in 1929), but they also drew support from another unlikely source. Major US gun manufacturers were keen to avoid being undercut by cheaper competitors. A Supreme Court case in 1939, the first and, for a long time, the *only* Supreme Court judgement on gun control and the Second Amendment, *United States v Miller* (the outcome of which is still subject to contrasting interpretations) appeared to uphold a prohibition against 'gangster' weapons (in this case a short-barrelled shotgun transported across state lines) by adopting the 'police powers' interpretation referred to earlier: that sensible crime prevention measures did not interfere with Second Amendment rights. In more recent years, this interpretation has been stretched to its limits, some might say broken entirely, by a renewed phase of gun rights activism.

The next federal gun controls, prompting criticism that the evolution of gun controls in the USA has been largely 'event driven' in the wake of tragedies, occurred in the late 1960s following the assassinations of President Kennedy, Robert Kennedy and Martin Luther King in, respectively, 1963 and 1968. The 1968 Gun Control Act, much watered down after five years of debate, sought to establish a federal firearms licensing system for dealers, manufacturers and importers, through which to regulate inter-state sales and distribution of firearms. It became illegal for any person without a licence to engage in any substantial firearm sales business. Second, a number of groups (minors, convicted felons, persons with a history of mental illness and users of illegal drugs) were prohibited from owning or possessing firearms. Finally, the importation of surplus military firearms was prohibited unless they were considered to have a primary 'sporting purpose'. Enforcement of these provisions was vested in the Alcohol, Tobacco, Firearms and Explosives Division of the Internal Revenue Service (IRS) (becoming the Bureau of ATF in 1972). The Act itself was something of a compromise and by the time it passed, the social context had changed dramatically. Rising crime, riots and disorder were prompting growing demand for self-defence firearms; sales of handguns had quadrupled to 2.4 million weapon purchases per year by 1968 (Zimring, 1975). Existing doubts about the ability of the IRS to exercise effective oversight of firearms commerce and trafficking were renewed. Even though additional resources were allocated, the ATF lacked capacity to scrutinize more than 2 per cent of the total annual trade in firearms.

Franklin Zimring made a detailed study of the impact of the 1968 Gun Control Act (Zimring, 1975), a time when the market for cheap handguns was expanding rapidly and gun violence increasing. Between 1964 and 1968 gun homicide increased by 89 per cent in the USA. By 1969, a majority of urban homicides were committed with handguns. Even so, Zimring concluded that, despite the limitations of the 1968 Act, it had curtailed, somewhat, the supply of cheap handguns and could be said to have moderated the steeply rising trend in handgun violence evident during the 1960s. Following these developments some liberal commentators, Zimring included, predicted that the 1970s would begin to see an end to America's gun violence problems as public safety policy-making gained the upper hand. In 1977, following New York's lead, Washington, DC banned handguns and established licensing arrangements for rifles and shotguns. In 1982, Chicago followed suit, banning handguns (both laws have recently been struck down by the Supreme Court). Yet the commentators could hardly have been more wrong. During the 1970s, the gun lobby began to shift the focus of its gun rights advocacy towards the defence of civilian ownership of personal protection handguns and this became a key gun control battleground in the final decades of the twentieth century – although not the only one.

A further catalogue of largely 'event-driven' issues surfaced during the 1970s and 1980s preoccupying federal legislators. The issues arising began to reflect the new political contours of the gun control debate. Tougher penalties were established for the use of firearms in crime and for firearm possession by prohibited persons (the Armed Career Criminal Act 1986) and banning the sale of so-called 'cop killer' bullets, capable of penetrating bullet-proof vests (the Law Enforcement Officers Protection Act 1986). Finally, following the killing of five children in Stockton, California, in 1989 (school shootings becoming a growing issue in the mid-1990s and especially after Columbine, in 1999), the 1980s and early 1990s saw the opening rounds of a debate about the appropriateness of civilian ownership of so-called military assault rifles. California banned these weapons after 1989 and federal legislation followed in 1990 (the Crime Control Act 1990), banning the manufacture or importation of such weapons for the civilian market in the USA. In 1994 (the Violent Crime Control and Law Enforcement Act 1994) prohibited a series of specified military assault weapons. The federal assault weapons ban expired in 2004 and although new bills have been introduced from time to time, the assault weapon prohibitions have not been reinstated.

Concurrent with these developments, the main gun control debate of the 1980s and early 1990s followed the shooting of President Reagan in March 1981. It concerned the campaign to introduce a national instant firearms sales check system (NICS) for would-be purchasers of a handgun from a federally licensed firearm dealer. The campaign was named in honour of James Brady, Reagan's press secretary, who was seriously wounded during the assassination attempt. After years of debate, the Brady Handgun Violence Prevention Act was eventually passed in 1994, requiring a national instant check system to be established by 1998. In the interim, a five-day waiting and checking period was established. An immediate weakness was that it impacted only upon the primary handgun sales market; subsequent sales (around 40 per cent of handgun sales annually) including so-called 'gun-show' firearms deals, went largely unregulated (Burbick, 2006). A second weakness was that the funds and facilities to enable the appropriate checks to take place were often either unavailable or insufficiently prioritized by police departments. Furthermore, record systems were not always fit for purpose. In the event, the case *Printz v USA* (Supreme Court, 1997), deemed certain aspects of the Brady Law unconstitutional. By then, however, not only had many states implemented their own versions of a gun purchase check system, but the long awaited NICS hosted by the FBI was almost ready. NICS now operates in over 30 states (some states retaining their own system) checking on would-be firearm buyers. In the decade since 1998, the FBI reported having run over 100 million checks resulting in some 700,000 gun sale refusals. As we have seen, however, there remain substantial gaps in the system, many states failing to make available the mental health and other records to make the system effective (MAIG, 2011).

In the 1980s, initially under the Reagan presidency, gun control and crime control began to develop their more contemporary disconnected and dual-track character. While federal level debates about NICS and assault weapons bans continued, a number of parallel developments were taking shape. Reflecting this duality, at the federal level, the 1986 Firearms Owners Protection Act had relaxed some of the 1968 restrictions on gun and ammunition sales while introducing tougher mandatory penalties for use of firearms during the commission of a crime. A number of states were also beginning to legislate to permit the carrying of concealed firearms for personal protection. Over 40 states now issue concealed carry permits to entitled applicants, some requiring prior participation in gun safety courses. This trend towards liberalizing gun availability, further embodied in so-called 'Castle Doctrine' laws (that attacked persons have no 'duty to retreat' before resorting to potentially lethal force) was accompanied by laws demanding greater responsibility from gun owners, for example requiring guns to be sold with trigger locks or kept in domestic gun safes, and strengthening penalties for firearm misuse. Enforcement-led initiatives such as *Project Exile* and *Operation Ceasefire* (Kennedy, 2011), both addressing firearm-involved criminal gang violence, also embraced this underlying, dual-track strategy seeking to control gun crime rather than controlling guns and permitting responsible citizens to keep guns for their own personal protection.

A further development in the 1990s saw gun control groups and victims' representatives bringing class action cases against particular gun manufacturers, retailers or dealers for irresponsibly producing, marketing or otherwise supplying firearms in ways which were alleged to have facilitated their uptake by offenders (Lytton, 2006). Such lawsuits have not generally been especially successful and have more recently faced congressional prohibition. The attention of gun control researchers and the law enforcement community then shifted to tracing weapons back to dangerous sales practices by negligent firearms dealers. When firearm trace information suggested that a particular gun dealership was linked to an unusually high number of weapons retrieved from crime scenes, police might investigate further and even undertake 'buy-bust' or 'sting' operations against suspected dealers. Vernick and Webster (2013) describe just such a police operation against a prominent gun dealer in the Milwaukee area. Following police intervention, the dealership announced that it would no longer be selling the small, cheap handguns (junk weapons) upon which it had built its dubious reputation. As a result, by 2005, around five years later, a 71 per cent reduction in 'Saturday Night Special' crime guns was being claimed in Milwaukee and a 44 per cent reduction in secondary sales of crime guns (guns sold to an offender within one year of original purchase). Since 2003, however, a number of NRA supported congressional provisions (the Tiahrt Amendments) have effectively limited the ability of law enforcement agencies to access, use and share firearm tracing data to prosecute negligent firearm dealers. MAIG has campaigned against these provisions, with some success. Vernick and Webster (2013: 139) argue that the amendments should be repealed.

Three final issues in the developing story of US firearms controls merit brief attention at this stage, each representing different strands in the contemporary politics of gun control. One concerns the so-called 'gun-show loophole'

(Burbick, 2006). The NICS system has largely targeted gun sales in the primary market involving federally licensed dealers, whereas private sales and sales at gun shows (40 per cent of the market, around three million sales per year) were often excluded from legal oversight. Gun control advocates have attempted to bring gun shows and private sales further into the regulatory system; another bill, the Gun Show Loophole Closing Act, was introduced into the House of Representatives in 2009 although, in fact, many states already regulate gun-show firearm purchases in various ways. Wintemute (2013: 104) has recently argued that there really is no gun-show loophole at all. So far as federal law is concerned, gun-show sales are not 'exempt', just poorly regulated. The real problem is what he calls the 'Federal Double Standard'. It is always illegal 'for a prohibited person to buy a firearm', but a firearm seller is only committing an offence if he knowingly sells a firearm to a prohibited person (Wintemute, 2013: 97).

A second issue concerns school shootings, which have increased in prominence especially after the Columbine (1999) and Virginia Tec (2007) atrocities (although none more so than Sandy Hook in December 2012), and inevitably these raise questions about school security; they have also brought gun control and Second Amendment politics head to head. Schools and colleges have long been places where weapon carrying has been prohibited. In the wake of such tragedies in a context where a majority of states permit concealed weapon carrying, firearm advocates have come to question why college campuses should be places where the claimed benefits of Second Amendment protection do not apply. An NRA-supported student campaign Concealed Campus has begun to campaign on this issue. I discuss the issues raised in school and rampage shootings in greater length in Chapter 6.

Finally, as we have noted, two recent rulings of the US Supreme Court have extended the distance between discourses on gun control and public safety and that concerning the meaning of the Second Amendment even further still by striking down fairly long-established handgun bans in both Washington, DC and Chicago. With the gun lobby in political and legal ascendancy, further legal attacks on hand-gun prohibitions in other cities, including New York, are anticipated. For the foreseeable future protection from the crimogenic consequences of widespread firearm availability in the USA seems likely to be sought only via control of the criminal or irresponsible *misuse* of firearms rather than controls over firearms – gun control – themselves. Yet this would primarily represent a political resolution, rather than a legal or judicial one. In their contribution to the *Reducing Gun Violence* summit report of 2013, Rosenthal and Winkler (2013) see no constitutional prohi-bition under the Second Amendment to rule out universal background checks for firearm purchasers, tighter regulation of firearm dealers, and prohibitions on both 'assault weapons' and high-capacity ammunition magazines. When the US Senate voted against precisely these provisions in President Obama's gun control package in April 2013, it confirmed that the chief obstacles to gun law reform were political rather more than legal or constitutional (Tushnet, 2007; Roberts, 2013).

The present not the past: politics not policy

Having outlined these developing themes in the gun control debate, noting how each finds its degree of purchase, even in a particular incident, we will now explore a number of them a little more thoroughly. These issues resonate both within the USA and beyond, they have truly global significance. First, however, it is important to establish the very contemporaneous nature of America's gun question which, as Cook and Ludwig (2000) have calculated, now entails a total financial cost of around some $100 billion per year in the USA. Above all, America's gun question is fundamentally rooted in and driven by modern fears and anxieties about crime, race and violence.

In this sense, as Melzer (2009; see also Tushnet, 2007) has argued, gun politics represent a *modern* culture war. Its advocates ('crusaders') certainly employ the past – the Constitution, Hollywood and other myths and traditions – but the conflict itself is firmly rooted in modernity. It is important to emphasize this point, that America's gun problems and the politics in which US gun policy is ensnared are a product of the final decades of the twentieth century, certainly since the 1960s, rather than some cultural hangover from a violent cowboy and frontier past. On the contrary what establishes the 'American exceptionalism' (Lipset, 1996; Garland, 2005; Ignatieff, 2005) as far as firearm laws, policies and practices are concerned is not the historical legacy of the 'wild west', even though some scholars would credit this (Brown, 1975; Tonso,1982) but, rather, a very contemporary set of economic, cultural, political and racial divisions. To be absolutely clear, history, culture and tradition are not irrelevant to these debates, but the question here is more properly one concerning the ways in which history is both used and abused, an issue that was manifestly exposed in the sorry saga of Michael Bellesiles' book *Arming America: The Origins of a National Gun Culture* (Bellesiles, 2000; Lindgren, 2002; Lindgren and Heather, 2002; Winkler, 2011), although this was far from being the only such occasion.

This use and abuse of history is also evident in the way that dozens of constitutional and legal scholars, rather like Victorian explorers scouring Africa for the true source of the Nile, have returned to the dusty archives in search of the 'true meaning' of the Second Amendment (Bogus, 2000). This is not the place to embark upon an exercise in US constitutional theory except to note, briefly, the variety of political positions and guises these debates have thrown up. It is never *just* a constitutional argument, however, for the pro-gun argument does not simply make a constitutional case for gun ownership, it also claims that utilitarian benefits for society derive from widespread gun ownership. Yet, whenever the 'net benefit' argument flounders, the argument shifts to the legal sphere, and vice versa. This might give us a clue to the shifting paradigms of the arguments themselves: in the wake of the 1960s following political assassinations, rising crime and racial tensions, the social and utilitarian case for gun control was gaining credibility (Kennett and Anderson, 1975) so the pro-gun groups shifted the argument to a terrain on which a different argument could be developed. In time, of course, recognizing that legal history alone might not be a sufficient support, academic researchers have also sought to underpin the newer revisionist, historical and constitutional arguments with cautionary tales of gun control (Kleck, 1991, 1997; Kleck and Kates, 2001) and concerning the benefits of widespread gun ownership (Lott, 1998).

Turning briefly to those constitutional arguments, in the first place there exists a simple distinction between individualist or collectivist readings of the Second Amendment, with disagreements concerning whether (or not) it guarantees an absolute individual right to bear arms (Squires, 2000: 70–75). The next layer to this debate concerns arguments about 'original intent' (what did the framers of the Constitution actually have in mind?); interpretation (how should the Second Amendment be interpreted by judges and how has it been influenced by established legal precedent?); and 'judicial activism' (is the Constitution a 'living' or 'dead' document? That is to say, should contemporary jurists be attempting to apply the law *creatively* to new circumstances, as opposed to sticking rigidly to the meaning of the text as they see it?). Here, a third position arises, this closer to Tushnet's view (2007), with the suggestion that the Second Amendment is an anachronism and what it *might* have meant over two centuries ago is unlikely to help us much today (see also Heyman, 2000: 206). Rather, somewhat akin to Lazare's (1996) judgement on the Constitution as a whole, the Second Amendment is, perhaps, part of today's problem.

The debate about the Second Amendment is obviously more complex than these outline positions imply, not least by virtue of the fact that, prompted by a resurgence of politically motivated scholarly endeavour, the meaning of the Second Amendment became more controversial around the time of its 200-year anniversary than at any previous point in its history. In the process, what had been a settled interpretation (the collective view), which was thought to have been endorsed by the Supreme Court in 1939, was displaced by the individualist interpretation. In one sense it was a paradoxical shift: embracing judicial activism to reinstate 'original intent', or simply a newer revisionism replacing an older one.

Drawing upon research by Carl Bogus (2000), Lepore (2012a) argues that

> at least sixteen of the twenty-seven law-review articles published between 1970 and 1989 that were favorable to the N.R.A.'s interpretation of the Second Amendment were 'written by lawyers who had been directly employed by or represented the N.R.A. or other gun-rights organizations'.
>
> *(Lepore, 2012a; see also Winkler, 2011: 96–97)*

Demonstrating the unusually highly charged nature of these debates, she cites a 1991 interview with former Supreme Court Justice, Warren Burger, who commented that the individual rights interpretation of the Second Amendment was 'one of the greatest pieces of fraud, I repeat the word "fraud", on the American public by special-interest groups that I have ever seen in my lifetime' (cited in Lepore, 2012a; see also Tushnet, 2007). The venerable judge went even further in a speech in 1992, declaring that 'the Second Amendment doesn't guarantee the right to have firearms at all'. His argument was that the purpose of the Second Amendment was 'to ensure that the "state armies" – "the militia" – would be maintained for the defense of the state' (Sunstein, 2007). In other words, this is the collectivist interpretation (Squires, 2000: 73–75).

The judge's remarks pose a dilemma for any 'absolutist' stance on this controversial amendment, as they raise a question, notwithstanding the Fourteenth Amendment's civil rights protections, introduced in 1868 following the Civil War,[5] regarding the constitutional basis for disarming anyone, even convicted felons. Indeed, some of the more extreme gun advocacy groups do argue that only offenders *actually serving a prison sentence* should be denied firearms, while others would extend the right to bear arms to children (Winkler, 2011: 82). The suggestion that it is only 'common sense' to attempt to deny violent criminals any access to firearms cuts no ice in a constitutional sense because such a view already entails the necessity of interpreting to whom, precisely, the amendment ought to apply.

Gun advocacy groups and pro-Second Amendment constitutional historians base their arguments in favour of unrestricted gun ownership upon what they argue were the 'original intentions' of the framers of the constitutional amendments. However, they achieve this, supposedly interpreting this controversial sentence in the context of its time, even while bringing to bear a far more individualist and libertarian conception of rights of much more recent pedigree (Spitzer, 2000). Finally, they often imply that the Fourteenth Amendment offers a reinterpretation of the Second for, as Amar (1998: 259) argues, the 'Reconstruction Republicans' of 1868 accomplished a 'remarkable re-reading of the arms right'. Over an 80-year period the meaning of gun ownership rights had shifted:

> Creation-era arms bearing was collective, exercised in a well-regulated militia embodying a public right of the people, collectively understood. Reconstruction gun-toting was individualistic, accentuating not group rights of the citizenry, but self-regarding 'privileges' of discrete 'citizens' to individual self-protection. The Creation vision was public, with the militia muster on the town square. The Reconstruction vision was private, with individual freedmen keeping guns at home to ward off Klansmen and other ruffians.
>
> *(Amar, 1998: 259)*

And this, of course, provides the basis for the contemporary conception of neoliberal individualism which sanctions the mutually 'armed and dangerous' citizenry of concealed carry America. These are quite different conceptions of right, sitting in quite different relation to public safety and security (Winkler, 2011: 287–288). As Ulliver and Merkel argue, such an *individual* right is far removed from the principle concerns of the Second Amendment's architects over 200 years ago: 'the *personal right* expressed in the neoclassical language of the Second Amendment was understood … to serve the interests of the commonweal by buttressing *community security* and reducing the sway of a dangerous, potentially usurpatory standing army' (Ulliver and Merkel, 2000: 149). Many contemporary individual gun rights advocates also continue to adhere to this 'collective defence against the state' argu-ment (sometimes referred to as the 'insurrectionist argument'; Henigan, 2009; Horwitz and Anderson, 2009); a classic case of wanting it both ways.

It is true that, as Winkler describes (2011: 108–109, 140), many individual states subsequently adopted constitutions echoing or closely resembling the provi-sions of the Second Amendment, prompting more recent scholars to argue that these, taken together, amount to evidence of a kind of rolling presumption that unrestricted firearm ownership was precisely the 'original intention'. For other commentators, this is to go too far – on two fronts. As Finkelman (2000: 146–147) notes, the Second Amendment was neither a constitutional 'suicide clause' allow-ing rebels, revolutionaries or terrorists to establish private militias to overthrow the Government,[6] nor an abdication of responsibility for the establishment of public safety policies 'within the constitutional limits of general federal police and com-merce powers'. Yet it was this potential evisceration of public safety policy by libertarian gun rights activism that so angered Justice Warren Burger in 1991. Perhaps it also parallels the wider failure of 'Great Society' optimism; poverty and the return of the underclass, mass unemployment, racialized inequality, hyper-ghettoization, the war of drugs, spiraling crime figures and an effectively marketed epidemic of fear predicated on the idea that the police could not protect everyone, everywhere, all the time. Late modernity's new frontiers seemed undefended, fear-ful citizens sought personal protection when calling 911 seemed second best to self reliance (Carlson, 2012). From Justice Burger's perspective, worse was to follow.

In due course, reflecting the weight of revisionist scholarship devoted to the Second Amendment – 'part of a larger movement by conservatives to reclaim the Constitution' (Winkler, 2011: 97) – the NRA version of the contested con-stitutional amendment, which had been enshrined in the 1986 Firearm Owners Protection Act, passed during the Reagan presidency, became the dominant ('standard') version (Lepore, 2012a).[7] This was further confirmed in 2001 by let-ters from John Ashcroft, as US Attorney General, to the NRA and all US federal prosecutors (Winkler, 2011: 46, 308fn). And finally, Supreme Court judgements in 2008 and 2010, striking down the handgun prohibitions of Washington, DC and Chicago, established the new precedent potentially opening up a whole raft of state and city-level gun control ordinances to a claim that they are now 'unconstitutional'.

Although gun advocates would like to consider this issue 'settled', the debates continue, with Rakove arguing for a contemporary interpretation acknowledging the dangers arising from widely available firearms. 'It is reasonable to conclude that the most compelling arguments for [firearm] regulation presuppose that this is one realm of behaviour where the concerns of the present have every right to supersede the obsolescent understandings of generations past' (Rakove, 2000: 75). Even that does not end the debate, of course, for it is precisely the 'concerns of the present' that persuaded large numbers of urban self-defence gun owners to join the queues at the gun stores in the first place. Winkler is rather more sanguine, for in the wake of the Supreme Court judgement in the Washington, DC case, although there have been upwards of 150 federal court rulings on the constitutionality of gun laws, the Supreme Court had not opened the floodgates 'at least in the short term' (Winkler, 2011: 289). Instead, the lower courts have frequently pointed to the *Heller* ruling to find in favour of many existing gun controls. Such assurances were repeated by the Supreme Court in relation to the 2010 case of *McDonald v City of Chicago* and so 'most gun control laws currently on the books [remain] constitutional regardless of the 2nd Amendment' (Winkler, 2011: 290).

As Lepore (2012a) suggests, the revisionist endeavours of constitutional historians have largely been about vindicating and historically endorsing a latter-day reinterpretation of the Second Amendment which has also served as a platform for the contemporary neo-liberal politics that would have each citizen armed, equating this with freedom, republican individualism and a minimal state – in much the same way as the right wing of the Republican Movement (the 'Tea Party') has sought to redefine and reclaim 'American Tradition' (Lepore, 2010). The work of the historians and federalists coincided with the neo-conservative legal activists who have sought to overturn gun control legislation as un-American and contrary to individual freedom. For many years, as Winkler has shown, 'debates over gun control proposals didn't focus upon their merits as matters of policy but instead became ensnared in arguments about … the 2nd Amendment' (2011: 294). His central claim is that the Supreme Court has now shifted this ideological logjam, establishing a compromise position favourable to gun ownership and thereby allowing a more focussed debate to develop upon the types of pragmatic policies that might go some way to reduce gun violence. Winkler now sees the baton passing from the lawyers, historians and constitutional scholars to the criminologists whose 'empirical work on gun crime' might provide us with tools to keep guns 'out of the hands of gang members and recidivist offenders responsible for the bulk of gun crime' (2011: 295). It is a tall order and probably entails something of a poisoned chalice for criminology for it potentially resurrects the 'good guy/bad guy' dualism upon which much gun rights mythology is founded. More to the point, it neglects the evidence of violence facilitation effects and the pronounced aggregated victimization rates found in most high gun-possession societies – especially the more unequal ones. The very idea that, once the legal and constitutional niceties of gun ownership are resolved, we merely need to concern ourselves with a few 'technical' control issues is a beguiling fiction the like of which no real criminologist could endorse. Furthermore, the NRA's robust response to President Obama's January 2013 gun control proposals,[8] formulated in the wake of the Sandy Hook school shooting in the days before Christmas 2012, hardly suggests that the US culture war over guns has *necessarily* reached any kind of consensus. After keeping its powder dry for a week but with its website promising 'meaningful contributions' to the proposed Obama gun control plan, Wayne La Pierre (NRA Executive President) used the NRA press conference to propose armed guards at all schools. Echoing the masculine hegemony of a 1950s western, 'the only way to stop a bad guy with a gun is a good guy with a gun', he said.

And yet, if the polling evidence is to be believed, 'large majorities back most general measures for controlling guns, policies to increase gun safety, laws to restrict criminals from acquiring firearms, and measures to enforce gun laws and punish offenders' (Smith, 2001a). While not all of those proposals raise the same highly charged 'gun control' sticking points (for example, tough sentencing policies are more readily supported by gun advocates as 'criminal control' policies), such findings are not unlike more recent polling results from MAIG (MAIG, 2012). Its evidence has suggested that even NRA members would support 'sensible gun control policies' intended to improve public safety, even though a great deal still hangs on those four apparently simple words. The central insistence of Winkler's complex and nuanced argument is that 'Americans *have always had* both gun rights and gun control' (2011: 296, emphasis added) and that today is really no different. Except, of course, that it is; for the chronic problems of gun violence at the heart of ostensibly civilized America, amongst the marginalized ghetto under-classes, point to a major failure of contemporary US politics. 'Sensible policies', 'individualism' 'constitutional freedoms', 'personal safety', 'gun rights' and 'gun controls' and a host of other symbolic slogans serve to conceal the true character of weaponized violence in the USA. Presented in neutral, generic and universal terms, the problem appears as a dilemma of the historical evolution of human society and civilization; of safety, law and progress. In fact it is a far more contingent outcome of inequality, fear and racism.

Miller's recent work (2008), in particular, has illustrated how the apparently neutral and generic framing of the 'law and order' agenda (and the institutions that support it and the rhetorics that animate it) has typically served to effectively 'de-couple' the problem of crime and violence – and perceived solutions to them – 'from broader concerns about class and race stratification' thereby simplifying and disaggregating complex social and historical processes, 'including white supremacy and systematic racial hierarchy' where contemporary problems of crime and violence have their roots (Miller, 2008: 50, 82). Tonry similarly argues that 'neglect of the interests of black Americans continues to characterize American crime policies' (2009: 386; 2011). In fact, in addition to this 'racial neglect', Tonry also includes: the 'paranoid style' of American politics, the 'Manichean moralism' of political activists and the 'obsolete constitution' amongst a quartet of factors establishing American punitive exceptionalism – it is noticeable how all four also bear directly upon Second Amendment politics (Tonry, 2009).

In a number of important ways, Miller's analysis empirically underpins, applies and develops the analysis of the contemporary 'crime complex' offered by David Garland (Garland, 2000, 2001a). This is so in both general theoretical and political terms, and also in a very specific policy sense. Garland's argument was that the contemporary punitiveness of Anglo-American penal policy (although in the present case, of US criminal justice policy especially) is currently sustained by both a particular configuration of political institutions and practices and by a series of ideas, attitudes and states of mind (fears, insecurities, intolerances). Both together comprise the contemporary 'crime complex'. In turn, these two dimensions of the crime complex are shaped by a series of social changes (globalization, social mobility, inequality and commodification) characteristic of late modernity and by the influence of the neo-liberal and socially conservative politics that dominated the developed economies both during and since the final decades of the twentieth century. Under the hegemony of these neo-liberal political values, a series of 'deeply conflicted' political strategies have emerged which, on the one hand, seek to manage pragmatically a failing state sovereignty: managing – rather than eliminating – crime; reasserting the power to punish (though not necessarily apprehending all of the guilty); upholding law and order (but not necessarily both at once) – while at the same time acting out an expressive and symbolic politics of law and order 'that is concerned not so much with controlling crime as with expressing the anger and outrage that crime provokes' (Garland, 2001a: 110). The analysis here is not dissimilar to Simon's conception of 'governing through crime' (Simon, 20067) or even the mobilization of punitiveness explored by Wacquant (Wacquant, 2009).

Garland develops his analysis in relation to a specific instance of American criminal justice policy, moreover one that is directly germane to our own present focus upon gun control and which similarly presents the USA in a seemingly 'exceptional' light, namely the death penalty (Garland, 2002, 2005, 2010). Garland's account contrasts with the contributions of many scholars who have invoked a culturalist interpretation of the death penalty (Zimring and Hawkins, 1986; Zimring, 2003; Whitman, 2005), and who account for the lethally punitive 'exceptionalism' of US criminal justice by reference to a strain of violent retributivism in US history (Brown, 1975). This they evidence by reference to vigilantism, the code of masculine honour (Nisbett and Cohen, 1996), violent frontier justice and extra judicial lynchings which, especially in the southern states in the aftermath of the Civil War, formed part of the region's local politics of race control. According to Garland, history and tradition are merely a cultural backdrop to some more contemporary reasons for the resurgence in the use of the death penalty after the mid-1970s, and these have to do with rising fear of crime, latent racism, political vested interests, the emergence of an increasingly punitive climate of opinion and the increasing politicization of crime control itself (Garland, 2005). My argument here is that essentially the same forces that fostered the return of the US death penalty are primarily responsible for the nature, extent and character of contemporary US advocacy of gun rights and the legal and political ascendancy of the Second Amendment. In other words, to adopt Garland's remark, the primacy of gun rights today 'is a contingent outcome of political, legal and cultural developments that occurred in the last 30 years' (Garland, 2005: 362).

A crucial distinction, for Garland, between the USA and countries that have abolished the death penalty relates to the federal structure of the American government. So, for example, the US Congress can no more bring the practice of capital punishment to an end in all of the 50 states than it can, in the absence of a constitutional amendment achieving the support of three-quarters of the states, abolish the Second Amendment's 'right to bear arms'. Furthermore, a central driver of the US politics of law and order occurs at the local level where a range of populist political processes (including voter ballot initiatives, local referenda and recall provisions) puts pressure on local criminal justice officials not to take positions that are unpopular with local electorates. The fact that many of these officials (for example governors, chief prosecutors, police chiefs) are directly elected and therefore thoroughly immersed in partisan political contests adds further bite to the pressure of local political interests. As regards the death penalty, in particular, popular support for capital punishment finds direct expression in the local political process and it is, likewise, at the state and municipal levels where gun rights advocates have won their successive incremental battles to establish, in state after state and municipality after municipality, 'Castle Doctrine' type laws[9] and concealed firearm entitlements (Diaz, 2013). These piecemeal local steps have coincided, in a kind of pincer-movement politics, with the constitutional/legal effort to force a particular reading of the Second Amendment as validating an individual right to possess firearms and which culminated in the Supreme Court decisions of 2008 and 2009 overthrowing the handgun control laws of both Washington, DC and Chicago. At the local level, Garland argues, debate about crime and its consequences and concerning the means for addressing it are not discussed in broad public policy generalities as part of a package of policies, bipartisan agreements or matters of conscience, rather, they assume the shape of often highly politicized and populist, single-issue struggles between competing interests. This is some way from a conception of high politics and may help explain the particular salience of short slogans or the simple bumper sticker half-truths that the NRA, in particular, has been effective in deploying.

Yet it takes more than a groundswell of public attitudes to change policy, for these attitudes require some means of articulation through the policy-making process; and such opportunities exist at the state level in US politics allowing popular and often populist sentiments to be translated into official policy. In these ways, the contemporary 'crime complex' in the USA has facilitated a fatal simplification of popular understandings of criminal justice and public safety where sound bites and slogans have decentred evidence and argument: for example in the one-line manifestoes supporting 'wars' on drugs and terror, 'truth in sentencing', 'three strikes', 'no-frills prisons', 'life means life' and so on. And, in this hothouse of political sloganizing, the gun rights advocates have been no slouches, supplying probably more sound bites, slogans and half-truths than most other political campaigns put together: 'the right to bear arms', 'the Second Amendment *is* Homeland Security', 'call 911 and die', 'if guns are outlawed only outlaws will have guns', 'rape prevention kit', 'refuse to be a victim', 'more guns, less crime', 'armed gays don't get bashed', 'guns don't kill people, people kill people', 'self-defense is a human right' and so on and on.

Perhaps there should be no surprise that single-issue political interests should be effective in mobilizing such simple, single-idea slogans. The key issue is that such ideas gain direct access to local political processes in the USA where they take on the power of simple truths, articles of faith and sometimes even embracing the 'populist myths' (Williams, 2003) with which the Second Amendment is frequently draped. Against such ideas there can often be little real debate, for these are fundamental ideals that resonate emotionally, morally and politically (Vizzard, 2000); aspects of identity and personal conviction (Kohn, 2004b), rather more than evidenced research. By contrast, as Goss (2006: 93) has noted, the gun control lobby groups have typically attempted to campaign 'rationally and nationally', and as a result have been criticized for being both 'elite' and 'expert' (i.e. out of touch).

Especially since the establishment, in 1975, of its Institute for Legislative Action (ILA), a proactive lobbying and advocacy branch of the NRA (C. Allen, 2006), and particularly following the hard-line leadership coup within the organization in 1977 – the so-called 'Cincinnati revolt' (Davidson, 1993; 34–36; Winkler, 2011: 66–67) – the organization itself has become especially adept at exploiting the federal US political system and tailoring its simple messages to the specific local political arenas in which it found itself (Goss, 2006; Miller, 2008). It has built from the ground up, expressed its politics in simple but absolute notions, 'pursued in principle as opposed to research and evidence' (Vizzard, 2000: 9) while playing to its core constituency's fears and concerns about crime in the streets, violence and racial conflict. More complex 'collective' or 'sociological' analyses of the causes of urban violence emerging from a 'policy and evidence discourse' become sidelined by a political rhetoric that puts a putative 'solution' to the problem of crime in the hands of 'sovereign' individuals with sovereign principles: 'the people' rather than 'the government' (Goss, 2006: 193–195).

A personal philosophy of 'rugged individualism' and a political philosophy of independence and state minimalism dovetail together neatly, and by this means (aside from a profound distrust of government) any conception of collective public safety benefits to be derived from even 'sensible' gun control measures appears as an alien ideal to the committed gun rights activist. Many of the dangers inherent in these paradoxes of law-and-order populism lie here. For not only does the gun advocacy politics described here frustrate many of the measures that might help policy-makers gain some further purchase on the proliferation of firearms in American society, the neo-liberal premise upon which self-arming rests simultaneously corrodes wider conceptions of civic responsibility and public safety while promoting and stimulating the levels of firearm acquisition which (for much of the period we are considering) sustain the levels of violence in the first place. But perhaps there is yet scope for progress, for as the 2012 poll by MAIG revealed, many Americans harbor somewhat more ambivalent and even moderate feelings about certain aspects of gun ownership, even despite the simplistic equation of guns with freedom retaining a powerful ideological influence (Gabbatt, 2012a). However, as Saad (2012) has noted, even though Americans express support for selected gun controls when polled, they continue to vote for pro-gun political representatives at election time.

The degree to which, since the mid-1970s, the NRA and its gun rights advocacy has been able to successfully turn the tables and seize the momentum in the politics of firearms might best be grasped if we compare what passed for the academic and policy orthodoxy regarding firearms and public safety in the 1970s with the position today. It is undeniable that the gun rights movement in the 1970s was galvanized into action through the passage in 1968 of the Federal Gun Control Act. Although this legislation was only passed in the wake of the assassinations of JFK, Robert Kennedy and Martin Luther King, it had been bitterly contested through Congress and emerged as only a pale shadow of its proponents' intentions. Notwithstanding this apparent 'heating up' of the gun debate, American social scientists Lee Kennett and James Anderson (1975) expounded a version of the 'civilizing thesis' (Elias, 1982) and felt confident enough to predict the end of the gun. The gun, they argued, was part of America's past; it formed part of a series of 'traditional attitudes' concerning 'government, society and the individual'. And, they continued, these attitudes run 'like so many threads, through the tapestry of the national past. In its essence, the gun controversy is a struggle between these attitudes and new ones' (Kennett and Anderson, 1975: 254). Thus the gun, frontier violence and the western culture (despite Hollywood's reverence for the cowboy) was part of the world America had left behind; there were no more frontiers, civilization and urbanization had done for the gun. Of course, they could not have been more wrong; in many respects the gun was about to turn the tables on civilization.

The timing was impeccable, establishing a further parallel with Garland's analysis of the US death penalty. Between the late 1960s and 1976, there was a de facto moratorium on the application of the death penalty in the USA following the Supreme Court decision in the case of *Furman v Georgia*. In this case the court had held that, taken together, the relative infrequency with which the death penalty was actually applied, concerns about racial discrimination in its use and the manner of its application, were such as to render the death penalty arbitrary, 'cruel and unusual' and therefore contrary to the Constitution. In other words, it was not the death penalty itself that was unacceptable and contrary to law, just the fairness with which it was applied. In the wake of the Supreme Court judgement, many US states began to pass new death penalty laws intended to overcome the criticisms of procedural unfairness in order to resurrect the death penalty. A series of Supreme Court judgements in 1976 eventually held that the state's death penalty statutes now satisfied the constitutional standards and executions resumed. From the perspective of the 'civilizing thesis', the resumption of executions jolted the clock backwards, coinciding with the rise of neo-liberal politics across the western world, unprecedented levels of crime and violence accompanied by the first stirrings of a renewed punitiveness in matters of law and order and, not least, a new politics of race.

In this political climate the gun lobby had already begun to mobilize, in doing so they caught Kennett and Anderson completely off guard. For these authors the gun was part of the American past and they could not see a place for it in America's future. It is worth citing their words at length: 'In the long run', they argued,

> time works against the gun. Increased social consciousness finds its excesses intolerable, whereas they were once accepted without thought ... The war against crime has mobilised the computer and other sophisticated techniques. Moreover, the police have come to regard the armed citizen more as a hazard than an ally. The city is the enemy of the gun, and the city is growing ... In megalopolis the gun as necessity seems doomed.
>
> *(Kennett and Anderson, 1975: 255–256)*

More astute observers might have noticed that the inhabitants of the big American cities, now preoccupied by violence, disorder and crime in the streets, were beginning to buy guns in larger numbers than ever before and increasingly for personal protection in the here and now rather than for leisure pursuits (such as hunting or target shooting) or as some kind of personal homage to the 'Old West'. Likewise, gun industry advertising began to switch increasingly towards the self-defence market.

Numbers games

It is inevitably difficult to provide absolutely accurate estimates on the numbers of firearms in a given society. Furthermore, the relation between firearm numbers and violent crime is difficult to analyse precisely because it is invariably the illegally held firearms that are the most likely to be used in criminal activities. Nevertheless, both government agencies and social scientists have devised a number of fairly reliable methods of estimate (Kleck, 1991). Estimates suggesting an increasing number of handgun owners, during the closing decades of the twentieth century, have been presented by Wellford *et al.* (2004). By 1999, the civilian firearm inventory for the USA comprised almost 260 million firearms of which almost 95 million were handguns (Wellford *et al.*, 2004). Such evidence tends to confirm that the influences prompting US citizens to invest in personal protection handguns were associated primarily with the late twentieth century; specifically, according to this evidence, handgun ownership seems to have more than tripled since the early 1960s. This is consistent with the ambitions of the NRA's 'concealed weapon' advocacy in the early 1990s – if not what actually happened.

Many scholars have contested what they have called the 'exaggerated' claims made about the expansion of handgun ownership – especially amongst non-traditional gun owning groups such as women (Glick, 1995b; Smith and Smith, 1995). A survey by Cook and Ludwig for the National Institute of Justice in 1997 found that only 25 per cent of adults actually owned firearms but that, generally, those who owned firearms tended to have more than one (Cook and Ludwig, 1997). Estimates for the Small Arms Survey project suggested that by

2007 there were 270 million privately owned firearms in the USA, roughly 88 guns for every 100 people (Karp, 2007). Differences in the findings are some-times attributed to distinctions between guns owned *by individuals* as opposed to guns owned *within households*; similarly, in a society where 40 per cent of firearm transactions occur away from public oversight, legality may also be a factor. Willingness to be honest with pollsters is also an issue. Yearly Gallup polling often throws up implausibly large year-on-year fluctuations in the percentage of people willing to declare themselves gun owners (Saad, 2011) sufficient to raise profound questions about data derived by a phone poll (Enten, 2012). Even so, some kind of consensus appears to be emerging, at least in certain academic cir-cles, that while the numbers of gun owners may not be growing, it may not be falling dramatically either.

Rather more reliable is the evidence that more guns appear to be owned by fewer people (Brennan, 2012); that people flock to buy guns following major incidents or disturbances and that they buy guns that appear threatened with prohibition (assault weapons in the mid-1990s (Chivers, 2010); Glock pistols in the late 1990s (Barrett, 2012) and assault rifles, once again, at Christmas 2012). FBI data (cited by Enten, 2012) indicates that for *every year* since 2000 in excess of eight million firearm purchase background checks were undertaken, with over 16 million in 2011. As Enten notes, this *could* mean a number of things:

> First, more people are getting concealed carry permits. Second, more people who already have a gun are deciding to get another. Third, more people are getting guns than a few years ago. Fourth, more people are deciding to legalize their gun transactions instead of buying them on the black market.
>
> *(Enten, 2012)*

The US General Social Survey (GSS) data rather points against Enten's third hypothesis, the GSS reports *household* gun ownership rates falling from around 50 per cent in the early 1970s to around 32 per cent in 2010. Gun owner-ship also seems more concentrated amongst middle-aged to older sections of the population; people born after 1960 are less likely to be gun owners, those born after 1980 less likely still (Waldman, 2012b). Support for mandatory gun permits (gun licensing) has remained consistently around 70 per cent too. The Violence Policy Center reports data suggesting falling *individual* gun ownership rates between 1980 and 2010 – from 29 per cent to 20 per cent. Methodological issues arise here too, it matters *who* your survey samples and where they live. Silver adds to a 'culturalist' appreciation of gun ownership and gun rights advo-cacy, he employs GSS data to show that 'gun ownership has declined over the past 40 years, but almost all of the decrease has come from Democrats' (Silver, 2012) (see Figure 4.1).

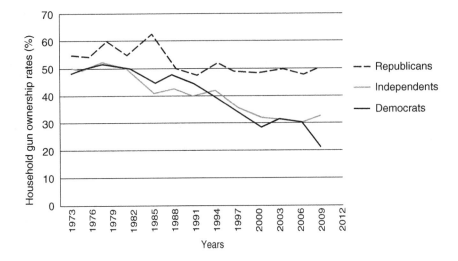

Figure 4.1   Household gun ownership rates (%) by party affiliation, 1973–2010

Source: GSS data cited in Silver (2012).

Such evidence lends further support to the cultural divide that attitudes to firearms crystallize. What is more, these partisan differences become more pronounced in suburban areas, with 58 per cent of Republican voters saying they had a gun in their household, compared with just 27 per cent of Democrats. Furthermore gun ownership rates are highest amongst the middle class, as compared with the poorest or the richest, finally 'gun ownership rates are inversely correlated with educational attainment' (Silver, 2012). Of course, it is not that party political affiliation causes anti-gun sentiments, but rather that certain identities, philosophies and outlooks are associated with values and relationships that disincline individuals to put their trust in personal firepower. In so far as the 'gun question' indicates the gap between Democrats and Republicans widening on these issues, it is perhaps further evidence of the hardening edges of a cultural rift in contemporary USA.

As we have seen, there is considerable ambiguity in the 'gun numbers game' but if Kennett and Anderson (1975) were caught out by how the politics of guns were to change in the 1980s and 1990s, so was Franklin Zimring. Even as late as 1981, criminologist Franklin Zimring, who has been one of the USA's most respected and persistent gun control commentators (Zimring, 1968, 1975, 1981; Zimring and Hawkins, 1987, 1997), as well as a relentless critic of the death penalty (Zimring and Hawkins, 1986; Zimring, 2003), tried to predict the future of American gun policy. 'If history is an appropriate guide,' he remarked, 'the next thirty years will bring a national handgun strategy' (Zimring, 1981). If anything remotely resembling a US national handgun (control) strategy were ever a serious proposition it might plausibly be argued, in 2012, that, at the federal level, such an aspiration lies in tatters even though some states have adopted more stringent firearms controls and background checks (Gerney *et al.*, 2013).[10] An overwhelming majority of states license private citizens to carry concealed firearms and a majority have adopted 'Castle Doctrine' laws. The USA's 'national handgun strategy', such as it is, would appear to entail the untrammeled right of law abiding and mentally capable adults to own as many firearms as they choose. Even so there are still signs, despite an abiding scepticism (Jacobs, 2002) that not all has been lost. The gun control lobbies might learn to counter the tactics of the gun rights activists; rational (evidence-based) and pragmatic ('common-sense') gun policies (Ludwig and Cook, 2003; Brady Center, 2008) might come to persuade the US electorate, and even the shifting demographics of the US electorate itself (Lee, 2012) might generate a renewed political will to tackle the proliferation of firearms. Much like Garland's optimistic conclusion that the USA may still be on a journey from 'exceptionalism' in matters of capital punishment, the country might still be similarly travelling as regards the politics of guns and gun control (even if the precise direction is unclear). I return to these issues later in Chapter 8, in the course of a discussion of the prospects of global gun control.

New politics, new precedents?

Somewhat contrarily, however, one of the elements that Zimring identified in 1981 as a component of an emerging national gun strategy entailed efforts to enforce tighter gun control policies, going beyond the 'national minimum', in 'states and cities where gun violence problems were especially acute' (Zimring, 1981). Despite Zimring's confidence, however, two recent court cases help reveal just how far the balance of forces has shifted, and perhaps how far we have come, in gun politics, over the past three decades. They also confirm a renewed conservative political activism in the US Supreme Court. It is also worthy of note, following Garland's death penalty parallel, that these judgements were exclusively concerned with contemporary demands for and rights to firearm ownership. A historic constitutional principle was being called upon, not for its own sake but for its *contemporary utility*. The cases were as we have already argued, about the present, not the past.

In 2008, as the culmination of a long-standing and concerted campaign of legal activism sustained by gun rights enthusiasts and libertarian lawyers (Doherty, 2008; Winkler, 2011) and, not least, capitalizing upon the political composition of the judicial bench of the US Supreme Court, the court agreed, in a landmark judgement in the case of *District of Columbia v. Heller*, to strike down the Washington, DC (near total) prohibition on civilian handgun ownership (first instituted in 1975) as contrary to the US Second Amendment. As commentators have noted, the judgement marked 'a new chapter in Second Amendment jurisprudence' (De Leeuw *et al.*, 2009) after nearly 70 years of Supreme Court silence on Second Amendment matters, one with potentially fundamental consequences for high-crime, inner-urban and suburban African–American neighbourhoods. The Washington, DC case was followed, within two years, by a second bout of Supreme Court activism, this time, judging the case of *McDonald v. City of Chicago* in June 2010, the Supreme Court justices voted 5:4 to rule that the city's 28-year-old handgun prohibition laws were 'unconstitutional'. Taken together, the two Supreme Court rulings appeared to drive a veritable coach and horses through a sequence of 'gun control as crime prevention' and public safety legislation dating back to the nineteenth century and, as we have seen, opened up a potential hornets' nest of issues concerning state and federal jurisdiction over firearms, judicial 'activism', 'sensible' gun laws, public safety and the right of self-defence. As always, these issues are closely shadowed by a politics of race, crime and fear.

However, as the dust has settled following these seemingly 'enormously significant' Supreme Court judgements, more considered appraisals (neither euphoric nor despairing) have surfaced as commentators searched, in the wording of the published judgements, for what they would mean for present and future gun laws and the parameters of future legislative manoeuvre at state and federal level. The Supreme Court's rulings, it is argued, are constructed in a very specific fashion. They have established that particular, supposedly over-embracing, firearms prohibitions, in Washington, DC and Chicago, overstepped the Second Amendment mark, but that they did not lay down precisely what future laws would be possible. In other words, they struck down a couple of exceptions but avoided framing a new template for gun control policy. Even though gun rights advocates gleefully celebrated the judgements and gun controllers preached dire warnings about a virtual 'meltdown' of gun controls as the gun lobby took impetus from their courtroom victories to challenge other gun laws in other states, this has not happened.

And reading Justice Scalia's verdict it is clear that the Supreme Court did not intend to prevent the state or federal legislatures from prohibiting certain types of firearms, or imposing other restrictions on who could purchase them, or the circumstances in which they could carry them (visible or concealed). In particular, there seems nothing in the Supreme Court judgement itself to prevent the Obama administration following through with a ban on assault weapons or restricting the magazine capacity of firearms in the wake of the Sandy Hook, Connecticut, shooting. As Justice Scalia put it:

> Like most rights, the right secured by the Second Amendment is not unlimited ... From Blackstone [eighteenth-century legal philosopher] through to the 19th-century cases, commentators and courts routinely explained that the right was not a right to keep and carry *any weapon whatsoever* in *any manner whatsoever* and for *whatever* purpose.
>
> *(Scalia, 2008: 54, emphasis added)*

Furthermore, he went on to add,

> nothing in our opinion should be taken to cast doubt on longstanding prohibitions on the possession of firearms by felons and the mentally ill, or laws

forbidding the carrying of firearms in sensitive places such as schools and government buildings, or laws imposing conditions and qualifications on the commercial sale of arms.

(Scalia, 2008: 54–55)

As our preceding discussion on the Second Amendment has noted, this interpretation offers no clarification as to precisely whom and under what circumstances any one in particular might be permitted to own and carry a firearm. At the very least, this rather more 'pragmatic' clarification is not to be found in the Second Amendment itself for here the proposition is simply that 'the right of the people to keep and bear arms *shall not be infringed*' (emphasis added). Scalia, by contrast, was allowing for at least four areas of potential 'infringement': the categories of permitted persons; the types of permissible firearms; the places in which firearms carriage might be inappropriate or ill-advised; and the circumstances relating to sale, transfer, registration or licensing. Legislative action on any of these issues is not ruled out of court by either the Heller or MacDonald judgements, but neither are these decisions especially helpful to legislators looking to develop future gun control and public safety policies. Even so, there are those who argue that Scalia's Heller judgement may even come to represent something of a 'Pyrrhic victory' for the gun rights movement (Winkler, 2011).

Gun tragedy and political farce

Having now introduced some of the broader social, political and historical issues impinging upon the discussion of gun control in the USA and, having tried to sketch the broad contemporary outlines of the culture and politics of recent US gun debates, it is important to develop a number of these issues in a little more detail in order to connect these American themes to a series of rather more global perspectives on gun crime, self-defence and gun control. A central issue, not least because of the ways that such events have kick-started and often fundamentally shifted prevailing trajectories of debate around guns, violence and gun control in a wide variety of societies (see Chapter 8), concerns the tragedies we have come to know as school or 'rampage' shootings. The ways in which the 14 December killings at Sandy Hook elementary school in Connecticut also transformed and energized the American gun debate also make this an essential topic.

On the other hand, for example, it is often suggested (mostly by the complacent or those who would prefer to do nothing) that legislative, media and public responses following tragedies are little more than unthinking, 'knee-jerk' reactions. Aside from an implication that it might be wrong to learn lessons from tragedies and to try and prevent them recurring, this is hardly the case in US gun control, for the timeline presented in Chapter 6 tells of over 70, multiple-victim school shootings, and many more gun rampages besides. This is a mightily slow and long-delayed 'knee jerk'. Karl Marx once commented on the tendency of history to repeat itself, 'the first time as tragedy, the second time as farce' (Marx, 1963); we might pause to reflect upon just what he might have made of America's eightieth school shooting.

The re-igniting of the gun debate in December 2012, however, reflected a number of difficult silences around American gun violence to which we have already referred. While American gun violence victims are overwhelmingly black, the Sandy Hook victims (and the victims of most other school or rampage shootings) have been almost entirely white. A terrible suburban school shooting in which six-year-old white girls were the majority victims had achieved what nearly three decades of firearm carnage in the ghettos had largely been unable to do: mobilize another major federal gun control effort. And yet, to echo an earlier theme, gun violence in the ghetto is marginalized around the symbolism of crime and, in American political discourse, that tends to surreptitiously bracket the discussion around a barely articulated politics of race, where white rights nearly always trump black victims. By contrast, 20 dead children (and six murdered teachers) in a suburban school is a 'tragedy', and although tragedies might happen anytime, anywhere, thereby, for some, making planned prevention potentially futile, unrealistic or simply insufficiently cost-effective, other people set to work on what *might* be preventable about them as a way of lowering the risk of further incidents.

Notes

1 As I discuss later, more extensive proposals of this nature did follow the Sandy Hook shooting in December 2012.
2 Mass shootings with assault weapons before the 1994 ban included the murder of 21 people and the wounding of 19 others in 1984, by James Huberty, using an Uzi assault pistol in a San Ysidro MacDonald's burger restaurant; the killing of seven people and the wounding of 13 more by Joseph Wesbecker using a collection of firearms including an AK-47 and 2 MAC-11 assault pistols in Kentucky in 1989; Patrick Purdy killing five children and wounding 29 others, firing over 100 rounds in under two minutes into a school yard in Stockton, California, in January 1989; and Gian Luigi Ferri, using two TEC-DC9s, killing eight people and wounding six others shooting in an office block in San Francisco in 1993.
3 In early 2013 the British MoD announced that British forces in Afghanistan were also to be issued with new Glock 17 pistols for personal defence, replacing the Browning pistol used since the 1960s.
4 Michael Bellesiles' book, *Arming America: The Origins of a National Gun Culture* garnered enormous praise when it was first published, even picking up academic prizes for its historical scholarship. Subsequently criticism began to mount. At first the criticism was political rather than scholarly, then definitional – what, exactly, might it mean to say a 'gun culture' does or does not exist? Finally the criticism turned to questions of scholarship and academic credibility. As Lindgren (2002: 2232) wrote, 'even from the beginning, there were … disturbing differences between *Arming America* and its sources … What is unprecedented in such a prominent book is how many errors it contains and how systematically the errors are in the direction of the thesis'.
5 The Fourteenth Amendment, one of the post-Civil War 'reconstruction' amendments, was drafted to ensure the application of universal civil rights to all American citizens, irrespective of race:

> No State shall make or enforce any law which shall abridge the privileges or immunities of citizens of the United States; nor shall any State deprive any person of life, liberty, or property, without due process of law; nor deny to any person within its jurisdiction the equal protection of the laws.

6 Even so, courts in southern jurisdictions continued to interpret the law in perverse and exclusive ways to uphold racist and discriminatory laws and practices. Or even resist it by impeding the due process of law, as the resolution of the Ruby Ridge (1992) or Waco siege (1993) incidents, amongst others, would appear to suggest.

7 Critics of the 'individualist' reading of the Second Amendment have frequently objected to the implied legitimacy entailed in referring to this interpretation as the 'standard model' but the label has seemingly stuck, if only by weight of numbers.

8 The president's January 2013 package of gun control proposals included: reintroducing an expired ban on new purchases of 'military-style' assault weapons' limiting ammunition magazines to ten rounds and a ban on possession and sale of armour-piercing bullets; background checks on all gun sales; closing the so-called 'gun-show loophole'; harsher penalties for gun traffickers, especially unlicensed dealers buying weapons for criminals; and ending the ban on gun violence research by federally funded agencies.

9 Castle Doctrine laws, based upon a principle rather similar to the notion that 'an Englishman's home is his castle', embrace the idea that an attacked person has no duty to retreat, but may use reasonable (including lethal) force, as necessary, to defend him or herself. The laws, sometimes referred to by supporters as 'Stand Your Ground' laws, or 'shoot first' (ask questions later) laws, by opponents, come in strong or weaker versions, depending upon the nature of crime threats they are intended to cover or the scope (in the home, in a vehicle, workplace or in public) of their intended application. Many states have now adopted such laws. As a nod to Hollywood, some of these laws (e.g. in Colorado) are referred to as 'Make my Day' laws in reference to a comment by Detective 'Dirty' Harry Callahan (played by Clint Eastwood in the 1983 film, *Sudden Impact*). Callahan ironically urges a suspect to attack him with the words: 'Go ahead, punk, make my day', implying thereby the sinister delight he will derive from shooting him, should he attempt to resist arrest.

10 President Obama's gun control package, developed in response to the December 2012 Sandy Hook school shooting in Connecticut, was blocked by senators in April 2013 (Roberts, 2013). Amongst the proposals are background checks for all gun sales, a measure that has long been a core component of a national handgun control strategy. The NRA leadership declared its fundamental opposition to the proposals.

5

AMERICAN GUN CRIME

Themes and issues, violences and silences

The bipolar sensitivities of the mainstream US media, and public attention at large, were starkly exposed following the forty-third homicide in Chicago during January 2013. January was still not over, but 2013 was already shaping up to exceed the 506 Chicago homicides of 2012, only 25 per cent of these were reported to have been solved (Gray, 2013). While gun crime in New York had fallen by almost 20 per cent during 2012 (a cause of great celebration for the Bloomberg administration), in Chicago it had risen by over 15 per cent. Chicago residents were nearly four times more likely to become homicide victims compared with New Yorkers (Johnson, 2012). Yet none of Chicago's previous 42 killings during January 2013 had achieved much more than a few lines in the local press; victim 43 was different.

Hadiya Pendleton, aged 15, had been shot in the back by a 16 year old. She had been in a Chicago park talking with friends, some of whom may have had 'gang affiliations' when another teenager jumped a fence and began firing indiscriminately at her group. As the shooter jumped back into a car and was driven away, Hadiya's group scattered, she managed to run a short distance before collapsing, and was pronounced dead on arrival at the hospital emergency room. Just another story of the gangs and the streets; of young men seeking reputations and loose friendship networks understood as 'gangs'; and non-cooperation with the police; and drive-by shootings as 'grounded action' (Sanders, 1994); and guns and anonymous young black victims. Not this time.

Just a week before she was shot, Hadiya had sung as a member of her school band at President Obama's inauguration. Now she was dead. The First Lady came to her funeral to pay respects; the president was busy with a heavy agenda, high on that list were soliciting and consolidating support for the package of gun control proposals emerging following the Sandy Hook shooting a few weeks earlier. Too late for Hadiya, but her death reached the national and international media.

US gun violence trends

Before I turn to school or 'rampage' shootings, and the incidents that do shape and sometimes redirect the event-driven US gun debate (the tragedies), it is important to spend some time examining and reflecting upon the chronic patterns of relentless gun violence that change nothing and, as noted, generally do not shape the news agenda. It is useful to outline, briefly, something of the scale of the gun crime problems facing the USA, as the landscape against which gun control issues get debated, even if that landscape is regarded in political terms as 'inert' and unchanging, the terrain over which the battle for gun control (or gun rights) is fought, as opposed to a reason for advocating any particular policy shift. On the contrary, 'events' shape politics and policies, and routine urban shootings are just 'business as usual'. So what follows is not intended to be a thorough analysis of the nuances of American gun crime trends but simply a sketch of the backdrop against which a series of specific issues are fought out. In Chapter 4, I have already considered the changing profile of US handgun ownership and the issues to which this gives rise; here I look at the patterns of firearm crime to which those gun purchases may well have contributed – or to which they may have been a response.

Figure 5.1 shows the handgun homicide trend and total firearm homicide trend from 1976–2010. This, by now familiar, pattern reveals a steep climb in gun-involved violence throughout the 1980s and peaking in1993 (with handgun homicides clearly dominating the picture as well as being overwhelmingly responsible for the increase to 1993) (Wintemute, 2000: 53). An equally steep decline follows until 1999–2000, after which the trend stabilizes continuing to decline after 2002. Handgun homicide continues to account for around 60 per cent of US homicides, although, in the period since 1993, the percentage of *non-fatal* violence attributable to firearms fell by almost half (from 11 per cent in 1993 to 6 per cent in 2004), while the rate of *non-fatal* firearm victimization has similarly fallen from 6 per thousand to 1.4 per thousand during the same time period (Bureau of Justice Statistics, 2010; Planty and Truman, 2013).

Although the decline in gun homicide in the USA since 1993 is substantial, it is worth taking a slightly closer look at the wider gun victimization figures from the most recent decade where the story is not quite so positive. Thus, as Figure 5.1 confirms, while the middle years of the recent decade saw a brief upturn in gun homicides, falling back again towards 2010, Figure 5.2 suggests a more persistently upward trend in *non-fatal* gun violence since 2000. Currie notes that there are as many as 4:5 non-fatal gun assaults as fatal ones (2005: 35). According to DiPoala *et al.* (2013: 7), the diverging trends for fatal and non-fatal gunshot victimization may be attributable, in part, 'to advances in the medical field, as hospitals are able to produce more viable outcomes for gunshot wound patients', an argument that contrasts with that regarding the rising lethality of gunshot victimization a decade or so earlier (refer to the discussion preceding Figure 5.3), improvements that may not ultimately be sustainable in the face of the relentless increases in the militarization of the civilian gun stock, the newer ammunition calibres, the greater accuracy, the 'assault-mode' semi-automatic functioning of the weapons and the increasing magazine capacities (Diaz, 2013). The mid-decade increases in firearm victimization described in Figures 5.1 and 5.2 also coincide with the increasing production of handguns in the USA from 2005 onwards revealed by Figure 5.3. More guns on the streets do seem to mean more gun violence victims. Moreover, while gun homicide decreases are measured in thousands, non-fatal shooting increases are measured in *tens of thousands*.

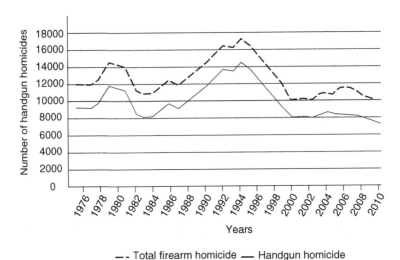

FIGURE 5.1 USA handgun homicides and total firearm homicides, 1976–2010

Sources: UNODC (2011); Wellford *et al.* (2004).

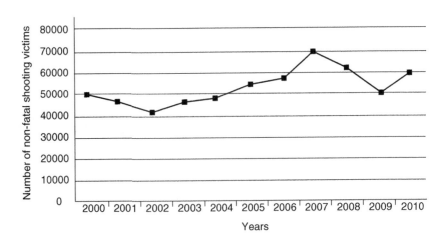

FIGURE 5.2 Non-fatal shooting victims in the USA, 2000–2010

Sources: Data from the Department of Health and Human Services; Centers for Disease Control and Prevention (CDC); DiPoala *et al.* (2012: 6).

There have been protracted debates concerning both the rapid increase and the subsequent (although now somewhat qualified) steep decline in gun crime in the USA since the early 1990s (Blumstein and Wallman, 2000; Wintemute, 2000; Zimring, 2007). The factors responsible for the initial fall in gun violence after 1993 have been the subject of both domestic and international analysis, commentary and speculation (Karmen, 2000). That said, the aim here is not to engage in a lengthy reiteration of these arguments but simply to sketch the broad contours of the major lines of analysis. This discussion echoes some of the themes that have already begun to arise in the analysis of British gun crime providing context for the issues raised in Chapter 6 and also anticipating both criminologically and analytically the many similar debates played out in other parts of the world where serious gun crime problems have arisen. Setting those issues aside, for one moment, it is revealing to compare the trends in US firearm homicide with those for handgun production. Accordingly, Figure 5.3 presents the US handgun production trends, collated by the ATF between 1986 and 2009.

It is immediately apparent that the 1993 peak in handgun homicides revealed in Figure 5.1 coincides exactly with the 1993 peak in US handgun production revealed in Figure 5.3. Furthermore, the increase in gun purchases during 1986–1993 seems primarily driven by an expanding market for the new semi-automatic pistol designs rather than the older revolvers. As Wintemute (2000: 53–55) argues, for example, almost the entire increase in gun homicides in Chicago in the two decades leading to 1995 was attributable to semi-automatic pistols. The new pistols also tended to have larger calibres and larger magazines (bigger bullets and more of them) thereby having more so-called 'stopping power' (Marshall and Sanow, 1992, 1996) and greater potential lethality. Wintemute (2000) cites data from hospital emergency room studies in different US cities, which not only revealed higher proportions of gunshot victims dying at the scene of the crime (despite improved paramedic responses) but also victims arriving at the ER with both larger and more numerous bullet wounds (McGonigal, 1993; Caruso et al., 1999).

Figure 5.3, however, only details new handgun production and not handguns purchased and, therefore, in circulation in the USA. It also fails to take account of firearms manufactured in the USA for export. However, the numbers involved are insufficient to counter the trend observable in the graph. Rather more significant, however, are the firearm importation figures and the evidence (Diaz, 1999) that from the late 1980s onwards, sales of higher calibre, larger magazine capacity, military specification pistols (and also assault rifles) came to dominate the civilian handgun market. As they did so, these same semi-automatic weapons began to percolate down into criminal hands (Wintemute, 1998, 2004) and then to appear more frequently in ATF crime gun traces (Koper and Shelley, 2007).

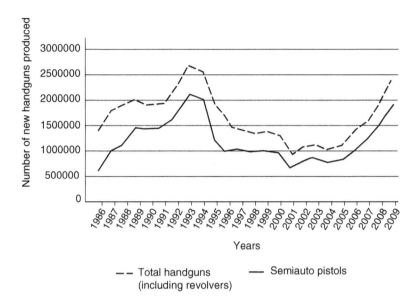

FIGURE 5.3 New handgun production in the USA, 1986–2009

Source: US Department of Justice (2011).

Although the sources of criminal firearms are many and various (see Figure 5.4) and some commentators have cautioned against using gun crime traces as a simple surrogate indicator of illegal firearms (Kopel, 1999), the available evidence does reveal that particular firearm types appear more frequently in ATF firearm traces; while certain gun dealers (Wintemute *et al.*, 2005; Webster *et al.*, 2006a, b) and, indeed, certain US states (Koper and Shelley, 2007), appear to supply more than their fair share of weapons to the criminal community. A study by the campaign organization MAIG (2010) found that ten states have a consistently higher pattern of inter-state firearm sales. These ten states, with relatively lax firearm sales laws, are responsible for half the crime guns traced by the ATF. These same states also have a shorter 'time to crime' on guns sold, which is to say a shorter period between the date upon which the gun is first sold and its first recorded use in a criminal offence.

Figure 5.4 makes it clear that firearms reach the criminal fraternity by a variety of routes; many of these channels are entirely informal and some are quite clearly illegal. It is well understood that a large minority of legal gun sales in the USA, as much as 40 per cent, occurs through what is known as the 'secondary gun market' (Jacobs, 2002). The primary firearm market is regulated; a purchase of a firearm is made from a federally licensed firearms dealer and is usually subject to a background check. However, the re-sale of firearms (from 'gun shows', markets, car-boot sales or other private purchasers) are not consistently regulated (Burbick, 2006).

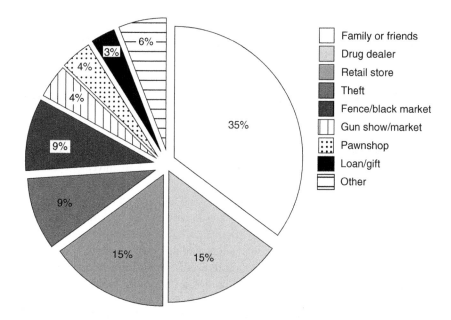

FIGURE 5.4 The sources of supply of criminal firearms in the USA

Source: Federal Firearm Offenders, 1992–98, Bureau of Justice Statistics, http://www.
bjs.gov/index.cfm?ty=pbdetail&iid=860, accessed 10 March 2014.

In this light, the very clear picture presented in Figure 5.4 shows that, as far as
firearm transactions leading to gun misuse in crimes are concerned, only a very
small minority of these firearm transactions fall within the formally transparent or
officially regulated sector, the rest occur well below the radar of public scrutiny or
accountability (Sheley and Wright, 1993a). As we have already seen in respect of
the British case study (Chapter 2), the degree to which the illegal firearm economy
is causally related to the legal supply of firearms is contested; it is contested the
world over (as we shall see; Collier, 2009; Greene and Marsh, 2012), although the
evidence presented above certainly suggests that wherever there is an abundant
supply of legal weapons, there will also be a thriving illegal firearm economy. For
example, as has been acknowledged already as regards firearm marketing in the late
twentieth century, the purchase of self-defence handguns may be a consequence
of a rising fear of crime and violence (Diaz, 1999; Zimring and Hawkins, 1997).

Whereas the illegal gun market in the UK, described as a 'junk-gun' market
because of the ways in which illegal weapon supply has been effectively restricted,
the supply of firearms is nowhere quite so restricted in most US jurisdictions. As
Cook *et al.* (2007) describe, however, this does not always mean that everyone
finds it easy to access any kind of firearm they want. Cook and his colleagues
found that many years of handgun restrictions in Chicago had made handguns
significantly harder to come by, especially new, factory-quality, high-performance

weapons. Younger people also found serviceable firearms harder to come by, the laws had made a difference, the illegal handgun market in Chicago was closer to the cheap 'junk-firearm' market apparent in mainland Britain than might have been assumed. It is precisely this illegal market suppression effect that the Supreme Court ruling in *Macdonald v Chicago* (Supreme Court, 2010) liberalizing handgun ownership and weaponizing the city seems likely to jeopardize. Other research, studying the effect of illegal market restrictions in the USA, has shown that weapons regulations can impact the nature, quality and quantity of weapons supply, especially to young people (Braga and Kennedy, 2001), or can otherwise reduce opportunities to purchase, given that young people seldom travel outside their own communities to acquire firearms (Webster *et al.*, 2002). Restrictions can also slow down rates of inter-state weapon trafficking and extend the 'time to crime' between a weapon leaving the arena of legal transactions and entering criminal hands or turning up at crime scenes (Brandl and Stroshine, 2011). Furthermore, market restrictions, alongside ballistic tracing and intelligence gathering, could help focus policing interventions onto the more problematic of licensed firearm dealers given that the evidence shows that 'crime gun traces are highly concentrated among a few federally licensed dealers' (Pierce *et al.*, 2004).

Returning to the trends depicted in Figures 5.1 and 5.2, just as firearm advocates become unconvincing when they try to suggest that gun ownership for personal self-defense is the main influence upon crime suppression (or even a restraint upon levels of crime at all (see for example Lott, 1998; Malcolm, 2002)), it is equally unlikely that *gun supply* is the only important factor influencing levels of firearm-related violence. The USA, by virtue of the coincidence there of a substantial civilian gun market, exceptional rates of gun violence (for a developed modern society) and a preponderance of academic research, provides a useful (although not necessarily conclusive) illustration of the wider issues at stake. Amongst these issues, the factors sustaining the *demand* for criminal firearms need to be carefully explored.

What goes up, might come down, somewhere

We have seen already that the wider politics of law and order in the USA interact with a number of other influences relating to particular patterns of criminal activity and perceptions about criminal perpetrators. Especially important here have been concerns about the street distribution of drugs in deprived urban areas and the 'war on drugs' as a policy response. Such questions are closely related to the role of armed street gangs in these same urban areas, the increasingly 'institutional' (Hagedorn, 1988, 2008) hold they come to assert upon the more marginalized youth of these poorer communities and the violent and 'lethal ecologies' they are said to sustain (Fagan and Wilkinson, 1998, 2002; Wilkinson, 2003). These concerns about crime, violence and disorder are, in turn, directly related to the politicization of law and order questions that feed through into discussions of criminal justice effectiveness, policing numbers and strategies, sentencing policy and incarceration rates. In the USA, all of these issues are thoroughly shot through by a politics of race (Miller, 2008; Alexander, 2010). To put it simply, the war on drugs (Tonry, 1995), the widespread adoption of paramilitary policing tactics against gangs (the new 'enemy within') (Kraska and Kappeler, 1997; Kraska, 2001; Balko, 2006; Greene and Pranis, 2007), the (related) over-criminalization of a black underclass (Miller, 1996; Tonry, 2009), the increasing punitiveness of American culture (Garland, 2001a; Simon, 2007) and the hyper-incarceration that society continues to experience (Wacquant, 2009), the increasing problematization of youth violence of the late twentieth century (Zimring, 1998) and the unrelenting growth in both supply of and demand for guns, setting in motion the vicious circles that peaked in the early 1990s, are all systemically (socially, politically and culturally) related. In the following few paragraphs, I consider the various elements and relationships thought to be responsible for this rise and fall of gun violence even while acknowledging, with Franklin Zimring (2007) and Jock Young (2011), that explanations for these trends are hotly contested and that criminology has hardly excelled itself, thus far, in explaining such crime trend fluctuations, still less in anticipating or predicting them.

The discussion that follows, therefore, is certainly not a detailed statistical analysis of the multiple variables that may have impacted American (and, for that matter, many other) national crime profiles, but a rather more limited overview of key themes that have arisen in these debates. For, as other, even more quantitatively inclined, criminologists have noted (Rosenfeld, 2000: 157; Young, 2011), the really important changes may not be readily reducible to simple statistical computation.

A wide range of factors have been put forward to explain the rise and, subsequently, the equally spectacular fall in violent (and especially gun-involved) crime in the USA. There is little agreement, as Zimring has noted, about the most significant factors, still less about the precise sequences or combinations of influences impacting the US violent crime trends. That said, one of the key commentaries intent upon explaining the 'crime drop' of the 1990s was provided by Steven Levitt (2004) and his colleagues. He itemized ten factors, even listing them according to the frequency with which they were cited in the media.[1] Levitt divided his factors into six, which he suggested had achieved little or no impact upon the crime rate and four others that may have had *some* effect. Amongst the former he listed: the growth in the economy; demographic changes; more effective policing strategies; gun control laws; and, conversely, concealed carry laws and the increased use of capital punishment. The factors he concluded had been more influential were: increases in the number of police officers; the rising prison population; the 'receding crack epidemic'; and the legalization of abortion following the *Roe vs Wade* Supreme Court decision in 1973 (Levitt, 2004: 176–183).

Franklin Zimring has subjected these analyses to a book-length criminological critique (Zimring, 2007) and his cautionary remarks are worth noting in the present context. In the first place he warns us against the lure of the opposing siren voices of optimism and pessimism. For the latter, with echoes of Martinson from 1974, nothing much will work, criminal justice policy merely scratches the surface of entrenched social problems and, as often as not, makes things worse (not unlike Kleck's (1991) commentary on hitherto existing gun control efforts; see also Polsby, 1994) or is inappropriate for other reasons (like Jacobs's (2002) rejection of gun control as a US political priority). For the optimists, especially for those who decide, implement or take political responsibility, criminal justice policies nearly always 'work' – that is to say – the political pressure is such that new initiatives (policing strategies, tougher sentencing, gang programmes) often cannot be allowed to appear to fail. David Kennedy's fascinating account (2011) of the story of the Boston Ceasefire project and of the conflicting array of jurisdictional politics, law enforcement agency reputations and entrenched attitudes and traditions that it had to negotiate *and compete with* is ample testimony to the problems associated with taking evaluation reports at face value.

Zimring turns first to consider three relatively long-standing sets of arguments about the factors that cause crime to rise or fall: imprisonment rates, demographic changes and the state of the economy. The debate about mass incarceration and its effectiveness as crime reduction has been a major debate in the US (Garland, 2001b; Parenti, 1999), and beyond (Sim, 2009; Drake, 2012), for well over a decade. In some respects, Zimring's analysis coincides more directly with that of Wacquant (2009), by arguing that the chronology of mass incarceration does not consistently fit the crime reduction achieved while, for Wacquant in particular, the increase in US punitiveness had the character of an independent variable, driving up incarceration rates irrespective of their impact upon crime. As Zimring noted, the late 1990s were the least likely point in America's penal expansion 'to expect major crime reductions from incapacitation' (2007: 51) and he concluded by noting that few analysts credit tough penal policy with anything more than a modest impact upon the falling crime figures. Economic growth and demographic changes offer Zimring no more plausible explanations for falling violent crime, thus 'demography all by itself will never be a major explanation for crime rates dropping ... because the changes in population groups are more gradual' (2007: 62), whereas economic growth is known to be related to *some* falling crime trends but also some rising ones (Field, 1990; Hale, 1998). As Zimring notes, what is good for General Motors may also be good for cocaine sales, firearm purchases and alcohol consumption (Zimring, 2007: 65). However, the fact that falling crime in developed societies is now a truly international phenomenon adds further complications (van Dijk *et al.*, 2012); characteristics that are too nation specific may not be very transferable.

A series of more recent 'candidate explanations' for the USA's declining aggregate crime trends from the mid-1990s attracted Zimring's attention next. These included changing patterns in drug use (specifically the decline in crack cocaine use – discussed later in this chapter, changes in gun availability (whether these entailed *restrictions* resulting from gun control policies or *increased availability* following the passage of concealed carry laws) and changes in the effectiveness of offender rehabilitation programmes. As Zimring argued, part of the problem with each putative explanation was the lack of reliable, national-level data on any of the three factors that might be used to demonstrate an impact on national violent crime trends (2007: 69–70).

As might be expected, given the 'hot politics' of firearm rights in the USA, the particular question of firearm availability (for crime *or* for self-defence) resonates particularly loudly in these discussions. I have discussed these issues before (Squires, 1999, 2000: 81–86), in particular John Lott's controversial book *More Guns, Less Crime* (1998), although, it has to be said, rather earlier in the developing debate. Controversy erupted when the research study, and the basis for the book, was first published in the *Journal of Legal Studies* in early 1997. Lott's central argument neatly, although rather misleadingly, summarized in his book's title consisted in the claim asserted, directly repudiating the conventional wisdom on rates of firearm ownership and firearm-involved violence, that higher rates of gun ownership actually prevented crime. In simple terms, weapon proliferation could be a force for good, especially when any additional weaponization was overwhelmingly concentrated in the hands of 'law-abiding citizens' or, more colloquially, 'good guys'. If only it were so simple.

Defensive gun use: crime control by private armed force

The question of defensive gun use by private citizens has been one of those issues that have raised a great deal of heat in the US gun debate and yet, often, rather more questions than answers. Nevertheless, the issue stands at the interface of several arguments linking the Second Amendment and core principles of personal freedom, individual rights, safety and security, frontier 'backs to the wall' culture, public commitments to the prevention of crime and confidence in the police. Evidence of defensive gun use also forms the wellspring from which the practical justifications of 'concealed carry', 'Stand Your Ground' and 'Castle Doctrine' laws flow.

In 1991, Kleck had estimated that gun-owning citizens employ their own firearms in a defensive capacity as many as a million times a year (1991: xiii). Having reviewed a series of 'defensive gun use' surveys, by 1995 Kleck and Gertz (1995, 1997) had increased the estimate of the number of times householders had used a firearm to defend themselves against an attacker or deter a criminal attempt to between 2.1 to 2.5 million times per year. They noted that, given some 220 million guns in private ownership, then it was not implausible to suggest that around 1 per cent of these were used self-defensively in any one year. The authors also added that, based upon research respondents' own claims, anything up to 400,000 of these defensive gun uses involved a potentially life-threatening challenge – that is, the use of a gun saved a life (Kleck and Gertz, 1995). Figures such as this are obviously critical to the debate, as a significant number of defensive uses might suggest a widespread public benefit to offset the numbers of lives lost to firearms. Not only would those individuals with firearms be defending their own life, liberty and property, they would also be contributing to the common good as well, the essence of Lott's claim in *More Guns, Less Crime*. Neo-liberal market economics finds its direct parallel in unrestricted citizen gun ownership for 'rational economic man'. Armed pursuit of rational self-interests apparently makes society as a whole safer and more secure; this is not so much a case of the 'hidden hand' working for communal benefit as the hidden trigger finger. Once more, using language more conventionally employed in economic debates, Lott also suggests criticism of those 'freeloaders' who refuse to carry firearms themselves but nevertheless derive a benefit from the 'umbrella of security' provided by concealed gun carriers (Lott, 1998: 110).

However, like many evidential claims arising in the US gun debate, these claims about the numbers of defensive gun uses have been challenged by a variety of commentators, while gun owners, as a group, have been associated, not with public benefits and additional security, but with greater risks (to themselves and others) and as a source of gun supply to offenders. Other researchers, for example Hemenway (1997), have put the figure at around 55,000 defensive gun uses per year, while Cook and Ludwig (1997) suggest a figure of around 108,000 defensive gun uses. Other commentators suggest that the highest figures are too high and the lowest estimates are too low (Smith, 1997). Throughout the entire debate, however, what becomes most apparent are the ways in which, first, sampling errors and 'false positives', extrapolated into national estimates, can produce wildly varying numbers of supposed defensive firearms uses. Cook and Ludwig refer to one respondent who reported 52 defensive gun uses in a single year (1997: 8). Second, the definition of 'defensive gun use' can be highly subjective – from brandishing a gun, even shooting, at an aggressor, to simply letting another person, considered suspicious, know that you are armed. It might also involve picking up a gun and peering around the curtain on hearing a strange noise outside, perhaps a 'reassurance' gun use rather more than a defensive one. Third, it is difficult to know whether 'defensive' gun uses are reported by aggressive persons who themselves may have initiated a confrontation; we might see this kind of 'self-defensive' gun use in quite a different light. Finally, Cook and Ludwig note that self-reported data on defensive gun use suffers from a kind of 'respondent motivated bias' in which gun owners seek to vindicate their gun ownership. They cite a number of anomalous findings produced by the National Survey of Private Ownership and Use of Firearms (NSPOF). For example, they note that 'the NSPOF estimate of the number of rapes in which a woman defended herself with a firearm was higher than the total number of rapes estimated from the National Crime Victimisation Survey', while the NSPOF estimate of 130,000 offenders either killed or injured by civilian gun defenders is 'completely out of line with more reliable statistics' on gunshot death and injury (1997: 9). Perhaps it goes without saying but other commentators have challenged such criticisms (Kleck and Gertz, 1997).

Smith (1997), for one, has called for more rigorous 'validation' research to better evidence the arguments underpinning various claims about firearms, public policy, community safety and crime prevention, but it is difficult to see evidence alone resolving these issues. Facts, as they say, do not speak for themselves. The intensity with which such arguments are fought out underpins the importance that such evidence *might* have in supporting a case either for, or against, gun ownership for self-defence. Unfortunately, however, like socio-legal historical scholarship supposedly re-interpreting what the Founding Fathers 'really intended', or historical work on the numbers of firearms held by colonists in the eighteenth century, contemporary gun policies seem to have become so entrenched, in principle, that nothing so mundane or arbitrary as research evidence can be allowed to influence matters. The gun debate in the USA has become all the more ideology driven and selectively evidenced as a consequence.

Yet if extravagant estimates of defensive gun use have formed one side of a debate in which firearm advocates have sought to underpin the public policy benefits of gun ownership, researchers with a public health orientation have frequently hit back with the other – dangerous and crimogenic – side of the story. Evidence appears to show guns kept at home are often more dangerous to family members, household occupants or acquaintances than they are to would-be criminal assailants or strangers (Wintemute *et al.*, 1987; Drinan, 1990; Schwarz, 1999).

Kellerman and Reay (1986) examined 743 gunshot deaths in King County, Washington, between 1978 and 1983, concluding that keeping firearms at home is a high-risk behaviour. The risks include 'injury or death from unintentional gunshot wounds, homicide during domestic quarrels, and the ready availability of an immediate, highly lethal means of suicide' (Kellerman and Reay, 1986: 1557). Firearms were involved in the deaths of friends or acquaintances 12 times more frequently than in the case of strangers. Even excluding suicides, guns kept at home were 18 times more likely to be involved in the death of family members than in the death of strangers. Most firearm deaths in the home occurred during the course of arguments or altercations, hence easy access to firearms seemed to be especially problematic in volatile households prone to domestic violence. Overall, therefore, Kellerman and Reay found 43 suicides, criminal homicides or accidental firearm deaths involving a gun kept in the home for every case of homicide for self-protection. Later studies have also confirmed that guns kept in the home increase the risk of homicide, while providing little help in resisting criminal assailants (Kellerman, 1993). McDowell and Wiersma also found relatively few instances of successful self-defence with a firearm and concluded their own study as follows: 'Coupled with the risks of keeping a gun for protection, [our] results raise questions about the collective benefits of civilian firearm ownership for crime control' (McDowell and Wiersma, 1994).

A community in which firearms are freely available and in which citizens are armed and dangerous to one another also tends to be a community in which violent, firearm-related deaths are significantly more likely. The risks attached to widespread firearm availability are not borne equally by all members of the community. Responding to the 'innocent victim' cases of children shot and killed while playing with their parent's loaded and unlocked 'self-defence handguns' left in readiness in bedside cabinets or under mattresses, gun lobby commentators express the ambition that training programmes in responsible gun ownership should reduce the frequency of preventable domestic firearm accidents. As firearm safety advocates have argued, 'the responsible use and safe storage of any kind of firearm causes no social ill and leaves no victims' (Suter, 1994). Likewise, NRA spokesmen argue that 'good' gun owners in America are 'safe, sane and careful in the use of firearms'. However, research evidence suggests a rather more troubling picture. A significant proportion of gun owners disregard basic safety procedures. Over one-third of gun owners surveyed kept their guns loaded and over a half left them in unlocked drawers or cupboards (Hemenway and Solnick, 1995). People who owned guns for defensive purposes were most likely to keep firearms loaded and unlocked – in readiness. The presence of children in a home did tend to increase the likelihood that some safety procedures were followed but whether a gun owner had undertaken a course in safe gun handling appeared to make no difference (Weil and Hemenway, 1992). In 2000, Azrael and Hemenway reported findings of a survey in which female respondents reported on the brandishing of firearms against them in their own homes, thereby linking masculine ownership and possession of firearms in the USA with wider and more global evidence of armed domestic violence against women around the world (see Chapter 7).

A final, often overlooked, aspect of the defensive gun use debate concerns the extent to which ostensibly 'defensive' gun owners use their firearms *aggressively or illegally*. A series of studies reported by Glick (1995a, 1996, 1998) reported upon the frequency with which 'concealed carriers' used their weapons aggressively or to commit offences. The first study concluded that 'Florida's concealed weapons law puts guns into the hands of criminals'; the second study found that one year after the passage of the Florida 'concealed carry law' the rate of firearm offending by concealed carry licensees had increased by nearly 30 per cent. The third study, this time undertaken in Texas, found that during 1996–1997, after the passage of the Texas concealed carry law, nearly 950 concealed carry licensed gun owners were arrested by police (including 263 felony arrests). Apparently concealed carry licensees were arrested for weapon offences at twice the rate of non-licensees. This question of the apparent licence granted to civilian firearm owners to 'take the law into their own hands', even a delegated right to kill, carries profound echoes of vigilantism (Brown, 1975; Johnston, 1996; Abrahams, 1998; Pratten and Sen, 2007), privatized law enforcement with all its worryingly *selective* characteristics. These issues surfaced again in 2012 and exposed, once more, the racialized over-tones of the policy and practice of 'concealed carry', 'Castle Doctrine' laws or 'Stand Your Ground' principles.

Licence to kill: '… and the all-white jury agreed'

As ever, however, real world tragedies often intervene to give a powerful edge and urgency to the rarefied debates and intellectual formulations of the jurists. The fatal shooting, in February 2012, of an unarmed, African–American 17 year old, Trayvon Martin, by an armed neighbourhood watch supervisor working in a gated residential community in Florida, struck deep into the local politics of race, fear, crime and guns. The incident highlighted many of the complex issues often obscured by elite Second Amendment scholarship. The law as it is played out on the streets by real people, as it were, rather than in the reified atmosphere of court-rooms, jurists' studies and constitutional scholarship.

Trayvon Martin was apparently returning to a relative's apartment in the gated housing development when he was observed by the neighbourhood watch super-visor. Following protocol, the supervisor (George Zimmerman) reported Martin as 'a suspicious person' to the local Sanford Police Department; however, entirely contrary to protocol *and* the advice of the Sanford Police telephone dispatcher, he then followed Martin whereupon a confrontation occurred (the precise details of which are both unclear and contested) culminating in a single fatal gunshot. The police initially detained and questioned the neighbourhood watch supervisor but later released him implying that there were insufficient grounds for charges to be brought. This triggered an angry reaction from family members of Mr Martin and members of the African–American community. The resulting national con-troversy led to further inquiries undertaken by the Florida Department of Law Enforcement, the Justice Department and the FBI. In due course a decision was taken to prosecute the neighbourhood watch supervisor with second degree mur-der, an offence carrying a mandatory minimum sentence of 25 years.

Somewhat complicating the picture further, Florida Law, embracing the so-called 'Castle Doctrine' or the 'Stand Your Ground' principle did not require a person to retreat in the face of an aggressor (Brown, 1991). Around half of US states have adopted such laws, Florida introducing its own in 2005. Such laws relate closely to civilian 'concealed firearm' provisions as part of contemporary citizen self-defences against crime but, as in the present case, they are often regarded by critics as providing a screen of legitimacy for affluent white Americans who shoot first and ask questions later (Diaz, 2013) in encounters with young African–Americans. Boyle (2004: 65) provides some fascinating historical perspective to this phenomenon; racist violence, he argues, was part of a 'way of life' under the Jim Crow laws, 'whites *learned* to have hair-trigger tempers' to keep blacks in their sup-posed place. Now, perhaps instead, they just have legally protected hair-triggers. Between 2000 and 2010, over 20 US states passed similar 'Stand Your Ground' laws and in those states so-called 'justifiable homicides' increased by 8 per cent, around 600 additional killings. Furthermore, it seems that white people are signifi-cantly more successful in claiming self-defence when their attacker is black than blacks are when they defend themselves against an aggressor who is white (Cheng and Hoekstra, 2013). McClellan and Tekin's findings (2012), on the other hand, revealed that in the 18 state jurisdictions that had expanded their 'Stand Your Ground' provisions between 2005 and 2010, the increase in homicides was largely confined to white males. They concluded, therefore, that the laws did not have the 'crime deterrent' effect claimed for them and that, all things considered, the findings 'raise serious doubts against the argument that Stand Your Ground laws make America safer' (2012: 2).

According to a 2013 study of race and 'justifiable homicide' (Roman, 2013), incidents with a white perpetrator and a black victim were considered 'justifiable' in 17 per cent of cases, whereas incidents with a black perpetrator and white victim were seen as 'justifiable' only 1 per cent of the time. Similarly, white-on-black shootings were nearly three times more likely to be considered 'justified' than white-on-white shootings. This all rather suggests that juries (especially white ones) do not find it difficult to accept the claims of shooters who testify in court that they felt they needed to defend themselves against 'persons of colour'. Professor of Law at the University of Southern California, Jody Armour, argues that this perceptual bias makes 'Castle Doctrine' and 'Stand Your Ground' types of laws potentially unconstitutional on grounds of racism. He opened his own book, *Negrophobia and Reasonable Racism*, published back in 1997, describing a shooting scenario in which a non-aggressive gesture by a black male was misunderstood by a white woman, with fatal consequences.

In the 2012 Florida case, of course, the vital questions about who really was the victim and who the aggressor are contested and shifting. Undoubtedly the Castle Doctrine laws are sustained, in part at least, by prevailing racialized fears and assumptions about a criminal black underclass (Meeks, 2006), in this case, Trayvon Martin, the object of the neighbourhood watch supervisor's suspicions. On the other hand, a young black man returning home from a trip to the local convenience store, confronted and killed by an armed aggressor, might well have a much stronger claim to victim identity when facing the armed and licensed representative of public authority whose first apparent instinct, even while Martin was not engaged in any apparent criminal activity, was to profile him as suspicious: a criminal risk and a personal threat. Much to the anger and consternation of campaigners against the law and members of the African–American community at large, the predominantly white jury trying the case eventually decided to acquit the defendant.

While the Trayvon Martin/George Zimmerman case, no doubt for its 'innocence aspect', has received the most media attention, other significant cases expose further potential repercussions of the Stand Your Ground laws. In 2007, for example, a 61-year-old Houston man, Joe Horn, became an NRA *cause célèbre* after he confronted two black men leaving his neighbour's property following a break-in. The parallels with the Martin case are significant. Having called 911 to alert the police, Horn, contrary to the explicit instructions of the police dispatcher, went out to confront the two men armed with a pump action shotgun. Before doing so he remarked to the dispatcher that he would shoot the men: 'I ain't going to let them go … I have a right to protect myself too, sir. The laws have been changed in this country since September the first, and you know it.' In Horn's case, however, the right to 'stand his ground' turned into an apparent 'right to confront' as the Harris County Grand Jury refused to agree the indictment brought against Horn for double homicide. Another incident occurred in Louisiana in February 2012, when a 21-year-old man fired into a moving SUV, killing one 15-year-old boy and injuring a 17 year old. A drug transaction broke down into a dispute and the boys quickly drove away, the shooter firing into the departing vehicle. It was initially suggested that the boys in the vehicle were armed but police found no firearms. A Grand Jury refused to indict the shooter, although the surviving boys were charged with drug and gang offences.

Finally, in March 2012, a 20-year-old man was shot and killed by a Wisconsin householder on whose front porch he was hiding. The man had been evading police officers who had responded to a noise complaint concerning an underage drinking party taking place nearby. A new Wisconsin 'intruders law' empowers householders to shoot trespassers provided they can show that their use of deadly force was 'reasonable'; prior to the new law householders could only employ potentially deadly force if they perceived their own lives to be at risk. What all these cases have in common, however, is the set of perceptions they carry about race and class and, in particular, who, apparently, can shoot whom, with relative impunity on the basis of contestable assumptions about violent crime, gangs and African–American communities. However, the direction of travel – from slavery and Jim Crow and, now, apparently, to 'open season' – has been made possible by the weaponized self-defence ethos that has become part of neo-liberal law and order politics, especially, but not exclusively, in North America.

The controversy ignited by such cases obviously polarizes around issues of race, crime, violence and safety. An opinion poll study published in the wake of the Trayvon Martin killing found clear evidence of the 'racial gradient' theory in matters of public opinion on law and order and concluded that 'the "racial divide" in public opinion is alive and well' (Gabbidon and Jordan, 2013: 13). Black people were far more disinclined to accept the allegedly 'justified' premise on which the shooting was based or confident that the criminal justice system would right the perceived wrongs. It also reawakened wider community concerns about a historic racial bias in police shootings and the police use of force (see for example Fyfe, 1988; Sparger and Giacopassi, 1992; Plant and Peruche, 2005; Payne, 2006; Correll *et al.*, 2007; Lloyd, 2012), and the prior existence of so-called 'fleeing felon' laws (a police officer's right to shoot a 'fleeing felon') which once appeared to contribute to the disproportionate risk of black offenders being shot by police officers relative to either their proportion in the local population or their arrest rate (Sparger and Giacopassi, 1992). Such laws, and the police and crime control practices still deriving from them, appear to delegate the power to kill to armed whites while perpetuating racialized suspicion (or perhaps 'racialized common sense'; Haney-Lopez, 2003; Fleury-Steiner *et al.*, 2009), mistrust and discrimination (and the patterns of civilian self-armament which follow). They represent one of the ways in which the gun question crosscuts the politics of race in contemporary America.

Such racialized attitudes are clear reactions to the ways in which dominant traditions in crime reporting define urban crime problems 'in terms of "thugs", "super predators", "gangsters" and other racialised code words for the inhabitants of "criminalised spaces"' (Fleury-Steiner *et al.*, 2009: 7). So when fearful white self-defence gun owners vote for tough law and order, or re-join, once more, the queue at the gun store, they are (simply?) but personally and viscerally re-committing to the war against crime 'aggressively waged against the threatening outsiders (poor, non-whites) and their disorderly territories (ghettos, barrios etc.)' (Fleury-Steiner *et al.*, 2009: 7). Carlson, for example, cites research that shows that 'white Detroit males who espouse racist views are also more likely to own firearms for self-protection against crime' (2012: 1115). Carlson goes further, suggesting that 'guns are socially deployed to express anxieties among white, male, conservative gun owners ... [providing] a means for white, conservative heterosexual men to reclaim masculine privilege as part of a broader conservative "backlash" against New Deal politics' (2012: 1115–1116); see also Melzer, 2009).[2] Furthermore, as Allen has acknowledged in her insightful ethnographic study of the NRA as a campaign organization, even while the firearm death and injury rate is considerably higher for African–Americans (especially young males), with homicide the leading cause of death for black males aged between 15–17 (handguns accounting for 78 per cent of these killings), black households are significantly less likely to contain firearms (Forjuoh *et al.*, 1996). The NRA also remains a largely white-dominated organization (C. Allen, 2006). However, most gun control lobby organizations, in particular, in Allen's study, the 'Million Mom March', were themselves also largely white dominated, 'responding to incidents of gun violence whose victims are not black', typically discussing urban gun violence in terms that were, almost always, racially coded (C. Allen, 2006: 222–223; Miller, 2008). These issues assume a further significance, as we have seen, when we reflect upon the ways in which different types of gun violence incident galvanise gun control initiatives.

Guns and the 'crime drop' enigma

Returning to Lott's arguments about the impact of gun ownership on crime rates, three propositions seem sufficient to capture his argument: 'allowing citizens to carry concealed handguns reduces violent crimes' (1998: 15), 'mass shootings in public places are reduced when law-abiding citizens are allowed to carry concealed handguns' (1998: 19) and permissive 'concealed carry' laws are 'the most cost effective means of reducing crime' (1998: 159). In the years after the book's publication the title – as slogan – became something of a mantra for gun lobbyists. As was noted over a decade ago (Squires, 1999), Lott concerns himself exclusively with firearms carried by law abiding citizens, in other words, '*good guns* owned by good people in areas with strongly established and "civilising" gun cultures' (1999: 320). He appeared less willing to acknowledge the crime facilitation effect of widespread gun availability in deprived, high-crime, troubled or socially disrupted areas or the slippage of guns from the hands of the law abiding and into the possession of the more criminally inclined. Lott's position was famously reiterated, some 15 years later and by Wayne La Pierre, Executive Vice-President of the NRA. La Pierre laid out the NRA position on school safety policy, 'the only way to stop a bad guy with a gun is a good guy with a gun' (see Stroud, 2012). In the wake of the Trayvon Martin killing, and the fatally accumulating legacy of the new 'Stand Your Ground' laws, such simple 'good guy – bad guy' illusions are a poor foundation for public safety policy.

Subsequently, Lott's methodology, analyses and conclusions have been found wanting by a wide range of academics and commentators. As Ayres and Donohue noted, 'their results have not withstood the test of time' (2003: 1296). Rebuttal of the argument, however, has done little to staunch the vigour with which Lott and many other gun rights enthusiasts have continued to assert it. Amongst the criticisms developed of the work are concerns about the timing and location of the analysis (very soon after the first concealed carry laws were introduced in untypical states which were already high in gun ownership) (Ayres and Donohue, 1999); the questionable search for a single-factor explanation of complex social changes delivering falling crime trends (Zimring, 2007); lack of attention to *illegal* firearm possession (Sugarman, 2001); the failure to show that increasing numbers of concealed carry permits had any relation to increasing numbers of actual weapons owned or carried (Duggan, 2001); and theoretical questions regarding Lott's rationalist conception of deterrence (Squires, 1999). Black and Nagin went further, undertaking a re-analysis of Lott's own data, and concluding that the particular selection of non-typical US states skewed his findings. They noted that

> the seemingly salutary impacts of Right to Carry (RTC) laws on murder and rape depend entirely on the data for Florida. Without Florida in the sample, there is no detectable impact for these two crimes ... [the] results cannot be used responsibly to formulate [national] public policy.
>
> *(Black and Nagin, 1998: 218–219)*

Ayres and Donohue (2003) make a similar point, noting that Florida and Texas both passed RTC laws in response to significant upsurges in violent crime and that 'as crime reverted of its own accord to its normal levels, the regression inappropriately attributed this reversion to the passage of the [new RTC laws]' (2003: 1287).

Ludwig (1998) drew particular attention to the discrepancy in age-related firearm offending, noting that, because juveniles were not permitted to carry concealed firearms in any of the states with RTC laws, any deterrent benefits of these laws ought to be concentrated amongst adults, whereas, in fact, his analysis suggested that the 'shall-issue laws have resulted, if anything, in an *increase* in adult homicide rates' (Ludwig, 1998: 239). Furthermore, as the data in Figures 5.6 and 5.7 indicate, both the rapid increase and, subsequently, the equally rapid decline in firearm violence are largely concentrated amongst those aged under 18 and African–Americans, neither group being foremost amongst concealed carry licence holders. Donohue agrees, 'the overwhelming story that leaps out ... is that most states experienced *increases* in crime from the "shall issue" laws' (2003: 324). However, even though the very raison d'être for the scholarship discussed here is precisely to provide sound evidence for better public policy-making, the political processes have proven relatively impervious. If ever there were a case of the evidence failing to spoil a good story, the self-defence gun ownership story is probably it. In other words, to anticipate the argument, culture rather than social science or evidence might seem to be the really influential factor in social life and change. But before developing this point, we need to conclude our consideration of Zimring's *Great American Crime Decline* factors.

The final sequence of factors often put forward to account for the US crime drop and to which Zimring gives his attention – police strategies and deployments, the rise and fall of crack cocaine and the legalisation of abortion after 1973 – were all, as we have seen, cited by Levitt (2004). Zimring addresses them, as he puts it, 'in increasing order of novelty' (2007: 73). He begins an assessment of the policing evidence in the wake of a discussion of Bayley's (1994) argument regarding the 'myth of the police' in which the author established how research had 'consistently failed to find any connection between the numbers of police and crime rates' and likewise how 'the primary strategies adopted by modern police have been shown to have little or no effect on crime' (Bayley, 1994, cited in Zimring, 2007: 75). In the wake of a veritable onslaught of police science and policing advocacy research claiming to show how, from *broken windows* and *problem-oriented policing* to *zero tolerance*, policing might now make an impact, Zimring concedes that the 1990s may, indeed, be different and proceeds to assess the evidence relating to the police contribution to the US crime drop. He cites a meta-analysis of 41 policing studies by Eck and Maguire (2000) which found that 'police strength' (numbers) had no impact on crime in 55 per cent of the analyses, a positive impact in 15 per cent and a negative impact (that is, extra officers appeared to generate *more* crime recording) in 30 per cent of the studies. Turning to the quality of policing, and policing strategies, Zimring acknowledges that the story here is especially dominated by the so-called 'New York miracle' (Bowling, 1999; Karmen, 2000; Young, 2011: 111–130) in which crime, in seven major offence categories, fell by between 52 per cent and 73 per cent during the 1990s and serious crime dropped by three-quarters in 15 years (Zimring, 2007: 137). Unfortunately, while he acknowledges that the substantial re-engineering of New York City policing may have contributed to something 'between a quarter and a half' of the New York crime drop,[3] it is extremely difficult to draw such conclusions for crime reduction across the USA as a whole. The major reason for such reticence concerns the organization of policing itself, which is 'decentralised into thousands of local departments, including hundreds of city departments' and jurisdictions (2007: 80), making it highly unlikely that national level changes in policing strategies will have impacted over the relatively short duration of the US crime drop.

Zimring turns next to the 'crack epidemic' argument. In the following section, I discuss the ways in which street-level crack distribution markets impacted especially the African–American community and, in particular, the street level violence within which its youth became embroiled (see Figures 5.5 and 5.6). At this point, I merely note Zimring's observation that the rapid rises in criminal violence, often associated with the crack epidemic of the late 1980s and early 1990s (Blumstein and Wallman, 2000) from 1993–1994, turn sharply into significant decreases, though not just in gun violence, but in a wide range of other, seemingly unrelated, offence types as well. In other words, crack's role might be considerable in sparking gun violence amongst young African–Americans living in deprived urban communities, which already had inflated rates of violence. As the crack epidemic receded and while rates of violence have since fallen, those same communities still have grossly inflated gun violence profiles.

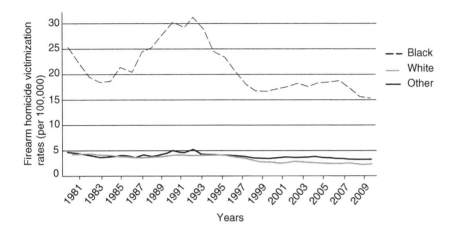

FIGURE 5.5 Firearm homicide victimization rates (per 100,000) by race, 1981–1999

Sources: Planty and Truman (2013); US Department of Justice; US National Vital Statistics data (WISQARS).

Note: In this graph 'other' comprises an aggregate for Hispanic, American–Indian/Alaskan and Asian/Pacific.

Zimring finally turns to the 'most novel' of the explanations offered up for the crime drop. It concerns what he terms the 'abortion policy crime reduction dividend'. Put simply, the arguments made by a number of commentators (Donohue and Levitt, 2001; Levitt and Dubner, 2005) comprise the suggestion that the legalization of abortion policy from 1973 effectively prevented the birth of a significant number of potentially high crime risk babies, who, in due course, would likely grow into career offenders. The invidious assumptions here, translated into research factors, entailed that 'teenagers, unmarried women and the economically disadvantaged' (the latter also being a proxy variable for 'race') would be more likely to seek abortions. As Zimring shows, however, there were no birth rate declines in these 'most risky' population groups, and he concludes, therefore, that the available evidence 'is not strongly supportive of abortion dividends' for crime reduction (2007: 102).

Having dispensed with this catalogue of contending explanations for the US crime drop, Zimring also looks northwards to Canada, acknowledging that there are 'extraordinary parallels in timing, breadth and magnitude between the crime declines of the USA and Canada' (2007: 132). For that matter we might also include the crime reductions in the wider world (van Dijk *et al.* 2012), Europe (Aebi and Lind, 2012), Australia and New Zealand (Mayhew, 2012) and other non-westernized societies (del Frate and Mugellini, 2012). The global character of the 'crime drop' phenomenon would throw doubt upon the significance of any single society changes (such as US abortion laws, US gun policies (liberal or restrictive) or changes in sentencing policies, police numbers, deployments or strategies).

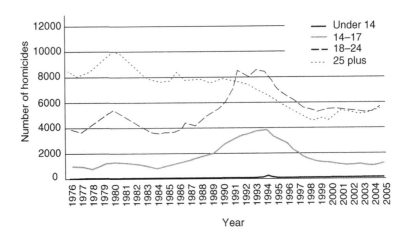

FIGURE 5.6 Firearm homicides by age of offender, 1976–2005

Source: Department of Justice, Bureau of Justice Statistics.

The evidence suggests, Zimring argues, that the crime drop phenomenon does not have 'discrete policy or economic causes' (2007: 133), so we might usefully direct our gaze towards a number of more general social and cultural changes.[4]

So we arrive at what Young describes as the 'enigma of the crime drop' (2011: 113), which the blinkered positivism of much American social science has encountered such difficulty in explaining. Young describes himself perplexed by Zimring's failure to discern the social and cultural changes, cultural changes *behind* the crime drop story, 'hyperpluralism', globalization, immigration and the 'increased feminization of the public sphere' which shape crime *responses* just as much as they shape crime itself. As Young notes, 'the inability of social science to predict the future is legendary' (2011: 127), and we have been here before. For example, Zimring's ill-fated prediction in 1981 that 'the next thirty years will bring a national handgun strategy' (Zimring, 1981, in Squires, 2000: 63). He penned this prediction on the very eve of the dramatic increases in gun violence encountered during the 1980s and before the de facto national firearm liberalization strategy inaugurated by the NRA, in the 'concealed carry' states. This firearm liberalization was itself a response to the culture of fear resulting from rapidly increasing crime and disorder and sharpening racial tensions. Having been trumped by cultural changes once, Zimring has become a little more cautious but still concludes his discussion with the observation that 'the most important lesson of the 1990s was that major social changes in rates of crime can happen without major social changes in the social fabric' (2007: 206).[5] And yet, this very decade, which geared up its 'war on crime' (Simon, 2007) and deployed its punitive language (Steinert, 2004), the consequences of which have been painstakingly elaborated by Wacquant and others (Wacquant, 2001, 2009; Pratt *et al.*, 2005), experienced many major social and cultural changes. I have already begun to suggest just how much of this war on

crime is shot through with an implicit politics of race, victimization and gun violence (see Tonry, 1995, 2009; Miller, 2008); it is now time to develop these points.

Young, victimized and black

As the earlier comments have suggested and as Figure 5.5 clearly shows, whatever
'drivers' were influencing the sharp upsurge in firearm-related violence in the USA
in the critical years between the mid-1980s and the mid-1990s, these were especially significant for African–American communities. It is equally clear that changes
affecting these same communities are equally relevant to the sharp decline in gun-
related violence between 1993 and the end of the twentieth century. Except that
this decline has not been sustained, the gap between rates of white and black gun
violence victimization has not closed and the latest evidence points to an increasing
racial polarization of gunshot victimization.

It would appear that if we are to understand the rise and fall of American gun
violence during these critical years it is, above all, the particular social and cultural changes impacting especially within the black community that we need to
explore. It should not to be overlooked, however, that some commentators (King,
1997) also relate this 'black violence' phenomenon to African–American historical experiences of 'chattel slavery, institutional racism, and intransigent poverty
and economic deprivation' (1997: 80). Yet, much as the historical experience of
black Americans is deeply scoured by these extremes of institutionalized violence
(Wacquant, 2001), as in Garland's critique of American cultural exceptionalism
and urban white America's relatively recent resort to the self-defence handgun, our
concern is not so much with the *overall* racial profile of twentieth-century criminal
violence and victimization in the USA but rather with the steep apparent fluctuations in this weaponized violence during the 1980s and 1990s.

Figure 5.5 details only the disproportionate rise and fall of gun violence victimization by skin colour until 1999; but ten years later in 2009 the homicide rate for black
teenagers was still over 18 times the rate for white teenagers, and double the rate for
Hispanic teenagers (Child Trends, 2010). Kennedy (2011) also makes the point that
even as the country, not to mention a number of key cities, have celebrated the crime
drop as a national success story, falling homicide and declining overall rates of gun violence, young black men are still 'dying more'. Even as gun homicide fell for whites,

> black men are dying, overwhelmingly by gunshot, at a horrendous pace …
> between 2000 and 2007 the gun homicide rate for black men aged fourteen
> to seventeen went up 40 per cent; eighteen to twenty four, up 18 per cent;
> twenty five and over, up almost 27 per cent.
>
> *(Kennedy, 2011: 12)*

Developing the picture, Braga (2003) provides complementary evidence of the
youthful nature of firearm-involved violence (see Figure 5.6). For example,
between 1984 and 1994 juvenile homicides (offenders aged under 18) committed

with handguns increased by 418 per cent, although adolescents (those aged 14–17) had the largest proportional increase in homicide *commission and victimization*, whereas young adults (aged 18–24) experienced the largest numerical increase. Furthermore, he adds, 'there was much crossfire between the two age groups'. The point underscores findings reported in respect of gang-related youth violence in the UK by Bullock and Tilley (2002) and highlighted by Pitts (2007b, 2008), that there is a substantial *social symmetry* between perpetrators and victims of gun violence. The point is reiterated in Ander *et al*.'s study of *Gun Violence Among School-Age Youth in Chicago*: 'Both victims and offenders are disproportionately likely to be young African American males; to come from poor, single-parent households; and to hail from some of the city's most disadvantaged neighborhoods' (2009: 2), and they go on to identify further factors – drug and alcohol misuse, mental health problems and especially school failure – that compound the problems associated with being young and black and poor in contemporary America (even as these issues throw up opportunities for potential intervention).

Taken together, these findings point to the issue of young people's involvement in gangs as a particular driver of risks associated with criminalization and victimization: nearly three-quarters of homicides of teens are attributed to gang violence (Finkerhor and Ormrod, 2001, Kennedy, 2011). Braga also argues that: 'Youth gun violence is concentrated among feuding gangs and criminally active groups' (2003: 5), even though employing the constructed notion of 'the gang' brings considerable conceptual and ideological baggage into play (Hagedorn, 1988; Hallsworth and Young, 2008), and the notion of 'gang-related' violence itself also begs many questions. What, exactly, is the 'gang relation'? Braga acknowledges, in common with Fagan and Wilkinson's New York study (1998, 2000), that most gun violence is not related to drug dealing or other gang-involved 'commercial interests' but rather resulted from 'relatively long-standing gang feuds' or involved issues of identity, respect, reputation, hierarchy or girlfriends. Despite this, he continues to deploy the phrase, for example, he notes, 'in Minneapolis, nearly two-thirds of youth murders between 1994 and 1997 were gang-related' (Braga, 2003; Kennedy, 2011: 40,104).

When two young men draw and shoot firearms in an altercation, their past or present gang affiliations are frequently employed to define the violent incident as 'gang related' even though their particular dispute may have nothing to do with gangs. For example, the fact that they may both be unemployed, has never (apparently) generated a concept of 'unemployment-related violence'. In the case of notions of 'gang-related violence', however, a cultural identifier (gang culture) derived from an essentially qualitative and ethnographic understanding of the contexts, meanings and purposes of behaviour is wrenched free of its surroundings and stretched and fitted to serve as the only meaningful account of weaponized conflict, thereby setting aside other, potentially quite plausible, acceptable and mainstream explanations: masculinity, honour, fear, American vigilantism, Hollywood role models, weapon facilitation effects. As an explanation, 'gang culture', released from its origins and moorings in the gang, has similarly been employed (although not without contestation: Hallsworth and Brotherton, 2011; Squires, 2011a) to explain the British 2011 riots (HM Government, 2011, 2012). Relatively few of the arrested rioters (10–15 per cent) were said to be 'gang affiliated' but 'gang culture' was blamed. The significance of this attribution of crime and violence – and, in the present discussion, firearm use in particular – to gang membership, gang affiliations or 'gang culture' is that it locates the problem firmly with the gang itself (treated as an independent and uncontested 'clean' variable), while requiring that we look no further. Gang members are violent because they are gang members; they carry weapons to protect themselves from other violent gang members. Simple criminality indeed. In the process attention is drawn away from the factors (poverty, unemployment, social and political marginality, lack of opportunity, racism – the underclass life) that produce the gang as a means of social, economic and psychological adjustment (indeed, for some a solution) to deprived and hostile circumstances (Thrasher, 1927; Hagedorn, 2008).

Despite their use of an 'epidemic' concept of youth violence, with guns playing the role of a 'virus' 'initiating, sustaining, and elevating the epidemic of youth violence' (Fagan and Wilkinson, 1998: 1; see also 2000: 1–2, 7–2), Fagan and Wilkinson helpfully describe the situational contexts of gun misuse in a fascinating study of weapon-involved violence in New York (1998, 2000). In particular their notion of the 'lethal ecology' of the disadvantaged inner city where many young men live explains the adaptations they make and the behaviours they adopt (gun carrying included) in order to safeguard themselves. The researchers interviewed active, former or incarcerated gun offenders in different New York locations, employing a narrative analysis in order to develop an understanding of both the facilitators and inhibitors of shootings. In other words, what, during or surrounding an altercation, led young men to draw their guns and shoot or, conversely, what was it about the context and dynamic of an altercation that led to the incident being resolved without resorting to potentially lethal violence. Fully two-thirds of the altercations described by the authors were prompted by 'identity, status or "respect" issues' (see also Stretesky and Pogrebin, 2007). It is worth noting that police involvement seldom had much impact upon the course of most of the incidents; respondents described the police as usually not there when they were needed most and typically unhelpful when they were present. Furthermore, encounters with the police were generally described as 'hostile, abusive and oppressive' and, to compound matters, cooperation with the police was viewed as disloyalty to the street and likely to attract retribution (Fagan and Wilkinson, 2000: 118).

Fagan and Wilkinson deployed their ecological perspective to understand the violence patterns identified in the incident narratives described to them. They argued that the behavioural adaptations made by their respondents were seen as necessary adjustments in order to survive when 'living in a war zone' and, as they recognize, the stark reality of such a life 'shapes attitudes, perceptions, behaviour, and social identity' (2000: 6–i). The important point about this 'lethal ecology' is that it is rooted in a cultural context, explaining behaviour produced (maybe co-produced) in that context. As Pogrebin *et al.* note, 'in street gang culture … the gun [is] a potent symbol of power and a ready remedy for all manner of conflicts and disputes' (2009: 20). But this does not mean that gun violence everywhere is 'gang related' any more or any less than it is always 'poverty related' or 'racism related'. What it does show, consistent with a tradition of gang research stretching back to Thrasher (1927) and the Chicago School, is that gang violence and shootings are a product of the American ghettos and, now, following Wacquant (2009), the hyper-ghetto: they are truly 'Born in the USA'.

Malcolm Klein (1995) shows that between the early 1960s and the mid-1990s serious criminal gang activities were being identified in more and more US cities. In 1961, 54 cities reported significant gang crime problems, a decade later it was 94 cities, and by 1980, 172 cities. During the 1980s the figure more than quadrupled, with 766 cities reporting 'serious gang problems'. This gang context reflects the racialized and age-delineated patterns of criminal firearm violence and victimization we have already seen and to this picture we must also add the wave of illegal crack cocaine distribution across America's cities which itself prompted the Reagan era 'war on drugs' (Inciardi, 1986) and the rolling out of tough policing interventions and disproportionate sentencing strategies (Alexander and Gyamerah, 1997) targeting the youthful black populations of urban America.

According to Grogger and Willis (2000: 528), comparing crime data from 27 metropolitan areas in the US, 'the arrival of crack cocaine led crime to rise substantially in the late 1980s and early 1990s' and this was especially significant as regards aggravated (weapon-involved) assault. Many commentators discuss the prevalence of crack cocaine use in black areas (Kennedy, 2011) and especially the role of street gangs in low-level drug distribution, as Joseph and Pearson remark:

> [M]any of the Black youths who sell drugs are from an inner-city economic structure with high unemployment, underemployment, and joblessness and where [the] 'juvenilization of poverty' prevails. The meager wages earned in unskilled jobs at fast food restaurants are, therefore, not as attractive to an inner-city youth who can make much more money from selling drugs. The crack-cocaine trade provides many inner-city youths with job opportunities.
>
> *(2002: 425)*

Yet while the 'crack wave' itself has often been credited in the media with promoting the high rates of urban violence reflected in the steep gun crime increases of the 1980s (Reinarman and Levine, 1997), other commentators relate the rising violence to urban political economy and especially the profound social exclusion, poverty and destabilization of communities. As Adler and Adler have noted,

> the circumstances surrounding and framing the behavior of [crack] users is more desperate and disenfranchised than found in previous drug scenes. This is related ... to the increasingly polarized distribution of income and resources, to the diminished and ineffective nature of treatment programs and facilities, and to the senseless nature of our government's recent drug policies.
>
> *(1993: 951; see also Blumstein, 1995)*

According to Kennedy, '[c]rack blew through America's poor black neighbourhoods like the Four Horsemen of the Apocalypse had traded their steeds for supercharged bulldozers' (2011: 10) and although different commentators across the social sciences have, more or less, emphasized different features of the phenomenon, Blumstein (1995) has captured many of the key characteristics of the urban crack market and its lethal consequences for inner city black communities. To begin, crack dealing was often a lower-priced, frequent-transaction, street-based activity in African–American communities. This rendered it both more visible and territorial and more readily targeted by the police; recruitment of juveniles was also facilitated by this neighbourhood visibility but also especially because of limited employment opportunities in the legitimate economy (Inciardi *et al.*, 1993). In turn visibility and territoriality gave rise to 'turf' disputes which prompted young men to arm themselves 'for protection' (and also to rob other dealers). The processes, occurring here in a developed modern context, are not unlike the consequences of weaponization described in less developed, second or third world, societies (discussed in Chapter 7). Increasing violence and perceived vulnerability facilitate the growth of a more widespread culture of youth gun carrying as firearms became 'diffused' to

> other teenagers who walked the same streets … because possession of a weapon may become a means of status-seeking in the community. This initiated an escalating process: as more guns appear in the community, the incentive for any single individual to arm himself increased.
>
> *(Blumstein, 1995: 30)*

As Kennedy put it, 'kids not involved in the drug trade were getting, carrying, and using guns because their world had become so objectively dangerous' (2011: 29). Research by Sheley and Wright (1993b) confirmed this picture, almost one-quarter of the young, urban-living people they surveyed carried a gun *some* of the time and gave 'personal protection' as their major reason.[6] More recently Pogrebin and his colleagues (2009: 83–91) found that protection-based arguments continued to dominate young men's explanations for gun carrying, although the more criminally involved these young people were, the more likely they were to attribute gun carrying to maintaining power and authority. This is often explained in terms of the 'recklessness and bravado' often typical of young men and, not least, the highly masculinized cultures of identity and 'respect' to which they belonged (Bourgois, 2003, Mullins, 2006) and their lack of maturity or relatively limited social skills for settling disputes other than through violence. Wacquant, however, insists on a contextual understanding of this violence for 'everyone must protect themselves from violence by being ready to wield it at any time' (2008a: 69). It is not surprising, therefore, that conflicts often result in high and self-perpetuating rates of retaliatory gun violence, in a 'grotesque theatre of aggressive masculinity on whose stage violent confrontation serves as the currency of honour' (Wacquant, 2008a: 211), particularly so as these young men generally mistrusted the police and certainly did not see them as a solution to their difficulties.

Such attitudes were substantially exacerbated by cultural socialization issues associated with high levels of poverty, high rates of single parenthood and family disorganization, educational failure, joblessness, economic hopelessness, racism and discrimination – not to mention police enforcement actions themselves (Kennedy, 2011). For, as Wacquant has argued, the police themselves are both feared and mistrusted, not because they represent the secular arm of law and state but because 'they are an additional vector of violence and insecurity' (Wacquant, 2008a: 129; Brunson, 2007).

Accordingly, even as overall gun-related homicide has fallen significantly across the USA, it has remained stubbornly persistent in the US hyper-ghettos and amongst the marginalized African–American communities resident there; just as it has in other parts of the world where rapid social changes, exacerbated by the ravages of neo-liberalism and weaponization, are most keenly felt. Places where unregulated gun supplies are most prevalent and where young men experience the worst of – and see the least to gain from – mainstream legitimate economic opportunities. Instead, these armed and angry young men become immersed instead in gangs, groups and associations and often fundamentally brutalizing illegal economies (Squires, 2012). It is not that these contexts are necessarily always *only* criminal and abusive, they also represent safety in numbers, resistance, community defence, political mobilization, economic lifeline and social solidarity and, sometimes, also contexts of terrorist radicalization (Nightingale, 1995; Anderson, 1999; Venkatash, 2006; Hagedorn, 2008; Kahn, 2010) as we shall see in Chapter 7. Yet the combination of poverty, criminal networks, an oversupply of firearms and oppressive (often paramilitary, often unaccountable) styles of policing are seldom conducive to the fostering of peaceful and orderly communities (Brunson, 2007; Kennedy, 2011).

Yet despite the headline issue, that the overall levels of firearm homicide have fallen in the USA, some of the most violent gun crime hotspots in the world remain the derelicted centres or depressed suburbs of America's cities (Binelli, 2013). A direct consequence of these growing inequalities and what Currie (1997) terms the 'progressive destruction of livelihood' is the fragmentation of community and the production of social insecurities, the seedbeds from which conflict and violence grow (Currie, 2005). In Chapter 1, we saw how Wilkinson and Pickett (2010) detailed these vicious circles – breakdowns of trust, mutuality and of community – and their relationship to rising violence and homicide. Wacquant (2009) has similarly described the rolling back of welfare and the criminalization of poverty, contrasting the insularity of affluent and white communities with marginalized poor and black ones. Few of the benefits of community crime reduction have trickled down to the 'dark ghettoes' (Wacquant, 2008a).

So it is really no surprise that, as McWhirter and Fields, writing in the *Wall St. Journal* (2012) remark, 'killings remain stubbornly high in the poorest pockets of cities large and small. In some cases, the rate is rising sharply'. Furthermore, 'because black-on-black violence tends to stay concentrated within poorer, inner-city areas, there is a lack of wider awareness of the depth of the problem'. As the rest of America celebrated its 'Great American crime decline', 94 per cent of black murder victims were being killed by other black males. Indeed, it is suggested that one of the reasons for the killing of Trayvon Martin in 2012 being particularly newsworthy (aside from the way it put Florida's 'Stand Your Ground' law in the national spotlight) was the fact that Martin was killed by a non-black shooter. Philadelphia's Police Commissioner Charles Ramsey noted, somewhat dismissively, 'nobody would even know the name Trayvon Martin if it had been a black kid who shot [him]' (cited in McWhirter and Fields, 2012). A Chicago police officer interviewed rather earlier by Wacquant likewise commented on the essential anonymity of the black gunshot victims: 'we have murders on a daily basis that never make the news. No-one really knows or cares' (Wacquant, 2008a: 210), leading Wacquant to reflect on the finding that (while homicide rates are generally regarded as amongst the firmest of criminological data) 'an unknown but not negligible number of homicides committed in the ghetto are not reported, even to the police, because the bodies do not turn up or because residents fail to inform authorities ... for fear of reprisals or judicial complications' (Wacquant, 2008a: 210, n17). Even when the crimes are reported and the victims found, the media, as Diaz (2013) has discovered, often fail to report them. Gunshot victims, especially black ones, are no longer newsworthy.

A paper by Fox and Swatt (2008), academics from Northeastern University, Boston, found that the proportion of homicides involving a firearm had increased since 2000, especially for young black offenders. The percentage of firearm homicides for black offenders aged less than 18 reached nearly 85 per cent by 2007. Similarly, between 2002 and 2007, the number of gun homicides involving young black male perpetrators increased by 47 per cent while homicides involving black male juveniles as victims grew by 54 per cent. The authors attribute these rising rates of gun violence to a combination of: political complacency (following the violence reductions beginning in the 1990s); changing priorities (after 9/11, 'much of the federal support for law enforcement shifted from hometown security and patrolling high crime neighborhoods to homeland security in protecting the nation's transportation, government and financial centers'); budget cuts (federal support for law enforcement, after-school projects, youth diversion and community crime prevention programmes have, they argue, 'been slashed' in the economic downturn since the beginning of the decade, see Lichtblau, 2004); and, finally, reflecting the NRA war of attrition against gun control, politically motivated legislative restrictions, upon the ATF undertaking and disseminating gun tracing information alongside other pro-gun legislation passed by Congress has, they suggest, made it more difficult for police agencies to identify and intercept illegal supplies of crime guns. They conclude, 'a triple whammy at the federal level – related to cops, guns and kids – has hampered proven strategies for crime control' (Fox and Swatt, 2008: 5). Like many other critical commentators (Miller, 2008; Wacquant, 2009; Gilligan, 2011) they advocate a return to proven strategies of social crime prevention rather than the vicious cycle of failing neo-liberal populist punitiveness and bumper-sticker rhetoric which, while it may win votes, does little to address the problems of crime and violence even as it further marginalizes the most deeply deprived and victimized communities.

The sharp increase (by 31 per cent) in African–American homicide victimization in New York in 2010 accounted for nearly all of the city's 14 per cent increase in murder that year, accounting for over two-thirds of the 536 New York murders in that year. Black men aged 15–29 years old were most likely to be the victims. This group comprises less than 3 per cent of the city's population but in 2010 accounted for 33 per cent of all homicide victims (Gardiner, 2011). Evidence of this nature reinforces an important reassessment of US crime data. It is not, as Fox and Swatt argue, that the crime figures tell an incorrect story about crime trends in contemporary America, but rather that 'they obscure the divergent tale of two communities – one prosperous and safe, the other poor and crime-ridden' (2008: 1). Evidence of these increasingly discrepant and unequal rates of violent victimization had also been uncovered by Klofas and his colleagues (2005) in their Rochester, NY, study. Rates of gun-involved violence and homicide had escalated even during the 'great American crime drop', they were concentrated amongst African–American males, had a strong 'group connection', with 37 per cent of the killings involving multiple assailants, one-quarter were linked to illegal drug dealing and fully two-thirds of them said to be spurred on by 'group dynamics'. The research presented a picture very similar to the 'lethal ecology' described by Fagan and Wilkinson (1998, 2000), the homicide rate for young black men (aged 15–19) in the research area was 65 times the national rate. In turn, this more specifically neighbourhood-based appreciation of the concentration of gun-involved violence has also contributed to new conceptions of localized public safety strategies and interventions (Kennedy, 2011). This has also involved greater attention to the particular workings of localized underground and illegal gun markets (Cook *et al.*, 2007) where both pragmatic gun control at the policy level (Ludwig and Cook, 2003) and targeted enforcement and deterrence in the neighbourhood (Braga and Pierce, 2005; Kennedy, 2011) can achieve some positive impacts – when not undermined by other (legal or statutory) developments. Certainly such initiatives have a far better purchase upon the gun crime problems of deprived US neighbourhoods than the rote sound-bites of much contemporary gun rights advocacy.

Overall, the evidence referred to above has brought two central themes of the US debates about gun violence to the fore. On the one hand, connecting with the themes in the earlier pages of this chapter, it reaffirms the centrality of race, neighbourhood and racialized disadvantage to the debates about gun violence, public safety and gun control; on the other hand, it demonstrates, as Miller (2008) has convincingly shown, that the almost abstract and formulaic manner in which the debates about gun rights, self-defence and personal protection are conducted are substantially irrelevant to the conditions of life, death and violence in the hyper-ghetto. People certainly carry guns 'for protection', whether affluent whites or poor African–American youth, the former are particularly likely to assert their constitutional right to do so (while for the latter, like being in a gang or dealing drugs, it forms part of a more complex negotiation of risk, identity and status – 'respect':

Bourgois, 2003; Harcourt, 2006; Pogrebin *et al.*, 2009). In this sense, we might even say that the ghetto gun carrier approaches the gun question with a greater degree of honest realism. At least he or she acknowledges that the gun represents a risk, whereas an aura of denial often appears to prevail for self-defence gun owners. Hemenway, for example, reviews a wide range of evidence relating to private citizens keeping guns at home, concluding that 'in most households a gun makes the home less safe' and 'researchers found that a gun in the home was much more likely to kill innocent victims than criminals' (2004: 79–80). But whatever the gun carrier's motives, whether white or black, in city slum or upmarket neighbourhood, as even combat-experienced police officers testify (Klinger, 2004), when pitched into the visceral and ignoble chaos and confusion of a gunfight, a firearm offers little protection especially when surprised, outnumbered or outgunned. As Klofas *et al.* (2005) noted, over one-third of homicides involved group assailants and fully two-thirds were rooted in group dynamics. In this context, the contemporary articulation of the Second Amendment, the 'right to bear arms' and its 'self-defence' principle has all the longevity of military battle plans which, infamously, seldom survive first contact with the enemy. In a similar manner, the rhetorics of contemporary gun advocacy scarcely survive first contact with reality (Henigan, 2009) and, like Johnny Cash's young protagonist discovers in *The Devil's Right Hand*, they can get you into trouble, but they cannot get you out.

Having devoted this chapter to a series of the main contextual, political and criminological debates surrounding firearms and culture in US society, detailing the many issues that arise and ways in which these are addressed, Chapter 6 turns to a more specific US phenomenon which points the way towards a series of more global and international dilemmas involving gun crime and gun control. In recognition of the ways in which these issues manifest themselves in the US debates, one aspect of the following discussions entails some unpacking of the discourses, or what Zimring refers to as (2003: 443) as the 'symbolic dominances' within which these issues are framed, while also developing an understanding of the socially (and ideologically, and legally) constructed character of these debates in US gun politics. The key starting point here concerns school or 'rampage' mass shootings. As we have noted already, in a gun debate that often goes nowhere, and which chronic levels of 'ordinary criminal violence' typically fail to shift, such incidents can sometimes achieve a little movement. The direction of travel, however, as we have seen in the wake of the Sandy Hook tragedy, is a whole other matter.

Notes

1   The media favoured 'innovative policing strategies', tough prison sentencing and changes in the drug market as their top three explanations followed by the aging population, 'tougher' gun control laws, the stronger economy and increased numbers of police (Levitt and Dubner, 2005: 164). In fact, Levitt's (2004) discussion of 'tougher' gun control laws also included an examination of the new 'concealed carry' firearm laws passed during the 1990s.

2 As we will see in Chapters 6 and 7, these issues also relate to a significant gender politics associated with firearm ownership with important consequences for patterns of sexual abuse, domestic violence and intimate partner homicide.

3 See Young's more sceptically informed judgement on the New York 'miracle':

> [T]he philosophy of zero-tolerance was a post-hoc rationalization of already existing practices … the rise in misdemeanour arrests started in 1993 – the year before the supposed introduction of zero tolerance … Zero tolerance arose as a result of the drop in crime, rather than the fall in crime being the result of zero tolerance. Bratton's magic was to reverse the causality of the process, to step in and claim the miracle.
>
> *(Young, 2011: 121–122; see also Curtis, 1998)*

4 It should be noted that the 'international' crime drop discussed here relates entirely to 'developed' although not always 'western' societies, but it is not therefore a fully global phenomenon. In that sense a gap persists between the wide range of violence regimes considered in Chapter 1 and the governance capacity necessary to establish reliable figures of crime trends, even including firearm homicides deemed criminal or conflict related. The global 'crime drop' may yet be as selective and concentrated globally as it is nationally.

5 A conclusion drawn, perhaps prematurely, by Goertzel and his colleagues in respect of Brazil (Goertzel and Kahn, 2009; Goertzel *et al.*, 2013); see Chapter 8.

6 Such attitudes – and the behaviours they sustain and reflect – can hardly be considered surprising in a culture that specifically endorses the right of private adult citizens to carry firearms for personal protection. These are hardly 'anti-American' attitudes. Indeed, it appears that it is not just possession of the guns themselves that has been 'diffused' to teenagers, so has the principle of arming for self-protection.

6

'TELL ME WHY I DON'T LIKE MONDAYS'

School and 'rampage' shootings

Having discussed the chronic landscapes of gun violence in US cities that have *not* tended to generate momentum within the national gun debate, we now turn to consider the events that do; the particular directions in which they shift and buffet the gun control/gun rights political agendas and the issues that arise when these debates are joined. As I have already indicated, however, with an emotive topic such as firearm violence, the issues are never confined to the numbers and the trends. Gun crime is especially important for *what* it is seen to represent, *who* it affects and *how* it affects them. Yet there are no simple or straightforward relationships between 'shooting tragedies' and policy solutions. Even as the global media awaited the US response to the 2012 Newtown shooting incident, largely buying into the 'never again' narrative, voiced from the bereaved families all the way up to the White House, research evidence and political experience suggested a different story. For as Haider-Markel and Joslyn (2001) noted over a decade earlier, established attitudes, whether pro-gun or pro-control, influence not just the acceptability of particular firearms laws, they also frame the way in which people understand and attribute responsibility – or 'blame' – for shooting incidents, thereby also shaping the political imperatives about 'what is to be done' (Lawrence and Birkland, 2004).

As Figure 6.1 shows, mass shootings in schools or at other venues have become increasingly frequent, especially since 2007. The marketing of high-performance, military-specification, semi-automatic rifles and pistols with large capacity ammunition magazines has undoubtedly contributed to the body count once an incident has commenced. Explaining why anyone would choose to launch an attack on innocent children, citizens or work colleagues is quite another matter. In the wake of such shootings, many questions arise. But two recur with unerring regularity: 'why?' and 'how can we stop it happening again?'

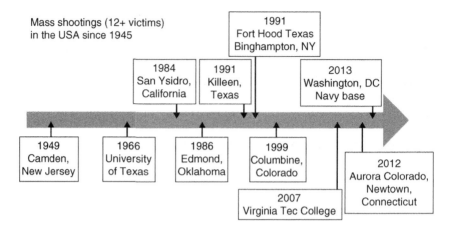

FIGURE 6.1   Timeline of mass shootings involving 12 or more victims since 1945

Source: Author's own work, compiled from media reports.

Neither question is easily answered but, given the intense media attention such incidents bring, and the 'copy-cat' potential (Sullivan and Guerette, 2003) which is thereby triggered, a number of commentators have begun to refer to the cycles of incident and incident reporting as conforming to 'cultural scripts', 'behaviour models that can arise out of violent films, other media products, and earlier school shootings' which perpetrators might adopt, learn and within which media and audience alike are joined (Larkin, 2009; Newman and Fox, 2009; Raittila *et al.*, 2010). Anyone seeking the 'dark celebrity' associated with mass killing is assured of instant notoriety, many recent mass killers have obliged this process by leaving extensive diaries, archives or manifestos, not always justifying, but more accurately 'celebrating' or 'communicating' their actions, accompanied by *YouTube* footage, soundtracks and images (Kiilakoski and Oksanan, 2011). These are not suicide notes but cultural statements for a personalized media age (Kellner, 2008; Muschert and Sumiala, 2012).

Rampage shootings

On 21 December 2012, exactly one week following the Sandy Hook school shooting where 20 children and six teaching staff were shot and killed by a lone gunman carrying a Bushmaster semi-automatic rifle, Wayne La Pierre, spokesman for the NRA, used his long-awaited press conference to give the assembled journalists a belligerent lecture on American gun rights. The world's media had gathered for the event because, in the intervening seven days, a consensus, of sorts, had formed, following President Obama's own emotional press conference appeal, that 'something' had to be done. Experienced NRA watchers urged caution, 'the NRA never comments directly on shooting tragedies', and, true to form, the organization had kept its powder dry for a week; its website simply promising 'meaningful contributions' to the proposed Obama gun control plan. But in fact Wayne La Pierre, ignoring hecklers, his flow only briefly interrupted by a scuffle involving protesters who had unveiled a banner exclaiming 'NRA KILLING OUR KIDS', seemed to be intent on hectoring the world's media for having the temerity to believe that the NRA might compromise its stance on US gun rights, even in the wake of a terrible massacre.

And now, here it was: the NRA's solution, armed guards at all schools. In La Pierre's words, echoing the masculine hegemony of a 1950s western (Stroud, 2012), 'the only way to stop a bad guy with a gun is a good guy with a gun'. And he would take no questions from the floor. Deputy Neil Gardner, a 15-year veteran of the Jefferson County, Colorado, Sheriff's Office might have told a different story; he was on duty at Columbine High School when Harris and Klebold began their murderous rampage *inside* the school. He raised the alarm: 'shots fired in the building' and was quickly joined by another officer. Both officers faced the same difficulty: 'There was an unknown inside a school. We didn't know who the "bad guy" was but we soon realized the sophistication of their weapons … We didn't have a clue who "they" were' (quoted in Terkel, 2012). Armed guards are really only part of the answer. La Pierre's remark is concrete confirmation of the accuracy of O'Neill's (2007) observations on the NRA's recurring depictions of 'terror', 'vulnerability' and 'salvation'; gun ownership is vital because 'each and every American citizen can become a victim at *any given moment*'. O'Neill undertook a review of 'self-defensive' gun use in NRA publications. Guns, as the story goes, are terror's only antidote (O'Neill, 2007: 467). Even having a cop, or an armed guard, nearby is never enough, *every* 'good guy' must carry a gun.

Opening out these issues of 'manhood', 'goodness' and 'responsible firepower', Stroud (2012) has demonstrated how contemporary discourses of hegemonic masculinity (Connell, 1995) underpin men's rationale's for owning self-defensive firearms. The men she interviewed in her study of self-defence firearm owners justified their gun ownership by reference to motivations such as protecting their wives and children, compensating for declining strength as they grew older and defending themselves against people and places considered dangerous 'especially those involving racial/ethnic minority men' (Stroud, 2012: 216). As we have already seen, the choice to carry a firearm is also influenced by the degree of confidence in the protection afforded by the police, especially the expectation that, in an emergency, they will arrive in time. However, as Carlson (2012) has argued, the discourses supporting gun ownership are seldom simply instrumental; they are also deeply symbolic, as a range of research, more usually undertaken with gang members and criminal gun carriers, confirms (Fagan and Wilkinson, 1998, 2000; Kimmel and Mahler, 2003; Harcourt, 2006; Stretesky and Pogrebin, 2007, Pogrebin *et al.*, 2009). However, whether the individual is a legal self-defence gun owner or criminal gun carrier, self-defence still entails the creation and maintenance of a 'defensive self'. As Stange and Oyster argue, 'in [the hands of men], the gun has served a symbolic function that exceeds any practical utility. It has become the symbol par excellence of masculinity: of power, force, aggressiveness, decisiveness, deadly accuracy, cold rationality' (2000: 22). They conclude that it therefore seems entirely logical to argue that men employ firearms to *perform* masculinity. And only a week after one man's dysfunctional performance of masculinity had ended the lives of 20 young children and six teaching staff, more masculinity and more guns were posited as the NRA's answer to the crisis.

In the debates and discussions that followed it became clear that some schools had already adopted NRA-style precautions. In the wake of the Virginia Tec shooting of 2007 (America's most murderous campus shooting in which 32 students and staff lost their lives), the NRA had begun targeting the types of campus firearm bans that, just like Virginia Tec, it claimed, left students and staff unprotected should a rampage shooter strike. NRA-backed campaigns 'Concealed Campus' and later 'Students for Concealed Carry' began to agitate to strike down campus firearm bans, and they were successful in a number of states and jurisdictions. A favoured form of protest was the 'empty holster' protest, with student firearm advocates attending lectures and classes in their universities and colleges with empty holsters, thereby signifying both their support for the 'right to self-defence' and their vulnerability on campus. Of course, the flip side of the 'empty holster' style of protest was the growing evidence that some school students already, although covertly and illegally, carried firearms to school. May (1999) reviewed a range of evidence that suggested that anything from less than 0.5 per cent to as many as 9 per cent of school students took a firearm to school occasionally (Sheley and Wright, 1993b: 5), although his concern was primarily with the reasons they gave for doing so. Chief amongst the reasons put forward were a cluster of issues concerned with fear, self-protection, anxieties about victimization and peer group pressure. May acknowledges, such reasons are not a million miles from those similarly provided by adults for their own investment in firearm protection, an observation carrying important implications for the dissemination of gun culture values. As Lebrun has confirmed: 'Children and youths taking weapons to school have the same motivations as their parents' (2009: 14). Most significantly, however, were the findings that the students *most* likely to carry guns to school were those living in high crime, disorderly and uncivil neighbourhoods: 'students carry guns to school because of the fear of classmates and the perceived crimogenic conditions of their neighbourhoods' (May, 1999: 117). Furthermore, he notes, 'with the prevalence of guns in our society, guns are readily available to juveniles ... a majority of students know where to get a gun if they desire' (May 1999: 117; see also Gaughan *et al.*, 2001; Lebrun, 2009). However, as I discuss later, notwithstanding the wider evidence of rates of student firearm carriage, the strikingly counter-intuitive finding is that school rampage shootings most frequently occur in relatively affluent, white, rural and suburban schools: the American 'heartlands' rather than the American ghettos. White, rather than African–American, boys appear more likely to indulge in random displays of gunfire (Kimmel and Mahler, 2003). Later in the chapter, I consider some of the reasons for this, although recognizing that gun rampages are a different kind of phenomenon compared to ghetto violence, for the moment it is enough to note that gun prevalence is not the only factor here.

Following La Pierre's NRA advocacy for armed school guards, a discussion on the BBC Radio's World Service also confirmed that schools in a number of US jurisdictions were beginning to take their own precautions. A British contributor (myself) raised a range of familiar doubts and concerns both about the need to provide armed guards at schools and the practical problems of doing so. Above all was the question regarding what armed school guards implied about public safety and schooling in the USA. The radio show host then turned to another interviewee, initially described only as the head teacher at a Texas school. What did he think about the NRA's recent proposal? In a gruff and resonant Texas accent he replied, 'All my staff carry side-arms', before pausing, to add 'and *we've* had no trouble'.

A few weeks later the news broke that South Dakota's legislature had passed a law allowing school districts to arm school teachers and other staff. Sponsored by Republican party gun advocates, the law would not require school districts or the teachers in them to carry firearms, but school districts would decide for themselves as a matter of policy and individual teachers would be given the choice. Armed teachers would be known as 'school sentinels' and would commence their additional responsibilities once they had successfully completed a state-financed training programme. Even as the Obama White House was continuing to press for tighter gun control measures in the wake of the Sandy Hook shooting, the new law's supporters argued that the sentinels would help to prevent and deter potential rampage shooting incidents in South Dakota schools.

Media themes and dominant interpretations

Whereas the routine, crime-related, gang-involved gun violence of urban streets has not tended to have much purchase on the US gun debate, some rampage shootings, for a range of often quite circumstantial reasons (the number or type of victims, characteristics associated with the offender, the nature of the attack, the weapon(s) employed or other factors that might give an incident an edge in the 'newsworthiness' stakes) have significantly impacted the debate. Muschert (2007b) argues that the spate of late 1990s school shootings, culminating in Columbine, attracted the attention they did by virtue of the way they helped build the myth of the dangerous juvenile 'super-predator' already gaining attention in the popular media (see also Zimring, 1998). Muschert suggested that the particular combination of 'perfect villains', 'perfect victims', 'tragic victims'[1] and the threats to 'cherished values' singled school attacks out for special attention (Muschert, 2007b). Some commentators have argued that the only reason that school shooting incidents received the media attention they did, had to do with the fact that both the shooters and most of their victims were white. 'To many it seemed that suddenly, mysteriously, the scourge of youth violence had burst free of the poor and minority neighbourhoods and came calling in the kinds of comfortable communities that residents believe are perfect places to raise kids' (Newman, 2006: 10).

A number of studies have criticized the distorting effect that high-profile but quite rare shooting incidents in schools can have on popular understandings of school and youth violence (Donohue *et al.*, 1998; Brooks *et al.*, 2000; Hagan *et al.*, 2002;

Lawrence and Mueller, 2003). Burns and Crawford (1999) have further suggested that the reaction to the 1990s school shootings bore all the hallmarks of a classic 'moral panic', where violent criminal incidents are exploited by moral entrepreneurs and other interest groups to further their own policy agendas. Likewise, although often for different reasons, some gun advocates are critical of policy-makers jumping to what they consider to be 'premature conclusions' about the need for new gun control measures after every incident; other commentators argue that the relentless media coverage makes it difficult to clearly articulate what lessons might be learned, although few criminologists would perhaps go quite so far as Kleck who ventured the view that 'no lessons' could be learned from Columbine (Kleck, 1999).

The attack at Columbine school, on the outskirts of Denver in April 1999, however, was one incident that did propel the debate forwards, although not necessarily as far as, or in the particular directions, first anticipated. Perhaps this was because Columbine was, at the time, the deadliest school shooting rampage, by adolescents, within their own school. Perhaps it was more to do with their elaborate plan, not simply to shoot fellow students, but to attempt to blow up the entire school and thereby kill substantially more people. As Cullen (2009) makes clear, shooting fellow students was just the back-up plan. Alternatively, the Columbine incident was read as deeply symbolic of contemporary US difficulties with 'disaffected youth', with the finger of blame pointed variously at dysfunctional families, violent media, music cultures or violent video games. One commentator (Stein, 2000) even cites Columbine as the definitive metaphor for the contemporary crisis of American youth culture.

Cullen cites many of the myths that quickly blew up during and after the Columbine incident: 'many of the most notorious myths took root before the killers' bodies were even found' (Cullen, 2009: 149); they are, above all a product of the voracious appetite of the media and the public need to know, to make sense and understand why something so awful could happen. And they feed into so many a priori narratives – problem youth, violent media, school cultures, easy access to guns – within which such incidents are often wrapped. One reason why these incidents are able to change the shape and character of wider debates about school safety, disaffected youth or gun control, is precisely their fit with existing presumptions and problem definitions. So when America began to experience what Kellner (2008: 19) terms 'a minor epidemic' of school shootings, culminating in Columbine in 1999, there already existed a series of ready-made discourses within which such events might be fitted.

In fact, as Muschert (2007a: 60) argues,

> cutting through the hype and public emotion about school shootings [and] despite the widely diffused recognition and fear associated with violence in schools, empirical evidence indicates that schools are among the safest places for children, compared to their homes and neighborhoods. The high level of attention given to school shootings ... is potentially misleading.

Only one in two million school-aged youth will either be killed or commit suicide at school in any given year and, in Figure 6.2, while only 1.2 per cent of youth homicides took place in school in the first year shown, 1992–1993, this had fallen to 1.07 per cent by 2009–2010. Best (2006) has noted how school shooting incidents have masked an underlying trend, that school violence has actually been declining in recent years. While noting that school shootings were rare, Figure 6.2 also reveals that they fell sharply after Columbine in 1999 a result, in part, as Newman *et al.* (2004) point out, of the alerts and 'early warning' measures put in place in school districts across the country.

Acknowledging that although these 'rampage', 'spree' or 'amok' incidents have become particularly associated with school or educational campuses, they have also occurred in workplaces, public areas and leisure facilities. It is also important to acknowledge that, although the USA may have experienced relatively more of these incidents, they are far from being a uniquely American experience.

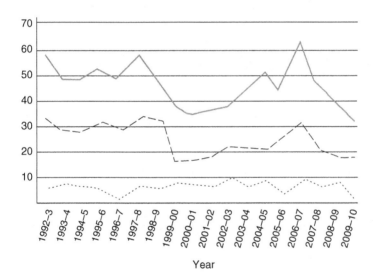

FIGURE 6.2 School-related deaths (suicide/homicide), students aged 5–18 and staff, 1992–2010

Source: National Centre for Education Statistics – Indicators of School Safety (2011), https://nces.ed.gov/pubsearch/pubsinfo.asp?pubid=2012002rev, accessed 10 March 2014.

Note: It should also be acknowledged that this figure only details school-related deaths where the student victims were aged 5–18 years old. During the time period covered by the graph, at least 60 further killings occurred on university campuses, roughly half of them during a single incident – America's deadliest campus shooting – at Virginia Tec in 2007.

They are however rare, but perhaps because of armed attacks on children in schools (the most innocent of victims in what ought to be the most secure and nurturing of environments) they acquire additional symbolic political significance. Even more broadly there have been attempts to link school shootings to a bitter strain of violence characterizing and comprising American history and culture itself (Luke, 2008). Attacks upon schools, special places of innocence and safety, where the most grotesque murders of children and young people are carried out, have been likened to the American pioneer stories of child abductions, murders and massacres by American 'Indian savages' from the days of the old frontier (Slotkin, 1973). These stories, which DuClos likens to what he terms a 'werewolf complex' (DuClos, 1998) have become part of a dark narrative – of an uncivilized evil which must be kept at bay – by which American society and culture understands itself and against which it arms itself. This narrative lies, for example, at the heart of the John Ford western, *The Searchers*, amongst many others, but it is a story that has its roots in true stories of 'frontier violence' (Dixon, 2005). However, notwithstanding the terror presumed to be lurking in the wild, untamed 'badlands', any examination of even the most historical catalogues of violent rampages in schools would reveal that the horror lies overwhelmingly within, rather than beyond, the civilized frontiers. This is a theme to which I will be returning in Chapters 7 and 8.

As the list which follows might suggest, rampage shootings defy any simple, single explanation. An FBI Academy report from 2000 (Blackman *et al.*, 2000) took up the 'school shooter' theme, proposing a fourfold categorization of school shooting 'types': (1) shootings involving personal disputes or seeking revenge against a particular target; (2) shootings that were 'gang-related'; and (3) shootings that were targeted *apparently* randomly in order to express strong feelings or 'send a message' to society. Notwithstanding the relative imprecision of these three categories, category (4) simply noted, shootings that had no apparent motive. Later their 'composite portrait' of school shooter types noted that all of the boys involved had 'troubled histories' (2000: 176).

In time a wide range of studies have come to confirm that rampage perpetrators often appeared to be embittered loners with psychological difficulties, and they are typically male. They are people, seemingly, with a grudge against the world or, apparently, against some of the people in it, or especially some of the people in the institution, a school or former workplace, at which they launch their attack. Gaughan *et al.*'s (2001) study of adolescent attitudes to school shootings confirmed that 87 per cent thought revenge was the strongest motive for a school shooting, closely followed by shootings as retaliation for persistent bullying or victimization. Shooting perpetrators may be employees (sometimes dismissed former employees or those overlooked for promotion), or bullied pupils, jilted lovers, the mentally ill or simply those who have been ostracized or rejected by the major cliques and social networks in their particular communities and against which they wreak a terrible revenge. As Newman *et al.* (2004: 111) remark, rampage shootings reflect the dark 'underbelly' of social capital. It is important, however, not to oversimplify the different contexts and motivations and, in any event, other lists are possible.

There is a long list to be compiled of other mass shootings in the USA and a second, rather shorter list, and probably the most difficult to complete, comprising the phenomenon gone global, other mass shootings around the world.

The incidents to be listed all involve the primary use of firearms and the shootings all occurred during 'peacetime' and exclude 'terrorist' incidents. Accordingly, Andrew Kehoe's bombing of the Bath School in Michigan in 1927 (killing 44); Timothy McVeigh's bombing of the Oklahoma federal building in 1995 (killing 168 including a large number of young children in a pre-school playgroup); the My Lai massacre, perpetrated by US soldiers in 1968 during the Vietnam war, where over 400 people are thought to have been killed; and the Beslan siege and eventual massacre in 2004 (when some 400 children and adults were killed) would not be included, even though they bear some important parallels to the incidents considered here (Kellner, 2008: 17). By contrast, Anders Breivik's murderous rampage at a youth summer camp in Norway in 2011, when 69 young people were shot and killed (the perpetrator having previously detonated a car bomb in central Oslo, killing eight), might be added to a troubling list of global gun rampages despite the 'neo-Nazi', lone-wolf terrorist, label Breivik himself sought to embrace.

TABLE 6.1 US school shootings, 1966–2012

Date	Killed	Injured	Details
1 Aug 1966	16	31	During a 96-minute rampage Charles Whitman shoots students from a tower at the University of Texas (Austin)
17 Jan 1969	2	0	Two students shot and killed during a student meeting at the University of California
4 May 1970	4	9	Ohio National Guard troops open fire on a student Anti-Vietnam war demonstration at Ohio's Kent State University
30 Dec 1974	3	11	A 17-year-old student attacked his school, closed during the Xmas vacation, shooting adults on the campus
22 Feb 1978	1	1	Neo-Nazi supporter kills classmates who taunted him with Luger-type pistol, in Lansing Michigan
29 Jan 1979	2	9	Girl shoots at school and kills two, injuring nine. She shows no remorse and her only explanation is: 'I don't like Mondays'
23 Oct 1985	0	1	Maine College dean shot by sniper, he survived the attack. The captain of the school's swimming team arrested
26 Nov 1985	3	0	A high school student in Washington State kills two 14-year-old boys (one a former boyfriend) before shooting herself
12 Aug 1986	1	4	Student at New York Technical College, in Brooklyn, shoots five fellow students, killing one
1 Nov 1991	6	2	Physics graduate at the University of Iowa kills five college staff, wound a further two, before killing himself
18 Jan 1993	2	0	Student kills teacher (with family member's gun) in revenge for poor marks, takes class hostage and then kills janitor who tried to intervene

Date	Killed	Injured	Details
23 Mar 1994	1	0	A gang-related drive-by shooting at a school in Seattle kills one student
23 Jan 1995	1	1	A 13-year-old boy goes home to fetch shotgun and injures principal who had reprimanded him. Kills himself
15 Nov 1995	1	1	Angry 17-year-old boy shoots two teachers, killing one, following a road accident he was involved in
2 Feb 1996	3	0	Two students and a teacher killed in a maths class when a 14-year-old student opens fire with rifle (Moses Lake, Washington). Killer had allegedly earlier confided in classmates about how 'cool' it would be to go on a shooting rampage as in the film *Natural Born Killers*
15 Aug 1996	3	0	Three professors killed by a graduate student during his viva thesis defence at San Diego State University
19 Feb 1997	2	2	College principal and one student killed, two injured (Bethel, Alaska) by student who took a shotgun to school
1 Oct 1997	2	7	Having earlier killed his mother, 16-year-old student in Mississippi starts shooting fellow students, killing two
1 Dec 1997	2	5	A 14-year-old student opens fire on fellow students at school in West Paducah, Kentucky. He had, apparently, earlier warned friends what he might do
15 Dec 1997	0	2	Two students shot by 14-year-old outside their college in Arkansas
24 Mar 1998	5	10	Two boys aged 11 and 13, hiding in nearby trees, open fire on their school playground, killing four girls and a teacher in Jonesboro, Arkansas
25 Apr 1998	1	2	A 15-year-old Pennsylvania pupil opens fire at a school dance, killing one teacher and wounding two students. He had earlier shown friends his 'secret' handgun and told them what he might do
19 May 1998	1	0	An 18-year-old student in Fayetteville, Tennessee, opens fire at his college killing a classmate who was dating his ex-girlfriend
21 May 1998	2	20	A teenage boy opens fire at a high school in Springfield, Oregon, after earlier having killed his parents. The day before he had been suspended for taking a gun to school
15 June 1998	0	2	A 14-year-old student shoots two staff in a school in Richmond, Virginia
20 Apr 1999	15	23	Columbine: two students, aged 17 and 18, plant bombs in their school, when these fail to ignite they start shooting throughout the school eventually also killing themselves (Littleton, Colorado)
20 May 1999	0	6	A 15-year-old boy in a Georgia high school shoots fellow pupils following break-up with his girlfriend

Date	Killed	Injured	Details
19 Nov 1999	1	0	A 12-year-old boy shoots a 13-year-old girl at a school in Deming, New Mexico
6 Dec 1999	0	4	Four students wounded after 13-year-old pupil opens fire with 9mm handgun in an Oklahoma school
29 Feb 2000	1	0	A six-year-old boy shoots a classmate at an elementary school in Michigan
10 Mar 2000	2	0	Two students shot and killed by classmate while leaving school dance in Savannah, Georgia
26 May 2000	1	0	A 13-year-old student killed his English teacher during a confrontation in class on the last day of term
28 Aug 2000	2	0	Graduate student killed himself and his professor in murder/suicide at the University of Arkansas
26 Sep 2000	0	2	Two students wounded by the same gun during a fight in a New Orleans middle school
17 Jan 2001	1	0	One student shot and killed outside a Baltimore high school
5 Mar 2001	2	12	A 15-year-old student shoots at fellow students at a high school in San Diego, California
7 Mar 2001	0	1	Bullied 14-year-old student at a school in Pennsylvania brings a gun to class and shoots one of the female classmates who had been tormenting her
22 Mar 2001	0	4	A teacher and three students wounded at a California high school, police shoot and stop the perpetrator
30 Mar 2001	1	0	An expelled student from a school in Gary, Indiana, returns to his college and shoots another student
15 Jan 2002	0	2	A teenage student shoots two classmates at a New York high school
16 Jan 2002	3	3	A graduate law student kills the college dean, a professor and a student, wounding others at the Appalachian Law School
28 Oct 2002	4	0	A nursing student kills three staff, then shoots himself, at the Arizona School of Nursing
14 Apr 2003	1	3	A gang-related attack by four teenagers at a school in New Orleans. The student killed was 15 years old
24 Apr 2003	2	0	A 14-year-old student kills the college principal and then himself in South-Central Pennsylvania
24 Sep 2003	2	0	A 15-year-old in Cold Spring, Minnesota, shoots two fellow students
21 Mar 2005	10	0	A 16-year-old student, having already killed members of his own family, shoots college staff and students, and then kills himself, in Red Lake, Minnesota
8 Nov 2005	1	2	A new student at a high school in eastern Tennessee kills the college principal and injures two administrators

Date	Killed	Injured	Details
24 Aug 2006	2	1	A 27-year-old man looking for his ex-girlfriend at a school in Vermont shoots two teachers, having already killed the girlfriend's mother
2 Sep 2006	3	0	A father visiting his two sons at university in West Virginia, kills them both, then himself
17 Sep 2006	0	5	Five members of a Duquesne university basketball team are injured by a shooter following a campus social evening
27 Sep 2006	2	0	A 53-year-old gunman takes girls hostage in Bailey, Colorado. He uses the girls as human shields for several hours in a stand-off with police before killing one of the girls and then himself
29 Sep 2006	1	0	Angry at being disciplined for smoking at school, a 15-year-old Wisconsin pupil fetches a gun and shoots his school principal
2 Oct 2006	6	5	A gunman shoots ten pupils (all girls aged 10–13) and then himself at an Amish school in Lancaster, Pennsylvania
3 Jan 2007	1	0	A 17-year-old student killed another in a school in Tacoma, Washington State
2 Apr 2007	2	0	A University of Washington, College of architecture, administrator is shot and killed by a man in a murder/suicide incident
16 Apr 2007	33	15	Virginia Tec: 23-year-old student kills students and staff, then himself. Deadliest campus shooting
5 Aug 2007	3	1	Four students shot in the head at close range, three killed and one critically wounded, in the parking lot of a New Jersey high school
21 Sep 2007	0	2	Two students wounded in a shooting on the campus of Delaware State University
30 Sep 2007	1	0	Student killed during a robbery attempt at the University of Memphis
10 Oct 2007	1	4	A 14-year-old student opens fire on staff and fellow students at a Cleveland academy, then shoots himself
24 Oct 2007	0	4	Four students injured by high school shooter during a college football game
10 Dec 2007	5	4	A 24-year-old man goes on shooting spree at a Denver religious college, ends by killing himself
13 Dec 2007	2	0	Two research students shot and killed at halls of residence at Louisiana State University
16 Jan 2008	0	1	Student wounded by gunfire leaving a school in Charlotte, North Carolina
4 Feb 2008	0	1	A 16-year-old student shot following an argument with a classmate in a Memphis high school

Date	Killed	Injured	Details
7 Feb 2008	1	0	A man shoots his ex-wife who was working at a school in Ohio
8 Feb 2008	3	0	A nursing student shoots two colleagues and herself at a Louisiana technical college
11 Feb 2008	1	0	A 17-year-old student shoots a classmate in a Memphis school gymnasium following an earlier argument
12 Feb 2008	1	0	A school feud between two teenagers ends when one shoots the other at school in Oxnard, California
12 Nov 2008	1	0	A 15-year-old female student shot by a classmate in Fort Lauderdale, Florida
11 Mar 2009	1	0	An Alabama middle school student shot in the head while walking along a school corridor
12 Feb 2010	3	3	A junior professor, earlier denied tenure, started shooting her colleagues
9 Mar 2010	2	1	An Ohio State University employee threatened with dismissal shoots three of his colleagues
5 Jan 2011	3	2	At a high school in Omaha, Nebraska, a suspended student returned and shot the school principal and other staff. The perpetrator then shot himself
5 Jan 2011	1	5	Two shooters open fire at a school football game in Houston, Texas
10 May 2011	3	0	Three killed in the car park of San Jose State University, in a murder/suicide incident
8 Dec 2011	1	0	A college security officer was killed by a 22-year-old student on the Virginia Tech University campus
10 Feb 2012	1	0	A 14-year-old New Hampshire student shot himself in front of around 70 of his fellow students
27 Feb 2012	3	6	A former Ohio high school student returns to his former college, shooting randomly at students
6 Mar 2012	1	0	A recently dismissed teacher returns to the school in Jacksonville, Florida, at which he had worked with an assault rifle and kills the headteacher
2 Apr 2012	7	5+	A former student, now in his 40s, returned to the Christian school in Oakland, California, he had once attended and started shooting current students
14 Dec 2012	28	2	Man with mental health issues killed his mother then took her assault rifle to a local school in Newtown, Connecticut where he killed 20, five-year-old children, six staff members, then himself

Source: Author's own compilation, drawn from media reports.

Having acknowledged that it is important not to simplify our accounting for these types of incident, it is also important to try to understand and, perhaps especially, to consider the kinds of explanations already offered, particularly with a view to attempting to make such incidents rather less likely. As Agger and Luke (2008) have remarked, when any particular incident occurs, the questions typically come thick and fast. They usually start with the perpetrator: was he evil or insane or was he otherwise driven to his terrible vengeance (the perpetrators are usually male). Sometimes the commentaries start and finish with the perpetrator, for example Altheide (2009) has argued that an exclusive focus upon the 'evil' or 'pathology' of the perpetrator often entails the attempt to submerge broader accounts and explanations, equating school shootings with terrorism. But other explanations dig deeper: what happened to produce such murderous fury; could the rampage have been predicted or prevented? What was it about his school, workplace or community; was there, indeed, something 'toxic' about the immediate social environment, institutional context or the peer relationships experienced by the shooter that led to him 'going postal' (Fox and Harding, 2005; Ames, 2007; Tonso, 2009); is it the 'seductive' attraction of guns or 'gun culture' (Webber, 2003); or even the wider American culture itself, the dark undertow of a broken 'American dream', the violent legacy of US history or the embittered endgame of a dysfunctional, aggrieved and anachronistic masculinity (Kellner, 2008; Kimmel, 2008)?

Constructing answers?

In classic criminological problem analysis, explanation might begin with the perpetrator (means, motive and opportunity). Such factors are often the focus of a 'what made them do it?' literature that can verge towards the 'true crime' genre. On occasion, these can be exceptional exercises in investigative journalism cum ethnography, such as Cullen's painstaking study *Columbine* (Cullen, 2009) outlining the tortured and anti-social relationships surrounding the Littleton High School where 15 people died, even leaving the reader to ponder, not 'why did it happen?' but rather, 'why does it not happen more often?'

Explanation must also take on board (from situational crime prevention or routine activity theory) the vulnerability of the victim(s) or 'target(s)' and the relationship between the perpetrators and the victims, including the presence or absence of 'guardianship' (the NRA's preferred response, the *National School Shield*); the degree of exposure endured by potential victims; or the institutionally protective factors in place. As Newman has argued, these issues are important in view of what we can learn about shootings that are prevented by effective 'listening' and intelligence gathering systems: 'between 1999 and 2001', she reveals, 'at least seven school shootings were prevented when peers reported the plans [of their school mates] to school or law enforcement authorities' (Newman, 2006: 17). Finally, moving the explanation on, we might borrow from left-realist criminological theory to set the incidents within their material, social and political contexts, acknowledging the ways in which wider cultural and ideological factors (the law, patterns of gun ownership and use, policing practices and other urban processes and, not least, the role of the media) play their part in spree shooting incidents. As Muschert (2007a: 65; Muschert and Sumiala, 2012) has argued, specifically in relation to school shootings, although his points relate more generally to the wider rampage killing phenomenon, the media are important in mass shooting incidents given that most people experience them as a mass-mediated phenomenon. In this case, aside from suggestions that the media may incite 'copy-cat' incidents (Webber, 2003; Larkin, 2007), it is also claimed that inaccurate perceptions that levels of school violence were increasing were largely a result of the intense media attention given to a series of incidents during the late 1990s (Muschert, 2007a).

In a neo-liberal culture that prefers to understand events through the lens of individual choice and motivation it is, perhaps, not surprising that the majority of spree shooter explanations have tended to focus upon the perpetrator, *his* decision, motives, reasoning and so on. The freedoms of neo-liberalism entail a heavy burden of theoretical responsibility. In many respects, though, this can be a convenient means of closing off discussion, for not only does the identification of individual responsibility correspond with the legal requirements of individual culpability under criminal law, it also firmly attaches the explanation for the event to the 'flawed' individual, thereby exonerating other potential factors (the community, peer groups, the school or workplace). Both aspects of this individualized 'bracketing' of the legal and symbolic attachment of responsibility are important because in many cases, where the perpetrator has committed suicide at the end of his rampage (a not uncommon outcome), there may be no-one else left to be judged criminally responsible. Of course, that might not be how it feels to parents and family members left behind. Lionel Shriver's insightful but painful novel, *We Need to Talk About Kevin*, written from the perspective of a mother of a school spree killer, explores at length the conflicted dynamics of guilt, misunderstanding, anger, loss and hindsight, that might give anyone sleepless nights.

Muschert (2007a) tries to distinguish between what he calls 'rampage' shootings, where the defining characteristic seems to be that the perpetrator is a member of the community (fellow pupils) he is targeting and 'mass murders' associated with schools where the perpetrator is an outsider. The phrase 'classroom avenger' (McGee and DeBernardo, 2002) is sometimes employed in respect of the former type. In practice these differentiated perpetrator motivations often tend to collapse and overlap. In either case particular individuals within the school community, or the institution itself, are targeted for revenge. The Columbine killers, Harris and Klebold, and Seung-Hui Cho, the Virginia Tech killer, it has been claimed, each targeted individuals and groups who had bullied, rejected or otherwise excluded them – or from which they withdrew themselves. In the case of Columbine it was said to be the popular, 'macho' sports students, the 'jocks', who had triggered the shooters' anger, although Cullen expresses his scepticism: 'there is no evidence that bullying led to murder' (Cullen, 2009: 158). As much as anything, Cullen argues, school bullying was singled out because it was, at least, a problem about which something might be done. Seung-Hui Cho, by contrast, began his rampage by shooting a female student who had, apparently, rejected his advances (he had earlier faced accusations of stalking female students). On the other hand there are 'outsider' attacks by, for example, Thomas Hamilton, who killed 16 five- and six-year-old children and their teacher at Dunblane Primary School (in Scotland, 1996); Mark Lepine at the École Politechnique de Montréal in Canada in 1989 (he entered the college and, in one classroom, having separated the male and female students, ordered the former to leave before beginning to shoot the young women, shouting 'you're all a bunch of feminists, I hate feminists', eventually killing 14 and then himself) (Rathjen and Montpetit,1999; Eglin and Hester, 2003); and finally, and most recent of all, Adam Lanza at Sandy Hook School, Connecticut, in December 2012.

In each of the cases, the attacks involved a combination of outrage, symbolism and revenge, seeking to hurt individuals, groups, an institution, a community or even 'authority'. Harter *et al.*, summarizing the findings from ten prominent school shootings in the late 1990s concluded,

> a common feature in the histories of school shooters has been that they each had a history of being humiliated by peers, a romantic other, or a teacher. In certain cases, the actual precipitating event was such victimization, leading to revenge.
>
> *(2003: 5; see also Kidd and Meyer, 2000; Burgess et al., 2006)*

Leary *et al.* (2003) in a study of 15 school shootings similarly identify 'acute or chronic rejection – in the form of ostracism, bullying and/or romantic rejection' as precipitating factors, factors that were especially influential where the excluded person had psychological problems, a history of depression or poor impulse controls. The authors remark,

> from reading descriptions of their peer relationships, our sense is that most of the shooters had experienced an unusually high amount of bullying or ostracism that was particularly relentless, humiliating, and cruel. Furthermore, when an individual has psychological difficulties, an affinity for guns and explosives, or a fascination with death and gore, such peer mistreatment may evoke a catastrophic reaction.
>
> *(2003: 212)*

Arguing the need for learning lessons – to facilitate future prevention – the particular complaint against social science in relation to school shootings advanced by Muschert (2007a) concerns the lack of integration of existing accounts. The dominant social scientific explanations he identifies operate at three levels: the individual; the school and community; and wider society and culture. Only one factor stands, as it were, outside this three-way classification and this, in itself, is often seen as both a necessary and a sufficient condition for mass shootings to occur: the (relatively easy) availability of firearms. Of course, even this issue breaks down into distinct dimensions, for even in a society in which firearms are plentiful, it does not necessarily follow that particular individuals will find them easy to obtain. While there are plenty of school shooters who stole firearms from their parents (who may or may not have practised appropriate security in their own homes, for example, Adam Lanza took his mother's guns and killed her first), other perpetrators, for example the Columbine pair, needed to solicit the help of an older friend to purchase guns for them from a local gun show (Cullen, 2009).

The individual factors that have been associated with mass shootings include a range of conditions under the generic heading of mental illnesses, depression or personality disorders. As McGee and DeBernardo argue, while reviewing a number of 'classroom avenger' case studies, such shooters are typically

> depressed and suicidal, usually Caucasian, adolescent males from a rural, suburban or small community who perpetrate a non-traditional multi-victim homicide in a school or classroom setting. Unlike more conventional adolescent shooting incidents, the Classroom Avenger's motive is personal vengeance and achievement of notoriety rather than being drug, inner city, or juvenile gang related.
>
> *(McGee and DeBernardo, 1999)*

The sample of 18 shooting incidents they analysed (17 from the USA and one from Canada) revealed white, pre-adolescent males, from lower-middle-class/blue-collar households, living in smaller, semi-rural communities to be the exclusive perpetrators. Apparently, all 18 had voiced explicit threats or declared their intentions to peers prior to their attacks (see also Newman *et al.*, 2004) and, rather than any of them having any specific or clinically diagnosed mental disorders, all of the shooters had experienced bullying, rejection and significant parental disciplining, and all felt themselves to be 'victimized' and 'outcast' from their main local peer groups. Meloy *et al.* (2001) have published the results of their review of adolescent mass murders over a 40-year period which broadly confirmed this emerging profile; a majority of perpetrators were described as 'loners' and, although most did not display explicitly 'psychotic' behaviours at the time of their incidents, they were known for 'depressive' symptoms as well as violent or anti-social behaviours. Furthermore, most of their 'attacks' had a precipitating cause and most communicated their intentions, or made threats, to third parties. Lebrun (2009: 17–32) develops this analysis by outlining a 'typical' profile of a school shooter before moving on to catalogue, in some precise detail, the various checklists and inventories developed by, amongst others, the FBI, educational psychologists and family dynamics therapists anxious to 'predict' dysfunctional adolescents with an unhealthy attachment to guns and violence. Perhaps it goes without saying, but the inventories illustrated seem far more likely to deepen contemporary anxieties, contributing to the moral panic rather more than they afford a means for alleviating it.

Sullivan and Guerette's (2003) analysis of a school shooting one month to the day following Columbine also pointed to evidence of the shooter as relatively withdrawn from key peer groups and enduring a fragmented and unstable family life which led to depression and emotional distancing. As in many, semi-rural, southern white communities, guns were common and the 15-year-old shooter's attitude to them was described in the following terms by the psychologist who had interviewed the perpetrator prior to his eventual trial. '[G]uns were the love of his life. He [also] enjoyed watching animals die and looking into their eyes and trying to figure out what it's like ... He enjoyed that' (Sullivan *et al.*, 2003: 45). In this case, however, the nature of the shooting as a 'copy-cat' incident, perpetrated by a disturbed young man keen to make a mark on his school community, was also noted.

Harding *et al.* (2003) likewise undertook a detailed study of a shooting case from 1997 in which eight students were shot (three fatally). They found that the evident insecurities of the perpetrator (for example, his small stature meant he found it difficult to gain acceptance in male peer groups while girls disregarded him) led him to steal money from home while circulating internet porn and other 'contraband' to his peers in order to gain acceptance. He came to resent this exclusion, reportedly seeming 'uncomfortable and self-conscious' around others and 'constantly looking for approval and respect from other youth' (2003: 136). His victims were predominantly older successful females (six victims) or popular sporting males (two victims). Like all of McGee and DeBernardo's sample he had what were described as significant interests in the military and weaponry as well as in violent TV, films, music and video-games and, also like them, had exhibited signs of 'chronic anger' or bitter resentments. Just like 88 per cent of McGee and DeBernardo's sample, he had obtained his firearms from home (McGee and DeBernardo, 1999). Of course, just how 'exceptional' an interest in music, violent films, video games and pornography really is amongst male adolescents remains an open question (Ferguson, 2008).

I move now from an initial focus upon mental and psychological problems to the wider questions of masculine identity, violent performance and patriarchal behaviour codes and rationalizations and a cultural context experiencing new uncertainties for what Kellner (2008: 90) calls 'white male identity politics'. For example, Harter *et al.* (2003: 8) revealed how many school shooters are described as 'inadequate in terms of their social skills, physical appearance, or athletic ability', while 'many were teased, taunted, or harassed by peers'. Feminist researchers have likewise sought to understand how school shooters, typically male adolescents, adopt and enact violent resolutions for their insecurities and vulnerabilities (Tonso, 2009). The Columbine shooters were more 'vulnerable to rage and violence' and precisely because they did not 'fit into the "myth" of masculinity, they may have been more likely than their peers to attempt to prove their manhood through active violence' (Mai and Alpert, 2000). Newman *et al.* (2004) expressed the issue starkly; all the rampage shooters in her study were boys. 'This is no accident', they remarked, 'for in addition to failing at adolescence, they were – at least in their own eyes – failing at manhood'

(2004: 143). Melzer (2009) argues that such interpretations broadly mirror the cultural politics of the NRA more generally, engaged as it is in a rear-guard defence of a beleaguered conception of American 'frontier masculinity': 'a form of collective action in response to perceived challenges to conservative men's status and identities' (Melzer, 2009: xii; De Foster, 2010). It is in this vein of argument that Schiele and Stewart (2001) connect this revanchist and aggrieved masculinity to conceptions of race, recognizing that most of the mass shooters have been white. Frontier masculinity was almost exclusively white, violently defended often in the face of the 'racialized other' and, accordingly, the burden of manhood it entails is also typically white. Three elements combine, they argue, to structure the violence of the rampage shooter: first the broader cultural endorsement of violence, second what they call the 'spiritual isolation' of hegemonic *individualism* and, third, the acute stresses associated with maintaining this desired status.

Neroni (2000), likewise, situates her analysis of school shootings within a broader cultural perspective on American attitudes to violence, especially the ways that this is celebrated in mainstream Hollywood films. The violence of school shootings, Neroni argues, 'has its genesis in the ideas and ideals of masculinity that continue to inform contemporary American culture' and the primary function of this violence lies in establishing and sustaining masculine and feminine roles and identities. Accordingly,

> it is no surprise that boys in their adolescence – the transition between boyhood and manhood – might see violence as a way to leave their mark on the world. Although no one surrounding the recent teen shootings mentions 'manhood', it is nonetheless the kernel of what is at stake.
>
> *(Neroni, 2000)*

Klein (2005) agrees, her analysis of the media coverage following 12 school shootings studied between 1997 and 2002 argues that although a masculine 'romantic rejection' motive was evident in the shootings, this was systematically downplayed by the media. She argues, 'the killings of girls who rejected their assailants can be explained as an effort to reverse the effects of subordination and inadequacy the assailants experienced as a result of their rejection' (2005: 94). Most worryingly of all, she argues, were the ways in which a seeming 'boys will be boys' tolerance in mainstream media reporting appeared to normalize masculine gender violence and minimize, or at least render 'understandable', female victimization. One youthful avenger shot and killed his ex-girlfriend with a group of his 'approving peers' egging him on. When he hesitated, one of his contemporaries reportedly told him to, 'stop whining and kill the bitch' (2005: 94). In the case of the Jonesboro shootings of March 1998, little was made of the fact that the two teenage killers had only killed females (girl students and a female teacher); according to Webber (2003: 55) the gendered targeting was 'rationalized' away by reference to a claim that there were simply more girls (members of the school choir) to be shot at in the relevant part of the school grounds.

For Klein, the iteration of masculine 'entitlement' to women played out in 'adolescent revenge' shootings is the same as found in more routine sexual harassment, date rape and domestic violence. Kimmel (2008: 72–73) likewise adds that such toxic, bitterly misogynistic and homophobic school environments bolster a sense of 'aggrieved entitlement' in which young men feel able to 'assert their faltering sense of manhood' by going out and killing someone. But as he goes on to recognize, in this case discussing the Virginia Tec shooting, this is far from being just an individual narrative, but rather 'the time honoured script of the American western: the lone gunman retaliates … destroys others to restore the self … It is *Gunfighter Nation* [Slotkin, 1992] … American men don't get mad they get even. It is *Grand Theft Auto* and hundreds of other violent video games. It's not just some westerns or action movies – it is virtually *every* western or action movie.' Evidence that Seung-Hui Cho, the killer of 32 students and staff at Virginia Tec in 2007, tormented and racially abused in class, experienced such values and validations can be found in the pictures and videos he posted of himself prior to his violent rampage. The images show him posing with firearms, aping many of the poses struck by another lone avenger, Travis Bickle (Robert de Niro), in the film *Taxi Driver*.

A Finnish analysis (Kantola *et al.*, 2011) also made an important contribution to the ways in which both school shootings, the debates about them and the reactions to them deployed powerfully gendered discourses. Kantola *et al.*'s study focussed explicitly upon two Finnish campus shootings in 2007 and 2008 in which 19 victims, plus the two perpetrators, died, as two singular, angry young men sought to make their own 'marks on the world'. Their examples are Finnish, although they situate their discussion within a developing commentary on US school shootings. The authors make the point that the predominantly gendered character of illegal firearm violence (in Finland as much as anywhere else) was not a theme much developed in the popular and media commentaries following the Finnish killings (even though such analyses *do* arise in the US context). Their explanation for this discrepancy centres upon Finland's self-censored official discourse as a supposedly gender-equal 'welfare society'. Although both shooters were male and the majority of victims in the second incident were female, 'gender was a silenced issue in the public debate, reflecting the difficulties of addressing remaining gender inequalities in society … The discourse of Finland as a gender equal country firmly upheld the silence on gender as a problem' (Kantola *et al.*, 2011: 184, 194).

They develop their argument via an analysis of three competing discourses in which the supposed qualities of the state, society and social institutions are juxtaposed. In the 'welfare discourse', the supportive and nurturing institutions of education are encapsulated, likewise women *and* victims. This discourse is contrasted by an assertive neo-liberal language of masculinity, aggressive competition and markets which, in their terms, confront the supposed 'welfare-dependency culture' with an ethic of individualism, responsibility and self-reliance. Unfortunately, although neo-liberalism embraces a high threshold of 'responsibility' it also fosters and aggressive risk-taking mentality and a strong conception of individual entitlement that only the third discourse of the 'realist/rationalist state' can hold in check.

Thus, individuals who put themselves above the social interest (criminals) or those who, for whatever self-delusional narratives of revenge and frustration, feel entitled to wreak havoc for others (rampage shooters; lone-wolf terrorists) must be neutralized by the forces of the state. In effect, as Kantola *et al.*, argue, while the aberrations of neo-liberal masculinity pose a risk to the well-being of all, only the righteous violence of the state – the police, military and criminal justice operatives – can hold the line. Therefore,

> the masculinity of the realist state, embodied by the police and the military, put on a pedestal a masculinity that was disciplinary and regulatory of these gender identities, bringing order to the chaos at the shooting scenes, investigating them and most importantly, providing a proper model for 'responsible' and 'rational' violence.
>
> *(2011: 195)*

The NRA's Wayne La Pierre could hardly have put it better, 'the only way to stop a bad guy with a gun is a good guy with a gun'.

As a model for understanding, Kantola *et al.*'s account captures very effectively the dilemmas facing the 'safe European homes' encountering for the first time the dangers of domestic firearm proliferation, new masculinities and suicide terrorism. It also points to the difficulties for restoring civic order and guaranteeing personal security in an avowedly dangerous world. For who, worried about 'bad guys', would *not* want to take appropriate precautions? Their analysis, not surprisingly, also provides important insights for exploring the July 2011 attacks in Norway (another Scandinavian welfare society) where 77 people were killed by Anders Behring Breivik, a 32-year-old Norwegian neo-Nazi extremist. Although separated by culture, continents and oceans, the 'white male identity politics' exercises a tenacious global grip. It is, as O'Neill (2007) has argued, a politics that the NRA itself has done a great deal to sustain.

Since 1926, the NRA's magazine, *The American Rifleman*, in an ongoing feature entitled 'Armed Citizen', has featured stories depicting apparently true incidents in which ordinary American gun owners have used their firearms to defend themselves or others. O'Neill has examined the discourse of masculinity mobilized in these incident descriptions in order to capture the particular construction of manhood occurring. He points to the production of a vision of an 'active, especially vigilant, kind of citizen who is distinctly masculine in character [and] … achieving this masculinity through heroic struggles' (O'Neill, 2007: 459). Importantly, for O'Neill, following Connell's work (Connell, 1995: 77) this construction of masculinity establishes and affirms 'a positive correlation between a masculinated cultural ideal and institutionalised power'. It is this connection that gives such a strong cutting edge to the challenge apparently faced by so many of the victimized young adolescents in American schools and which fires up some of them to vent their frustrations and animosities against their tormentors in a blaze of 'masculine firepower' – just like the hegemonic armed citizens of NRA mythology.

This point is reinforced in Pascoe's discussion of the ways in which contemporary American adolescent males assume their masculinity 'through the continual repudiation of a "fag" identity' (2005) given the manner in which male adolescent bullying is frequently articulated through homophobic insults and insinuations. The corollary may be that marginalized young males, experiencing this kind of homophobic victimization, might find recourse in the symbols and practices of symbolic masculine hegemony in order to accomplish their masculinity in violent retribution. Klein (2006) makes a similar point in relation to the struggle for status and recognition (social capital) in the competitive environment of a contemporary US high school. This 'cultural capital', akin to Sandberg's notion of 'street capital' (Sandberg, 2008: Sandberg and Pederson, 2011) and Anderson's (1999) knowledge of the 'behaviour codes', concerns how young males have to perform their masculinity in order to negotiate contested territories. Fighting and other acts of physical superiority, especially performed with an audience,[2] serve to confer the sought-after status and respect. As Adler *et al.* (1992) have argued, displaying 'physical prowess, athletic ability and belligerency' is vitally important in the testing ground of the school. On the other hand boys who display more 'effeminate' behaviour become referred to in negative terms as 'fag', 'pussy' and 'homo'. This can be a competition, successful boys demean the less successful precisely to establish their own hetero-normal status and authority. Applying this analysis to school shootings, Klein (2006: 60) shows how perpetrators of school shootings were often described as 'short, little, fat, chubby, pudgy, slight, skinny and scrawny' and instead of playing sports like the popular boys they participated in so-called 'feminized' activities, such as music. Klein specifically reviewed the case of one school shooter who, tormented by the tougher, smarter and sporty boys, shot and killed three girls who also played in the school band (as if to reject and repudiate them) and 'he then targeted the preps and jocks who had called him a faggot' (2006: 60). Such evidence underpins Katz and Jhally's observation, 'what these school shootings reveal is not a crisis of youth culture, but a crisis in masculinity'; the problems lie in our concepts of 'manhood', 'power' and 'respect' (Katz and Jhally, 1999). In such a setting Klein (2006: 61) depicts the choice of guns and shooting by the marginal, vulnerable and victimized as a fast-track route to a version of masculinity that compensated for their other social failures. Kellner (2008) similarly describes Seung-Hui Cho's murderous rampage at Virginia Tec in 2007 as motivated, in part, by his frustration at being repeatedly rejected by female classmates. In a culture of perceived 'easy-sex' he was seen as a 'nerd' and a 'loser' and 'when it was impossible for him to create a normative male sexual identity, he went amok constructing an ultra-violent masculine identity, with tragic results' (Kellner, 2008: 133). The irony about such essentially self-defeating strategies of 'masculinization' is that the weaker and more marginal boys attempted to adopt these symbolic trappings of a valued masculinity in order to achieve an often temporary and suicidally doomed identity: fighting bullies by becoming a bully. In other words, they tried to become what they could not be and thereby guaranteed their own failure: the school shooters, 'low status boys perpetuated the hyper-masculine values, internalising hatred of their own feminine attributes, and using symbolic masculinity (violence and domination) to prove that they could conform to social expectations' (Klein, 2006: 67). Klein argues that school staff, wider communities and institutions were also often complicit in sustaining such pathological power structures and inequalities. To this extent Kimmel and Mahler (2003: 1450) have argued that as homophobic bullying was such a recurring theme in the 28 incidents of random school shooting between 1982 and 2001, the precipitating stories, they note, are 'tales of boys who did not measure up to the norms of hegemonic masculinity'. In that light, they suggest, the issue is not one of 'psychopathological deviance', but rather of '*over-conformists* to a particular normative construction of masculinity, a construction that defines violence as a legitimate response to a perceived humiliation' (Kimmel and Mahler, 2003: 1440, emphasis added; Kimmel, 2008). Consalvo (2003) draws particular attention to the difficulty that mainstream media reporting has with such conceptions of dangerous, violent and abusive masculinity; hence killers become demonized as 'monsters' rather than opening up questions about the aspects of normative masculine behaviour they embody. As many sociological commentators on American youth sub-cultures have noted (from Albert Cohen (1955), Walter Miller through to Cloward and Ohlin, (1960)), however, these are *mainstream* constructions of dominant masculinity rather than marginal ones, reflected in both criminalized street sub-cultures and amongst conformist high-school students.

With this in mind we must also shift the explanation beyond the simple personal characteristics of the shooters themselves, of their victims and of the peer group relationships sustained within the fateful schools. At the very least, an analysis needs to move beyond an account pitched primarily at the immediate personal and inter-personal level. Accordingly a number of studies have focussed upon the school context itself, or the school in the context of the local community. Inevitably, issues at this level impinge on broader questions of youth culture, masculinity, social and community cohesion and peer groups, issues close to those I have already explored. Many of these issues are addressed directly by DeJong *et al.* (2003), *Bad Things Happen in Good Communities*, and although the 14-year-old shooter in this incident ticked many of the boxes we have already noted (mental illness issues became exposed, reclusiveness, withdrawal from confiding in parents, increasing peer group competition, gender rejection issues, a copy-cat factor, early use of alcohol and drugs – not to mention a gun-owning household), relatively little was likely to trigger any early warning. The school was thought to be a good one and the community fairly small, close knit and supportive; this was, like the site of many school shootings, white, professional, affluent, rural, 'God-fearing', 'vintage, small town America' (DeJong *et al.*, 2003). What perplexed many local residents was 'how could this happen here?' In the troubled aftermath of the shooting, attention focussed on a number of issues such as: parent–child relationships (parents spending enough 'quality time' with their children); the competitive environment of the school; youth-related social facilities; and in-group/out-group cliques. The authors of the report noted, however, that

> relatively few Edinboro residents appear to have given much thought to the
> fact that [the 14-year-old shooter] had such easy access to his father's semi-
> automatic handgun ... many people reminded us that the Edinboro area has
> many hunters, and that having guns of all types in the home is accepted as a
> matter of course. Reminders of the gun culture are everywhere. One school
> official told us that there is no school on the Monday after Thanksgiving
> because it is the first day of deer season. [On the other hand] some residents
> have called the Edinboro region's gun culture into question, especially after
> the shooting, but most remain largely silent. Gun ownership is just too much
> a part of the community's social fabric.
>
> *(DeJong et al., 2003)*

Kimmel (2008; Kimmel and Mahler, 2003) has also picked up this theme; his
research demonstrates that school shootings are unevenly distributed, with rural
republican areas having significantly more. He comments that local political cultures develop differently, their salient features may include 'gun culture' (the
proportion of homes with firearms, levels of NRA membership) as well as local
gender cultures and local school cultures – 'attitudes about gender non-conform-
ity, tolerance of bullying, teacher attitudes' (Kimmel, 2008: 70), all of which may
either exacerbate or mediate the climates that mobilize harassment, homophobia
and marginalization while simultaneously arming and equipping the revengeful
masculinity to which these give rise.

And yet, DeJong concludes his report on the Edinboro school shooting with an
observation seemingly guaranteed to vindicate the NRA's recent policy line.

> In support of gun ownership, people had only to point at gun shop owner
> James Strand, who had grabbed his shotgun and forced [the shooter] to drop
> his weapon. How many more teachers and children may have died, they
> asked, if Strand had not owned a gun?
>
> *(DeJong et al., 2003)*

In turning to these questions about the wider communities, families and cultures,
we have already noted concerns arising after a number of school shooting incidents
regarding the supposed effects of young men repeatedly playing violent video-games
– especially so-called 'first person shooter' games. These games, it is claimed, either
desensitize young people to the activity of killing or, at the very least, train them
in precision shooting. David Grossman, a former military psychologist, has argued
that video game-makers have effectively repackaged military training materials into
firearms training simulators specifically designed to encourage recruits to overcome
their natural inhibitions about shooting at other humans (Grossman, 1995). These
'murder simulators' are subsequently marketed to both children and adolescents. In
their book *Stop Teaching our Kids to Kill*, Grossman and Degaetano (1999) argue
that through repeatedly playing the games, young people are becoming increasingly
desensitized to the act of killing. They describes an incident from 1997:

prior to stealing the gun [the shooter] had never shot a real handgun in his life
... [Yet] he fired eight shots; he got eight hits on eight different kids. Five of
them were head shots, and the other three were upper torso.

(Grossman and Degaetano, 1999: 4)

Such unerring accuracy, according to Grossman, was extraordinary even by law
enforcement standards. Accordingly he has argued that such levels of skill had
been finely tuned 'for hundreds of hours' on point and shoot video-games, essentially military-style killing simulators (Newman, 2006: 8). According to Thompson
(2006) FBI research has shown that violent video entertainment 'invariably plays
a role in school shootings ... [and that] dozens of incidents since Columbine have
confirmed this' (Thompson, 2006: 29). Other commentators, however, are not
persuaded by the video-game evidence, indeed 'the overwhelming majority of kids
who play [violent] video games do not go on to commit anti-social acts' (Jenkins,
2006: 33). Jenkins also goes on to argue that the emphasis upon video-games has
been positively harmful insofar as it has drawn attention away from other factors
that are more important, but in many ways harder to address. The video-game
industry itself appears to avoid being drawn into these debates, the balance of the
academic research (Ferguson, 2008) appears to suggest that there is no evidence of
direct causal links between game playing and real world violence. Such conclusions
underpinned a series of legal judgements in the USA, ending up in the Supreme
Court, which acknowledged the First Amendment rights of the game industry.
The industry appears to be happy with that, although there are suggestions that the
relentless inter-personal violence of many game formats is not sustainable, while
consumers are beginning to demand more. Games industry researcher Steven
Poole concluded his book *Trigger Happy: The Inner Life of Videogames* (Poole, 2000)
with a discussion of the moral and ethical dilemmas of violent game playing for
the game industry itself. He argues that, on the one hand, computer gaming provides an ultimate opportunity to eliminate regret, 'regret is an easily vanquishable
phantom' (2000: 234), simply lock and load and start afresh, but this is not the real
world, and there are both opportunities and dangers in the way that video games
are 'rewiring our minds'. So, he argues, let us challenge the video-game design-
ers, 'don't bore us, don't alienate us ... if videogames continue to plough clichéd
visual and formal ruts they will furnish the anomic landscape of an impoverished
and unimaginative future generation' (Poole, 2000: 240–241).

Yet if Poole raises his concerns about the anomic and morally impoverished
landscapes of contemporary America represented in violent and dystopian video
games, Ames (2007) points an even more accusatory finger at the tensions and
injustices of real, contemporary US lives, communities and workplaces. Ames'
book *Going Postal* addresses both school shootings, workplace shootings and other
gun rampage incidents in contemporary America. His argument, reflected in the
subtitle of the book, *Rage, Murder and Rebellion in America* is that, while the perpetrators of particular shootings undoubtedly had their own individual issues,
problems or demons, the phenomenon itself is a distinct product of a confluence

of pressures in contemporary USA. Other employees become 'collateral damage' in what amounts to an attempt to destroy the repressive and demeaning ethos of the school or workplace itself; some people rebel, others seek specific revenge, others 'snap' (2007: 16). Ames describes an interview with a police officer following a particularly bloody workplace rampage, to underscore his argument that the rampage phenomenon is not centrally about individuals. According to the police officer, co-workers of the shooter were able to cite a list of colleagues they thought *more likely* to 'snap' and perpetrate an outrage than their stressed-out fellow employee (2007: 15). It is, Ames contends, no accident that the first workplace rampage shootings took place in US Post Office depots (hence, 'going postal') for this industry is thought to have spearheaded a brutal new corporate and business culture – Reaganomics – characterized by authoritarian business management practices comprising: employee harassment and intimidation; widening pay inequalities and differentials; diminishing job satisfaction and security; and an intense competitive culture of contractual outsourcing (so-called workforce 'flexibility'), resulting in stress, more demanding work regimes, longer hours, declining real living standards and increasing debt (Ames, 2007: 9, 45).

The growing similarities between competitive business environments and competitive school cultures account, says Ames, for the striking similarities between the shooting rampages perpetrated. According to Ames, schools have become 'compressed microcosms of the larger culture' (2007: 173). Rather than devoting our energies to profiling the type(s) of person who might perpetrate such crimes, he argues we should profile the institutions and communities that *produce* these tragedies (2007: 171); office, workplace and school culture, he claims, are causing the 'new violence' (2007: 73), yet commentators tend to blame 'everything but the schools themselves for schoolyard massacres' (2007: 46). And yet, just as business has become cut-throat and competitive, with all the consequences described above for individual employees, so, in schools, bullying, harassment and aggression had been allowed to become 'culturally normative' whether tolerated, ignored or overlooked by teachers and other staff. For example, 'students and parents all complained of Columbine High's exceptionally brutal culture, but the administration did nothing about it' (Ames, 2007: 212; Kimmel, 2008). Relatedly, Arcus (2002) has demonstrated that, after controlling for other relevant factors, school shootings are more common in schools still practising corporal punishment. Clabaugh and Clabaugh (2005) go further, arguing that not only is rampant and unchecked bullying often a feature of high-school life, the macho athletic culture is often promoted by school administrations as a sign of 'success'. A final irony then, as other commentators have already noted, is that in the wake of a tragedy, 'toxic school culture is further reinforced by repressive [security and discipline] measures' (Ames, 2007: 202). Fox and Levin (2005) have similarly argued that over-reactions to school shootings can further intensify the underlying sense of alienation felt by many pupils. Ramping up security, intensifying surveillance, installing metal detectors and turning schools into fortresses or, worse, semi-penal establishments, only reinforces the sense of anonymity and depersonalization within which animosities and bullying will thrive (Webber, 2003: 195), just as it does in prisons; in turn the most excluded and alienated pupils might come to identify more with school shooters as 'resistance heroes'.

The concluding twist in Ames' argument concerns the ways in which school and workplace shootings, 'in their details and circumstances, are remarkably similar to [many of the] doomed rebellions we have seen throughout American history – in their goriness, and in the way they are totally misrepresented at the time [as] the mentally unbalanced psychology of the rebel' (2007: 19); tragedies turned into farces by constant repetition. As we have seen, however, Ames is not the only commentator to pitch his analysis, of this or any number of other issues, at the level of American 'cultural exceptionalism', even if he does push the argument to its most extreme. In one sense, this is the 'dark side' to the American dream, in another, as Agger and Luke (2008: 14–15) concur, 'violence and brutality are as American as apple pie'; school shootings gone viral 'disclose some disturbing truths about America today' (Agger and Luke, 2008: ix). Simply *because* violence has long been regarded as 'an acceptable and rational means of solving conflicts' in contemporary America (Webber, 2003: 33), the only strategies open to schools are precisely to ramp up the security (deploying the 'good guys with guns'), maintaining close surveillance, while scanning the student body for the tell-tale traces of malicious intent.

Yet, just as angry young men reach for their firearms to get even with their arrogant, adolescent persecutors or the young women, to whom they felt entitled, who refused them, finding their American responses to the vicissitudes (stresses and strains) of American life, so American law and justice brings its own closures. These are not isolated and distinct criticisms of the broader contexts of American violence. They take us directly back to the prevalence of firearms, the particular ways in which easily available, high-power, high-capacity firearms so effectively facilitate mass killing – and the reasons gun advocates think them necessary. Other societies have had gun rampages, but no society has had so many, nor has any other society become so intransigently reluctant to address either the prevalence or the management of firearms for enhancing public safety. Kellner, writing in 2008, in the aftermath of the Virginia Tec shooting, America's most lethal campus shooting where 33 students and staff were killed and another 15 injured, describes how the official report into the incident chaired by State Governor Tim Kaine 'managed' the gun control agenda. In the first place an executive order was drafted, closing a Virginia loophole, in order to ban the sale of firearms to 'people involuntarily committed to in-patient and out-patient mental health treatment' (Kellner, 2008: 142). Although, the order still had to be ratified by the state legislature, itself historically rather sceptical of gun control. Nevertheless, this manoeuvre effectively shifted the debate away from the broader question of gun availability and into a series of distinct areas: the performance of the first responder units to arrive at the scene and the ensuing police actions; the management of students with mental health difficulties, including the college's support systems; and school and campus security. As Kellner noted, 'a whitewash was coming' (2008: 143). However, despite this official attempt to close down the agenda, Kellner refers to 'one positive outcome' from the incident: the renewed national debate 'about gun control and the role of guns in US society', even though he concluded that 'it is not certain that there will be much progress on this issue in the foreseeable future' (2008: 145).

It is notable that, still further from progress, Virginia Tec appears to have been a catalyst for the NRA-backed 'Concealed on Campus' campaign which has advocated for students to be permitted to carry concealed firearms on university and college campuses. In the wake of the Virginia Tec, the NRA weighed in with a range of hard-hitting gun rights propaganda claiming that the decision of the college authorities to disallow students from bringing weapons to class had effectively disarmed the victims and rendered them especially vulnerable to deranged killers running amok. Around a dozen college and university campuses now permit concealed firearms on campus, another dimension to the wider self-defence-as-human-right argument reflected in the contemporary politics of concealed carry and gun rights activism.

It may be the second tragedy of Sandy Hook school which, by April 2013, had turned, inexorably, into the long-running farce of American gun politics.

Notes

1 Often the 'tragic heroes' are teachers or other school staff who put themselves in harm's way, being killed or seriously injured, to protect children or students. Many school rampage shootings feature such heroes. A particular example might be Professor Liviu Librescu at Virginia Tec, a 76-year-old aeronautics professor and holocaust survivor who was killed while barring the door to his classroom and allowing time for his students to escape.
2 In a similar fashion much research on gang violence points to the importance of the 'audience' for whom the violent acts are performed (Fagan and Wilkinson, 2000; Wilkinson, 2003; Stretesky and Pogrebin, 2007). Zimring (1998) makes an essentially similar point about the group process and social character of most juvenile delinquency.

PART 4

Global dimensions

7

THE 'AMERICAN DREAM' AND THE KALASHNIKOV NIGHTMARE

A number of themes concerning gun ownership, marketing, distribution, use and misuse and the contexts and cultures in which firearm proliferation occurs have arisen during the foregoing chapters. The aim of the remaining two chapters is to draw these themes together within a more explicitly *global* context. However, the aim is not to develop a detailed empirical commentary on global dimensions of arms trafficking, of conflicts in the poorest parts of the world sustained by SALW proliferation or of local, national and international arms control initiatives; there are now substantial literatures on each of these topics. Rather, the ambition here, writing from predominantly sociological and criminological perspectives, is to define and address a number of the main themes relating to globalization, weaponization, gun cultures and their control. The aim is not to suggest, however, that everywhere is the same or even subject to identical processes. Arms researchers or NGO development workers and project evaluators in different countries on different continents are often quick to point out the importance of local cultures, histories, resources, circumstances, politics, factions and disputes that differentiate one chronic and hyper-violent 'conflict complex' (Bourne, 2007) from another. This is fair enough. The argument here is simply premised on the recognition that whatever the reason for the poverty, state failure, corruption or compromised governance suffered by any given region, the arrival and dispersal of tens of thousands of assault rifles is pretty much guaranteed to trample all over local specificities and change things for the worse. Of course, it makes a difference to whom the weapons are distributed, as well as how their new owners employ them – but these 'local' variables are likely to change. The key point is that, whatever was unique or different about a region *prior to* its weaponization is now likely to be less important than the fact that the areas is awash with, for example, AK-47s. Thankfully, however, everywhere is not the same; all gun cultures do not descend into chaos and bloodshed (a kind of dangerous sameness) – though many do, and it is important to be able to work out how and why, and what can be done about it.

As the argument has been developed throughout the book, however, the problem of the gun is seldom *only* about 'the gun', it also profoundly concerns the social relations and culture – the different types of 'gun control regimes' discussed earlier – surrounding firearm possession and use and the various 'gun cultures' that have emerged either despite – or because – of them. That said, there are relatively few scenarios where large-scale community weaponization – an unrestricted supply and an indiscriminate proliferation of firearms – would represent positive contributions to public safety or social progress. On the contrary, a core argument of the chapter, and of the book, concerns the ways in which weapon proliferation, militarization – or weaponization (or even perhaps 'pistolization') – the routine practice of significant numbers of people carrying firearms around with them, or having them reasonably to hand, perhaps because of their fear of attack, or maybe because they have some attacking of their own in mind, fundamentally transforms the social relations of the society and culture in which this weaponization occurs. As Carr reiterates in his piercing analysis of *Kalashnikov Culture*,

> when a society or part of society becomes 'weaponised', that is to say, when military style arms become freely available to the general public, notions of control, stability and security must undergo radical redefinition … a proliferation of arms down to the individual level, in all but the most structurally stable of political entities, can itself create political eddies of insecurity that either exacerbate existing problems or, in extreme cases, actually eclipse the authority of centralised governance.
>
> *(Carr, 2008: 2)*

Cukier and Sheptycki, developing Latour's work (Latour, 1999) similarly discuss how 'access to the gun transforms the "good guy" into a potential killer' (Cukier and Sheptycki, 2012: 4). It might be suggested that it is not the firearm itself, but merely the fear or the aggressive intent prompting its carriage, which effects the real social transformation, except that it is only when guns are present that these perceptions, or the motivations based upon them, can be put into effect. Personal firearms bring change; they facilitate self-defensiveness or aggression, what Muggah (2001) has referred to as 'mental militarization', especially so when broader social changes are transforming traditional solidarities and identities, eroding the more communal ways of living and producing by which people sustain themselves, detaching peoples from their land rights, rendering old skills and loyalties redundant and producing marginality and new inequalities. As Louise (1995: 14–15) has argued,

> widespread proliferation of light weapons and small arms has often led to the acceptance of weapons as a normal part of life and of violent conflict as an everyday occurrence … The most overt consequence of societal militarization has been the creation of a culture of militarism and the horizontal diffusion of weapons throughout communities … the excessive militarization of a society leads to a 'mental militarization', in which violent responses to social problems become the norm.

He goes on to argue that 'highly militarized cultures' can colour people's perceptions of reality, replacing concepts of justice and human rights with crudely utilitarian conceptions of force and power, making consent and inclusive governance increasingly difficult.

> The dual sense of fear and empowerment that the widespread use of armaments brings to groups and individuals can disrupt rational decision-making processes and destroy perceptions of non-violent options for conflict resolution. The result is societal brutalization and the collapse of traditional value systems.
>
> *(Louise, 1995: 14–16)*

Finally, the 'social disintegration linked to gun culture is most … poignantly illustrated in the behaviour and response of children' and he cites an article on children – child soldiers – in Uganda.

> Some children [have] spent the whole of their formative years carrying a gun. When the war ends, they've never been to school. All they know is how to shoot. You can't just expect them to put down the guns and start being kids again.
>
> *(Newton, 1993, cited in Louise, 1995: 16–17)*

In the first place, it is often 'under the gun' that profound transformations are *first* wrought, so it should be no surprise to see indigenous or displaced peoples acquiring weapons to fight back, and realizing the power they entail. Second, whatever wider social changes are ongoing, the gun itself is an agent of change. It is, as we have said, loaded with meaning and potential. This is especially so in an age of global media when firearm advertising, not to mention Hollywood, has indoctrinated the world in armed, primarily masculine, heroism: guns are equalizers, peacemakers, they make the man and they might set you free.

Finally, as Kunkeler and Peters (2011), and a wide range of other commentators have argued (Koonings and Kruijt, 2004; Dowdney, 2003; Arias, 2006; Hagedorn, 2008; Rodgers, 2009), it is often in the hands of young men, who as soldiers (child soldiers), gang members or street drug runners, relatively detached from families or lacking ties of property or access to political representation, that firearms are brought into action. For Kunkeler and Peters, the future is not bright, they conclude by describing an armed global 'precariat' (see Standing, 2011):

> [T]he number of young people who find themselves in extremely challenging circumstances in weak or post-conflict third world states where state support and provision are already limited is only likely to increase in the future. Responses vary, but can include active participation in armed violence (including urban violence) … the dichotomy between youth as 'perpetrators' or 'victims' is not very useful here (often they are both, or become perpetrators

only after their human rights have been violated in the first place) and other dichotomies – such as 'political versus criminal violence' or 'new war versus old war' are equally problematic and unhelpful.

(Kunkeler and Peters, 2011: 289)

These points are reflected in the four key themes addressed in this and the following chapter. The present chapter will focus upon the practices and patterns of illegal weapon trafficking before turning to the regional conflict traps and cultures of endemic violence thereby established and sustained. Chapter 8 will then consider how gun violence problems and *especially* multiple-victim rampage killings have been followed by gun control initiatives at the national level and how these, in turn, have led to potentially global arms control initiatives. Perhaps it goes without saying, but these four themes are closely connected. More weapons in a given community almost invariably increases rates of weapon misuse, while many of the neo-liberal, social and economic changes the globalizing world is currently undergoing (to say nothing of the rapid changes faced by the world's more violent regions) are likely to make even the safest 'gun cultures' appear rather more divided, dangerous, precarious and conflict ridden (Taylor, 1999). And, just as Findlay (1999) described, while crime itself is a force for globalization, so too are weapon trafficking and 'weaponization', they represent powerful vectors of neo-liberal globalization by virtue of the enhanced capacities of sovereign individualism they entail. Where the weapon travels so too will aspects of 'gun culture' and 'cultures of violence' and while, in dangerous societies, the gun may indeed appear to set you free, at a price, this version of weaponized modernization is nowadays perhaps less the 'American Dream' than the 'Kalashnikov nightmare'. For, as Miller and Cukier note,

> once guns become widely available, the problems can become hard to reverse, as "gun cultures" develop that are reinforced by violent movies and television which tend to link heroism with guns and violence, and by sub-cultures where displays of guns become symbols of social status.
>
> *(Miller and Cukier, no date: 9)*

The argument being broadly developed in the course of the two sections of this chapter concerns how the arms trade represents a weaponization vector of contemporary global neo-liberalism (Muggah, 2001). Crimogenic neo-liberal policies, and especially the social and individual consequences of tough 'law and order' strategies, play a vital role in incentivising the acquisition of firearms by offenders and thereby legitimating gun ownership by law-abiding citizens, especially in high crime societies, where a vicious circle of weapon diffusion then begins' (Meek, 1997, 2000). Cukier and Sheptycki have recently argued that the 'carriers of gun culture' by which they refer to 'technology, media and ideology' have helped to '(re)produce the links between masculinity, affluence and firearms' (2012: 10); in this chapter we are simply recognizing the corollary, that the carriers of market liberalism have also diffused gun culture.

There is no particular priority or sequence to the following themes, although this chapter will deal with a number of observations on weapon trafficking and then turn to the consequences of this trafficking in the global gun crime hotspots and 'conflict complexes' (Bourne, 2007) where the proliferation of SALW helps to sustain chronic patterns of violence, condemning millions to live in insecurity, constant fear and poverty, turning children into soldiers and whole communities into victims and refugees. Chapter 8 will then pick up from a discussion begun earlier, in chapter 6, in order to explore the actions taken by a number of societies which have experienced 'spree' or 'rampage', multiple-victim shootings. The commentary will focus less upon the incidents themselves, than upon the debates and ensuing policy processes through which the various societies sought to address and reform their domestic gun laws – or, conversely, chose not to do so. The discussion will reflect upon why it may be that a single firearm 'rampage' can prompt social and political reactions in ways that the regular toll of 'routine' gun crime victims never can; it will also explore what became of these new laws, whether they 'worked', how or why they were effective and how they formed part of a wider process of social change through which the various societies were passing. Finally, the second half of the chapter, recognizing that global firearm trafficking, not to mention broader global and 'gun cultural' influences, can erode domestic and national firearm control policies (especially those of smaller and weaker states), will address recent efforts to address the illegal proliferation of SALW and the debates leading the UN programme of action on SALW and the UN adoption of a global Arms Trade Treaty (ATT).

Weapons proliferation/small arms smuggling

The issue of weapon trafficking generates a particular debate in international relations and security studies. In their domestic debates, gun advocates often argue that 'Guns don't kill people; people kill people', or that 'the trigger doesn't pull the finger' (cited in Sampson, 1977), reflecting a long history of denial in the arms development and distribution business. Writing even earlier, Thayer argued, 'the gun is the bride of war ... the trade in arms encourages arms races and transforms political conflicts into war', before describing a dozen or more instances of imported weaponized conflict, almost entirely in the 'under-developed areas of the world'. In the absence of these arms supplies, he concluded, 'most of these conflicts would have been channelled into diplomatic and political channels for negotiation and solution' (Thayer, 1969: 351–352). However, across the international arena, things are seldom clear cut, for commentators also distinguish between *direct* consequences of weapon proliferation, killings and injuries, and the *indirect* consequences such as exacerbating the length and ferocity of armed conflicts, producing thousands of homeless refugees, recruiting children as soldiers, blocking humanitarian aid and assistance and abusing human rights while also placing relief and development workers in peril. Over the longer term, weapon proliferation and the resulting conflicts can undermine regional security, discourage investment and frustrate employment projects, disrupt harvests and food supplies, overwhelm health and medical facilities, destroy education systems (by killing teachers and conscripting children into militias), perpetuating poverty and political instability, eroding civilian protection and undermining economic development (Buchanan, 2004; Pattugalan, 2004; Ginnifer, 2005). Furthermore, periods of civic conflict also provide numerous criminal opportunities, as Ginnifer has commented, during the violence in Sierra Leone combatants from all sides 'used the power of the gun to rob individuals, groups, and plunder the state'; only those who were themselves armed, or were members of armed groups, were able to protect their homes and property (Ginnifer, 2005: 29; Austin, 1999).

Some commentators may argue that supplies of SALW in themselves 'do not cause the outbreak of violence' (Bourne, 2007: 4)[1] rather weapons are simply supplied according to the logic of the market economy; that weapon demand (the real issue) from conflict areas will inevitably be met by a shady world of brokers and dealers, or simply other states seeking geo-political advantages and alliances (Austin, 1999: 33). A focus upon SALW is critical here because these are the weapons most often used to perpetrate the violent killings associated with both conflict and crime: indeed they cross the increasingly hazy dividing lines between weapons of military conflict and weapons of civilian and criminal misuse. As Boutwell and Klare remark, introducing their 1999 collection of essays on the international trade in light weapons,

> the widespread global diffusion of assault rifles, machine guns, mortars, rocket-propelled grenades, and other light weapons that can be easily carried by an individual or transported by a light vehicle has greatly intensified the scale of conflict in countries and societies around the world. In the 1990s alone, such weapons have accounted for the vast majority of the four million deaths that have occurred in forty-nine major ethnic and sectarian conflicts. From Bosnia to Zaire, Rwanda to Afghanistan, and Tajikistan to Somalia.
>
> *(1999: 1–2)*

Laurance went even further, arguing, in 1999, that there was no longer any doubt that a net increase in the global supply of small arms was directly responsible for the perpetuation of conflicts 'carried out by criminals, terrorists, and irregular militia and armed bands', culminating in a global security threat, and thereby making the case for more coordinated international action (presaging the UN's efforts towards an ATT) to tackle the indiscriminate supply of small arms (Laurance, 1999: 185–186). Amongst a number of concerns he identified was the diffusion of military specification weapons into civilian possession. He noted that 'in the end, people kill people, but when modern military weapons are used, the lethality escalates to inhumane levels' (1999: 193), an observation with considerable contemporary significance (see Diaz (2013) on the militarization of the civilian gun inventory).

That said, conflict and violence are never just an issue of the hardware; violence is emphatically a *social* relation. This is so in the sense described by Jennings (2007);

a supposed 'war zone' is still a social space, sites of intensified 'destruction, chaos and ruin', although that is only half of the story, they also represent 'continuity, destruction, adaptation, and innovation', although 'conflict is the new normal'. Immediacy and survival may become pressing concerns and social relations can become transformed by violent necessity, but these need not be the only issues. As we have argued already, trafficked weapons travel with something other than ammunition and their acquisition is largely inseparable from the intention, the will or merely just the potential to use them aggressively, murderously, to inflict violence and suffering. In one sense this *deus ex machina*, the received cultures of gun use, firearm performance or weaponized identity, rather than the flying bullets (gods *from* the machine; a power over life and death), directly reflect the ways in which 'fire power' augments the lethal capacity of men, how it fosters the aura of the 'gunman', soldier or 'warrior'. In another sense, however, these men were, arguably, there all along, awaiting the arms that could transform them (Gibson, 1994). Accordingly, it is in this sense that African development economists (Collier, 2009) and small arms analysts have likened arms proliferation to 'a cancer' or a chronic disease vector, bringing 'social and economic development in reverse', sustaining the weaponization of impoverished communities, producing and perpetuating the endemic violence that grips underdeveloped countries and entire regions in dire poverty. As the Small Arms Survey (2002) has noted, firearm supplies have to be seen as an 'independent variable' in conflict zones, or 'situational facilitators' of a range of forms of violence, spanning from domestic abuse, gang-related and misogynistic violence, all the way to terrorism and civil war.

Generally speaking, illegal weapon trafficking takes one or more of the following forms: leakage (theft and fraud) directly from points of production or military stockpiles, or police sources; fake export arrangements sometimes involving governments or other well-placed intermediaries (ex-military or security personnel); conversion of non-lethal firearms; recycling of discarded or surplus weapons; theft, fraud and leakage from legal dealers or private owners; fraud by private owners. There seems, on a global scale, relatively little outright illegal firearm production (Bourne, 2007: 66–67), but plenty of illegal weapon conversion and the reactivation of deactivated firearms and some unregulated and unlicensed production (for example in China and Croatia, particularly of AK-47 variants; Chivers, 2010), although illegal manufacture is not entirely unknown. For example, during 2013 the Indian news media featured reports of illegally manufactured firearms found in the possession of criminals and terrorists and, during early September, police raided a small metal-works unit in Biharsharif, unearthing what was described as a 'huge cache of firearms, ammunition and gun components' (Nadim, 2013). Differences of scale in production and distribution are clearly entailed here, from states to private individuals but, as we shall see, each plays a part. Figures vary as to the scale of global annual small arms production, but Dimitrov and Hall (2012: 208) report estimates that over 800,000 military small arms were produced globally in 2000, but that around seven million commercial firearms were manufactured in the same year. Diaz (2013) has suggested that such distinctions may be collapsing in the USA where some of the most enthusiastic firearm marketing and purchasing occurs; one key consumer trend involves the 'militarization' of the civilian market.

Until relatively recently little consistent empirical evidence existed joining up what was known about SALW trafficking at the various (global, regional and local) levels and despite sporadic efforts by international law enforcement agencies (such as Interpol) there is even less clear and consistent evidence of effective enforcement at the international level. What is known tends to reflect the work of a limited number of specialist security studies research organizations and NGOs such as: the Graduate Institute of International Studies in Geneva, which has conducted an annual Small Arms Survey (an annual review of global small arms issues including production, stockpiling, brokering, legal and illicit arms transfers, the impact of small arms, and national, bilateral and multilateral strategies to tackle the problems associated with small arms) since 1999; the Institute for Security Studies (originally established in South Africa but now networked across 17 African countries); the Stockholm International Peace Research Institute (SIPRI); organizations such as IANSA; and Saferworld. There are also a number of, generally smaller, research institutes attached to universities in different countries around the world. A great deal of the evidence of illegal weapon trafficking has been particularistic and often anecdotal, coming to light, like the visible tip of an iceberg, when an illegal shipment, large or small, is discovered. As Marsh has noted, despite a great deal of work to quantify the flows of small arms, licit and illicit, the research community has found it difficult to document adequately the proliferation and diffusion of small arms into the hands of insurgency groups, armed militias and criminal gangs; work on the acquisition of such weapons 'remains dominated by case studies and anecdotes' (Marsh, 2012: 26). And, as Greene has added, even as some NGOs and the international arms community began to get to grips with the proliferation of guns in particular regions, for a long while the supply of ammunition 'arguably the most lethal part of any weapons system' went somewhat overlooked (Greene, 2006). Drawing largely upon the work of a relatively limited range of research institutes and NGOs, it is possible to draw some conclusions about the scale, structure and nature of contemporary small arms smuggling and trafficking, weapon proliferation and diffusion.

There are important distinctions of scale and organization within the weapon trafficking arena. Larger-scale items such as tanks and military vehicles, planes and even warships are generally traded, directly or indirectly, by governments – although often cloaked by the involvement of layers of brokerage companies and networks of contractors and sub-contractors. Griffiths and Wilkinson (2007), in their report on *Clandestine Arms Transfers* for SSESAC (the south-eastern and eastern Europe Clearinghouse for the Control of Small Arms and Light Weapons) point out that relatively few illegal weapon shipments have been detected or intercepted in transit and that this is often attributable to a combination of 'inefficiency, lack of resources and high-level complicity and corruption'. The systematic analysis and detection of clandestine arms shipments, they claim, remains 'still in its infancy'. Professional arms dealers often operate on the fringes of legality and financial accountability, perhaps rarely contravening the laws of their 'base countries' but utilizing a range of covert connections, under-regulated off-shore banking systems and contacts with military and governmental personnel, to evade proper scrutiny (perhaps underpinned by bribes and other inducements to regulators). The expansion of global trade, changing international business practice and, not least, the advent of private military companies, consultants and trainers providing and delivering military services and supplies, have further complicated these complex and often opaque international markets.

Alternatively, governmental arms transfers may be shielded by the systems of export licensing and 'end-user certification' which supposedly guarantees the legality and credibility of arms transfers between states. For example, in 1997 the Organization of American States (OAS) Inter-American Convention Against the Illicit Manufacturing of and Trafficking in Firearms, Ammunition, Explosives, and Other Related Materials emphasized the need for government-issued end-user certificates (EUCs) and related documentation in the weapons export licensing process and this was endorsed by the 2001 UN Programme of Action to Prevent, Combat and Eradicate the Illicit Trade in Small Arms and Light Weapons which encouraged states to employ 'authenticated end-user certificates and effective legal and enforcement measures' when controlling the export of SALW. Unfortunately, these systems of scrutiny and accountancy become subject to the same pressures of illegality and corruption as the original arms transactions. Bourne (2007: 131) has described many EUC processes as simple 'veils of legality' designed to conceal covert military aid or bypass trade embargoes and he cites Naylor's dismissive summary of EUCs:

> obtaining a passable end-user certificate is about as difficult as getting an American gun-dealer's license, an honour seemingly denied only to convicted serial killers (who can get around that obstacle by applying in the name of their pet dog). Sometimes end-user certificates are completely faked … more commonly they are completely real.
>
> *(Naylor, 1995: 14)*

Problems with EUCs can fall into a number of types: EUCs can be forged, original documents can be altered and re-used, misleading or incomplete information can be provided on them, weapons can be diverted in transit to putative 'end users' and the 'end user' described in the documentation can fail to comply with the agreements and re-sell the weapons to a further party. Another weakness is the failure by export country authorities to verify that weapons reach the intended recipients. Goldring (1999) describes how, between 1989 and 1993, the US Department of State's Office of Defense Trade Controls verified EUCs for only 21 of the 1,632 licences issued for small arms transfers to eight Latin American countries (see also Lumpe, 1999b).

A study of end-user certification processes by SIPRI in 2010 (Bromley and Griffiths, 2010), found examples of forged, fabricated or altered EUCs issued in respect of arms transfers involving Equatorial Guinea, Chad and Tanzania. The same study found examples of privately issued EUCs which have, since 1945, allowed considerable discretion and limited documentary regulation to British arms dealers presumed to be operating 'on behalf of' government. Between 2003 and 2005, a series of private EUCs were used to permit the export of 200,000 AK-47 assault rifles from eastern European states, including 100,000 from Bosnia. The overall purpose of the transaction is unspecified (but *might* have involved the intended destruction of the weapons), although at least one consignment of the Bosnian-sourced rifles, numbering between 25,000–30,000 weapons, was diverted to Iraqi government forces. A subsequent British parliamentary committee on Arms Export Controls has since recommended that the arrangements for monitoring and controlling large volume weapon transfers should be tightened.

If not manipulating the end-user certification processes, states can deploy other methods to evade scrutiny of their more dubious arms deals. Cramer (2006), for instance, describes how companies, in this case Heckler & Koch (HK), a subsidiary of British Aerospace, licensed the production of its popular semi-automatic carbine (essentially an assault rifle), a version of which is extensively deployed as the standard firearm of British police forces, to Turkey. The virtue of this deal was that Turkey could directly export the weapons to Indonesia which, because of arms sales embargoes, would not have been possible for HK based in the UK. Similar, off-shore arrangements were in place in 1994 in the wake of a UN embargo to enable arms brokering deals via the Isle of Man supplying weapons to Rwanda (in the wake of the Rwandan genocide). The weapons could not have been directly supplied from Britain but the British Government's implementation of the embargo did not extend to Crown Dependencies or the Isle of Man, thereby subverting the explicit intention of the UN embargo (Cramer, 2006: 20). Widening this picture of weak oversight, in 2006, Control Arms issued a damning indictment of the effect of the past decade's arms embargoes:

> [E]very one of the 13 United Nations arms embargoes imposed in the last decade has been systematically violated, [but] only a handful of the many arms embargo breakers named in UN sanctions reports has been successfully prosecuted. According to SIPRI (the Stockholm International Peace Research Institute), between 1990 and 2001 there were fifty-seven separate major armed conflicts raging around the globe, yet only eight of them were subject to UN arms embargoes … embargoes are usually late and blunt instruments, [they] have to rely largely on Member States to monitor and implement them … These controls are woefully inadequate.
>
> *(Sprague, 2006)*

A somewhat more positive picture of arms embargoes achieving a net reduction in the quantity of weapons supplied (rather than a complete elimination of supply) and securing improvements in the behaviour of states subject to embargo, might be found in a 2007 SIPRI report (Strandow and Wallensteen, 2007). Marsh (2012: 22) also notes that 'some arms embargoes are effective and many more are partially effective', a crucial factor being enforcement capacity (often lacking) and the role of campaigning NGOs.

Such observations underpin Bourne's (2007) central complaint against much of the existing academic research on firearm proliferation and diffusion,[2] the study of which, he argues, is unhelpfully fragmented according to whether the weapon transfers are notionally 'legal' or 'illegal' or movements within a vast unaccounted for stock of 'grey market' weapons. Most academic and policy literature on SALW, he argues, 'focuses on the *supply* side of the phenomenon and gives relatively less attention to the *dynamics of the demand*' (2007: 5, emphasis added), and operates with only a rather generic and somewhat homogenized understanding of weapon diffusion, whereas, in fact, as we have already seen, legality is often only a thinly veiled fiction, while legally acquired weapons are also often misused and virtually all illegal firearms originate in legal production. Accordingly, amongst others, he calls for a more sophisticated, contextualized understanding of the 'structures of weapon availability' and the factors that 'shape the arming of conflict' (2007: 8) and a better situated understanding of the production of a *demand for* firearms (Atwood *et al.*, 2006).

So far we have mainly considered the weapon trafficking issues in relation to warfare and militarized violence – political conflicts by other means – whereas, for the most part, the book has been primarily concerned with civil conflict and the criminal misuse of weapons. Even here, however, the legacies of war do play a massive and continuing role especially in terms of the ways that wars are particularly good at facilitating the indiscriminate proliferation of firearms, while the endings of wars typically expose huge weapon surpluses that are frequently dispersed amongst civilian populations. While most of this book has been written from within a broadly 'criminological' perspective, a lot of the time it has also been looking outwards. It is, accordingly, important to acknowledge the intersection of different disciplines that contribute to our developing understanding of weapon proliferation; although this is not to suggest that the 'fragmentation of perspective' which once affected the subject matter has been wholly overcome. So significant are the security issues posed by the proliferation of SALW that it might be assumed that the whole question of international weapon smuggling and trafficking would be subject to the most comprehensive scrutiny and analysis. Unfortunately, until relatively recently, for a number of reasons ('fragmentation of perspective' being one, but also secrecy, politics, criminality, danger and difficulty), this has not been the case. Even now, as a number of powerful organizations have begun to engage with the global question of small arms proliferation, not least the United Nations (which commenced its Programme of Action on Small Arms and Light Weapons in 2001), these difficulties remain, frustrating the efforts of researchers, law enforcement, DDR specialists, aid agencies and peace-builders alike. To take the first issue, the fragmentation of perspective, the applied social sciences' collective grasp upon SALW proliferation still tends to be somewhat divided between criminologists (whose interest lies primarily upon the criminal misuse of firearms on the streets or the connections between firearm use and supply and other forms of illegal criminal organization); defense and security studies (often preoccupied by the supply of weapons to terrorist or organized criminal groups); conflict and war studies (the role of weapons used by militias and armed groups to organize insurgencies and military coups or to destabilize countries or regions, and perpetrate war crimes or genocide); international relations (the licit and illicit use of arms brokerage to establish or sustain geo-political alliances); and development and peace studies (the study of disarmament and demobilization processes). There are relatively few attempts to take in the whole picture; different disciplines have tended to tackle the issues from their own particular perspectives and, furthermore, these perspectives can often be very localized or regionalized. They can also emphasize either 'top-down' or 'bottom-up' strategies of weaponization (Bourne, 2007) and, while the former account for most of the major flows of weapon supply, the latter comprise the more usual forms of weapon trafficking for civilian and criminal uses as opposed to military supply. For that reason these will be the main focus in the following discussions, always remembering that top-down supply of military weapons is often a necessary precursor of wider patterns of civilian weaponization.

A number of developments involving globalization and the changing shape of international conflict have made the aspects of fragmented perspective referred to above increasingly problematic. These include collapsing distinctions between areas of activity once thought discrete, for example civil war, ethnic conflicts and 'warlordism' (Newman, 2009), or the rise of narco-terrorism and insurgency (Bourne, 2007: 167; Peters, 2009); the nature of 'new' and asymmetric warfare and the roles of 'private military organizations' and non-state actors within this (Leander, 2005; Kunkeler and Peters, 2011); the increasing attempt to 'normalize' – or criminalize – war crime and the conduct of war, with all that this entails about bringing conflict and war-related activities including the notion of 'crimes against humanity' within the purview of international jurisprudence and the International Criminal Court (Power, 2003; Bekou and Cryer, 2004; T. Allen, 2006); the growing recognition that peace building, governance development and aid arrangements are being routinely hampered by continuing legacies of weaponization and that fostering refugee settlement and civil society development is incompatible with a proliferation of 'post-conflict' firearms (Reno, 1999); the ending of the major structures of geo-political hegemony associated with the Cold War and these being superceded by persistently failing states and corrupt regimes in which legal and illegal arms brokering forms part of wider commercial arrangements for extraction of raw materials (diamonds, oil, precious minerals) (Richards, 1996; Cramer, 2006); the recognition that, in terms of 'dollar value', the outright *illegal* trade in SALW amounts to only some 10–20 per cent of the global weapons trade (Bourne, 2007: 36); and the changing nature of small arms brokering itself, which is no longer said to be about the fostering of geo-political alliances but rather, according to Naylor (1995, 1997), mainly concerns the profitability of criminal enterprise. Naylor, one of the leading analysts of the modern arms black market, describes a critical shift in the 'new' international weapons trafficking. Compared to the Cold War era, dominated by a few big suppliers who understood what their merchandise could do for their *customer's political ambitions* and who used arms transfers to cement political alliances, the new fragmented, criminal weapons market has become increasingly colonized at the regional and local level by mercenaries and criminal traffickers who are chiefly interested in what their lethal merchandise might do for their own *financial* ambitions (Naylor, 1995). Furthermore, at the regional level, the problem of weapon proliferation has primarily come to be defined as an issue of corruption and weak enforcement in failed and failing states rather than as a problem of powerful offenders with global reach (Karp, 1994). Finally, increasing global mobility – both people movement and reduced barriers to international trade – has also facilitated the 'blowback loops' which have brought a variety of converted firearms to Britain, trafficked, for example, through the trans-national diaspora connections of Cape Verdean and Turkish communities resident in Portugal and the Netherlands (De Vries, 2011) and Makarov semi-automatic pistols, transported along drug smuggling routes from eastern Europe and the Balkans region (Sagramoso, 2001) to the streets of Moss Side.

This blowback phenomenon is not unknown in the USA. Perhaps the world's most infamous assassination weapon, the 6.5mm Carcano rifle use by Lee Harvey Oswald to shoot President Kennedy in 1963, was an Italian military surplus weapon, dumped onto the American market via an advertisement in *American Rifleman*, the magazine of the NRA. More recently evidence of the penetration of Latin American drug-trafficking organizations (DTOs) and trans-national criminal enterprises into North American organized crime, street gangs and suburban communities, have begun to feature more prominently in FBI Annual Serious Crime Threat Assessment (FBI, 2009). Yet in their northern Mexico heartland, the drug cartels and DTOs are sustained by a constant flow of North American weapons (Vulliamy, 2010); a supply of firepower which has enabled them to progress from being relatively simple criminal trafficking organizations into real social and political powerbases in the region, capable of physically confronting the civil and military authorities, subverting, corrupting or assassinating judicial and political authorities while developing more explicitly political ambitions as terrorist, guerrilla or paramilitary organizations (Goodman and Marizco, 2010: 171–172).

What is true in the US/Mexico context is true in many other parts of the world – chronic patterns of armed conflict are frequently sustained, more than anything else, by supplies of SALW. The trade in SALW represents one of the major security threats facing the twenty-first century. The trade in small arms is especially important as it represents the types of weapons most often actually used, contributing to problems of terrorism, regional instability, failed states, international drug trafficking, urban gang 'weaponization' (Squires, 2011a) or 'pistolisation' (Sheptycki, 2009; Cukier and Sheptycki, 2012) and empowering cartels, warlords, insurgents, pirates and many other organized or disorganized criminal groups and gangs. And, as the most recent Small Arms Survey (2013b) yearbook demonstrates, community weaponization also sustains patriarchal relations of dominance or hyper-aggressive masculinity which frequently reaps a terrible burden upon the lives of women and girls. As the Small Arms Survey (2013b: 2) report noted, 'countries with high rates of violence and gun possession tend to have high rates of gender inequality and tolerance of inter-personal violence against women'. Furthermore local cultures may reinforce conceptions of tough masculinity that 'embrace gun possession' or, alternatively, as Turshen describes in respect of Algeria, patriarchal 'islamist' insurgent groups may use their power of arms in targeting women and girls in order to reinforce their own strict ideological agendas (Turshen, 2004). The majority of civilian-owned weapons are, not surprisingly, owned and used by men; this helps sustain practices of 'routine violence' and intimidation. Such men's firearms, often *including* those in the possession of members of the armed services, the police and private security guards are 'employed to threaten and intimidate far more frequently than they are used to kill'. Accordingly there seems relatively little evidence that 'owning or having access to a gun protects a woman from attack by her partner', quite the contrary; the risks of keeping a firearm in the home significantly outweighs the benefits – especially for women (Small Arms Survey, 2013b). I develop these themes further in the second half of this chapter.

While, as I have noted, a proportion of arms trafficking – the weaponization of conflict – is undoubtedly based upon illicit deals, Bourne (2007: 71), in one of relatively few attempts to analyse the proliferation of firearms, globally and regionally, has insisted that the supply of SALW is still largely organized around the structures and processes of the legal or 'quasi-legal' firearms market. Bourne has detailed different historical phases of the SALW market supply structures. These correspond loosely to the period immediately following WW2 when international trade was 'dominated by the transfer of WW2 surplus arms by the USA and the UK'. Large quantities of small arms were shipped to the British colonies, to NATO and other westward-leaning allies under military assistance programmes designed to reinforce spheres of influence and contain and confront the perceived threat of communist infiltration (Bourne 2007: 71). In the Communist bloc, weapon proliferation was facilitated through geo-political alliances in which weapons production licensing and technology transfer agreements were secured. One of the chief reasons for the rapid distribution of the AK-47 assault rifle around the world, aside from questions of its technical attributes (simplicity, reliability and durability in a range of conflict conditions), concerned the large number of Soviet bloc countries and allies licensed to produce it by the 1960s. The AK-47 was intended to be the standard Soviet military rifle, designed to facilitate military collaboration, rearmament and supply between Soviet forces (Carr, 2008; Chivers, 2010).

In the second, Cold War, phase of global arms dealing, the two opposing blocs of countries, and their second-tier allies, dominated the arms transaction picture. Moving upscale in the black market it becomes clear how the supplies of arms during the Cold War years established durable international networks for the subsequent clandestine distribution of weapons to all manner of groups and organizations. Illegal gun running was often an aspect of covert foreign policy. For example, CIA involvement with the Air America airline allowed covert weapon distribution throughout Vietnam, Laos and Cambodia. Top-down 'dependency' armament strategies generally dominated, with arms transfers playing the role of political tools to cement alliances, bolster former colonial relationships and influence non-aligned states (Krause, 1992). After the Cold War, the global trade in small arms came to be described more as a 'buyer's market' compared to the seller's market it had been before.

Lumpe, writing in 1999, described this new 'buyer's market' as the 'global arms bazaar at century's end' (Lumpe, 1999a) pointing out that fully 80 per cent of global weapon supplies were produced by the five permanent members of the UN security council – Britain, China, France, Russia and the USA. 'The end of the Cold War left these and other states with large stocks of surplus weapons, as they downsized their militaries. It also left them with massive arms industries that needed to produce ever more weapons [for export] in order to stay alive' (Lumpe, 1999a, 1999b; Eavis and Benson, 1999). The ending of the Cold War also led to more open borders, and the weakening of the structures for controlling arms production and distribution. More particularly, the victory of the global free market saw a shift in the significance of weapons as they became less obviously the instruments of vicarious foreign policy and increasingly tradeable commodities. Whether this distinction made any substantial difference to the lives of the people living in the developing world, and directly or indirectly victimized by the arms bazaar's newest customers (where 75 per cent of the arms were destined to end up), remains an open question.

According to Greene,

> with the end of the Cold War, the armed forces of NATO and the former Warsaw Pact were downsized, releasing vast quantities of surplus arms and ammunition onto the international market at bargain prices. Much of this weaponry ended up in areas of conflict, where demand is highest. Weapons transferred to the military forces of 'responsible' governments in relatively peaceful areas displaced older weapons which then became available for transfer.
>
> *(Greene, 1999)*

Thus, large surpluses, particularly of former Soviet bloc weapons, found their way to buyers in the world's new conflict zones. As economic opportunities in eastern Europe declined, both states and criminal entrepreneurs discovered that former military weapon stocks were amongst their most saleable commodities: governments sold weapons, individual politician criminal entrepreneurs sold weapons and soldiers and entire Soviet regiments sold their weapons. As Chivers (2010) has noted, with no little irony, it took the global triumph of neo-liberalism to make a global commodity of communism's best gun.

Controlling second-hand or 'surplus' weapons is of critical significance in efforts to prevent SALW proliferation. These munitions undermine distinctions between military, police and civilian firearm types, specifications, ownership and use (I have already discussed this 'militarization' of the civilian gun market (Diaz, 2013) in earlier chapters on the USA). In practice, as Greene (1999) acknowledges, 'surplus "military" small arms are often sold on to civilians, at home and abroad' and these now 'civilian' firearms often enter the 'grey pool', the ante-room to the illicit arms trade, ultimately ending up in the hands of criminals, terrorists or insurgents. Surplus weapons are also vulnerable in dispersed government stockpiles, for example it is estimated that over 500,000 small arms were plundered from government armouries and army depots during the crisis in Albania in 1996, finding their way to gangs, organized criminal groups and terrorist cells.

Generally, the post-Cold War era, our third phase, is characterized by far greater diversity, fragmentation and regionalization of weapon trafficking networks and arrangements, which have become increasingly commercialized and privatized or represented as military aid, although, for Bourne (2007), these still remain dominated by a legacy of formal, legal and quasi-legal, state level supplies which continue to provide a degree of 'cover' for illicit small arms supply arrangements. In turn, both the war on drugs and the war on terror have provided continuing and renewable rationales for US weapon supplies to Latin America: the justifications may have changed but the weapon supplies continued. The USA supplied SALW to insurgent and rebel groups in Angola, to the Contras in Nicaragua (Stohl and Tuttle, 2008) and, during the period of Soviet occupation, to the Mujahedeen in Afghanistan. When, even following the scandal of Colonel Oliver North and the Iran-Contra affair, the scale of the misappropriation of funds devoted to weapons smuggling was exposed, the CIA still continued to run a weapons supply pipeline to Nicaragua through a number of front companies (Klare and Anderson, 1996).

Bourne's efforts to characterize the particular distribution process at work during the three phases of post-war weapons trafficking provides an important insight, in particular, he argues, because it shifts emphasis away from a perception of an amorphous, homogenized and global 'grey' market in firearms – a world simply awash in illegal firearms – gravitating ineluctably to the highest bidder. Rather he argues the real picture is more varied, nuanced and, especially, regionalized.

> The dominant global structures that shape both legal and illicit flows [of small arms] to conflicts are the legal market. This is clearly demonstrated by the legal trade, the patterns of covert aid, and the lack of distinct systems of illicit SALW spread: thus, trends in the legal market have shaped the legal flow of SALW to conflicts.
>
> *(2007: 239)*

At the same time, leakage and slippage from the legal trade have been a significant influence in provoking, sustaining and re-igniting regional conflicts. The substantial advantage of Bourne's approach, unpacking the predominantly regional structures, channels and processes through which SALW flow to conflict destinations and criminal end-users, is akin to the developments described earlier in terms of new approaches to understanding domestic criminal gun markets (Pierce *et al.*, 2004; Cook *et al.*, 2007). For if the gun supply networks can be identified and exposed, then, so the argument goes, the points of intervention in these markets can be more effectively identified and they can be controlled. Supply-side constraints can have a significant impact, restricting weapons purchasers to bottom–up sources of supply can restrict both the number and quality (and therefore also the relative lethality) of the weapons that can be obtained. On the other hand, Bourne argues, black (explicitly criminal) and grey firearms markets do undoubtedly exist and these operate predominantly at the regional and 'conflict complex' levels (Bourne, 2007: 244). Bourne is also doubtful about the extent to which the problem of small arms proliferation can be laid at the door of battalions of shady, but globally active, and criminally inclined, brokers. The scope of black-market and grey-market weapon supply processes 'is very limited beyond the regional level … globalisation appears to have failed to generate a global black market'. Accordingly, he concludes, 'there is little reason to see [illegal arms brokers] as the representatives of illicit globalisation' (Bourne, 2007: 117; see also Bourne, 2012). Insofar as this is a conclusion about illegal brokers as less than primary movers in the global small arms market place, it is surely fair enough. But if, as we have argued, weapon supply is not just about the hardware, but also about the attitudes, the propensity to use and misuse and the dissemination of a neo-liberal 'kill or be killed' individual sovereignty of the self, then anything that facilitates the supply promulgates the values. Evidence I will discuss later will show how once pastoral, peasant or communitarian cultures have become ravaged by conflict spurred on by gun-driven modernization, a new power in the land (Alpers, 2005; Mkutu, 2008).

Although poorer societies typically bear the brunt of these problems, more developed societies (amongst which we often find the leading producers and exporters of SALW – the USA, Russia, France, Germany and the UK and, increasingly, China; Dimitrov and Hall, 2012) are not immune from the problems of the gun. Indeed, it is in the very nature of weapons trafficking that scarcity can drive up the price that trafficked weapons can command. Countries with relatively successful gun control regimes, but still a demand for weapons, can see their control efforts undermined by bad neighbours as weapon scarcity renders even small-scale smuggling more lucrative. The notorious *trafico de la hormiga* ('trail of ants') routinely smuggles firearms across the Mexico border from the USA where legally entitled or 'straw purchasers' can make multiple gun purchasers from gun stores and gun shows in states such as Arizona and Texas. The guns are then passed on to traffickers who shift them across the border in small consignments hidden either in private vehicles or a variety of trade goods. Another, essentially small-scale, dimension of this smuggling activity has seen British and American troops bringing home 'battlefield souvenirs' from their tours of duty in Iraq and Afghanistan. Some of these weapons undoubtedly remain as battlefield trophies and mementoes; others are sold on to criminal contacts. Although technically 'small scale', the quantities of weapons involved can, over time, amount to very substantial numbers. Over half of the illegal handguns recovered in Canada and around 80 per cent of illegal firearms recovered in Mexico and successfully submitted for tracing (some 68,000 weapons, many being high-specification military assault rifles) were primarily designed for the US domestic market and sourced from within the United States (Goodman and Marizco, 2010; Small Arms Survey,

2013a). An ATF 'intelligence-led', test-purchase, firearm-tracing operation, *Project Gunrunner*, and its successor operation, *Operation Fast and Furious*, ran into major political difficulties in late 2010 when a US Border Patrol agent was shot and killed by an alleged Mexican trafficker firing an AK-47, purchased in the USA, as part of the ATF operation to trace the distribution of weapons to the Mexican cartels. The tragedy of the officer's death was turned into high political farce as pro-gun politicians sought to exploit the circumstance that bullets from one particular smuggled firearm, amongst the many tens of thousands trafficked over the years, were responsible for the killing (Pavlich, 2012). Above the confused cluster of denials, document redaction and agency heads running for cover all the way to Washington, the gun lobby politicians are likely to have nullified the surveillance of firearm sales in US border states and killed off the proactive policing of illicit firearm trafficking into Mexico.[3] Along with, in an election year, implicating the president in the controversy, this is just what they would have wanted.

Although the concept of 'ant-trade trafficking' first originated in respect of the USA–Mexico border crossing, it continues as a familiar practice across, into and out of many of the world's conflict complexes, including Liberia and the Cote d'Ivoire (Reno, 1999), Mozambique, Swaziland and South Africa (Chingono, 1996; Meek, 1999; Macgregor, 1998), Sierra Leone (Richards, 1996; Denov and Maclure, 2009), the Horn of Africa region (Kenya, Sudan, Ethiopia and Somalia), (Africa Peace Forum, 2006; Mkutu, 2008), Afghanistan (Pirseyedi, 2000) and Colombia (Franco, 2000), amongst a host of other examples, where violence itself often functions as a direct primary means of production (via theft, pillage and extortion). Small-scale, 'bottom-up' weapon trafficking arrangements are also closely associated with wider criminal enterprises in south-central and eastern Europe, especially drug and firearm trafficking routes moving through the Balkans region. Sagramoso commented on the

> regular trickle of small arms primarily from the Balkan region, as well as from eastern Europe … the collapse of the Soviet Union, the end of the Warsaw Pact and the wars in former Yugoslavia have resulted in a relaxation of border controls and an excess supply of light weapons, some of which found their way into Europe. Small arms and light weapons have fed local criminal underworlds as well as European terrorist groups.
>
> *(2001: 1–2)*

France, Spain, the Netherlands and Britain all felt the impact of these newer, trans-European criminal networks, the UK National Criminal Intelligence Service (NCIS) attributing Britain's 1998–2002 spike in gun violence (see Chapter 2) to these new trafficking routes (Davis *et al.*, 2001).

In his recent expose of the global arms trade, *The Shadow World*, Feinstein (2011: xxv) argues that international arms dealing accounts for fully '40% of the corruption in all world trade' and details 502 investigated and documented breaches of UN arms embargoes since the 1970s, only one of which resulted in legal action.

A number of closely-related conclusions would seem to follow. First, the arms trade and marketized weapon supply are major contributors to the globalization of crime and corruption; second, both illicit arms deals and firearm proliferation both serve to undermine good and accountable governance, both narrowing conceptions of the role of government while increasing global insecurity (Greene and Marsh, 2012d); third, increasing global insecurity itself works to generate demand for defensive firearms; fourth, the proliferation of firearms stimulates conflict and violence which further weakens social, economic and political securities; and, fifth, when social, economic and political security, that is, family and community structures, are weakened, young men often appear at the greatest risk of marginalization and subject to the lure of gangs and weaponization, apparently willing to embrace the norms of the gun culture. Finally, at both the individual and personal, and the collective and governmental levels, a corrosive neo-liberalism has the effect of mobilizing both personal behaviour and public policy around narrow conceptions of 'risk' and 'security interests'.

The weaknesses of the existing UN arms embargo system are amongst the reasons explaining the decision taken by a number of development and disarmament NGOs (Oxfam, Amnesty International, Control Arms) to press for a new international ATT, via the UN, in the late 1990s (Sprague, 2006). Feinstein explains the fraud and corruption in international arms dealing as resulting, in part, from the 'all-encompassing secrecy that often characterizes arms deals' and which 'hides corruption, conflicts of interest, poor decision-making and inappropriate national security choices'. As a consequence, he concludes, 'this trade, which should be amongst the most highly controlled and regulated, is one of the least scrutinized and accountable areas of government and private activity' (Feinstein, 2011: xxv). In particular, he points to a continuing 'revolving door' process whereby people move seamlessly through the ranks of government, military procurement and the arms industry thereby ensuring that the aims and priorities of weapons manufacturers are never far from the priorities of elected officials. In 1961, President Eisenhower coined the phrase 'military industrial complex' to warn against the dangers posed by an arms industry grown too powerful, and dictating political choices. The phrase has fallen out of use in more recent times but still captures the dilemma:

> supplying conflicts from world wars to the Cold War to the War on Terror, from small insurgencies to large scale revolutions, arms dealers, weapons manufacturers and even governments have fuelled and perpetuated tensions in pursuit of profit, on occasion selling to all sides in the same conflict.
>
> *(Feinstein, 2011: xxiv)*

Acknowledgement of such a powerful economic motive at the heart of small arms proliferation serves as a timely reminder to social scientists, and criminologists in particular, who have only recently begun to grapple with the complications that a simultaneous blurring of war, crime and conflict and the increasing interpenetration of the public and the private in policing, peacekeeping and soldiering, have brought to their discipline. An idea that criminologists have only relatively lately grown comfortable with – governing through crime (Simon, 2007) – implying that powerful social and economic interests might be deeply invested in reproducing and sustaining our crime and disorder problems is very much part of the conventional wisdom of arms control and conflict studies. Without violence and recurring conflicts there would be few profits in weapons production and brokering.

The fact that such insights might surface in a study of the vicious circle of weapons proliferation should come as no surprise. For, as Diaz (1999, 2013) has noted, firearms are sold to the police and military as loss leaders and for their advertising potential in the much bigger and ultimately more lucrative civilian markets. Once acquired by civilians, weapons (including the old, off-loaded, military stock[4]) inevitably leak into criminal hands, where their frequent misuse serves to remind those citizens who have not yet invested in personal protection weaponry, of the urgent need to do so. Arms control commentators employ a concept, 'blowback', which describes the process by which firearms supplied by one country, to an ally, end up being employed against the originating country. One of the most celebrated examples involved the weapons supplied by the USA during the 1980s to the Afghan Mujahedeen to help resist the Russian occupation, and which eventually came to be used against US troops by the Taliban. But rather than 'blowback' being an exceptional outcome of time, illicit trafficking and changing geo-political alliances, weapon proliferation and the weaponization of communities represents an institutionalized 'blowback' process in which firearms and military hardware, not to mention the hard attitudes of the gun culture, are disseminated and universalized. Like it or not, we are all living in a 'blowback culture' to some extent.

Yet notwithstanding the scale of the problems of weapon proliferation in the world, the international arms control movements would certainly point to important progress: for example on international treaties against cluster munitions and landmines. They might point to the expansion of research; greater transparency and improved accountability; enhanced international cooperation, information exchange and enforcement coordination on illicit arms transfers and the host of international treaties and agreements designed to give effect to these principles (Greene and Marsh, 2012d: 169–174); and growing respect for human rights and an increased willingness to hold the perpetrators and facilitators of violence to account (Sikkink, 2011). The UN PoA on Small Arms and Light Weapons, agreed and launched in 2001, and the subsequent ATT, agreed in 2013, are part of the process. As we shall see, however, these remain incomplete and contested and not just in the USA where, as we have seen, the ownership of firearms is often taken to be a constitutional – indeed, a *human* – right.

Where the guns go: violent conflict traps

This brings us to our second theme for the chapter, the uniquely violent conflict traps (Collier, 2008; Greene and Marsh, 2012c) and hotspots where firearm-related violence is rife, guns plentiful and weaponization intensifying. It should be recognized, weaponization is understood here as a process and it operates in different ways in different 'violence regimes' (to recall the typology developed in Chapter 1). War zones, conflict traps, failing states and high-violence areas in developed societies are all different, even as they share certain fundamental social and cultural characteristics and especially, above all, unacceptably high rates of gun violence. The discussion, therefore, will not comprise a simple cataloguing of the 'worst of the worst' – the cities, districts or regions that have, at one time or another, borne the unenviable title 'murder capitol' (Bowden, 2010; Carroll, 2011). Instead, the discussion will try to identify some of the key characteristics of violent and weaponizing areas, especially those features that appear to drive their decline, deterioration and de-civilization.

To this end, I will address these themes and issues in a number of areas where chronic armed violence has persisted. The areas are diverse and plentiful, and I cannot cover each in any detail but they include, for example, northern Mexico, Brazil and many parts of Latin America, southern Africa, Kenya and its immediate neighbours in the Horn of Africa, Central Africa and the Great Lakes region, West Africa, the Philippines, the 'Middle-East' region, Afghanistan, India, South East Asia and parts of central and eastern Europe (the former Yugoslavia), and Russia. What such areas often have in common are the sharp social, economic or political transformations they have lately undergone (post-apartheid; post-colonial; post-dictatorship; post-communist; even post-pastoral) and related transitions, transitions that are also typically associated with varying degrees of state failure and highly exploitative relations of social production but have a rather limited embrace of political accountabilities or human rights in their diverse governance processes. Instead the proliferation of firearms in such regions, especially the particular patterns and forms of weapon possession, often impede the development of more democratic and accountable governance processes, while simultaneously threatening the sustainability of peace building initiatives and those engaged in them (ICRC, 1999). They are also often characterized by aggressive, non-accountable forms of militarized policing or peacekeeping (Chevigny, 1995; Huguet and de Carvalho, 2008) which further exacerbate conflicts, hostilities and social division. For example, some Central and Latin American countries

> have adopted so-called *mano dura* (iron-fist) policies, criminalizing membership in youth gangs and resorting to extensive imprisonment ... [Others] have resorted to armed police or military forces to retake territories with weak state presence, which are essentially governed by criminal groups or illegal militias or, in the case of Colombia, by an insurgent group.
>
> *(Felbab-Brown, 2011b; see also Wacquant, 2003, 2008b)*

One significant, although rather counter-productive, outcome of these policies, detailed in the United Nations Office on Drugs and Crime (UNODC) Global Homicide Report (2011), in respect of Mexico, Costa Rica and Panama, has been that, as police and military campaigns have been stepped up against DTOs and cartels, criminal gangs or insurgent groups, disrupting both trafficking supply lines and regional sources of authority and leadership, so homicide rates in these countries have risen significantly (UNODC, 2011: 52).

Furthermore, plentiful supplies of small arms invariably help to either cultivate or sustain 'warrior' or 'gangsta' cultures (Hagedorn, 2008) or forms of patriarchal 'warlordism' or 'islamist insurgency' frequently to the especial detriment of women and children living in these regions (Turshen, 2004). Small arms proliferation often transforms the nature of conflict, embedding chronic violence and blurring distinctions between new and old wars, small insurgencies, conflict and post-conflict societies, civilian and combatant, while facilitating interpersonal crime and violence (Rogers, 2009). The war in El Salvador during the 1980s, for example, profoundly accelerated the poverty, economic disruption and marked inequality of the country, weaponizing and militarizing society as a direct legacy of the conflict. El Salvador is now one of the most violent countries in Latin America (see Figure 7.1), with high levels of violent street crime, extensive armed gang networks (or *Maras*, providing substantial illegal employment opportunities, initially for demobilized ex-combatants, and subsequently becoming institutionalized in communities) and major issues of domestic violence. Hume (2004) has argued that 'fear and insecurity still characterise everyday life for many citizens', while 'violence has become part of everyday neighbourhood interaction ... [Disputes] between neighbours are aggravated by the use of small arms, as are traffic incidents'. Estimates suggest that 86 per cent of murders are caused by everyday 'social violence', including family and neighbour disputes, and peer group (gang) conflicts, which are often still influenced by a legacy of grievances and social divisions going back to the war. Police reports indicate that firearms are used in as many as 85 per cent of homicides (refer to Figure 7.2 below) (Hume, 2004: 2–3). Governmental responses to the gangs tend towards the populist and repressive (*Super Mano Dura* or 'heavy hand' policing, since 2003), with fairly predictable results in escalating levels of violence and further cementing gang solidarities and perpetuating conflicts. In this turbulent context, weapon possession has both instrumental and expressive features, with guns seen as essential for personal and family protection but also as a way of embodying tough aggressive maleness or 'militarized masculinity'; carrying weapons apparently made some men 'feel more like men'. Taken together these attitudes to masculinity, firearms and self-protection underpin dominant discourses of 'righteous' violence, honour and legitimate retribution as an appropriate way to solve problems and restore respect, and they are reported in other parts of central and South America (Koonings and Kruijt, 2007; Rotker, 2002; Savenije and van der Borgh, 2004; Zubillaga, 2009; Cukier and Sheptycki, 2012).

A Small Arms Survey regional trends analysis of Central America (Godnick *et al.*, 2002: vii) notes that

> social violence and armed criminality are on the rise in the aftermath of the conflicts that have plagued most countries of the region ... the politicized factions are giving way to criminal gangs and organized civilian militia groups that are taking advantage of left-over military-style weapons [while] disenfranchised ex-combatants and unemployed or otherwise marginalized male youths are easily recruited into such groups.

Furthermore, 'military-style weapons and commercial firearms' have spread from the formerly conflict-affected countries of El Salvador, Guatemala and Nicaragua, to the previously peaceful countries of Costa Rica, Honduras, Mexico and Panama (refer to Figures 7.1 and 7.2). Thus, 'recycled Central American weapons are finding new, more profitable markets throughout the region and beyond'. Finally, the proportion of homicides committed with firearms is rising (Godnick *et al.*, 2002: vii).

Given the range of the different areas under consideration here, the commentary can only be something of an overview, but an overview specifically concerned with the ways in which the dynamics of weaponization impact upon social relationships and economic development in the affected regions – and often with profound 'blowback' consequences for the countries of the developed world. Figure 7.1, drawing upon data from the excellent gun policy news website resource (GunPolicy. org), presents a range of societies, based upon the latest available data, with the highest international rates of gun homicide.[5] An immediate contrast with most similar diagrams featuring *first world* societies is the position of the USA towards the lowest end of the distribution. One important qualification needs to be introduced, as I noted in Chapter 1, the ability of a society to compile reasonably reliable crime and homicide data is often compromised in failed and failing states; the ability to collate homicide data is itself a mark of governmental capacity (Soares, 2004).

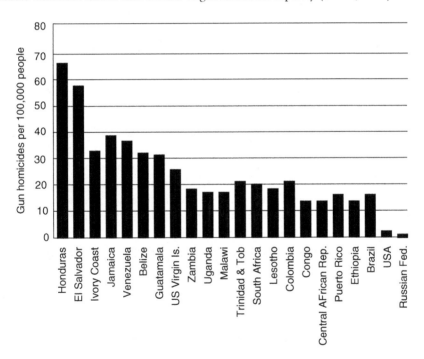

FIGURE 7.1 Gun homicides per 100,000 people in the most violent societies

Sources: Alpers *et al.* (2013); UNODC (2011).

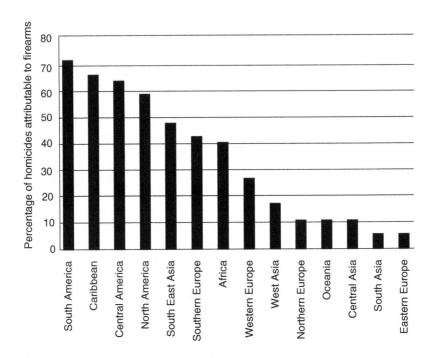

FIGURE 7.2 Percentage of homicides attributable to firearms in differing regions of the world

Source: UNODC (2011: 40).

In societies with the highest gun violence records, questions of data reliability are likely to arise, whereas societies with the very worst problems, in particular a number of conflict societies in Africa, as indicated in Figure 7.2 from the UNODC, may well be excluded by virtue of their inability to maintain an effective count. Pattugalan (2004: 66), here discussing firearm-related deaths in South East Asia, argues that there are often better records of 'conflict-related' deaths and that 'statistics could considerably increase if the number of deaths due to armed criminality is accounted for. Unfortunately, there is [often] poor national reporting on this.'

One further important issue revealed by the UNODC Global Homicide study and which has a direct bearing upon *overall* homicide figures, concerns the proportions of homicides attributable to firearms in different parts of the world. As Figure 7.2 indicates, these rates can vary considerably, suggesting that restrictions on firearm proliferation can, in the context of other social and cultural factors, have a significant influence upon a society's overall homicide rate.

The central dynamics at the heart of many of the world's worst conflict complexes appear to comprise rapid social and economic changes, social and economic dislocations which result in rising inequalities and insecurities, the growing marginality of significant sections of the population and the breakdown of law and order. In turn, rising criminalization, fears and insecurities, foster a demand for firearms, while nar-row principles of neo-liberal governance appear to prevail and these become reflected in a highly individualistic, competitive and, in the case of armed young men, increas-ingly non-compliant aggressive cultures of expressive self-interest. Weaponization typically features as both cause and consequence of this cycle of events. As Buchanan (2004: 4–5) has argued, tackling these perceived security deficits can create what she calls a 'freedom from fear dividend', which can help create a more favourable climate for de-weaponization and civilian disarmament policies – although it can just as easily persuade people that acquiring their own weapons is a 'sensible' precaution to take. In the context of our discussions of firearm trafficking, I have already referred to a number of these dilemmas insofar as they relate to the northern regions of Mexico, so here I will develop that commentary.

Central America/Mexico

The US–Mexico border region and its deeply conflicted social relations has been graphically described by journalist Ed Vulliamy in his book *Amexica* (2010). Juárez, one of the principle Mexican cities of the region, embodies many of the worst aspects of the conflict complexes outlined by Bourne (2007). According to Felbab-Brown,

> more than any other place in Mexico, Ciudad Juárez has become a symbol of the drug-related violence of the 2000s and a test and proving ground of the effectiveness of Mexico's national security strategy to combat its powerful drug trafficking organizations … Some of Mexico's most dramatic violence has taken place in the city. With 3,097 homicides in 2010, Juárez was not only one of the most violent cities in the world, but its murder rate alone was on par with violence in Afghanistan, a country with an intense insurgency and counterinsurgency campaign.
>
> *(Felbab-Brown, 2011a: 8)*

To the north it has one of the most unforgiving neighbours possible, the USA, for which Juárez serves as little more than a combined junction, workshop and labour supply depot on one of the world's major land-based trade transportation routes. The huge volume of trade traffic passing through the city provides plentiful and lucrative opportunities for cocaine trafficking to the insatiable market in the north, thereby explaining the increasingly bitter, violent struggles between rival drug car-tels seeking to control these key trade routes and the traffic running along them.

As we have seen, however, paralleling the northern flow of cocaine, is a south-ern flow of high grade automatic and semi-automatic arms and ammunition – the river of steel – from the gun stores and rather less well-regulated gun-shows of states such as Texas, Arizona, California and New Mexico, augmenting the fire-power of the cartels. This illegal trade in firearms, the original *trafico de la hormiga* ('trail of ants' weapon smuggling) entails the regular and routine smuggling of firearms across the Mexican border from the USA. Over 68,000 firearms sold in the USA have been subsequently traced to Mexico and around some 90 per cent of successfully traced illegal firearms recovered in Mexico originate within the United States (Chu and Krause, 2009; Goodman and Marizco, 2010: 171–172). Diaz (2013) cites a Violence Policy Centre publication from 2009 which details, on a case-by-case basis and drawn from court and prosecution records, the range and variety of firearms smuggled south from the USA. Both US and Mexican government officials appear to agree:

> large numbers of military style firearms from the U.S. civilian gun market are fuelling criminal violence in Mexico. A series of Congressional hearings and public policy reports have made clear that the U.S. gun industry – manufacturers, importers, distributors, retailers, and so-called 'gun shows' – plays an instrumental role in making readily available to illegal gun traffickers the types and numbers of weapons that facilitate drug lords' confrontations with the Mexican government and its people.
>
> *(VPC, 2009: 1)*

Dube *et al.* (2012) treated the ending of the US assault weapons sales ban in 2004 as a 'natural experiment' to assess the extent to which the renewed availability of powerful, military-style assault rifles, known to be smuggled into Mexico in large numbers, had an impact on rates of firearm violence in Mexico. They found that the Mexican areas located closest to the assault weapon supply states in the USA did encounter increases in gun-related violence and homicides after 2004, although the violence rates were also influenced by local cartel–political conflicts and levels of drug trafficking.

The demand for powerful, military-style American weapons is a direct consequence of the conflict both between rival drug cartels, and between the cartels and the police and military units deployed by the Mexican president Calderon (Abu-Hamdeh, 2011). The military were deployed precisely because the regular local police forces in Mexico were considered 'so corrupt and hollowed out that they [were] unable to respond effectively to the violence and do not have the capacity to reduce the power of the cartels' (Felbab-Brown, 2011b: 3). A US special agent in charge of Arizona's Phoenix ATF field office, directly involved in tackling the cross-border weapon trafficking fuelling what he called the 'drug cartel war', described the range of firearms intercepted. These included Barrett 50-caliber long range sniper rifles, Colt AR-15 .223-caliber assault rifles, AK-47 7.62-caliber assault rifles and their variants, and FN 5.57-caliber pistols, now better known in Mexico as the *mata policia,* or 'cop killer', semi-automatic pistol with armour piercing capability.[6] The point was not lost on the ATF agent that military specification weapons, to fight a drug war, were being sourced from US *civilian* markets (VPC, 2009).

Even though the prevalence of firearms, lucrative drug supply routes to be defended, a protracted drug cartel war, police corruption, failing government and a profound militarization of law and order exert a profound influence upon the crime complex of northern Mexico and the Juárez region, they certainly do not exhaust the troubles besetting the area. The dramatic changes impacting upon Mexico during the past two-to-three decades largely mark an acceleration of longer run social and economic trends that have seen a concentration of land-holding in Mexican agriculture, the increased proletarianization of small and subsistence farmers and growing numbers of landless and dispossessed workers (Chacon and Davis, 2006). Many of these gravitated northwards hoping, perhaps, to cross into the USA or to work as cheap and dispensable labour in the Border Industrialisation Programme factories, later the North American Free Trade Agreement (NAFTA) production plants, which formalized the neo-liberal 'super-exploitative' conditions conferring no workplace rights, little security of employment and wages barely hovering above a legal minimum, established from the mid-1990s onwards (Bacon, 2008).

The proximity to the USA border accounts for the large number of would-be (illegal) transients and emigrants frustrated and piled up at the border in their quest for the American Dream. Instead they frequently found themselves ensnared by its opposites, either, along with 35 per cent of the Mexican population, 'eking out a living in hardscrabble poverty' (Grayson, 2010: 4), or as the cheap disposable labour of the sweatshop *maquiladora* factory systems, the vulnerable prey of US Border Patrols and vigilantes (Walker, 2007), or members of a vast surplus population, reluctant foot-soldiers of the cartels or denizens of the dangerous and depleted contraband economies. The NAFTA factories and assembly plants were given free access to the cheap, non-unionised labour of northern Mexico; in turn Mexico gained some much needed economic investment and the people some promise of employment and opportunity. Unfortunately the benefits of this arrangement were far from equally distributed, for Vulliamy, the *maquiladoras* perfectly symbolize Mexico's 'subjugated but dependent relationship to the US economy' (2010: 200).

The *maquiladora* factory units offer long hours, gruelling and highly exploitative working conditions for a largely female-dominated, and seemingly expendable, labour force. Like many of the neo-liberalizing strategies of economic development the world over, the new factory units further intensified what Bourgois (2003: 292) has termed the long 'historical crisis' of masculinity. That is to say, the traditional status and respect attached to masculinity, rooted in producer, worker, provider and, in some parts of the world, as we shall see, 'hunter' and 'warrior' identities which men are often reluctant to relinquish, are sharply confronted by what the men perceive to be 'feminized' factory working conditions. The phenomenon has been reported in many parts of the world (Campbell, 1993); it can be exacerbated at the personal level by cultural and gendered relations of respect involved when, for example, being publicly disrespected in front of female onlookers (Fagan and Wilkinson, 1998) or, as in examples provided by Bourgois, having to take orders from female supervisors at work (2003: 148–149). Such reflections merely provide a broad sociological backdrop for the micro-politics of 'respect', status and identity which often seem to lie behind much street level violence between young men or directed at young women. It can help to explain the apparently scripted 'hair trigger' sensitivities (Short, 1997; Squires, 2011a) played out around conceptions of respect and identity and enacted between young men at ground level and the ways in which possession of firearms and the performance of violence can amount to compensatory strategies for their 'defence of self' – not to mention self-defence (Harcourt, 2006; Cukier and Sheptycki, 2012).

For many commentators, the marginality of these young men and the seeming dispensability of the largely female labour force are reflected in another of the cruel realities of Juárez: the spate of so-called *femicido* murders of over 500 young women and the hundreds more missing or lost since 1994. According to Alba and Guzman (2010) and Staudt (2008), the Juárez border area establishes a worst case scenario of weaponized, hyper-violent, misogynistic masculinity in crisis. The drug cartel conflicts, the firearms and the para-militarization bring a certain empowerment to many unattached young men, as in so many gang cultures around the world (Totten, 1999; Batchelor, 2009), and have cultivated a culture of violent masculine impunity (see Bourgois, 2003: 205) often further sustained by police corruption and ineptitude. According to Olivera, the alarming rate of female murders, spreading across the whole of Mexico since the 1990s, 'in direct relation to the expansion of neo-liberalism' needs to be viewed 'as an expression of the country's current crises of governability, internal security, and respect for human rights' (Olivera, 2006). At the same time the predominantly female employment opportunities in the new factory system have allowed the resentments of displaced males to fester even as the social needs and human rights of this vast, nameless, transient and abused female workforce are ground down to the minimum on American assembly lines. South African researchers describe similar gendered violence relations:

> [G]un ownership is mainly a male phenomenon, a means to demonstrate manhood, particularly among young men. While men are the predominating victims of gun violence, women are most vulnerable behind closed doors, where guns are used to intimidate, control, hurt and kill intimate partners. An association between gun availability and homicides and suicides has been shown. A gun in the home is more likely to be used against a family member than in providing protection. Femicide studies have shown that gun availability is a major risk factor in intimate femicide.
>
> *(Abrahams* et al., *2010: 586)*

As Arriola has explained, the missing element in many of the official discussions of the Juárez murders

> is the multi-national corporations' complicity with Mexican officials in disregarding the health, safety and security needs of the Mexican women and girls who work in the *maquiladoras* ... the factories run twenty-four hours a day, [but] pay no taxes, and do very little to ensure that their workers will have a roof over their heads, beds to sleep in and enough money to feed their families ... such employment has not enhanced peace and prosperity amongst the working class, instead hostility against the poor working women has increased.
>
> *(Arriola, 2010: 27–28)*

Or, as one of Vulliamy's interviewees has put it, rather more forcefully:

> The *maquilas* see women who work much as they see our city, as something expendable. So what if a woman is murdered? Ten or a hundred? There are always plenty more If you want to beat, rape or kill a woman, there is no better place than Juárez, there are thousands to choose from, plenty of opportunities and, thirdly, you can get away with it. The lives of women, especially poor women, have no value.
>
> *(Vulliamy, 2010: 164)*

Grayson (2010), amongst others, has argued that the violence, the collapse of the rule of law, the sheer un-governability of large areas, the subversion of democracy – including the emergence of 'narco sub-states' where the authority of the central state is displaced by that of the cartels (Manwaring, 2007), the poverty and the absence of rights or social infrastructure, not to mention the many thousands of desperate people aiming to leave, conspire to make Mexico a prime candidate for a 'failed' or certainly 'failing state'. By contrast, the final irony, for Vulliamy, is that Juárez – the scorched-earth, neo-liberal trap where the American Dream turns nightmare – marks not the breakdown of the late capitalist social order, or perhaps some failing state, rather, Vulliamy suggests, this *is* the neo-liberal order of the future (2010: 106).

Hyper-aggressive, macho and misogynist behaviours are often familiar in highly weaponized, para-militarized and 'gangsta' cultures (Hagedorn, 2008) and, confronted by the violence, it may seem a rather moot point, whether the destructive environments or 'lethal ecologies' (Fagan and Wilkinson, 1998, 2000; Wilkinson, 2003) inhabited by these young men, working through their peer influences, their desperate struggles for survival, elaborate rituals of respect or 'anticipatory retaliations' (Collins, 2008), or perhaps just the simple power of firearms, are most responsible for driving their violences. Diaz (2013) even speculates about whether this capacity for violence is 'inherent' in the nature of the gun itself. In one sense, this may simply be part of the gun's design; the modern, semi-automatic, high-performance firearm does what it is designed to do – discharge ammunition quickly and accurately killing or wounding many people. This is a deliberate design feature. But he goes further, 'to the denizens of this dark universe, a gun is an amulet that magically transforms the bearer into a righteous and invulnerable defender of all that is good and right' (Diaz, 2013: 58, 66). All irony aside, his point is that the gun has the potential to transform human and social relations; producing a world in which citizens are all 'armed and dangerous' to one another fundamentally transforms sociability. It does not create a 'polite society', as an old NRA bumper sticker used to proclaim,[7] it establishes a highly dangerous one, where raw human emotions (stupidity, anger, jealousy) can tip easily into lethal violence. The world's conflict zones are manifestly not 'polite societies'; but societies where the well-armed dominate the rest. They are characterized, as Muggah and Batchelor argue, by 'terror and suffering': yet terror and suffering … are neither discussed nor documented as extensively as death and injury, but the fear engendered by the use of small arms and the rapid breakdown of informal norms of trust and co-operation are far-reaching. As civilians have become strategic targets in many conflicts, through summary and mass executions, brutal intimidation and criminality, small arms have come to represent a potent and ubiquitous instrument of terror. Small arms availability and misuse also has a measurable impact on decisions relating to personal mobility, social cohesion, political participation, child-schooling, employment and personal-protection.

(Muggah and Batchelor, 2002: 22)

Guns underpin a certain kind of toxic political power, both personally and collectively, as the NRA's Wayne La Pierre let slip in a seemingly unguarded moment 'the guys with the guns make the rules', he noted (cited in Diaz, 2013: 194). Although he was only partly correct, the guys with the guns do the killing, the guys who *supply* the guns make the rules. But the personal is political; the armed individual thereby becomes a temporary sovereign of neo-liberalism, living, albeit very briefly, in a nasty and brutish world (Squires, 2012).

Nothing in the foregoing commentary is intended to suggest that weaponization, armed groups and individuals necessarily, absolutely and everywhere, fundamentally transform societies, cultures, communities and social relationships. Still less are any ensuing changes universally the same, although societies in conflict, flux and change, where communities and vital social institutions have the least resilience, in other words, failing states and broken societies, are likely to be impacted the most. Even so, weaponized social relationships are still contextualized *social* relationships, the neighbourhood gangs, the drug dealing and contraband distribution networks, the protection racketeers, corrupt officials and organized criminals, still negotiate forms of sub-political 'governance from below' (Beck, 1996 in Rodgers, 2009: 39), but with an additional 'edge' assured by their means of violence; after all conflict traps are typically found in failed or failing states which, by definition, no longer have a monopoly of violence. Hagedorn, for instance, specifically associates the rise of gang cultures with neo-liberalism and the *retreat* or *failure* of the once inclusive state: 'Gangs and other groups of armed young men occupy the vacuum created by the retreat of the social welfare policies of the state' (Hagedorn, 2005: 154). And a wide range of academic commentators have drawn attention to the roles undertaken by these agents, perhaps 'armed actors', 'drug trafficking networks', 'violence entrepreneurs', street activists or gangs, in establishing forms of order, economy, social structure and even security (DiChiara and Chabot, 2003; Koonings and Kruijt, 2004; Savenije and van der Borgh, 2004; Arias, 2006; Rodgers, 2009; Rodgers and Jensen, 2009; Sonnevelt, 2009). Many would subscribe to Davis' (2008) observation that gangs, as exemplars of these otherwise marginalized groups, establish a powerbase for the relatively powerless through their control of spaces and resources (including violence).

For poor youth lacking other resources, these informal spatial monopolies if successfully defended and consolidated, provide some measure of entrepreneurial opportunity as well as local prestige and warrior glamour. Gangs also frequently act as neighbourhood militias to police public space, enforce (or resist) ethnic or racial borders and thereby control access to jobs and housing.

(Davis, 2008: xi)

And he continued by emphasizing the double-edged character of the gang phenomenon. 'If some gangs are vampire-like parasites on their own communities, others play Robin Hood or employer of last resort; most combine elements of both predation and welfare' (Davis, 2008: xi). The same essential variety applies also to the joining of gangs and violence groups: some elect to join gangs, others have gangs thrust upon them by residence or kinship, some are 'wannabes', others more reluctant (Pitts, 2008); in a more extreme context Somasundaram (2002) catalogues a range of 'push and pull' factors under which children become soldiers or fighters – from fear and poverty, desperation and survival to kidnap, indoctrination and brutalization (Honwana, 2006). Perhaps there is a terrible parallel here, where poor young women become the dispensable labour power of the new, neo-liberal economic order and poor young men the equally dispensable shock troops and bullet catchers of its dark underside (Muggah and Batchelor, 2002: 17).[8]

Discussing her interviews with Mexican youth workers, Felbab-Brown describes this resort to cheap 'dispensable youth' as the foot-soldiers of the new 'narco-liberalism':

In order to reduce the group's visibility to law enforcement agencies and rivals, the DTOs increasingly recruit among youth gangs or hire young people for one-time hits. An NGO worker operating a reintegration program for gang members in one of Ciudad Juárez southern *colonías* described to me how young boys are currently given an assault weapon for a hit and end up spraying a target with bullets, no matter how many bystanders get caught in the crossfire, because they have never been trained to operate the weapon. If they fail to kill their target, they risk being killed themselves by the criminal group that hired them.

(Felbab-Brown, 2011a: 11)

One consequence of this conscription of young children into weaponized gang violence is described by Godnick *et al.* (2002), namely the number of young children killed or injured by 'stray bullets':

[C]hildren are frequently caught in the middle of violent assaults or gang fights. Four hundred and nineteen children were admitted to Benjamín Bloom Hospital in San Salvador as a result of wounds caused by stray bullets between 1990 and 2000 not one of which has resulted in a criminal prosecution. Forty per cent of the child victims of stray bullets were girls, compared to the six per cent female incidence in all homicides.

(Godnick et al., 2002: 13)

But perhaps one of the most revealing aspects of this weaponization of youth is the sense that it reflects the further transformation of law, order and community, and the destabilization of social relations, in the face of the increasingly militarized campaigns against the traffickers and cartels. Often such transformation could be read as 'breakdown', but not always. Brazil, Colombia, Mexico and Jamaica have adopted tough military tactics to physically retake territories, favelas or communities; territories in a practical sense controlled by criminal or insurgent groups. In Rio de Janeiro, Brazil, similar patterns of youth conscription into violence and youthful victimization are apparent; the story has been powerfully conveyed in Lins' portrait of the *City of God* (Lins, 2006) and by Dowdney's book *Children of the Drug Trade* (2003). Likewise, at the beginning of a fascinating ethnography of drugs and democracy in Rio, Arias describes his first trip into a favela, driving past the virtual gang checkpoint stationed at the entrance to the community. '[W]e had to turn down our headlights so as not to provoke a hail of bullets from the traffickers who had positioned themselves at the entrance' of the favela. Further on, 'we passed the occasional *boca de fuma* (drug sales point), where a group of adolescents and young men would sit with automatic rifles and other weapons selling cocaine' (Arias, 2006: ix). But another dimension of this armed order is revealed in Goldstein's anthropology of a Rio favela – governance from below – where the gangs themselves exercised a form of gun control on the community:

> The Amigos dos Amigos (friends of friends) prohibited anyone who was not part of the gang from owning a gun ... Breno's brother-in-law, a resident, owned a gun that the new gang insisted he give up. After numerous verbal threats, members of the gang resorted to force and one evening entered his home with the goal of confiscating his gun.
>
> *(Goldstein, 2003: 192)*

Unfortunately, gang governance had its familiar, brutal, patriarchal side. Breno was not there and his wife was home alone, and was brutally beaten 'for being unable or unwilling to tell them where the gun was hidden' (Goldstein, 2003: 192).

Not surprisingly, 'the main homicide victims are young black men or male members of other underprivileged groups and residents of low income communities'. Furthermore, because of the perceived connections between these high death rates and the criminal activities of the networks involved in the sale of drugs, the residents of these areas are easily stigmatized and criminalized (Ribeiro and Oliveira, 2010: 9). And yet, in Rio, one seemingly perverse consequence of the militarization of law and order made necessary by the epidemic crime levels associated with the lucrative and highly weaponized drug trade has been the addition of a further layer of violence. New militia groups have subsequently emerged, 'modernized versions of more traditional vigilante groups' which attempt to rationalize their violence by promising 'to remove drug gangs and the need to respond to the violence caused by the competition between these gangs over drug trafficking free zones' (Ribeiro and Oliveira, 2010: 9–10) but they do so as old-fashioned protection rackets, their ultimate motivation is economic; security at a price. The supposed legitimacy of such gangs comes from the absence of regular law enforcement but the

> perverse reality Rio is witnessing today is that – on top of the violence between drug gangs and between drugs gangs and police – the militias have added yet another wave of violence; of militias against drug gangs, militias against militias and militias against police.
>
> *(Blickman, 2010: 5)*

Such arguments go some way to underpin the arguments by Kunkeler and Peters (2011: 283) that although '[u]rban youth violence and armed conflict are clearly separated – conceptually – in [academic] conflict literature through a "political versus criminal violence" dichotomy … the extremely high levels of (youth) violence in South Africa or Brazil' are now embedded within complex weaponized conflict dynamics which actually reveal more similarities than differences.

Small arms and Africa

For Solomon (1999), discussing conflict and weapon proliferation in the southern Africa region, it matters less how the conflict began than how it is currently sustained and perpetuated. As Barker and Ricardo note, mid-way through the first decade of the twenty-first century, 'approximately half of Africa's countries and about one in three persons … were affected either directly or indirectly by conflict' (2005: 24). Many of the original wars in the southern Africa region, and there have been plenty ('anticolonial struggles, the warfare by liberation movements against minority regimes, Cold War "proxy wars", destabilization operations conducted by the apartheid regime in South Africa, and the effects of postcolonial civil and ethnic strife' (Solomon, 1999: 147-8)), have left a legacy in the diffusion of weapons, civil strife, cultures of violence, historic grievances, poor governance processes, oppressive policing tactics and, not least, the racist inequalities of the apartheid regime in South Africa itself, which have proven a fertile recruiting ground for criminal gangs and organized crime groups (Standing, 2005, 2006). Solomon continues by noting that

> there are today in the region some 400 regional crime syndicates whose activities range from the smuggling of illegal immigrants to narco-trafficking, money laundering, and arms trafficking. Ordinary crime is also threatening human security … The ready availability of light weapons also provides the means to transform ethnic differences into open conflict.
>
> *(Solomon, 1999: 148)*

Berman and Florquin (2005) describe similar problems in the ECOWAS region (Economic Community of West African States), where they identified 35 separate armed groups representing a direct threat to regional and human security. The groups originally comprised both 'pro-state, and anti-state groups, and a wide range of vigilante groups established to safeguard various financial (both individual and commercial), religious, communal, and ethnic interests' but over the course of time have become 'armed and aimless – but no less deadly' as 'regardless of original motives ... original "ideology" tends to evaporate rapidly in the face of temptations to engage in financial or political aggrandizement – usually at the point of a gun'. Rape, murder and human rights violations 'typically forms part of the groups' mode of operating, tens of thousands of children being press-ganged into joining them. Disaffected youth were said to form the greater part of the membership of the groups. Unemployment and lack of alternative economic options made membership a particularly attractive option for the region's youth. Interviews suggest that a majority had voluntarily joined the armed groups primarily because it represented their best – if not only – opportunity to 'earn' a living. As Berman and Florquin conclude: 'Gangs of untrained, inexperienced youth would be less threatening were it not for easy access to a wide variety of small arms and light weapons' (Berman and Florquin, 2005: 385–387).

Just as young men appear the most susceptible to the lure of guns and gang involvements in Rio de Janeiro and West Africa, so too, in Nigeria itself, Ginnifer and Ismail (2005) describe young men – often unemployed youths, sometimes referred to as 'area' or 'rarray' boys (footloose youth) (Barker and Ricardo, 2005: 2) amongst a number of similarly pejorative references to apparently unattached male adolescents – as the primary disposable combatant members of gangs, vigilante and militia groups (Peters *et al.*, 2003; Jennings, 2007: 16). Sometimes these groups reflect ethnic and tribal loyalties, at other times they serve political interests, 'manipulating electoral outcomes by kidnapping or killing political opponents, threatening and intimidating electorates, destroying lives and properties, and disrupting election campaigns' (Barker and Ricardo, 2005: 3–4); at other times they simply form part of a violent criminal economy, sometimes preying upon, or taxing, the business and communities amongst which they live, sometimes protecting them, at a price. Barker and Ricardo warn against oversimplification, they note that

> there is no typical young man in sub-Saharan Africa and no single African version of manhood. There are numerous African masculinities, urban and rural and changing historically, including versions of manhood associated with war, or being warriors and others associated with farming or cattle-herding.
>
> *(2005: v)*

Nevertheless, they emphasize the combination of factors: rapid social and economic change and the social dislocations to which they are related, poverty, AIDS, unemployment and marginality, weak or failing government, civil unrest and, not least, a proliferation of firearms for accelerating 'the socialization of boys into rigid gender norms, and violence and conflict' (2005: vi). Accordingly, they argue that there are fairly direct connections between violence and conflict and the ways in which contemporary manhoods or masculinities are constructed in Africa (2005: 24–25). For, just as excluded young men join gangs in first-world societies, so African adolescents find both material and emotional support in groups:

> [B]oth income and social recognition is linked to young men's participation in armed conflicts ... conflict and the use of violence become ways to obtain empowerment ... for young men who perceive no other way to achieve it. Young men may also find camaraderie with male peers in some armed insurgency groups, and in some cases, male role models or surrogate fathers, and substitute families.
>
> *(Barker and Ricardo, 2005: vi)*

They report how the weaponization of youth, child soldiers with AK-47s, permits the performance (bolstered by violent initiation rites, threats, drugs and indoctrination), by adolescents, of a violently unrestrained version of manhood taken to its extreme, before a terrified audience of adults. In the context of her ethnography of Mohajir militancy in Pakistan, another 'Kalashnikov culture', Khan also describes how boys as young as 13 and 14, 'roaming the streets with automatic weapons' and engaging in targeted killings, kidnapping and robbery, were both establishing strongly masculine gendered selves and also transforming a broader cultural politics through their violence (Khan, 2010: 7–9). Such performances of violence both (re)produce, confront and disrupt traditional relations of age, experience, hierarchy and authority (Barker and Ricardo, 2005: 25). A much acclaimed recent novel, *Beasts of No Nation* (perhaps *Catcher in the Rye* for the post-colonial world) centring upon the experience of child soldiers in Africa, engages directly with these themes. The author Uzodinma Iweala (2005) describes the brutal atrocities committed by the boys, empowered by their weapons. Only towards the end of the story, when the boy breaks free from his captivity and, crucially, throws away his heavy black machine gun, does he find real manhood and redemption. This may only be a novel, but everything about Africa's dilemma was centred here upon the gun: both liberator and millstone.

A number of civil wars in West Africa have contributed greatly to a fairly familiar vicious cycle of weapon proliferation in the region, supplemented by extensive cross-border arms smuggling and mercenary actions. This, as Ginnifer and Ismail describe, has led to an increasing 'self-help' attitude with regard to firearms, with civilians arming, as and when they can, for self-defence, whereas the criminal gangs and vigilante groups perceive a need for ever more weapons with which to protect themselves or launch attacks on rival groups. All told, this has contributed to a substantial 'normalisation of the gun culture among youths' (2005: 13).

The widespread availability of small arms in Nigeria has reputedly

> transformed existing social, cultural, ethnic, political and environmental cleavages into violent confrontations ... increasing the scale of lethality, the degree of intensity, the numbers of casualties and the extent of livelihood destruction.

> SALW were freely used in the more than 50 identifiable outbreaks of ethno-religious violence occurring [between 1999 and 2005], in which more than 100,000 people were thought to have died.
>
> *(Ginnifer and Ismail, 2005: 4)*

One response to this escalating weaponized violence has been the resort to tough and militarized, but often highly fallible and sometimes politically corrupt, law enforcement. At the same time, the wealthy and major businesses, for example oil and gas extraction businesses of the Niger delta, have invested extensively in private security companies, and sometimes local militia groups, offering a full range of militarized security options, to defend their operations against criminal gangs, smugglers, pirates and local resistance militias. According to Ikelegbe (2005) the 'political economy of conflict' surrounding resource extraction in Nigeria perpetuates the vicious cycles of weaponization and violence in the region. It has already 'fuelled a deadly regime of violence and crime ... it has supported a massive arms trade [comprising] thousands of sophisticated assault rifles ... it underpins crime and violence in the region'. It is compounded by organized criminal and militia resistance in the region, and 'it is further sustaining it' (Ikelegbe, 2005: 226–230).

Macha (2006), discussing weaponization, rising violence and militancy in the Horn of Africa region (Somalia, Ethiopia and Kenya) describes a similar sequence of originating factors constituting the region's violence complex: impoverished, marginalized and frustrated youth and young men lacking jobs, opportunities or other meaningful activities become susceptible to the lure of plentiful firearms and the power and criminal opportunities these confer. Increasingly, he argues, especially in the more rapidly urbanized areas, young Somali men, former refugees, have turned to violent gang and militia activities and, more recently, Islamist jihadi insurgent groups which, in turn, intensify the regional demand for weapons.[9] Sang (2009) describes the rapid urbanization of Mogadishu and Nairobi, where some 60 per cent of citizens are said to live in poverty-stricken and overcrowded slum areas to which regional refugees often gravitate. Like the squatter settlements of many of the world's fastest growing 'southern' cities (Davis, 2006), these areas are often high crime areas with weapons in abundance, although also no-go zones for the police. Nairobi is also described by Bartolucci and Kanneworff (2012: 130) as 'one of the most violent cities in sub-Saharan Africa' and frequently referred to as 'Nairobbery'. The Small Arms Survey (2002) saw weapon proliferation as one of the chief security threats facing Nairobi, although not just weapons in the hands of gangs , but also in possession of organized criminal groups which appeared to target the homes and businesses of the city's more affluent citizens in the form of armed robberies, home invasions, rapes, kidnappings and car-jackings (Sang, 2009: 10–11). The net effect of this weaponization, including police and security responses, has been the establishment of a violent gun culture, creating further social trauma and instability which, in turn, polarizes communities, fosters social division and distrust, thereby further eroding social cohesion and creating, as Witsenberg and Zahl (2012) describe, 'spaces of insecurity'. In Kenya, they suggest, these spaces of insecurity are rendered ever more dangerous by 'the criminal nature of the post-colonial state, the exploitative nature of the market, the scarce natural resources and the fact that otherwise illegal small arms are almost openly found in the possession of local people' (Witsenberg and Zahl, 2012: 5). These conditions, they argue, do not make violent conflict inevitable, but they make it ever more likely; violence and the potential for violence thoroughly shape the life-worlds of both the powerful and the powerless. Francis and Nyamongo (2005) describe the weaponized crime and violence permeating rural Kenya adding to the instability and insecurity:

> The new wave of rural crime is also associated with unprecedented levels of brutality, robbery increasingly being accompanied by murder, rape, and the wanton destruction of property … In Bungoma district just before our fieldwork, a gang had attacked ten households, gang raping women and girls, assaulting men and destroying property, but stealing nothing. As one inform-ant observed: 'it is as if they wanted to humiliate their victims'. With changing patterns of rural crime, the weapons, too have evolved … now they came with guns, making resistance by victims or neighbours futile or fatal.
>
> *(Francis and Nyamongo, 2005)*

In the more rural areas commentators describe the transformation of tribal pastoral relations that weapon proliferation has facilitated. While, as Mburu (2007) has argued, arms bearing and cattle rustling predated the proliferation of modern mili-tary firearms, these have certainly intensified and diversified the violent conflicts as the opportunities for pastoral subsistence have diminished and young men face increasingly bitter struggles, using firearms to fight and steal livestock to achieve their rites of passage to a new warrior manhood (Mburu, 2007: 72–73). 'The proliferation of firearms along the borders between Kenya and Uganda, Sudan, Ethiopia and Somalia, and the inability of these states to control cross-border raids have created a situation of permanent insecurity in the borderlands' (Osamba, 2000: 21). According to Mkutu,

> cattle rustling has been a mode of demonstrating the courage of new warriors and acquiring 'bride wealth' … rustling has undergone a major transforma-tion in the last four decades to become an illicit, violent commercial activity precipitated and maintained by small arms.
>
> *(2008: 13)*

In turn as 'economic' opportunities open up around the commercial rustling activity, more unemployed youth join the growing bandit groups which begin, increasingly, to resemble criminal militias, often with their own political and sub-political agendas linked to feuds and retaliations sustaining themselves by a range of criminal activities and exceeding the capacity of local policing resources to respond (Eaton, 2012). Almost inevitably, these escalating conflict relations centring upon

land, livestock, inter-ethnic rivalries, political power and related resources generate further demands for weapons (Mkutu, 2008: 51). One further consequence of
these developing gun cultures, a feature that has often been observed when small
arms filter into more traditional cultures (Alpers, 2005), has been a shift in the balance of authority within tribal societies; armed and powerful, the younger men are
able to extract themselves from the more measured authority of tribal elders.

These vicious cycles of weaponization, the conflicts, social and economic dis-
ruptions, collapsing institutions and deteriorating social relationships, state failures,
youth marginality, criminalizations, alternative economies and repressions, might
describe many of the violence complexes, the violent, failing regimes, depicted in
Table 1.1 and which I have referred to around the world. As I have argued, they
are not all the same and they do not all have the same causes, nor are they all at
a same point on the violence cycle. But it is manifestly clear that weaponization
induces its own violent sameness, melting away civility, security, reciprocity and
traditional authority while ceding a power over life and death to the chaotic criminal aspirations of the well-armed. In the case of a number of African 'failed states',
Musah (2002) identifies militias, private military companies working for resource
extractors, their partner arms brokers and local warlords, as 'the major cause of
on-going asymmetric warfare in Africa – and the proliferation of weapons' as the
principal 'incendiary elements' in these wars. Firearms trafficking and weaponization facilitate the globalization of a version of sovereign personal impunity, the
perfect global representative of neo-liberal individualism, with 'gun culture' as
corrosive criminal neo-liberalism writ large. For example, in an analysis of armed
violence in Bangladesh, the misuse of small arms

> has been identified in virtually all types of violence including political con-
> flict, drug and arms trading, trafficking in women and children, smuggling,
> prostitution, abduction, rape, extortion, election rigging, mugging, vehicle
> hijacking, carjacking, highway robbery, shrimp cultivation, illegal occupation
> of land, auctioning of woodlots, tender and contracting enforcement, street
> violence, campus violence, attacks on journalists, slum eviction and settlement
> and poaching.
>
> (Sharif, 2001, in Muggah and Batchelor, 2002: 22)

In turn, the growing fear of armed violence prompts private citizens in violence
cultures to purchase weapons for their own self-defence, turning the cycle of
weaponization further still.

South Africa: guns, gangs and self-defence

While much of Africa is still coping with the consequences of past conflicts, if not
still experiencing the increasingly weaponized violence of today, South Africa still
reflects the legacy of a different kind of conflict and manifests a violence problem of a rather more conventionally criminal kind (Schönteich and Louw, 2001;

Super, 2010). South Africa even had its own rampage killer incident in 1988 when Barend Strydom, a self-styled 'white wolf' racist avenger, killed eight black people and attempted to murder 25 more. He was sentenced to death but released under the post-apartheid amnesty arrangements in 1992. Unlike other countries (UK, Canada, Australia – see Chapter 8) the incident is not generally seen as shaping the country's emerging gun control agenda; for instance, South Africa's major Firearms Control Act did not appear until 2000.

As Lemanski has argued, a great deal of the continuing 'apartheid-style segregation' in South Africa ' is fuelled by a fear-of-crime rhetoric' (Lemanski, 2004: 103; Super, 2010). In a sense, sustaining this 'criminal' definition of South Africa's violence has much to do with the power and authority of the South African 'security state', capacities that many other African states cannot claim. As Peters *et al.* (2003) note, the annual homicide rate in South Africa at the coming of the twenty-first century was nearly twice that estimated for the conflicts in war torn Sierra Leone, and 'interpersonal violence' is the leading risk factor for death and injury (Seedat *et al.*, 2009) with access to firearms a central aspect of the 'social dynamics that support violence'. Seedat *et al.* continue: 'South Africa's violent history has resulted in an entrenched gun culture' (2009: 1016), while a wide range of research points to the scale of gang activity in the Western Cape Region of South Africa (Standing, 2005, 2006) where as many as 90,000 young people are said to be members of criminal gangs (Barker and Ricardo, 2005: 30). These gangs now share many of the features of the globalized 'gangsta' phenomenon (Hagedorn, 2008), even as they have their roots in an apartheid society, providing a powerful sense of 'heroic' or 'resistance identity' linked to the struggle against apartheid (Pinnock, 1984; Hagedorn, 2005: 158) and youth opportunities in townships where 'the use of violence to achieve political and personal aims became endemic' (Shaw, 1997: 2).

Some commentators began to speak of South Africa as a ticking, crime 'time bomb' given that, especially in the poorest and squatter township areas, significantly over half of the population were below the age of 25 (Schönteich, 1999), while the gang phenomenon has already begun to overlap with South African concerns regarding organized crime. Even as 'young black men' continue to represent the most potent manifestation of urban menace in South Africa (Jensen, 2008; Samara, 2005: 211), 'street gangs are no longer characterised by youngsters who hang around the streets of local communities to "defend" the community from rival gangsters. They have developed into organised criminal empires' (Kinnes, 2000: 2). With other commentators, Kinnes attributes this entrenchment of criminal gang culture to the social context of racialized poverty and exclusion, the violence traditions of the Western Cape, and new cultural influences, including the globalization of youth gang and gun culture, including gangsta rap and hip-hop music from the USA (Standing, 2005: 13). These influences have then played out in a 'democratic transition' society which, along with major social and political changes, has seen a significant liberalization of criminal opportunity structures (mobility, trade, commerce) into which the criminal groups have been able to move. Not unlike the way that Hagedorn (1988, 2005: 7) describes the 'institutionalization' of gangs in the ghetto and the illegal 'shadow' economies of the USA during the 1980s, so South African gangs have been able to use their community bases and their capacity for violence while moving from disorganized to more 'organized' criminal activities (Standing, 2003). Shaw notes that many of the gangs operate primarily in the 'most destitute' areas of the Western Cape, 'and often provide the only means of livelihood for whole communities' (Shaw, 1998: 3). According to Kinnes, the gangs 'have become more organised and have embarked on an organised campaign of criminality intended to build up their legitimacy within the communities where they are active', and they have moved into the drug trade, weapon trafficking, protection rackets, armed robberies, car-jackings, assassinations and the sex, entertainment, fishing, diamond and property businesses (2000: 8–9). As I have noted of gang cultures in other parts of the world,

> young gang members are favoured for carrying out 'hits' on other gangsters as they are believed to be less likely to receive long prison sentences ... [while] gang wars have turned communities into battlegrounds and stray gunshots have claimed the lives of innocent bystanders.
>
> *(Standing, 2005: 9–11)*

Most homicide victims are black, while gun homicide victims are noticeably younger, and disproportionately so (Seedat *et al.*, 2009: 1012).

Shaw describes the growth in South African organized crime, finding the law enforcement and security services 'unprepared' (Shaw, 1998) as they shifted from an essentially authoritarian style of order and containment to an ostensibly more democratic and accountable policing system. The new opportunity seeking criminal entrepreneurs (especially Nigerian Organised Crime Groups (OCGs,) Russian Mafia and Chinese Triads) connecting with the more organized gang structures (Williams, 1997) were, reportedly, 'extremely well financed and superbly armed' (Shaw: 1998). As Samara (2005: 212) has noted, a 'fear of the urban poor' has long been a feature of urban politics in South Africa, but in the wake of apartheid it has become reconfigured on a more international neo-liberal model (Bond, 2000). As the South African economy and society have opened up to global capitalism, there has been great pressure to develop both urban and business security, on the understanding that serious and organized crime is both a security threat and an impediment to continued economic development. This has generated familiar policy pressures in terms of securing the city through fortified urban renewal, security privatization, so-called 'zero-tolerance' community policing initiatives and tough 'war on crime' or 'war on gangs' strategies (Samara, 2003) that have collided uncomfortably with the reform of the South African police service. These policies then have predictable consequences in terms of heightened rates of incarceration, prisonization and gang recruitment – the kinds of strategies that have fundamentally consolidated and sustained gang formation the world over (Greene and Pranis, 2007; Rodgers and Jensen, 2009: 231). In turn, as Samara notes, the emerging role of urban renewal in this struggle is to forge an elite consensus around the city's future, by weaving together a discourse of post-apartheid anxieties around race (the moral panic around street children and crime) with a political and economic programme of neoliberal reform that, at least in the short and medium term, is unlikely to meet the basic needs of the majority of urban poor.

(2005: 223)

In this sense, the gangs and organized crime groups of South Africa are as much a part of the neo-liberal reforms as the reconfigured public–private security state, the weapons they deploy and the tough law and order strategies they have come to legitimate. For Rodgers and Jensen, the gun violence they commit in furtherance of their criminal activities represents the globalization of essentially neo-liberal interest, a fight for themselves:

[G]angs in Cape Town are really not fighting 'for' anything but themselves. Although they can plausibly be said to be fighting 'against' wider structural circumstances of economic exclusion and racism, most of the time the behaviour patterns of gang members are clearly motivated principally by their own interests rather than the active promotion of any form of collective good.

(Rodgers and Jensen, 2009: 231)

These findings are perhaps most emphatically borne out by the 'epidemic' rates of rape and sexual assault which we consider later in the chapter. Not unlike the misogynistic gang cultures of Mexico that I have already considered, much of the violence of South African men is profoundly structured through a performance of armed masculinity: 'women are integrally connected to small arms violence in their daily lives … [they] pay the price for gun violence in both household and community spaces' (Fish and Mncayi, 2009: 291).

Seedat *et al.* (2009) present a grim, but not uncommon, picture of this masculine violence:

The dominant ideals of masculinity, across racial groups, are predicated on a striking gender hierarchy; with demonstrations of toughness, bravery, and defence of honour … Men tend to be highly competitive about power, respect, and status. With common carrying of weapons, fights in defence of honour and for status often occur, resulting in serious injuries and deaths.

(Seedat et al., 2009: 1015)

These dominant notions of armed masculinity – celebrated by some as 'honourable' South African tradition (De Groot, 2002) – are predicated on the control of women, and infused with ideas of male sexual entitlement.

Physical violence is used to manufacture gender hierarchy (i.e. teach women their place) and to enforce this hierarchy through punishment of transgression. Rape is often used as punishment for infidelity, attempts to end a relationship, refusal of sexual advances, or behaviour that is deemed to show insufficient respect for men … Likewise, the raping and killing of homosexual women, which is becoming increasingly common, is often enacted as corrective action.

(2009: 1015)

Like many other areas of the world where gangs and guns are prevalent, gang membership in South Africa helps young men achieve a number of social, emotional and material needs (Daniels and Adams, 2010). At the same time commentators have particularly drawn attention to perceptions concerning the greater propensity for criminal violence which is attributed now to the new violent gang culture and the prevalence of illegal firearms. Although, in South Africa, another 'frontier culture' with its own hunting traditions (Keegan, 2005: 28; Storey, 2008), carrying a gun has long been regarded as 'a sign of status, male affluence and power', accordingly the gun, a key component of masculine identity politics in South Africa, 'remains a convenient peg on which to hang traditional notions of masculine power' (Cock, 1997, 2001). Keegan's interviews also unearthed a profound commitment to gun carrying on both sides of the South African racial divide. She refers to a Zulu song which insists, 'a boy who doesn't have a gun must get one', while noting common values relating to gun ownership including protecting one's family, and maintaining one's own power and dignity. One participant in a focus group remarked that real men did not want to be ruled by fear: 'It's all about power', he asserted, 'men get guns to get power, and to make themselves feel powerful'. Another young man took up the theme: 'Men are afraid of men. If a man sees another man with a gun, he feels he has to have one to restore his dignity, to maintain his sense of self-esteem … the gun-owner thinks that other people will respect him' (Keegan, 2005: 28–29). As Cukier and Sheptycki confirm, 'in highly weaponised societies, the pistol is a mark of manhood, a symbol of the ability to forcefully intervene in the everyday making of social order, and a perceived tool for solving problems of conflict' (2012: 6). Bartolucci and Kanneworff (2012: 127) describe essentially the same identity construction amongst the Camorra in Naples: violence, weapons and the public display of both are the foundations of the power of the Camorra, 'a Neapolitan is only a real man if he possesses a gun'.

Researchers have also unearthed testimony to the effect that the presence of guns has apparently been increasing amongst criminal gangs. Thaler's interviewees reported that while they used to be robbed by offenders with knives now, 'they've progressed to guns'. Others noted that 'you see more violence today because these young boys have access to guns'. Another admitted: 'Guns are very central to today's violence. I mean we never had guns during our times. But now guns are free for anyone who wants one' (Thaler, 2011: 9). Such findings echo those reported in an earlier study by Kynoch (2003: 10) to the effect that, before the 1990s, the criminals mainly carried knives, but 'nowadays the townships are awash with firearms and shootings are a daily occurrence'. An earlier research project on behalf of the South African Police in 2001 had confirmed the widespread use of firearms in crime (Hennop *et al.*, 2001) and pointed to a number of difficulties, including civilian loss and negligence leading to the loss or theft of many weapons and the degree to which police were overburdened and able to investigate only the most serious or apparently 'solvable' offences. In reflection of this, a high degree of perceived 'criminal impunity' regarding minor gun offences, such as illegal possession, was noted, and very limited cooperation from the community when the police were dealing with gun crime; not surprisingly the police only achieved a particularly low rate of successful prosecution.

As Figure 7.1 has shown, South Africa is very close to the top ten most violent societies in the world. Although the gun homicide rate has lately been falling (amongst a range of declining crime trends) (see Figure 7.3), at least until 2012–2013, in the wake of the tough new laws to tackle gangs, organized crime and weapon proliferation (the Prevention of Organised Crime Act 1998 and the Firearms Control Act 2000). Some critics have disputed that any direct relation exists between the new legislation and the falling violent crime, in part because it is recognized that most gun violence in South Africa is committed with *illegal* firearms (primarily handguns) and the recorded incidence of illegal firearm *possession* was higher in 2007 than it had been a decade earlier (Lamb, 2008). This may tell us relatively little, however, for records of firearm possession offences are more reliable indicators of police proactivity than they may be of underlying rates of illegal gun possession. Nevertheless, following the package of gun control measures in place by 2004,[10] gun homicide rates fell significantly faster than non-gun homicides (Abrahams *et al.*, 2010; Lamb, 2008). Even so, some 8,000–9,000 people are still being killed, each year, as a result of gun violence; as of 2013 this amounts to around 20 gun murders per day (ISS, 2013). And, reflecting patterns we have early discussed concerning weaponization, violence and masculinity, South Africa still has a firearm femicide rate seven times higher than that of the USA, namely that a woman is killed by her intimate partner every eight hours (Abrahams *et al.*, 2012). There are also 55,000 rapes of women and girls reported to the police every year, a figure that is estimated to be nine times lower than the actual number (Jewkes *et al.*, 2006).

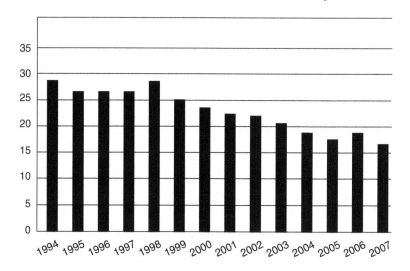

FIGURE 7.3 Gun homicide in South Africa (rate per 100,000)

Source: Alpers *et al.* (2013).

In response to the rates of violence already described, the number of licenced guns in private hands are reported to have increased from some 2.5 million in 1986 to 3.7 million in 2004 (Keegan, 2005), when the new gun control laws became fully operational. In addition it is estimated that, despite UN arms embargoes, anything up to four million made their way into southern Africa 'as a result of the wars of independence and the civil wars in Mozambique and Angola and the democratic struggle in South Africa' itself (Keegan, 2005: 1; see also Hennop, 1997). There are several seeming contradictions associated with South Africa's post-apartheid embrace of neo-liberalism; no sooner were the arms embargoes lifted than guns, both licit and illicit, began flooding into the country (Meek, 2000), dominating the domestic market and overwhelming police efforts at containment and thereby prompting the new government's gun control initiative (Keegan, 2005). But just as South Africa was beginning to acknowledge that privately owned firearms were also part of the problem of gun proliferation (Meek, 1997) and the country was embarking upon its own gun control measures, the white demand for self-defensive firearms began to take off. In this sense, 'gun control' might be seen an administrative means of responsibilizing white rearmament. As Keegan has noted,

> the forces driving the growing demand for guns since 1994 have been equally contradictory, for while many want guns to undertake crime, others want guns to protect themselves from crime … as a result, there were not only more firearms in civilian hands, but more were being carried on the streets.
>
> *(2005: 28, 30)*

As Meek put it in 1997,

> the criminal use of guns, and especially in violent crime, is inhibiting the development of security among citizens and resulting in a vicious circle in which people arm themselves against armed criminals. In South Africa, the ironic twist is that many of the weapons used by criminals are those which have been stolen from licenced owners.
>
> *(Meek, 1997: 35)*

Thaler concurs, 'gun possession and use has been increasing since the transition to democracy in 1994 … [and] weapons are used primarily by criminals' (Thaler, 2011).

As in the USA where demands for self-defensive firearms are couched explicitly in terms of crime prevention and implicitly in terms of race, the weaponization of South Africa prompts wider questions about firearms and social change and narrower, perhaps even 'situational', questions about violence and consequences. Keegan's research respondents voiced concerns about widespread firearm carrying that referred to a profound 'suspension of normality'; conversely other commentators have referred to the 'normalisation of violence' for South African youth (Pelser, 2008). Holding a gun, you were powerful and able to act with impunity;

having it pointed at you made you powerless, it was that simple: everything or nothing. Guns were currency, as one young man exclaimed, 'if you've got a gun, you've got a credit card'. These ideas were reflected in the views of younger children who were interviewed about joining gangs, even the younger children

> were remarkably consistent in what they viewed as the reasons for joining gangs. Every group mentioned the greater wealth of gangs, with money, guns, brand name clothing, and nice cars being consistently mentioned as part of what made gangs attractive. For young men, one of the attractions suggested was access to women.

On the other hand, girls outlined 'a particularly gendered approach to relations with gangs in terms of both material goods and the need for protection' (Ward, 2007: 24, 30).

At the same time, guns subverted normal social interactions, values, property relations, the conventional reciprocities of daily life. The old came to fear the young. One of Keegan's Cape Town focus group members told how 'a local gangster had forced her family at gun point to let him into their house to watch a soccer match on television. It was a small incident, but it traumatized her family'. His expressed attitude was 'there's nothing you can do about it' (Keegan, 2005: 99). Gun proliferation in formerly social spaces encouraged people – those who could – to retreat from normal interactions, to avoid so-called risky places, to retreat behind walls and fortified residential communities and armed guards, and their own defensive weapons. In South Africa, as in other profoundly weaponized environments, and whether carried for aggressive or defensive purposes, Thaler argues that firearms are technologies that 'change the balance of power in violent situations'. For criminal aggressors, these imbalances are 'frequently used to aid in the extraction of material goods or sexual compliance, or in interpersonal disputes' (2011: 3). Personal firearms are used to obtain what Arendt (1970: 41) has termed the 'unquestioning obedience' that a threat of violence can secure (Thaler, 2011: 22). A report by Oxfam and Amnesty International in 2003 reported testimony from a villager from Papua New Guinea: 'In my village, everyone has a gun', he said, 'a gun of his own … if you don't have one for yourself then … you don't have a name in this village. Your wife can be raped. They can steal. They can do anything to you' (Oxfam and Amnesty International, 2003: 49). So fundamentally does gun ownership transform social relations? So embedded has gun ownership become to notions of masculine power, status and identity that in some cultures the questions we asked become reversed: how can men exist without guns? According to Carr, 'in rural areas of Kenya and Uganda young women will not countenance courtship with a man who does not own an automatic rifle' (Carr, 2008: 2).

Thaler's research comprised an attempt to explore the consequences of weapon carrying, how it altered perceptions of personal security and whether gun carriers felt safer or more confident and empowered; whether carrying a firearm changed people's outlooks in other ways; or, finally, whether people, who generally led law abiding lives, behaved more aggressively or were more likely to face victimization if they carried a gun. Other research has acknowledged that 'carrying a weapon may also lead to greater risk-taking and more aggressive and confrontational behavior' (Thaler, 2011: 22). Keegan, for example, remarked that her respondents felt that 'a person's comportment changed when he got a gun ... he also can become more aggressive, less ready to cooperate or compromise and far more ready to take risks' (2005: 96). Having a gun, apparently, made you feel 'like no one can do anything to you' ((2005: 96). This argument wraps together notions of both empowerment and facilitation (Squires, 2000: 10, 176), for guns make possible forms of lethal intervention – shootings driven by spontaneous anger, retaliation killings – that simply could not take place without them. For, as Blumstein has noted, when guns are involved, 'even transitory violent impulses can have lethal consequences' (2002: 8). Furthermore, firearms can and do 'escalate the extent of crime and the types of crime that youth get involved in' (Keegan, 2005: 94–95), they can also establish a sequence to conflict relations, for example in patterns of revenge and retaliation shootings or the dangerous choreography of the 'drive-by'. Thaler concludes that 'for non-criminal weapon carriers, it is unclear that the protective benefits of weapon carrying outweigh the potential personal and societal costs' (2011: 22). This conclusion is consistent with Kellerman's earlier research in the USA which found that 'for every time a gun in the home was used in a self-defence or legally justifiable shooting, there were four unintentional shootings, seven criminal assaults or homicides, and 11 attempted or completed suicides' (Kellerman *et al.*, 1998: 263). In other words, as I have already discussed at some length in respect of the USA, although the point is no less valid in other parts of the world, a gun kept at home is, statistically, far more dangerous to the home's occupants than any potential aggressor, while male gun ownership is especially dangerous to women (Farr *et al.*, 2009). And as Johnston *et al.* 2005 have noted, referring specifically to data from South Africa and Brazil, but making the more generic point, 'in places not characterised by armed conflict in the traditional sense, those who use weapons are more likely to die by them' (2005: 12).

Such issues were forcefully brought to the world's attention in February 2013 when news broke that gold medal winning South African Paralympic athlete Oscar Pistorius had been arrested at home after a shooting incident in which his girlfriend had been shot and killed. The incident drew attention onto the role of fear of crime in encouraging not only the acquisition of self-defence firearms by private citizens but also, for the white elites who can afford them, the construction of high-security residential complexes, surrounded by electrified fences and patrolled by private armed response companies. As we have seen, South Africa now has one of the world's highest rates of firearm-related violence, a continuing legacy of the apartheid system, with around 50 people a day being killed or injured by gunfire. This, in turn, prompts the high rates of supposedly 'protective' gun ownership. There are now thought to be around six million legally owned firearms in South Africa with around 13 per cent of the population being a gun owner (Karp, 2007). And wherever there is a large legal market in firearms, there is invariably a thriving illegal firearm economy.

So, although the acquisition of self-defence firearms by civilians is primarily associated with the USA, where, in some states, the right to shoot strangers is creeping ever closer to becoming constitutionally protected (Diaz, 2013), as we have seen, it has nonetheless become a truly global phenomenon. Evidence has emerged of the civilian gun ownership issue surfacing in Latin America, for example, Brazil, as well as Europe, Russia and Australia, and, lately, even India's middle classes are reputed to be purchasing firearms for self-defence in the face of a growing (although not always accurate) perception of rising crime and a concern that the police cannot be relied upon to provide protection. The recent gang rape and murder of a young Indian woman apparently prompted significant numbers of middle-class householders and female professionals to enquire about obtaining firearm licences, nearly 31,300 arms firearm licences were issued to women in the Punjab and over 31,000 firearms were actually purchased (Burke, 2012). As one report in the *Times of India* recounted, 'a sense of insecurity has gripped the female population in parts of India … Since the news of the brutal gang rape and murder in December, 274 New Delhi women have applied for gun licenses, Delhi police said. Some 1,200 more have called the licensing department to inquire how to obtain one' (Ghosh, 2013).

Whether, in a country with an already estimated 40 million illegal firearms, greater safety and security will be the outcome of all this defensive gun buying, seems rather doubtful. Yet defensive gun buyers should be careful about what they wish for and especially about what they keep at home. Pistorius' story is really all too familiar and, like too many women, his girlfriend paid the ultimate price for his firearm enthusiasms. The cases of India and South Africa, like our earlier discussion of defensive firearm acquisition in the USA, demonstrate clearly that contemporary civilian defensive gun ownership is a product of late modernity and neo-liberal culture. Governments are discredited, the streets are not safe, law and order ineffectual, and collective policy responses rejected. Emboldened by ideologies of self-reliant individualism, like the sorcerer's apprentice making off with the magician's wand, personal firepower has come to represent a troubling augmentation of individual capacity in a dangerous world. Creating a society of armed and dangerous co-existence suggests a dangerous and ill-advised road to public safety, prioritizing the 'right to kill' over tackling the conditions producing risk and insecurity. A tougher line, however, is apparently still being held in Russia. Following a mass shooting in Belgorod, southwest Russia in April 2013 in which six people were killed, discussion focussed upon self-defence, but at a press conference President Putin said he opposed the idea of allowing Russians to buy guns freely for self-defence purposes. He added that 'it is dangerous to artificially stimulate this process' (Von Eggert, 2013). The issue gained extra traction following the sentencing of a 21-year-old Moscow student to three years imprisonment for shooting and injuring two men with a travmatichesky pistol (also referred to as 'traumatic pistols') firing hard rubber bullets. The student had claimed self-defence but the court found her guilty of aggressive behaviour. Apparently, opinion polls suggest that the number of Russians advocating the right to carry defensive firearms has been steadily growing over recent years, with more than 50 per cent now in agreement. Russian nationalists are reputed to be at the forefront of the self-defence movement, 'they are convinced that only free citizens with real guns can quell the wave of criminality, which they blame on people from the North Caucasus and migrants from Central Asia' (Von Eggert, 2013). Like so many other crime complexes around the world, inequalities and ethnic tensions map onto security concerns stimulating self-defence, yet the very conditions that generate the demand make any influx of personal firepower a profoundly dangerous step to take.

Despite the 2013 verdict and continuing official reticence, it was estimated in 2005 that over five million Russians already owned firearms for self-defence, although the classes of weapons, 'smoothbore hunting rifles, CS gas pistols, or revolvers shooting rubber bullets', are very restricted, in accordance with a weapons law passed in 1996 (Simonov, 2005). Once citizens have undergone extensive checks and then demonstrated their capacity to handle such firearms safely for five years, they are entitled to apply to purchase a wider class of rifles or shotguns. Even so there still seems little enthusiasm for liberalizing gun ownership laws in Russia. A spokesman for the Russian interior ministry commented, in stark contrast to 'American thinking':

> If we throw 10 to 12 million guns into the streets, any teenager will be able to seize a pistol from a woman. He will start shooting whenever he can. Guns will be stolen from cars and desk drawers. The number of lost weapons will go up hundreds of times, and they will be beyond control and ready for crimes. This would be a dream come true for Russian criminals.
>
> *(Simonov, 2005)*

In Russian terms, therefore, civilian firearm ownership is still small arms proliferation.

Conclusion

Taken as a whole, these Russian dilemmas take us to the heart of one of the most pointed contradictions of contemporary neo-liberalism under which *both* free market economic policies *and* individually self-interested strategies of welfare maximization prosper. Yet the global regime transformations brought forth by neo-liberalism – especially where they have been most rapid, dramatic and productive of the greatest inequalities, relative deprivations or 'advanced marginalities' – have, almost everywhere, been associated with rapidly increasing rates of crime and violence (Findlay, 1999). In turn, this crime and violence has been responded to by policies that have, in Wacquant's (2009) terms, involved a rolling out of the 'penal state', the power to criminalize and a rolling back of the social welfare state (Squires and Lea, 2012a). These policies have typically accelerated and intensified the criminalization of 'outcast' groups, even as global crime rates may have appeared to fall, all of which has served to convince the global urban middle classes of their heightened insecurity. More than at any other time, these insecurities are reinforced by the practice of contemporary democracies increasingly 'governing through crime' (Simon, 2007) and a rapidly growing private security industry with a direct financial incentive in marketing the idea that no-one should feel too comfortable. It is now indisputable, however, that another powerful global vector of this emerging neo-liberalization of the self comprises the demand for self-defence firearms and the doubtful promise of security and tough empowerment they are thought to bring (Muggah, 2001). Muggah cites Lock's gloomy predictions regarding the future of urban security, itself not a million miles from Tony Bottoms' pessimistic vision of the future referred to by Squires (2000: 4),[11] for as the affluent retreat to their private security complexes protected by armed guards, those unable to afford 'protected castles and the ... commodification of their security are forced to organise their self-defence outside legal parameters'. We are witnessing, he suggests, a profound privatization of security, a 'mutually reinforcing system of multi-polar re-armament' of the self and the social, 'cascading down the social ladder where it amounts to an informal militarisation ... at the lower end of the social pyramid' (Lock, 1999, cited in Muggah, 2001: 73–74).

Krause and Milliken (2009) also project an increasingly bleak picture 'for the future of armed violence' for although, as they suggest, major wars and civil wars are becoming increasingly less frequent, weapon proliferation in large parts of the global South has made it easier for armed groups to keep a complex host of (ethnic, drug war, diaspora, religious, economic, territorial, terrorist *and criminal*) conflicts going as 'low-intensity conflicts', insurgencies, organized crime or 'gang wars'. Weak and failing states will find it difficult to contain such persistent armed struggles, they argue, while militarily more powerful western states will probably be no more able to achieve lasting victories than domestic states might eliminate crime. This raises some important lessons regarding the corrosive power of weaponization and the future of the neo-liberal state where it no longer has a monopoly of armed force, or 'post-conflict' societies, where restoring that monopoly and reclaiming the weapons distributed in the course of the conflict (from armed actors often rather unwilling to give them up) are vital political priorities (Kreutz *et al.*, 2012). In Chapter 9, I will consider various attempts to redress this balance, domestically and internationally.

Notes

1 Bourne (2007: 4) continues:
     While there is no clear, causal relationship between arms and violence, as Edward Laurance (1999: 12) contends, there is 'an undeniable mass of "correlational" evidence'. This relates to catalytic implications of SALW availability on potential or already violent environments. In such circumstances – that are complexly constructed – the availability of SALW may make violence more feasible (by providing tools), more likely (by contributing to dynamics of insecurity, polarisation, and fear), and more destructive (by expanding the scope of violence, by expanding the lethal capacity of actors involved, by diffusing violence and its tools throughout a society, and by contributing to the challenges of post-conflict peace building and development).

2 Some commentators, for example Klare (1999), prefer to speak of the 'diffusion' of small arms in societies and communities in order to capture something distinctive about the social mechanisms by which firearms are often spread from hand to hand. Other commentators such as Laurance (1996) describe a 'circulation' of weapons between combatants, a notion that has also been used to describe the circulation of weapons within and between criminal gangs in the UK. As Klare concludes: 'Whichever term is used, it is important to accurately portray the complexity of the distribution system for small arms and light weapons' (1999: 21).

3 As Diaz (2013) has shown, pro-gun legislators have sought to frustrate the intelligence gathering and enforcement capabilities of regulatory agencies – especially the ATF and the Department of Defence – in respect of firearms ownership and sale within the USA, while also choking off funding for research into the consequences of gun violence. As Chapter 8 documents, this 'interference' has also extended to undermining global efforts towards the development of international norms and treaties for the curtailment of small arms proliferation.

4 In addition, it is not unknown in the USA for resource-stretched local police departments to re-sell confiscated criminal firearms back into the civilian market (Olinger, 1999; Thayer, 2013).

5 The gun homicide rates reflected in Figure 7.1 may not all represent data from the same year, although the UNODC (2011) study draws upon figures from 2010 or the most recent available year. The chart is intended to depict broad comparisons, reflecting the 'mosaic approach' (Jackson and Marsh, 2012) referred to in Chapter 1, which is often utilized in approaching this question, comparing societies based upon the latest available national data, not absolute snap-shot accuracy. For more information refer to the GunPolicy.org website.

6 The FN 5.57 machine pistol achieved a certain notoriety in November 2009 when Major Nidal Hasan used one to fatally shoot 13 people and injure more than 30 others at the Fort Hood army base in Texas. This was the worst mass shooting to take place at a US military base.

7 The slogan claimed: 'An armed society is a polite society'.

8 As Muggah and Batchelor write,

> most of those civilians doing the killing, as well as those killed and injured, are male youth – though women and children also suffer disproportionately from forced recruitment, psychological trauma and sexual violence. According to some estimates from UNICEF, in the past decade more than two million children were killed during warfare, five million disabled and 12 million made homeless. Third, the rates of firearm related casualties often only marginally declined following armed conflict – a result of the legacy of small arms proliferation among civilians during the wars.
>
> *(2002: 17)*

9 At the time of writing, Kenyan security forces were still dealing with the consequences of the Islamist terrorist attack on the West Gate shopping mall in Nairobi during which over 60 people were shot and killed.

10 The new measures included background checks on the mental health of applicants and whether they have any history of substance misuse or criminal records, and stricter eligibility and competency requirements for obtaining firearm licences which can now only be granted to persons over 21. There is mandatory training and a test on firearm safety, and more stringent storage requirements. The screening of would-be gun owners can also include interviews with intimate partners. There are also limits on the numbers of firearms any person can own.

11 > I profoundly hope that this ... interpretation of our own situation is an over-pessimistic one. For if individualism really is unstoppable, the end result, or nightmare, could ultimately be a society with massive security hardware protecting individual homes, streets, and shops, while all adult citizens would carry personal alarms, and perhaps guns, for individual protection while moving from place to place.
>
> *(Bottoms, 1990: 20)*

8

WHEN THE SHOOTING STOPS

From national responses to global arms control

Picking up from the discussion begun in Chapter 6, I turn now to consider the occurrence of 'rampage' or 'spree' shootings around the world, and their social and political consequences, particularly the gun control laws that societies sought to pass in the wake of these tragedies; and whether and why they were effective – or not. From the national sphere, I then move to the global, looking at the ways in which localized gun control efforts opened up a series of questions about global firearm supply and proliferation more generally and, allied with peace building (DDR projects) and development projects, in some of the world's most chronically violent and unstable regions came together to press for a more concerted international effort to curtail the 'Illicit trade in Small Arms and Light Weapons'. This resulted in the establishment of a UN PoA on SALW in 2001, paving the way for the eventual adoption by the UN of a comprehensive Arms Trade Treaty, during April 2013. Although this was by no means a smooth and simple process.

America may have had rather more rampage shootings and it may have come to see them as a particularly American phenomenon; the 'price' paid for the continued existence of a certain kind of 'gun culture' and its associated legacy of violence (Brown, 1975), but it certainly has no monopoly on mass civilian shootings nor does it have the dubious distinction of the *most* lethal mass shooting. For this we must look to Norway, to recall our regime table in Chapter 1 (Table 1.1), an affluent, 'high-trust' Nordic welfare state with a 'civilized' gun culture based predominantly upon hunting and sports shooting.

Certainly Norway has a relatively high per capita rate of firearm ownership (rated eleventh of 178 countries by the Small Arms Survey in 2007) but also one of the lowest gun violence rates in the world. However Norway, along with other Scandinavian countries, has also begun to experience dimensions of ethnic marginalization, growing inequalities and host society racism (Andersson, 2003, 2005; Sandberg and Pederson, 2008). And on 22 July 2011, having first detonated home-made bombs in central Oslo (killing eight), Anders Behring Breivik, a self-proclaimed neo-Nazi enthusiast with a deep-seated grudge against the Norwegian Labour party, which he held responsible for encouraging migration to Norway, disguised himself as a police officer and made his way to a Youth League Summer Camp. Once there, armed with a Mini-Ruger 14 carbine and a Glock 34 pistol, he relentlessly gunned down teenagers at the summer resort, killing 69 and injuring many more, before finally surrendering to police. The most murderous single shooter gun rampage ever recorded. Prior to launching his attacks, Breivik released onto the internet his own personal neo-Nazi and Christian fundamentalist 'manifesto' attacking, in turn, Marxism, feminism and Islam. At his trial he was found to be sane and guilty of mass murder before being sentenced to 21 years of preventive detention, though subject to risk assessments meaning he is unlikely to ever be released.

Surprisingly, perhaps, Australia experienced the second most murderous single person rampage shooting in April 1996, just six weeks after Thomas Hamilton's killing spree at Dunblane Primary School in Scotland. Martin Bryant, variously described as autistic, mentally retarded and borderline schizophrenic, killed 35 people (injuring 21 more) in Port Arthur, Tasmania, with a Colt AR-15 semi-automatic rifle and an L1A1 self-loading rifle. Bryant had a childhood history including shooting passers-by with his air rifle, animal cruelty and was, until withdrawn from school, a victim of bullying by fellow students. He was eventually sentenced to 35 life sentences. Following the shooting (although having experienced several previous 'multiple victim shooting incidents' involving semi-automatic rifles and shotguns[1]), Australia embarked upon a series of fiercely contested firearm control reforms. I will discuss these changes to the Australian gun control regime, the debates about them and their consequences, in more detail later in the chapter, for the moment it is sufficient to note that, in common with many of the US rampage shootings already considered, the attacks in Norway, Scotland and Tasmania were all perpetrated with legally owned firearms. Aside from questions of weaponization amongst the criminal fraternity, which has often driven the 'gun crime' debates of many societies, also influencing the patterns of police armed response, tactics and weapon use, it is notable that some of the world's most 'signal' and 'symbolic' firearm incidents have involved perpetrators using firearms that were legally held at the time of the incident in question. Despite the bullish complacency of the NRA, it has not always been easy to separate the 'good guys' from the 'bad guys'; civilian weaponization has also been a critical issue. In a world full of weapons, shooting atrocities can occur anywhere, even affluent and well-integrated societies; and they have (Oksanen *et al.*, 2010). This is theme to which I will return as I discuss the weapon control debates that have often followed major shooting outrages.

Accordingly, the second theme of the chapter shifts the analysis from the national to the global as I explore the ways in which particular gun control initiatives by nation states inevitably drew attention to the patterns of licit and illicit firearm supply around the world, the connections with organized crime and terrorism and the scale of civilian weapon ownership, especially in some of the world's most conflict-ridden locations. Here the discussion also connects with the developing academic commentary, and emerging academic and political engagements with the problems of these regional conflict traps and the SALW weapon trafficking to which they are frequently subject. That is to say it concerns peace building and peacekeeping, the work of DDR organizations, and social and economic development initiatives. Often the frontline work in DDR projects is undertaken through collaborations between non-governmental aid organizations (Oxfam, the International Red Cross, Christian Aid, Médecins Sans Frontières, Save the Children) and the United Nations. Increasingly, recognizing the role of SALW proliferation in frustrating peace and economic development – small arms, the weapons most widely used – aid organizations have come to collaborate with a range of SALW control, research and lobbying organizations or 'think tanks' (Amnesty International, IANSA, Campaign against the Arms Trade (CAAT), ControlArms, Human Rights Watch, the Institute for Security Studies (South Africa) and SaferWorld). Amongst the benefits of this engagement has been: the emergence over many years of a detailed evidence base relating to the supply, distribution and misuse of weapons and of effective strategies for DDR.[2] Much of this evidence has been collated by SIPRI and the publication, every year since 2001, of the Small Arms Survey,[3] a detailed accounting of small arms distribution and misuse around the world. As I noted in Chapter 1, part of the brief of the Small Arms Survey consists in providing a global overview of the scale of civilian weaponization and of the deaths, injuries and harms that thereby result. As well as providing robust and comprehensive global evidence of small arms proliferation, stockpiling and misuse, particular editions of the Survey have a specific regional or thematic focus. For example, the 2007 focus was on 'guns and the city'; the 2010 edition featured 'gangs, groups and guns'; while the most recent edition, 2013, explored 'everyday dangers', the multiple dimensions of gun violence beyond the direct context of armed conflict itself, including, for example, weapon use in intimate partner violence, gun use by street gangs, and guns in drug trafficking and organized crime.

However, the most significant political outcome of the collaboration between NGOs, researchers, think tanks and the United Nations has arguably been the adoption by the UN, during April 2013, of a comprehensive ATT to address the illegal trafficking of conventional arms including SALW. The treaty failed to reach a consensus at the UN, three countries (North Korea, Iran and Syria) voted against the treaty and 23 abstained (including China and the Russian Federation) but the treaty will come into force 90 days after being ratified by a fiftieth state (at the time of writing, 83 have signed). Importantly, the USA, under the Obama presidency, came on board, in marked contrast to the attitude of the previous US administration. However, the treaty remains an inherently weak and compromised agreement, offering only an essentially voluntary arms control regime governed by agreed international principles; it lacks both a monitoring system and any enforcement capacity beyond any actions that independent states might take themselves.

A consortium of NGOs began to lobby the UN, becoming successful in securing, in 2001, an agreement to a UN PoA on Small Arms and Light Weapons (The Programme of Action to Prevent, Combat and Eradicate the Illicit Trade in Small Arms and Light Weapons in all its Aspects; UN, 2001), to complement international agreements on nuclear and chemical weapons, land mines and cluster munitions, although at the time the Bush administration was vehemently opposed to the measure. A United Nations project on arms control was perceived by gun rights advocacy groups, the NRA and the US Republican Party as 'global gun control', a threat to civilian firearm ownership, contrary to the Second Amendment and an attack on the US Constitution (La Pierre, 2006). In fact it was nothing of the sort, as a statement by Secretary of State Hillary Clinton (14 October 2009) had established.

In the wake of rampage 1: Europe

As we have seen in the discussion of school shootings in the USA in Chapter 6, multiple victim shooting incidents, once the debate has moved beyond the incredulous: 'how or why could this happen here?' (Oksanen *et al.*, 2010), occasion a great deal of commentary, reflection and political debate. However this need not imply that any substantial legal changes follow. As a comparative examination of the UK after Dunblane and the USA after Columbine has shown (Squires, 2000) while Britain moved quickly towards the prohibition of handguns in the wake of the Dunblane shooting, no such fundamental policy shift occurred in the USA,[4] and as the more recent Sandy Hook (December 2012) tragedy has revealed, thus far, despite the investment of substantial political resources and the explicit support of the President, gun law reform has stalled in the US political process. However, as we have already demonstrated, the character of any particular gun tragedy may not define the entirety of a society's gun problems. In the USA for instance, as many inner city African–American children may die as a result of gun violence *every week* as are killed in any particular school shooting (as discussed extensively in Chapter 5), tackling the problem of school shootings may have little bearing upon gun deaths in the ghetto. Putative solutions to gun violence incidents might not address the underlying problems.

There has been an element of this in the evolution of British gun control policy, changes to gun laws following tragedies are often criticized for being 'event driven', but this may be only part of the story. After the 1987 shootings in Hungerford, Berkshire, when 16 people were killed, the media focus, perhaps understandably, was on Michael Ryan's 'Rambo-like' camouflaged appearance – and his AK-47 assault rifle – which many people in the UK did not imagine could be legally owned (Josephs, 1993). In the wake of Hungerford, the 1988 Firearms (Amendment) Act prohibited semi-automatic, centre-fire rifles (but not .22 calibre rim-fire weapons, a type of assault weapon popular in the USA and bearing an uncanny resemblance to the Bushmaster rifle used by Adam Lanza at Sandy Hook school). The 1988 legislation also prohibited pump-action shotguns with a capacity for more than two rounds of ammunition, even though this type of weapon played no part in the Hungerford shooting (gun lobby commentators voiced the view that such weapons had been on a government 'hit list' since 1973, Hungerford merely providing a prohibition opportunity; Harding, 1979; Squires, 2000). Overlooked entirely in 1997–1988 was the semi-automatic handgun with which Ryan killed a number of his victims. It was not until ten years later, after the Dunblane school shooting, that handguns became prohibited but even then it took a number of subsequent political inquiries, legislative changes, changes in police practice and firearm licensing guidance, border security developments and new forensic systems before the complex of issues comprising the UK gun problem was fully appreciated (Squires, 2000, 2008; Squires and Kennison, 2010). Many of the changes made were contested; undoubtedly loopholes still remain.

The reason for making these points about post-shooting-incident legislating, especially the major contrast between Britain and America is to acknowledge that, whether a great deal of policy development follows a tragedy, or very little, similar questions are likely to arise, concerning public safety, responsibility, causality, effectiveness, proportionality and culture, in other countries. Often these issues are the vehicles around which competing interests mobilize and the different ways in which different societies answer these questions shape the gun policies that emerge.

In the wake of the Norway shooting massacre in 2011, for example, a wholesale reform of Norwegian gun laws was not undertaken (although an independent panel of advisors did recommend a broad prohibition on individual ownership of pistols and semi-automatic weapons, and mental health checks). Norway has relatively high rates of gun ownership; chiefly for hunting and sports shooting (some types of firearms not conforming to these purposes are banned). Firearms are tightly controlled, gun ownership is not a right, a licensing system operates, licensees have to undergo background and suitability checks and they must specify their reason for wanting firearms and each weapon has to be registered. Even so, there are estimated to be anything up to half a million illegal weapons in Norway (Alpers and Wilson, nd). Norway's gun regulations had been tightened in 2009 but in the wake of Breivik's shooting rampage, the public and political focus centred upon Breivik's Nazi-inspired views, his questionable mental health and the necessity for effective due process in his prosecution and conviction. One exceptional incident, it was implied, was not a reason for changing laws established over many years. In Switzerland, likewise, although long regarded by gun advocates the world over as the very epitome of a civilized gun culture (Kopel, 1992; Munday, 1996) a disturbed man with a longstanding grudge against the local political authorities entered the regional parliament building in the city of Zug in 2001 disguised as a police man and carrying four firearms. He killed 14 people, injuring 18 more, before detonating a small bomb, and then killing himself. In part because of its militia system which permits militia members to keep their weapons (but not ammunition) at home (locked away), Switzerland has one of the highest rates of gun ownership in the developed world (Small Arms Survey, 2007). Gun purchase regulations in Switzerland were tightened in the late 1990s and again in 2008 as a result of Switzerland joining the Schengen

European security agreement. However, Switzerland still has a popular culture of sports shooting, a relatively low rate of firearm homicide and fairly low (but rising) rates of violent street crime, although relatively higher rates of domestic, firearm-involved homicide and suicide. Professor Martin Killias, director of criminology at Zurich University, interviewed for the BBC in 2013, commented that 'there is a strong correlation between guns kept in private homes and incidences occurring at home – like private disputes involving the husband shooting the wife and maybe the children, and then committing suicide' (Killias, quoted in Kirby, 2013). Such issues sustained a Swiss campaign to hold a referendum on tighter gun ownership which was eventually successful in 2011, but 56 per cent of voters rejected the proposed gun control package. Two more recent multiple victim shootings in early 2013, in which seven people were killed, further tarnishing the country's 'safe gun culture' reputation, seem likely to maintain the pressure for better information sharing about gun ownership between Switzerland's distinct cantons (Freedman, 2013).

In contrast to European cultures where gun legislation *failed* to change substantially following mass shooting incidents, Finland, typically regarded as a high-trust, gender-equal, affluent, progressive and safe, high gun-ownership culture (Lappi-Seppala, 2007; Kantola *et al.*, 2011) *did* eventually overhaul its gun laws following two mass shooting incidents in 2007 and 2008 during which 21 people (including both perpetrators) were killed. Both incidents involved perpetrators with licensed firearms. The Finnish shootings closely follow the US 'school shooter' phenomenon with significant 'copycat' elements (Lindberg *et al.*, 2012), with a school and a college being targeted by perpetrators with a history of bullying, personality disorders and alleged anti-social behaviour traits (Raittila *et al.*, 2010: 23; Kiilakoski and Oksanan, 2011). The 2007 incident involved the 18-year-old perpetrator prefacing his rampage by posting images of himself, posing with his new gun, on the internet and in film clips on YouTube. He wore a T-shirt bearing the phrase 'humanity is over-rated', a sentiment corresponding with comments in an 'anti-humanist manifesto' he had prepared prior to the incident. Less than a year later, a 22-year-old college student also posted images and films of himself on social networking sites in aggressive gun handling postures before carrying out his own attack. These images had prompted the Finnish police to interview him about his gun licence in the week before the shooting tragedy, although, concluding that he had broken no laws; they did not revoke his weapons permit (Raittila *et al.*, 2010: 24). A suicide note subsequently discovered by police expressed a supposed 'hatred for mankind' and alluded to the fact that he had been planning his massacre for years. He also kept a collection of materials relating to US school shootings. The 2008 incident involved mainly female victims, but police, who argued that there were significant 'copy-cat' elements in the second shooting, denied that women had been specifically targeted, pointing out that the victims were members of a catering class containing mainly female students. As we have seen, however, Finnish social scientists have contested the down-playing of gender and power in both incidents, remarking that the apparently 'self-righteous violence' of armed neo-liberal masculinity has to be seen as a central feature of the rampage shooter phenomenon (Kantola *et al.*, 2011).

As we have seen earlier, Finland has one of the world's highest rates of *legal* firearm ownership, chiefly rifles and shotguns, for hunting and sports shooting, although there are also thought to be almost a quarter of a million handguns in circulation (Alpers and Wilson, nd). Despite the prevalence of gun ownership Finland had fairly restrictive firearms laws. Gun ownership, for instance, was not a 'right', firearm licence applicants had to establish a legitimate reason for owning a gun, references were required and extensive background checks are carried out. Driving convictions and a record for drunkenness might be used to reject a licence application. Widespread lawful firearm ownership has tended to obscure the issue of illegal weapons in Finland, until recently many were thought to be a legacy of WW2 and related Finnish/Soviet conflicts, although a different picture has lately begun to emerge. An illegal .9mm handgun found employment in December 2009 when a 43-year-old man of Kosovan–Albanian origin shot his former partner at her home before moving on to kill four of her colleagues working in a shopping mall (Mutanen, 2009). Finland has a fairly high rate of homicide, three times higher than similar Nordic countries, but despite the rate of gun ownership, knives remain the most common murder weapon and alcohol is reported to be a factor in three-quarters of Finnish homicides (Nurmi, 2012). That said, 45 per cent of firearm homicides involved a legal firearm (therefore 55 per cent of the homicide firearms were illegal). However, as much concern, from a public health perspective, has been the fact that almost 60 per cent of adolescent suicides (compared with 29 per cent of adults) in Finland are carried out with firearms (Lahti *et al.*, 2006). In recent years, Finnish police have been reporting greater numbers of illegal firearm seizures (mainly handguns but also a number of automatic weapons), especially relating to the activities of criminal gangs. The seizures have also included reactivated and converted weapons and significant numbers of the Russian-made 'traumatic guns' which fire a rubber projectile.

Although the campus shootings of 2007 and 2008 initiated the most recent reforms of Finland's gun laws, the policy shift was by no means smooth and uncontested. While some commentators condemned Finland's allegedly 'primitive' gun laws, others sought to celebrate the country's hunting legacy. A continuing sequence of shooting incidents kept the gun question live until late 2012 when, undoubtedly also prompted by the Norway massacre the year before, a new Gun Control Act was passed, bringing Finland closer into line with EU gun control norms. The age at which citizens could legally own a firearm was raised from 15 to 20, and gun licenses became renewable after five years. Applicants would be required to undergo a safety test, referees and medical practitioners would henceforth have to certify the suitability of all applicants (as well as being required to report to the police any relevant changes in a gun owner's health and personal circumstances).

Another relatively high gun ownership European society prompted to reform its gun laws in the wake of rampage shooting incidents is Germany. Germany is thought to have some 25 million privately owned firearms, putting it in the top five 'most armed' societies, and fifteenth in terms of the rate of gun ownership (gun ownership per 100 citizens). However, only some 7.2 million of the German firearms are legally registered, the remaining 17 million being unregistered and therefore unlawfully held (although estimates of illegal weapon numbers are inevitably imprecise) (Alpers and Wilson, nd). This anomaly results from a number of factors: the consolidation of federal German gun control policies in the 1970s, an unforeseen consequence of large numbers of firearms disappearing from the official records as owners failed to register them as required; German reunification added further to the illegal weapon inventory; likewise illegal weapon trafficking from former Eastern bloc societies; and German police sources now describe a 'thriving black market' in illegal weapons in Germany.

Germany experienced two major school shooting incidents since 2000, at Erfurt in 2002 and Winnenden in 2009.[5] Seventeen people (including the shooter, a 19-year-old expelled former student) were killed in the first incident, the killer mainly targeting teachers and administrators; at Winnenden, 16 people were fatally shot (including the perpetrator) and nine seriously injured. Parallels with American and Finnish school shootings were clear; in both cases the majority of victims were female. Eleven of the victims at Winnenden were female students, eyewitnesses suggesting that females had been specifically targeted (Hall, 2009). The perpetrators were both angry young men with grievances and emotional issues about their perceived 'persecution'; their enthusiasms for firearms were well known; the shooter in the 2009 incident had articulated his intentions in ways that might have prompted preventive intervention (Davies and Pidd, 2009); the weapon employed in the 2009 incident had not been adequately secured by its owner, the shooter's father, who was subsequently prosecuted for negligence and his 14 other firearms were confiscated (Yeoman and Charter, 2009). Tighter gun control measures followed both of the German school shootings, including tighter registration arrangements and more intensive monitoring of the safe storage of weapons in private homes. A National Firearms Register was also proposed to become operational by 2013, a year earlier than required by the EU Firearms Directive (Council Directive 91/477/EEC of 18 June 1991). German gun control policy now exceeds the public safety requirements set by the EU. Firearm homicide in Germany has fallen significantly since the mid-1990s; the overall rate of gun homicide appears slightly higher than that of England and Wales, the rate of *handgun* homicide, slightly lower (Alpers and Wilson, nd).

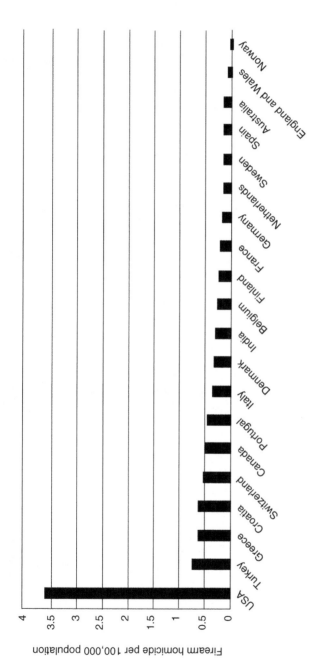

FIGURE 8.1 Firearm homicide rates in selected societies: firearm homicide per 100,000 population

Note: The data for this chart is drawn from Alpers *et al.* (2013). The societies are selected to demonstrate the European range of gun homicide rates as compared with the two 'post-frontier' societies (Australia and Canada) we are about to consider, and the USA. India, which we considered briefly earlier, is also included. For purposes of further comparison, the relevant figures for South Africa and Mexico, both of which featured in the discussion of chronic gun violence in conflict zones in Chapter 7, are 17 and 10 per 100,000, respectively, both of them soaring way off the chart.

In the wake of rampage 2: post 'frontier' societies

While European societies (England and Wales, Norway, Finland, Switzerland and Germany) have, in their own ways, demonstrated varieties of action and inaction following major shooting incidents, two societies, in particular, Australia and Canada have featured significantly in global debates about gun control in the wake of their own post-incident gun control initiatives. As we have noted already, in both cases it was a major incident, or several major incidents, rather than underlying levels of 'ordinary' gun crime that prompted the key reforms. What follows is not, in any sense, a direct or exhaustive comparison between the two countries, but merely an attempt to draw out some of the issues relating to gun control politics, the measures undertaken and their impacts and consequences in two societies that do share some important cultural and historical characteristics.

Both societies are relatively high gun ownership cultures with similar proportions of citizens participating in gun ownership and shooting activities (see Table 8.1). Yet both societies appear to contain substantial numbers of illegal and unregistered firearms, in each case, numbers substantially exceeding the quantity of legal weapons. As we have already seen, the tragedy at Port Arthur in April 1996, when 35 people were killed, although it was not the first Australian rampage killing, was the major event that led to a significant tightening of Australian gun laws. Canada, likewise, was jolted towards gun control by the École Polytechnic massacre in Montreal, 1989, at which 14 female students were fatally shot (and 14 injured) by a deluded misogynist who believed he was 'fighting feminism' (Rathjen and Montpetit, 1999).[6] Aside from such similarities, however, each society politically engaged with the question of gun control in different ways, the ensuing debates took different shapes as public safety advocates employed different control strategies (although a number of similar issues surfaced), with different outcomes and longer-term consequences.

TABLE 8.1 Canada and Australia: selected firearms evidence

	Canada	Australia
Rate of civilian gun possession (legal and illegal) (per 100 citizens)	23.8	15
Rate of *legal* gun ownership (per 100 citizens)	5.42	3.96
World ranking for number of legal guns	12th	25th
World ranking for rate of legal gun ownership	13th	42nd
Estimated total number of legal civilian firearms	10 million	3 million
Number of gun owners	1.8 million	730,000

Source: Alpers *et al.* (2013).

Canada

As Cook *et al.* (2009) have pointed out, in common with Mexico, Canada's major problem with regard to illegal firearms has much to do with the long, undefended border it shares with the USA (over 5,500 miles). Yet borders are porous, during the USA's ill-fated experiment with alcohol prohibition in the 1920s, large quantities of alcohol travelled south from Canada (Behr: 1996), and when Canada imposed high tobacco taxes in the 1990s, cigarettes made their way northwards. Now it is guns, for cross-border contraband follows a number of simple rules of illegal supply and demand relating, ultimately, to risks, incentives and price differentials (Taylor, 1999; Chettleburgh, 2007: 82–87). Although sharing many 'frontier society' characteristics with its neighbour to the south, Canada is often distinguished from the USA by reference to key criminal justice policies, including its attitude to gun control. Michael Moore, in his partly satirical film about US attitudes to firearms, *Bowling for Columbine* (Moore, 2002) drew some invidious comparisons between firearms and violence north and south of the 49th parallel. Likewise, in his historical study of guns and gun control in Canada, Blake Brown (2012) reviews the memoirs of former Canadian Prime Minister, Jean Chretien (1993–2003), who suggests that 'gun control is a "core value" that helps "define the difference between Canadians and Americans"'. Blake Brown continues, 'while the United States is allegedly filled with "gun nuts" defended by the all-powerful NRA, Canada is a place of "peace, order and good government" – a nation whose citizens tolerate firearm regulation to ensure public safety' (2012: 3).

Inevitably, perhaps, such starkly drawn contrasts overstate the differences between the two societies for both share important cultural and historical characteristics: both (and Australia likewise) were former 'frontier societies' where expanding patterns of white settlement conflicted with indigenous peoples, and government authority was often, at best, remote. Shooting, as in hunting, was part of natural tradition but, especially in the second half of the nineteenth century (although Canada had no civil war accelerating the mass proliferation of firearms), just as in the USA, the areas of inward migration on the eastern seaboard began to experience increasing concerns about 'aliens', crime, disorder and violence whereby firearms, particularly handguns, began to be subject to often discriminatory forms of regulation – arming Britons and disarming immigrants and indigenous peoples (Blake Brown, 2012: 63–80). From the turn of the century while, just as in the USA, rifle shooting came to be celebrated in Canada for its 'manly', recreational and disciplining virtues (even for women) as well as good military preparedness, handguns began to become subject to increasingly strict regulation after WW1 and from the 1930s onwards (Cook *et al.*, 2009). In many respects the incremental regulation of weapons in Canada, notwithstanding the locally nuanced ways in which the 'gun question' was perceived and the particular groups upon whom greater or lesser degrees of 'gun control' were imposed (Irish 'fenians', Italians, indigenous peoples, Bolsheviks, Germans and Italians), makes for an interesting application of the civilization thesis as far as weapons, governance capacity, urbanization and democratizing legitimacy are concerned (Elias, 1939; Smith, 2006). However, no sooner was peaceable and civilized modernity attained than (also echoing the USA in the

1960s and 1970s) a number of counter tendencies surfaced which began to increasingly associate firearms with crime and violence, leading politicians to contemplate tighter restrictions on firearm availability and prompting representatives of shooting groups or 'angry white men' (Blake Brown, 2012: 159) to mobilize to safeguard their firearm ownership. By the late 1970s, attempts had been made to restrict certain types of firearms (including versions of the AR-15 military assault rifle) and prevent access to weapons by unsuitable people (criminals and the mentally ill). Penalties were increased for weapons offences and a new licensing and purchase screening system was proposed. The latter initiative, in particular, began to galvanize an emerging Canadian 'gun lobby' into action. Taken as a whole, this legislation was thought to have had relatively limited impact as, during the period, the actual availability of firearms in Canada had increased (Mundt, 1990). When the Montreal massacre occurred, in 1989, the gun debate in Canada had already become very polarized.

After the tragedy a tougher screening process was introduced for all gun purchases and the age for obtaining a firearm acquisition certificate was raised to 18. New risk assessments and background checks were introduced as well as training courses, a thorough questionnaire, a photograph of the gun owner and the submission of suitable references (Cukier and Sidel, 2006). In the wake of the massacre, such changes did not go far enough for many gun control advocates, they impacted upon new gun acquisition, not firearms already privately owned; it was estimated that only around one-third of Canadian gun owners had valid acquisition certificates (having been through the screening process). Accordingly another Firearms Act was introduced in 1995 which sought to further restrict classes of firearms 'not reasonably used in hunting' (a means of prohibiting semi-automatic assault weapons); it proposed a ban on certain classes of handguns; required the five-yearly licensing of all gun owners (by 2001) and the registration of all firearms (by 2003). Finally, anyone seeking to purchase ammunition would need to produce their firearm licence in order to do so. Passage of the new law was highly contested, the new legislation then faced some (ultimately unsuccessful) legal challenges in the courts, the Canadian Supreme Court finding eventually that regulation of firearms, as a matter of public safety, fell well within the jurisdiction of the Federal Government. Fierce and protracted opposition from gun lobby groups followed, especially concerns about the considerable expense and cost overruns of the licensing and gun registry systems (Mauser, 2001), the invasion of privacy and the alleged imposition of 'urban sensibilities' onto rural and hunting cultures (Blake Brown, 2012: 240–241). The supposed excessive annual cost of the gun registry – $66 million in 2010–2011 – was frequently cited by opponents, although this has to be set against the estimated financial costs resulting from misuse of firearms, $6.6 billion per year even in the 1990s (Chapdelaine, 1996).

Nevertheless, according to Cook et al. (2009: 6–7) the 1995 measures were operational by 2003 with an estimated 90 per cent of Canadian gun owners complying and a similar percentage of Canada's seven million guns registered (estimates that suggest some variance in relation to the proportion of gun owners and the numbers of guns referred to in Table 8.1). As it turned out, however, this was not the end of the story. The Conservative Government elected in 2011 scrapped the federal gun registry for long guns (rifles and shotguns) in 2012, although it will continue to monitor handguns. According to Blake Brown, the gun registry fell foul of an emerging neo-liberal political agenda in Canada which

> connected gun control to the problems of an expanding government bureaucracy, interventionist economic and social policies, and high taxes. Gun owners voiced a powerful neo-liberal critique of the interventionist state … [This] combination of neo-liberal political ideology, regional bitterness, well-organised lobby groups, the urban-versus-rural divide and competing conceptions of masculinity explain the ferocious resistance to gun control since the 1970s.
>
> *(2012: 240)*

Perhaps things were not so different to the USA after all.

While the registry existed it achieved support from the police and the majority of urban Canadians; the police found the registry a useful intelligence back-up, accessing the system around 2,000 times a day, when dealing with potentially armed offenders. Academics and public safety advocates argued that the registry had been the latest in a line of gun control measures that had seen firearm deaths and injuries – especially those carried out with long guns, the focus of the legislation – fall to a 30-year low by 2007 (see Figure 8.2) (Cukier and Sidel, 2006). Domestic firearm homicides fell by 80 per cent during this period, while the number of women killed by firearms fell by two-thirds. Unfortunately, homicides with handguns increased over the same period (Dauvergne and De Socio, 2006), driven by illegal firearm trafficking, the drug economy and a growing urban street gang culture.

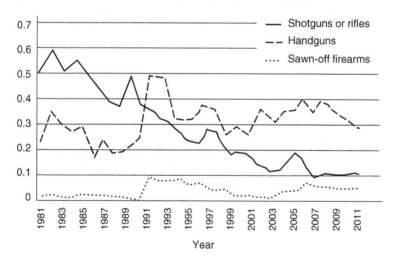

FIGURE 8.2 Firearm-related homicides (by 100,000 population), by type of firearm, Canada, 1981–2011

Source: Perreault (2012).

There were an unprecedented 52 killings in Toronto in 2005, the final victim of the year, a 15-year-old white girl, was killed on Boxing Day while out shopping with friends, 'an entirely innocent victim caught in a cross-fire of street gun-play between rival factions of ethnic minority youth' (Sheptycki, 2009: 309), although, as Sheptycki continued, 'the majority of victims of gun-crime in Toronto that year, and indeed every other recent year, had been ethnic minority people … [accordingly] media discourse was considerably shaped by a surreptitiously and routinely racialised discourse' (2009: 310). These changing patterns of gun crime and urban gun cultures in Canada have led commentators to describe a process of 'pistolization' embracing the demand for, and casual resort to, weapon carrying (and use) as the performance of a certain masculinity in a world perceived as dangerous (Hagedorn, 2008; Sheptycki, 2009; Cukier and Sheptycki, 2012). Pistolization, perhaps inevitably, resonates globally with notions of 'gun culture' (Bascuñán and Pearce, 2008) and necessarily demands a given level of, legal or illegal, firearm supply. In the Toronto case, where criminologists have begun to recognize this phenomenon, the source of supply is, and for many years has been (Dandurand, 1998; Frappier *et al.*, 2005), the liberal and illegal gun markets of the USA. Cook *et al.* (2009) cite a number of Royal Canadian Mounted Police (RCMP) firearm tracing initiatives revealing that, of prohibited criminally involved firearms (primarily handguns) successfully traced, between two-thirds to 70 per cent originated in the USA. Chettleburgh adds a cautionary note, however, still reluctant to exclusively blame the USA for Canada's gang and gun crime problems: while globalizing 'gang culture' and a plentiful supply of weapons are not irrelevant, he contends, 'deteriorating economic conditions for marginalised people, combined with the brutal competition that results when people sell illicit drugs for huge profits … have much more to do with gang violence and gang expansion in Canada than guns ever have, and ever will'. Gang culture, gun violence and aggression, he concludes, originates in the social conditions of contemporary urban Canada, in racism, inequality, marginality, unemployment and the drug culture. It does not somehow surge forth, seemingly fully formed 'from the hunk of metal that is the American handgun' (Chettleburgh, 2007: 87–88). But this, of course, is precisely the debate.

As we have noted, borders are porous, especially in an age of globalization, and a bad neighbour can significantly undermine a country's gun control efforts. For Canada this has been so in two senses, not only have illegal weapons been traded northwards by small-scale illegal entrepreneurs and organized criminals, the US gun lobby also weighed in. The NRA was keen to support Canadian gun rights and the political ambitions of its subsidiary organization in the north; they celebrated the demise of the gun registry, anxious, as ever, to show (in the run-up to the 2012 presidential elections, and while the NRA was still fighting the UN ATT) that gun control measures could be overturned and neo-liberal gun culture globalized (Kopel, 2012). In one respect at least, without a land border with any other society, especially the USA, Australia might have an 'enormous advantage' in gun control (Harding, 1981: 161). As Reuter and Mouzos note: 'It is more difficult to import prohibited guns into Australia than into the United States or any western European country because there are no land borders' (Reuter and Mouzos, 2003: 125).

Australia

That said, the gun control measures proposed in the wake of the 1996 Port Arthur shootings prompted no less argument and controversy. As I have already noted, the Port Arthur massacre was not Australia's first multiple victim shooting tragedy, the country had previously experienced 11 such incidents since 1980. As a result, the Federal Government had already banned the importation of 'military-style', semi-automatic weapons in 1991 (whereas handguns had been strictly regulated since the 1930s), but by then there were thought to be many tens – possibly hundreds – of thousands of these weapons in civilian circulation. No-one knew where they were, three of Australia's states had no gun registration at all implying there was no consistent regulation or monitoring of secondary weapon sales. Tasmania, where the shooting had occurred, had the weakest gun laws of all (Chapman, 1998/2013). Harding noted that 'nearly half of all gun owners obtained their guns through private sales, gifts, as heirlooms or other means' (Harding, 1981: 84). There was growing dissatisfaction at this state of affairs; Chapman describes opinion poll data during the 1990s showing significant majorities – as much as 90 per cent (Peters and Watson, 1996) – consistently in favour of tighter federal- and state-level gun laws. Some states had already introduced their own legislation, but a uniform federal firearm registration system still seemed some way off, especially given the reluctance of the political leaderships in New South Wales, Queensland and Tasmania to cooperate, 'this left Australia with a legal patchwork of astonishing inconsistency' (Chapman, 1998/2013: 103). Richard Harding, an academic criminologist, had begun to outline an Australian gun control strategy to address these inconsistencies back in 1981. Uppermost in his mind was the 'inexorable' growth in Australian firearms ownership and the emergence of a number of issues which, given time, might grow into a gun problem 'of the American kind' (Harding, 1981: 158). He proposed a tighter system of firearms licensing and registration, the single most important objective of which 'should be to keep the handgun inventory down to the bare minimum', although he did acknowledge that, so far, the police authorities had been 'reasonably successful' at this (1981: 163). He urged action, above all, to address the rising profiles of gun violence, including assault, homicide, robbery and suicide, the impact these would have on police resort to firearms and in order to prevent firearm violence becoming part of everyday life in Australia, 'and the quality of life … poisoned by anxiety and fear' (1981: 166).

It is arguable to say that Port Arthur, in 1996, marked the most critical turning point (but neither the first nor the only one) in Australian attitudes to firearms. Chapman's book, *Over our Dead Bodies*, first published in 1998 (republished in 2013), tells the story of the 'fight for gun control' in Australia which followed. Several themes are addressed in the course of the book: the importance of effective political leadership (especially the role of the recently elected Premier, John Howard) and coordinated gun control advocacy (see also Peters, 2013: 197); the framing of the debate in the media; and the rhetoric and arguments employed by gun lobby advocates to resist the changing laws. A final section of the book explores the ways in which (and why and how) some of the original proposals were watered down or subsequently amended, including a number of instances where 'state law reform fell disturbingly short of the original Howard plan' (1998/2013: 28). Finally, Chapman turns to a couple of areas of 'unfinished business' for Australian gun control: the safe storage of firearms and the need for tighter controls on semi-automatic handguns. His aim, in part, was that the book should serve as a guide for other gun control lobbyists around the world. His core observation, prescient if disturbing, was that the massacre was a *necessary* but, of itself, not a *sufficient* cause for fundamental firearm safety reform. The initial publication date of the book implies that it was unable to make an assessment of the impact and effectiveness of the laws, but subsequently many analysts and commentators have sought to engage with this issue.

The Port Arthur shooting occurred only one month after the election of the John Howard Liberal/National Coalition Government. The new prime minister acted quickly, summoning the Australian Police Ministers Council (APMC) and they quickly hammered out a 'uniform firearm agreement' for adoption by the Federal Government and the eight states and territories of Australia. The main components of these proposals were: (1) a ban on the importation, ownership, sale, resale, transfer, possession, manufacture or use of semi-automatic rifles and pump-action shotguns; (2) a compensatory 'buyback' scheme in which gun owners would be paid the market value of any prohibited guns they surrendered; (3) the registration of all firearms as part of a national gun owner licensing scheme; (4) the requirement that all gun licence applicants prove a 'genuine reason' for owning a firearm; (5) requirements that all guns be stored securely; and (6) uniform national gun laws.

Most of these provisions faced serious opposition but, according to Chapman, the various measures were not always objected to by the gun lobbies in relation to their potential for effectiveness. Most commentators are also agreed that the reforms, including the buyback, were thoroughly and effectively carried out (Leigh and Neill, 2010). The ban on semi-automatic rifles and national registration was fiercely opposed, although it was the requirement to show 'genuine need' for a firearm that, potentially, could have been the most restrictive measure. Much would depend upon how tightly these definitions were applied, in other words, the potential gap 'between the spirit of the new agreement and its translation into state and territory law and ... the extent to which the various provisions would be actually implemented' (1998/2013: 253). In the past (as in England, Scotland and Wales), this issue, the membership of a shooting club, had been something of a 'flag of convenience' for gun owners (Squires, 2000). In Australia, Chapman points to a similar phenomenon, for even before 1996,

> self or family defence was not officially recognised as a justifiable reason for being granted a firearms licence in any jurisdiction ... But it was certainly the case that many applicants for licences acquired them with this reason in mind and simply ticked a box on gun licensing forms indicating that they wanted a gun for other purposes, like hunting.
>
> *(1998/2013: 149)*

By contrast, Kohn found that *none* of her Australian sports-shooter interviewees admitted to keeping their guns for self-defence; as they reminded her, gun
ownership for self-defence was not lawful in Australia (Kohn, 2004b). Even more
tellingly, few Australian shooters voiced opinions even remotely supportive of
what they termed 'the American way' with regard to gun ownership, although
McCarthy, having conducted his own ethnographic works with Australian shooters, feels they may have been rather circumspect and 'economical' in how much
they told her (McCarthy, 2011). In Australia the issue of 'genuineness' became
primarily focussed upon the supposed need for semi-automatic rifles (Chapman,
1998/2013: 149) and for which financial compensation was available. Before 1996
handguns (revolvers and pistols) were already restrictively licensed, they were
available only to members of handgun clubs and those employed in the security
industry. Besides, the weapon that had done the damage at Port Arthur was an
assault rifle so this was where the public and political gun control agenda focussed.

The gun 'buyback' from 1996 until September 1997 is said to have netted
some 650,000 semi-automatic rifles for which market-level compensation was
made. This figure needs setting against a police estimate that there were almost
1.5 million such weapons in circulation. Compliance with the requirements of the
buyback is thought to have varied somewhat on a state-by-state basis (Reuter and
Mouzos, 2003: 131). The Australian gun lobby rather confused issues by simultaneously arguing that there were more (soon to be illegal) firearms in circulation
than estimated; that most committed shooters would not give them up; that the
shooting fraternity was essentially law abiding; and that the money made available
for compensation was insufficient (Chapman, 1998/2013: 229). Official estimates
had suggested that some 800,000–900,000 illegal firearms (semi-automatic rifles
and pump-action shotguns) remained unaccounted for, but on the positive side the
new firearm registration system was now beginning to reject significant numbers of
'unsafe' gun licence applications. All told, following a more rigorous recent analysis
of amnesties, buybacks and gun surrender programmes in Australia, including the
handgun buyback of 2003,[7] Alpers (2013) has argued that well over one million
firearms (approximately one-third of the national civilian gun stock) were surrendered for destruction since 1988. This bore witness to a sea change in attitudes
to firearms in Australia while contributing to falling rates of homicide, specifically
gun homicide (see Figure 8.3) and as much as an 80 per cent reduction in firearm
suicides (Leigh and Neill, 2010). By 2012, however, it was clear that Australian
shooters had been restocking, buying legal firearms to replace those restricted after
1996. By 2012, there were once again as many firearms in Australia as there had
been in 1996 (Alpers, 2013).

Yet the uniform firearm agreement, hammered out shortly after the Port Arthur
shooting, was not uniformly implemented, in different states concessions were struck
and exceptions made, reflecting specific local interests and political balances. And,
over the years, as Peters has noted, 'individual states and territories have amended
their laws … and some cracks are beginning to emerge' (2013: 202). New South
Wales relaxed its laws on unlicensed persons using handguns at gun clubs and in

2011 someone smuggled a pistol out of a club's shooting range to fatally shoot her father. There was also evidence that the laws specifying the requirement for safe and secure domestic gun storage were only being very variably and rather cursorily enforced by the police. The strategic aim of the gun control lobby had been the removal of domestic firearm storage altogether. Such arrangements had an enormous potential for making the overall gun control package more effective. After all, fully 81 per cent of Australian gun deaths were suicides and a significant proportion of domestic gun misuse formed part of a pattern of domestic violence. For example, victim surveys confirmed widespread anecdotal evidence from domestic violence projects that firearms were often brandished in the home to intimidate women and children; 14 per cent of domestic violence victims surveyed revealed that they had been threatened or injured with a gun, and a survey in Sydney reported that 15 per cent of domestic violence clients reported that their partners owned a gun. Major shooting tragedies may command all the media attention, but in terms of over-all rates of gun misuse they are statistically overshadowed by suicides and domestic violence (Chapman, 1998/2013: 92–94). If firearms were not stored at home they would not be instantly available to the violent, impetuous or suicidal. Furthermore, guns cannot be fired legally in residential settings, they are not permitted for self-defence and, if they are not kept at home (where they are the most prone to theft), they may be less likely to be stolen or accidentally fired (perhaps by a child). In the event, the proposals for non-domestic firearm storage, similar to those proposed by the Cullen enquiry after Dunblane (Cullen, 1996) were not taken up.

Before moving to consider the evaluation of the effectiveness of the Australian gun control measures after 1996, it is instructive to consider the role and politics of the Australian shooting lobby in these debates. In many respects their spokesmen appeared to have been cut from similar reactionary masculinist cloth as their US or Canadian fellows (Melzer, 2009; Blake Brown, 2012), and largely championing

> a reactionary, right-wing political agenda including advocacy of individual liberty in the face of perceptions of excessive government, opposition to immigration, opposition to multiculturalism, rabid opposition to any group whose moral or sexual perspectives deviate from anything the far right consid-ers normal, and claims that law and order is breaking down to the extent that citizens need weapons to defend themselves.
>
> *(Economou, cited in Chapman, 1998/2013: 156)*

The Australian shooters also scored something of an own goal by admitting to the receipt of donations from the US NRA to help fight their cause. If that had been their only error, things might not have gone so badly but, above all, whether by virtue of their evident paranoia, their on-air jokes about domestic violence and their intimidating behaviour which seemingly confirmed everything the 'gun nut' stereotype embraced, then a strain of outright redneck craziness shone right through their 'foot-in-mouth' politics, further alienating mainstream political support.

Supporters of the package of gun reforms claimed the measures a success. An analysis after ten years (Chapman *et al.*, 2006) argued that, following the gun control package implemented in 1996, there had been no further mass shootings in Australia (whereas there had been 13 in the previous two decades) and the new controls appeared to have accelerated already falling trends in firearm suicides and homicides. During the two years of the gun buyback, firearm homicide fell 46 per cent and firearm suicide by 43 per cent (Hemenway, 2009: 267). In any event, the homicide rate has been falling significantly in Australia since 1990 and, in 2010, stood at an historic 20-year low. Within that overall picture, firearms appear to be responsible for a diminishing proportion of homicides (see Figure 8.3). During 2008–2010, only 13 per cent of homicides involved a firearm and, of these, only 14 per cent were handguns. Having risen after 1996, handgun use in Australian homicides has fallen sharply, by over two-thirds, since 2005 (Chan and Payne, 2013).

Critics of the view that the Australian gun buyback made a significant contribution to preventing gun violence (crimes involving firearms and especially homicide and suicide) in Australia have ranged from the academic, political and polemical, advancing arguments of varying quality, rigour and insight. Carcach *et al.* (2002), treating the Port Arthur shootings as a 'quasi experiment' to test the impact of the incident, conclude that neither the shooting nor the gun control measures that followed had any 'lasting impact' on firearm homicide in Australia, although, subsequently, homicide has resumed its 'long-term downward trend'. Reuter and Mouzos (2003), in another of the earlier academic evaluations, concluded that 'the buyback alone was an implausible candidate for reducing crime rates because the targeted gun type was one not much used in homicides or, presumably, other types of violent crime' (2003: 141).

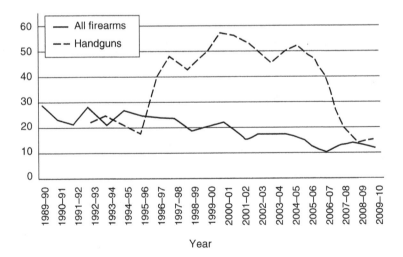

FIGURE 8.3   Use of firearms in Australian homicides, 1989–2010 (%)

Sources: Bricknell (2008); Chan and Payne (2013: 14).

A later complex predictive statistical analysis by Baker and McPhedran (2007) disputed any significant impact on firearm homicide and found only that the rate of gun suicides appeared to have been significantly affected by the buyback and the new regulations, although they questioned the reliability of the evidence – suicide determination as cause of death (McPhedran and Baker, 2008) – upon which even this finding was reached. In turn, this critical assessment was also challenged by Neill and Leigh (2007) who concluded 'our re-analysis shows a statistically significant reduction in deaths due to both firearm homicides and suicides' and so, 'to the extent that the time series evidence points anywhere, it is towards the conclusion that the [Australian] National Firearms Agreement reduced gun deaths' (Neill and Leigh, 2007).

Amongst other arguments, Reuter and Mouzos (2003) noted the fact that the decline in firearm violence in Australia had begun prior to the buyback. In fact, different Australian states, such as Victoria, embarked upon significant firearm control interventions long before 1996 as a result of shooting incidents they had experienced (Ozanne-Smith et al., 2004). Indeed, according to Lee and Suardi (2010), this already falling trend in firearm death rates, which began before 1996, may well have obscured any possible impacts that the gun control measures, arising from the 1996 National Firearms Agreement, might have had on both gun suicide and gun homicide rates. In passing they comment that, although the incident and the ensuing firearm policies might appear a relatively clear-cut example of before-and-after policy impact assessment, appropriate evaluation of the measures is by no means a straightforward exercise (Lee and Suardi, 2010: 66).

As if confirming these difficulties, Reuter and Mouzos (2003) pointed out that handgun-involved crime rose immediately after 1996 in Australia (before falling again, dramatically, after 2005), and they rehearsed the arguments that buybacks and amnesties usually only recover the lowest risk firearms; criminals usually being the least inclined to give up their weapons (Kennedy et al., 1996). They acknowledged, however, that in the five-year period following the new laws, no multiple victim shootings had occurred. However the extent to which the gun crime reduction impacts might be attributable to the firearm buyback as opposed to other aspects of the Australian gun control package, indeed, whether it is possible to attribute specific violence reduction outcomes to the buyback *alone*, remain rather more open questions (Leitzel, 2003). Whether the large-scale and exceedingly expensive firearm buyback exercise was a *necessary* aspect of the reform programme (or simply useful to grease the political process and compensate gun owners) and whether it is something other societies might usefully follow may be less clear cut (although civilian firearm buybacks – combined with other gun control measures – have been successfully reported in Brazil (Rio de Janeiro) and, although rather less positively, in Argentina; Dreyfus et al., 2008; Lenis et al., 2010). Also less clear cut is the distinction alluded to in Baker and McPhedran's conclusion, 'there is insufficient evidence to support the simple premise that reducing the stockpile of licitly held civilian firearms will result in a reduction in either firearm or overall sudden death rates' (2007: 467) for if the Australian evidence tells us anything it is that, just as it is not always easy in the USA to tell the 'good guys with guns' apart from the bad guys, so licit and illicit firearm stocks are not necessarily the watertight categories we might assume. Accordingly, it follows that the gun rights discourse that frames the issue of gun safety as exclusively something to do with 'good guys' and firearms in the 'right hands' is largely missing the point.

One abiding impression gained from many of the analyses critical of the impact of the new Australian gun laws concerns how counter-intuitive some of their claims have been, invoking highly complex statistical and time-series tests to, effectively, 'prove' – following any tightly specified 'gun control measure', in a complex, shifting field and, more often than not, a highly charged and fast moving social context – that nothing happened (Hemenway, 2009), even as gun death trends plummeted to the lower right corner of their charts. In one sense this is a familiar, though limited reflection of the statistical war of attrition that often passes for *half* of the US gun control debate.[8] In one sense representatives of the Australian gun control lobbies might care less, for firearm homicide had been falling consistently for over two decades. In fact, that is to say, just as is apparent in the USA (where advances in emergency medical care and a growing racial disproportion in gun crime victimization may be a more central part of the story than gun control measures of the nature and scale of those pioneered in Australia). When pressed, statistically inclined gun researchers seeking to explain these comparable trends often turn to 'other' social and cultural factors that were insufficiently quantifiable to be modelled effectively in their study. As Baker and McPhedran (2007) note, 'societal factors could also have influenced observed changes', and thereby, as Young notes, relinquishing their blinkered and myopic statistical empiricism and falling back on largely unexplored social and cultural explanations, perhaps the last refuge of the frustrated positivist (Rosenfeld, 2000: 157; see Young, 2011: 113). Except that, generally speaking, they do not pursue these other arguments or undertake the research to explore them, being content to have found the test measures 'not proven': science as impediment. As Alpers (2013: 209) has noted, we have seen all of this before: industry and self-interest lobbying, scientific obfuscation, fear, denial and ideological – sometimes even quasi-religious – objection, have often resisted policies for delivering vehicle-related safety, tackling drink driving and tobacco-related illness, HIV/AIDS transmission and global warming. And now the same has become true of reducing firearm-related deaths but, on the positive side, the solutions *are* out there.

As the overall rate of homicide has fallen and firearm homicide has become a declining proportion of this, attention has shifted increasingly to the handgun violence problem in Australia. In that sense Australia's problem of gun-involved criminal violence has come, increasingly, to more closely resemble the problem in the rest of the world, with a focus on handguns. As we have seen, handguns have historically been more tightly controlled than most other 'civilian' firearms in Australia. A study of handgun use in crime during 1997–1999 found that some 90 per cent of the handguns used by criminals were not registered and those in possession of them were not licensed (Mouzos, 2000). While the number of illicit handguns in Australia is difficult to estimate, evidence still suggests that the overwhelming majority are illegally acquired (Bricknell, 2008). Mouzos has argued that the patterns of firearm trafficking (a key source of criminal handguns, along with theft and 'leakage' from legal sources) was relatively small scale, 'unorganized and opportunistic' (Mouzos, 2000). The ways in which firearms are acquired, the reasons for which they are acquired (transport, ease of use, concealability) and the roles in which they are employed (for protection, drug trade enforcement, armed robbery – not to mention displays of hard masculinity; 'respect') are thought to reflect the international evidence about certain types of offenders' predilections for handguns (Wright and Rossi, 1994; Lizotte *et al.*, 2000; Hales *et al.*, 2006; Williams and Poynton, 2006). As Figure 8.3 shows, while the proportion of homicides committed by offenders with handguns grew significantly after 1996, it fell again, even more dramatically, after 2005. Some 22 per cent of armed robberies are committed with a firearm, handguns accounting for around two-thirds of these (Bricknell, 2008).

The rising significance of handgun involved crime prompted a more contemporary review of firearm trafficking and 'serious and organised crime gangs', this was concluded in 2012 (Bricknell, 2008; 2012) and revealed that, judging by firearms seized from offenders, these groups appeared to have a near monopoly on prohibited weapons in Australia. Nearly 50 per cent of weapons seized from organized crime groups and gangs were prohibited weapons while, of prohibited, semi-automatic rifles and handguns, between 70 per cent and three-quarters of the total seized were taken from serious and organized offenders. Overall the review concluded that, based upon police intelligence and court records 'the trafficking network is not considered to be overly organised in structure, but largely dominated by serious and organised criminal entities (such as outlaw motorcycle gangs (OMCGs)) who traffic illicit firearms as a side venture' and smaller operators or corrupt dealers, with the 'grey pool' of semi-automatic rifles not surrendered after 1996 (Bricknell, 2012: 26) continuing as a significant source of supply. Regarding handguns, deactivation/reactivation has been a significant source of supply (39 per cent of firearms seized),[9] as well as theft (31 per cent), although illegal importation appears to be a minor contributor to the criminal armoury. Between 2004 and 2009, an annual average of some 1,500 firearm thefts were reported to the police each year, although this represents less than half the annual average during the previous decade (Borzycki and Mouzos, 2007).

The discussion of handguns has, seemingly inevitably, brought us to a discussion of the forms of criminality most commonly associated with seemingly reckless handgun violence. As in Canada and the UK, this entails a comment on Australian gangs (Squires, 2011a). Until relatively recently, with the exception of the OMCGs (Ayling, 2011),[10] Australian politics and law enforcement interests appeared not to have been especially preoccupied with the gang phenomenon, yet now, firearm trafficking and gun violence have apparently become one of the strands of the contemporary gang problem: 'demand for illicit firearms comes from lower-level criminal individuals – for example, members of street-level gangs … [who] use illicit firearms for self-protection, protection of assets and enabling of other crime types, and to enhance their perceived image' (Australian Crime Commission, 2013: 46). This 'complex' and often 'symbolic' pattern of illegal gun use (Hales *et al.*, 2006) is, according to Bricknell (2012), coming increasingly to characterize the use of handguns by Australian street gangs.

Yet in common with research in the UK and other European societies, much of earlier research in Australia tended to reject the existence of 'American-style' street gangs in Australian cities (Perrone and White, 2000). At the same time, however, commentators acknowledged that police and media reports, and public and political commentaries, were increasingly referring to 'gang problems' (White, 2004). By contrast researchers tended to draw distinctions between 'gangs' and various gang-related behaviours (styles of dress, speech, street socializing, anti-social behaviours) being adopted by groups of young people (White and Mason, 2006). In any event, it appears that a full cycle 'gangsterization' process (Squires, 2011a), akin to the 'pistolization' dynamic described by Sheptycki and Cukier (Sheptycki, 2009; Cukier and Sheptycki, 2012), is now developing in Australia whereby many of the 'risk-averse' and 'profile-driven' interventions effectively net-widen and exacerbate the very issues of youth marginality with which they purport to deal (White, 2008a) – just as they have in the US and UK (Hallsworth and Young, 2008; Goldson, 2011). As White has also confirmed (2008b), ethnicity and masculinity are also deeply implicated within these processes of gang construction.

The issues manifested in the 'new' Australian criminal gun culture are undeniably global, even as they emerge from a very local series of tragedies (particular mass shootings) and the processes of political debate surrounding Australian gun law reform. In a sense, it might be fair to say that the 'local' has here been substantially outflanked by the 'global' ('gangsta' culture, racism and racialization, immigration, Islamaphobia, youth marginality, gang moral panics, fear, weaponization and weapon trafficking and, partly in response, the familiar repertoire of new neo-liberal 'law and order' politics). After all, as we have seen, having eliminated nearly one-third of the weapons in civilian ownership following 1996 and restricting the classes of firearm available to private citizens, Australia has fully restocked, and now it has an emerging gang problem as well. Just like Canada in fact; just like many other developed parts of the world. Fortunately, unlike Canada, Australia does not share a highly porous 5,000 mile border with 'guntopia', the USA, although this certainly does not imply that it is immune to the consequences of weapons trafficking in the Pacific region. Indeed, Mouzos reported in 1999 that the largest numbers of firearms smuggled into Australia were imported from the USA (Mouzos, 1999). This continues – in 2013 New South Wales police found evidence of a smuggling operation running between Nashville and NSW. Handguns purchased by straw purchasers or from Tennessee gun shows were smuggled to Australia in a consignment of used engine parts. As the ATF officer in charge of the case explained, 'strict gun laws in other countries make guns very valuable on the black market' (Hall, 2013).

Subsequently a number of research reports, surveys and intelligence briefings over the past two decades have begun to address this phenomenon. Initially the evidence base was rather ad hoc and largely anecdotal relating to occasional weapons seizures or prosecutions. Subsequently, however, a rather more strategic and regional overview approach began to emerge (Alpers and Twyford, 2003; Capie, 2003; Alpers,

2005; LeBrun and Muggah, 2005). Taken as a whole the globally connected patterns regarding weapon supplies and trafficking demand that, in order to develop a more upscale, upstream and supply-side perspective on the phenomenon, we also move beyond the national level to consider the efforts by the United Nations to bring the trafficking of SALW under greater scrutiny and control. Having considered the various gun control initiatives of a number of countries visited by shooting tragedies, the second half of the chapter will address the efforts to join these together globally.

Brazil: gun control and the 2005 referendum

Brazil provides a different kind of gun control country comparison for, although it witnessed its own rampage killing in 1997 when a man, reputed to be disturbed and depressed and prone to voicing death threats, killed 14 people before, having been surrounded by police, committing suicide, this incident is not usually regarded as significant in prompting Brazil's own efforts at gun control.[11] Part of the reason for this might be gleaned from Figure 7.1 in the previous chapter. Brazil is one of the top 20 countries in the world for gun violence; around 34,000 people each year are killed by firearms. As Figure 8.4 reveals, Brazil's problems with the gun are far more chronic and entrenched than a question of occasional spree killings. Historian Luis Mir has referred to Brazilian major conurbations as the 'metropolises of death' (Mir, 2004), while Mota (2006: 6) has suggested, 'in Brazilian society, urban violence has taken on the characteristics of a social epidemic with firearms as the main vector, which aggravates the problem as well as symbolizes it'. Perlman has likewise added, 'high levels of inequality are associated with the epidemic of violence that is countering the conviviality and trust needed to keep the social contract alive' (2010: 8).

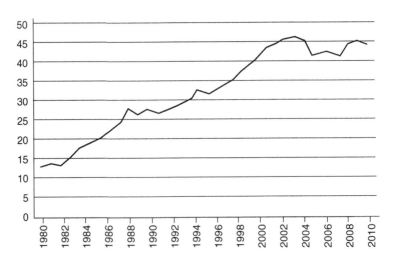

FIGURE 8.4 Firearm mortality rates in Brazil, 1980–2010 (deaths per 100,000)

Source: Waiselfisz (2013).

We have already considered many aspects of the issues relating to young men – even children – guns and masculinity, gangs, organized crime and the drug trade in Brazil (see Dowdney, 2003). As Goertzel *et al.* argue in their cross-national analysis of homicide trends, in Brazil 'homicide rates were highest among poor urban youth often involved in drug gangs … economic stagnation exacerbated these problems, as did the easy availability of firearms' (Goertzel *et al.*, 2012: 66; see also Holzmann, 2006: 34–36). Two further factors exerting an upward pressure on weaponization and violence have also been cited; in the first place the gross inefficiencies in the way that policing and security functions were carried out, at times compromised by corruption, led some criminal entrepreneurs to foster an aura of impunity around their activities. As Huguet and de Carvalho note, in their discussion of violence, crime and the policing of the favelas, '[s]tructural violence and direct violence are highly interdependent' (2008: 93). At the same time, private citizens, lacking confidence in and feeling unprotected by the police and criminal justice system, adopted their own 'solutions' or retaliations, sometimes involving weapons (Barata *et al.*, 1999). Rivero (2004) has painted a particularly daunting portrait of the crime problems of Brazil's major cities as characterized by an essentially *criminally deregulated* market, where firearms have replaced contract and legality in the ordering of social and economic relations.

Accordingly, guns are routinely employed in the favelas by gangs and drug-trafficking factions

> as a way to guarantee and affirm their territorial power, which in turn permits them to trade freely in drugs. To do this, they must confront both the police and other drug-trafficking factions. This situation leaves the favelas of Rio de Janeiro in a state of permanent armed conflict.
>
> *(Rivero, 2004: 58)*

A direct consequence of this being that parts of Rio experience rates of firearm related death paralleled only by states embroiled in civil war. The complicated picture of social order maintenance in the Brazilian favelas adds another dimension to the portrait of uneven reciprocity and contested 'gang-governance from below', in the absence of the state (Holzmann, 2006: 31). Perlman notes how the favelas have become 'trapped between drug gangs, extortionist militias and corrupt police' (2010: 21). Goldstein likewise emphasizes the complex distinctions between gangs, traffickers, vigilantes, police (including police 'death squads'[12]) and private security agencies, 'the categories were used interchangeably … suggesting that the "players" had become hybridized to such an extent that nobody was certain who were bandits, who were police, or who were both' (Goldstein, 2003). The gangs' violence, or their threat of violence, allowed them to both profit from the community and be protected by the community in exchange for services and facilities such as 'the maintenance of social order, support, economic stimulation and provision of leisure activities' (Rivero, 2004), including fuel and power, and especially drugs.

Holzmann, for instance, describes the practice 'governance through drugs' which shapes the life of favela residents:

> This dangerous life, full of armed disputes with other gangs or the police, regularly results in an early death. In the world of drug traffickers, violence becomes ordinary business, and killings out of revenge or as a punishment for behaviour that deviates from established rules, are frequent ... this war-like situation does not leave the vast majority of the *favela* residents, uninvolved in drug trafficking, unaffected. All too often during times of invasion by rival factions or when police curfews are imposed, innocent bystanders are killed by stray bullets. Residents also have to follow clear rules of conduct, in some *favelas* even needing the permission of the drug chief to invite guests.
>
> *(Holzmann, 2006: 30–31)*

Over half of the gun homicides have been directly or indirectly attributed to the drug trade (Rivero, 2004). Problems of violence were also exacerbated by poverty, inequality and state neglect of the favelas which permitted the conflation of class, race, stigma and criminality (Huguet and de Carvalho, 2008; De Souza and Miller, 2012), a legacy of corruption, political and resistance movements turned into criminal rackets, and by traditions of aggressively militaristic policing having their origins in the pre-democracy repressive era before 1985 (Koonings and Kruijt, 2004; Zaluar, 2004; Brinks, 2008; Arias and Goldstein, 2010). On top of this, the widespread availability of firearms, over three-quarters of which were estimated to be illegally held, made for a highly dangerous environment (Rivero, 2004: 61).

Gun violence rates accelerated sharply during the 1980s as Brazil was experiencing its own neo-liberal miracle of highly uneven economic growth (Therborn, 1989) and as the cocaine trafficking economy expanded. According to Goldstein, it was in the midst of this neo-liberal miracle of economic de-control that 'the diversion of firearms to criminal elements reached its peak ... increases in the drug trade coincide with increases in gun related crimes and with diversion of weapons from legal to illegal markets' (Goldstein, 2007a: 34). Perlman also voices profound scepticism about the social and economic strategies that followed the return to democracy in the 1980s, over four decades she has charted the changing character of life in Rio's favelas (1976, 2010). The neo-liberal austerity measures of the 1980s were supposed to inaugurate the fabled 'trickle down' of opportunities, employment and prosperity, instead it has compounded the social exclusion of the poorest and entrenched their 'advanced marginality'. The only things that 'trickled down', she suggests, were drugs and guns. 'The most devastating change that has occurred over four decades is the increase in the drug and arms traffic in the favelas and the take-over of community control by organised narco traffic or self-appointed militias – or both' (2010: 21). The weaponization of these communities has eroded 'social capital', trust and collective association, increasingly replacing it with a fearful individualism. In the gang cultures that emerged in this society in transition, familiar relations of masculine 'warrior' respect and honour dominated social interactions with expendable younger gang members bearing the brunt of the violent retaliation as gangs sought to 'dominate local populations with extremely ruthless security rules' (Zaluar, 2004: 148). Some part of this increasing homicide rate was attributed to the increasing numbers of guns in criminal hands and the growing lethality of the military-style firearms used by the gangs and criminal groups (semi-automatic firepower, higher calibre, greater magazine capacity) (Rivero, 2004: 62)[13] but another significant aspect was routine domestic misuse of firearms (amongst neighbours, partners and ex-partners, family members, peer groups). As Mota (2006) has argued while a popular, and in some ways convenient, perception in Brazil held that the greater part of the gun violence was attributable to criminal groups using illegally trafficked weapons, by the 1990s it was clear that fully 85 per cent of firearms used in homicide were of domestic origin: manufactured, purchased and fired in Brazil (Dreyfus *et al.*, 2005). This new evidence changed the picture entirely:

> [L]ight firearms in the hands of civilians were responsible for the majority of 'close proximity' crimes, affecting indiscriminately women, young people, neighbours, friends, parents, and a significant number of people who, if it weren't for this mortal weapon, would still be with us. These impressive figures, and the firearms that were relatively cheap and easy to obtain, increasingly reinforce a 'culture of violence' … killing innocent victims, destroying families and having a damaging effect on the fabric of society.
>
> *(Crespo, 2006: 3)*

The evidence also reshaped perceptions of the gun crime problem and influenced the subsequent direction of gun control strategy in Brazil. Furthermore, growing evidence of the impact of gun violence upon women and girls, particularly, as we have seen already, emphasizing the ways in which the weaponization of men in communities and the resulting socialization of boys in armed, violent cultures (Barker, 2005), facilitated a kind of violent masculine impunity ('hyper-masculinity') which rendered women's lives all the more violent, abusive and victimized (Holzmann, 2006: 38–63).[14] When Perlman returned, 40 years on, to the favelas she had first researched in the 1970s she found profoundly transformed communities.

> Where there had been hope, there was now fear and uncertainty. People were afraid of getting killed in the crossfire during a drug war between competing gangs; afraid that their children would not return alive after school, or that a stray bullet would kill their toddlers playing on their verandas. They felt more marginalised than ever.
>
> *(Perlman, 2010: xxii)*

Subsequently these issues came to shape the nature of developing gun control campaign in Brazil's urban areas and particularly the leading roles of many women, and communities, within it. A peace and disarmament campaign by the Viva Rio community organization, which was so central to mobilizing the Brazilian gun control movement, was very much centred around a gendered perspective on armed violence and female vulnerability: 'Choose gun-free! It's your gun or me' was the message that the campaign's women attempted to get across to their partners, lovers and boyfriends (Bandeira and Bourgois, nd: 50). Women's organizations played leading roles in many of Brazil's gun control initiatives.

A number of important parallels with the USA are reflected here, as Goldstein notes, during the 1970s and 1980s Brazil was becoming 'a dominant regional player in firearms production' (Goldstein, 2007a: 33) and by the mid-1980s it had become the second largest producer of guns in the western hemisphere. While much of this new handgun production was being exported to the USA, the prices undercutting those of US manufacturers, many were also sold within Brazil (Dreyfus et al., 2005). This influx of civilian handguns (as in the USA) had the predictable consequence of accelerating rates of domestic death and injury, in particular as 'the purchase and use of firearms and by civilians remained unregulated until 1980' (Dreyfus and Nascimento, 2005: 96). After 1980 new regulations restricted the types of firearms a civilian might purchase, made registration of the weapon a condition of sale and established an age limit of 20 for firearm purchase and possession. A weakness of the new registration system concerned the fact that weapons were registered with the police of different states (not nationally), leaving large loopholes for inter-state trafficking.

As in many of the adolescent gang cultures already considered, access to firearms is seen by many young men as a short-cut to rapid promotion and the achievement of 'masculinity' (Holzmann, 2006) as well as to obtaining valued consumer goods, status and access 'prestige, power, money, women, and respect' (Rivero, 2004: 96). Relatedly, firearm ownership also permitted the adoption of the component identities of 'guerrilla warrior, virility, and courage, firearms are [therefore] a fundamental element in the construction of masculinity'. Rivero concluded, 'for some people from the favelas this represented the development of a way of leaving their mark – the predatory mark of a violent death – within their social network', whilst also underpinning the argument that policies for tackling the proliferation of increasingly lethal small arms in Rio especially must necessarily address the underlying causes of the *demand* for firearms (Lessing, 2005). This suggests not just a need for gun control but also for the development of educational and work opportunities for excluded young people. Brazil began to address its firearms proliferation in the mid-1990s, when the Federal Government effectively nationalized the firearms registration system established in the early 1980s.

The impetus for gun control reflects the influence of new NGOs in Brazil, especially Viva Rio and Instituto Sou da Paz (ISP). The former having its origins in 1993 as a community campaign to address growing violence in the city and launching the 'Rio Disarm Yourself' campaign in 1994; the latter originating as a student campaign in São Paulo in 1997 focussing upon the voluntary surrender of firearms. These, essentially community-based, projects eventually gained national political support and, in a number of areas, were also complemented by municipal community policing initiatives designed to suppress and discourage illegal gun carrying in public. Between 1996 and 1999 quarterly rates of firearm confiscation in São Paulo had almost doubled (Goertzel and Kahn, 2009: 405). As the local campaigns gathered pace and mobilized nationally, as many as 60 separate legislative proposals for gun control were submitted to state legislatures and the Brazilian Congress. By the presidential elections of 2002, gun control had become a firm part of the Workers' Party political agenda and what became known as the Disarmament Statute followed in 2003 on the back of a substantial wave of public activism, political lobbying and marches and demonstrations in many cities (Bandeira and Bourgois, nd: 81).

The new legislation, finally passed in December 2003, contained a number of provisions: raising the age of gun purchase to 25; prohibiting the carrying of firearms in public; strict controls on the purchase of firearms (including criminal records checks, mental health assessments, residency, employment and competency tests); registration of sales; purchase taxes; and safe storage requirements. There were also to be bans on replica firearms, periodic inspections of the weapons held by private security agencies and tougher penalties for firearms offences and trafficking. The legislation also established a national firearms buyback programme (Dreyfus *et al.*, 2008) and firearm surrender amnesties while paving the way for what would be the world's first national referendum on firearm prohibition. The question the referendum posed was: 'Should the sale of firearms and munitions be prohibited in Brazil?'

For Mota and Crespo (Mota, 2006) the referendum provided an opportunity for a fascinating case study of lobbying and political influence and of the power of elite groups, firearms manufacturers and international interests to mobilize fear and insecurity to thwart the momentum of the Brazilian gun control initiative. When the referendum campaigns began, an overwhelming number of opinion poll respondents declared themselves in favour of a prohibition on civilian firearm ownership and therefore likely to vote 'YES' in the referendum, for example a poll conducted in São Paulo showed that 83 per cent of residents were against the sale of firearms to civilians, only 14 per cent stated they were in favour of civilians being able to purchase firearms (Lissovsky, 2006: 26). However by the time of the referendum itself, held in October 2005, the substantial majorities apparently supporting the measure had evaporated, just under 64 per cent of those voting opposed firearm prohibition, slightly over one-third (36 per cent) were in favour.

Detailed analysis of the results and related polling appeared to show that class, age, gender and region of residence influenced voting choices. Women were more in favour of prohibition than men, older people more in favour than younger people (Soares, 2006). The more affluent citizens were less enthusiastic about gun control than the poorest, while the strongest areas of support for the prohibition proposal could be found in the north-east of the country and the state of Pernambuco (which voted 45.5 per cent for the proposal). By contrast, the more affluent (also more starkly unequal) areas, especially Rio de Janeiro, the south and the southernmost state of Rio Grande do Sul were more opposed, the latter recording a vote of almost 87 per cent *against* firearm prohibition (Mota, 2006).

As the Institute for Religious Studies (ISER) noted, it seemed that those who had experienced most intimately the destructive power of firearms in their communities were more enthusiastic for the ban (Mota, 2006).

Analysis of the campaigning during the referendum process threw up a number of explanations for the collapse in support for the firearm prohibition, some of these related to the professionalism of the contrasting 'YES' and 'NO' campaigns, others alluded to the power of commercial and lobbying organizations, especially the National Arm Owners and Traders Association (Sorj, 2006). Above all, however, and especially when the 'NO' campaign organization began to draw upon the assistance of (US) NRA resources and expertise, and started to craft their campaign arguments around fear of crime, confidence in the police and law and order, and personal insecurities, their messages began to resonate more persuasively with the electorate. According to Lissovsky (2006), the 'NO' campaign proved itself able to shift the terms of the debate and turn a 'public safety' strategy into a 'rights' issue centred upon the idea that, although most citizens did not own firearms, and had not even contemplated buying them, they could, given the recent history of crime and violence in Brazil, the many very familiar vulnerabilities of poor communities and the well-known failings of the local police (Da Cunha, 2006), anticipate they might need to do so in the future. In other words, the message: 'prohibition will not solve a single problem. It will only strip a citizen of his right', proved most persuasive (Lissovsky, 2006: 38). Such NRA-inflected arguments echo the presentation of gun advocacy in the USA, the anti-prohibition campaign couched its message in terms of a discourse of rights, individualism and responsibility which connected well with dominant Brazilian associations between manhood, masculinity, freedom and patriarchal authority (Morton, 2006). As Cunha (2006) has demonstrated in her analysis of the 'NO' campaign broadcasts, the question of civil rights and especially the right of a man to protect his life and his duty to defend his family was heavily plugged during the media campaign.

Confronting these ideas, the gun control arguments, even supported by the aggregated social scientific evidence, could not sufficiently disrupt the individualist ideology of masculine control (that guns will not be misused by responsible men) and a dichotomized perception of gun violence (firearm-related violence is embodied in and perpetrated by others – criminals – against whom it is prudent to take precautions). As we have seen, both of these ideas have played out powerfully in recent US gun advocacy rhetorics (Stroud, 2012). In a sense, voting against these powerfully constructed pro-gun positions became tantamount to a declaration that: 'I am not careful, I am not responsible' and, perhaps above all, 'I am not a man', a step too far for many relatively affluent Brazilian men who, apparently, saw gun control as a threat from which they could lose.

The loss of the referendum vote was a major blow to the Brazilian gun control movement but it was celebrated as a major victory by NRA leaders who had seen the Brazilian developments through the lens of 'domino theory', a viewpoint no doubt heightened by the negotiations regarding the PoA on SALW and a global ATT concurrently taking place at the United Nations. NRA Director of Public

Affairs, Andrew Arulanandam, deploying language regularly invoked by the NRA leadership, for whom gun control anywhere is a threat to gun freedom everywhere, remarked: '[W]e view Brazil as the opening salvo for the global gun control movement. If gun control proponents succeed in Brazil, America will be next' (Sorj, 2006: 23). Despite the loss of the referendum vote, the package of other gun control measures introduced from 2003 appear to have helped to halt the relentless increasing in gun violence in Brazil (see Figure 8.4), briefly reversing and then stabilizing the gun homicide trend. Goertzel and Kahn (2009: 405, 2012) attribute the sharp decline in gun homicide in São Paulo, specifically the steepest fall in murder rates in a major city ever recorded, exceeding even the renowned 'New York miracle', to both the gun control package, the increased penalties for carrying firearms in public (deterrence) and the more proactive efforts of local police to get guns off the street (confiscations). Brazil's improving economic situation also played its part; economic growth and new opportunities were associated with a number of improving social indicators after 2005.

Not unlike the picture we obtained for the USA, however, national trends often conceal a number of opposing regional or counter-trends. In the case of Brazil, the stabilization of the rising gun homicide rate after 2004 was also associated with divergent regional trends and a stronger concentration of gun deaths amongst young males. The *Mapa da Violencia* study (Waiselfisz, 2013) produced evidence showing that while national rates of gun homicide had fallen after 2005, a number of states in northern Brazil had experienced significant increases in gun deaths, especially amongst youth and young men. For example, north-eastern states such as Alagoas, Paraiba, Bahia and the northern state of Para experienced the greatest increases in gun-related deaths. A 215 per cent *increase* in gun homicide occurred in Alagoas between 2000–2010, resulting in a firearm death rate of 55 per 100,000 inhabitants, now the highest in the country. By contrast the states in Brazil's south-eastern economic hub, Rio de Janeiro and São Paulo, saw major reductions in gun homicide, a 67.5 per cent drop in São Paulo and a 44 per cent fall in Rio (Waiselfisz, 2013). Police commentators attributed the changes, in part, to the influxes of young men into the northern cities looking for work, and the dispersal of drug trafficking from the São Paulo/Rio de Janeiro region. Goertzel and Kahn had taken some comfort, in 2009, from 'the great São Paulo homicide drop' suggesting that it showed how 'effective measures can be taken to reduce lethal crime without waiting to solve underlying socio-economic problems' (2009: 407), a judgement that might, now, need some qualification.

Global small arms control

Gun control campaign groups in societies suffering the consequences of global small arms proliferation recognized that national solutions for gun crime would need to be complemented by international action. Likewise NGO disarmament and development workers in the conflict zones where most of the killing took place appreciated the need for more effective regulation of the supply side to stem the flows of weapons which were, daily, undermining their efforts and threatening their lives. DDR could not just be about fire-fighting and peacekeeping, important as that was, but needed to look forwards to security and development (Bourne and Greene, 2012). And the arms control and international relations research communities increasingly recognized the rather porous character of much existing arms control. As Greene and Marsh (2012d) have noted of the research base, policy-making in the field of SALW governance (including DDR, post-conflict management, security sector and arms trade reform, the removal of weapon surpluses and regulation of stockpiles, criminal trafficking and domestic law enforcement) needed to be more effectively 'joined-up'.

In many respects, progress on the global arms control agenda and the research base has been impressively rapid during the past two decades, with a number of important signal achievements to which I will shortly turn. Although progress was not without some difficult and protracted arguments, not least, as I have already noted, the implacable opposition mounted by the US Bush administration. Things changed after 2008 following the election of President Obama. Implementation at ground level, however, where the problems of firearm victimization are at their most acute, is typically dependent upon local political resources and governance capacities and may be quite limited in practice. As *Saferworld* remarked in July 2008 in its position statement following the third biennial meeting to review UN progress on SALW controls, 'progress in taking practical action has been slower than desired' (Saferworld, 2008).

The development of international action against SALW proliferation forms part of an increasing emphasis at the UN level on international or 'trans-national' crime, including the establishment, in 1997, of the UN Office on Drugs and Crime and the United Nations Convention against Transnational Organized Crime, adopted by General Assembly resolution 55/25 of 15 November 2000 (UN, 2004). In respect of SALW, specifically, these developments were complemented by the UN protocol against the Illicit Manufacturing of and Trafficking in Firearms, Their Parts and Components and Ammunition, agreed on 31 May 2001 (General Assembly resolution 55/255, 2001) and the UN PoA on the Illicit Trade in Small Arms and Light Weapons in All its Aspects agreed later the same year. Under the PoA, state signatories committed themselves to a two-yearly meeting cycle to review domestic and international progress towards sharing information, experience and expertise and developing effective regulatory methods for small arms (for instance, in 2008, the biennial meeting of states focused upon more effective regulation of weapon brokering, the control of weapon stockpiles and surpluses and the development of systems for tracing firearm movements from production to end use). The work following the 2001 PoA eventually concluded with the adoption of the ATT agreed at the UN in April 2013.

A meeting of the UN General Assembly during August–September 2012 had reaffirmed the purpose of the PoA as follows:

3   We affirm the continued relevance and vital importance of the PoA as the global framework to prevent, combat and eradicate the illicit trade in small arms and light weapons in all its aspects, as reiterated annually in the General Assembly resolution entitled 'The illicit trade in small arms and light weapons in all its aspects', and remain convinced that its full and effective implementation is essential for furthering peace, reconciliation and security, protecting lives and promoting sustainable development.

4   We emphasize that the illicit trade in small arms and light weapons in all its aspects continues to sustain conflicts, exacerbate armed violence, undermine respect for international humanitarian law and international human rights law, aid terrorism and illegal armed groups and facilitate increasing levels of transnational organized crime, as well as trafficking in humans, drugs and certain natural resources.

5   We acknowledge that by threatening security, safety and stability, the illicit trade in small arms and light weapons continues to have devastating humanitarian and socioeconomic consequences, including by impeding the provision of humanitarian assistance to victims of armed conflict, contributing to the displacement of civilians and undermining sustainable development and poverty eradication efforts.

6   We continue to recognize the primary responsibility of Governments for preventing, combating and eradicating the illicit trade in small arms and light weapons in all its aspects and for identifying and solving the problems associated with such trade, and to recognize the importance of regional and international cooperation in supporting and reinforcing national implementation.

(UN General Assembly, 2012: 8)

Amongst other priorities, the meeting then went on to commit signatories for the period 2012–2018, to

support the development and implementation of adequate laws, regulations and administrative procedures to prevent, combat and eradicate the illicit trade in small arms and light weapons in all its aspects, including the diversion of small arms and light weapons to unauthorized recipients.

(UN General Assembly, 2012: 8)

This included national and international coordination to address 'the illicit manufacture, control, trafficking, circulation, brokering and trade, as well as tracing, finance, collection and destruction of small arms and light weapons' and to implement 'adequate laws, regulations and administrative procedures' so as to control the production, export and import of small arms and to introduce 'effective disarmament, demobilization and reintegration programmes' including peacekeeping in post-conflict situations (2012: 8–9). Special reference was also made to exploring 'means to eliminate the negative impact of the illicit trade in small arms and light weapons on women' and to address 'the special needs of children affected by armed conflict, in particular their reunification with their families, reintegration into civil society and appropriate rehabilitation' (2012: 9).

This agenda for action remains consistent with one of the earliest UN statements of intent on international small arms control uttered by Secretary General Boutros Boutros-Ghali's comments to the UN Security Council in 1995:

> I wish to concentrate on what might be called 'micro-disarmament', by this I mean practical disarmament in the context of the conflicts the United Nations is actually dealing with, and of the weapons, most of them light weapons, that are actually killing people in their hundreds of thousands.
>
> *(cited in Klare, 1999)*

A resolution (50/70 B of 12 December 1995) of the UN general assembly then empowered the Secretary General to compile a report, drawn up by a 'panel of experts', into small arms proliferation and disarmament. In fact these commitments were already being pioneered by researchers and NGOs exploring the ramifications of small arms proliferation in different parts of the world. The American Academy of Arts and Sciences convened a workshop in 1994 on the international trade in light weapons, comprising both a global overview of arms trafficking and weaponization and regional case studies featuring South Asia, Angola, Columbia and the former Soviet Union (Boutwell *et al.*, 1995). The following year Klare and Anderson published *Scourge of Guns: The Diffusion of Small Arms and Light Weapons in Latin America* (Klare and Anderson, 1996) while work progressed on the South African Institute for Security Studies project *Society under Siege* (Gamba and Meek, 1997–2000). In 1997 the EU agreed a Programme for Preventing and Combating Illicit Trafficking in Conventional Arms and, in 1998, while the UK held the presidency of the EU, an agreement was secured amongst EU member states for an EU Code of Conduct on arms exports (Eavis and Benson, 1999). In 1996, mass shootings in Britain and Australia had galvanized the arms control community and, a year later, the UN Panel of Experts reported.

Focussing its attention on small arms developed to military specification but dispersed into civilian hands, the report began by reviewing evidence on the scale of small arms distribution and reiterating the contribution of small arms to violence and conflict. It acknowledged that although these were the types of weapons 'increasingly used as primary instruments of violence in the internal conflicts dealt with by the United Nations … responsible for large numbers of deaths and the displacement of citizens … and [consuming] large amounts of United Nations resources', there were currently no internationally agreed norms by which the proliferation of small arms might be regulated (UN Panel, 1997: para. 13). Tackling the accumulation, trafficking and misuse of weapons was recommended for UN priority precisely because, as it appeared to the UN Panel, 'the illicit trafficking in such weapons by drug cartels, criminals and traders in contraband goods has also been on the increase', fuelling organized crime, gang activity, terrorism, insurgency, civil conflict and war in many parts of the world (1997: para.14). The UN

Panel foregrounded the impact of small arms misuse on civilian populations, especially women and children, noting that, as of 1996 'over 35 million people in 23
different countries … were at risk owing to on-going humanitarian crises' resulting
from the proliferation of small arms (1997: para 15).[15] They concluded by drawing
a, by now, familiar picture of the vicious circle of weaponization and violence:

> In one way or another, virtually every part of the United Nations system is
> dealing with the direct and indirect consequences of recent armed conflicts
> fought mostly with small arms and light weapons. Some of the most intracta-
> ble armed conflicts being dealt with by the United Nations are those in which
> a recurring cycle of violence, an erosion of political legitimacy and a loss of
> economic viability have deprived a State of its authority to cope either with
> the causes or the consequences of the excessive accumulation, proliferation
> and use of small arms and light weapons.
>
> *(UN Panel, 1997: para 20)*

Subsequent sections of the report reviewed the types of weapons most frequently
employed in these recurring patterns of violence, and presented a series of regional
weaponization and conflict profiles, before embarking upon a series of recommendations suggesting to the UN a comprehensive and urgent package of proposals to
'reduce the excessive and destabilizing accumulation and transfer of small arms and
light weapons' (UN Panel, 1997: para 78). This included support to post-conflict
initiatives involving disarmament; demobilization and weapon collection; strengthening international police cooperation to prevent weapon circulation; retrieving
and destroying all weapons not under legal ownership by civilians (and which are
not required for the purposes of national defence and internal security); encouraging all states to 'determine in their national laws and regulations which arms
are permitted for civilian possession and the conditions under which they can be
used'; exercising effective control (perhaps, even, by licensing arrangements) over
the civilian ownership of firearms; exploring the feasibility of international firearm
marking and trafficking systems; and establishing a global register of authorized
firearm producers and dealers (UN Panel, 1997: para 80).

The UN continued to develop a broad work programme on 'firearms controls'
commissioning an international study on firearm regulation which reported in
1997 and devoting a session of the Economic and Social Council, Commission
on Crime Prevention and Criminal Justice to a review of the results and
recommendations of the study. The report recognized that import and export
controls alone would not eliminate all illegal trafficking and that one society's
lack of effective regulation could undermine another's security, that manufacture
and trade in firearms for civilian and domestic use required effective domestic
regulation and effective cooperation between all levels of law enforcement and
government. Accordingly, amongst the Commission's recommendations were
regulatory proposals including:

Appropriate penalties for serious offences involving the misuse of firearms; amnesty programmes to encourage citizens to surrender illegal, unsafe or unnecessary firearms; licensing systems to ensure that persons who are at high risk of misusing firearms are prevented from possessing and using firearms; and a record-keeping system for firearms, including a requirement for appropriate marking of firearms at manufacture and at import to assist criminal investigations, discourage theft and ensure the accountability of owners

(UN ESC, 1997: 7–8)

By 1997, as Philip Alpers had noted, the international gun lobby, in the form of the American NRA, had already begun to refer to the UN initiative as 'global gun grabbing' (Chapman, 1998/2013: 264) so proposals for gun licensing and registration to 'ensure the accountability' of gun owners, something that the US gun lobby had always steadfastly refused to countenance, was bound to lead to debate and controversy (Defensor, 1970; La Pierre, 2006).

Although unable to persuade any other country to support its position, the NRA submitted a statement to the 1997 Commission on Crime Prevention and Criminal Justice arguing that its research was 'incomplete and inconclusive' and that the proposals were 'not warranted at this time' (Goldring, 1999: 109). The NRA and the America problem went to the heart of the Commission's ambitions: gun lobbyists and their political representatives on Washington's Capitol Hill had blocked legislation to introduce licensing and gun registration and bring accountability to gun ownership in the USA; American firearms dealers sold guns around the world; US governments had a poor track record on subordinating arms control to their foreign policy ambitions in Central and Latin America; lax American gun laws led to serious crime and security problems for its immediate neighbours, north and south (Lumpe, 1999b); and, finally, as we have seen in the case of Brazil, the NRA were not averse to intervening in the domestic politics of other nations to push the gun rights message. As the emerging UN gun control proposals moved towards New York for the UN meeting, they garnered support from a range of regional governance organizations (the Organisation for Security and Co-Operation in Europe; the Brasilia Declaration of Latin American and Caribbean States; and the Organisation of African Unity and the European Union).[16] And as the UN prepared to debate global gun control, the NRA began to mobilize its own international resistance.

The armed resistance

The principal forum through which the gun lobbies of a variety of countries sought to articulate their opposition to the UN proposals was the World Forum on the Future of Sport Shooting Activities (WFSA), the origins of which go back to the early 1990s. Its first meeting, in Australia in 1993, hosted delegates from the USA, Canada, South Africa, New Zealand and Australia. Leading sponsors of the organization are the NRA and SAMMI (the Sporting Arms and Ammunition Manufacturers Institute), a US firearms industry lobbying body. Alert to the developments within the UN, the WFSA organized its own meeting in 1997 where it committed itself to 'work jointly to establish a presence during discussions of global gun control to insure that correct and unbiased information is available to international decision makers' (WFSA, cited in Goldring, 1999: 112). The organization gave notice that it intended to apply for NGO status in order to gain access to UN deliberations.

Prominent amongst the concerns of the WFSA were a series of specific issues dear to the heart of the NRA in particular and firearms advocates the world over. First they sought to establish sharp distinctions between 'civilian' and 'military' weapons, irrespective of the fact that these categories had become increasingly blurred, that the USA civilian market had already opened up to military assault rifles and semi-automatic pistols and that the Federal Government had already instituted a ban (lasting between 1994–2004) on assault weapons. They rejected the argument that weak gun control regimes in some countries had security implications for others and saw 'gun laws' through the lens of national sovereignty, referring to the US Constitution and Second Amendment in their argument that 'UN bureaucrats' and 'gun grabbers' had no right or mandate to dictate laws to sovereign states. From such arguments it was but a short step to the more ideological and culturally inflected claims that appear with predictable regularity in the tirades of NRA executive vice-president, Wayne La Pierre, associating 'armed Americans' with free people and the UN bureaucrats with an elitist, socialist, and intellectual global conspiracy to subvert the US Constitution (La Pierre, 2006; Melzer, 2009; Squires, 2013). In like fashion, an NRA spokesman at a UN Commission on Crime Prevention and Criminal Justice, Firearms Panel, meeting in Tanzania in 1997, voiced the view that 'non-hunting societies should not seek to impose their values on hunting societies' (cited in Goldring, 1999: 113). And as Melzer (2009) has shown, the NRA has been very adept at using the threat of global disarmament to raise funds and recruit new, conservative-leaning members, depicting the UN initiative as a direct threat to American tradition and firearm rights. In similar rhetoric designed primarily for US domestic consumption, gun advocacy groups described the UN agenda as 'a tourniquet that is slowly being drawn around gun owners' necks' and which sympathetic 'liberal' US politicians (Clinton Democrats) were helping the UN to tie (in Goldring, 1999: 115). After 2008, the Obama administration, which re-committed the US to the UN cause (after the Bush administration had blocked and prevaricated for eight years), was attacked in similar terms.

Even prior to the initial UN Small Arms conference of July 2001, the WFSA Manufacturer's Advisory Group convened a meeting in April 2001 at the Imperial War Museum, London, to develop its response. While some of the organization's work has undoubtedly remained close to a 'sports shooting' agenda, from 1997 a significant part of their activities appear motivated towards developing a much wider advocacy on behalf of firearms: on the one hand seeking to refute any links drawn between firearms, crime and political instability; on the other attempting to validate the case for firearms for self-defence and an international 'right to bear arms'. WFSA representatives frequently represent themselves as the only real experts in any debates on firearms, occasionally betraying some resentment that supposedly less well-informed persons should be so presumptuous as to propose gun control policies. WFSA delegates (directors of Sturm-Ruger & Co and Glock firearms manufacturers) derided the loose, unsophisticated and imprecise language of gun control proponents who, they claimed, 'sought to confine the language of the debate to "guns", having little if any knowledge of the range of sporting shooting'. Even more worrying, they argued, was the conference's apparent desire to 'extend beyond the illicit so as to include all firearms', sports shooting weapons included (Peroni, 2001).

The outcome of this meeting, the 'London Definitions' report, comprised an attempt to strictly define the types of firearms to which the upcoming UN conference on 'Small Arms and Light Weapons' ought to confine its attentions. For David Penn, of the Imperial War Museum, the focus of the international community should entirely be upon 'what can be termed "weapons of war"', for want of a better term' (Penn, 2001: 6). Penn then proceeded to provide a historical overview of the development and design characteristics of personal use firearms which was intended to serve as a basis for distinguishing between these 'weapons of war' about which the UN ought to be concerned and genuine 'sporting firearms' which it ought to leave alone. This 'history' consisted almost entirely of a narrow chronology of technical development, largely ignoring the fact that many of the hunting or marksmanship rifles in use today are originally based upon military-designed, bolt-action weapons from the late nineteenth and early twentieth centuries (wartime being a great innovator in weapon design). Furthermore, while, in the post WW2 era, the design of military and sporting rifles had begun to diverge, the global proliferation of military assault weapons in civilian hands – the Kalashnikov cultures (Carr, 2008) – and the burgeoning demand for 'assault type' weapons in the US civilian market (the social and cultural relations of firearm diffusion, ownership and use), largely eclipsed any purely 'technical' demarcation between weapon types. In the end and, no doubt, reflecting the US and manufacturer influence at the meeting (Penn, 2001: 14), the delegates finally settled upon the 'fully automatic firing' criterion as the solitary relevant distinguishing feature of a 'weapon of war', perhaps the most restrictive definition of military weapons possible.[17] This left all semi-automatic handguns, semi-auto and assault rifles in the 'civilian' firearms category; just as it had before, sports shooting, firearm marketing and the purchase preferences of American gun owners were serving as the 'flag of convenience' for the continued expansion of a definition of the 'modern sporting firearm' (Squires, 2000).

If the first WFSA meeting in London had concentrated its energies on rifles, a subsequent meeting held at the Royal Armouries Education Centre at the Tower of London turned to discuss the question of handgun ownership and use, under the theme 'Legal, Economic and Human Rights Implications of Civilian Firearms Ownership and Regulation'. The meeting was attended by a number of leading US firearm advocates, such as David Kopel and Don Kates, who began by developing a relationship between a right to self-defence and armed self-determination in the face of oppression, tyranny or threats of genocide. Accordingly, in contrast to the UN aspiration, they defended the appropriateness of permitting the sale or transfer of arms to oppressed peoples – that is, non-state actors . Similarly, with 9/11 still fresh in the mind, Gary Perlstein put the case for civilian firearms ownership as a defence against terrorism. Historian Joyce Lee Malcolm, developing themes from her recent book (Malcolm, 2002), perhaps the most distorted single-factor interpretation of crime trends in English history ever written, advanced her argument that the progressive disarming of the English working class after 1918 was largely responsible for the high rates of crime (even though, by 2002, they had begun to fall) in the British Isles. She was supported in this argument, that prohibiting firearms disarms only the law abiding, and is therefore profoundly crimogenic, by Austrian criminologist and WFSA member Franz Csaszar (Csaszar, 2000) and by Juan de Groot, a South African firearms lobbyist who referred to the Rwandan massacres of the early 1990s as evidence of the 'disastrous results of disarming a civil population' (de Groot, 2002). Back in the USA, the Second Amendment itself was gathering hubris as a supposed beacon of freedom in a dangerous world, seemingly acquiring the form of a 'human right' (Cerone, 2006; Stell, 2006), not to mention a specifically *feminist* right to domestic self-protection (Stange, 2006).

Yet even such extreme and made-in-the-USA 'rights-based' or 'self-defence' arguments were unlikely to disturb the emerging consensus in the WFSA for, at the earlier London meeting, Penn had carefully crafted his arguments around the need for the organization to be inclusive of significant cultural variations in its appreciation of firearm ownership and use and this included the embrace of American orientations towards the (dubious) reassurance of – and enthusiasm for – the 'self-defence handgun'. In the end, therefore, the supposed WFSA distinction between 'civilian appropriate' or 'military' firearms ultimately collapsed behind the largely subjective individual choice made by American men (who had the right) to be armed or not. In effect, the WFSA, while setting out to propound a definition of those weapons falling appropriately within the UN 'small arms and light weapons' mandate, ended up by propounding a global right to bear arms on the US model. In the WFSA's view, shooting and individual firearms ownership represented a legitimate civil right, 'more or less strongly entrenched in different societies and not about to be wished away. In a fair, liberal and truly civil society', Penn had concluded, 'these interests need to be accommodated' (Penn, 2001: 16). These issues, and more, were to resurface when the UN itself debated the adoption of the PoA on SALW, in New York, during July 2001.

'Lowest common denominator' gun control?

The arms control conference convened, at the UN building, in New York in early July 2001 with a draft PoA on the Illicit Trade in Small Arms and Light Weapons to discuss. Two weeks of intense debate, disagreement, argument and haggling were to follow. By 21 July, a compromise PoA to 'prevent, combat and eradicate' the illicit small arms trade had been achieved. Many participants were pleased that a compromise had been achieved at all, others felt that the proposals had been so watered down that they amounted to a 'lowest common denominator' strategy (Atwood and Greene, 2002: 203) from which many key elements had been omitted. Nevertheless the agreement did enable continued momentum on the global arms control agenda – delegates would reconvene to monitor progress every two years and hold a further conference, by 2006, to review the implementation of the programme.

From the first day of the conference, the US Bush administration, represented by US Under-Secretary of State John Bolton, laid its cards on the table. In a robust, no-nonsense speech he made clear the issues at stake. The proposed programme was defective, he argued, because it conflated issues that should properly be dealt with by sovereign governments with those appropriate to the UN. The USA, he announced, defined SALW, strictly, as *military* weapons and would not support measures to restrict the legal manufacture of SALW or their legal trade, any measures prohibiting civilian firearm ownership; or any proposals to prevent the trade in SALW to non-state actors. He opposed the idea of a mandatory review conference and urged the UN to restrict the arms control advocacy role of NGOs (Bolton, 2002). The positions articulated by Bolton were no surprise to seasoned arms control advocates, as we have seen they were similar to the positions adopted within the WFSA, furthermore his speech was prefaced by a reference to the US Second Amendment and he was accompanied in the US delegation by a number of senior members of the NRA (Atwood and Greene, 2002: 219).

In the event, as the discussions and negotiations proceeded, disagreements came to focus upon two core principles – both of them *distributional* issues, both of them meaningful as components of the advanced neo-liberal agenda – civilian possession of firearms and arms transfers to non-state actors. Given the intransigence of various delegations at the conference, in particular the USA, China and some Arabic states, the final PoA document contained a number of silences and compromises. Because the US delegation would not accept a definition of SALW that went beyond exclusively 'military weapons' and most of the delegates wanted a more inclusive definition, in the end, no definition was provided. While most countries accepted the connections between the illicit weapons trade and human rights violations, a number of states, including China, made sure that any language linking these issues was excluded from the final programme. The issue of selling/transferring weapons to non-state groups was fudged, raising the issue but doing nothing about it. The same was true of ensuring transparency in international firearms dealing – no measures were proposed and, facing objections from China, there was no real pressure to introduce international firearms marking and tracing systems. The US objected to any recommendations stating or implying that the programme would apply to 'civilian possession' so, after much debate, the whole paragraph was dropped from the final document. Finally a number of states objected to the idea that they should destroy surplus and confiscated weapons, preferring to recycle them for use by their own military or security forces or, rather more perversely, selling them on to other states or armed groups and, thereby, presumably, merely recycling the problem (Atwood and Greene, 2002: 220–225).

While the conference failed to resolve many issues and left a great deal still to be decided – and even more still to be done – it generated a great deal of attention for the cause of global small arms control and put the issue firmly on the international agenda. It went some way towards the establishment of a number of international norms (unfortunately not legally binding) for the governance of global small arms proliferation, and established that tackling conflict, armed violence and human rights abuses required attention to their underlying causes, the availability of the weapons by which much of the violence was inflicted. Finally, through the arrangements for the biennial follow-up meetings and a review conference in 2006, it left a way forwards.

In July 2008, the third biennial review conference on the UN PoA was held, the review conference having taken place two years earlier. Commentators described the process as afflicted by 'paralysis' and, at best, only 'inching forwards'.

> The first Review Conference ... characterized by much political wrangling, reached no substantive agreement of any kind ... [and] independent evaluations of progress made by states in fulfilling their commitments under the *Programme* had consistently shown that, while not entirely idle, they were by and large falling short [while] ... the meetings in 2003, 2005, and 2006, had done relatively little to advance *Programme* implementation
>
> *(Bevan* et al.*, 2009)*

The 2006 review conference was said to have reflected a 'fragmenting' of the global arms control effort, with dissent, lack of consensus and conflicting geo-political interests over weapons transfer controls hampering progress. The obstructive stance taken by the USA, in particular, was referred to by a number of commentators (Macdonald *et al.*, 2007: 118–120). The third review conference, however, according to Bevan *et al.*, (2009), represented 'two steps forwards' for the UN small arms control process. It levered the process back on track in the course of developing discussions for a comprehensive UN ATT and, despite slow progress towards developing methods for international firearms tracing, it also revived a focus upon the issue of surplus ammunition stocks which had become somewhat neglected. The priority, however, as Bevan *et al.* (2009) noted, was still one of turning carefully – and sometimes rather too cautiously – negotiated words and principles into effective national action. In late 2008, however, the outcome of the US presidential election altered the attitude of the US administration to the UN PoA and Small Arms control process. There were still issues, but rather than blocking the process, US negotiators were cooperating with it. A statement by Secretary of State Hillary Clinton (14 October 2009)[18] had sought to undercut gun lobby opposition in the USA. She reiterated that the purpose of the UN process was to control *illegal* weapon trafficking and proliferation, the supply of weapons to 'rogue states', terrorists and other non-state insurgency groups or militias rather than interfere with legitimate trade. The treaty specifically excluded domestic gun transfers or civilian weapon ownership and exercises no authority over the firearms control laws of sovereign states; in any event the US already had a number of essentially similar arms control provisions in its own 1976 Arms Export Control Act. This forced a significant change of tack by the NRA lobby vis-à-vis their own government, but also allowed the UN process to move forwards with some greater consensus. However, even late in the process, during the fourth Biennial meeting in 2010, gun trade and shooting lobbyists were still fighting their rearguard action against disarming citizens, and in favour of the gun trade, hunting, sports shooting and firearms for personal self-defence. They consistently rejected arguments that any available evidence suggested a relationship between 'civilian access to small arms and light weapons [and] criminal or terrorist violence'. Despite their efforts, however, by now the real debate had moved on.

By 2011, a conference of 'governmental experts' had been convened to consider practically the international implementation of a firearm tracing instrument including, amongst other issues, weapon marking, import and export recording, record-keeping, and information sharing through technical and law enforcement cooperation. The meeting was described as 'action oriented'; progress, of a sort, was being made (Macdonald, 2012). The following year, a second PoA review conference took place which, according to Macdonald, avoided many of the problems that had beset the earlier deliberations: 'UN member states reached consensus agreement … committing themselves to a series of measures designed to bolster implementation of the Programme and International Tracing instrument during the period up to 2018' (2013: 173). Ultimately, during April 2013, as I noted at the beginning of the chapter, the UN General Assembly finally agreed a comprehensive Arms Trade Treaty to address the illegal trafficking of conventional arms including SALW. The treaty was not unanimous but is currently being ratified by supporting countries. At the time of writing it has been signed by 114 countries (including the USA); full ratification and adoption into existing national law is a different matter, thus far only eight states have achieved this.

Unfortunately, in many respects the treaty remains a weak and compromised agreement, providing, essentially, only a voluntary arms control regime governed by agreed international norms; it lacks an effective monitoring system or any implementation or enforcement mechanisms beyond actions that independent states might take themselves. As far as the UN is concerned, that may be its weakness, but it could equally be its strength: for *action* is for national governments to take, within a framework of international norms governing the distribution of weapons around the world. For the first time there exists a statement of international principles on weapon distribution, agreed by 154 of the United Nation's constituent members seeking to: 'Establish the highest possible common international standards for regulating the international trade in conventional arms; and prevent and eradicate the illicit trade in conventional arms' (UN General Assembly, 2013), in order to 'contribute to international and regional peace, security and stability and reduce human suffering; [and] promote cooperation, transparency and responsible action by States in the international trade in conventional arms' (UN ATT, 2013: Article 1).

And in order to achieve this:

> No state shall authorize any transfer of conventional arms if it has knowledge at the time of authorization that the arms or items would be used in the commission of genocide, crimes against humanity, grave breaches of the Geneva Conventions of 1949, attacks directed against civilians … or other war crimes, including –
>
> - undermining peace and security;
> - committing or facilitating a serious violation of international humanitarian law or international human rights law;
> - committing or facilitating an act constituting an offence under international conventions to which the exporting State is a Party;
> - committing or facilitating an act constituting an offence under international conventions or protocols relating to transnational organized crime or terrorism; or
> - committing or facilitating serious acts of gender-based violence or serious acts of violence against women and children.
>
> *(UN ATT, 2013: Articles 6 and 7)*

Macdonald's (2013) verdict upon the 2012 second PoA review conference remains optimistic – it supported the tracing of 'conflict firearms' and established a structured process for moving forwards, even though gaps remain resulting from the intransigence of certain states. For example, the phrase 'small arms and light weapons' has still not been firmly defined (states will apply their own definitions) and ammunition still sits 'in some kind of political limbo' outside the arms control process. As Macdonald concludes:

> Despite the apparent preference of a few states for a weaker PoA and ITI [International Tracing Instrument], there was no dilution of existing norms. With or without an Arms Trade Treaty, the PoA will remain the only comprehensive global framework for small arms control, covering almost all stages of the small arms life cycle from cradle (manufacture) to grave (final disposal). 'Control' is more difficult than prohibition. The long life span and complex ownership chains of many small arms make the task harder. Yet, building on preceding UN meetings … the 2nd Review Conference offers an extensive road map for meeting these challenges. What is essential, obviously, is not simply to have the map, but to use it to move forward.
>
> *(Macdonald, 2013: 174)*

As he recognized, a number of states continued to view UN small arms policymaking with profound suspicion. Even so, something useful was wrested from the conference. Accordingly, 'while a future embracing "the full and effective implementation" of the PoA and ITI remains to be written, for the moment the UN small arms process has a spring in its step' (Macdonald, 2013: 174).

Still doubtful and suspicious, however, the Republican-controlled Senate vowed to vote against ratification of the treaty, while the NRA, in typical fashion, has been milking the issue for all it is worth to secure new members and financial contributions to fight what they represent as the latest threat to 'Freedom and the American Way' (Melzer, 2009). Given that, despite the NRA arguments, the ATT will have no bearing on firearm *ownership* in the USA, thereby suggesting that the NRA opposition is more effectively representing the interests of the firearm *industry* rather than those of its mass membership.[19] In this case the core problem is not one of weapon 'blowback', but rather one of neo-liberal 'blow-out', where US domestic firearm priorities – or, unrestricted civilian weaponization; free markets in firearms; in other words, weaponization as a *solution*, and 'an assault weapon in every home' – are, both counter-intuitively and contrary to the best available evidence, represented as the most effective guarantees of personal security and global freedoms (Kopel *et al.*, 2008).

The adoption of the ATT and the projection of future activities to 2018 (the 'map'), under the UN PoA on SALW, meant that processes of international governance had become thoroughly engaged (ideologically, institutionally, and at the level of policy, practice and intervention) within a global culture war over firearm proliferation, just as gun control advocates had worked at the national level following shooting tragedies. The gun debate had become an irretrievably 'global politics', pitting those who felt that freedom, self-determination, individual rights and personal security flowed from the barrel of a gun against those who harboured rather higher aspirations for civilized co-existence. In the final chapter, I will review the arguments bringing us to this point while exploring what this new global politics of the gun might have in store for crime, violence and conflict, and human rights, freedom and social justice.

Notes

1 For example, Julian Knight killed seven people and injured 19 in what became known as the Hoddle Street massacre, in Victoria, in August 1987; Frank Vitkovic killed nine people (including himself) and injured five in Melbourne in December 1987; and Malcolm Baker killed six and injured one in a rampage attack with a 12 gauge pump-action shotgun in New South Wales in October 1992.

2 According to Kofi Annan, the UN Secretary General in 2000,

   a process of disarmament, demobilization, and reintegration has *repeatedly proved to be vital* to stability in a post-conflict situation; to reducing the likelihood of renewed violence, either because of a relapse into war or outbreaks of banditry; and to facilitating a society's transition from conflict to normalcy and development.

   (United Nations, 2000)

3 Published by the Graduate Institute of Postgraduate Studies, Geneva, Switzerland.

4 This however, is not quite the same as saying that nothing happened. The US prioritized a range of school safety and school defence initiatives after 1999 (including armed guards and, in some states, arming teachers), pupils were schooled in lockdown

and evacuation routines as well as fire drills (Webber, 2003). The new fortress schools developed 'listening' networks, hoping to spot early signs of disaffection and danger and by such methods, it is claimed, further shooting disasters were averted (Newman, 2006). Police armed response units developed 'active shooter' tactics which required officers to forcibly engage intruders rather than simply 'containing' them within a secure perimeter (a tactic much criticized after Columbine).

5 Germany had also experienced a number of much earlier school shootings: at Bremen in 1913 when five girls were killed by an unemployed teacher; at Cologne in 1964 a man killed ten people and himself with a home-made flame thrower, amongst other weapons; and at Eppstein, in 1983, six people were killed, including the shooter (and 14 injured), by a man armed with two semi-automatic pistols.

6 Refer also to Chapter 6. Canada has experienced half a dozen school or college 'rampage' shootings, two in 1975 and the remainder following the Montreal incident, although none resulted in quite so many victims. The key perpetrator characteristics (masculinity issues, mental illness, rejection, isolation, bullying) reflect many of those we have already discussed.

7 A student with mental health issues killed two fellow students, injuring a lecturer and four fellow students in a shooting at Monash University, Melbourne, in October 2002. He was found to be carrying six legally acquired handguns. Tougher penalties for handgun offences, tighter regulations for handgun calibres and ammunition capacity and a handgun buyback followed.

8 Only half of this debate is evidence led, as was argued in Chapter 1. The other half of the debate, which operates as a 'double safety catch' on the Second Amendment, concerns the legal and constitutional arguments whereby gun controls that do 'work' are deemed (often rather contentiously) 'unconstitutional' and either weakened or scrapped.

9 Firearm deactivation standards were not rendered generally compatible across states and territories until after 2006, implying that states with the weakest weapon deactivation standards provided a loophole through which the 'reactivated firearm market' operated.

10 According to the 2013 report *Organised Crime in Australia* by the Australian Crime Commission, OMCGs have a significant role in perpetuating a culture of armed violence, but this may be changing:

> Some organised crime groups in Australia, such as outlaw motorcycle gangs (OMCGs), have a long-standing association with a culture of violence. In the past this violence has typically been conducted out of the public view. There are, however, some indications that this may be changing. The bludgeoning and stabbing death of an OMCG member at Sydney Airport in 2009 and the shooting death of Giovanni Focarelli in South Australia in January 2012 are examples of cases in which OMCG-related violence is being played out in public. The drive-by shootings that have occurred in a number of Australian states are other examples. If violence between crime groups is increasingly played out in the public space, the risk increases that members of the public will become unintended 'collateral' victims of this violence.
>
> *(Australian Crime Commission, 2013: 28)*

11 Brazil also suffered a school shooting in April 2011, when a former pupil killed 12 children (aged 12–14) and injured 12 more at a school in Rio de Janeiro. The incident closely fits a pattern we have already explored. As a pupil, the perpetrator had been bullied and harassed at the school; he had lately converted to Islam and appeared fascinated by terrorism. In a video he recorded shortly before his attack he appeared to conflate avenging his own victimization with a notion of terrorist jihad. Witnesses suggested he specifically targeted girls, ten of the 12 killed were young women.

12 There has been extensive discussion on the existence and activities of police 'death squads' in parts of Brazil and Latin America more generally. Holzmann (2006: 33) refers to the *Candelária* massacre of 1993, in which seven children and adolescents living on the street were killed and which gave rise to a UN investigation in 2004 (United Nations, 2004). A similar incident occurred in March 2005 when 30 people were shot,

apparently 'randomly' by police in the *Baixada Fluminense*, a poor area in Rio. For further discussion of these issues see Huggins (2002) and Brinks (2008).

13 Underpinning what we have already discovered about arms movements in the Americas, in particular regarding Mexico, Rivero notes that the major proportion of military-style firearms seized by the police in Brazil, especially 'automatic pistols and assault rifles', originated from the USA (2004: 64–66).

14 Holzmann (2006: 68) also describes the 'objectification of women within the hyper-masculine gang culture reinforces their role as "playthings" in factional conflicts'. She describes a protracted conflict between rival gangs in which women and girls associated with rival gang members and their families – including pregnant women – were targeted for killing (more easily targeted) as part of the ongoing feud between the rival factions.

15 The original UN estimates of firearm victimization initially stressed how indirect casualties, especially women and children, represented a majority of the indirect victims of firearm violence, the 1997 report suggesting that 'women and children account[ed] for nearly 80 per cent of the casualties' (UN Panel, 1997). While women and children may well have represented a majority of non-combatant and 'indirect' casualties, most firearm-involved violence, be it crime or conflict, involves young men shooting other young men.

> Most small-arms owners and users are male … while men die from gun violence in far greater numbers than women, the fact that women represent a very small proportion of gun owners means that they are disproportionately the victims of gun violence.
>
> *(Cukier, 2009: 7)*

16 Chinese political influence was sufficient to block similar regional agreements from the South Asian Association for Regional Cooperation, the Association of South East Asian Nations and the Asian Regional Forum (Atwood and Greene, 2002: 216).

17 Smith (2006: 718) has argued that 'insofar as a "pro-gun" lobby exists in Britain, it is really a lobby seeking the preservation of shooting sports rather than as a general "right" to gun ownership'. There is some truth in this, although, no doubt bolstered by the American influence, the WFSA certainly adopted an extremely liberal interpretation of sporting firearms.

18 http://www.reuters.com/article/2009/10/15/us-arms-usa-treaty-id USTRE59E0Q92 0091015, accessed 19 March 2014.

19 In March 2012, with a President Obama seeking re-election, and reluctant to pass up an opportunity to attack both the UN Arms Control Process and the Obama administration's record, while also galvanizing its own membership, the leadership of the NRA (Wayne La Pierre) journeyed to London, not for the first time, to film a live debate about the UN and Arms Control. During the sometimes heated exchanges, La Pierre derided the UN Arms Control process as a threat to 'American freedoms', linking possession of arms to freedom and the American birthright and castigating the UN as supposed 'arrogant elitists' who were enabling tyranny. 'The only free people who had ever walked the earth', he suggested, 'have been armed people'. An account of the debate can be found on www.petersquires.net.

9

CONCLUSION

Rock, paper, scissors … gun: neo-liberal weaponization?

As Chapter 1 outlined, one ambition for this book has concerned intellectual and academic synthesis. That is to say, the book has attempted to draw together five areas of academic endeavour which centred upon guns and gun proliferation. These have involved: first, where the book began, criminology and the misuse of firearms in gun crime; second, it has concerned conflict studies and the role of firearms in failed states, conflict complexes, civil wars, terrorist activities and insurgencies, or 'violences beyond crime' where the state (even the international community) lacks the legitimacy, authority or even the capacity to 'criminalize'; third, the book has embraced the study of weapon proliferation, arms trading, SALW diffusion, firearm trafficking and the control of illicit weapons markets, areas of endeavour that often fall within the purview of law and international relations; and fourth, it has concerned the ethnographies of violence and peace building, stories from the ground up, of survival, struggle and development. The book has also sought to examine gun control politics, both within particular societies and internationally.

At the centre of all these analytical endeavours sit the SALW that facilitate so much death and injury, trouble and trauma, around the world. There is no little irony in the fact that although the firearm sits so firmly at the centre of these various dimensions of academic research and analysis, the study of the gun, its history, design, use and misuse, travels, consequences and control, symbolic meanings and significances remains so essentially fragmented. Perhaps there is a case for a new, interdisciplinary project in 'firearm studies', although that is not quite what is being proposed here. Even so, the themes pursued within the book have embraced criminology, sociology, anthropology, international relations, socio-legal studies, political studies, race and gender studies, to name only the most obvious. In another sense the book has also sought to reflect the real-world overlaps and connections occurring between, for example, criminology and conflict studies, and the emergence of the new, asymmetric or 'fourth generation' warfare afflicting many regions of the world. In a more mundane sense, any global project on firearms studies would have to take seriously the growing *militarization* of the civilian gun inventory whether this is occurring through the consumer market place, as in the USA (Diaz, 2013), or through conflict-led diffusion of firearms in the many 'Kalashnikov cultures' (Carr, 2008) already established.

Yet while synthesis was a core aspect of this book's ambitions, the more critical theme has concerned the development of a new analysis of the problems of global gun violence around an exploration of neo-liberal weaponization. Hence a key focus of Chapter 1 concerned the social and political contexts within which firearms were used and deployed. These were contexts where the symbolic significances of firearms varied by reference to the cultures of use surrounding their ownership and distribution and the legal and political regimes pertaining to their control. Springwood refers to these contexts as 'gunscapes', and notes that 'guns prevail in both regulated and unregulated spaces, and they emerge with dangerous impact wherever borders are contested' (Springwood, 2007a: 21).[1] I return, inevitably, to the power, conferred or achieved, but certainly in the Foucauldian sense, *exercised* by the possession of a gun. As argued in Chapter 1, the legal status of a firearm matters not one jot in this respect. An illegal — or illegally possessed — firearm will kill just as effectively as a legal (legally possessed) one. Indeed, it is likely that, outside of formal 'conflicts', more people are killed or injured by firearms that are illegally held.

All of which brings us to the 'rock, paper, scissors' metaphor. Many thousands of people have played the game, either simply for its own sake or, like tossing a coin, as a means of making any number of minor decisions, or resolving small routine dilemmas (who buys the next round of drinks; who pays for the taxi). In its essence, because of the cyclical structure of priority built into the choice (scissors cut paper, paper wraps rock, rock crushes scissors), each element can be trumped by another, but each can 'win'. In that sense the three elements reflect a separation of powers 'in miniature'; representing authority (rock), legitimacy (paper) and agency (scissors). Taken together, but also in a very real sense, they reflect the form of contract at the heart of democratic governance: a balance is struck. Unfortunately this balance is entirely undermined by the arrival of a kind of 'super-agency', represented by the 'gun' that shoots and smashes rock, drills bullet-holes through paper and kills or incapacitates agency. If this all seems too far-fetched and metaphorical, consider other aspects of liberal-democratic theory, where the state (rock) is presumed to control the monopoly of legitimate force. The key to many of the conflict complexes, failed states and 'gunscapes' considered thus far in this book is that whatever states still exist in these regions often do not control even a majority of the local firepower. Furthermore, even in the more liberal gun ownership regimes where substantial 'security states' exist, this cult of super-agency (neo-liberalism) insists upon the right of free individuals to resist unwarranted state force with potentially lethal force: in simple terms, to shoot cops (Diaz, 2013). This, taken to its logical extension in the insurrectionist agenda (Horwitz and Anderson, 2009), implies that what is often presented as merely a 'defensive' human right ('Castle Doctrine', or 'Stand Your Ground' laws) is really rather more fundamental. The 'defence of the self' implied in much 'right to bear arms' political philosophy is also an assertion of the self, a demand for freedom and self-determination, the insurgent spirit of the smallest unit of political authority: the sovereign individual attacking and eroding, by constant attrition, the rock of political authority.[2]

Where states are small and weak, or not yet established (frontier societies) – or even where they have begun to delegate key areas of security of policing activities to private agencies, or armed individuals – the super-agency of armed protagonists carries even more potential. In the former frontier societies, failed states and war zones, this armed agency is especially dangerous and the rule of law perhaps a distant dream already shot full of holes. In the latter, where an increasingly private exercise of armed force may prevail, sub-contracted to the neo-liberal state, the exercise of armed agency may be increasingly selective just as, in America's suburbs, concealed carry provisions largely underpin white, neo-conservative masculinity (Lloyd, 2012). In such scenarios, the only check on the agency of the armed is an alternative armed force. In one sense 'good guys' or 'bad guys', like legal or illegal, scarcely matters, at best, as I argued in Chapter 7, they are but two sides of the 'weaponization' coin. There is only armed and unarmed, alive and dead; and history, as Machiavelli argued, is written by the victors (or survivors).

For now, it remains to show how the power of the firearm empowers and emboldens human agency, and how firearms become joined and *embodied* with human and social purposes. Second, we must next remind ourselves of the many consequences of this, as they have been described and elaborated throughout this book. And finally, we must reiterate how weaponization and neo-liberalism mutually reinforce, extend and facilitate one another and, ultimately, how the global proliferation of SALW represents, in its most starkly anti-humanist form, the global power of neo-liberalism.

The NRA never seems to tire from insisting along with Alan Ladd, playing *Shane*, in the title role of the 1953 film, that 'a gun is just a tool'. The NRA leaves it there, as if that was all there is to be said. In the course of the book we have already exposed this as a hopelessly limiting and 'un-sociological' point of view. But, as Ashkenazi (2012) has noted the observation has a certain truth, for in the same way that a spade enhances a human capacity to dig, a gun certainly enhances a human capacity to kill. It might be possible to develop this argument about the social significance of spades to another level, to the effect that with a spade a man might extend his dominion over land, and thereby acquire territory, and property, so that, in a fully Lockean sense, by using the spade to mix his labour with 'nature' he could accumulate the necessaries of subsistence and, later perhaps, a surplus, leading to wealth and power and, ultimately, dominion over other men, his servants or employees. Going back to our earlier, 'rock, paper, and scissors' metaphor, with his spade our man has exercised his agency, acquired legal title and now stands on the 'rock' of his property. So much for the unsung social significance of spades, yet while one tool facilitated this process of social production, another tool, the gun, could take it all away again, in a moment. The gun achieves a sudden and dramatic shift in social relations, empowering, in an instant, the gun owner and disempowering the disarmed. In the very simplest sense articulated by Latour, possession of a gun can turn the NRA's ubiquitous 'good guy' into a potential killer (Latour, 1999: 177).

This vital change in the nature of the relationship between citizens is both sudden and dramatic. One is reminded of a similarly dramatic transformation, depicted by Marx in *Capital Volume One*, when the once free contracting agents leave the 'sphere of simple commodity circulation' or 'contract' and enter instead the unequal and exploitative relations of capitalism. In like fashion, when our own spade owner and gun owner step from the sphere of governance, legality and justice and into the 'gunscape' or 'conflict complex' (or, simply, a more 'liberal' gun control regime) then *a sudden transformation occurs in the physiognomy of our dramatis personae. He, who before, was the gun owner, now strides in front as sovereign individual; the abject possessor of labour-power follows carrying a spade. The former with an air of importance, smirking, intent on business; the other, timid and holding back, like one who is bringing his own hide to market but with only a grave to dig.*[3] There is a further truth, of course, in another of Marx's observations that every social form of production, and in this sense quite literally, produces its own grave diggers.

Many tools and technologies extend man's dominion but few do so with such ease and simplicity and so instantaneously or, as Springwood (2007b) reminds us, *at a distance*. Guns extend men's power both practically and symbolically and effect a significant change in social relations; quite literally, guns in human hands embody power, effecting a redefinition of the boundary of the body and the relationship it sustains with others. Springwood continues:

> [G]uns too easily merge with bodies … dissolving into one's self … and transforming the psyches and boundaries of those whom they possess and of those at whom they are aimed. They also transform, and often reinforce, the psyches of national and ethnic communities.
>
> *(2007b: 22)*

Springwood develops his argument by suggesting that 'guns offer the illusion of consolidation and unification of one's body. Their presence works to shape, for those who "carry", a system of embodied dispositions, possibilities and potentialities' (2007b: 23). One might say, here paraphrasing Foucault (1977: 194), that the 'gun-man' is fabricated in an ideological representation of society: that is society as a war zone. Contextualized this way, the citizen becomes gun man, warrior, combatant, gang member, insurgent or terrorist. 'The gun … becomes, for many, what one is, rather than what one has, [it] becomes a medium for relating to people, things and ideas' (Springwood, 2007b: 23).

Likewise, King (2007) describes the transformative power of the gun in relation to its enhancement of masculinity, men being overwhelmingly the possessors, carriers and primary users of guns. Indeed, as we have already explored in relation to the gun culture of South Africa, '[m]en dominate gun cultures and gun cultures extend male domination' (King, 2007: 87) although, on the basis of a cultural unpacking of discourses and popular representations of firearms, King goes even further, insisting that 'guns amplify sexualised power, projecting masculinity and violence, which encourages dehumanisation and degradation' (King, 2007: 87). Holding a gun, the body is reconstituted as a weapon and, just as Marx depicted the factory proletariat reduced to its core productive essentials 'hands' and 'labour', so too the armed man becomes 'gun man'. In contemporary military terms, King describes how this process of 'soldierization' is completed, how the free citizen is transformed into an armed killer, through a brief examination of some of the basic training and indoctrination sequences of the Stanley Kubrick film, *Full Metal Jacket*, in which a strict drill sergeant runs his raw recruits through their basic weapons induction programme. As King notes, in boot camp, the recruits establish new selves, in the process becoming 'soldiers and men' (rather than the 'pukes and pussies' who disembarked from the bus a few weeks earlier). This is all achieved through the relationships they are required to foster with their rifles, reflected in the mantra they are required to recite every night before lights out: 'This is my rifle, there are many like it but this one is mine. Without me, my rifle is nothing; without my rifle, I am nothing.'

Other commentators have drawn attention to the cinematic representation of men with guns. Arjet (2007), for instance, explores the ways in which a series of 'gunplay' films, popular especially in the 1980s and 1990s,[4] depicted the deployment of hegemonic masculinity through an armed projection of the self. Through guns and violence, men negotiated homosocial relationships. In this way, despite the common critique that such films represented 'senseless violence', there was really no such thing. The violence was really saturated with meaning, the guns and the violence they permitted were 'artefacts of ideology'; such films played out the populist 'fantasies of masculine power that underlie US gun culture' (Arjet, 2007: 127), constructing both norms and male relationships predicated upon assertiveness, dominance and righteous violence. As Spencer has remarked, such films and their reference points in US history and culture 'remind us again how potent the idea of taking the law into one's own hands is in the American political imaginary' (Spencer, 2007). Class, wealth and status, in themselves, are nothing in the face of a decisive, action-oriented, clear-thinking man willing to take a chance for a just cause. In the past these were the virtues associated with the maverick cowboy figure, more contemporaneously they become associated with the maverick cop.[5] The juxtaposition of armed and unarmed agents in the gunplay film, depicted, for Arjet, as reality 'vigorously propagated by the gun culture at large' to the effect that 'nothing a man has, not his possessions, not his family, not his power – is truly his unless he can defend it in gun combat with other men' (Arjet, 2007: 129). In case these depictions are considered extreme or, perhaps, 'only in the movies', the testimonies of those having encountered gun-driven intimidation in South Africa (see Chapter 7) are worth recalling. Equipped with the magical power of the gun, all other benefits are possible – wealth, prestige, comfort, public vindication, moral redemption, sex with beautiful women, a happy family life. Nothing is beyond the capabilities of a man who can defeat other men in gunplay. Without this power, there is only death at best, humiliation and feminisation at worst ... Without a weapon, men simply don't count.

(Arjet, 2007: 131)

As we discovered in Chapter 1, even reflective sports shooting advocates will concede that firearms are empowering when possessed, permitting their owners a distinct sense of uniqueness and individuation, 'the ultimate extension of self' (McCarthy, 2011: 321). Perhaps this, after all, was Samuel Colt's dream: hand-held firearms transforming through empowerment, turning the passive subjects of the old world into the active agents and decision-makers fit for the new, in a dangerous new democracy of armed and dangerous equals.

In these ways possession of a firearm substantially 'makes the man', disciplines the spirit and projects purposeful masculinity. The process is not dissimilar to that described by former US army psychologist Dave Grossman, founder of the discipline he calls 'killology', a new science with which he describes the psychological processes that military recruits have to undergo in order to overcome their civilized reticence about killing other human beings and thereby becoming effective soldiers. Having studied the phenomenon in previous writings on military training and battle preparedness, he concluded 'the average soldier will not kill unless coerced and conditioned and provided with mechanical and mental leverage' (Grossman, 1995: 31). In this account, of course, it is less the gun *in isolation* that effects the vital transformation of the man, but the gun in its empowering cultural milieu, the relations of emotional hegemony sustained by a particular 'gun culture' as animated by regular fears, duties, values, intolerances and hatreds. In an earlier sense we have equated the gun man with the theoretical 'sovereign individual' of neo-liberalism and, in that guise, the individual gun man has tremendous lethal potential or capacity. The crazed and rampaging spree killers leaving death and destruction behind them in classrooms or workplaces (discussed in Chapter 6) point to a risk quite unique to modernity, but not one, apparently, capable of fundamentally changing society – they are the occasional 'price we pay for the way we live' (most spree killings, apparently, are carried out with firearms that are legally owned). On the contrary it is the gun *en masse*, or guns collectively and their antecedent cultures, and especially those 'in the wrong hands', that we are told we have most to fear.

Towards the end of his study of *Violent Crime in Global Perspective*, Currie sought to identify the defining characteristics of violent 'gun culture' societies. They were, he said,

neglectful societies that tend to ignore social problems until or unless they explode into conflict and violence. They are societies characterised by what we might call a *culture of disregard*, in which people feel little sense of responsibility

or solidarity towards others and a 'me-first' ethic of personal gain often domi-
nates public life.

(Currie, 2005: 111)

These were, he elaborated, 'harsh societies', harsh in many ways at the same time,
creating inequality and deprivation at the bottom while concentrating wealth,
opportunities and resources at the top, and providing few safeguards for the vulnerable. Such societies tended to allow misfortune to lie where it falls, and upon
whom it falls, largely blaming individuals for the problems they encounter. They
were, he continued, typically punitive in their treatment of offenders and discipli-
narian in their approaches to childrearing, frequently tolerating the economic and
social subordination of women, racially divisive and with a tendency to marginalise
minorities (Currie, 2005: 111). Other commentators have likewise drawn attention to the fact that the 'negative side of … neoliberalism is violence and conflict'
(Sen and Pratten, 2007: 4); 'neoliberal violence is both structural and undeniably physical', entailing inequitable distributions, rigid hierarchies and boundaries
secured by a combination of public/private armed force (Goldstein, 2007a: 241).

And this returns us to the consequences of guns and gun cultures for society,
civilization and human rights. As we have seen several times already throughout
the book, firearm rights advocates frequently portray gun violence as simply an
issue of guns in the 'wrong' hands, of dangerous people and dangerous places. This
rendition of the problem implicitly repeats the story of the 'sorcerer's apprentice',
who, to lighten his daily workload, steals his master's magic wand and commands
his broom to sweep and clean all by itself. While he knows the spell to animate the
broom into action, he has absolutely no idea about how to make it stop and the
demonic broom beats him endlessly around the house, relentlessly attacking the
apprentice himself as something 'out of place' in the tidiest of houses. Be careful
what you wish for. The story has been told in many variants, including the science
fiction film *RoboCop* (1987), featuring a 'robotic law enforcement unit' pro-
grammed to uphold law and order through the application of righteous violence
directed at eliminating anyone either resisting or failing to show instant compliance. The prototype, unveiled at a weapons conference, its 'tolerance' threshold
set too tightly, mistakes the audience reaction and despatches a whirlwind of bullets killing everyone in sight, until its supply of ammunition is exhausted. Around
the world, it seems, dangerous young apprentices in dangerously unstable places
are weaponizing themselves and their communities, running off with the sorcerer's
piece, and creating untold criminal havoc, entrenching and perpetuating conflict,
while making the lives of those around them nasty, brutish, dangerous and short.

In earlier chapters (Chapters 7 and 8) I have described places, broken societies,
failing states, 'gunscapes' (Springwood, 2007b) or 'conflict complexes' (Bourne,
2007), where the angry, young and dispossessed have acquired weapons and find
themselves wreaking chaos, compounding inequalities, over-turning traditional
cultures and practices, rejecting established authorities, or perhaps just confronting an older autocratic armed predation with a newly 'democratic' weaponized

predation. All too frequently, what accompanies such developments is an unleashing of collective misogynistic violence against women and girls. While the dangerous places of the world have fallen subject to relentless weaponization, more developed 'safe' states have likewise experienced problems as privatization, disinvestment and a withdrawal of governance have created localized security deficits and vulnerabilities – in ghettos, banlieu, no-go areas, shanty towns, slums and favelas. Even the substantially disciplined and controlled (gun) cultures of Europe have experienced a junk weaponization of their most reckless and marginalized masculinity which has unleashed terrible collateral injury upon young children, women and girls, in the wrong place at the wrong time, unwittingly stepping into the path of drive-by bullets or random exercises in ballistic messaging between groups of young men displaying their bravado and supposedly post-coded affiliations. In other societies whether weapon regulation has been more or less strict, no regime of control is ever so watertight (or clairvoyant) as to prevent random crazy people venting their frustrations on suitably symbolic targets; the women who have rejected them; the feminists who may have challenged them; the employers and colleagues who have disrespected them; or the young children in their schools (the most perfect victims) who embody the hope and cherished values of society and thereby represent, in the 'scripted' vengeance of mass killing, the most perfect of all targets (Raittila *et al.*, 2010).

In the USA, where the Second Amendment 'right to bear arms' has, under relentless ideological pressure since the 1960s, never ceased to evolve, becoming, first, an individual right, rather than the collective militia right first adopted in 1791, subsequently a 'constitutional right to self-defence' (Cerone, 2006; Lund, 2006; Stell, 2006) before morphing, finally, into a de facto 'right to kill', when confronted, challenged, or even sceptical of police diligence regarding due process or 'probable cause' (Diaz, 2013). In April 2012, at around the time the US Senate was blocking the Obama gun control package developed in the wake of the Sandy Hook School shooting tragedy, Newt Gingrich, former speaker of the US House of Representatives and one-time Republican presidential hopeful, bequeathed the Second Amendment to the world at large. 'The Second Amendment is an amendment for all mankind', he told an NRA annual meeting in St Louis (Lepore, 2012a), with more than just a hint towards a global, neo-liberal hegemony of armed masculinity.

Of course, Gingrich was not the first to do this for, as we saw in Chapter 8, just as the United Nations began to work towards the development of a POA on SALW and an ATT, so also the NRA-led global voice of gun advocacy, the WFSA, with representatives in many varieties of regimes where shooting is far more effectively regulated than the US (and which, accordingly, have substantially lower gun violence problems) found themselves quite incapable of crafting a definition of a 'civilian appropriate' firearm that excluded any weapon less lethal than a machine gun capable of fully automatic fire. The definition of 'sporting firearms' (or the 'myth' of sportization; Smith, 2006) evidently now embraces military specification semi-automatic handguns and assault rifles, a consequence of the fact that the heavily saturated, though demographically diminishing, industry-driven firearms market in the USA will only attract buyers if the weapons it can sell them enhances the lethal capacity they already own. Yet while US gun culture is sometimes represented as a centuries old and resolute foundation, celebrated historically, enshrined constitutionally, validated by contemporary experience and fears of crime and disorder and – for these reasons – formidably defended and promulgated by its political establishment, it might yet still fall victim to the shifting sands of American demographics and electoral politics. As Lee (2012) has argued, the re-election of President Obama marked a first occasion in which the majority white male vote was *not* decisive in electing a president. This, itself, might account for the rightwards shift of the republican neo-conservative establishment. Their increasingly strident embrace of neo-liberal values and their attempted re-writing of US history (Lepore, 2010) or re-interpretation of constitutional amendments, may be a sign of weakness, not strength; of marginality rather than core values (Melzer, 2009); and of the past rather than the present. New electoral constituencies may yet emerge which, less wedded to the gun culture, come to generate the political will to address the anachronism which is America's gun problem.

Nevertheless, locked and loaded, American gun culture still confronts the rest of the globe. We are reminded of the uniqueness of the USA, as a highly developed, substantially unequal and culturally diverse, neo-liberal and formally democratic society with a high gun violence regime, which celebrates a principle of armed self-defence as the ultimate guarantor of personal freedom. And yet, as has been argued, we also recognize that this defensiveness of the self is also an assertion of self-hood thoroughly steeped in the hard core of America values. This essential armed American self, the smallest unit of populist sovereignty, brings a corrosive spirit to bear upon society, social justice and human rights. It embraces a rampant individualism, formed around a 'lowest common denominator neo-liberalism', the right to kill others. Some societies, even as they are subjected to many of the 'global carriers of gun culture' (Cukier and Sheptycki, 2012), have achieved a robust democratic resistance to this ideological onslaught, but others, especially those in which social order is fragmentary, the state weak and compromised (or remote or non-existent), have seen (crimogenic) neo-liberal gun cultures take hold as a supposed solution for their deeper insecurities. Fragmented, insecure and violent societies are the least likely places in which to secure a commitment to citizen disarmament – a lesson, perhaps, from the Brazilian referendum of 2005, or the badlands of northern Mexico. And yet, like the paradox of America's simultaneous 'exceptionalism' and 'globalism' detailed by Ignatieff (2005), it is also necessary to acknowledge that, just as a globalizing American 'gun culture' has been a vital preoccupation for the neo-liberal agenda in matters of law, order and security (rolled out in Latin America, South Africa and the Middle-East) so, likewise, the global diffusion of neo-liberal values has hosted an effective dissemination of the American gun culture. And, as we have seen, this has developed its deepest roots where existing institutions and cultures of governance were at their weakest or most precarious, like the chronically poor 'conflict traps' of Africa described by

Collier (2008), heavily weaponized and endlessly recycling violences and retributions. Once community weaponization becomes established, gun violence is that much more difficult to prevent or control, as 'gun culture' takes hold, and young men in particular embracing that 'militarization of the mind' described by Muggah (2001) linking gun possession and use with manliness, status and success. Dinnen and Thompson (2009: 146–147) summarize much of the literature on the quality of lives lived in the weaponized conflict zones of the underdeveloped world, or 'Global South'. They draw particular attention to the gendered character of much of the ensuing armed violence: 'The introduction of modern weapons into society has reinforced and perpetuated traditions of militarised masculinity and tolerance of gender-based violence, while the lethality of the violence has greatly increased'.

This commentary on global weaponization and its violent consequences runs somewhat counter to one of the dominant, supposedly reassuring, apparently self-vindicating narratives on humanitarian progress. Perhaps the civilization thesis (Elias, 1982) needs a cautionary shadow, a reminder that there is nothing inevitable about progress, socialism or barbarism. It all depends. The civilization thesis has been given a new lease of life in the work by Stephen Pinker (2011), *The Better Angels of Our Nature*; I discussed this briefly in Chapter 1. In simple terms Pinker advances a view that violent deaths (he really means *conflict* deaths) have followed a downward track since the middle ages. The neo-liberal capitalist world, in other words, is following a long civilizing movement and becoming more peaceable. A world awash with personal firearms, over 650 million known firearms, up to 15 million more in illegal (gang-related or 'insurgent' hands), and some eight million more added, each year, to this global stockpile (Karp, 2010, 2011), is supposedly a safer place. To paraphrase another NRA bumper sticker: 'An Armed World is a *Polite* world'. Or maybe not.

The rapid global social changes ushered in by capitalist development and neo-liberal politics, particularly where these have been associated with the sharpest inequalities and most acute marginalities have, almost everywhere, come to be associated with significantly increasing rates of crime and violence (Sen and Pratten, 2007). Vulliamy's chilling descriptions, for instance, of Juárez, Mexico – the scorched-earth, neo-liberal trap – where the third world scrapes painfully against the barricades of the first and the American Dream bleeds – marks not a breakdown of the late capitalist social order, or just some dysfunctional state ravaged, quite coincidently, by narco-violence. On the contrary, Vulliamy insists, this *is* the violent neo-liberal order of the future (2010: 106). Is it conceivable that these levels of firearm proliferation, the trickle-down securitization and the weaponization of the self and the social in near permanent, low-intensity conflicts around the globe are consistent with civilizing? Weak and failing states, lacking even a monopoly of armed force, find it as difficult to eliminate chronic patterns of violence as developed societies find it to eliminate crime. We can only retain a faith in the civilizing possibilities of weaponized neo-liberalism if, shrouded by the gun smoke of violent conflict, we are unable even to count the bodies, nearly three-quarters of a million, direct and indirect, crime and conflict deaths, each year. In other words, the rhetoric and iconography of gun rights is profoundly out of sync with its realities. Pinker's civilizing trend may have substantially relegated gun violence to the margins, but there it remains sustained by a diet of neo-liberal economic and social policies and an abundance of surplus firearms trickling, trafficking and diffusing into angry, young, 'post-colonial' hands.

Pinker implies that a weaponized world can be, indeed *is*, a peaceful world. Surprisingly or not, he shares this viewpoint with leading lights of the NRA. Civilization, capitalism, neo-liberal governance and firearm proliferation, it seems, represent a virtuous circle of peace and human progress. Commenting on Joyce Lee Malcolm's book, *Guns and Violence: The English Experience* (2002), NRA reviewers Kopel *et al.* (2006) conclude that the book tells the story of 'a society's self-destruction' and of how government, in a few decades, 'managed to reverse six hundred years of social progress in violence reduction' (almost exactly the time frame for Pinker's civilizing process). The cause of this great decivilizing reversal, they claim, echoing Malcolm, has been the bipartisan efforts, in late twentieth-century Britain, to substantially reduce the civilian gun stock, tightly regulate firearm ownership and, finally, after the Dunblane killings in 1996, prohibit handguns (Kopel *et al.*, 2006: 424).

Yet judging from the respective positions of England and Wales in Figure 1.4, and acknowledging the diminishing frequency of recorded gun crime in Britain, a society already having one of the lowest rates of gun crime in the world, the subprime junk gun supply available to offenders and the (though perhaps optimistic) police intelligence estimates of only a thousand or so 'active' criminal firearms, one might wonder which society, Britain or America, is really closest to addressing its gun crime problems. In truth, however, that has never mattered much to the NRA and its supporters. Anyway their book review was directed towards their core American audience. What most preoccupied them, in 2006, in the light of the UN initiative on international gun control, was whether 'the rest of the world should follow the British agenda' on gun control (Kopel *et al.*, 2006: 424). If it did, if the ATT has a real impact upon the proliferation of small arms in the world, especially in the world's most conflict-prone areas, that might *really* represent a significant step forwards on the 'civilizing' path.

Notes

1 Springwood's definition of the 'gunscape' involves 'a dynamic yet delicate assemblage of firearm circuits, discourses, and practices that dominate a global region. In addition to the global economy of firearms, local and regional political relations shape these gun landscapes which always interpenetrate and inform one another' (2007a: 24). Echoing Carr's *Kalashnikov Culture* (2008) he specifically cites 'Central Asia, from Afghanistan to Tajikistan' as a violent gunscape, and also the USA. The 'gunscape' entails a geographically contextualized, materially rooted and specific 'gun culture'.

2 A contrasting argument, recently articulated by Carlson (2013) suggests that gun users 'participate in the sovereign power of the state' and that they exercise individual sovereignty 'within' the shaping and limiting purview of the state (2013: 2). Ultimately, she suggests, the state vindicates their role in suppressing crime. It may be, in some 'gunscapes' – or gun

control regimes – that this is precisely what happens, unfortunately, it is not necessarily the case for the gun culture about which she writes, the USA. After all, the theory – the political theory of the NRA and writers such as Lott and Kopel – is empirically testable, and relatively unfettered access to firearms seems not to suppress violent crime but to exacerbate it. The critical distinction here may be the vital difference between 'governing through crime' (Simon, 2007) and neo-liberal 'governance through guns'.

3 The original comment from Marx:

> When we leave this sphere of simple circulation or the exchange of commodities … a certain change takes place, or so it appears, in the physiognomy of our dramatis personae. He, who before was the money-owner, now strides in front as capitalist; the possessor of labour-power follows as his worker. The one smirks self-importantly and is intent on business; the other is timid and holds back, like someone who has brought his own hide to market and now has nothing to expect but – a tanning.
>
> *(Marx, 1976: 380)*

4 A number of writers have similarly explored the 'gunplay' film phenomenon, linking it – in part – to American moral and political rearmament in the post-Vietnam, Reagan era. Differing commentaries draw parallels between events depicted in popular Hollywood movies and hardening attitudes to US policies in relation to law and order, foreign policy as well as popular conceptions of crime, race and masculine virtue. See, for example, Hellman, 1986; Jeffords, 1989, 1994; Slotkin, 1992; and Gibson, 1994.

5 From 'Dirty Harry' Callahan (Clint Eastwood) in the *Dirty Harry* series, to John McClane (Bruce Willis) in the *Die Hard* series, and beyond. The vigilante phenomenon depicted in the films is even identified criminologically as a dilemma in relation to contemporary policing; see Klockars (1980); Nina, (2000). Somewhat ironically, what has been described as the 'new, smart, macho' has become a template for the 'new police leadership' (Silvestri, 2007).

BIBLIOGRAPHY

Abrahams, N., Jewkes, R. and Mathews, S. 2010 Guns and gender-based violence in South Africa. *South African Medical Journal* vol. 100: 586–588.

Abrahams, N., Mathews, M., Jewkes, R., Martin, L.J. and Lombard, C. 2012 Every eight hours: intimate femicide in South Africa 10 years later! South African Medical Research Council, Research Brief, August.

Abrahams, R.G. 1998 *Vigilant Citizens: Vigilantism and the State*. Cambridge, Cambridge University Press.

Abrahamsen, R. and Williams, M.C. 2010 *Security Beyond the State: Private Security in International Politics*. Cambridge, Cambridge University Press.

Abu-Hamdeh, S. 2011 The Merida Initiative: an effective way of reducing violence in Mexico? *Pepperdine Policy Review* vol. 4, article 5. http://publicpolicy.pepperdine.edu/policy-review/2011v4/content/merida-initiative.pdf (accessed 13 April 2014).

Adams, L. 2008 £5m bid to bring peace between city gangs, *Glasgow Herald*, 12 December.

Adler, P.A. and Adler, P. 1993 The coming of age of crack cocaine. *Contemporary Sociology* vol. 22 (6): 848–851.

Adler, P.A., Kless, S.J. and Adler, P. 1992 Socialisation to gender roles: popularity among elementary school boys and girls. *Sociology of Education* vol. 65: 169–187.

Aebi, M.F. and Lind, A. 2012 Crime trends in Western Europe according to official statistics from 1990–2007, in van Dijk, J., Tseloni, A. and Farrell, G. (eds) *The International Crime Drop: New Directions in Research*. Basingstoke, Palgrave Macmillan.

Africa Peace Forum 2006 *Controlling Small Arms in the Horn of Africa and the Great Lakes Region: Supporting the Implementation of the Nairobi Declaration*. Nairobi, Africa Peace Forum.

Agger, B. and Luke, T.W. 2008 *There is a Gunman on Campus: Tragedy and Terror at Virginia Tech*. Lanham, MD, Rowman and Littlefield.

Alba, A.G. and Guzman, G. (eds) 2010 *Making a Killing: Femicide, Free Trade and La Frontera*. Austin, TX, University of Texas Press.

Aldridge, J., Medina, J. and Ralphs, R. 2008 'Dangers and problems of doing "gang" research in the UK', in van Gemert, F., Peterson D. and Lein, I-l. (eds) *Street Gangs, Migration and Ethnicity*. Collumpton, Willan.

Aldridge, J., Shute, J., Ralphs, R. and Medina, J. 2011 Blame the parents? Challenges for parent-focussed programmes for families of gang-involved young people. *Children in Society* vol. 25 (5): 371–381.

Alexander, M. 2010 *The New Jim Crow: Mass Incarceration in the Age of Colour Blindness*. New York, The New Press.

Alexander, R. and Gyamerah, J. 1997 Differential punishing of African Americans who possess drugs: a just policy or a continuation of the past? *Journal of Black Studies* vol. 28 (1): 97–111.

All Party Parliamentary Group (APPG) (2003) *Combating the threat of gun violence: A report of Parliamentary Hearings*, November. London, Saferworld/GCN.

Allen, C. 2006 *Living the Second Amendment: An Ethnography of Gun Rights Activism in the United States*. Unpublished PhD Thesis, Department of Sociology, University of Essex.

Allen, C. 2007 'Gun rights are civil rights': racism and the right to keep and bear Arms in the United States, in Springwood, C.F. (ed.) *Open Fire: Understanding Global Gun Cultures*. New York, Berg.

Allen, J. and Ruparel, C. 2006 Reporting and recording crime, 4 in Walker, A., Kershaw, C. and Nicholas, S. (eds) *Crime in England and Wales 2005/06*. Home Office Statistical Bulletin 12/06. London, the Home Office, pp. 47–60.

Allen, T. 2006 *Trial Justice: The International Criminal Court and the Lord's Resistance Army*. London, Zed Books.

Allison, E. 2007 I will regret it till the day I die, *The Guardian* 7 November.

Alpers, P. 2005 *Gun-running in Papua New Guinea: From Arrows to Assault Weapons in the Southern Highlands*, Small Arms Survey, Special Report no. 5.

Alpers, P. 2013 The big melt: how one democracy changed after scrapping a third of its firearms, in Webster, D.W. and Vernick, J.S. (eds) *Reducing Gun Violence in America: Informing Policy with Evidence and Analysis*. Baltimore, MD, Johns Hopkins University Press.

Alpers, P. and Morgan, B. 1995 *Firearm Homicide in New Zealand: Victims, Perpetrators and their Weapons 1992–1994*. Paper to the National Conference of Public Health, Dunedin.

Alpers, P. and Twyford, C. 2003 *Small Arms in the Pacific*. Small Arms Survey Occasional Paper No. 8. http://www. smallarmssurvey.org/fileadmin/docs/B-Occasional-papers/SAS-OP08-Pacific.pdf

Alpers, P. and Wilson, M. (nd.) GunPolicy.org. Sydney School of Public Health, The University of Sydney. GunPolicy.org. http://www.gunpolicy.org/firearms/home

Alpers P., Wilson, M. and Rossetti, A. 2013 *Guns in Australia: Facts, Figures and Firearm Law*. Sydney School of Public Health, The University of Sydney.

Altheide, D.L. 2009 The Columbine shootings and the discourse of fear. *American Behavioural Scientist* vol. 52 (10): 1354–1370.

Amar, A.R. 1998 *The Bill of Rights: Creation and Reconstruction*, New Haven, CT, Yale University Press.

Ames, M. 2007 *Going Postal: Rage, Murder and Rebellion in America*. Brooklyn, NY, Soft Skull Press.

Ander, H., Cook, P.J., Ludwig, J. and Pollack, R. 2009 *Gun Violence Among School-Age Youth in Chicago*. Crimelab, The University of Chicago.

Anderson, E. 1999 *Code of the Street: Decency, Violence and the Moral Life of the Inner City*. New York, Norton & Co.

Anderson, J. 1996 *Inside the NRA: Armed and Dangerous, An Expose*, Beverly Hills, CA, Dove Books.

Andersson, M. 2003 Immigrant youth and the dynamics of marginalisation. *Young Nordic Journal of Youth Research* vol. 11: 74–89.

Andersson, M. 2005 *Urban Multi-culture in Norway*. Lewiston, NY, Edward Mellen Books.

Animal Aid 2012 *Gunning for Children* http://www.animalaid.org.uk/images/pdf/booklets/ gunningforchildrenreport.pdf.

Arcus, D. 2002 School shooting fatalities and school corporal punishment: a look at the States. *Aggressive Behavior* vol. 28: 173–183.

Arendt, H. 1970 *On Violence*. London, Allen Lane.

Arias, E.D. 2006 *Drugs and Democracy in Rio De Janeiro: Trafficking, Social Networks and Public Security*. Chapel Hill, NC, University of North Carolina Press.

Arias, E.D. and Goldstein, D.M. (eds) 2010 *Violent Democracies in Latin America*. Durham, NC, Duke University Press.

Arjet, R. 2007 'Man to man': power and male relationships in the gun play film, in Springwood, C.F. (ed.) *Open Fire: Understanding Global Gun Cultures*. New York, Berg.

Armour, J. 1997 *Negrophobia and Reasonable Racism: The Hidden Costs of Being Black in America*. New York, New York University Press.

Armstrong, E.G. 2001 Gangsta misogyny: a content analysis of the portrayals of violence against women in rap music, 1987–1993, *Journal of Criminal Justice and Popular Culture* vol. 8 (2): 96–126.

Arriola, E.R. 2010 Accountability for murder in the Maquiladoras: linking corporate indifference to gender violence at the US–Mexico border, in Alba, A.G. and Guzman, G. (eds) *Making a Killing: Femicide, Free Trade and La Frontera*. Austin, TX, University of Texas Press.

Ashkenazi, M. 2012 What do the natives know? Societal mechanisms for controlling small arms, in Greene, O. and Marsh, N. (eds) *Small Arms, Crime and Conflict: Global Governance and the Threat of Armed Violence*. London, Routledge.

Association of Principal Youth and Community Officers (APYCO) 2008 Report on a National Policy Round Table: Gang, Gun and Knife Crime: Seeking Solutions. 29 Feb. http://www.safecolleges.org.uk/sites/default/files/NYA_GFSR_2008.pdf

Atkinson, R. and Blandy, S. 2006 *Gated Communities: International Perspectives*. Abingdon, Routledge.

Atwood, D. and Greene, O. 2002 Reaching consensus in New York: the 2001 UN Small Arms Conference, *Small Arms Survey 2002: Counting the Human Cost*. Oxford, Oxford University Press.

Atwood, D., Glatz, A,-K. and Muggah, R. 2006 *Demanding Attention: Addressing the Dynamics of Small Arms Demand*. Geneva, Small Arms Survey and the Quaker United Nations Office.

Austin, K. 1999 Light weapons and conflict in the Great Lakes region of Africa, in Boutwell, J. and Klare, M. (eds) *Light Weapons and Civil Conflict: Controlling the Tools of Violence*, Oxford, Rowman and Littlefield.

Australian Crime Commission 2013 *Organised Crime in Australia*. Canberra, Commonwealth of Australia.

Ayling, J. 2011 Pre-emptive strike: how Australia is tackling outlaw motorcycle gangs, *American Journal of Criminal Justice* vol. 36: 250–264.

Ayres, I. and Donohue, J. 1999 Nondiscretionary concealed weapons law: a case study of statistics, standards of proof, and public policy, *American Law and Economics Review* vol. 1 (1): 436–470.

Ayres, I. and Donohue, J.J. III 2003 Shooting down the more guns, less crime hypothesis, *Stanford Law Review* vol. 55: 1193–1312.

Azrael, D. and Hemenway, D. 2000 'In the safety of your own home': results from a national survey on gun use at home, *Social Science & Medicine* vol. 50 (2), January: 285–291.

Bacon, D. 2008 *Illegal People: How Globalization Creates Migration and Criminalizes Immigrants*. Boston, MA, Beacon Press.

Baker, J. and McPhedran, S. 2007 Gun laws and sudden death: did the Australian Firearms Legislation of 1996 make a difference? *British Journal of Criminology* vol. 47: 455–469.

Balko, R. 2006 *Overkill: The Rise of Paramilitary Police Raids in America*. Washington, DC, Cato Institute.

Bamber, D. 2002 Gun crime trebles as weapons and drugs flood British cities, *Daily Telegraph* 24 February.

Bambra, C. 2007 Going beyond the three worlds of welfare capitalism: regime theory and public health research, *Journal of Epidemiology & Community Health* vol. 61 (12): 1098–1102.

Bandeira, A. and Bourgois, J. (no date) *Firearms: Protection or Risk? A Practical Guidebook*. Stockholm Parliamentary Forum on Small Arms And Light Weapons.

Bangalore, S. and Messerli, F.H. 2013 Gun ownership and firearm-related deaths, *The American Journal of Medicine* vol. 126: 873–876.

Barata, R., Ribeiro, M. and Morais, J. 1999 Temporal trend of mortality in homicides: city of Sao Paulo, Brazil 1979–1994, *Cadernos de Saude, Publica* vol. 15. www.scielosp.org/scielo.php?pid=S0102-311X1999000400005&script=sci_arttext&tlng=e (accessed 13 April 2014).

Barker, G. and Ricardo, C. 2005 *Young Men and the Construction of Masculinity in Sub-Saharan Africa: Implications for HIV/AIDS, Conflict and Violence, Social Development*. Working Paper No 26, World Bank, Washington, DC.

Barker, G.T. 2005 *Dying to be Men: Youth, Masculinity and Social Exclusion*. Oxford, Routledge.

Baroness Scotland 2007 Evidence to the Home Affairs Select Committee, 13 March 2007, Evidence page 119. House of Commons: Home Affairs Committee 2007, *Report on Young Black People and the Criminal Justice System*. HC 181-ii. London, The Stationery Office.

Barraclough, B. and Harris, E.C. 2003 Suicide preceded by murder: the epidemiology of homicide–suicide in England and Wales 1988–92, *Journal of Psychological Medicine* vol. 33 (2): 577–584.

Barrett, D. 2008 Gun crime 60% higher than official figures, *Daily Telegraph* 19 October.

Barrett, P.M. 2012 *Glock: The Rise of America's Gun*. New York, Random House.

Bartolucci, V. and Kanneworff, A.B. 2012 Armed violence taking place within societies: SALW and armed violence in urban areas, in Greene, O. and Marsh, N. (eds) *Small Arms, Crime and Conflict*. London, Routledge.

BASC (British Association for Shooting and Conservation) 2009 *Controls on Deactivated Firearms: A Consultation Paper from the Home Office*, 22 May.

Bascuñán, R. and Pearce, C. 2008 *Enter the Babylon System: Unpacking Gun Culture from Samuel Colt to 50 Cent*. Toronto, Random House.

Batchelor, S. 2009 Girls, gangs and violence: assessing the evidence, *Probation Journal* vol. 56, December: 399–414.

Bauman, Z. 1982 *Memories of Class*. London, Routledge.

Bauman, Z. 1989 *Modernity and the Holocaust*. Cambridge, Polity Press.

Bauman, Z. 2000 *Liquid Modernity*. Cambridge, Polity Press.

Bayley, D. 1994 *Police for the Future*, New York, Oxford University Press.

Bayley, D. and Shearing, C. 1996 The future of policing, *Law and Society Review* vol. 30 (3): 585–606.

BBC News 2003a Blunkett targets gangster gun culture, 6 January. http://news.bbc.co.uk/1/hi/uk_politics/2632343.stm

BBC News 2003b Gun crime growing like cancer, 21 May. http://news.bbc.co.uk/1/hi/england/3043701.stm

BBC News 2008 Men jailed over assassin kit guns, 1 August. http://news.bbc.co.uk/1/hi/england/manchester/7537286.stm (accessed 13 April 2014).

BBC Scotland 2002 Scottish gun crime soaring, 7 November. http://news.bbc.co.uk/1/hi/scotland/2413223.stm

Beckford, N. 2012 Almost 3,000 guns lost or stolen in UK, figures reveal. *BBC News Website* 29 August, http://www.bbc.co.uk/news/uk-19416579 (accessed 13 April 2014).

Behr, E. 1996 *Prohibition: Thirteen Years that Changed America*. New York, Arcade Publishing.

Bekou, O, and Cryer, R. (eds) 2004 *The International Criminal Court*. Plymouth, Ashgate.

Bell, E. 2011 *Criminal Justice and Neo-liberalism*. Basingstoke, Palgrave Macmillan.

Bellesiles, M.A. 2000 *Arming America: The Origins of a National Gun Culture*. New York, Knopf.

Bellis, M.A., Hughes, K., Wood, S., Wyke, S. and Perkins, C. 2011 National five-year examination of inequalities and trends in emergency hospital admission for violence across England. *Injury Prevention* vol. 17: 319–325.

Bellos, A. 2003 Where children rule with guns, *The Observer* 19 January.

Bennett, T. and Holloway, K. 2004 Gang membership, drugs and crime in the UK, *British Journal of Criminology* vol. 44 (3): 305–323.

Bennetto, J. 2004 New Year shooting that killed girls 'meant to hit rival', *The Independent* 10 November.

Berdal, M. and Malone, D.M. (eds) 2000 *Greed and Grievance: Economic Agendas and Civil Wars*. Boulder, CO, Lynne Rienner.

Berman, E.G. and Florquin, N. 2005 Armed and aimless: conclusion, in Florquin, N. and Berman, E.G. (eds) *Armed and Aimless: Armed Groups, Guns, and Human Security in the ECOWAS Region*. Geneva, Small Arms Survey.

Best, J. 2006 The media exaggerate the school shooting problem, in Hunnicutt, S. (ed.) *School Shootings*. New York, Greenhaven Press.

Bevan, J., Macdonald, G. and Parker, S. 2009 Two steps forward: UN measures update, *Small Arms Survey 2009: Shadows of War*. Cambridge, Cambridge University Press.

Binelli, M. 2013 *The Last Days of Detroit*. London, Bodley Head.

Black, D. and Nagin, D. 1998 Do 'right-to-carry' laws deter violent crime? *Journal of Legal Studies* vol. 27 (1): 209–219.

Blackman, P.H., Leggett, V.L., Olsen, B.L. and Jarvis, J.P. (eds) 2000 *The Varieties of Homicide and its Research: Proceedings of the 1999 Meeting of the Homicide Research Working Group*. Washington, DC, FBI.

Blake Brown, R. 2012 *Arming and Disarming: A History of Gun Control in Canada*. Toronto, University of Toronto Press.

Blickman, T. 2010 Human insecurity and markets of violence, *The Impact of Militia Actions on Public Security Policies in Rio de Janeiro*, Amsterdam, Transnational Institute, Crime and Globalisation Debate Paper Series.

Blumstein, A. 1995 Youth violence, guns and the illicit-drug industry, *Journal of Criminal Law and Criminology* vol. 86 (1): 10–36.

Blumstein, A. 2002 Youth, guns and violent crime, *Future of Children* vol.12 (2): 39–54.

Blumstein, A. and Wallman, J. (eds) 2000 *The Crime Drop in America*. Cambridge, Cambridge University Press.

Boffey, C. 2004 Failed by the system, executed aged seven, *Daily Telegraph* 30 April.

Bogus, C.T. 2000 The history and politics of the Second Amendment: a primer, in Bogus, C.T. (ed.) *The Second Amendment in Law and History: Historians and Constitutional Scholars on the Right to Bear Arms*. New York, The New Press.

Bolton, J. 2001 *Statement Made at the United Nations Conference on the Illicit Trade in Small Arms and Light Weapons in all its Aspects*, 9 July. http://2001-2009.state.gov/t/us/rm/janjuly/4038.htm (accessed 13 April 2014).

Bond, P. 2000 *Elite Transition: From Apartheid to Neoliberalism in South Africa*. London, Pluto Press.

Bonoli, J. 1997 Classifying welfare states: a two-dimension approach. *Journal of Social Policy* vol. 26 (3): 351–372.

Borchers, C. 2012 Mitt Romney in NBC interview: 'I don't happen to believe that America needs new gun laws', *Boston Globe* December.

Borzycki, M. and Mouzos, J. 2007 *Firearms Theft in Australia 2004–05*. Research and Public Policy Series no. 73. Canberra, Australian Institute of Criminology.

Bottoms, A.E. 1990 Crime prevention facing the 1990s, *Policing and Society* vol. 1: 3–22.

Bourgois, P. 2003 *In Search of Respect: Selling Crack in El Barrio*. Cambridge, Cambridge University Press, 2nd edition.

Bourne, M. 2007 *Arming Conflict: The Proliferation of Small Arms*, Basingstoke, Palgrave Macmillan.

Bourne, M. 2012 Small arms and light weapons spread and conflict, in Greene, O. and Marsh, N. (eds) *Small Arms, Crime and Conflict*. London, Routledge.

Bourne, M. and Greene, O. 2012 Governance and control of SALW after armed conflicts, in Greene, O. and Marsh, N. (eds) *Small Arms, Crime and Conflict*. London, Routledge.

Boutwell, J. and Klare, M.T. (eds) 1999 *Light Weapons and Civil Conflict: Controlling the Tools of Violence*. Oxford, Rowman and Littlefield.

Boutwell, J., Klare, M.T. and Reed, L.W. (eds) 1995 *Lethal Commerce: The Global Trade in Small Arms and Light Weapons*. Cambridge, MA, The American Academy of Arts and Sciences.

Bowden, C. 2010 *Murder City: Ciudad Juarez and the Global Economy's New Killing Fields*. Philadelphia, Nation Books.

Bowling, B. 1999 The rise and fall of New York murder: zero tolerance or crack's decline? *British Journal of Criminology* vol. 39 (4): 531–554.

Boyle, K. 2004 *Arc of Justice: A Saga of Race, Riots and Murder*. New York, Henry Holt & Co.

Brady Center to Prevent Gun Violence 2004 *On Target: The Impact of the 1994 Federal Assault Weapon Act*. Washington, DC, Brady Center.

Brady Center to Prevent Gun Violence 2008 *Common Sense Gun Laws Won, the NRA Lost and What it Means*. Washington, DC, Brady Center. http://www.prweb.com/releases/BradyCenter/Elections/prweb1586404.htm

Brady Center to Prevent Gun Violence 2011 *Officers Gunned Down*. Washington, DC, Brady Center.

Braga, A. 2003 Serious youth gun offenders and the epidemic of youth violence in Boston, *Journal of Quantitative Criminology* vol. 19 (1): 33–54.

Braga, A. 2008 *Gun Violence Among Serious Young Offenders*. Washington, DC: Center for Problem-Oriented Policing.

Braga, A. and Kennedy, D. 2001 The illicit acquisition of firearms by youth and juveniles, *Journal of Criminal Justice* vol. 29 (5): 379–388.

Braga, A. and Pierce, G.L. 2005 Disrupting illegal firearms markets in Boston: the effects of Operation Ceasefire on the supply of new handguns to criminals, *Criminology and Public Policy* vol. 4 (4): 201–233.

Brand, A. and Ollereanshaw, R. 2008 *Gangs at the Grassroots: Community Solutions to Street Violence*. London, National Local Government Network.

Brandl, S.G. and Stroshine, M.S. 2011 The relationship between gun and gun buyer characteristics and time-to-crime. *Criminal Justice Policy Review* vol. 22 (3): 285–300.

Brauer, J. and Van Tuyll, H. 2008 *Castles, Battles and Bombs: How Economics Explains Military Strategy*. Chicago, IL, Chicago University Press.

Brennan, A. 2012 Analysis: fewer U.S. gun owners own more guns, *CNN News website* 1 August.

Bricknell, S. 2008 Criminal use of handguns in Australia. *Trends and Issues in Crime and Criminal Justice*, No. 361. Australian Institute of Criminology. Canberra, Australian Government.

Bricknell, S. 2012 *Firearm Trafficking and Serious and Organised Criminal Gangs*. AIC Reports: Research and Public Policy Series No. 116. Canberra, Australian Government.

Brinks, D.M. 2008 *The Judicial Response to Police Killings in Latin America: Inequality and the Rule of Law*. Cambridge, Cambridge University Press.

Britten, N. 2003 We are overrun by gun crime, says police chief. *Daily Telegraph* 10 October.

Broadhurst, K. and Benyon, J. 2000 *Gun Law: The Continuing Debate About the Control of Firearms in Britain: Evidence to the Home Affairs Select Committee*. Occasional Paper no. 16. Leicester, University of Leicester Scarman Centre.

Bromley, M. and Griffiths, H. 2010 End-user certificates: improving standards to prevent diversion. *SIPRI Insights on Peace and Security 2010/3*, March.

Brooks, K., Schiraldi, V. and Zeidenberg, J. 2000 *School House Hype: Two Years Later*. Washington, DC, The Justice Policy Institute.

Brown, A. 2003 Tackling gun crime in London's black communities, unpublished presentation to *Guns, Gangs and Youth Culture*, Nexus Conferences, Local Government House, London, 8 April.

Brown, G. 2007 Speech to the ACPO Annual Conference, 19 June 2007.

Brown, M.L. 1981 *Firearms in Colonial America: The Impact on History and Technology, 1492–1792*. Washington, DC, The Smithsonian Institute.

Brown, R. 1975 *Strain of Violence: Historical Studies of American Violence and Vigilantism*. New York, Oxford University Press.

Brown, R. 2011 Gun stash in hands of thieves, *Cambridge News* 18 March.

Brown, R.M. 1991 *No Duty to Retreat: Violence and Values in American History and Society*. Norman, OK, University of Oklahoma Press.

Brown, M. and Bolling, K. 2007 *2006 Scottish Crime and Victimisation Survey: Main Findings*, Scottish Government Social Research.

Brunson, R.K. 2007 'Police don't like black people': African American young men's accumulated police experiences. *Criminology & Public Policy* vol. 6 (1): 71–102.

Bryson, A. and Jacobs, J. 1992 *Punishing the Workshy*. Aldershot, Avebury.

Buchanan, C. 2004 Armed violence, weapons availability and human security: a view of the state of play and options for action. Papers from the Helsinki Process on Globalisation and Democracy Track on Human Security. Human Security and Small Arms Programme, Centre for Humanitarian Dialogue, July.

Bullock, K. and Tilley, N. 2002 *Shootings, Gangs and Violent Incidents in Manchester*, Crime Reduction Series, Research Paper 13, London, the Home Office.

Bullock, K. and Tilley, N. 2008 Understanding and tackling gang violence. *Crime Prevention and Community Safety* vol. 10 (1): 36–47.

Burbick, J. 2006 *Gun Show Nation: Gun Ownership and American Democracy*. New York, The New Press.

Bureau of Justice Statistics *National Crime Victimization Survey, Nonfatal Firearm Incidents and Victims, 1993–2008*. US Department of Justice, Washington, DC. http://www.bjs.gov/index.cfm?ty=dcdetail&iid=245 (accessed 13 April 2014).

Burgess, A.W., Garbarino, C. and Carlson, M.I. 2006 Pathological teasing and bullying turned deadly: shooters and suicide. *Offenders and Victims* vol. 1 (1): 1–14.

Burke, J. 2012 Indian women turn to firearms against threat of violence, *The Guardian* 21 May.

Burke, J., Thompson, T., Bright, J., Hinsliff, M., Barnett, A. and Rowan, D. 2003 Where the gun rules and the innocent go in fear, *The Observer* 5 January.

Burnett, D. 2012 Colorado Supreme Court affirms campus carry, Students for Concealed Carry, 5 March. http://concealedcampus.org/2012/03/colorado-supreme-court-affirms-campus-carry (accessed 13 April 2014).

Burns, R. and Crawford, C. 1999 School shootings, the media and public fear: ingredients for a moral panic. *Crime, Law and Social Change* vol. 32 (2): 147–168.

Caldeira, T.P.R. 2000 *City of Walls: Crime, Segregation and Citizenship in Sao Paulo*. Berkeley, CA, California University Press.

Caless, B. 2011 *Policing at the Top: The Roles, Values and Attitudes of Chief Police Officers*, Bristol, Policy Press.

Campbell, B. 1993 *Goliath: Britain's Dangerous Places*. London, Methuen.

Campbell, J. 2010 Neoliberalism's penal and debtor states: a rejoinder to Loïc Wacquant, *Theoretical Criminology*, vol. 14 (1): 59–73.

Campsie, A. 2008 Glasgow looks stateside for ways to solve gang problems, *Glasgow Herald*, 25 October.

Capie, D. 2003 *Under the Gun: The Small Arms Challenge in the Pacific*. Wellington: Victoria University Press.

Carcach, C. and Graborsky, P.N. 1998 Murder–suicide in Australia, *Australian Institute of Criminology: Trends and Issues* May.

Carcach, C., Mouzos, J. and Grabosky, P. 2002 The mass murder as quasi-experiment: the impact of the 1996 Port Arthur Massacre. *Homicide Studies* vol. 6: 107–127.

Carlson, J. 2012 'I don't dial 911': American gun politics and the problem of policing, *British Journal of Criminology* vol. 52 (6): 1113–1132.

Carlson, J. 2013 States, subjects and sovereign power: lessons from the global gun culture. *Theoretical Criminology* 25 November. http://tcr.sagepub.com/content/early/2013/11/1 3/1362480613508424.full.pdf

Carr, C. 2008 *Kalashnikov Culture: Small Arms Proliferation and Irregular Warfare*. Westport, CT, Praeger Security International.

Carroll, R. 2011 Drugs, murder and redemption: the gangs of Caracas, *The Guardian, Special Report* 10 March.

Caruso, R.P., Jara, D.L. and Swan, K.G. 1999 Gunshot wounds: bullet calibre is increasing, *Journal of Trauma* vol. 46: 462–465.

Casciani, D. 2003 Gun crime: has anything changed? *BBC News Online* 29 April. http://news.bbc.co.uk/1/hi/uk_politics/3667985.stm (accessed 13 April 2014).

Castles, F. and Mitchell, D. 1993 Worlds of welfare and families of nations, in Castles, F. (ed.) *Families of Nations: Patterns of Public Policy in Western Democracies*. Aldershot, Dartmouth, pp. 93–128.

Cavadino, M. and Dignan, J. 2006 *Penal Systems: A Comparative Approach*. London, Sage.

Cavalcanti, R. 2013 Edge of a barrel: gun violence and the politics of gun control in Brazil, *British Society for Criminology Newsletter*, No. 72, Summer 2013.

Centre for Crime and Justice Studies (CCJS) 2008 *The Street Weapons Commission: Guns, Knives and Street Violence*. London: Centre for Crime and Justice Studies.

CDP 1977 *Gilding the Ghetto: The State and the Poverty Experiments*. London: Community Development Project Inter-project Editorial Team.

Centre for Social Justice 2009 *Dying to Belong: An In depth Review of Street Gangs in Britain*. London, Centre for Social Justice.

Cerone, J. 2006 Is there a human right of self defense? *Journal of Law, Economics and Policy* vol. 2 (2): 319–330.

Chacon, J.A. and Davis, M. 2006 *No-One is Illegal: Fighting Racism and State Violence on the US–Mexico Border*. Chicago, IL, Haymarket Books.

Chan, A. and Payne, J. 2013 *Homicide in Australia: 2008–09 to 2009–10*. National Homicide Monitoring Program annual report. AIC Monitoring Report no. 21. http://www.aic. gov.au/publications/current%20series/mr/21-40/mr21.html (accessed 13 April 2014).

Chapdelaine, A. 1996 Firearms injury prevention and gun control in Canada, *Canadian Medical Association Journal* vol. 155 (9): 1285–1289.

Chapman, S. 1998/2013 *Over our Dead Bodies: Port Arthur and Australia's Fight for Gun Control*. London and Sydney, Pluto Press/Sydney University Press.

Chapman, S., Alpers, P., Agha, K. and Jones, M. 2006 Australia's 1996 gun law reforms: faster falls in firearm deaths, firearm suicides, and a decade without mass shootings. *Injury Prevention* vol. 12: 365–372.

Chavez, L.R. 2007 Spectacle in the desert: the Minuteman Project on the US–Mexico border, in Pratten, D. and Sen, A. (ed.) *Global Vigilantes*. London, Hurst & Co.

Cheng, C. and Hoekstra, M. 2013 *Does Strengthening Self-defense Law Deter Crime or Escalate Violence? Evidence from Extensions to Castle Doctrine*. National Bureau of Economic Research, Cambridge, NBMA Working Paper no. 18134, June.

Chettleburgh, M.C. 2007 *Young Thugs: Inside the Dangerous World of Canadian Street Gangs*. Toronto, HarperCollins.

Chevigny, P. 1995 *Edge of the Knife: Police Violence in the Americas*. New York, Norton & Co.

Child Trends 2010 *Teen Homicide, Suicide, and Firearm Deaths*. http://www.childtrends. org/?indicators=teen-homicide-suicide-and-firearm-deaths (accessed 13 April 2014).

Chingono, M.F. 1996 *The State, Violence and Development: The Political Economy of War in Mozambique 1975–1992*. Aldershot, Avebury.

Chivers, C.J. 2010 *The Gun: The AK-47 and the Evolution of War*. London, Allen Lane.

Chu, V.S. and Krause, W.J. 2009 *Gun Trafficking and the South West Border*, Congressional Research Service: Report for Congress, 7-5700, 21 September.

Chua, R. 2013 Do we take our gun control legislations for granted? *The Singapore Law Review* 14 May.

Clabaugh, G.K. and Clabaugh, A.A. 2005 Bad apples or sour pickles? Fundamental attribution error and the Columbine massacre, *Educational Horizons* Winter.

Cloward, R.A. and Ohlin, L.1960 *Delinquency and Opportunity*. New York, The Free Press.

Cock, J. 1997 Fixing our sights: a sociological perspective on gun violence in contemporary South Africa, *Society in Transition* vol. 28 (1–4): 70–81.

Cock, J. 2000 Weaponry and the culture of violence in South Africa, in Gamba, V. (ed.) *Society under Siege*, vol. 3. Oxford, Institute for Security Studies.

Cock, J. 2001 Gun violence and masculinity in contemporary South Africa, in Morell, R. (ed.) *Changing Men in Southern Africa*. Pietermaritzburg and London, University of Natal Press/Zed Books.

Coffman, K. and Simon, S. 2012 Gunman kills 12, wounds 59, at 'Batman' premiere in Colorado, *Reuters USA*. www.reuters.com/article/2012/07/20/us-usa-shooting-denver -idUSBRE86J0AM20120720 (accessed 13 April 2014).

Cohen, A.K. 1955 *Delinquent Boys: The Culture of the Gang*. New York, The Free Press.

Cohen, S. 1972 *Folk Devils and Moral Panics*. St Albans, Paladin.

Coleman, K., Jansson, K., Kaiza, P. and Reed, E. 2007 *Homicides, Firearm Offences and Intimate Violence 2005/6*, Home Office Statistical Bulletin, London, the Home Office.

Collier, P. 2008 *The Bottom Billion: Why the Poorest Countries are Failing and What can be Done About it*. Oxford, Oxford University Press.

Collier, P. 2009 *Wars, Guns and Votes: Democracy in Dangerous Places*. London, Vintage Books.

Collier, R. 1998 *Masculinities, Crime and Criminology*. London, Sage.

Collins, R. 2008 *Violence: A Micro-Sociological Theory*. Princeton, NJ, Princeton University Press.

Connell, R.W. 1995 *Masculinities*. Cambridge, Polity Press.

Connolly, K. and Cobain, I. 2007 Lithuanian vet who put hundreds of guns on the streets of London and Manchester, *The Guardian* 24 February.

Consalvo, M. 2003 The monsters next door: media constructions of boys and masculinity, *Feminist Media Studies* vol. 3: 27–45.

Cook, P. and Ludwig, J. 1997 *Guns in America: National Survey on Private Ownership and Use of Firearms*. US Department of Justice, National Research Brief.

Cook, P. and Ludwig, J. 1998 Defensive gun uses: new evidence from a national survey, *Journal of Quantitative Criminology* vol. 14: 111–131.

Cook, P. and Ludwig, J. 2000 *Gun Violence: The Real Costs*. New York, Oxford University Press.

Cook, P. and Ludwig, J. 2004 Principles for effective gun policy, *Fordham Law Review* vol. 73 (2): 589–613.

Cook, P., Cukier, W. and Krause, K. 2009 The illicit firearms trade in North America, *Criminology and Criminal Justice* vol. 9 (3): 265–286.

Cook, P., Ludwig, J., Venkatesh, S. and Braga, A.S. 2007 Underground gun markets, *The Economic Journal* vol. 117, November: 588–618.

Correll, J., Park, B., Judd, C.M., Wittenbrink, B., Sadler, M.S. and Keesee, T. 2007 Across the thin blue line: police officers and racial bias in the decision to shoot, *Journal of Personality and Social Psychology* vol. 92 (6): 1006–1023.

Courtwright, D.T. 1996 *Violent Land: Single Men and Social Disorder from the Frontier to the Inner City*. Cambridge, MA, Harvard University Press.

Cowey, A., Mitchell, P., Gregory, J., Maclennan, I. and Pearson, R. 2004 A review of 187 gunshot wound admissions to a teaching hospital over a 54-month period: training and service implications, *Annals of the Royal College of Surgeons* vol. 86 (2): 104–107.

Cowling, M. 2012 Neoliberalism and crime in the United States and United Kingdom, in Whitehead, P. and Crawshaw, P. (eds) *Organising Neoliberalism: Markets, Privatisation and Justice*. London, Anthem Press.

Cramer, C. 2006 *Civil War is not a Stupid Thing: Accounting for Violence in Developing Countries*. London, Hurst & Co.

Crespo, S. 2006 Introduction, in Mota, M.A.R. and Crespo, S. (eds) *Referendum from Yes to No: A Brazilian Democracy Experience*. Rio de Janeiro, ISER (Institute for Religious Studies), Communication no. 62.

Csaszar, F. 2000 *Gun Control and the Reduction in the Number of Arms*. A WFSA White Paper, October 2000. WFSA Website.

Cukier, W. 2002 Gendered perspectives on small arms proliferation and misuse: effects and policies, in the Bonn International Centre for Conversion, Brief 24: *Gender Perspectives on Small Arms and Light Weapons: Regional and International Concerns*.

Cukier, W. and Cairns, J. 2009 Gender, attitudes and the regulation of small arms: implications for action, in Farr, V., Myrttinen, H. and A. Schnabel (eds) *Sexed Pistols: The Gendered Impacts of Small Arms and Light Weapons*. Tokyo, UN University Press.

Cukier, W. and Sheptycki, J. 2012 Globalization of gun culture: transnational reflections on pistolisation and masculinity, flows and resistance, *International Journal of Law, Crime and Justice* vol. 40: 3–19.

Cukier, W. and Sidel, V.W. 2006 *The Global Gun Epidemic: From Saturday Night Specials to AK-47s*. Westport, CT, Greenwood Publishing.

Cullen, D. 2009 *Columbine*. London, Old Street Publishing.

Cullen, Lord W.D. 1996 *The Public Inquiry into the Circumstances Leading up to and Surrounding the Events at Dunblane Primary School on Wednesday 13 March 1996*. The Scottish Office, Cm. 3386, HMSO.

Currie, E. 1997 Market, crime and community: toward a mid-range theory of post-industrial violence, *Theoretical Criminology* vol. 1 (2), May: 147–172.

Currie, E. 2005 *The Roots of Danger: Violent Crime in Global Perspective*. Columbus, OH, Prentice-Hall.

Curtis, R. 1998 The improbable transformation of inner-city neighborhoods: crime, violence and drugs in the 1990s. *Journal of Criminal Law and Criminology* vol. 88 (4): 1233–1276.

Da Cunha, C.V. 2006 The referendum: televised propaganda and perceptions of the public, in Mota, M.A.R. and Crespo, S. (eds) *Referendum from Yes to No: A Brazilian Democracy Experience*. Rio de Janeiro, ISER (Institute for Religious Studies), Communication Number 62.

Dandurand, Y. 1998 *Firearms, Accidental Deaths, Suicide and Violent Crime: An Updated Review of the Literature with Special Reference to the Canadian Situation*. Vancouver, International Centre for Law reform and Criminal Justice Policy.

Daniels, D. and Adams, Q. 2010 Breaking with township gangsterism: the struggle for place and voice. *African Studies Quarterly* vol. 11 (4): 45–57.

Dauvergne, M. and De Socio, L. 2006 *Firearms and Violent Crime*. Juristat: Statistics Canada – Catalogue no. 85-002-XIE, vol. 28, no. 2.

Davenport, J. 2009 Teenage 'respect' shootings send gun crime soaring, *Evening Standard* 19 October.

Davenport, J. 2013 London gangs use World War II guns as police crack down on weapons suppliers. *Evening Standard* 9 October.

Davidson, O.G. 1993 *Under Fire: The NRA and the Battle for Gun Control*. New York, Henry Holt.

Davies, L. and Pidd, H. 2009 Germany school killer gave warning in chatroom, *The Guardian* 12 March.

Davies, M., Kerins, M. and Glucksman, E. 2011 Inner-city gunshot wounds: 10 years on. *Injury* 42 (5): 488–491.

Davies, M., Wells, C., Squires, P.A., Hodgetts, T.J. and Lecky, F.E. 2012 Civilian firearm injury in England and Wales: Trauma Audit and Research Network, *Emergency Medicine Journal* vol. 29: 10–14.

Davis, I., Hirst, C. and Mariani, B. 2001 *Organised Crime, Corruption and Illicit Arms Trafficking in an Enlarged EU: Challenges and Perspectives*. London, Kings College, Institute for Defence Studies and Saferworld.

Davis, M. 1990 *City of Quartz: Excavating the Future in Los Angeles*. London, Verso.

Davis, M. 2006 *Planet of Slums*. London, Verso.

Davis, M. 2008 Foreword to Hagedorn, J. *A World of Gangs: Armed Young Men and Gangsta Culture*. Minneapolis, MN, University of Minnesota Press.

Davison, J. 1997 *Gangsta: The Sinister Spread of Yardie Gun Culture*. London, Vision Paperbacks.

De Foster, R. 2010 American gun culture, school shootings, and a 'frontier mentality': an ideological analysis of British editorial pages in the decade after Columbine, *Communication, Culture & Critique* vol. 3 (4): 466–484.

De Groot, J. 2002 The role of NGOs in the control of light weapons: a case study of the South African gun owners association, in Gamba, V. (ed.) *Society Under Siege*, vol. 3, Oxford, Institute for Security Studies.

De Koning, R. 2004 What warriors want: young men's perspectives on armed violence, peace and development in Najie, Karamoja, in Cappon, J. (ed.) *Civil Society Acting on Community Security*, vol. 4, Nairobi, Pax Christi Horn of Africa.

De Leeuw, M.B., Dale, E.H., Kim, J.K. and Kotler, D.S. 2009 Ready, aim, fire? District of Columbia v. Heller and communities of color, *Harvard Blackletter Law Journal* vol. 25: 133–179.

De Souza, E. and Miller, J. 2012 Homicide in the Brazilian favela: does opportunity make the killer? *British Journal of Criminology* vol. 52: 786–807.

De Vries, M.S. 2011 Converted firearms: a transnational problem with local harm, *European Journal of Criminal Policy Research* vol. 18 (2): 205–216.

Defensor, H.C. 1970 *Gun Registration Now – Confiscation Later*. New York, Vantage Press.

DeJong, W., Epstein, J.C. and Hart, T.E. 2003 Bad things happen in good communities: the rampage shooting in Edinboro, Pennsylvania, and its aftermath, in Moore, M.H., Petrie, C.V., Braga, A.A. and McLaughlin, B.L. (eds) *Deadly Lessons: Understanding Lethal School Violence*. Washington, DC, The National Academies Press.

del Frate, A.A. and Mugellini, G. 2012 The crime drop in non-Western countries, in van Dijk, J., Tseloni, A. and Farrell, G. (eds) *The International Crime Drop: New Directions in Research*. Basingstoke, Palgrave Macmillan.

Denham, J. 2002 *Building Cohesive Communities: A Report of the Ministerial Group on Public Order and Community Cohesion*. London, The Home Office.

Denov, M. and Maclure, R. 2009 Girls and small arms in Sierra Leone: victimisation, participation and resistance, in Farr, V., Myrttinen, H. and Schnabel, A. (eds) *Sexed Pistols*. Tokyo, United Nations University Press.

Department for Children, Schools and Families 2008 *Youth Taskforce Action Plan*. Nottingham, DCSF Publications.

Department of Health 2008a *Hospital Accident and Emergency Admissions for Gunshot Wounds and Stab Injuries*. Placed in the House of Commons Library, 16 June. www.theyworkforyou.com/wrans/?id=2008-06-16a.206489.h&s=hospital+admission+u (accessed 13 April 2014).

Department of Health 2008b *Hospital Accident and Emergency Admissions for Gunshot Wounds and Stab Injuries by Age*. Placed in the House of Commons Library, 25 June. www.theyworkforyou.com/wrans/?id=2008-06-25b.210404.h&s=stab+wounds#g (accessed 13 April 2014).

Department of Justice Canada and Canadian Association of Chiefs of Police 1997 *Firearms Recovered in Crime: A Multi-site Study*. Ottawa, Department of Justice/CACP.

Diaz, T. 1999 *Making a Killing: The Business of Guns in America*. New York, The New Press.

Diaz, T. 2013 *The Last Gun: How Changes in the Gun Industry are Killing Americans and What it Will Take to Stop it*. New York, The New Press.

DiChiara, A. and Chabot, R. 2003 Gangs and the contemporary urban struggle: an unappreciated aspect of gangs, in Kontos, L., Brotherton, D.C. and Barrios, L. (eds) *Gangs and Society: Alternative Perspectives*. Columbia University Press.

Dimitrov, D. and Hall, P. 2012 Small arms and light weapons production as part of a national and global defence industry, in Greene, O. and Marsh, N. (eds) *Small Arms, Crime and Conflict: Global Governance and the Threat of Armed Violence*. London, Routledge.

Dinnen, S. and Thompson, E. 2009 State, society and the gender of gun culture in Papua New Guinea, in Farr, V., Myrttinen, H. and Schnabel, A. (eds) *Sexed Pistols*. Tokyo, United Nations University Press.

DiPoala, A., Duda, J. and Klofas, J. 2013 *An Exploration of Gun Violence and Prevention: Toward the Development of an Inclusive Database.* Rochester Institute of Technology, Centre for Public Safety Initiatives.

Dixon, D. 2005 *Never Come to Peace Again: Pontiac's Uprising and the Fate of the British Empire in North America.* Norman, University of Oklahoma Press.

Dodd, V. 2011 New questions raised over Duggan shooting: investigators find no forensic evidence that man whose death triggered riots was holding gun, *The Guardian* 19 November.

Doherty, B. 2008 *Gun Control on Trial: Inside the Supreme Court Battle over the Second Amendment.* Washington, DC, Cato Institute.

Donohue, E., Schiraldi, V. and Zeidenberg, J. 1998 *School House Hype: The School Shootings and the Real Risks Kids Face in America.* Washington, DC, the Justice Policy Institute.

Donohue, J.J. 2003 The impact of concealed carry laws, in Ludwig, J. and Cook, P.J. (eds) *Evaluating Gun Policy: Effects on Crime and Violence.* Washington, DC, Brookings Institution Press.

Donohue, J.J. and Levitt, S. 2001 Legalized abortion and crime, *Quarterly Journal of Economics* vol. 116 (2): 379–420.

Dorling, D. 2005 Prime suspect: murder in Britain in Hillyard, P., Pantazis, C., Tombs, S., Gordon, D. and Dorling, D. (eds) *Criminal Obsessions: Why Harm Matters More than Crime.* London: Pluto Press.

Dowdney, L. 2003 *Children of the Drug Trade: A Case Study of Children in Organised Armed Violence in Rio de Janeiro.* Rio de Janeiro, 7 Letras.

Drake, D. 2012 *Prisons, Punishment and the Pursuit of Security.* Basingstoke, Palgrave Macmillan.

Dreyfus, P. and Nascimento M. de Sousa 2005 Small arms holdings in Brazil: towards a comprehensive mapping of guns and their owners, in *Brazil: The Arms and the Victims*, Rio de Janeiro: Viva Rio/ISER.

Dreyfus, P., Lessing, B. and Purcena, J.C. 2005 *The Brazilian Small Arms Industry: Legal Production and Trade, Geneva.* Viva Rio/ISER. http://www.smallarmssurvey.org/fileadmin/docs/C-Special-reports/SAS-SR11-Small-Arms-in-Brazil.pdf (accessed 13 April 2014).

Dreyfus, P., Guedes, L.E., Lessing, B., Bandeira, A.R., de Sousa Nascimento, M. and Silveira Rivero, P. 2008 *Small Arms in Rio de Janeiro: The Guns, the Buyback, and the Victims.* Geneva, Small Arms Survey, Viva Rio/ISER.

Drinan, R.F. 1990 The good outweighs the evil, in Nisbet, L. (ed.) *The Gun Control Debate.* New York, Prometheus Books.

Dube, A., Dube, O. and García-Ponce, O. 2012 *Cross-border Spillover: US Gun Laws and Violence in Mexico.* Discussion Paper Series, Forschungsinstitut zur Zukunft der Arbeit, no. 7098. http://hdl.handle.net/10419/69479 (accessed 13 April 2014).

DuClos, D. 1998 *The Werewolf Complex: America's Fascination with Violence.* Oxford, Berg.

Duggan, M. 2001 More guns, more crime, *Journal of Political Economy* vol. 109 (5): 1086–1114.

Eades, C., Grimshaw, R., Silvestri, A. and Solomon, E. 2007 *'Knife Crime': A Review of Evidence and Policy.* London, CCJS, 2nd edition.

Eaton, D. 2012 Revenge, ethnicity and cattle raiding in north-western Kenya, in Witsenberg, K. and Zahl, F. (eds) *Spaces of Insecurity: Human Agency in Violent Conflicts in Kenya.* Leiden, Africa Studies Centre, vol. 45.

Eavis, P. and Benson, W. 1999 The European Union and the light weapons trade, in Boutwell, J. and Klare, M.T. (eds) *Light Weapons and Civil Conflict: Controlling the Tools of Violence.* Oxford, Rowman and Littlefield.

Eck, J. and Maguire, R. 2000 Have changes in policing reduced violent crime?, in Blumstein, A. and Wallman, J. (eds) *The Crime Drop in America.* New York, Cambridge University Press.

Eglin, P. and Hester, S. 2003 *The Montreal Massacre: A Story of Membership Categorization Analysis*. Waterloo, ON, Wilfrid Laurier University Press.

Elias, N. 1939 *The Civilizing Process*. [Translated from German] (1939/1969). Oxford, Basil Blackwell 1994.

Elias, N. 1982 *State Formation and Civilisation*. Oxford, Blackwell.

Enten, H. 2012 Gun ownership in the US: what the data can tell us, *The Guardian* 25 July.

Esping-Anderson, G. 1990 *Three Worlds of Welfare Capitalism*. Cambridge, Polity Press.

European Commission 2008 Directive 2008/51/EC of the European Parliament and of the Council of 21 May 2008 amending Council Directive 91/477/EEC on control of the acquisition and possession of weapons. http://eur-lex.europa.eu/legal-content/EN/ALL/?uri=CELEX:32008L0051 (accessed 13 April 2014).

European Commission 2010 Report from the Commission to the European Parliament and the Council: the placing on the market of replica firearms. http://eur-lex.europa.eu/legal-content/EN/ALL/?uri=CELEX:52010DC0404 (accessed 13 April 2014).

Fagan, J. and Wilkinson, D. 1998 Guns, youth violence and social identity in inner cities, *Youth Violence* vol. 24: 105–188.

Fagan, J. and Wilkinson, D. 2000 *Situational Contexts of Gun Use by Young Males in Inner Cities*. US Department of Justice, National Criminal Justice Reference Service (NCJRS).

Faiola, A. 2013 After shooting tragedies, Britain goes after guns. *The Washington Post* 1 February.

Fallouh, H.B., Venugopal, P.S. and Newton, A. 2009 Occult gunshot wounds in an emergency department, *The Lancet* vol. 373 (9664), 21 February: 631–632.

Farr, V., Myrttinen, H. and Schnabel, A. 2009 *Sexed Pistols: The Gendered Impact of Small Arms and Light Weapons*. Tokyo, United Nations University Press.

Farrington, D. 1996 Understanding and Preventing Youth Crime, Social Policy Research Findings No. 93. York, The Joseph Rowntree Foundation.

Farrington, D. 2002 Developmental criminology and risk-focussed prevention, in Maguire, M., Morgan, R. and Reiner, R. (eds) *The Oxford Handbook of Criminology*. Oxford, OUP, 3rd edition.

FBI 2009 National Gang Threat Assessment: http://www.fbi.gov/stats-services/publications/national-gang-threat-assessment-2009-pdf

Feinstein, A. 2011 *The Shadow World: Inside the Global Arms Trade*. London, Hamish Hamilton.

Felbab-Brown, V. 2011a *Calderón's Caldron: Lessons from Mexico's Battle Against Organized Crime and Drug Trafficking in Tijuana, Ciudad Juárez, and Michoacán*. Brookings Institute, Latin America Initiative.

Felbab-Brown, V. 2011b *Bringing the State to the Slum: Confronting Organized Crime and Urban Violence in Latin America. Lessons for Law Enforcement and Policymakers*. Brookings Institute, Latin America Initiative.

Ferguson, C.J. 2008 The school shooting/violent video game link: causal relationship or moral panic? *Journal of Investigative Psychology and Offender Profiling* vol. 5: 25–37.

Field, F. 1981 *Inequality in Britain: Freedom, Welfare and the State*. London, Fontana.

Field, S. 1990 *Trends in Crime and their Interpretation*. Home Office Research Study, London, the Stationery Office.

Findlay, M. 1999 *The Globalisation of Crime: Understanding Transitional Relationships in Context*. Cambridge, Cambridge University Press.

Fine, B. 2001 *Social Capital versus Social Theory: Political Economy and Social Science at the Turn of the Millennium*. Abingdon, Taylor & Francis.

Fine, B. 2010 *Theories of Social Capital: Researchers Behaving Badly*. London, Pluto Press.

Finkelman, P. 2000 'A well-regulated militia': the Second Amendment in historical perspective, in Bogus, C.T. (ed.) *The Second Amendment in Law and History: Historians and Constitutional Scholars on the Right to bear Arms*. New York, The New Press.

Finkerhor, D. and Ormrod, R. 2001 *Homicides of Children and Youth*. Office of Juvenile Justice and Delinquency Prevention, U.S. Department of Justice. https://www.ncjrs. gov/pdffiles1/ojjdp/187239.pdf (accessed 13 April 2014).

Fish, J.N. and Mncayi, P. 2009 Securing private spaces: gendered labour, violence and democratization in South Africa, in Farr, V., Myrttinen, H. and Schnabel, A. (eds) *Sexed Pistols*. Tokyo, United Nations University Press.

Fisher, D. and Gruescu, S. 2011 *Children and the Big Society: Backing Communities to Keep the Next Generation Safe and Happy*. ResPublica: Children and Families Unit.

Fitch, K. 2009 *Teenagers at Risk: The Safeguarding Needs of Young People in Gangs and Violent Peer Groups*. NSPCC. http://www.nspcc.org.uk/Inform/research/findings/Teenagers AtRisk_wda64009.html (accessed 13 April 2014).

Fitzgerald, M. and Hale, C. 2006 Ethnic minorities and community safety, in P. Squires (ed.) *Community Safety: Critical Perspective on Policy and Practice*. Bristol, The Policy Press.

Fletcher, J. 1997 *Violence and Civilisation: An Introduction to the Work of Norbert Elias*. Cambridge, Polity Press.

Fleury-Steiner, B.D., Dunn, K. and Fleury-Steiner, R. 2009 Governing through crime as commonsense racism: race, space, and death penalty 'reform' in Delaware, *Punishment & Society* 11 January: 5–24.

Florida, R. 2011 The geography of gun deaths, *The Atlantic* 13 January. www.theatlantic.com/ national/archive/2011/01/the-geography-of-gun-deaths/69354 (accessed 13 April 2014).

Flint, J. and D. Robinson (eds) 2008 *Community Cohesion in Crisis: New Dimensions of Diversity and Difference*. Bristol, Policy Press.

Forjuoh, S.N., Coben, J.H. and Dearwater, S.R. 1996 Firearm ownership and storage practices in Pennsylvania homes, *Injury Prevention* vol. 2: 278–282.

Foucault, M. 1977 *Discipline and Punish*. Harmondsworth, Allen Lane.

Fox, C. and Harding, D.J. 2005 School shootings as organisational deviance. *Sociology of Education* vol. 78: 69–97.

Fox, J.A. and Levin, J. 2005 Overreacting to school shootings intensifies the problem, in Hunnicutt, S. (ed.) *School Shootings*. Detroit, Greenhaven Press.

Fox, J.A. and Swatt, M.L. 2008 *The Recent Surge in Homicides involving Young Black Males and Guns: Time to Reinvest in Prevention and Crime Control*. Boston, MA, Northeastern University.

Francis, P. and Nyamongo, M. 2005 Bitter harvest: the social costs of state failure in rural Kenya. Arusha Conference, *New Frontiers of Social Policy*. 12–15 December.

Franco, G.H. 2000 Their darkest hour: Colombia's government and the narco-insurgency, *Parameters* Summer: 83–93.

Frappier, J.Y., Leonard, K.A. and Sacks, D. 2005 Youth and firearms in Canada, *Paediatric Child Health* vol. 10 (8): 473–477.

Freedman, J.M. 2013 Swiss killings raise pressure for stricter gun-control laws, *Bloomberg. com/news* 8 February.

Fry, C. 1989 Dangerous imitations, *Police Review* 29 September.

Fry, C. 1991 Real or replica: do you shoot first? *Police Review* 13 September.

Fyfe, J.J. 1988 Police use of lethal force: research and reform, *Justice Quarterly* vol. 5: 164–205.

Gabbatt, A. 2012a Poll finds gun owners in favour of tighter restrictions on buying weapons, *The Guardian* 24 July.

Gabbatt, A. 2012b Obama calls for US gun control laws to be tightened in wake of Aurora shooting, *The Guardian* 26 July.

Gabbidon, S.L. and Jordan, K.L. 2013 Public opinion on the killing of Trayvon Martin: a test of the racial gradient thesis, *Journal of Crime and Justice* vol. 36 (3): 1–13.

Gamba, V. and Meek, S. (eds) 1997–2000 *Society under Siege*, three volumes. Oxford, Institute for Security Studies.

Gamble, A. 1988 *The Free Economy and the Strong State*. Basingstoke, Macmillan.

Gardiner, R. 2011 Rise seen in black victims, *Wall Street Journal* 9 March.

Garland, D. 1996 The limits of the sovereign state: strategies of crime control in contemporary society, *British Journal of Criminology* vol. 36: (4) 445–471.

Garland, D. 2000 The culture of high crime societies: some preconditions of recent 'law and order' policies, *British Journal of Criminology* vol. 40 (3): 347–375.

Garland, D. 2001a *The Culture of Control: Crime and Social Order in Contemporary Society*. Oxford, Oxford University Press.

Garland, D. (ed.) 2001b *Mass Imprisonment: Social Causes and Consequences*. London, Sage.

Garland, D. 2002 The cultural uses of capital punishment, *Punishment & Society: The International Journal of Penology* vol. 4 (4): 459–487.

Garland, D. 2005 Capital punishment and American culture, *Punishment & Society: The International Journal of Penology* vol. 7 (4): 347–376.

Garland, D. 2010 *Peculiar Institution: America's Death Penalty in an Age of Abolition*. Cambridge, MA, Harvard University Press.

Garot, R. 2010 *Who You Claim: Performing Gang Identity in School and on the Street*. New York, New York University Press.

Garside, R. 2006 Right for the wrong reasons: making sense of criminal justice failure, in Garside, R. and McMahon, W. (eds) *Does Criminal Justice Work? The 'Right for the Wrong Reasons' Debate*. London, Crime and Society Foundation.

Gaughan, E., Cerio, J.D. and Myers, R.A. 2001 *Lethal Violence in Schools: A National Study*. New York, Alfred University.

Gerney, A., Parsons, C. and Posner, C. 2013 *America Under the Gun: A 50-State Analysis of Gun Violence and its Link to Weak State Gun Laws*. Washington, DC, Center for American Progress.

Ghosh, D. 2013 Delhi women gun for licences; rape triggers big rush to acquire arms, 1 January. http://timesofindia.indiatimes.com/city/delhi/Delhi-women-gun-for-licences-rape-triggers-big-rush-to-acquire-arms/articleshow/17836320.cms

Gibbons, F. 2003 Minister labelled racist after attack on rap 'idiots', *The Guardian* 6 January.

Gibson, J.W. 1994 *Warrior Dreams: Violence and Manhood in Post-Vietnam America*. New York, Wang & Hill.

Gibson, K.A. 2012 'Have gun – will travel': the movement and re-use of firearms in England and Wales. Masters Thesis. UCL/NABIS.

Gill, C. 2008 Schoolboy, 13, becomes the youngest ever person charged with possession of a gun, *Daily Mail* 13 August.

Gill, M.L. 2000 *Commercial Robbery: Offenders' Perspectives on Security and Crime Prevention*. London, Blackstone Press.

Gilligan, J. 2011 *Why Some Politicians are More Dangerous to Your Health Than Others*. Cambridge, Polity Press.

Gilroy, P. 2003 A new crime, but the same old culprits, *The Guardian* 8 January.

Ginnifer, J. 2005 *Armed Violence and Poverty in Sierra Leone: A Case Study for the Armed Violence and Poverty Initiative*. University of Bradford, Centre for International Cooperation and Security, Department of Peace Studies.

Ginnifer, J. and Ismail, O. 2005 *Armed Violence and Poverty in Nigeria: A Case Study for the Armed Violence and Poverty Initiative*. University of Bradford, Centre for International Cooperation and Security, Department of Peace Studies.

Glick, S. 1995a *Concealed Carry: The Criminal's Companion: Florida's Concealed Carry Weapons Law*. Washington, DC, Violence Policy Center.

Glick, S. 1995b *Female Persuasion: A Study of How the Firearms Industry Markets to Women and the Reality of Women and Guns*. Working Papers, Violence Policy Center.

Glick, S. 1996 *Concealing the Risk: Real-World Effects of Lax Concealed Weapons Laws*. Washington, DC, Violence Policy Center.

Glick, S. 1998 *License to Kill: Arrests Involving Texas Concealed Handgun License Holders*. Washington, DC, Violence Policy Center.

GMP (Greater Manchester Police) 2006 *Operation Xcalibre Intelligence Briefing*, Powerpoint presentation. Manchester, GMP.

Godnick, W., Muggah, R. and Waszink, C. 2002 *Stray Bullets: The Impact of Small Arms Misuse in Central America*. Geneva, Small Arms Survey.

Goertzel, T. and Kahn, T. 2009 The great São Paulo homicide drop. *Homicide Studies* vol. 13: 398–410.

Goertzel, T., Shohat, E., Kahn, T., Zanetic, A. and Bogoyavlenskiy, D. 2012 Homicide booms and busts: a small-n comparative historical study, *Homicide Studies* vol. 17: 59–74.

Golding, B., McClory, J. and Lockhart, G. 2008 *Going Ballistic: Dealing with Guns, Gangs and Knives*. London, The Policy Exchange.

Golding, P. and Middleton, S. 1982 *Images of Welfare*, Oxford, Martin Roberston.

Goldring, N.J. 1999 Domestic laws and international controls, in Boutwell, J. and Klare, M.T. (eds) *Light Weapons and Civil Conflict. Controlling the Tools of Violence*. Oxford: Rowman and Littlefield Publishers.

Goldson, B. (ed.) 2000 *The New Youth Justice*. Dorset, Russell House.

Goldson, B. 2001 The demonisation of children: from the symbolic to the institutiona, in Foley, P., Roche, J. and Tucker, S. (eds) *Children in Society: Contemporary Theory, Policy and Practice*. Basingstoke, Palgrave.

Goldson, B. 2003 New punitiveness: the politics of child incarceration, in Muncie, J., Hughes, G. and McLaughlin, E. (eds) *Youth Justice: Critical Readings*. London, Sage.

Goldson, B. (ed.) 2011 *Youth in Crisis: Gangs, Territoriality and Violence*. London, Routledge.

Goldstein, D.M. 2003 *Laughter out of Place: Race, Class, Violence, and Sexuality in a Rio Shantytown*. Berkeley, CA, University of California Press.

Goldstein, D.M. 2007a Gun politics: reflections on Brazil's failed gun ban referendum in the Rio de Janeiro context, in Springwood, C.F. (ed.) *Open Fire: Understanding Global Gun Cultures*. Oxford, Berg.

Goldstein, D.M. 2007b Flexible justice: neo-liberal violence and 'self-help' security in Bolivia, in Pratten, D. and Sen, A. (eds) *Global Vigilantes*. London, Hurst & Co.

Goodchild, S. 2003, Rap stars and record companies to blame for gun culture, say police, *Independent on Sunday* 5 January.

Goodman, C. and Marizco, M. 2010 *US Firearm Trafficking to Mexico: New Data and Insights Illuminate Key Trends and Challenges*. Woodrow Wilson International Centre, Working paper series on US–Mexico Security Co-operation, pp. 167–203.

Gorman, S. 2012 Utah boy charged with bringing gun to school, cites fears of Newtown attack. *Chicago Tribune* 18 December. http://articles.chicagotribune.com/2012-12-18/news/sns-rt-us-usa-gun-utahbre8bi051-20121218_1_utah-boy-gun-school-day

Goss, K.A. 2006 *Disarmed: The Missing Movement for Gun Control in America*. Princeton, NJ, Princeton University Press.

Graef, R. 2009 Revealed: why millionaire Christopher Foster slaughtered his family, *Daily Mail* 4 April.

Graham, G. and Bowling, B. 1995 *Young People and Crime*. Home Office Research Study No. 145. London, HMSO.

Gray, P. 2013 Chicago girl who performed at Obama's inauguration killed in shooting, *Time Magazine* 30 January.

Grayson, G.W. 2010 *Mexico: Narco-Violence and a Failed State?* New Brunswick, Transaction Books.

Greene, J. and Pranis, K. 2007 *Gang Wars: The Failure of Enforcement Tactics and the Need for Effective Public Safety Strategies*. Washington, DC, Justice Policy Institute.

Greene, O. 1999 Small arms, global challenge: the scourge of light weapons, *Global Dialogue* vol. 1 (2), Autumn. www.worlddialogue.org/content.php?id=37 (accessed 13 April 2014).

Greene, O. 2006 Ammunition for small arms and light weapons: understanding the issues and addressing the challenges, in Pezard, S. and Anders, H. (eds) *Targeting Ammunition: A Primer*. Geneva, Small Arms Survey.

Greene, O. and Marsh, N. (eds) 2012a *Small Arms, Crime and Conflict: Global Governance and the Threat of Armed Violence*. London, Routledge.

Greene, O. and Marsh, N. 2012b Introduction, in Greene, O. and Marsh, N. (eds) *Small Arms, Crime and Conflict: Global Governance and the Threat of Armed Violence*. London, Routledge.

Greene, O. and Marsh, N. 2012c Armed violence within societies, in Greene, O. and Marsh, N. (eds) *Small Arms, Crime and Conflict: Global Governance and the Threat of Armed Violence*. London, Routledge.

Greene, O. and Marsh, N. 2012d Governance and small arms and light weapons, in Greene, O. and Marsh, N. (eds) *Small Arms, Crime and Conflict: Global Governance and the Threat of Armed Violence*. London, Routledge.

Greene, O. and Penetrante, A.M. 2012 Arms, private militias and fragile state dynamics, in Greene, O. and Marsh, N. (eds) *Small Arms, Crime and Conflict: Global Governance and the Threat of Armed Violence*. London, Routledge.

Greene, J. and Pranis, K. (2007) *Gang Wars: The Failure of Enforcement Tactics and the Need for Effective Public Safety Strategies*. Justice Policy Institute, USA.

Greenwood, C. 1999 Verbal evidence to the Select Committee, 17 December.

Gregory, K. 2007 Drawing a virtual gun, in Springwood, C.F. (ed.) *Open Fire: Understanding Global Gun Cultures*. New York, Berg.

Griffiths, H. and Wilkinson, A. 2007 *Guns, Planes and Ships: Identification and Disruption of Clandestine Arms Transfers*. SEESAC, United Nations Development Program.

Grogger, J. and Willis, M. 2000 *The Introduction of Crack Cocaine and the Rise in Urban Crime Rates*. National Bureau of Economic Research, NBER Working Paper no. 6353.

Grossman, D. 1995 *On Killing: The Psychological Cost of Learning to Kill in War and Society*. Boston, Little, Brown & Co.

Grossman, D. and Degaetano, G. 1999 *Stop Teaching our Kids to Kill*. New York, Crown Publishers.

Gurr, T.R. 1981 Historical trends in violent crime: a critical review of the evidence, in Morris, N. and Tonry, M. (eds) *Crime and Justice*, vol. 3. Chicago, University of Chicago Press.

Gurr, T.R. 1989 Historical trends in violent crime: Europe and the United States, in T.R. Gurr (ed.) *Violence in America Vol 1: The History of Crime*, Thousand Oaks, CA, Sage.

Gustafson, K.S. 2011 *Cheating Welfare: Public Assistance and the Criminalization of Poverty*. New York, New York University Press.

Gutierrez, F. 2010 Mechanisms, in Gutierrez, F. and Schonwalder, G. (eds) *Economic Liberalization and Political Violence: Utopia or Dystopia*. London, Pluto Press.

Hagan, J., Hirschfield, P. and Shedd, C. 2002 First and last words: apprehending the social and legal facts of an urban high school shooting, *Sociological Methods Research* vol. 31 (2): 218–254.

Hagedorn, J. 1988 *People and Folks: Gangs, Crime and the Underclass in a Rustbelt City*. Chicago, Lakeview Press.

Hagedorn, J. 2005 The global impact of gangs, *Journal of Contemporary Criminal Justice* vol. 21 (2): 153–169.

Hagedorn, J. 2008 *A World of Gangs: Armed Young Men and Gangsta Culture*. Minneapolis, MN, University of Minnesota Press.

Haider-Markel, D.P. and Joslyn, M.R. 2001 Gun policy, opinion, tragedy, and blame attribution: the conditional influence of issue frames, *Journal of Politics* vol. 63: 520–543.

Hale, C. 1998 Crime and the business cycle in post-war Britain revisited, *British Journal of Criminology* vol. 38 (4): 681–698.

Hales, G. 2006 *A Guide to and Review of Home Office Gun Crime Statistics*. Institute of Criminal Justice Studies, University of Portsmouth.

Hales, G., Lewis, C. and Silverstone, D. 2006 *Gun Crime: The Market in and Use of Illegal Firearms*. Home Office Research Study 298. London, the Home Office.

Hall, A. 2009 Police uncover astonishing weapons cache of another German teenager as country is hit by wave of copycat threats. *Daily Mail* 13 March.

Hall, B. 2013 Smuggling ring sent guns from Nashville to Australia. News Channel 5.com http://www.newschannel5.com/story/22738028/smuggling-ring-sent-guns-from -nashville-to-australia

Hall, S. and Jacques, M. (eds) 1983 *The Politics of Thatcherism*. London, Lawrence & Wishart.

Hall, S., Critcher, C., Jefferson, T., Clarke, J. and Roberts, B. 1978 *Policing the Crisis: Mugging, the State, and Law and Order*. London, Hutchinson.

Hallsworth, S. and Brotherton, D. 2011 *Urban Disorders and Gangs: A Critique and a Warning*. London, The Runnymede Trust.

Hallsworth, S. and Young, T. 2008 Gang talk and gang talkers: a critique, *Crime Media Culture* vol. 4 (2): 175–195.

Hamid, A. 1990 The political economy of crack-related violence, *Journal of Contemporary Drug Problems* vol. 17: 31–78.

Hamm, M.S. and Ferrell, J. 1998 Rap, cops, and crime: clarifying the 'cop killer' controversy, in Monk, R.C. (ed.) *Taking Sides: Clashing Views on Controversial Issues in Crime and Criminology*. Guilford, CT: Dushkin/McGraw-Hill, pp. 23–28.

Haney-Lopez, I. 2003 *Racism on Trial: The Chicano Fight for Justice*. Cambridge, MA: Belknapp Press of Harvard University Press.

Hannam, A.G. 2010 Trends in converted firearms in England and Wales as identified by the National Firearms Forensic Intelligence Database (NFFID) between September 2003 and September 2008, *Journal of Forensic Sciences* vol. 55 (3): 756–766.

Harcourt, B.E. 2006 *Language of the Gun: Youth Crime and Public Policy*. Chicago, IL, University of Chicago Press.

Harding, D., Metha, J. and Newman, K. 2003 No exit: mental illness, marginality, and school violence in West Paducah, Kentucky, in Moore, M.H., Petrie, C.V., Braga, A.A. and McLaughlin, B.L. (eds) *Deadly Lessons: Understanding Lethal School Violence*. Washington, DC, The National Academies Press, pp. 132–162.

Harding, R. 1979 Firearms use in crime, *Criminal Law Review*, 765–774.

Harding, R. 1981 *Firearms and Violence in Australian Life*. Perth, University of Western Australia Press.

Harriman, B. and Perring, M. 2012 *Consultation on Legislative Changes to Firearms Control: A Response by the British Association for Shooting and Conservation*. Wrexham, BASC, 7 May.

Harter, S., Low, S.M. and Whitesell, N.R. 2003 What have we learned from Columbine: the impact of self-system on suicidal and violent ideation among adolescents, *Journal of School Violence* vol. 2: 3–26.

Harvey, D. 2005 *A Brief History of Neo-liberalism*. Oxford, Oxford University Press.

Hayden, C., Hales, G., Lewis, C. and Silverstone, D. 2008 Young men convicted of firearms offences in England and Wales: an exploration of family and educational background as opportunities for prevention, *Policy Studies* vol. 29 (2): 163–178.

Hazen, J.M. 2010 Gangs, groups and guns: an overview, *Small Arms Survey 2010: Gangs, Guns and Groups*. Geneva and Cambridge, Graduate Institute of International Studies and Oxford University Press.

Heal, R. 1991 Laws that shoot from the hip, *Police Review* 28 June.

Heale, J. 2008 *One Blood: Inside Britain's New Street Gangs*. London and New York, Simon & Schuster.

Healy, G. (ed.) 2004 *Go Directly to Jail: The Criminalisation of Almost Everything*. New York, Cato Institute.

Heide, K.M., Eyles, C.H. and Spencer, E. 2000 School shootings in the USA: a typology of lethal and non-lethal injury, in Blackman, P.H., Leggett, V.L., Olsen, B.L. and Jarvis, J.P. (eds) *The Varieties of Homicide and its Research: Proceedings of the 1999 Meeting of the Homicide Research Working Group*. Washington, DC, FBI.

Hellman, J. 1986 *American Myth and the Legacy of Vietnam*. Columbia, NY, Columbia University Press.

Helmer, W.J. 1970 *The Gun that Made the Twenties Roar*. New York, Macmillan.

Hemenway, D. 1997 Survey research and self-defense gun use: an explanation of extreme over-estimates, *Journal of Criminal Law and Criminology* vol. 87: 1430.

Hemenway, D. 2004 *Private Guns, Public Health*. Ann Arbor, MI, University of Michigan Press.

Hemenway, D. 2009 How to find nothing, *Journal of Public Health Policy* vol. 30 (3): 260–268.

Hemenway, D. and Solnick, S.J. 1995 Firearm training and storage, *Journal of the American Medical Association* vol. 273 (1): 46–50.

Hemenway, D., Prothrow-Stith, D., Bergstein, J.M., Ander, R. and Kennedy, B. 1996 Gun carrying among adolescents, *Law and Contemporary Problems* vol. 59 (1): 39–53.

Henigan, D.A. 2009 *Lethal Logic: Exploding the Myths that Paralyze American Gun Policy*. Dulles, VA, Potomac Books.

Hennop, E. 1997 Illegal firearms in circulation in South Africa, in Gamba, V. (ed.) *Society under Siege*, vol. 1. Oxford, Institute for Security Studies.

Hennop, E., Potgieter, J. and Jefferson, C. 2001 *The Role of Firearms in Crime in South Africa: A Detailed Analysis of Police Dockets*. Pretoria, ISS Monograph no. 55.

Henry, S. 2009 School violence beyond Columbine: a complex problem in need of an interdisciplinary analysis, *American Behavioral Scientists* vol. 52 (9): 1246–1265.

Heyman, S.J. 2000 Natural rights and the Second Amendment, in Bogus, C.T. (ed.) *The Second Amendment in Law and History: Historians and Constitutional Scholars on the Right to Bear Arms*. New York, The New Press.

Himmelfarb, G. 1996 *The De-moralization of Society: From Victorian Virtues to Modern Values*. London, Vintage Books.

HM Government 2008 *Youth Crime Action Plan*. London, Central Office for Information.

HM Government 2011a *Ending Gang and Youth Violence*. A cross-government report including further evidence and good practice case studies. London, The Stationery Office.

HM Government 2011b *The Government Response to the Third Report From the Home Affairs Committee Session 2010–11 HC 447, Firearms Control*. Cm 8155. London, The Stationery Office.

HM Government 2012 *Ending Gang and Youth Violence Report: One Year On*. Cm 8493 (Session 2012–2013). London, The Stationery Office.

Hodgson, D.L. 2004 *Once Intrepid Warriors: Gender, Ethnicity and the Cultural Politics of Maasai Development*. Bloomington, CT, Indiana University Press.

Holland, C. 2013 *The Report of the Azelle Rodney Inquiry*. House of Commons, HC 552. London, The Stationery Office.

Holzmann, N. 2006 *Missing Men, Waking Women: A Gender Perspective on Organised Armed Violence in Brazil*, the International Yearbook of Regional Human Rights Master's Programmes, Centre for Human Rights, Faculty of Law, University of Pretoria.

Home Office 2004 *Connected: Together We Can Tackle Gun Crime*. Birmingham Botanical Gardens, 19 and 20 January.

Home Office 2006 *The Second Connected Conference: Building on our Work Together to Tackle Guns, Knives and Gang-related Crime in England and Wales*. Oxford, 24 May.

Home Office 2008 *Saving Lives. Reducing Harm. Protecting the Public: An Action Plan for Tackling Violence 2008–11*. London, the Home Office.

Home Office 2008b *Violent Crime Action Plan*. Home Office, London, The Stationery Office.

Home Office 2008c *Tackling Gangs Action Plan*. Home Office, London, The Stationery Office.

Home Office, Research and Statistics Directorate 1996 Annex G: Gun Availability and Violent Crime: Research Evidence, Appendix 21 in Volume II of the House of Commons: Home Affairs Committee, *Fifth Report: The Possession of Handguns*. Minutes of Evidence, HMSO HC 393-ii.

Honwana, A. 2006 *Child Soldiers in Africa*. Philadelphia, PA, University of Pennsylvania Press.

Horovitz, B. 2013 Starbucks CEO says guns not welcome in stores, *USA Today* 18 September.

Horwitz, J. and Anderson, C. 2009 *Guns, Democracy and the Insurrectionist Idea*. Ann Arbor, MI, University of Michigan Press.

House of Commons: European Scrutiny Committee 2010 *The Marketing of Replica Firearms: Commission Report Considered by the Committee on 27 October 2010*. London, The Stationery Office, COM(10) 404.

House of Commons: Home Affairs Committee 1996 *Fifth Report: The Possession of Handguns*. Volume I, Report and Proceedings, Volume II, Minutes of Evidence, HMSO HC 393-i/ii.

House of Commons: Home Affairs Committee 2000 *Second Report: Controls over Firearms*. HC 95 i-ii. London, The Stationery Office.

House of Commons: Home Affairs Committee 2010 *Third Report: Firearms Control*. HC 447-i. London, The Stationery Office.

House of Commons: Home Affairs Select Committee 2007 *Second Report: Young Black People and the Criminal Justice System*. HC 181-i. London, The Stationery Office.

Hsieh, C.C. and Pugh, M.D. 1993 Poverty, income inequality, and violent crime: a meta-analysis of recent aggregate data studies, *Criminal Justice Review*, vol. 18 (2): 182–202.

Huggins, M.K. 2002 Modernity and devolution: the making of police death squads in modern Brazil, in Campbell, B.B. and Brenner, A.D. (eds) *Death Squads in Global Perspective: Murder with Deniability*. Basingstoke, Palgrave-Macmillan.

Hughes, G. 2007 *The Politics of Crime and Community*. Basingstoke, Palgrave MacMillan.

Huguet, C. and de Carvalho, I.S. 2008 Violence in the Brazilian *Favelas* and the role of the police, *New Directions for Youth Development* vol. 119, Fall: 93–109.

Hume, M. 2004 *Armed Violence and Poverty in El Salvador: A Case Study for the Armed Violence and Poverty Initiative*. University of Bradford, Centre for International Co-operation and Security.

Hutchinson, A. 2013 *The National School Shield: Report of the National School Shield Task Force*. 2 April.

ICRC (International Committee of the Red Cross) 1999 *Arms Availability and the Situation of Civilians in Armed Conflict*. Geneva, ICRC.

Ignatieff, M. 2005 Introduction: American exceptionalism and human rights, in Ignatieff, M. (ed.) *American Exceptionalism and Human Rights*. Princeton, NJ, Princeton University Press.

Ikelegbe, A. 2005 The economy of conflict in the oil rich Niger Delta region of Nigeria, *Nordic Journal of African Studies* vol. 14 (2): 208–234.

Inciardi, J.A. 1986 *The War on Drugs: Heroin, Cocaine, Crime, and Public Policy*. Palo Alto, CA, Mayfield Publishing Company.

Inciardi, J.A., Horowitz, R. and Pottieger, A.E. 1993 *Street Kids, Street Drugs, Street Crime: An Examination of Drug Use and Serious Delinquency in Miami*. Belmont, CA, Wadsworth.

Innes, M. 2004 Signal crimes and signal disorders: notes on deviance as communicative action, *British Journal of Sociology* vol. 55: 335.

IPCC 2009 *Report Following the IPCC Independent Investigation into the Fatal Shooting of Terry Nicholas at Hanger Green, London on Tuesday 15 May 2007*. London, IPCC.

IPCC 2010 *Independent Investigation into the Fatal Shooting of Mark Saunders on 6 May 2008*. London, IPCC.

ISS (Institute for Security Studies) 2013 *Factsheet: South Africa's Official Crime Statistics for 2012/13*. Pretoria, ISS.

Iweala, U. 2005 *Beasts of No Nation*. London, John Murray Publishers.

Jackson, T. and Marsh, N. 2012 Guns and deaths: a critical review, in Greene, O. and Marsh, N. (eds) *Small Arms, Crime and Conflict: Global Governance and the Threat of Armed Violence*. London, Routledge.

Jacobs, J. 2002 *Can Gun Control Work?* Oxford and New York, Oxford University Press.

Jeffords, S. 1989 *The Re-masculinisation of America: Gender and the Vietnam War*. Bloomington, IN, Indiana University Press.

Jeffords, S. 1994 *Hard Bodies: Hollywood Masculinity in the Reagan Era*. New Brunswick, NJ, Rutgers University Press.

Jenkins, H. 2006 Violent video games do not create school shooters, in Hunnicutt, S. (ed.) *School Shootings*. Detroit, MI, Greenhaven Press.

Jennings, K.M. 2007 *The War Zone as Social Space: Social Research in Conflict Zones*. Oslo, New Security Programme, FAFO Report 08.

Jensen, S. 2008 *Gangs, Politics and Dignity in Cape Town*. Chicago, IL, University of Chicago Press.

Jewkes, R., Dunkle, K., Koss, M.P., Levin, J.B., Nduna, M., Jama, N. and Sikweyiya, Y. 2006 Rape perpetration by young, rural South African men: prevalence, patterns and risk factors, *Social Science and Medicine* vol. 63: 2949–2961.

Johnson, M.A. 2012 Tale of two cities: homicides plummet in New York, leap in Chicago, *NBC News* 29 December.

Johnston, L. 1996 What is vigilantism? *British Journal of Criminology* vol. 36 (2): 220–236.

Johnston, N., Godnick, W., Watson, C. and von Tangen Page, M. 2005 *Putting a Human Face to the Problem of Small Arms Proliferation: Gender Implications for the Effective Implementation of the UN Programme of Action to Prevent, Combat and Eradicate the Illicit Trade in Small Arms and Light Weapons in all its Aspects*. London, International Alert.

Jones, G. and Rodgers, D. (eds) 2009 *Youth Violence in Latin America*. New York, Palgrave Macmillan.

Jones, T. and Newburn, T. 2002 The transformation of policing: understanding current trends in policing systems, *British Journal of Criminology* vol. 42: 129–146.

Joseph, J. and Pearson, P.G. 2002 Black youth and illegal drugs, *Journal of Black Studies* March, vol. 32 (4): 422–438.

Josephs, J. 1993 *Hungerford: One Man's Massacre*. London, Smith Gryphon Publishers.

Justice Policy Institute 2002 *Cell-blocks or Classrooms: The Funding of Higher Education and Corrections and its Impact on African American Men*. Washington, DC, Justice Policy Institute.

Jutersonke, O., Krause, K. and Muggah, R. 2007 Guns in the city: urban landscapes of armed violence, *Small Arms Survey 2007: Guns and the City*. Cambridge, Cambridge University Press.

Kahn, N. 2010 *Mojahir Militancy in Pakistan: Violence and Transformation in the Karachi Conflict*. London, Routledge.

Kaiza, P. 2008 Homicides, recorded crimes involving firearms, in Povey, D., Coleman, K., Kaiza, P., Hoare, J. and Jansson, K. (eds) *Homicides, Firearm Offences and Intimate Violence 2006/07* (Supplementary Volume 2 to Crime in England and Wales 2006/07), 31 January, Home Office online report 03/08. www.homeoffice.gov.uk/rds/pdfs08/hosb0308.pdf (accessed 13 April 2014).

Kangas, O. 1994 The politics of social security: on regressions, qualitative comparisons and cluster analysis, in Janoski, T. and Hicks, A. (eds) *The Comparative Political Economy of the Welfare State*. Cambridge, Cambridge University Press, pp. 346–365.

Kantola, J., Norocel, O.C. and Repo, J. 2011 Gendering violence in the school shootings in Finland. *European Journal of Women's Studies* vol. 18 (2): 183–197.

Karmen, A. 2000 *New York Murder Mystery: The True Story Behind the Crime Crash of the 1990s*. New York, New York University Press.

Karp, A. 1994 The rise of black and gray markets, *The Annals of the American Academy of Political and Social Science* vol. 535: 175–189.

Karp, A. 2007 Completing the count: civilian firearms: annexes online, *Small Arms Survey 2007: Guns and the City*. Cambridge, Cambridge University Press.

Karp, A. 2010 Elusive arsenals: gang and group firearms, *Small Arms Survey 2010: Gangs Groups and Guns*. Cambridge, Cambridge University Press.

Karp, A. 2011 Estimating civilian owned firearms, *Small Arms Survey Research Note*, Number 9 September. www.smallarmssurvey.org/fileadmin/docs/H-Research_Notes/SAS-Research-Note-9.pdf (accessed 13 April 2014).

Katz, J. and Jhally, S. 1999 The national conversation in the wake of Littleton is missing the mark, *The Boston Globe* 2 May, p. E1.

Kau, I. 2012 Firearms offences, in Smith, K. (ed.) *Homicides, Firearm Offences and Intimate Violence, Supplementary Volume 2 to Crime in England and Wales 2010/11*. London, the Stationery Office.

Keegan, M. 2005 *The Proliferation of Firearms in South Africa, 1994–2004*. Braamfontein, Gun Free South Africa.

Kellerman, A.L. 1993 Gun ownership as a risk factor for homicide in the home, *New England Journal of Medicine* vol. 329: October.

Kellerman, A.L. and Reay, D.T. 1986 Protection or peril, *New England Journal of Medicine* vol. 314 (24): June.

Kellerman, A.L., Somes, G., Rivara, F.P., Lee, R.K. and Banton, J.G. 1998 Injuries and death due to firearms in the home, *The Journal of Trauma: Injury, Infection and Critical Care* vol. 45 (2): 263–267.

Kellner, D. 2008 *Guys and Guns Amok: Domestic Terrorism and School Shootings from the Oklahoma City Bombing to the Virginia Tech Massacre*. Boulder, CO, Paradigm Books.

Kennedy, D. 2011 *Don't Shoot: One Man, a Street Fellowship and the End of Violence in Inner City America*. London, Bloomsbury.

Kennedy, D., Braga, A. and Piehl, A.M. 1996 Gun buy-backs: where do we stand and where do we go?, in Plotkin, M.R. (ed.) *Under Fire: Gun Buy-Backs, Exchanges and Amnesty Programs*. Washington, DC, Police Executive Research Forum.

Kennett, L. and Anderson, J.L. 1975 *The Gun in America: The Origins of a National Dilemma*. Westport, CT, Greenwood Press.

Khan, N. 2010 *Mohajir Militancy in Pakistan: Violence and Transformation in the Karachi Conflict*. Abingdon, Routledge.

Kidd, S.T. and Meyer, C. 2000 *Similarities of School Shootings in Rural and Small Town Communities*. Unpublished, Academy of Criminal Justice Sciences, 38th Annual Meeting, Washington, DC.

Kiilakoski, T. and Oksanan, A. 2011 Soundtrack of the school shootings: cultural script, music and male rage, *Young* vol. 19 (3): 247–369.

Killias, M. 1993 Gun ownership, suicide and homicide: an international perspective, in del Frate, A., Zvekic, U. and van Dijk J.J. (eds) *Understanding Crime and Experiences of Crime and Crime Control*. Rome, UNICRI Publication no. 49.

Killias, M., van Kesteren, J. and Rindlisbacher, M. 2001 Guns, violent crime and suicide in 21 countries, *Canadian Journal of Criminology* vol. 43: 429–448.

Kimmel, M. 2008 Profiling school shooters and shooter's schools: the cultural contexts of aggrieved entitlement and restorative masculinity, in Agger, B. and Luke, T.W. (eds) *There is a Gunman on Campus: Tragedy and Terror at Virginia Tech*. Lanham, MD, Rowman and Littlefield.

Kimmel, M. and Mahler, M. 2003 Adolescent masculinity, homophobia and violence: random school shootings, 1982–2001, *American Behavioural Scientist* vol. 46 (10): 1439–1458.

King, A.E.O. 1997 Understanding violence among young African American males: an Afrocentric perspective, *Journal of Black Studies* vol. 28 (1), September: 79–96.

King, C.R. 2007 Arming desire: the sexual force of guns in the United States, in Springwood, C.F. (ed.) *Open Fire: Understanding Global Gun Cultures*. New York, Berg.

Kingsbury, K. 2012 Firearm homicides vs. gun prevalence. http://aphyr.com/posts/261-firearm-homicides-vs-gun-prevalence (accessed 2 August 2013).

Kinnes, I. 2000 *From Urban Street Gangs to Criminal Empires*. Cape Town, Institute for Security Studies (ISS).

Kirby, E.J. 2013 Switzerland guns: Living with firearms the Swiss way. *BBC News Magazine* 11 February.

Klare, M. 1999 The international trade in light weapons: what have we learned?, in Boutwell, J. and Klare, M.T. (eds) *Light Weapons and Civil Conflict: Controlling the Tools of Violence*. New York, Rowman and Littlefield.

Klare, M. and Anderson, D. 1996 A *Scourge of Guns: The Diffusion of Small Arms and Light Weapons in Latin America*. Washington, DC, The Arms Sales Monitoring Project, Federation of American Scientists.

Kleck, G. 1991 *Point Blank: Guns and Violence in America*. New York, Aldine De Gruyter.

Kleck, G. 1997 *Targeting Guns: Firearms and their Control*. New York, Aldine De Gruyter.

Kleck, G. 1999 There are no lessons to be learned from Littleton, *Criminal Justice Ethics* vol. 18: 60–63.

Kleck, G. and Gertz, M. 1995 Armed resistance to crime: the prevalence and nature of self-defence with a gun, *Journal of Criminal Law and Criminology* vol. 86: 150.

Kleck, G. and Gertz, M. 1997 The illegitimacy of one-sided speculation: getting the defensive gun use estimate down, *Journal of Criminal Law and Criminology* vol. 87: 1446.

Kleck, G. and Kates, D. 2001 *Armed: New Perspectives on Gun Control*. New York, Prometheus Books.

Klein, J. 2005 Teaching her a lesson: media misses boys' rage relating to girls in school shootings, *Crime Media Culture* vol. 1; 91–97.

Klein, J. 2006 Cultural capital and high school bullies, *Men and Masculinities* vol. 9 (1): 53–75.

Klein, M. 1995 *The American Street Gang: Its Nature, Prevalence and Control*. Oxford: Oxford University Press.

Klein, M., Kerner, H-J., Maxson, C. and Weitekamp, E. (eds) 2000 *The Eurogang Paradox: Street Gangs and Youth Groups in the US and Europe*. Dordrecht, Kluwer Academic Publishers.

Klockars, C.B. 1980 The dirty Harry problem, *The ANNALS of the American Academy of Political and Social Science* vol. 452 (1): 22–47.

Klofas, J.M., Delaney, C. and Smith, T. 2007 *Strategic Approaches to Community Safety Initiative (SACSI) in Rochester, NY*. U.S. Department of Justice/ NCJRS. Document No. 220488. https://www.ncjrs.gov/pdffiles1/nij/grants/220488.pdf (accessed 13 April 2014).

Knight, G. 2010 *Hood Rat: Britain's Lost Generation*. London, Pan-MacMillan.

Kohn, A. 2004a *The Wild West Down Under: Comparing American and Australian Expressions of Gun Enthusiasm*. Unpublished paper.

Kohn, A. 2004b *Shooters: Myths and Realities of America's Gun Cultures*. Oxford, Oxford University Press.

Koonings, K. and Kruijt, D. 2004 Armed actors, organised violence and state failure in Latin America: a survey of issues and arguments, in Koonings, K. and Kruijt, D. (eds) *Armed Actors: Organised Violence and State Failure in Latin America*. London, Zed Books.

Koonings, K and Kruijt, D. (eds) 2007 *Fractured Cities: Social Exclusion, Urban Violence and Contested Spaces in Latin America*. London, Zed Books.

Kopel, D.B. 1992 Switzerland: the armed society, in Kopel, D.B. (ed.) *The Samurai, The Mountie and the Cowboy*. New York, Prometheus Books.

Kopel, D.B. 1999 '*Clueless': The Misuse of BATF Firearms Tracing Data*. Michigan State University, Detroit College of Law Review, pp. 171–180.

Kopel, D.B. 2009 Pretend – gun-free school zones: a deadly legal fiction, *Connecticut Law Review* vol. 42 (2), December: 515–584.

Kopel, D.B. 2012 Canada abolishes long gun registry, *The Volokh Conspiracy* 5 April. www.volokh.com/2012/04/05/canada-abolishes-long-gun-registry (accessed 13 April 2014).

Kopel, D.B., Gallant, P. and Eisen, J.D. 2003 Global deaths from firearms: searching for plausible estimates, *Texas Review of Law and Politics* vol. 114 (1).

Kopel, D.B., Gallant, P. and Eisen, J.D. 2006 Review of Malcolm 'guns and violence: the English experience', *Journal of Law, Economics and Policy* vol. 2 (2): 417–425.

Kopel, D.B., Gallant, P. and Eisen, J.D. 2008 Human rights and gun confiscation 26, *Quinnipiac Law Review* vol. 2: 385–438.

Kopel, D.B., Gallant, P. and Eisen, J.D. 2010 How many global deaths from arms: reasons to question the 740,000 factoid being used to promote the arms trade treaty, *NYU Journal of Law and Liberty* vol. 5: 674–715.

Koper, C.S. 2004 *Updated Assessment of the Federal Assault Weapons Ban: Impacts on Gun Markets and Gun Violence, 1994–2003*. Report to the National Institute of Justice, United States Department of Justice. Jerry Lee Center of Criminology, University of Pennsylvania.

Koper, C.S. 2013 America's experience with the federal assault weapons ban, 1994–2004: key findings and implications, in Webster, D.W. and Vernick, J.S. (eds) *Reducing Gun Violence in America: Informing Policy with Evidence and Analysis*. Baltimore, MD, Johns Hopkins University Press.

Koper, C. and Reuter, P. 1996 Suppressing illegal gun markets: lessons from drug enforcement, *Law and Contemporary Problems* vol. 59 (1): 119–146.

Koper, C. and Shelley, M. 2007 *Gun Crime Risk Factors: Buyer, Seller, Firearm and Transaction Characteristics Associated with Gun Trafficking and Criminal Gun Use*. US DOJ, Report to the National Institute of Justice.

Korpi, W. and Palme, J. 1998 The paradox of redistribution and strategies of equality: welfare state institutions, inequality, and poverty in the Western countries, *American Sociological Review* vol. 63 (5): 661–687.

Kraska, P. 2001 Playing war: masculinity, militarism and their real-world consequences, in Kraska, P. (ed.) *Militarizing the American Criminal Justice System: The Changing Roles of the Armed Forces and the Police*, Boston, Northeastern University Press, pp. 141–147.

Kraska, P. and Kappeler, V.E. 1997 Militarizing American police: the rise and normalization of paramilitary units, *Social Problems* vol. 44 (1): 1–18.

Krause, K. 1992 *Arms and the State: Patterns of Military Production and Trade*. Cambridge, Cambridge University Press.

Krause, K. and Milliken, J. 2009 The challenge of non-state armed groups, *Contemporary Security Policy* vol. 30 (2): 202–220.

Kreutz, J. and Marsh, N. 2012 Lethal instruments: small arms and deaths in armed conflict, in Greene, O. and Marsh, N. (eds) *Small Arms, Crime and Conflict: Global Governance and the Threat of Armed Violence*. London, Routledge.

Kreutz, J., Marsh, N. and Torre, M. 2012 Regaining state control: arms and violence in post conflict countries, in Greene, O. and Marsh, N. (eds) *Small Arms, Crime and Conflict: Global Governance and the Threat of Armed Violence*. London, Routledge.

Krug, E.G., Mercy, J.A., Dahlberg, L.L., Zwi, A.B. and Lozano, R. (eds) *2002 World Report on Violence and Health*. Geneva, World Health Organization.

Kunkeler, J. and Peters, K. 2011 'The boys are coming to town': youth, armed conflict and urban violence in developing countries, *International Journal of Conflict and Violence* vol. 5 (2): 277–291.

Kynoch, G. 2003 Apartheid nostalgia: personal security concerns in South African townships, *South Africa Crime Quarterly* vol. 5 (3): 7–10.

La Pierre, W. 2006 *The Global War on Your Guns: Inside the UN Plan to Destroy the Bill of Rights*. Nashville, TN, Nelson Current.

Lacey, N. 2008 *The Prisoners' Dilemma: Political Economy and Punishment in Contemporary Democracies*. Cambridge, Cambridge University Press.

LaFree, G. and Tseloni, A. 2006 Democracy and crime: a multi-level analysis of homicide in 44 different countries, *The Annals of the American Academy of Political and Social Science* vol. 605: 25–49.

Lahti, A., Räsänen, P., Karvonen, K., Särkioja, T., Meyer-Rochow, V.B. and Hakko, H. 2006 Autumn peak in shooting suicides of children and adolescents from Northern Finland, *Neuropsychobiology* vol. 54: 140–146.

Lamb, G. 2008 *'Under the Gun': An Assessment of Firearm Crime and Violence in South Africa*. Report compiled for the Office of the President, Pretoria, South Africa, Institute for Security Studies.

Lappi-Seppala, T. 2007 Trust, welfare and political economy: cross-comparative perspectives in penal severity, in Traskman, P. (ed.) *Rationality and Emotion in European Penal Policy: Nordic Perspectives*. Unpublished.

Lappi-Seppala, T. 2012 Criminology, crime and criminal justice in Finland, *European Journal in Criminology* vol. 9: 206–222.

Larkin, R.W. 2007 *Comprehending Columbine*. Philadelphia, PA: Temple University Press.

Larkin, R.W. 2009 The Columbine legacy: rampage shootings as political acts, *American Behavioral Scientists* vol. 52 (9): 1309–1326.

Latour, B. 1999 *Pandora's Hope: Essays on the Reality of Science Studies*. Cambridge, MA, Harvard University Press.

Lau, I. 2012 Recorded offences involving the use of firearms, in Smith, K. (ed.) *Homicides, Firearm Offences and Intimate Violence 2010/11: Supplementary Volume 2 to Crime in England and Wales 2010/11*. Home Office 02/12.

Laurance, E.J. 1996 *The New Field of Micro-Disarmament*. Briefing 7. Bonn, Bonn International Center for Conversion, September.

Laurance, E.J. 1999 Light weapons and human development: the need for transparency and early warning, in Boutwell, J. and Klare, M.T. (eds) 1999 *Light Weapons and Civil Conflict: Controlling the Tools of Violence*. Oxford, Rowman and Littlefield.

Lawrence, R.G. and Birkland, T.A. 2004 Guns, Hollywood, and school safety: defining the school-shooting problem across the public arenas, *Social Science Quarterly* vol. 85: 1193–1207.

Lawrence, R.G. and Mueller, D. 2003 School shootings and the man-bites-dog criterion of newsworthiness, *Youth Violence and Juvenile Justice* vol. 1 (4): 330–345.

Lazare, D. 1996 *The Frozen Republic: How the Constitution is Paralyzing Democracy*. Orlando, FL Harcourt, Brace & Co.

Lea, J. 1999 Social crime revisited, *Theoretical Criminology* vol. 3 (3): 307–325.

Leander, A. 2005 The market for force and public security: the destabilizing consequences of private military companies, *Journal of Peace Research* vol. 42 (5): 605–622.

Leary, M.R., Kowalski, R.M., Smith, L. and Philips, S. 2003 Teasing, rejection and violence: case studies of the school shootings, *Aggressive Behaviour* vol. 29: 202–214.

LeBrun, E. and Muggah, R. (eds) 2005 *Silencing Guns: Local Perspectives on Small Arms and Armed Violence in Rural South Pacific Islands Communities*. Geneva, Small Arms Survey, Occasional Paper no. 15.

Lebrun, M. 2009 *Books, Blackboards and Bullets: School Shootings and Violence in America*. New York, Rowman and Littlefield.

Lee, T. 2012 America's race: what effect will demographic shifts, made unavoidably clear in the 2012 presidential election, have on US politics in the long term? *Royal Society of the Arts Journal* Winter: 10–15.

Lee, W.-S. and Suardi, S. 2010 The Australian firearms buyback and its effect on gun deaths, *Contemporary Economic Policy* vol. 28 (1) January: 65–79.

Legge, J. 2013 US government orders Cody Wilson and defense distributed to remove blueprint for 3D-printed handgun from the web, *The Independent* 10 May.

Leibfreid, S. 1992 Towards a European welfare state, in Ferge, Z. and Kolberg, J.E. (eds) *Social Policy in a Changing Europe*. Frankfurt, Campus-Verlag, pp. 245–279.

Leigh, A. and Neill, C. 2010 Do gun buybacks save lives? Evidence from panel data. Discussion paper series *Forschungsinstitut zur Zukunft der Arbeit*, no. 4995. http://www.econstor.eu/handle/10419/36943 (accessed 13 April 2014).

Leitzel, J. 2003 Comment on Reuter and Mouzos, in Ludwig, J. and Cook, P. (eds) *Evaluating Gun Policy: Effects on Crime and Violence*. Washington, DC, The Brookings Institute.

Lemanski, C. 2004 A new apartheid? The spatial implications of fear of crime in Cape Town, South Africa, *Environment and Urbanization* vol. 16 (2): 101–112.

Lenis, D., Ronconi, L. and Schargrodsky, E. 2010 *The Effect of the Argentine Gun Buy-Back Program on Crime and Violence.* Unpublished paper, Universidad Torcuato Di Tella. http://socrates.berkeley.edu/~raphael/IGERT/Workshop/PEVAF_September_27_2010.pdf (accessed 13 April 2014).

Lepore, J. 2010 *The Whites of their Eyes: The Tea Party's Revolution and the Battle over American History.* Princeton, NJ and Oxford, Princeton University Press.

Lepore, J. 2012a The Lost Amendment, *New Yorker Magazine* 19 April.

Lepore, J. 2012b Battleground America: one nation, under the gun, *New Yorker Magazine* 23 April.

Lerner, R.L. 2006 The worldwide popular revolt against proportionality in self defense law, *Journal of Law, Economics and Policy* vol. 2 (2): 213–220.

Lessing, B. 2005 The demand for firearms in Brazil's urban periphery: a comparative study, in Dreyfus, P., Guedes, L.E., Lessing, B., Bandeira, A.R., de Sousa Nascimento, M. and Rivero, P. (eds) *Small Arms in Rio de Janeiro: The Guns, the Buyback, and the Victims,* Geneva, Small Arms Survey, Viva Rio/ISER.

Levitas, R. 1996 The concept of social exclusion and the new Durkheimian hegemony, *Critical Social Policy* vol. 16 (46): 5–20.

Levitt, S. 2004 Understanding why crime fell in the 1990s: four factors that explain the decline and six that do not, *The Journal of Economic Perspectives* vol. 18 (1): 163–190.

Levitt, S. and Dubner, S.J. 2005 *Freakonomics: A Rogue Economist Explores the Hidden Side of Everything.* Harmondsworth, Penguin.

Lichtblau, E. 2004 Key antigun program loses direct financing, *New York Times* 2 December.

Lindberg, N., Sailas, E. and Kaltiala-Heino, R. 2012 The copycat phenomenon after two Finnish school shootings: an adolescent psychiatric perspective, *BMC Psychiatry* vol. 12: 91–106.

Lindgren, J. 2002 Fall from grace: arming America and the Bellesiles scandal, *Yale Law Journal* vol. 111: 2195–2249.

Lindgren, J. and Heather, J.L. 2002 Counting guns in early America, *William & Mary Law Review* vol. 43 (5): 1777–1842.

Lins, P. 2006 *City of God.* London, Bloomsbury.

Lipset, S.M. 1996 *American Exceptionalism: A Double-edged Sword.* New York, W.W. Norton.

Lissovsky, M. 2006 Television campaign and the disadventure of the YES that was NO, in Mota, M.A.R. and Crespo, S. (eds) *Referendum from Yes to No: A Brazilian Democracy Experience.* Rio de Janeiro, ISER (Institute for Religious Studies), Communication Number 62.

Lizotte, A.J., Krohn, M.D., Howell, J.C., Tobin, K. and Howard, G.J. 2000 Factors influencing gun carrying among young urban males over the adolescent-young adult life course, *Criminology* vol. 38 (3): 811–834.

Lloyd, J.M. 2012 The fire next time, *City* vol. 16 (4): 431–438.

Loeber, R. and Farrington, D.P. (eds) 1998 *Serious and Violent Juvenile Offenders: Risk Factors and Successful Interventions.* Thousand Oaks, CA, Sage.

Loney, M. 1983 *Community Against Government. The British Community Development Project 1968–78: A Study of Government Incompetence.* London, Heinemann.

Lott, J.R. 1998 *More Guns, Less Crime: Understanding Crime and Gun Control Laws.* Chicago, IL, University of Chicago Press.

Louise, C. 1995 *The Social Impacts of Light Weapons Availability and Proliferation.* Discussion Paper DP59. Geneva, United Nations Research Institute for Social Development, March. http://www.essex.ac.uk/armedcon/story_id/Social%20Impact%20.pdf (accessed 13 April 2014).

Luck, A. 2009 The 'usual suspects': how the Baikal became Britain's favourite killing machine, *Daily Mail* 11 January.

Ludwig, J. 1998 Concealed-gun-carrying laws and violent crime: evidence from state panel data, *International Review of Law and Economics* vol. 18 (3) September: 239–254.

Ludwig, J. and Cook, P. (eds) 2003 *Evaluating Gun Policy: Effects on Crime and Violence*. Washington, DC, Brookings Institute Press.

Luke, T.W. 2008 'April 16 2007, at Virginia Tech – To: Multiple Recipients: "A Gunman is loose on Campus…"' in Agger, B. and Luke, T.W. 2008 *There is a Gunman on Campus: Tragedy and Terror at Virginia Tech*. Lanham, MD, Rowman and Littlefield.

Lumpe, L. 1999a Global arms bazaar at century's end, *Global Dialogue* vol. 1 (2) Autumn. www.worlddialogue.org/content.php?id=34 (accessed 13 April 2014).

Lumpe, L. 1999b U.S. policy and the export of light weapons, in Boutwell, J. and Klare, M.T. (eds) *Light Weapons and Civil Conflict: Controlling the Tools of Violence*. New York, Rowman and Littlefield.

Lumpe, L. (ed.) 2000 *Running Guns: The Global Black Market in Small Arms*. London, Zed Books.

Lund, N. 2006 A constitutional right to self-defense? *Journal of Law, Economics and Policy* vol. 2 (2): 213–220.

Lytton, T.D. 2006 *Suing the Gun Industry: A Battle at the Crossroads of Gun Control and Mass Torts*, Ann Arbor, MI, University of Michigan.

McAra, L. and McVie, S. 2010 Youth crime and justice: key messages from the Edinburgh study of youth transitions and crime, *Criminology and Criminal Justice* vol. 10: 211–230.

MacAskill, E. 2012 Obama vows to take on the gun lobby, *The Guardian* 20 December.

McCarthy, M. 2009 *Consuming Guns: Motives and Social Interaction of Australian Sports Shooters*. Saarbrucken, Germany, VDM Verlag.

McCarthy, M. 2011 Researching Australian gun ownership: respondents never lie … or do they?, in Ashwin, M. (ed.) *The Proceedings of the 10th European Conference on Research Methodology for Business and Management studies*. Caen, Normandy Business School.

McClellan, C. and Tekin, E. 2012 *Stand Your Ground Laws and Homicides*. Bonn, Institute for the Study of Labour, IZA Discussion Paper no. 6705, July.

Macdonald, G. 2012 Precedent in the making: the UN meeting of governmental experts, *Small Arms Survey 2012: Moving Targets*. Cambridge, Cambridge University Press.

Macdonald, G. 2013 Second wind: the PoA's 2012 review conference, *Small Arms Survey 2013: Everyday Dangers*. Cambridge, Cambridge University Press.

Macdonald, G., Hasan, S. and Stevenson, C. 2007 Back to basics: transfer controls in global perspective, *Small Arms Survey 2007: Guns and the City*. Cambridge, Cambridge University Press.

McDowall, D. and Loftin, C. 1983 Collective security and the demand for legal handguns, *American Journal of Sociology* vol. 88 (6): 1146–1161.

McDowell, D. and Wiersma, B. 1994 The incidence of defensive firearm use by U.S. crime victims, 1987 through 1990, *American Journal of Public Health*, vol. 84: 1982–1984.

McGee, J.P. and DeBernardo, C.R. 2002 The classroom avenger, in Ribner, N.G. (ed.) *Handbook of Juvenile Forensic Psychology*. San Francisco, CA, Jossey-Bass, pp. 230–249.

McGonigal, M.D. 1993 Urban firearm deaths: a five-year perspective, *The Journal of Trauma* vol. 35 (4): 532–537.

McGreal, C. 2012 Obama faces fierce pressure over gun control as senators call for weapons ban, *The Guardian* 16 December.

McGreal, C. and Pilkington, E. 2012 Pressure mounts on Obama to show leadership on tougher gun controls, *The Guardian* 17 December.

Macgregor, J. 1998 Violence and social change in a border economy: war in the Maputo hinterland, *Journal of Southern African Studies* vol. 24 (1): 37–60.

Macha, T. 2006 The proliferation and effects of small arms and light weapons in urban centres in Tanzania: a case study of Dar es Salaam, in the Africa Peace Forum, *Controlling Small Arms in the Horn of Africa and the Great Lakes Region: Supporting Implementation of the Nairobi Declaration*. Nairobi, Africa Peace Forum and Project Ploughshares.

Mackay, B. 2004 Gunshot wounds: the new public health issue, *Canadian Medical Association Journal* vol. 170 (5): 780.

Mackie, P. 2013 'Antique guns' adapted by criminals facing weapons shortage, *BBC News Website* 22 October. http://www.bbc.co.uk/news/uk-england-24626158

McKinley, 2008 In Texas schools, teachers carry books and guns, *New York Times* 28 August.

McLagan, G. 2005 *Guns and Gangs: Inside Black Gun Crime*. London, Allison & Busby.

McPhedran, S. and Baker, J. 2008 Australian firearms legislation and unintentional firearm deaths: a theoretical explanation for the absence of decline following the 1996 gun laws, *Public Health* vol. 122: 297–299.

McWhirter, C. and Fields, G 2012 Communities struggle to break a grim cycle of killing, *Wall Street Journal* 18 August.

Mai, R. and Alpert, J. 2000 Separation and socialization: a feminist analysis of the school shootings at Columbine, *Journal for the Psychoanalysis of Culture and Society* vol. 5: 264–275.

Malcolm, J.L. 1994 *To Keep and Bear Arms: The Evolution of an Anglo-American Right*. Cambridge, MA, Harvard University Press.

Malcolm, J.L. 2002 *Guns and Violence: The English Experience*. Cambridge, MA, Harvard University Press.

Manwaring, M.G. 2007 *A Contemporary Challenge to State Sovereignty: Gangs and Other Illicit Transnational Criminal Organizations in Central America, El Salvador, Mexico, Jamaica, and Brazil*. Strategic Studies Institute, Carlisle, PA. http://www.StrategicStudiesInstitute.army.mil/

Marfleet, N. 2008 *Why Carry a Weapon? A Study of Knife Crime Amongst 15–17 Year Old Males in London*. London, Howard League for Penal Reform.

Marshall, B., Webb, B. and Tilley, N. 2005, *Rationalisation of Current Research on Guns, Gangs and Other Weapons: Phase 1*. University College, London, Jill Dando Institute of Crime Science.

Marshall, T.H. 1963 Citizenship and social class, in Marshall, T.H. (ed.) *Sociology at the Crossroads*. London, Heinemann.

Marx, K. 1976 *Capital, Volume 1*. Harmondsworth, Penguin.

Matthews, R. 1996 *Armed Robbery: Two Police Responses*. Home Office, Police Research Group, Crime Detection and Prevention Series, paper 78.

Matthews, R. 2002 *Armed Robbery*. Cullompton, Willan Publishing.

Mayer, M. 2010 Punishing the poor a debate: some questions on Wacquant's theorizing the neoliberal state, *Theoretical Criminology* vol. 14 (1): 93–103.

Marsh, N. 2012 The tools of insurgency: A review of small arms and light weapons in warfare, in Greene, O. and Marsh, N. (eds) *Small Arms, Crime and Conflict*. London, Routledge.

Marshall, E.P. and Sanow, E.J. 1992 *Handgun Stopping Power: The Definitive Study*. Boulder, CO, Paladin Press.

Marshall, E.P. and Sanow, E.J. 1996 *Street Stoppers: The Latest Handgun Stopping Power Street Results*. Boulder, CO, Paladin Press.

Marx, K. 1963 *The Eighteenth Brumaire of Louis Napoleon*. New York, International Publishers.

Mauser, G. 2001 *Misfire: Firearm Registration in Canada*. Simon Fraser University, Public Policy Sources no. 48.

May, D.C. 1999 Scared kids, unattached kids, or peer pressure: why do students carry firearms to school? *Youth and Society* vol. 31 (1): 100–127.

Mayhew, P. 2012 The case of Australia and New Zealand, in van Dijk, J., Tseloni, A. and Farrell, G. (eds) *The International Crime Drop: New Directions in Research*. Basingstoke, Palgrave Macmillan.

Mayors Against Illegal Guns (MAIG) 2010 *Trace the Guns: The Link Between Gun Laws and Interstate Gun Trafficking*. www.mayorsagainstillegalguns.org/downloads/pdf/trace_the_guns_report.pdf (accessed 13 April 2014).

Mayors Against Illegal Guns (MAIG) 2011 *Fatal Gaps: How Missing Records in the Federal Background Check System Put Guns in the Hands of Killers*. MAIG, November.

Mayors Against Illegal Guns (MAIG) 2012 *Gun Owners Poll: Results*, July. www.mayorsagainstillegalguns.org (accessed 13 April 2014).

Mburu, N. 2007 Warriors and guns: the anthropology of cattle rustling in North Eastern Africa, in Springwood, C.F. (ed.) *Open Fire: Understanding Global Gun Cultures*. New York, Berg.

Medina, J., Aldridge, J.A. and Ralphs, R. 2009 'Chimera' or 'Super Gangs'? Studying Youth Gangs in an English City. Unpublished paper. Centre for Criminological and Socio-Legal Research, University of Manchester.

Medina, J., Ralphs, R. and Aldridge, J.A. 2010 Mentoring siblings of gang members: a template for reaching families of gang members? *Children in Society* vol. 26 (1): 14–24.

Meek, S. 1997 Legal firearms in South Africa: a part of the problem?, in Gamba, V. (ed.) *Society under Siege*, vol. 1. Oxford, Institute for Security Studies.

Meek, S. 1999 Illegal weapons proliferation in Swaziland, in Nkwaine, T.C., Chaciua, M. and Meek, S. (eds) *Weapons Flows in Zimbabwe, Mozambique and Swaziland*. ISS monograph 34, Cape Town, Institute for Security Studies.

Meek, S. 2000 Transition and illegal weapons in South Africa: an overview, in Gamba, V. (ed.) *Society under Siege*, vol. 3. Oxford, Institute for Security Studies.

Meeks, D. 2006 Police militarization in urban areas: the obscure war against the underclass, *The Black Scholar* vol. 35, (4) Winter.

Meikle, J. 2013 Boy of five feared shot by eight-year-old, *The Guardian* 6 November.

Mellor, D. 1996a Why handguns must be banned, *Mail on Sunday* 17 March.

Mellor, D. 1996b No guns in the house, *The Guardian* 14 October.

Meloy, J.R., Hempel, A., Mohandie, K., Shive, A.A. and Gray, B.T. 2001 Offender and offence characteristics of a non-random sample of adolescent mass murderers, *Journal of the American Academy of Child and Adolescent Psychiatry* vol. 40: 719–728.

Melzer, S. 2009 *Gun Crusaders: The NRA's Culture War*. New York, New York University Press.

Merton, R.K. 1957 Social structure and anomie, in Merton, M.K. *Social Theory and Social Structure* (revised edition). Glencoe, Free Press.

Metropolitan Police Authority 2004 *Gun Crime Scrutiny: Final Report*. London, MPA, February.

Mieth, F. 2012 In between cattle raids and peace meetings: voices from the Kenya/Ugandan border region, in Witsenburg, K. and Zaal, F. (eds) *Spaces of Insecurity: Human Agency in Violent Conflicts in Kenya*. Leiden, The Africa Studies Centre.

Migeot, G. and De Kinder, J. 1999 Reactivating deactivated firearms, *Forensic Science International* vol. 103 (3): 173–179.

Miller, D. and Cukier, W. no date *Regulation of Civilian Possession of Small Arms and Light Weapons*. Biting the Bullet Report 16. London, International Alert.

Miller, J.G. 1996 *Search and Destroy: African–American Males in the Criminal Justice System.* Cambridge, Cambridge University Press.

Miller, L. 2008 *The Perils of Federalism: Race, Poverty, and the Politics of Crime Control.* Oxford and New York, Oxford University Press.

Millie, A. (ed.) 2009 *Securing Respect.* Bristol, Policy Press.

Milroy, C.M. 1993 Homicide followed by suicide (dyadic death) in Yorkshire and Humberside, *Medicine Science and Law* vol. 33 (2): 167–171.

Milroy, C.M. 1998 Homicide followed by suicide: remorse or revenge? *Journal of Clinical Forensic Medicine* vol. 5: 61–64.

Mir, L. 2004 *Civil War: State and Trauma.* Sao Paulo, Geracao Editora.

Mkutu, K.A. 2008 *Guns and Governance in the Rift Valley: Pastoralist Conflict and Small Arms.* Bloomington, IN, Indiana University Press.

Moore, M. 2002 *Bowling for Columbine* (documentary film).

Morris, L. 1994 *Dangerous Classes: The Underclass and Social Citizenship.* London, Routledge.

Morrison, S. and O'Donnell, I. 1994 *Armed Robbery: A Study in London.* Occasional Paper no. 15. Oxford, Centre for Criminological Research.

Morrison, S. and O'Donnell, I. 1997 Armed and dangerous? The use of firearms in robbery, *Howard Journal of Criminal Justice* vol. 36 (3): 305–320.

Morselli, C. 2012 Assessing network patterns in illegal firearm markets, *Crime Law and Social Change* vol. 57 (2): 129–149.

Morton, D. 2006 *Gunning for the World Foreign Policy.* January–February. www.alternet.org/ story/38268/gunning_for_the_world (accessed 13 April 2014).

Mota, M.A.R. 2006 The October 2005 referendum: from many conquests to unexpected defeat, in Mota, M.A.R. and Crespo, S. (eds) *Referendum from Yes to No: A Brazilian Democracy Experience.* Rio de Janeiro, ISER (Institute for Religious Studies), Communication Number 62.

Mouzos, J. 1999 International traffic in small arms: an Australian perspective. *Trends & Issues in Crime and Criminal Justice,* no. 104. Canberra: Australian Institute of Criminology.

Mouzos, J. 2000 The licensing and registration status of firearms used in homicide, *Trends & issues in Crime and Criminal Justice,* no. 151. http://www.aic.gov.au/documents/6/2/ A/%7B62AD9B59-92FB-43A1-8848-F1EFA8042F98%7Dti151.pdf (accessed 13 April 2014).

Muchembled, R. 2012 *A History of Violence.* Cambridge, Polity Press.

Muggah, H.C.R. 2001 Globalisation and insecurity: the direct and indirect effects of small arms availability. *University of Sussex IDS Bulletin* vol. 32 (2).

Muggah, R. and Batchelor, P. 2002 *Development Held Hostage: Assessing the Effects of Small Arms on Human Development – A Preliminary Study of the Socio-Economic Impacts and Development Linkages of Small Arms Proliferation, Availability and Use.* A report of the United Nations Development Programme, New York.

Mullins, C.W. 2006 *Holding Your Square: Masculinities, Streetlife and Violence.* Cullompton, Willan Publishing.

Munday, R. 1996 *Most Armed and Most Free.* Brightlingsea, Piedmont Publishing.

Mundt, R.J. 1990 Gun control and rates of firearms violence in Canada and the United States, *Canadian Journal of Criminology* vol. 32 (1): 137–154.

Musah, A.-F. 2002 Privatization of security, arms proliferation and the process of state collapse in Africa, *Development and Change* vol. 33 (5): 911–933.

Muschert, G.W. 2007a Research in school shootings, *Sociology Compass* vol. 1 (1): 60–80.

Muschert, G.W. 2007b The Columbine victims and the myth of the juvenile superpredator, *Youth Violence and Juvenile Justice* vol. 5 (4): 351–366.

Muschert, G. and Sumiala, J. (eds) 2012 *School Shootings: Mediatized Violence in a Global Age.* Bingley, UK, Emerald Group Publishing Limited.

Mutanen, A. 2009 Finnish gun laws under fire, *The Guardian* 31 December.

NABIS (National Ballistics Intelligence Service) 2011 Operational debrief: Olympic .380 BBM programme of activity [restricted document]. www.nabis.police.uk.

Nadim, F. 2013 Cops bust gun factory in Biharsharif, *The Times of India* 4 September.

National Alliance of Gang Investigators Associations 2005 *National Gang Threat Assessment.* Washington, DC, Bureau of Justice Assistance.

National Centre for Education Statistics – Indicators of School Safety 2011 https://nces. ed.gov/pubsearch/pubsinfo.asp?pubid=2012002rev (accessed 10 March 2014).

Navarro, V. and Shi, L. 2001 The political context of social inequalities and health, *Social Science and Medicine* vol. 52: 481–491.

Naylor, R.T. 1995 Loose cannons: covert commerce and underground finance in the modern arms black market, *Crime, Law and Social Change* vol. 22: 1–57.

Naylor, R.T. 1997 The rise of the modern arms black market and the failure of supply side controls, in Gamba, V. (ed.) *Society under Siege*, vol. 1. Oxford, Institute for Security Studies.

Neate, R. 2012 A week on from Newtown, business as usual for gun manufacturers and sellers, *The Guardian* 20 December.

Neill, C. and Leigh, A. 2007 *Weak Tests and Strong Conclusions: A Re-Analysis of Gun Deaths and the Australian Firearms Buyback.* The Australian National University, Centre for Economic Policy Research Discussion paper 555.

Nelken, D. 2010 Denouncing the penal state, *Criminology and Criminal Justice* vol. 10 (4): 331–340.

Neroni, H. 2000 The men of Columbine: violence and masculinity in American culture and film, *Journal for the Psychoanalysis of Culture and Society* vol. 5: 256–263.

Newburn, T. 1991 *Permission and Regulation: Law and Morals in Post-war Britain.* London, Routledge.

Newman, E. 2004 The 'New Wars' debate: a historical perspective is needed. *Security Dialogue* vol. 35 (2): 173–189.

Newman, E. 2009 Conflict research and the 'decline' of civil war, *Civil Wars* vol. 11 (3): 255–278.

Newman, K. 2006 School shootings are a serious problem, in Hunnicutt, S. (ed.) *School Shootings*. Detroit, MI, Thomson Gale.

Newman, K. and Fox, C. 2009 Repeat tragedy: rampage shootings in American high school and college settings, 2002–2008, *American Behavioral Scientists* vol. 52 (9): 1286–1308.

Newman, K.S., Fox, S., Harding, D.J., Mehta, J. and Roth, W. 2004 *Rampage: The Social Roots of School Shootings.* New York, Basic Books.

Nightingale, C. 1995 *On the Edge: A History of Poor Black Children and Their American Dreams.* New York, Basic Books.

Nina, D. 2000 Dirty Harry is back: vigilantism in South Africa – the (re)emergence of the 'good' and 'bad' community, *African Security Review* vol. 9 (1): 18–28.

Nisbett, R.E. and Cohen, D. 1996 *Culture of Honor: The Psychology of Violence in the South.* Boulder, CO, Westview Press.

North, M. 2000 *Dunblane: Never Forget.* London, Mainstream Publishing.

Nozick, R. 1974 *Anarchy, State and Utopia.* New York, Basic Books.

Nurmi, J. 2012 Making sense of school shootings: comparing local narratives of solidarity and conflict in Finland, *Traumatology* vol. 18: 16–28.

Obama, B. 2007 *The Audacity of Hope.* New York, Random House.

Obama, B. 2008 Acceptance Speech. http://uspolitics.about.com/od/speeches/a/obama_accept_4.htm (accessed 13 April 2014).

O'Connor, J.F., O'Connor, J.S. and Lizotte, A. 1978 The 'southern subculture of violence' thesis and patterns of gun ownership, *Social Problems* vol. 4 (1): 420–429.

O'Hare, P. 2012 Crime clan gun dealer jailed after 90 weapons seized from him were linked to Ulster terror groups, *Daily Record* 21 December.

Oksanen, A., Rasanen, P., Nurmi, J. and Lindstrom, K. 2010 'This can't happen here!': community reactions to school shootings in Finland, *Research on Finnish Society* vol. 3: 19–27.

Olinger, D. 1999 Police guns in the hands of criminals, *Denver Post* 20 September.

Oliver, M. 2003 Birmingham shooting victims named, *The Guardian* 3 January.

Olivera, M. 2006 Violencia femicida: violence against women and Mexico's structural crisis, *Latin American Perspectives* vol. 33: 104–114.

O'Neill, K.L. 2007 Armed citizens and the stories they tell: the National Rifle Association's achievement of terror and masculinity, *Men and Masculinities* vol. 9: 457–475.

O'Neill, S. 2008 Baikal: the gangsters' gun, *The Times* 21 July.

Osamba, J.O. 2000 The sociology of insecurity: cattle rustling and banditry in north-western Kenya, *African Journal on Conflict Resolution* vol. 1 (2): 11–37.

Ousely, H. 2001 *Community Pride – Not Prejudice.* Bradford, 20/20 Vision.

Oxfam and Amnesty International 2003 *Shattered Lives: The Case for Tough International Arms Control.* London, Amnesty International and Oxfam International.

Ozanne-Smith, J., Ashby, K., Newstead, S., Stathakis, V.Z. and Clapperton, A. 2004 Firearm related deaths: the impact of regulatory reform, *Injury Prevention* vol. 10: 280–286.

Parenti, C. 1999 *Lockdown America: Police and Prisons in an Age of Crisis.* London, Verso.

Pallister, D. 2006 Cold-blooded killer of Toni-Ann jailed for at least 40 years, *The Guardian* 5 August.

Palmer, S. and Pitts, J. 2006 'Othering' the brothers: black youth, racial solidarity and gun crime. *Youth & Policy* vol. 91.

Pascoe, C.I. 2005 'Dude, you're a fag': adolescent masculinity and the fag discourse, *Sexualities* vol. 8 (3): 329–346.

Pattugalan, G.R. 2004 Small arms proliferation and misuse: human security impact and policy actions in Southeast Asia, *Philippine Journal of Third World Studies* vol. 19 (1): 62–91.

Pauls, M.A. and Downie, J. 2004 Shooting ourselves in the foot: why mandatory reporting of gunshot wounds is a bad idea, *Canadian Medical Association Journal* vol. 170 (8): 1255–1256.

Pavlich, K. 2012 *Fast and Furious: Barack Obama's Bloodiest Scandal and its Shameless Cover-up.* Washington, DC, Regnery Publishing.

Payne, B.K. 2006 Weapon bias: split-second decisions and unintended stereotyping, *Current Directions in Psychological Science* vol. 15 (6): 287–291.

Peachey, P. 2013 Police winning battle against inner city gun crime, *The Independent* 24 January.

Pelser, E. 2008 *Learning to be Lost – Youth Crime in South Africa.* Discussion Paper for the HSRC youth policy initiative. Cape Town, Centre for justice and crime prevention.

Penn, D. 2001 *Basic Firearm Types: Common and Distinctive Operational and Design Characteristics between Categories of Firearms,* in WFSA, London, London Definitions Report.

Pepper, L.V. and Petrie, C.V. (eds) 2004 *Firearms and Violence: A Critical Review.* Washington, DC, The National Academy.

Pereira, A. 2005 *Political (In)justice: Authoritarianism and the Rule of Law in Brazil, Chile, and Argentina.* Pittsburgh, PA, Pittsburgh University Press.

Perlman, J. 1976 *The Myth of Marginality: Urban Poverty and Politics in Rio de Janeiro*. Berkeley, CA, University of California Press.

Perlman, J. 2010 *Favela: Four Decades of Living on the Edge*. New York, Oxford University Press.

Peroni, C. 2001 WFSA Report on United Nations Conference on the Illicit Trade in Small Arms and Light Weapons in all its Aspects. New York 9–20 July. www.wfsa.net

Perreault, S. 2012 *Homicide in Canada*. www.statcan.gc.ca/pub/85-002-x/2012001/article/11738-eng.htm (accessed 13 April 2014).

Perrone, S. and White, R. 2000 *Young People and Gangs*. Canberra, Australian Institute of Criminology. Trends and Issues paper no. 167.

Persad, I.J., Srinivas-Reddy, R., Saunders, M.A. and Patel, J. 2005 Gunshot injuries to the extremities: experience of a U.K. trauma centre, *Injury* vol. 36 (3), March: 407–411.

Peters, G. 2009 *Seeds of Terror: How Heroin is Bankrolling the Taliban and Al Qaeda*. Oxford, One World Books.

Peters, K., Richards, P. and Vlassenroot, K. 2003 *What Happens to Youth During and After Wars? A Preliminary Review of Literature on Africa and an Assessment of the Debate*. Netherlands Development Assistance Research Council, RAWOO Working Paper.

Peters, R. 2013 Rational firearm regulation: evidence based gun laws in Australia, in Webster, D.W. and Vernick, J.S. (eds) *Reducing Gun Violence in America: Informing Policy with Evidence and Analysis*. Baltimore, MD, Johns Hopkins University Press.

Peters, R. and Watson, C. 1996 A breakthrough in gun control in Australia after Port Arthur, *Injury Prevention* vol. 2: 253–254.

Pierce, G.L., Braga, A.A., Koper, C., McDevitt, J., Carlson, D., Roth, J., Saiz, A., Hyatt, R. and Griffith, R.E. 2004 *Characteristics and Dynamics of Crime Gun Markets: Implications for Supply-Side Focused Enforcement Strategies*. US Department of Justice, NCJRS Document number 208079.

Pinker, S. 2011 *The Better Angels of our Nature: A History of Violence and Humanity*. London, Penguin Books.

Pinnock, D. 1984 *The Brotherhoods: Street Gangs and State Control in Cape Town*. Cape Town, David Philip.

Pirseyedi, B. 2000 *The Small Arms Problem in Central Asia: Features and Implications*. Geneva, UNIDIR.

Pitts, J. 2007a *Reluctant Gangsters: Youth Gangs in Waltham Forest*. Luton, University of Bedfordshire.

Pitts J. 2007b Americanisation, the third way and the racialization of youth crime and disorder, in Hagedorn J. (ed.) *Gangs in the Global City*. Chicago, IL, University of Illinois Press.

Pitts, J. 2008 *Reluctant Gangsters: The Changing Face of Youth Crime*. Cullompton, Willan Publishing.

Plant, E.A. and Peruche B.M. 2005 The consequences of race for police officers' responses to criminal suspects, *Psychological Science* vol. 16 (3): 180–183.

Planty, M. and Truman, J.L. 2013 *Firearm Violence, 1993–2011: Special Report*. US Department of Justice, Bureau of Justice Statistics.

Pogrebin, M.R., Stretesky, P.B. and Unnithan, N.P. 2009 *Guns, Violence and Criminal Behaviour: The Offender's Perspective*. Boulder, CO, Lynne Rienner Publishers.

Police Complaints Authority (2003) *Review of Shootings by Police in England and Wales from 1998 to 2001*. House of Commons HC 313. London, The Stationery Office.

Polsby, D.P. 1994 The false promise of gun control, *Atlantic Monthly* March.

Poole, S. 2000 *Trigger Happy: The Inner Life of Videogames*. London, Fourth Estate.

Porteus, M.J., Edwards, S.A. and Groom, A.F. 1997 Inner-city gunshot wounds, *Injury* vol. 28 (5–6), June–July: 385–387.

Power, S. 2003 *A Problem from Hell: America and the Age of Genocide*. London, HarperCollins/ Flamingo Books.

Pratt, J. 2011 The international diffusion of punitive penality: or penal exceptionalism in the United States? Wacquant v Whitman, *Australian & New Zealand Journal of Criminology* vol. 44 (1): 116–128.

Pratt, J., Brown, D., Brown, B., Hallsworth, S. and Morrison, W. 2005 *The New Punitiveness: Trends, Theories, Perspectives*. Cullompton, Willan Publishing.

Pratten, D. and Sen, A. (eds) *Global Vigilantes*. London, Hurst Publishers.

Prince, R. and Whitehead, T. 2010 David Cameron: burglars leave human rights at the door. *Daily Telegraph* 1 February.

Punch, M. 2010 *Shoot to Kill*. Bristol, The Policy Press.

Ragin C. 1994 A qualitative comparative analysis of pension systems, in Janoski, T. and Hicks, A. (eds) *The Comparative Political Economy of the Welfare State*. Cambridge, Cambridge University Press, pp. 320–345.

Raittila, P., Koljonen, K. and Väliverronen, J. 2010 *Journalism and School Shootings in Finland 2007–2008*. Finland, University of Tampere.

Rakove, J.N. 2000 The Second Amendment: the highest stage of originalism, in Bogus, C.T. (ed.) *The Second Amendment in Law and History: Historians and Constitutional Scholars on the Right to Bear Arms*. New York, The New Press.

Ralphs, R., Medina, J. and Aldridge, J. 2009 Who needs enemies with friends like these? The importance of place for young people living in known gang areas, *Journal of Youth Studies* vol. 12 (5): 483–500.

Rathjen, H. and Montpetit, C. 1999 *December 6: From the Montreal Massacre to Gun Control*. Toronto, McClelland & Stewart.

Rawlinson, P. 2010 *From Fear to Fraternity: A Russian Tale of Crime, Economy and Modernity*. London, Pluto Press.

Reid, M. 2012 Gun deaths vs. gun prevalence. http://mark.reid.name/blog/gun-deaths-vs-gun-ownership.html (accessed 2 August 2013).

Reinarman, C. and Levine, H.G. (eds) 1997 *Crack in America: Demon Drugs and Social Justice*. Berkeley and Los Angeles, CA, University of California Press.

Reiner, R. 1991 *Chief Constables: Bobbies, Bosses or Bureaucrats?* Oxford, Clarendon Press.

Reiner, R. 1997 Media made criminality: the representation of crime in the mass media, in Maguire, M., Morgan, R. and Reiner, R. (eds) *The Oxford Handbook of Criminology*. Oxford, Oxford University Press, 2nd edition.

Reiner, R. 2007 *An Honest Citizen's Guide to Crime and Control*. Cambridge, Polity Press.

Reiner, R., Livingstone, S. and Allen, J. 2003 From law and order to lynch and mobs: crime news since the Second World War, in Mason, P. (ed.) *Criminal Visions*. Cullompton, Willan Publishing.

Reno, W. 1999 *Warlord Politics and African States*. London, Lynne Rienner Publishers.

Reuter, P. and Mouzos, J. 2003 Australia: a massive buy back of low risk guns, in Ludwig, J. and Cook, P. (eds) *Evaluating Gun Policy: Effects on Crime and Violence*. Washington, DC, The Brookings Institute.

Ribeiro, P.J. and Oliveira, R. 2010 *The Impact of Militia Actions on Public Security Policies in Rio de Janeiro*. Amsterdam, Transnational Institute, Crime and Globalisation Debate Paper Series.

Richards, P. 1996 *Fighting for the Rain Forest: War, Youth and Resources in Sierra Leone*. Oxford, The International Africa Institute.

Richmond, T., Cheney, R. and Schwab, W. 2005 The global burden on no-conflict related firearm mortality, *Injury Prevention* vol. 11 (6): 348–352.

Rivero, P.S. 2004 The value of the illegal firearms market in Rio de Janeiro City: the economic and symbolic value of guns in crime, in Dreyfus, P., Guedes, L.E., Lessing, B., Bandeira, A.R., de Sousa Nascimento, M. and Silveira Rivero, P. 2008 *Small Arms in Rio de Janeiro: The Guns, the Buyback, and the Victims*. Geneva, Small Arms Survey, Viva Rio/ISER.

Rix, B., Walker, D. and Ward, D. 1998 *The Criminal Use of Firearms*. Home Office, Police Research Group.

Roberts, D. 2013 Gun control: Barack Obama condemns 'shameful' failure to pass reform, *The Guardian* 18 April.

Rodger, J. 2008 *Criminalising Social Policy: Anti-Social Behaviour and Welfare in a De-civilised Society*. Cullompton, Willan Publishing.

Rodger, J. 2012 Loic Wacquant and Norbert Elias: advanced marginality and the theory of the de-civilising process, in Squires, P. and Lea, J. (eds) *Criminalisation and Advanced Marginality*. Bristol, Policy Press.

Rodgers, D. 2009 Living in the shadow of death: gangs violence and social order in urban Nicaragua: 1996–2002, in Jones, G. and Rodgers, D. (eds) *Youth Violence in Latin America*. New York, Palgrave Macmillan.

Rodgers, D. and Jensen, S. 2009 Revolutionaries, barbarians or war machines? Gangs in Nicaragua and South Africa, *Socialist Register* vol. 45: 220–238.

Rogers, D. 2009 *Post-internationalism and Small Arms Control: Theory, Politics, Security*. Farnham, Ashgate Publishing.

Roman, J. 2013 *Race, Justifiable Homicide, and Stand Your Ground Laws: Analysis of FBI Supplementary Homicide Report Data*. The Urban Institute. www.urban.org/UploadedPDF/412873-stand-your-ground.pdf (accessed 13 April 2014).

Rose, N. 1999 *Powers of Freedom: Reframing Political Thought*. Cambridge, Cambridge University Press.

Rosenfeld, R. 2000 Patterns of adult homicide: 1980–1995, in Blumstein, A. and Wallman, J. (eds) *The Crime Drop in America*. Cambridge and New York, Cambridge University Press.

Rosenthal, L.E. and Winkler, A. 2013 The scope of regulatory authority under the Second Amendment, in Webster, D.W. and Vernick, J.S. (eds) *Reducing Gun Violence in America: Informing Policy with Evidence and Analysis*. Baltimore, MD, Johns Hopkins University Press.

Rotker, S. (ed.) 2002 *Citizens of Fear: Urban Violence in Latin America*. New Brunswick, Rutgers University Press.

Rowe, M. 2013 Just like a TV show: public criminology and the media coverage of 'hunt for Britain's most wanted man', *Crime, Media Culture* vol. 9 (1): 23–38.

Saad, L. 2011 Self-reported gun ownership in U.S. is highest since 1993: majority of men, Republicans, and southerners report having a gun in their households, *Gallup Politics* 26 October.

Saad, L. 2012 *Americans Want Stricter Gun Laws, Still Oppose Bans*, Gallup Politics, 27 December. www.gallup.com/poll/159569/americans-stricter-gun-laws-oppose-bans.aspx (accessed 13 April 2014).

Saferworld 2008 Briefing: Third Biennial Meeting of States to Consider the Implementation of the UN Programme of Action. saferworld.org.uk

Sagramoso, D. 2001 *The Proliferation of Illegal Small Arms and Light Weapons in and around the European Union: Instability, Organised Crime and Terrorist Groups*. London, Kings College, Institute for Defence Studies and Saferworld.

Samara, T.R. 2003 State security in transition: the war on crime in post-apartheid South Africa, *Social Identities* vol. 9 (2): 277–312.

Samara, T.R. 2005 Youth, crime and urban renewal in the Western Cape, *Journal of Southern African Studies* vol. 31 (1): 209–227.

Sampson, A. 1977 *The Arms Bazaar : From Lebanon to Lockheed*. New York, Viking Books.

Sandberg, S. 2008 Street capital: ethnicity and violence on the streets of Oslo, *Theoretical Criminology* vol. 12 (2): 153–171.

Sandberg, S. and Pedersen, W. 2008 *Street Capital: Black Cannabis Dealers in a White Welfare State*. Bristol, Policy Press.

Sandbrook, D. 2011 *Mad as Hell: The Crisis of the 1970s and the Rise of the Populist Right*. New York, Random House.

Sanders, W.B. 1994 *Gang-bangs and Drive-bys: Grounded Culture and Juvenile Gang Violence*. New York, De Gruyter.

Sands, P. 2005 *Lawless World: America and the Making and Breaking of Global Rules*. Harmondsworth, Allen Lane.

Sandys-Winsch, G. 1999 *Gun Law in England and Wales*. Crayford, Shaw and Sons, 6th edition.

Sang, F.K. 2009 *Gun Violence and its Impact on Human Security in Nairobi*. Milton Keynes, AuthorHouse Publications.

Savenije, W. and van der Borgh, C. 2004 Youth gangs, social exclusion and the transformation of violence in El Salvador, in Koonings and D. Kruijt, D. (eds) *Armed Actors: Organised Violence and State Failure in Latin America*. London, Zed Books.

Scalia (Justice), A. 2008 *Opinion of the Supreme Court: District of Columbia, et al., Petitioners v. Dick Anthony Heller*. 128 Supreme Court 2783: 54.

Schiele, J.H. and Stewart, R. 2001 When white boys kill: an Afrocentric analysis, *Journal of Human Behavior in the Social Environment* vol. 4 (1): 253–273.

Schneider, J., Rowe, N., Forrest, S. and Tilley, N. 2004 *Biting the Bullet: Gun Crime in Greater Nottingham*. Unpublished report for Nottinghamshire Police.

Schönteich, M. 1999 Age and aids: South Africa's crime time bomb, *African Security Review* vol. 8 (4): 34–44.

Schönteich, M. and Louw, A. 2001 *Crime in South Africa: A Country and Cities Profile*. Pretoria, Institute for Security Studies, Occasional Paper no. 49.

Schwarz, T. 1999 *Kids and Guns: The History, the Present, the Dangers and the Remedies*, New York, Franklin Watts.

Seedat, M., van Niekerk, A., Jewkes, R., Suffla, S. and Ratele, K. 2009 Violence and injuries in South Africa: prioritising an agenda for prevention, *Lancet* vol. 374: 1011–1022.

Seiber, M. 2011 *Gunfire Graffiti: Overlooked Gun Crime in the UK*. Hampshire, Waterside Press.

Sen, A. and Pratten, D. 2007 Introduction: global vigilantes, perspectives on justice and violence, in Pratten, D. and Sen, A. 2007 *Global Vigilantes*. London, Hurst Publishers.

Sharif, A. 2001 *Illegal Small Arms in Bangladesh and South Asian Perspective*. United Nations, March PrepCom: Regional Briefing (Background Paper).

Shaw, M. 1997 South Africa: crime in transition, *Terrorism and Political Violence* vol. 8 (4): 156–175.

Shaw, M. 1998 *Organised Crime in Post-Apartheid South Africa*. Pretoria, Institute for Security Studies, Occasional Paper no. 28.

Sheley, J.F. and Wright, J.D. 1993a *Gun Acquisition and Possession in Selected Juvenile Samples*. Washington, DC, National Institute of Justice.

Sheley, J.F. and Wright, J.D. 1993b Motivations for gun possession and carrying among serious juvenile offenders, *Behavioural Sciences and the Law* vol. 11 (4), Autumn.

Sheptycki, J. 2009 Guns, crime and social order: a Canadian perspective, *Criminology & Criminal Justice* vol. 9 (3): 307–336.

Short, J.R.F. 1997 *Poverty, Ethnicity and Violent Crime.* Boulder, CO, Westview Press/ HarperCollins.

Shropshire, S. and McFarquhar, M. 2002 *Developing Multi-Agency Strategies to Address the Street Gang Culture and Reduce Gun Violence among Young People.* Briefing No. 4. Manchester: Steve Shropshire and Michael McFarquhar Consultancy Group.

Sikkink, K. 2011 *The Justice Cascade: How Human Rights Prosecutions are Changing World Politics.* New York, Norton & Co.

Silver, N. 2012 Party identity in a gun cabinet, *New York Times* 18 December.

Silverman, J. 1994 *Crack of Doom.* London, Headline Books.

Silvestri, M. 2007 'Doing' police leadership: enter the 'new smart macho', *Policing and Society* vol. 17 (1): 38–58.

Sim, J. 2009 *Punishment and Prisons: Power and the Carceral State.* London, Sage.

Simon, J. 2007 *Governing Through Crime: How the War on Crime Transformed American Democracy and Created a Culture of Fear.* Oxford and New York, Oxford University Press.

Simonov, V. 2005 How I bought a rifle for self-defence in Russia, *RiaNovosti* 11 August. http://en.rian.ru/analysis/20050811/41139012.html (accessed 13 April 2014).

Singer, P.W. 2007 *Corporate Warriors: The Rise of the Privatised Military Industry.* Ithaca, NJ, Cornell University Press, 2nd edition.

Slotkin, R. 1973 *Regeneration through Violence: The Mythology of the American Frontier, 1600–1860.* Middletown, CT, Wesleyan University Press.

Slotkin, R. 1992 *Gunfighter Nation: The Myth of the Frontier in Twentieth Century America.* New York, Athaeneum.

Small, G. 1995 *Ruthless: The Global Rise of the Yardies.* London, Warner Books, Little, Brown & Co.

Small Arms Survey 2002 *Counting the Human Cost.* Oxford, Oxford University Press.

Small Arms Survey 2007 *Guns and the City.* Graduate Institute of Geneva, Cambridge University Press.

Small Arms Survey 2008 *Geneva Declaration: The Global Burden of Armed Violence 2008.* Cambridge, Cambridge University Press.

Small Arms Survey 2010 *Gangs, Groups and Guns.* Graduate Institute of Geneva, Cambridge University Press.

Small Arms Survey 2011 *Geneva Declaration: The Global Burden of Armed Violence 2011.* Cambridge, Cambridge University Press.

Small Arms Survey 2013a *Captured and Counted: Illicit Weapons in Mexico and the Philippines.* Geneva, Everyday Dangers: Small Arms Survey Yearbook.

Small Arms Survey 2013b *Too Close to Home: Guns and Intimate Partner Violence.* Geneva, Everyday Danger: Small Arms Survey Yearbook.

Smith, D. and McVie, S. 2003 Theory and method in the Edinburgh study of youth transitions and crime, *British Journal of Criminology* vol. 43: 169–195.

Smith, K., Osborne, S., Lau, I. and Britton, A. 2012 Homicides, firearm offences and intimate violence, *Supplementary Volume 2 to Crime in England and Wales 2010/11.* London, The Stationery Office.

Smith, S. 2004 Clay shooting: civilization in the line of fire, in Dunning, E., Malcolm, D. and Waddington, I. (eds) *Sport Histories: Figurational Studies of the Development of Modern Sports.* London, Routledge.

Smith, S. 2006 Theorising gun control: the development of regulation and shooting sports in Britain, *Sociological Review* vol. 54 (4): 717–733.

Smith, T.W. 1997 A call for a truce in the defensive gun use war, *Journal of Criminal Law and Criminology* vol. 87: 1462.

Smith, T.W. 2001a Public opinion about gun policies, *Public Opinion* vol. 12 (2): 155–163.

Smith, T.W. 2001b *National Gun Policy Survey of the National Opinion Research Center: Research Findings*. Chicago, IL, University of Chicago, National Opinion Research Center.

Smith, T.W. and Smith, R.J. 1995 Changes in firearms ownership among women, 1980–1994, *Journal of Criminal Law and Criminology* vol. 88 (1): 133–149.

Snowden, C. 2010 *The Spirit-level Delusion: Fact Checking the Left's New Theory of Everything*. London, The Democracy Institute.

Soares, G.A.D. 2006 From yes to no: an analysis of tracking surveys, in Mota, M.A.R. and Crespo, S. (eds) *Referendum from Yes to No: A Brazilian Democracy Experience*. Rio de Janeiro, ISER (Institute for Religious Studies), Communication no. 62.

Soares, R.R. 2004 Crime reporting as a measure of institutional development, *Economic Development and Cultural Change* vol. 52: 851–871.

Social Exclusion Unit 1998 *Bringing Britain Together: A National Strategy for Neighbourhood Renewal*. Cm. 4045. London, The Stationery Office.

Soderstrom, E. 2012a *Shooting Highlights Fallacy of Gun-free Schools*, 2 April. http://concealed campus.org/2012/04/shooting-highlights-fallacy-of-gun-free-schools (accessed 13 April 2014).

Soderstrom, E. 2012b *Students Take Aim at College Gun Bans*, 2 April. http://concealedcampus. org/2012/04/students-take-aim-at-college-gun-bans (accessed 13 April 2014).

Solomon, H. 1999 Controlling light weapons in Southern Africa, in Boutwell, J. and Klare, M.T. (eds) *Light Weapons and Civil Conflict: Controlling the Tools of Violence*. New York, Rowman and Littlefield.

Somasundaram, D. 2002 Child soldiers: understanding the context, *British Medical Journal* vol. 324: 1268–1271.

Sonnevelt, M. 2009 Dealing with violence and public (in)security in a popular neighbourhood in Guadalajara, Mexico, in Jones, G. and Rodgers, D. (eds) *Youth Violence in Latin America*. New York, Palgrave Macmillan.

Sorj, B. 2006 Internet, public sphere and political marketing: between the promotion of communication and moralist solipsism, in Mota, M.A.R. and Crespo, S. (eds) *Referendum from Yes to No: A Brazilian Democracy Experience*. Rio de Janeiro, ISER (Institute for Religious Studies), Communication no. 62.

Spapens, T. 2007 Trafficking in illicit firearms for criminal purposes within the European Union, *European Journal of Crime, Criminal Law and Criminal Justice* vol. 15 (3): 359–381.

Sparger, J.R. and Giacopassi, D.J. 1992 Memphis revisited: a re-examination of police shootings after the Garner decision, *Justice Quarterly* vol. 2, June.

Spencer, J. 2007 Foreword to D. Pratten and A. Sen (eds) *Global Vigilantes*, London, Hurst & Co.

Spitzer, R. 1998 *The Politics of Gun Control*. New York, Seven Bridges Press, 2nd edition.

Spitzer, R. 2000 Lost and found: researching the Second Amendment, in Bogus, C.T. (ed.) *The Second Amendment in Law and History: Historians and Constitutional Scholars on the Right to Bear Arms*. New York, The New Press.

Sprague, O. 2006 Briefing Note, UN arms embargoes: an overview of the last ten years. *Control Arms Campaign*, 16 March.

Springwood, C.F. 2007a The social life of guns: an introduction, in Springwood, C.F. (ed.) *Open Fire: Understanding Global Gun Cultures*. New York, Berg.

Springwood, C.F. 2007b Gunscapes: a global geography of the firearm, in Springwood, C.F. (ed.) *Open Fire: Understanding Global Gun Cultures*. New York, Berg.

Squires, P. 1990 *Anti-Social Policy: Welfare, Ideology and the Disciplinary State*. Hemel Hempstead, Harvester/Wheatsheaf Books.

Squires, P. 1999 Review of J. Lott: more guns, less crime, *British Journal of Criminology* vol. 39 (2): 318–320.

Squires, P. 2000 *Gun Culture or Gun Control?: Firearms, Violence and Society*. London, Routledge.

Squires, P. 2008a *'Gun Crime': A Review of Evidence and Policy*. Centre for Crime and Justice Studies. *Whose Justice?* Series (with E. Solomon and R. Grimshaw). London, Kings College.

Squires, P. (ed.) 2008b *ASBO Nation: The Criminalisation of Nuisance*. Bristol, The Policy Press.

Squires, P. 2009a 'You lookin' at me?' Discourses of respect and disrespect, identity and violence, in Millie, A. (ed.) *Securing Respect: Behaviour Expectations and Anti-Social Behaviour in the UK*. Bristol, Policy Press.

Squires, P. 2009b The knife crime 'epidemic' and British politics, *British Politics* vol. 4: 127–157.

Squires, P. 2011a Young people and weaponisation, in Goldson, B. (ed.) *Youth in Crisis: Gangs, Territoriality and Violence*. Abingdon, Routledge.

Squires, P. 2011b There's nothing simple about 'simple criminality', *UCU Magazine*, no. 2, Autumn. http://uc.web.ucu.org.uk/2011/10/theres-nothing-simple-about-simple-criminality (accessed 13 April 2014).

Squires, P. 2012 Gun control, in Miller, W.R. (ed.) *The Social History of Crime and Punishment in America*. New York, Sage.

Squires, P. 2013 Educating Wayne: debating gun control with the NRA, *British Society for Criminology Newsletter*, no. 72: 8–10.

Squires, P. and Goldsmith, C. 2010 Bullets, blades and mean streets: youth violence and criminal justice failure (with C. Goldsmith), in Barter, C. and Berridge, D. (eds) *Children Behaving Badly: Perspectives on Peer Violence*. Chichester, Wiley/Blackwell.

Squires, P. and Kennison, P. 2010 *Shooting to Kill: Policing, Firearms and Armed Response*. Oxford, Wiley/Blackwell.

Squires, P. and Lea, J. (eds) 2012a *Criminalisation and Advanced Marginality: Critically Exploring the Work of Loïc Wacquant*. Bristol, Policy Press.

Squires, P. and Lea, J. 2012b Introduction: reading Loïc Wacquant – opening questions and overview, in Squires, P. and Lea, J. (eds) *Criminalisation and Advanced Marginality: Critically Exploring the Work of Loïc Wacquant*. Bristol, Policy Press.

Squires, P. and Stephen, D. 2005 *Rougher Justice: Anti-Social Behaviour and Young People*. Cullompton, Willan.

Squires, P., Silvestri, A., Grimshaw, R. and Solomon, E. 2008 *The Street Weapons Commission: Guns, Knives and Street Violence*. London, Kings College, CCJS.

Standing, A. 2003 *The Social Contradictions of Organised Crime on the Cape Flats*. Institute for Security Studies Paper 74. Pretoria, ISS.

Standing, A. 2005 *The Threat of Gangs and Anti-gangs Policy*. Policy discussion paper no. 166. Pretoria, ISS.

Standing, A. 2006 *Organised Crime: A Study from the Cape Flats*. Pretoria, ISS.

Standing, G. 2009 *The Precariat: The New Dangerous Class*. London, Bloomsbury.

Standing, G. 2011 *The Precariat: The New Dangerous Class*. London, Bloomsbury Academic.

Stange, M.Z. 2006 From domestic terrorism to armed revolution: women's right to self-defence as an essential human right, *Journal of Law, Economics and Policy* vol. 2 (2): 213–220.

Stange, M.Z. and Oyster, C.K. 2000 *Gun Women: Firearms and Feminism in Contemporary America*. New York, New York University Press.

Staudt, K. 2008 *Violence and Activism at the Border: Gender, Fear and Everyday Life in Ciudad Jaurez*. Austin, TX, University of Texas Press.

Steele, J. 2003 Gun crime has doubled since Labour took office in 1997, *Daily Telegraph* 17 October.

Stein, H.F. 2000 Disposable youth: the 1999 Columbine high school massacre as American metaphor, *Journal for the Psychoanalysis of Culture and Society* vol. 5: 217–236.

Steinert, H. 2004 The indispensable metaphor of war: on populist politics and the contradictions of the state's monopoly of force, *Theoretical Criminology* vol. 7: 265–291.

Stell, L.K. 2006 Self defense and handgun rights, *Journal of Law, Economics and Policy* vol. 2 (2): 265–308.

Stewart, E.A., Schreck, C.J. and Simons, R.L. 2006 'I ain't gonna let no-one disrespect me'; does the code of the street reduce or increase violent victimisation among African American adolescents? *Journal of Research in Crime and Delinquency* vol. 43 (4): 427–458.

Stohl, R. and Tuttle, D. 2008 *The Small Arms Trade in Latin America*. NACLA report on the Americas, March–April.

Stohl, R., Schroeder, M. and Smith, D. 2007 *The Small Arms Trade: A Beginner's Guide*. Oxford, One World Publications.

Storey, W.K. 2008 *Guns, Race and Power in Colonial South Africa*. New York and Cambridge, Cambridge University Press.

Strandow, D. and Wallensteen, P. 2007 *United Nations Arms Embargoes: Their Impact on Arms Flows and Target Behaviour*. Stockholm, SIPRI.

Strathclyde Police, Public Performance Report 2006/07.

Street Weapons Commission (SWC) 2008 *Report and Recommendations*. London Channel 4 TV.

Stretesky, P.B. and Pogrebin, M.R. 2007 Gang-related gun violence: socialization, identity, and self, *Journal of Contemporary Ethnography* vol. 36: 85–114.

Stroud, A. 2012 Good guys with guns: hegemonic masculinity and concealed handguns, *Gender and Society* vol. 26 (2): 216–238.

Sugarman, J. 2001 *Every Handgun is Aimed at You: The Case for Banning Handguns*. New York, The New Press.

Sullivan, M.L. and Guerette, R.T. 2003 The copycat factor: mental illness, guns, and the shooting incident at Heritage high school, Rockdale County, Georgia, in Moore, M.H., Petrie, C.V., Braga, A.A. and McLaughlin, B.L. (eds) *Deadly Lessons: Understanding Lethal School Violence*. Washington, DC, The National Academies Press, pp 25–69.

Summers, C. 2011 Travels of a London gun: how the gun that killed Agnes had been traded by gangs, *BBC News Website* 12 April.

Summers, C. and Jackson, P. 2009 'Cunning plan' by police led to death, *BBC News Online* 2 October, http://news.bbc.co.uk/1/hi/8255598.stm (accessed 13 April 2014).

Sunstein, C. 2007 The most mysterious right, *The New Republic* 18 November.

Super, G. 2010 The spectacle of crime in the 'new' South Africa: a historical perspective (1976–2004), *British Journal of Criminology* vol. 50 (2): 165–184.

Supreme Court 1997 *Mack and Printz v. United States*, 521 U.S. 898.

Supreme Court 2010 *McDonald v. Chicago*, 561 U.S. 3025.

Suter, E.A. 1994 Guns in the medical literature: a failure of peer review, *Journal of the American Medical Association of Georgia* vol. 83, March: 133–147.

Taylor, D. 2003 Gun crime is soaring, *Evening Standard* 9 January.

Taylor, I. 1999 *Crime in Context: A Critical Criminology of Market Societies*. Cambridge, Polity Press.

Taylor, I. and Hornsby, R. 2000 *Replica Firearms: A New Frontier in the Gun Market*. University of Durham and Gun Control Network.

Taylor, I., Walton, P. and Young, J. 1973 *The New Criminology*. London, Routledge.

Taylor-Gooby, P. and Dean, H. 1992 *Dependency Culture: The Explosion of a Myth*. London, Routledge.

Terkel, A. 2012 Columbine high school had armed guard during massacre in 1999, *Huffington Post*, 21 December. www.huffingtonpost.com/2012/12/21/columbine-armed-guards_n_2347096.html (accessed 13 April 2014).

Thaler, K. 2011 *Weapons, Violence and the Perpetrator-Victim Nexus in South Africa*. University of Sussex, MICROCON Research Working Paper 51. Brighton, MICROCON.

Thayer, G. 1969 *The War Business*. London, Weidenfeld & Nicolson.

Thayer, K. 2013 Suburb plans gun sell-back, *Chicago Tribune* 31 May.

Therborn, G. 1989 The two-thirds – one-third society in Hall, S. and Jacques, M. (eds) *New Times: The Changing Face of Politics in the 1990s*. London, Lawrence & Wishart.

Thompson, J. 2006 Violent video games train school shooters, in Hunnicutt, S. (ed.) *School Shootings*. Detroit, MI, Greenhaven Press.

Thrasher, F.M. 1927 *The Gang: A Study of 1,313 Gangs in Chicago*. Chicago, IL, University of Chicago Press.

Titmuss, R.M. 1963 The social division of welfare, in Titmuss, R.M. (ed.) *Essays on the Welfare State*. London, Heinemann.

Tonry, M. 1995 *Malign Neglect: Race, Crime and Punishment in America*. New York, Oxford University Press.

Tonry, M. 2004 *Punishment and Politics: Evidence and Emulation in the Making of English Crime Control Policy*. Cullompton, Willan.

Tonry, M. 2009 Explanations of American punishment policies: a national history, *Punishment and Society* vol. 11 (3): 377–394.

Tonry, M. 2010 The costly consequences of populist posturing: ASBOs, victims, 'rebalancing' and diminution in support for civil liberties, *Punishment & Society* vol. 12 (4): 387–413.

Tonry, M. 2011 *Punishing Race: A Continuing American Dilemma*. New York, Oxford University Press.

Tonso, K.L. 2009 Violent masculinities as tropes for school shooters: the Montreal massacre, the Columbine attack, and rethinking schools, *American Behavioural Scientist* vol. 52 (9): 1266–1285.

Tonso, W.R. 1982 *Gun and Society: The Social and Existential Roots of the American Attachment to Firearms*. Lanham, MD, University Press of America.

Totten, M. 1999 *Guys, Gangs and Girlfriend Abuse*. Peterborough, Ontario, Broadview Press.

Townsend, M. 2007 The gun lords' deadly legacy, *The Observer* 9 December.

Travis, A. 2003 Judges get final say on gun crime sentencing, *The Guardian* 7 January.

Travis, A. 2007 Younger offenders, younger victims – a grim trend: 'From fists to knives, knives to guns – it's evolution', gang veteran tells researchers. *The Guardian* 24 August.

Travis, A., Johnson, L.J. and Milroy, C.M. 2007 Homicide–suicide (dyadic death) homicide and firearms use in England and Wales, *American Journal of Forensic Medicine* vol. 28 (4): 314–318.

Turshen, M. 2004 *Armed Violence and Poverty in Algeria: A Case Study for the Armed Violence and Poverty Initiative*. University of Bradford, Centre for International Co-operation and Security.

Tushnet, M. 2007 *Out of Range: Why the Constitution Can't End the Battle Over Guns*. Oxford and New York, Oxford University Press.

Ulliver, H.R. and Merkel, W.G. 2000 Muting the Second Amendment: the disappearance of the constitutional militia, in Bogus, C.T. (ed.) *The Second Amendment in Law and History: Historians and Constitutional Scholars on the Right to Bear Arms*. New York, The New Press.

United Nations 2001 Programme of Action to Prevent, Combat and Eradicate the Illicit Trade in Small Arms and Light Weapons in All Its Aspects. UN Document A/CONF.192/15. http://www.poa-iss.org/poa/poahtml.aspx

United Nations 2012 Conference to Review Progress Made in the Implementation of the Programme of Action to Prevent, Combat and Eradicate the Illicit Trade in Small Arms and Light Weapons in All Its Aspects. New York, 27 August–7 September 2012. Assembly/CONF.192/2012/RC/4

United Nations Economic and Social Council 1997 Report to the Secretary General: Criminal Justice Reform and Strengthening of Legal Institutions Measures to Regulate Firearms. Commission on Crime Prevention and Criminal Justice Sixth Session. Vienna, 28 April–9 May 1997. E/CN.15/1997

United Nations General Assembly 2013 68/31: The Arms Trade Treaty. Resolution adopted by the General Assembly on 5 December 2013. 68th SessionA/RES/68/31.

United Nations Panel of Governmental Experts on Small Arms 1997 Report on General and Complete Disarmament: Small Arms. UN General Assembly, 52nd Session. A/52/298. 27 August 1997.

United Nations Press Release 2000 Disarmament, Demobilization and Reintegration at Heart of Peacekeeping Efforts, Secretary-General Tells Security Council. Press Release SC/6830: 23 March.

United Nations (Special Rapporteur) 2004 *Civil and Political Rights, Including the Question of Disappearances and Summary Executions.* Extrajudicial, summary or arbitrary executions.

UNODC (UN Office of Drugs and Crime) 2011 *Global Study on Homicide: Trends, Contexts, Data.* Vienna, UNODC.

US Department of Justice (ATF) 2011 *Firearms Commerce in the USA.* http://www.atf.gov/files/publications/firearms/121611-firearms-commerce-2011.pdf (accessed 13 April 2014).

Van Dijk, J., Tseloni, A. and Farrell, G. 2012 *The International Crime Drop: New Directions in Research.* Basingstoke, Palgrave Macmillan.

van Kesteren, J.N. 2014 Revisiting the gun ownership and violence link, *British Journal of Criminology* vol 54: 53–72.

Venkatesh, S.A. 1997 The social organization of street gang activity in an urban ghetto, *AJS* vol. 103 (1), July: 82–111.

Venkatesh, S.A. 2006 *Off the Books: The Underground Economy of the Urban Poor.* Cambridge, MA, Harvard University Press.

Venkatesh, S.A. 2008 *Gang Leader for a Day.* New York, Penguin Group.

Vernick, J.S. and Webster, D.W. 2013 Curtailing dangerous sales practices by licensed firearm dealers: legal opportunities and obstacles, in Webster, D.W. and Vernick, J.S. (eds) *Reducing Gun Violence in America: Informing Policy with Evidence and Analysis.* Baltimore, MD, Johns Hopkins University Press.

Vincent, J. 2013 German police test the threat posed by 3D-printed guns by printing their own, *The Independent* 24 July.

Violence Policy Center (VPC) 2004 *A Further Examination of Data Contained in the Study On Target Regarding Effects of the 1994 Federal Assault Weapons Ban.* Washington, DC, VPC.

Violence Policy Center (VPC) 2009 *Briefing: Why Military-Style Guns Flow From the United States to Mexico.* Washington, DC, VPC.

Vizzard, W.J. 2000 *Shots in the Dark: The Policy, Politics, and Symbolism of Gun Control.* Lanham, MD, Rowman and Littlefield.

Von Eggert, K. 2013 Russians debate the right to bear arms, RIA Novosti. http://indrus.in/society/2013/03/26/russians_debate_the_right_to_bear_arms_23221.html (accessed 13 April 2014).

Vulliamy, E. 2010 *Amexica: War Along the Borderline*. London, Bodley Head Publishers.

Wacquant, L. 2001 Deadly symbiosis: when ghetto and prison meet and mesh, *Punishment and Society* vol. 3 (1): 95–133.

Wacquant, L. 2003 Toward a dictatorship over the poor? Notes on the penalization of poverty in Brazil, *Punishment and Society* vol. 5 (2): 197–205.

Wacquant L. 2008a *Urban Outcasts: A Comparative Sociology of Advanced Marginality*. Cambridge, Polity Press.

Wacquant, L. 2008b The militarization of urban marginality: lessons from the Brazilian metropolis, *International Political Sociology* vol. 2: 56–74.

Wacquant, L. 2009 *Punishing the Poor: The Neoliberal Government of Social Insecurity*. Durham, NC, Duke University Press.

Waddington, P.J. and Hamilton, M. 1997 The impotence of the powerful: recent British police weapons policy, *Sociology* vol. 31 (1): 91–109.

Waiselfisz, J.J. 2013 *Mapa da Violencia: Mortes Matadas par Armas de Fogo*. Brazil, CEBELA (Centro Brasileiro de Estudos Latino-Americanos).

Waldman, P. 2012a *The Myth of NRA Dominance: Part One (of Four)*. http://thinkprogress.org/justice/2012/02/09/421893/the-myth-of-nra-dominance-part-i-the-nras-ineffective-spending (accessed 13 April 2014).

Waldman, P. 2012b Not man enough? Buy a gun, *CNN News Website* 21 December. http://edition.cnn.com/2012/12/20/opinion/waldman-guns-manhood/ (accessed 13 April 2014).

Walker, A. 2009 Real IRA suspect on trial over Lithuania arms, *Sky News* 7 October. http://news.sky.com/story/730566/real-ira-suspect-on-trial-over-lithuania-arms (accessed 13 April 2014).

Walker, A., Kershaw, C. and Nicholas, S. 2006 *Crime in England and Wales: 2005/06*. Home Office Statistical Bulletin 12/06, HMSO.

Walker, C.J. 2007 Border vigilantism and comprehensive immigration reform, *Harvard Latino Law Review* vol. 10: 135–174.

Walsh, P. 1999 Lock, stock and barrel, *The Guardian* 9 September.

Walsh, P. 2003 *Gang War: The Inside Story of the Manchester Gangs*. Bidford on Avon, Milo Books.

Ward, C.L. 2007 *It Feels Like it's the End of the World: Cape Town's Youth Talk About Gangs and Community Violence*. ISS monograph series, no. 136. Pretoria, ISS.

Warlow T.A. 2007 The criminal use of improvised and re-activated firearms in Great Britain and Northern Ireland, *Science & Justice* vol. 47 (3), November: 111–119.

Washington Post (Editorial) 2009 President Obama should lead the fight for sensible gun laws, 13 May.

Watt, H., Winnett, R. and Newell, C. 2012 Offshore stash of man found with a house full of guns, *Daily Telegraph* 8 November.

Webber, C. 2007 Revaluating relative deprivation theory, *Theoretical Criminology* vol. 11 (1): 97–120.

Webber, J.A. 2003 *Failure to Hold: The Politics of School Violence*. New York, Rowman and Littlefield.

Webster, D.M. and Vernick, J.S. (eds) 2013 *Reducing Gun Violence in America: Informing Policy with Evidence and Analysis*. Baltimore, MD, Johns Hopkins University Press.

Webster, D.W., Vernick, J.S. and Bulzacchelli, M.T. 2006a Effect of a gun dealer's change in sales practices on the supply of guns to criminals, *Journal of Urban Health* vol. 83 (5): 778–787.

Webster, D.W., Bulzachelli, M.T., Zeoli, A.M. and Vernick, J.S. 2006b Effects of undercover police stings of gun dealers on the supply of new guns to criminals. *Injury Prevention* vol. 12 (4), August: 225–230.

Webster, D.W., Freed, L.H., Frattaroli, S. and Wilson, M.H. 2002 How delinquent youths acquire guns: initial versus most recent gun acquisitions, *Journal of Urban Health* vol. 79 (1): 60–69.

Weil, D.S. and Hemenway, D. 1992 Loaded guns in the home: Analysis of a national random survey of gun owners, reprinted in Dizard, J.E., Muth, R.M. and Andrews, S.P., Jr. (eds) 1999 *Guns in America: A Reader*. New York, New York University Press.

Weissner, P. 2006 From spears to M-16s: testing the imbalance of power hypothesis among the Enga, *Journal of Anthropological Research* vol. 62: 165–191.

Wellford, C.F., Pepper, J.V. and Petrie, C.V. 2004 *Firearms and Violence: A Critical Review*. Washington, DC, National Research Council, National Academies Press.

Wessells, M. 2006 *Child Soldiers: From Violence to Protection*. Cambridge, MA, Harvard University Press.

Western, B. 2002 The impact of incarceration on wage mobility and inequality, *American Sociological Review* vol. 67: 526–546.

Wheal, H. and Tilley, N. 2009 Imitation gun law: an assessment, *The Howard Journal of Criminal Justice* vol. 48 (2): 172–183.

White, R. 2004 *Police and Community Responses to Youth Gangs*. Canberra, Australian Institute of Criminology, Trends and Issues paper no. 274.

White, R, 2008a Disputed definitions and fluid identities: the limitations of social profiling in relation to ethnic youth gangs, *Youth Justice* vol. 8 (2): 149–161.

White, R. 2008b Weapons are for wimps: the social dynamics of ethnicity and violence in Australian gangs, in van Gemert, F., Peterson, D. and Lien, I.-L. (eds) *Street Gangs, Migration and Ethnicity*. Cullompton, Willan Publishing.

White, R. and Mason, R. 2006 Youth gangs and youth violence: charting the key dimensions, *Australian and New Zealand Journal of Criminology* vol. 39 (1): 54–70.

Whitehead, P. and Crawshaw, P. (eds) 2012 *Organising Neoliberalism: Markets, Privatisation and Justice*. London, Anthem Press.

Whiting, A. 2010 A report (Part 1) concerning the grant of a firearm certificate and a shotgun certificate to Derrick Bird by Cumbria Constabulary and (Part 2) observations regarding potential changes to the system of granting such certificates and related provisions in law. ACPO.

Whitman, J.Q. 2005 *Harsh Justice: Criminal Punishment and the Widening Divide Between America and Europe*. New York and Oxford, Oxford University Press.

Wiktor, S.Z, Gallaher, M.M., Baron, R.C., Watson, M.E. and Sewell, C.M. 1994 Firearms in New Mexico, *West(ern) Journal of Medicine* vol. 161 (2): 137–139.

Wilkinson, D.L. 2003 *Guns, Violence and Identity among African American and Latino Youth*. New York, LFB Publishing.

Wilkinson, R. and Pickett, K. 2010 *The Spirit Level: Why Equality is Better for Everyone*. Harmondsworth, Penguin.

Williams, D.C. 2003 *The Mythic Meanings of the Second Amendment: Taming Political Violence in a Constitutional Republic*. New Haven, CT, Yale University Press.

Williams, P. 1997 Transnational organised crime and national and international security: a global assessment, in Gamba, V. (ed.) *Society Under Siege*, vol. 1. Oxford, Institute of Security Studies.

Williams, S. and Poynton, S. 2006 Firearms and violent crime in New South Wales, 1995–2005, *Crime and Justice Bulletin* vol. 98: 1–7.

Wills, G. 2002 *A Necessary Evil: A History of American Distrust of Government*. New York, Simon & Schuster.

Wilson, J.Q. and Kelling, G.L. 1982 Broken windows, *Atlantic Monthly* March: 29–38.

Winkler, A. 2011 *Gunfight: The Battle over the Right to Bear Arms in America*. New York, Norton & Co.

Wintemute, G. 2000 Guns and gun violence, in Blumstein, A. and Wallman, J. (eds) *The Crime Drop in America*. Cambridge and New York, Cambridge University Press.

Wintemute, G. 2013 Comprehensive background checks for firearm sales: evidence from gun shows, in Webster, D.W. and Vernick, J.S. (eds) *Reducing Gun Violence in America: Informing Policy with Evidence and Analysis*. Baltimore, MD, Johns Hopkins University Press.

Wintemute, G., Cook, P.J. and Wright, M.A. 2005 Risk factors among handgun retailers for frequent and disproportionate sales of guns used in violent and firearm related crimes, *Injury Prevention* vol. 11: 357–363.

Wintemute, G.J., Teret, S.P., Kraus, J.F., Wright, M.A. and Bradfield, G. 1987 When children shoot children: 88 unintended deaths in California, *Journal of the American Medical Association* vol. 257: 3107–3109.

Wintemute, G.J., Wright, M.A., Parham, C.A., Drake, C.M. and Beaumont, J.J. 1998 Criminal Activity and Assault-Type Handguns: A Study of Young Adults. *Annals of Emergency Medicine* vol. 32: 44–50.

Wintour, P. and Dodd, V. 2007 Blair blames spate of murders on black culture, *The Guardian* 12 April.

Witsenberg, K. and Zahl, F. 2012 Spaces of insecurity, in Witsenberg, K. and Zahl, F. (eds) *Spaces of Insecurity: Human Agency in Violent Conflicts in Kenya*. Leiden, Africa Studies Centre, vol. 45.

Woollaston, V. and Murphy, S. 2013 The £16 gun: plastic firearm you can make at home from household items is created by 3D printer, *Daily Mail* 21 May.

Wright, J.D. and Rossi, P.H. 1986 *Armed and Considered Dangerous: A Survey of Felons and their Firearms*. New York, Aldine de Gruyter.

Wright, J.D. and Rossi, P.H. 1994 *Armed and Considered Dangerous: A Survey of Felons and their Firearms*. New York, Aldine de Gruyter, 2nd edition.

Yeoman, F. and Charter, D. 2009 Tim Kretschmer, the boy who killed 15 in school rampage, stole pistol from his father's arsenal, *The Times* 12 March.

Young, J. 1999 *The Exclusive Society*. London, Sage.

Young, J. 2011 *The Criminological Imagination*. Cambridge, Polity Press.

Zaluar, A. 2004 Urban violence and drug warfare in Brazil, in Koonings, K. and Kruijt, D. (eds) *Armed Actors: Organised Violence and State Failure in Latin America*. London, Zed Books.

Zimring, F.E. 1968 Is gun control likely to reduce violent killings? *University of Chicago Law Review* vol. 35: 721–737.

Zimring, F.E. 1975 Firearms and federal law: the Gun Control Act of 1968, *Journal of Legal Studies* vol. 4 (1): 133–198.

Zimring, F.E. 1981 Handguns in the twenty-first century: alternative policy futures, in Cook, P.J. (ed.) *Gun Control: The Annals of the American Academy of Political Science*. Philadelphia, Sage Publications, in association with the American Academy of Political and Social Science, pp. 1–10.

Zimring, F.E. 1998 *American Youth Violence*. New York: Oxford University Press.

Zimring, F.E. 2003 *The Contradictions of American Capital Punishment*. New York, Oxford University Press.

Zimring, F.E. 2007 *The Great American Crime Decline*. Oxford and New York, Oxford University Press.

Zimring, F.E. and Hawkins, G. 1986 *Capital Punishment and the American Agenda*. New York, Cambridge University Press.

Zimring, F.E. and Hawkins, G. 1987 *The Citizen's Guide to Gun Control*. New York, Macmillan.

Zimring, F.E. and Hawkins, G. 1997 *Crime is not the Problem: Lethal Violence in America*. New York, Oxford University Press.

Zubillaga, V. 2009 'Gaining respect': the logic of violence among young men in the Barrios of Caracas, Venezuela, in Jones, G. and Rodgers, D. (eds) *Youth Violence in Latin America*. New York, Palgrave Macmillan.

Zylinska, J. 2004 Guns n' rappers: moral panics and the ethics of cultural studies, *Culture Machine*, vol. 6. http://www.culturemachine.net/index.php/cm/article/viewArticle/7/6 (accessed 13 April 2014).

INDEX

386 Index

El Salvador: gun homicide in 38; gun homicides in 247; inequality in 38; war brought chronic conflict 246
Elias, Norbert: 'civilizing process' 13
Ellis, Charlene 90, 94, 106
empowerment by guns 18; of aggressors 21; in a neo-liberal world 8; for self-defence 19; trade to conflict and crime 237–8; US and UK gang research 108
end-user certification (EUC) 233–4
England and Wales: air weapons offences 53; gun homicide rate 283; illegal gun inventory 59–60; non-use offences 58
Enten, H. 157
Epstein, J. C. see DeJong, W.
Equality Trust 33, 35
Equatorial Guinea 233
Esping-Anderson, G. 28
Ethiopia: gun homicides in 247; trafficking into 242
European Union: Code of Conduct on arms export 308; governance of arms 6; gun control laws 281; Programme for Preventing and Combating Illicit Trafficking 308; proportion of gun homicides 248; reaction to rampage shootings 278–83; regulating weapon transfers 71; trade in replicas/conversions 70–1

Fagan, J.: imitation/replica weapons 64; lethal inner city ecology 187, 192; New York gang feuds 186
Faiola, A. 75
family: breakdown as cause of gangs 118, 122–3; conditions of violent crime 4
Federal Bureau of Investigation (FBI): Annual Serious Crime Assessment 237
Federal Gun Control Act, 1968, USA 155
Feinstein, A.: The Shadow World 242–3
Felbab-Brown, V.: iron fist policies 245; on Juárez 249; narco-liberalism and youth 255
Field, Frank 27–8
Fields, G. 190–1
films: dark frontier narratives 202; explanation for violence 186; Gunfighter Nation 214; masculinity and school shooters 213; men with guns 325; Natural Born Killers 204; Shane 22, 323; Taxi Driver and Virginia Tec 214
Findlay, M.: globalization and crime 228; neo-liberalism and crime 8
Fine, B. 117
Finkelman, P. 149

Finland: homicide rate 33, 38, 283; income equality in 35, 38; reaction to rampage shootings 280–1; silence of gender problem 214; social problems index 32
Firearm Owners Protection Act, 1986, USA 149
Firearms Act, Canada, 1995 286
Firearms (Amendment) Act, UK, 1988 278
Firearms Consultative Committee (FCC): Home Affairs Committee after Dunblane 92
Firearms Control Act, South Africa, 2000 263, 267
Firearms Forensic Intelligence Database 71
Firearms Owners Protection Act, 1986, USA 144
Fletcher, J. 13
Florquin, N. 257–8
Ford, John: The Searchers 202
Forensic Science Service 73
Foster, Christopher 95
Foucault, Michel: escape the prison 10; on military discipline 8
Fox, J. A.: gun homicides 191–2; school culture 220–1
Fox, S. see Newman, K.
France: arms trade 239; homicide rate 33, 38, 283; income equality in 35, 38; social problems index 32; trans-European criminal network 242
Francis, P.: criminal Kenya 261
freedom: balances of 34; guns equal 19, 20, 154
Full Metal Jacket (Kubrick) 325
Furman v Georgia 155

Gamba, V. 8
games and play: Grand Theft Auto 214; imitation weapons 61–2; violence and school shooters 218–19
gangs and criminal groups: Australia 296–8; 'black-on-black' shootings 66; Canadian 288; criminology and 9–10; explanation for violence 186–7; growth of 188; gun crime in UK 54; gun culture 5; Home Office programme 82; imitation/replica weapons 63–4; inequality and poverty in UK 119–26; intervention programmes 104; neo-liberalism and 125–6; personal responsibility and 104–5, 123; popular misunderstandings of 91; protection and 55; rap music and 102; South Africa 263–4; school shootings and 202; Scotland 51; settled/failing states and 8; South African 8; state controls 5; UK

Wilkinson, R. 35; community vicious
circles 190; homicide and inequality 38,
39; *The Spirit Level* (with Pickett) 32–3
Willis, M. 188
Wilson, J. Q.: 'Broken Windows' theory 23
Winkler, A. 145, 149–50, 151
Winnenden, Germany school shooting 282
Wintemute, G. 145, 167
Witsenberg, K. 260–1
women and girls: Australian shoots
'feminists' 284; Brazilian gun control
initiatives 302; Brazilian violence and
301; femicide in South Africa 267; gun
cultures and 327; with guns 271; guns
as feminist right 313; guns dangerous
for 270; Mexican murders and 251–2;
misogynism 41; rape in South Africa
265; South African men and 265–6;
victims of gunshots 84–6; violence
against 237–8, 328
Wood, S. *see* Bellis, M. A.
World Federation of Sports Shooting
Activities 17
World Forum on the Future of Sport
Shooting Activities (WFSA): Bush
administration and 314; civilian
appropriate firearms 328; resistance to
UN programme 310–13

World Health Organization (WHO) 11
Wyke, S. *see* Bellis, M. A.

Young, Jock 295; rise and fall of gun
violence 171; on Zimring 184
young men: beyond the statistics 90–1;
global corrosion marginalizes 243;
marginal young men and illegal guns
78–82; narco-liberalism of Mexico 255;
viewing with violence lens 103
Young, T.: gang talk 91; UK gangs and
102
Youth Crime Action Plan 116
Yugoslavia (former): chronic violence spots
245; firearm trafficking 70

Zahl, F. 260–1
Zambia 247
Zimmerman, George 35, 36, 177–9
Zimring, Franklin E. 92; 1968 Gun
Control Act 142; *Great American Crime
Decline* 181–4; predicting trends 158,
159; rise and fall of gun violence 171–2;
symbolic dominances 193; view of
youth culture 103